The Job Ladder

WIDER STUDIES IN DEVELOPMENT ECONOMICS

The United Nations University (UNU) World Institute for Development Economics Research (UNU-WIDER) was established by the United Nations University as its first research and training centre and started work in Helsinki, Finland, in 1985. The mandate of the Institute is to undertake applied research and policy analysis on structural changes affecting developing and transitional economies; to provide a forum for the advocacy of policies leading to robust, equitable, and environmentally sustainable growth; and to promote capacity strengthening and training in the field of economic and social policy-making. Its work is carried out by staff researchers and visiting scholars in Helsinki and via networks of collaborating scholars and institutions around the world.

United Nations University World Institute for
Development Economics Research – UNU-WIDER
Katajanokanlaituri 6B, 00160 Helsinki, Finland
www.wider.unu.edu

The Job Ladder

Transforming Informal Work and Livelihoods in Developing Countries

Edited by

GARY S. FIELDS
T. H. GINDLING
KUNAL SEN
MICHAEL DANQUAH
SIMONE SCHOTTE

A study prepared by the United Nations University World Institute for Development Economics Research – UNU-WIDER

OXFORD
UNIVERSITY PRESS

OXFORD
UNIVERSITY PRESS

Great Clarendon Street, Oxford, OX2 6DP,
United Kingdom

Oxford University Press is a department of the University of Oxford.
It furthers the University's objective of excellence in research, scholarship,
and education by publishing worldwide. Oxford is a registered trade mark of
Oxford University Press in the UK and in certain other countries

World Institute for Development Economics Research of the United Nations University (UNU-WIDER),
Katajanokanlaituri 6 B, 00160 Helsinki, Finland

Enquiries concerning reproduction outside the scope of this licence
should be sent to the Rights Department, Oxford University Press, at the address above

Published in the United States of America by Oxford University Press
198 Madison Avenue, New York, NY 10016, United States of America

British Library Cataloguing in Publication Data
Data available

Library of Congress Control Number: 2022946568

ISBN 978–0–19–286733–9

DOI: 10.1093/oso/9780192867339.001.0001

Printed and bound by
CPI Group (UK) Ltd, Croydon, CR0 4YY

Foreword

Policy-makers are sorely challenged by finding ways to encourage the movement of workers from the informal sector to the more productive formal sector and, concurrently, creating opportunities for more dynamic informal firms to flourish and grow while, at the same time, providing their workers with decent and remunerative work. Bringing in classical accounts of economic development, economic growth is seen to be accompanied by a decline in the informal sector, yet, in most developing countries, the informal sector remains a persistent phenomenon despite rapid economic growth in recent decades. With premature deindustrialization and the growth of the informal service sector, it seems likely that the trajectory towards informalization in low-income and middle-income countries may be intensified in the future.

To delve deeper into the patterns and drivers of informality, in 2019, UNU-WIDER launched a wide-ranging research project, Transforming Informal Work and Livelihoods, with a goal of gathering and providing knowledge for better policy-making by understanding the causes and consequences of informality feeding into the informal work sector. The project team spanned the globe, with contributions from country experts providing rich, at times granular, studies on the causes and consequences of the informality trend.

We enquire into what explains the high prevalence of informality in sub-Saharan Africa and South Asia compared to East Asia and Latin America. How can workers in the informal sector climb the job ladder and move on to better paid remunerations? How can the livelihoods of informal workers be transformed? What do we know about the policy interventions that can contribute to livelihood enhancement for informal workers and households?

This book contains the concentrated knowledge garnered from multidisciplinary research work conducted over three years. I wholeheartedly thank my fellow editors—Gary Fields, T. H. Gindling, Michael Danquah, and Simone Schotte—for their editorial skills in bringing this compilation to publication.

UNU-WIDER gratefully acknowledges the support and financial contribution received for this project from the governments of Finland, Sweden, and the United Kingdom. Without such vital funding, our research and policy advisory work would be impossible.

Kunal Sen
Director, UNU-WIDER
Helsinki, January 2023

Contents

List of figures

List of tables

List of abbreviations

AERC	African Economic Research Consortium
AFC	Asian Financial Crisis
CAPMAS	Central Agency for Public Mobilization and Statistics
CCP	Chinese Communist Party
CCSS	Costa Rica Social Security
CEDLAS	Center of Distributive, Labor, and Social Studies
CEPAL	United Nations Economic Commission for Latin America and the Caribbean
CFPS	China Family Panel Studies
CIDE	Centro de Investigación y Docencia Económicas (Centre for Research and Teaching in Economics)
CIEDUR	Interdisciplinary Centre for Development Studies Uruguay
CIRJE	Center for International Research on the Japanese Economy
CNY	Chinese yuan renminbi
CPI	consumer price index
DIGESTYC	General Directorate of Statistics and Census
DOS	Department of Statistics (Jordan)
ECE	Encuesta Continua de Empleo
ECINEQ	Society for the Study of Economic Inequality
ECLAC	United Nations Economic Commission for Latin America and the Caribbean
EGP	Egyptian pounds
EHMP	Encuesta de Hogares para Medir la Pobreza
EHPM	Encuesta de Hogares de Propósitos Múltiples
ELMPS	Economics, Law, Management, Politics and Sociology Ethics Committee
ENAHO	Encuesta Nacional de Hogares (Costa Rican National Household Survey)
ENDE	National Survey of Occupation and Employment
EPAR	Evans School Policy Analysis & Research Group
EPL	employment protection laws
EPH	Encuesta Permanente de Hogares
ERF	Economic Research Forum
ESCWA	UN Economic and Social Commission for Western Asia
FIDEG	Fundacíon Internacional par el Desafio Económico Global
FMLE	Federal Ministry of Labour and Employment (Nigeria)
FUSADES	Fundación Salvadoreno para el Deserrollo Económico y Social
GPD	gross domestic product
GHS	Global Human Settlement

GSPS	Ghana Socio-Economic Panel Survey
GSS	Ghana Statistical Service
IBGE	Instituto Brasileiro de Geografia e Estadística
ICLS	International Conference of Labor Statisticians
IDB	Inter-American Development Bank
IDRC	Canadian Development Research Center
IDS	Institute of Development Studies
IFLS	Indonesian Family Life Survey
IGC	International Growth Centre (Ghana)
IHDS	Indian Human Development Survey
IHS	inverse hyperbolic sine
ILO	International Labour Organization
INCO	Indian National Classification of Occupations
INDEC	Instituto Nacional de Estadística y Censos
INEC	Instituto Nacional de Estadística y Censos
INEGI	Instituto Nacional de Estadística y Geografía
INEI	Instituto Nacional de Estadística e Informática
ISCO	International Standard Classification of Occupations
ISTC	International Standard Text Code
ITUC	International Trade Union Confederation
IZA	Institute of Labor Economics
JD	Jordanian dollars
JLMPS	Jordan Labor Market Panel Survey
LEL	low earnings line
LSMS—ISA	Living Standards Measurement Study—Integrated Surveys on Agriculture
MENA	Middle East and North Africa
MHS	Multipurpose Household Surveys
NBS	National Bureau of Statistics
NBS GHS	National Bureau of Statistics General Household Survey
NCEUS	National Commission for Enterprises in the Unorganized Sector
NECA	Nigeria Employers Consultative Association
NGN	Nigerian naira
NHIS	National Health Insurance Scheme
NIDS	National Institute for Discovery Science
NLC	Nigeria Labour Congress
NSSF	national social security fund
NSSO	National Sample Survey Office (India)
OAMDI	Open Access Micro Data Initiative
OECD	Organisation for Economic Co-operation and Development
OLS	ordinary least squares
PME	Pesquisa Mensal de Emprego
PNADC	Pesquisa Nacional par Amostra de Domicilios Continua
PPP	purchasing power parity
SE	self-employment

SEDLAC	Socio-Economic Database for Latin America and the Caribbean
SSA	sub-Saharan Africa
TD	Tunisian dollars
TLMPS	Tunisia Labor Market Panel Survey
TUC	Trade Union Congress
TZNPS	Tanzania National Panel Survey
UNDP—IAP	United Nations Development Programme—International Recovery Platform
UNPS	United Nations Pacific Strategy
UNRISD	United Nations Research Institute for Social Development
UNU-MERIT	United Nations University Maastricht Economic and Social Research Institute on Innovation and Technology
UNU-WIDER	United Nations University World Institute for Development Economics Research
WE	wage-employment
WEF	World Economic Forum
WIEGO	Women in Informal Employment: Globalizing and Organizing
WTO	World Trade Organization

Notes on contributors

Enrique Alaniz is a Nicaraguan researcher devoted to the study of poverty, inequality, and the functioning of labour markets in Central America. He did his Bachelor's in Economics and Finance at Universidad Thomas More in Managua, and his Master's in Economics at Universitat Pompeu Fabra in Barcelona, Spain. Currently he is a lecturer at Universidad Thomas More, where he teaches courses on quantitative research methodology and statistics.

Shireen AlAzzawi is a lecturer in the economics department, Santa Clara University and Research Fellow at the Economic Research Forum, Cairo, Egypt. Her research is in the fields of development economics and international trade, particularly in the Middle East and North Africa. She has published in the fields of labour economics, gender, and poverty and inequality, with special emphasis on youth and women.

Didier Alia is a research associate at the Daniel J. Evans School of Public Policy and Governance at the University of Washington, where he is also the lead in data and analytics at the Evans School Policy Analysis & Research Group (EPAR). His current work focuses on the construction of agricultural development indicators, on assessing progress on inclusive agricultural transformation, and on measurement issues in agricultural economics with gender and risks and resilience as cross-cutting themes. Dr Alia has published in the area of rural non-farm enterprises dynamics and performance in Africa and their implications for rural development.

Michael Danquah, a development economist, is a Research Fellow at UNU-WIDER. Michael is a visiting Research Fellow at the Transfer Project and a Researcher for the International Growth Centre (IGC), Ghana. Previously, he worked at the Department of Economics, University of Ghana, Legon. His research interest is in economic development in sub-Saharan Africa, focusing on issues such as informality, poverty, and productivity growth, among others. Michael's research has been published in journals such as *Journal of Economic Behavior & Organization*, *Small Business Economics*, and *Energy Economics*, among others. He has been awarded the Most Promising Young Scholar and Best Researcher in the School of Social Sciences, University of Ghana. Michael has also been interviewed by the BBC World Service on issues related to poverty reduction as well as on the pandemic effects of COVID-19 in sub-Saharan Africa.

Sènakpon Fidèle Ange Dedehouanou is an assistant professor at the Faculty of Business and Economics, University of Abomey Calavi (UAC), Benin. His research focuses on microeconomic and macroeconomic issues of development. He has published in the fields of development economics, namely, employment, small business and entrepreneurship, microfinance, agriculture, governance and social service delivery, social protection, food security, and nutrition.

Robert Duval-Hernández is an assistant professor at the Faculty of Economics and Management at the Open University of Cyprus, a Research Fellow at the Institute of Labor Economics (IZA) and an External Affiliate Professor at the Centro de Investigación y Docencia Económicas (Centre for Research and Teaching in Economics) (CIDE), Mexico. His areas of interest are labour and development economics. He has studied the interrelationship between income mobility and inequality, the characteristics of informal labour markets, and labour supply topics in both developing and developed countries.

Alma Espino is an economist and researcher at the Institute of Economics, Faculty of Economics Sciences and Administration, University of the Republic, Uruguay. She is also the Coordinator of Development and Gender Area at the Interdisciplinary Centre for Development Studies, Uruguay (CIEDUR). She has worked as a consultant to government agencies and ministries in the country and the region as well as international organizations (World Bank, the United Nations Research Institute for Social Development (UNRISD), UNWomen, the Inter-American Development Bank (IDB), the United Nations Economic Commission for Latin America and the Caribbean (ECLAC) and others) and is the author or co-author of several journal articles in refereed and non-refereed publications and working papers and has participated in the drafting of several book chapters.

Gary S. Fields is the John P. Windmuller Professor of International and Comparative Labor and Professor of Economics at Cornell University, Program Coordinator of the IZA Institute for Labor Economics Program on Labor and Development, and a UNU-WIDER Non-Resident Senior Research Fellow. He is the 2014 winner of the IZA Prize in Labor Economics, the top worldwide award in the field. He has been an Ivy League teacher and professor for 50 years, first at Yale University and then at Cornell University. He teaches and conducts research on labour economics and development economics. Fields has published more than 200 books, articles, and book chapters. His most recent books are *Growth, Employment, and Poverty: Latin America in the 2000s* with Guillermo Cruces, David Jaume, and Mariana Viollaz (Oxford University Press 2017) and *Employment and Development* (Oxford University Press 2019).

Abiodun O. Folawewo is a professor at the Department of Economics, University of Ibadan, Nigeria. His research interest spreads across macroeconomic, labour, and development economics and he has published extensively in these areas. His current research focuses on understanding of household behaviour within the urban informal sector.

T. H. (Tim) Gindling is a professor in the Department of Economics and the 2020–2021 Lipitz Professor of Arts, Humanities, and Social Sciences at the University of Maryland, Baltimore County (UMBC). His research has focused on the study of factors influencing the distribution of wages, income, and work in developing economies. Dr Gindling is a Non-Resident Senior Research Fellow at UNU-WIDER, an IZA Research Fellow, and subject editor for economic development for the *IZA World of Labor*.

Vladimir Hlasny is an economic affairs officer with the poverty and inequality research team at the UN Economic and Social Commission for Western Asia (ESCWA) in Beirut. Prior to joining ESCWA, he taught Economics at Ewha Womens' University in Seoul. He conducts research in labour and welfare economics, particularly in relation to Asia and the Middle East region. He holds a doctorate in Economics from Michigan State University.

Carl Lin is an Associate Professor of Economics at Bucknell University, a liberal arts college located in Lewisburg, Pennsylvania. His research focuses on economic and public policies of minimum wages, immigration, and rural–urban migrants in China. He serves as a consultant to the World Bank and is also a Research Fellow at IZA (Institute for the Study of Labor) in Germany, a Research Fellow at the Global Labor Organization, and a Research Fellow at China Institute for Income Distribution in Beijing Normal University. He coedited and published the book *Minimum Wages in China: Evolution, Legislation, and Effects* in 2020.

Catherine Mata is a PhD candidate in economic public policy at the University of Maryland, Baltimore County (UMBC). She studies applied microeconomics with a focus on economic development, economics of education, and labour markets. Through her research, she evaluates public policies that aim to address economic inequalities faced by historically disadvantaged populations. Prior to joining the UMBC, Catherine was a researcher for the University of Costa Rica.

Roxana Maurizio is Regional Specialist on Labour Economics for Latin American and the Caribbean, International Labour Organization (ILO). Her areas of interest are labour economics, income distribution, poverty, and social policies in Latin America. She has published articles and books about labour informality, labour institutions, international migration, income mobility, inequality and poverty, and labour and social programmes. She holds an undergraduate degree in economics, a master's degree in economics, and a PhD in economics.

Ana Paula Monsalvo is a researcher and assistant professor at the University of General Sarmiento, Buenos Aires, Argentina, and Technical advisor at the Instituto Nacional de Estadistica y Censos. Her areas of interest are labour economics, income distribution, poverty, and social policies in Latin America.

Rajesh Raj Natarajan is Associate Professor at the Department of Economics, Sikkim University, Gangtok, India. His main research interests include labour and employment, industrialization and productivity, firm dynamics, and the informal sector. He has published widely in academic journals including *Small Business Economics*, *Journal of Comparative Economics*, *Manchester School*, *International Journal of Educational Development*, and *Oxford Development Studies*. His books include *Out of the Shadows? The Informal Manufacturing in Post-Reform India* (Oxford University Press 2016) and *Small Firm Ownership and Credit Constraints in India* (Routledge 2020). He is a co-editor of *Productivity in Indian Manufacturing: Measurement, Methods and Analysis* (Routledge 2014) and *The Routledge Handbook of Post-Reform Indian Economy* (Routledge 2021).

Olusegun A. Orija is a doctoral student in the Department of Economics, University of Ibadan, Nigeria. His research focus is in the areas of international finance and development economics.

Mayang Rizky is a researcher at the SMERU Research Institute in Jakarta, Indonesia. Her research interests are in the intersection of poverty, labour, and child wellbeing. Prior to joining SMERU, Mayang worked as a research assistant at the Demographic Institute, University of Indonesia. Mayang holds a master's degree in behavioural economics from the

University of Nottingham and a bachelor's degree in economics from the University of Indonesia.

Diego Rojas is a consultant for the Office of the Chief Economist for Latin America and the Caribbean region at the World Bank. Before joining the World Bank, he worked as lecturer and researcher at the University of Costa Rica. His most recent work has focused on labour markets, macroeconomics, and international trade. His work on trade and labour market interactions has been published in economic development journals.

Simone Schotte is Research Associate at UNU-WIDER. She is a development economist with research interests at the crossroads of inequality, social stratification, and labour markets research. At UNU-WIDER, Simone's main research focus is on horizontal inequalities and affirmative action, as well as questions related to understanding the drivers and livelihood implications of transitions between different types of formal and informal work and the interlinkage between occupational change and earnings inequality dynamics in developing countries. Simone's research has been published in journals such as *World Development*, *Journal of Economic Inequality*, *Journal of Development Studies*, *Kyklos*, and *International Migration Review*, among others.

Kunal Sen is Director of UNU-WIDER and Professor of Development Economics, Global Development Institute, University of Manchester (on leave). He has over three decades of experience in academic and applied development economics research. He is the author of eight books and the editor of five volumes on the economics and political economy of development. He has performed extensive research on international finance, the political economy determinants of inclusive growth, the dynamics of poverty, social exclusion, female labour force participation, and the informal sector in developing economies. His research has focused on India, East Asia, and sub-Saharan Africa. His books include *The Political Economy of India's Growth Episodes* (2016), *The Process of Financial Liberalization in India* (1997), and the *Economic Restructuring in East Asia and India: Perspectives on Policy Reform* (1995). His is a co-editor of *Deals and Development: The Political Dynamics of Growth Episodes* (2018) and *The Politics of Inclusive Development* (2016). He has also written twenty-five chapters in other volumes and published more than ninety peer-reviewed journal articles on topics in his field.

Daniel Suryadarma is a research fellow at the Asian Development Bank Institute in Tokyo. He conducts research on education, poverty, and social policies in Asia and the Pacific, in partnership with government and non-government agencies. His work has appeared in reputable international journals, including *American Economic Journal: Applied Economics* and *Journal of Development Economics*. Daniel has economics degrees from Brandon University, the University of Toronto, and the Australian National University.

Asep Suryahadi is a senior research fellow at the SMERU Research Institute in Jakarta, Indonesia. Previously, he was the director of the institute from 2009 to 2019 and the deputy director of research from 2003 to 2009. He is currently a visiting researcher at Bank Indonesia Institute. He currently serves as a member of the editorial board of the Bulletin of Indonesian Economic Studies and the advisory board of Indonesia Project, both at the Australian National University. He is a member of the advisory body of the Indonesian statistical agency. He holds a PhD in economics from the Australian National University.

Linxiang Ye is a Professor of Economics at Nanjing University of Finance and Economics in Nanjing, China. His research field mainly focuses on the Chinese labour market, including compliance and enforcement of the minimum wage policy, income distribution, and employment characteristics of the low-income population in China. He serves as a Research Fellow at China Institute for Income Distribution in Beijing Normal University and has published papers on the Chinese minimum wage policy, income, and opportunities of the low-income population in China.

Wei Zhang is a PhD student in Economics at Beijing Normal University in China. His research interests include income inequality, subjective well-being, and the labour market in China.

PART I
INTRODUCTION

1
The job ladder

Gary S. Fields, T. H. Gindling, Kunal Sen, Michael Danquah, and Simone Schotte

1. Introduction

In classical accounts of economic development, economic growth is seen to be accompanied by a decline in informal employment.[1] Yet, in most developing countries, particularly in sub-Saharan Africa and South Asia and less so in East Asia and Latin America, informal forms of economic activity remain a persistent phenomenon in spite of rapid economic growth in recent decades (Kanbur 2017). Informal employment now constitutes more than 60 per cent of total global employment (ILO 2018). In Africa, for instance, every 8 out of 10 work informally (ILO 2018). Micro, small, informal and household-run enterprises employ a large share of the workforce and provide livelihoods for the poor (La Porta and Shleifer 2014). Women are more likely to engage in precarious forms of informal work, such as contributing family/unpaid workers in the enterprises headed by the males in their households or in poorly paid casual jobs in the informal sector.

However, it is important to note that informal economic activity takes many different forms and plays different roles. In low- and middle-income countries, it is often a place of residual employment for impoverished, marginalized, and vulnerable workers, particularly at times of economic stress and crisis. It can, though, also act as a staging ground for household enterprises in their initial stage of growth. Accordingly, there is an increasing consensus in the existing literature that the analysis of informality cannot be performed without recognizing the extent of heterogeneity in informal work (see, inter alia, Chen 2012; De Vreyer and Roubaud 2013; Kanbur 2017). Informal workers range from multidimensionally deprived individuals in subsistence activities, including own-account workers, who are either single-person operators or heads of family units, and contributing family workers at the lower end (*lower-tier* informal workers and enterprises) to entrepreneurs and technical workers or professionals with high

[1] Informal employment is defined as consisting of 'all remunerative work (i.e. both self-employment and wage employment) that is not registered, regulated or protected by existing legal or regulatory frameworks, as well as non-remunerative work undertaken in an income-producing enterprise' (ILO 2019). See Chapter 2 for further details.

Gary S. Fields et al., *The job ladder*. In: *The Job Ladder*. Edited by Gary S. Fields, T. H. Gindling, Kunal Sen, Michael Danquah, and Simone Schotte, Oxford University Press. © UNU-WIDER (2023).
DOI: 10.1093/oso/9780192867339.003.0001

potential, who voluntarily choose to remain informal (non-registered) at the upper end (*upper-tier* informal workers and enterprises).

With 'premature deindustrialization' and the growth of the informal service sector, it seems likely that the trajectory towards informalization in low- and middle-income countries may be intensified in the future (Rodrik 2016). The challenge for policy-makers is then to find ways to encourage the movement of workers from informal to formal employment and, at the same time, to provide opportunities for more dynamic informal firms to grow and for those working in these firms to achieve remunerative work, even while remaining informal. However, in this effort, policy-makers are constrained by the lack of available evidence on the causes of informality and the most effective mechanisms to reduce low-paid, informal employment.

Using a range of countries from the Global South, this book examines heterogeneity within informal work by applying a common conceptual framework and empirical methodology. The country studies use panel data to study the dynamics of worker transitions between formal and heterogeneous informal work. The range of country studies (covering Asia, Latin America, Middle East and North Africa and sub-Saharan Africa) in the book allows us to present, in the concluding chapter, a comparative perspective across developing countries. The book is an outcome of a United Nations University World Institute for Development Economics Research (UNU-WIDER) project, *Transforming Informal Work and Livelihoods.*[2]

Early work in the 1970s and 1980s conceived of informal work as essentially a free-entry option at the bottom end of the employment distribution, where workers who cannot obtain limited and preferred formal employment can find at least low wage-employment.[3] Later research, however, distinguished a second category of informal employment: informal work that required human capital and/or financial capital and could not be entered freely. Fields 1990 (an excerpt of which was also published in Fields (2019)) advocated for the essential duality of informal employment along free-entry/restricted-entry lines. In this book, we will denote free-entry informal work as lower-tier informality and restricted-entry informal work as upper-tier informality.

Another source of heterogeneity in informality is the difference between wage-employment and self-employment, each with possible different working conditions and compensation mechanisms. There is evidence from Latin America that informal self-employment is largely voluntary while informal wage-employment is largely involuntary. Each country study provides a nuanced view of informality, dividing workers into six work status groups: formal wage-employees,

[2] See https://www.wider.unu.edu/project/transforming-informal-work-and-livelihoods for more details about the project.

[3] Highlighting the early literature were four book-length ILO country studies covering Ceylon, Colombia, Iran, and Kenya. See Thorbecke (1973) for a summary and review.

upper-tier informal wage-employees, lower-tier informal wage-employees, formal self-employed, upper-tier formal self-employed, and upper-tier informal self-employed. Based on this common conceptual framework, the country studies examine the distribution of workers between each of these work status groups.

All country studies analyse panel data, allowing the authors to document transition patterns across different formality and work status groups. One key question regarding transitions is the extent to which lower-tier informality is a dead end where workers are stuck once entered or whether lower-tier informality is a staging area for budding entrepreneurs that can provide experience and skills that allow workers to move on to better work status groups. The panel data analysed in each country study gives us a basis for making statements about labour market transitions that are not warranted when using comparable cross sections. To be able to make statements about gross flows between work status groups, we must have panel data.

In addition to measuring the distribution of workers and transitions between work status groups, each country study examines individual- and household-level characteristics associated with workers in each work status. Using these characteristics, each country study constructs a 'job ladder' that ranks each work status. The country studies then examine the characteristics of workers that are associate with transitions up (and down) the job ladder.

A key contribution of the book is that it offers a more nuanced view of informality that differentiates not only between formal and informal, self-employed, and wage-employment but also between upper-tier and lower-tier informality. In addition, the identification of workers in each work status in all the chapters uses similar data and follows the same conceptual framework. In identifying each work status, lower-tier informal work is understood as comprising activities which have low returns/are poorly paid, are easily accessible (no/low barriers to entry), and may be considered undesirable relative to formal-sector employment. Upper-tier informal work is understood as comprising activities which have higher returns/are better paid, exhibit barriers to entry (e.g. skill or capital requirements), and may sometimes be preferred to formal employment.

2. Heterogeneity in work status groups

The early literature on modelling labour markets in developing countries characterized the dualism inherent in these labour markets through two sector models, where the two sectors could be agriculture/manufacturing or rural/urban, or traditional/urban (Lewis 1954; Harris and Todaro 1970). More recent literature has pointed out the multilayered nature of labour markets in developing countries, arguing that two-sector models do not seem to be consistent with the empirical realities of labour markets in developing countries (Fields 2005,

2019). In particular, there are two distinct characteristics of work status that need to be captured in an empirically grounded model of the labour market in developing countries. First, workers can either be in wage-employment or self-employment, which can exist as both formal and informal employment.[4] Second, informal employment is characterized by its own internal duality, where both wage-employed and self-employed workers can be in upper-tier or lower-tier informal employment (Fields 1990). This implies that any particular individual who is employed can be in one of six possible work status groups at a given point of time: (i) formal self-employed, (ii) formal wage-employed, (iii) upper-tier informal self-employed, (iv) upper-tier informal wage-employed, (v) lower-tier informal self-employed, and (vi) lower-tier informal wage-employed. In this section, we discuss alternate approaches to classifying workers in different work status groups and propose our preferred approach operationalizing the six work status groups for the four countries in our study.

We first need to make a distinction between informal and formal employment. Here, the seventeenth International Conference of Labour Statisticians at the ILO has provided a consistent definition of informal employment which has been widely adopted in the literature and which we follow in our study (see ILO 2018). According to this definition, informal employment is understood as work that lacks any type of legal recognition or protection and where workers do not have secure employment contracts, workers' benefits, social protection, or workers' representation. This implies that within self-employment, formal self-employed are those enterprises that are registered with national state authorities (e.g. with social security, sales, or income tax authorities), while informal self-employment are those enterprises that are unregistered. Within wage-employment, formal wage-employed are workers who have secure employment contracts, workers' benefits, social protection, or workers' representation and informal wage-employees are those who do not.

On the distinction between upper-tier and lower-tier informal work, two different approaches have been commonly discussed in the literature. The first approach is to take upper-tier informal employment as being 'voluntary' in nature, where workers choose to be in jobs that offer more independence and better earnings and working conditions as compared to working in the formal sector (the so-called 'exit' view of informal work, see Maloney 1999, 2004). In contrast, lower-tier informal work is 'involuntary' and employment of last resort, when individuals cannot find employment in formal or upper-tier informal work (the 'exclusion' view of informality, see Fields 2005, 2019).

[4] The informal self-employed include employers, own-account workers, and contributing family workers (Gindling and Newhouse 2014). Own-account workers are self-employed individuals who do not employ others. Contributing family workers are those workers who hold self-employment jobs as own-account workers in a market-orientated establishment operated by a related person living in the same household.

To operationalize this approach, it would be best to ascertain directly from labour force surveys whether a worker is voluntarily or involuntarily engaged in informal work. An example of such an approach is provided by Maloney (1999), where workers who moved to informal jobs from formal jobs in Mexico were asked in the survey whether the reason for the move was due to a desire for greater independence, or for higher pay, or was the move involuntary (also see Duval, Chapter 9 in this volume). Such direct questions to workers on their motives for changing jobs are extremely rare in standard labour force surveys in developing countries, especially in the sub-Saharan African context. The lack of such information in most other countries on worker motives for changing jobs in the data we have for the countries in our study (we describe our data in greater detail in section 3) does not allow us to use an approach that can infer upper-tier and lower-tier work status from workers' self-reported reasons.

A second approach for classifying workers in upper-tier or lower-tier informality is to use outcome-based performance measures—such as earnings, business profits, or enterprise productivity—as the sorting criteria (see, e.g. Grimm et al. 2012). As outcomes in the upper tier are by definition superior to those in the lower tier, and sometimes comparable to the outcomes of formal units, this is interpreted as evidence for the voluntariness of upper-tier informal employment.[5] However, this approach has two limitations. First, income or earnings would not capture other characteristics and benefits that may be associated with a job (such as the intrinsic value in terms of autonomy and independence that workers may attach to being self-employed in upper-tier informal work as compared to being a wage-employee in a formal firm) (Maloney 2004). Second, if a key objective of the analysis of worker transition is to understand whether transitions from lower-tier to upper-tier informal work are welfare enhancing, using an income or earnings measure as the sorting criteria does not allow us to separate out the factors that may explain movements in work status from its consequences in terms of income gains or losses.

A third approach takes upper-tier informal work as 'restricted-entry' employment and lower-tier informal work as 'free entry' (Fields 1990). In the former case, there are barriers to entry to the job, which could be a certain level of capital if the worker is self-employed or some necessary professional training required for the job if the worker is wage-employed. In the latter case, by definition, 'free-entry' employment does not require sizeable accumulation of financial capital or any need for prior training. The advantage of this approach is that the classification of

[5] Similarly, Günther and Launov (2012) fit a finite mixture model to household survey data from Côte d'Ivoire to test for unobserved earnings heterogeneity in the informal sector. They identify an upper-tier segment that is superior to the lower-tier one in terms of significantly higher average earnings as well as higher returns to education and experience. Their results also indicate that those in the upper tier tend to have a comparative advantage in the informal sector, while for those in the lower tier, informality is a strategy of last resort to escape unemployment.

informal work as upper tier or lower tier is undertaken based on the *observable characteristics of the job* rather than the latent unobserved preferences of workers, as in the first approach, and outcome measures of job hierarchies as in the second approach. However, a limitation of this approach is that classifying informal workers as upper tier or lower tier does not permit a judgement about exit versus exclusion.

Our preferred approach in this book is to follow the third approach to classify upper-tier and lower-tier informal employment. We next discuss how we propose to operationalize the classification of all informal jobs as upper-tier informal self-employment, lower-tier informal self-employment, upper-tier informal wage-employment, and lower-tier informal wage-employment in the book.

Upper-tier informal self-employed are classified as self-employed workers with unregistered business activities who either employ at least one person (who is not a household member) or are in activities that require some type of professional training (defined as International Standard Classification of Occupations (ISCO) groups 1–4, covering managers, professionals, technicians, and clerks), while other non-professional, own-account workers with unregistered business activities are classified as lower-tier informal (examples of which are street venders and waste pickers). The rationale for classifying informal employers as upper-tier informal self-employment is that the hiring of non-family workers for a household enterprise involves an implicit 'barrier to entry' as these employers typically need to finance the wages of hired workers by borrowing from credit markets or through the profits of the enterprise (Banerjee et al. 2016).[6] All contributing family workers are classified as lower-tier informal, irrespective of the nature of the enterprise.

Among the wage-employees not covered by social protection provisions (who are classified as informal workers, in line with the ILO definition), those in professions that require some type of professional training (ISCO 1–4) are classified as upper-tier informal as they are 'restricted entry'. In addition, we check whether workers report having a written employment agreement and/or are entitled to de facto benefits such as paid sick or maternity leave. The remainder are classified as lower-tier informal.

In Table 1.1, we provide an illustration of the schema that is applied to a specific country context—in this case, Costa Rica. Not all country studies in the book were able to include all of the work status groups that were there in the Costa Rica case, given data limitations, but to the extent possible each country study mapped their work status groups onto the upper-tier informal and lower-tier informal framework.

In Fig. 1.1, we provide a diagrammatic overview of how a typical classification schema looks like in several of our country case studies. We start with the working-age population, where an individual may be employed, unemployed, or

[6] In their study of informal enterprises in West Africa, Grimm et al. (2011) find significant entry barriers in the form of large sunk costs (such as the purchase of raw materials and building up inventories) in some segments of informal self-employment but not in others.

Table 1.1 Work status definition and operationalization: the case of Costa Rica

Work status group	Definition/operationalization
Formal self-employed	We identify formal self-employed workers as the self-employed (own-account or owners) who follow all regulations: specifically, those who both contribute to social security *and* are registered. Workers are identified as registered if they are registered in the National Records or other public institution or keep formal accounts for reporting to the government.
Upper-tier informal self-employed	This group is identified as those who comply with some but not all regulations. Specifically, self-employed (own-account and owners) who are registered *or* receive some type of social security health insurance (including the special regime, as a direct dependent of an insured employee, insured by the government, or have private insurance) but are not both registered and have social security. Even if they are neither registered nor pay social security, other self-employed workers are classified as upper-tier informal self-employed if they are in a profession that requires post-secondary or vocational education, if they are employers with at least one employee, or if their place of work has a fixed premises.
Lower-tier informal self-employed	These are self-employed who have neither any type of health insurance nor are registered, have no paid employees, and are not professional or technical workers. These include those whose place of work has no fixed premises (i.e. in the owner's dwelling, itinerant, on construction sites, or on agricultural plots).
Formal wage-employees	These are wage-employees whose employers contribute to social security or who are public-sector employees.
Upper-tier informal wage-employees	These are wage-employees whose employers do not contribute to social security *but* who have social security health insurance as a dependent of a directly insured, pay through the 'special regime' or *cuota voluntaria*, are insured by the state or private insurance, or if the employee receives other mandated benefits such as paid annual leave, paid sick leave, work risk insurance, or *aguinaldo* (mandated one-month salary bonus in December), or if income taxes are deducted from their salary, or if they are professional or technical employees.
Lower-tier informal wage-employees	These are all other employees; that is, lower-tier informal wage-employees have neither health insurance nor receive any other labour protection benefits.

Source: authors' construct.

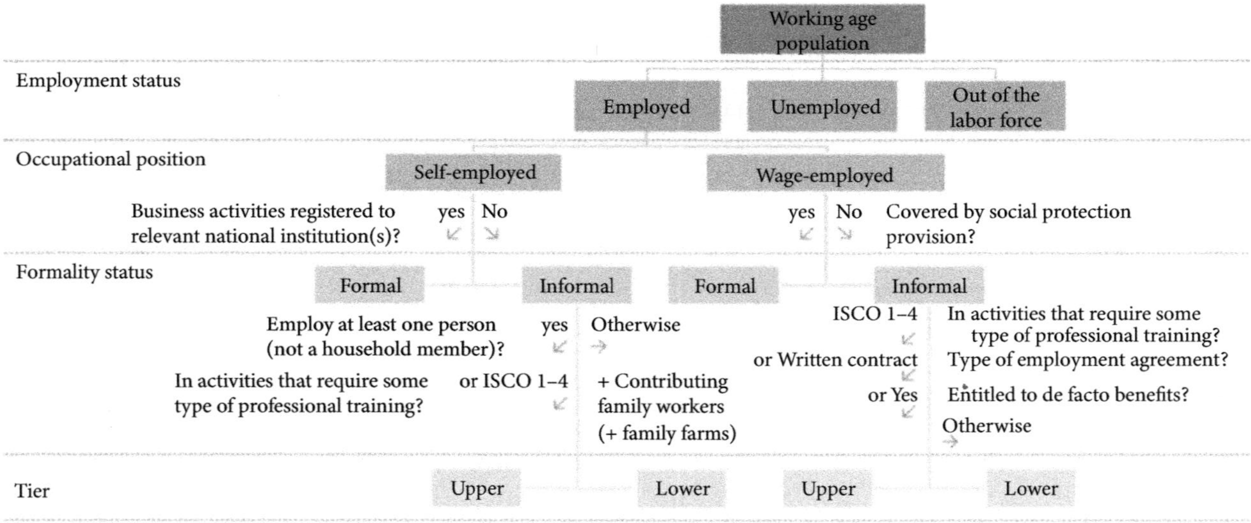

Fig. 1.1 Work status classification

Source: authors' construct.

out of the labour force. Among those employed, workers may be self-employed or wage-employed, depending on their occupational position. The self-employed and wage-employed can be in formal or informal work. Within informal employment, the characteristics of the job or activity allow us to classify workers in upper-tier or lower-tier work, as discussed earlier. Thus, any individual in employment will be uniquely assigned to one out of six possible work status groups discussed earlier in this section.

Workers can switch from one work status to another over time. The schema that we propose does not constrain the direction of movement and allows for a combination of movements across occupational positions, formality states, and tiers, thus allowing for a complex set of transition possibilities across all six work status groups. In the book, we will aim to quantify the magnitudes of these various transitions in the countries under study and to quantify the extent to which these transitions are associated with income gains or losses.

An important conceptual tool we use in this book is the job ladder, which tells us where workers are in different work status groups relative to each other with respect to mean real earnings (see Fields, Chapter 2 in this volume for an exposition). We provide an example of a job ladder in the case of Costa Rica (see Fig. 1.2).

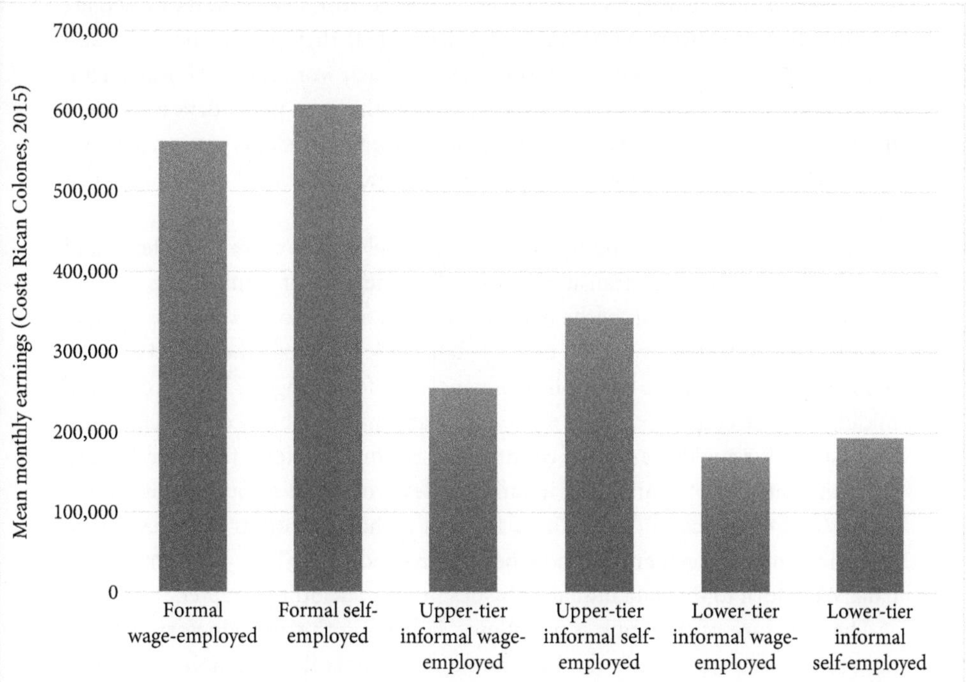

Fig. 1.2 The job ladder in the case of Costa Rica
Source: authors' construct; see Chapter 6.

3. The contribution and structure of the book

The intended intellectual contribution of the book is four-fold: first, to examine the distribution of workers in formal, upper-tier informal, and lower-tier informal wage-employees and self-employed in a wide range of developing economies using a common conceptual framework; second, to provide a comparative analysis of the patterns and correlates of worker mobility across lower-tier and upper-tier informal work and formal work status, and between self-employment and wage-employment; third, to understand the consequences of such movements for income gains and losses; and finally, to draw conclusions from the cases on what policies can be put in place to transform the livelihoods of workers in developing countries, especially those in informal work.

In choosing the country cases, we have sought to cover the different developing regions of the world and a mix of low-income and middle-income developing countries and regions. These cases include a range of middle-income developing countries in: (i) Central and Latin America: Argentina, Brazil, Costa Rica, Ecuador, Mexico, Nicaragua, Paraguay, and Peru; (ii) sub-Saharan Africa: Ghana, Mali, Niger, Nigeria, South Africa, and Tanzania; (iii) the Middle East and North Africa: Egypt, Jordan, and Tunisia; and (iv) Asia; China, India, and Indonesia.

Where data availability allows, each country study author has used the following structure: (i) they identify workers in each of the six work status, (ii) they calculate the distribution of workers in each work status, (iii) they present personal and family characteristics of workers associated with each work status, (iv) they construct a job ladder to rank each work status, (v) they use panel data to present transition matrices that measure movement between work status groups, and (vi) they present the personal and family characteristics correlated with transitions from lower-tier informal work up the job ladder.

As noted earlier, all the country studies use panel data to examine patterns and correlates of work status transitions (except in the case of Tunisia, see chapter Appendix). The time span of the panel data varies from two years to close to two decades (e.g. India has two waves of panel data while for Brazil, the period covered is 2002–2019). While the availability of panel data for a range of low-income and middle-income countries allows us to study patterns of mobility or persistence in work status for a wide variety of country and regional contexts for several countries, the data is not available at a sufficient level of detail to operationalize the work status classification as in Table 1.1, and authors of country studies had to make informed judgements on how best to proceed in the light of the imperfect data. We return to the data limitation issues in the concluding chapter.

The structure of the book is as follows. Following this introductory chapter, the second chapter reviews the literature and presents the common conceptual framework that the country studies use to examine heterogeneous informality. The conceptual chapter also presents the argument for why it is important for studies of informality to recognize this heterogeneity. These are followed by eleven country or multi-country case studies based on a common conceptual framework, common format, and analysis of panel data to the extent possible. The concluding chapter summarizes the main findings of the country studies and gleans insights from the comparative approach used in the book. It also provides options for policy, drawing from the findings of the country studies.

References

Banerjee, S., R. S. N. Raj, and K. Sen (2016). 'Monitoring Costs'. *Credit Constraints and Entrepreneurship, Manchester School*, 84(5): 573–599.

Chen, M. A. (2012). 'The Informal Economy: Definitions, Theories and Policies'. Women in Informal Employment: Globalizing and Organizing (WIEGO) Working Paper 1. Cambridge, MA: WIEGO.

De Vreyer, P., and F. Roubaud (eds) (2013). *Urban Labor Markets in sub-Saharan Africa*. Washington, DC: World Bank.

Fields, G. S. (1990). 'Labour Market Modelling and the Urban Informal Sector: Theory and Evidence' (electronic version). In D. Turnham, B. Salomé, and A. Schwarz (eds), *The Informal Sector Revisited*. Paris: Organisation for Economic Co-operation and Development (OECD). Available at: https://ecommons.cornell.edu/handle/1813/75798 (accessed 30 September 2022).

Fields, G. S. (2005). 'A Guide to Multisector Labor Market Models'. Social Protection Discussion Paper Series 0505. Washington, DC: World Bank.

Fields, G. S. (2019). *Employment and Development: How Work Can Lead from and into Poverty*. Oxford: Oxford University Press.

Gindling, T. H., and Newhouse, D. (2014). 'Self-Employment in the Developing World'. *World Development*, 56, 313–331.

Grimm, M., J. Krüger, and J. Lay (2011). 'Barriers to Entry and Returns to Capital in Informal Activities: Evidence from West Africa'. *Review of Income and Wealth*, 57: S27–1352–1368.

Grimm, M., P. Knorringa, and J. Lay (2012). 'Constrained Gazelles: High Potentials in West Africa's Informal Economy'. *World Development*, 40(7): 1352–1368.

Günther, I., and A. Launov (2012). 'Informal Employment in Developing Countries: Opportunity or Last Resort?' *Journal of Development Economics*, 97(1): 88–98.

Harris, J. R., and M. P. Todaro (1970). 'Migration, Unemployment and Development: A Two-Sector Analysis'. *American Economic Review*, 60(1): 126–142.

ILO (International Labour Organization) (2018). *Women and Men in the Informal Economy: A Statistical Picture* (3rd edn). Geneva: International Labour Office.

ILO (2019). 'ILO Thesaurus: Informal Employment'. Available at: https://www.ilo.org/inform/online-information-resources/terminology/thesaurus/lang--en/index.htm (accessed 30 September 2022).

Kanbur, R. (2017). 'Informality: Causes, Consequences and Policy Responses'. *Review of Development Economics*, 21(4): 939–961.

La Porta, R., and A. Shleifer (2014). 'Informality and Development'. *Journal of Economic Perspectives*, 28(3): 109–126.

Lewis, W. Arthur (1954). 'Economic Development with Unlimited Supplies of Labour'. *Credit Constraings and Entrepreneurship, Manchester School*, 22: 139–191.

Maloney, W. F. (1999). 'Does Informality Imply Segmentation in Urban Labor Markets? Evidence from Sectoral Transitions in Mexico'. *World Bank Economic Review*, 13: 275–302.
Maloney, W. F. (2004). 'Informality Revisited'. *World Development*, 32(7): 1159–1178.
Perry, G., W. Maloney, O. Arias, P. Fajnzylber, A. Mason, and J. Saavedra-Chanduvi (2007). *Informality: Exit and Exclusion*. Washington, DC: World Bank.
Rodrik, D. (2016). 'Premature Deindustrialization'. *Journal of Economic Growth*, 21(1): 1–33.
Thorbecke, E., (1973). 'The Employment Problem: A Critical Evaluation of Four ILO Comprehensive Country Reports'. *International Labor Review*, 107(5): 393–423.

Appendix
Years of coverage in panel data, individual chapters

Chapter number	Country	Region	Years	Panel
3	China	Asia	2014, 2016, 2018	Yes
4	India	Asia	2004/5, 2011/2	Yes
5	Indonesia	Asia	2000, 2007, 2014	Yes
6	Costa Rica	LAC	2011–2018	Yes
	Nicaragua	LAC	2009–2017	Yes
7	Argentina	LAC	2003–2019	Rotating
	Brazil	LAC	2002–2019	Rotating
	Ecuador	LAC	2003–2019	Rotating
	Mexico	LAC	2005–2019	Rotating
	Paraguay	LAC	2010–2017	Rotating
	Peru	LAC	2003–2019	Rotating
8	Nicaragua	LAC	2009–2012	Yes
	El Salvador	LAC	2008–2012	Rotating
9	Mexico	LAC	2015, 2016	Yes
10	Mali	SSA	2014, 2017	No
	Niger	SSA	2011, 2014	Yes
11	Nigeria	SSA	2010/11, 2012/13, 2015/16	Yes
12	Ghana	SSA	2009/10, 2013/14	Yes
	South Africa	SSA	2014/15, 2017	Yes
	Tanzania	SSA	2010/11, 2012/13	Yes
	Uganda	SSA	2010/11, 2011/12	Yes
13	Egypt	MENA	1998, 2006, 2012, 2018	Yes
	Jordan	MENA	2010, 2016	Yes
	Tunisia	MENA	2014	No

2

Informality and work status

Gary S. Fields

1. Informality and work status: what do we mean?

1.1 Informality and its components

For the purposes of this chapter, 'informality' is conceptualized as a general notion.[1] It can be thought of as a job-based concept or an enterprise-based concept (ILO 2019). Informality in this chapter is a catch-all term referring to the informal economy, informal sector, informal employment, and formality/informality status.

I am not alone in bemoaning the lack of terminological precision. Guha-Khasnobis et al. (2006: 2–3) write:

> Given the prominence of the formal–informal dichotomy in the development discourse, one might expect to see a clear definition of the concepts, consistently applied across the whole range of theoretical, empirical, and policy analyses. We find no such thing. Instead, it turns out that formal and informal are better thought of as metaphors that conjure up a mental picture of whatever the user has in mind at that particular time.

Still, we can clarify a number of ideas.

The definition of *informal economy* by Women in Informal Employment: Globalizing and Organizing (WIEGO), the International Conference of Labor Statisticians (ICLS), and the International Labor Organization (ILO) is 'the diversified set of economic activities, enterprises, jobs, and workers that are not regulated or protected by the state' (WIEGO 2020).

A second concept is the *informal sector*. The informal sector is defined as 'units or enterprises that are not registered in the statistical or tax institutions and do not keep written accounts' (Herrera et al. 2012).

[1] A presentation on an earlier version of this chapter was made at the UNU-WIDER workshop 'Transforming Informal Work and Livelihoods', on 23 October 2020 in Helsinki., Finland. I gratefully acknowledge invaluable comments and discussions with Tim Gindling, Kunal Sen, and Robert Duval-Hernández on earlier drafts.

Gary S. Fields, *Informality and work status*. In: *The Job Ladder*. Edited by Gary S. Fields, T. H. Gindling, Kunal Sen, Michael Danquah, and Simone Schotte, Oxford University Press. © UNU-WIDER (2023).
DOI: 10.1093/oso/9780192867339.003.0002

Because the *Transforming Informal Work and Livelihoods Project* of the United Nations University World Institute for Development Economics Research (UNU-WIDER) has adopted a job-based concept of informality rather than an enterprise-based one, the term 'informal sector' will be used only in passing in this chapter.

A third concept is *informal employment*. Informal employment is of two kinds (ILO 2018):

(1) self-employment in informal enterprises (small unregistered or unincorporated enterprises) including: employers, own-account operators, and unpaid family workers in informal enterprises; and
(2) paid employment (or what, in this chapter, is called wage-employment) in informal jobs (for informal enterprises, formal enterprises, households, or no fixed employer) including: casual or day labourers, industrial outworkers, unregistered or undeclared workers, contract workers, and unprotected temporary and part-time workers.

Accordingly, the UNU-WIDER project formulates informal employment as a job-based concept consisting of 'all remunerative work (i.e. both self-employment and wage-employment), that is not registered, regulated or protected by existing legal or regulatory frameworks, as well as non-remunerative work undertaken in an income-producing enterprise' (ILO 2019).

To illustrate the importance of choosing the precise notion of informality, take the case of India. There, the terms 'organized sector' and 'unorganized sector' are used in place of the more common 'formal sector' and 'informal sector', respectively. Data show that half the people working in formal-sector entities in India (including firms, government office, etc.) are themselves employed informally in the sense of not being registered with the government or receiving the protections that others in the same workplaces receive (NCEUS 2009).

The UNU-WIDER project is concerned with informal employment. Although many of the informally employed are in the informal sector, many others are in the formal sector. Conversely, many but not all of the formally employed are in the formal sector; some are formally employed in the informal sector. Since our concern is with people working informally, we should focus on informal employment, recognizing that not all of it is in the informal sector.

Data from ILO (2018) and WIEGO (see Bonnet et al. 2019) show that 2 billion of the world's employed population aged 15 years and above work informally. This represents 61.2 per cent of global employment. Regions with above-average rates of informal employment are Africa (85.8 per cent), Asia and the Pacific (68.2 per cent), and the Arab states (68.6 per cent).

1.2 Work status

The UNU-WIDER project uses the term 'work status' to denote the kind of employment in which a worker is engaged. This project adopts a multifaceted categorization scheme, not just a single classifying variable. Four variables—employment status, occupational position, formality status, and upper/lower tier—are used to determine work status. Each is defined in section 2.

As examples, the studies by Danquah et al. (2019) on four African countries and by Alaniz et al. (2020) on Costa Rica and Nicaragua adopt the schema shown in Fig. 2.1.

Using these variables, the result is a six-category work status variable:

- formally self-employed;
- formally wage-employed;
- upper-tier informally self-employed;
- lower-tier informally self-employed;
- upper-tier informally wage-employed;
- lower-tier informally wage-employed.

The remainder of this chapter discusses how these work status groups might be used fruitfully.

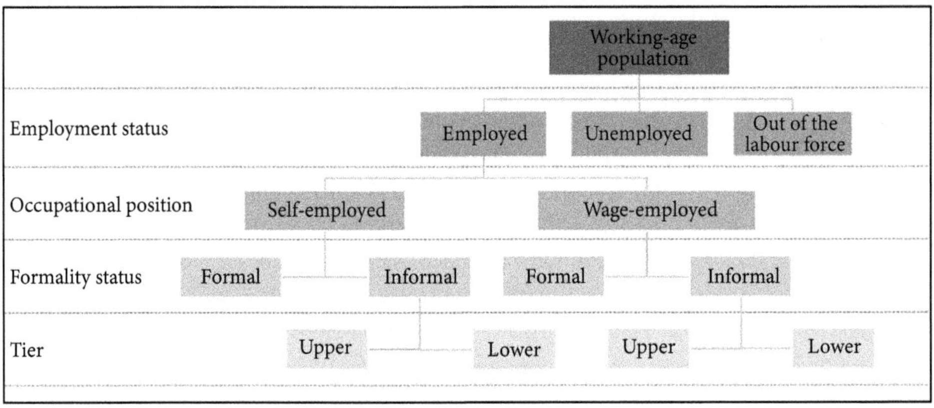

Fig. 2.1 A six-way work status classification

Source: reproduced from Raj et al. (2020: 4), under Creative Commons licence CC BY-NC-SA 3.0 IGO.

2. Differentiating between the work status groups

2.1 The limitations of employment versus unemployment

The usual starting points for assessing an individual's labour market status are whether or not that individual is in the labour force and whether or not that individual is employed. Individuals are defined as being in the labour force if they are working or looking for work. Individuals who are neither working nor looking for work are defined as being out of the labour force. This project focuses on individuals who are in the labour force.

For the labour market as a whole, the first measure reported by statistical offices and used by many analysts to indicate the goodness or badness of labour market conditions is the *unemployment rate*. The unemployment rate is the number unemployed taken as a percentage of the labour force (note that this is *not* the working-age population). At the time of writing, the unemployment rate tells a terrible story: in recent months, countries throughout the world have experienced unemployment rates not seen since the Great Depression of the early twentieth century, from which they are only slowly recovering.

The unemployment rate, as important as it is, is not the whole story. The reason becomes clear once one understands the definition of 'employment'. By ILO guidance and standard international statistical conventions, individuals are counted as employed if they worked one hour or more for pay or fifteen hours or more not for pay in the reference week covered by the survey. Thus, only some of those employed are fully and gainfully employed; others work less than full time, work fewer hours than they want to work, and/or earn so little per hour that, despite working a standard work week or more, they do not earn enough to be able to achieve an adequate standard of living. Thus, countries around the world, including the developing countries, face an *employment problem* consisting of unemployment plus inadequate quality of employment as gauged by the preceding indicators. The ILO reckons that the number of working poor in the world is far greater than the number of unemployed: 700 million working poor in 2018 compared with 173 million unemployed (ILO 2019).

A finer categorization of work status groups other than employed versus unemployed provides the kind of fine-grained picture needed to analyse the employment problem that countries throughout the world now face. This categorization is developed in section 3.

2.2 Key distinctions among work status groups

As already noted, the UNU-WIDER project defines work status categories according to employment status, occupational position, formality status, and tier. They are distinguished as follows.

Employment status and occupational position

The project classifies workers according to occupational position, separating the wage-employed from the self-employed. It is important to do this because (i) wage-employees experience an employer–employee relationship, which the self-employed do not and (ii) policy interventions that might be suited for one of these groups are inapplicable to others. For example, maximum hours and minimum wage legislation can perhaps be enacted for wage-employees but they cannot be applied to the self-employed. If I am self-employed, how can the government order me to pay myself a specified minimum amount?

Formality status

Formality status—whether formally or informally employed—matters most importantly for understanding which work status groups have more social protections than others. In the past, definitions and measurements varied widely across countries (Charmes 2009). More recently, though, attempts at standardization have been made (ILO 2019: 10–12). Still, most country studies operationalize the informality variable using what is available in the country's household surveys. Examples in the literature are whether the worker has a work card in Brazil, whether the worker is registered with the social security system in Mexico, and whether the job provides for pension benefits in Argentina. Following this lead, the country studies in this project use country-specific definitions.

It should be noted that formality status and occupational position are two different things. Formal does not equal wage-employed, nor does informal equal self-employed, as has been assumed in some previous research (e.g. Kucera and Roncolato 2008). Those of us who write about these things need to be careful to clarify which of them we are talking about.

Upper-tier informality versus lower-tier informality

A third key distinction is the division within informality between upper-tier and lower-tier informal employment. Early work in the 1970s and 1980s conceived of informal work as essentially a free-entry option at the bottom end of the employment distribution; examples are the four ILO country reports evaluated by Thorbecke (1973), the books by Turnham (1971) and Squire (1981), and the theoretical model by Fields (1975). Later research, however, distinguished a second category of informal employment: informal work that required human capital and/or financial capital and could not be entered freely (Fields 1990, an excerpt of which was also published in Fields 2019b), which advocated for the essential duality of informal employment along free-entry/restricted-entry lines.[2]

2.3 Underlying labour market models

Today, the bare minimum of four categories are necessary for understanding developing country labour markets. For example, a recent theoretical model has three employment states—wage-employment, free-entry self-employment, and high-wage self-employment—plus an unemployment category (Basu et al. 2019). Having two types of informal work (or, alternatively, two types of self-employment) is essential to capture the reality that some workers are engaged in informal employment not because they *have* to be but because they *want* to be.

The most important reason for drawing the distinction between upper- and lower-tier work is where they lie along a job ladder. The job ladder may be based on such factors as labour market earnings, non-wage benefits, workplace protections and regulations, or some combination of these. Regardless of which components one chooses to focus on, lower-tier work can be thought of as being *below* formal wage-employment on the job ladder, while upper-tier informal work may be *above* formal wage-employment for some (though not all) workers, for example, those with a particular skill or taste for entrepreneurship or self-employment.

At the very bottom of a typical job ladder in a developing country is unemployment, that is, not working at all. Many of those who work informally—the majority, I think—do so because, in the countries in which they live, unemployment insurance is limited or non-existent and, consequently, being unemployed means having no income. These workers have no choice but to take whatever they can. But there are some—primarily, the well-educated and young people in well-to-do families—who can afford to remain unemployed for longer periods of time while searching for good jobs. This was long ago termed the 'luxury unemployment hypothesis' (Turnham 1971) and has been re-established over the years (e.g. Udall and Sinclair 1982; Ghose 2003).

Lower-tier informal workers have been given a variety of names, including penniless entrepreneurs (Banerjee and Duflo 2007), reluctant entrepreneurs (Banerjee and Duflo 2011), entrepreneurs out of necessity (Poschke 2013), engaged in informality as a survival strategy (LaPorta and Shleifer 2014), and a strategy of last resort (Günther and Launov 2011).

[2] For a more recent review along similar lines, see Kanbur (2017).

The literature offers two competing views of why people are working informally. The free-choice view is that all workers can choose whether or not to work formally, and the division of workers between formal and informal employment reflects these choices. Reasons for choosing one versus another include comparative advantage, heterogeneous preferences for independent work, and the wish by some to avoid payroll taxes and other expensive regulations. The segmented labour market view is that the number of jobs in wage-employment is limited relative to the size of the labour force, and so even if all wage-employment jobs were to be filled, much of the labour force would be rationed out of such jobs. Maloney (1999, 2004) and Levy (2008, 2018) emphasize the first view, while Basu (1997) and Fields (2009, 2019c) emphasize the second.

Empirical studies support a mix of reasons, with the weight being about in the middle. Banerjee and Duflo (2011) studied poor workers in 18 developing countries and found that half of the extremely poor in urban areas operate a non-agricultural business. Their interpretation is this: 'Perhaps the many businesses of the poor are less a testimony to their entrepreneurial spirit than a symptom of the dramatic failure of the economies in which they live to provide them with something better' (Banerjee and Duflo 2011: 226). Another study concludes that two-thirds of self-employment in the developing world as a whole results from individuals having no better alternatives (Margolis 2014). Another finds an approximately equal split in non-Organisation for Economic Co-operation and Development (OECD) countries (Poschke 2013). Yet another study finds that about half of those working informally in the case of Côte d'Ivoire are doing so by choice and the other half not (Günther and Launov 2011). A World Bank study of Latin America concludes that the majority of independent workers are informal largely voluntarily, whereas the majority of informal salaried workers appear to be involuntary (Perry et al. 2007).[3]

2.4 Classifying workers into work status groups

The authors of the country studies for the UNU-WIDER project were given discretion on how to make use of the preceding variables to devise their own work status categories. Figure 2.2 is a flow chart displaying how Danquah et al. (2019) used occupational position, formality status, and tier to assign individuals to work status groups.

Now, let us turn to some of the lessons learned by analysing work status groups.

[3] See also the empirical studies reviewed in Basu et al. (2019).

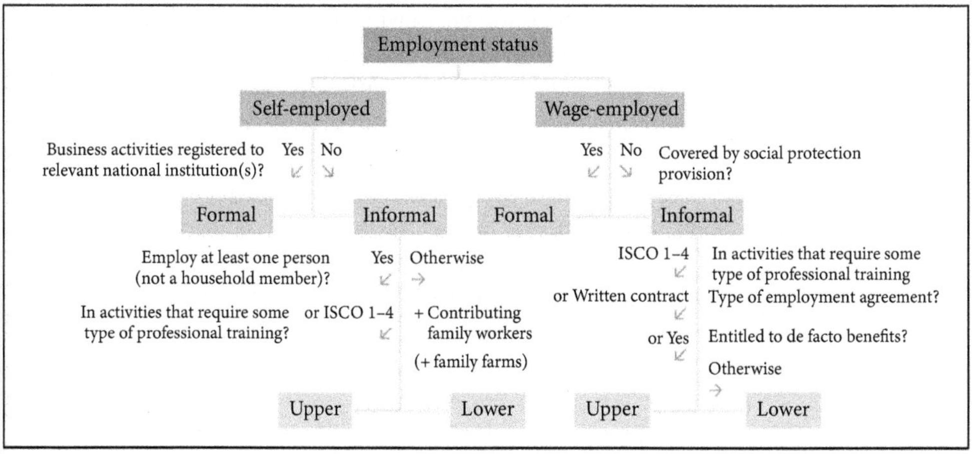

Fig. 2.2 Rules for assigning workers in Ghana, South Africa, Tanzania, and Uganda to work status groups

Source: reproduced from Danquah et al. (2019: 7), under Creative Commons licence CC BY-NC-SA 3.0 IGO.

3. Analysis of work status groups

3.1 Learning from a single cross section

In a typical labour market study, we know the percentage of workers in each work status. Knowledge of these so-called state probabilities provides an essential snapshot of the kinds of work people are doing at a point in time. We learn, for example, that most workers in developing countries are self-employed rather than wage-employed, that the percentage working in agriculture is much higher than the percentage working in services or manufacturing, and that the percentage working informally is much higher than the percentage working formally (Fields 2012, 2019c; ILO 2018). Note, though, that these patterns differ by region of the world, which links closely to per capita gross domestic product (GDP); differences between (i) East Asia, (ii) Latin America, and (iii) sub-Saharan Africa and South Asia can be understood accordingly (Gindling and Newhouse 2014; Merotto et al. 2018).

Of course, some job categories are better on average than others across a variety of measures, including earnings, social protection, and stability of employment. A single cross section for a given country can tell us which categories are the better ones. Note that different measures may give different rankings: for example, individuals working in the public sector may have greater job security but lower pay than they might have in the private sector. Revealed preference suggests that such rankings vary across individuals within the same country.

Taking Costa Rica as a case study and focusing on labour market earnings, let us look at six aggregate groups:

- formally employed, regardless of occupational position and tier;
- informally employed, regardless of occupational position and tier;
- wage-employed, regardless of formality status and tier;
- self-employed, regardless of formality status and tier;
- upper-tier informal workers, regardless of occupational position;
- lower-tier informal workers, regardless of occupational position.

Comparing these aggregates, we see the following in Fig. 2.3:

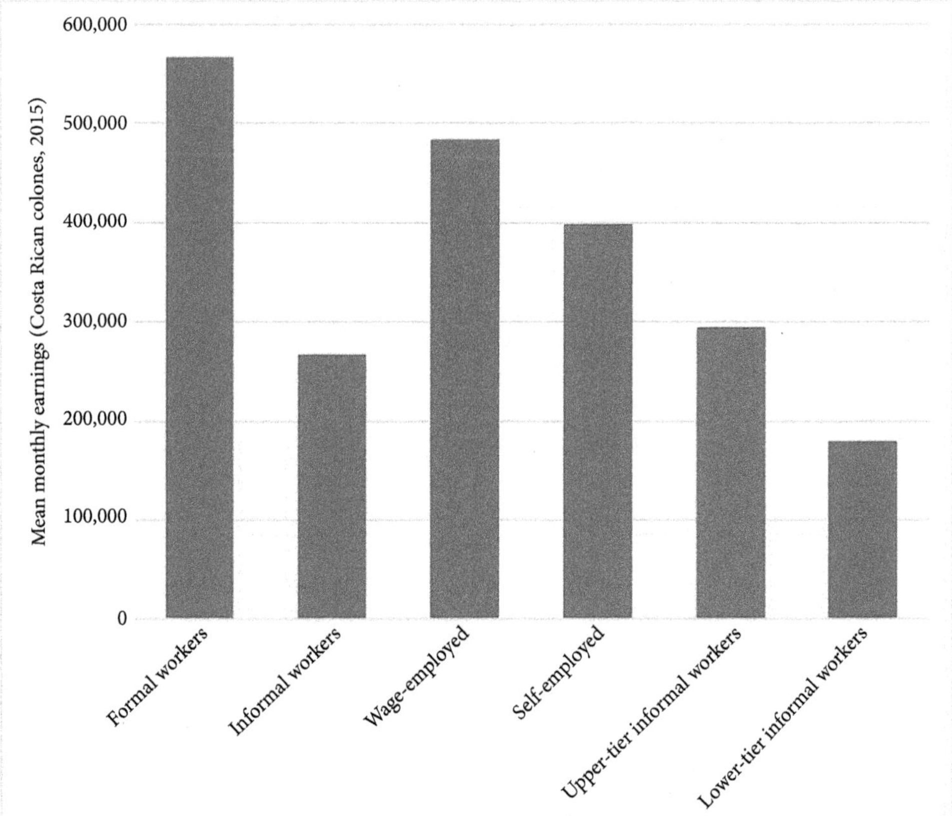

Fig. 2.3 Mean earnings across six aggregates, Costa Rica
Source: tabulation provided by Tim H. Gindling, reproduced here with permission.

- formally employed workers earn more than informally employed workers;
- wage-employed workers earn more on average than the self-employed;
- upper-tier informal workers earn more than lower-tier informal workers.

Then, using a six-way work status scheme similar to the previous one for Africa but different in some specifics, the Costa Rica study (Alaniz et al. 2020) reveals that the highest-earning category is the formally self-employed and the lowest-earning category is the lower-tier informally wage-employed (see Fig. 2.4).

This fine-grained pattern would not have been found if only the aggregates in Fig. 2.3 had been used instead.

In addition to examining which of the six work status groups pay more on average than others, we can also explore other questions at a point in time. How many

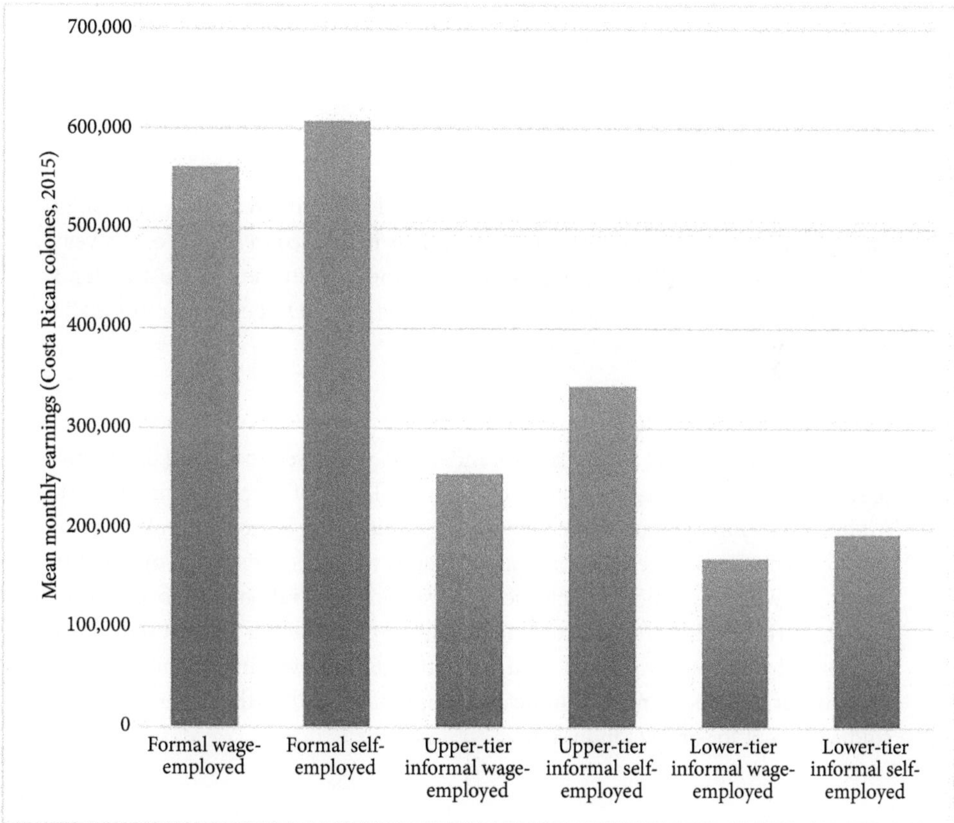

Fig. 2.4 Mean earnings across six work status groups, Costa Rica

Source: reproduced from Alaniz et al. (2020), under Creative Commons licence CC BY-NC-SA 3.0 IGO.

workers are found in each of the six work status groups? Which personal characteristics are associated with employment in the different work status groups? Apart from cash earnings, how do the different work status groups compare in terms of non-wage benefits? Other studies have been completed and are published here in this volume.

3.2 Analysing comparable cross sections

Moving from single cross sections to comparable cross sections, we can learn how the cross-sectional picture is changing over time. The results of a previous study (Cruces et al. 2017) are revealing, which includes research conducted for each of the 16 Latin America countries (Argentina, Bolivia, Brazil, Chile, Colombia, Costa Rica, Dominican Republic, Ecuador, Honduras, Mexico, Panama, Paraguay, Peru, El Salvador, Uruguay, and Venezuela) along with cross-country analysis. Remarkable progress was found in all three aspects of the growth–employment–poverty nexus across the Latin American region.

Growth

All 16 countries achieved positive rates of annual growth of real GDP per capita during the 2000s, ranging from 1 per cent a year in Mexico to 5.6 per cent a year in Panama and Peru. The regional average for the 16 countries was just under 3 per cent, well above the annualized rate of growth of GDP per capita in OECD countries, which was 1.0 per cent a year.

Labour market indicators

A number of traditional labour market indicators were used including the unemployment rate, mean earnings, the occupational mix of employment, the distribution of employment by occupational position, the sectoral breakdown of employment, workers' educational attainments, and the percentage of workers registered with the national social security system. The rate of improvement in labour market indicators was exceptional. All 16 of the labour market indicators improved in Bolivia, Brazil and Peru, 15 of the 16 improved in Panama, and the majority of the labour market indicators improved in all of the other countries studied except for one (Honduras).

Poverty rates

Using the 4 and 2.5 dollars-a-day poverty lines ('poverty' and 'extreme poverty'), reduced rates of poverty and extreme poverty were found in 15 of the 16 countries. On average, extreme poverty fell by 45 per cent while poverty declined by 37 per cent. Only one Latin American country registered an increase in its rate of poverty.

In short, the 2000s have been a time of strong improvement in the growth–employment–poverty nexus in the great majority of Latin American countries. It is precisely evidence like this that leads to the conclusion that economic growth of the right type is indispensable to improving labour market conditions and thereby reducing poverty.

As the reader will have noticed, these results are for the traditional labour market aggregates. It would be interesting to see what else can be learned by examining changes in employment and earnings for the six work status groups analysed in this project, not for Latin America alone but for other regions as well.

3.3 Examining transitions and changes using panel data

Panel data analysis gives us a basis for making statements about labour market transitions that are not warranted when using comparable cross sections. Suppose we were to find in comparable cross sections that the number of people in wage-employment in a country increased from 100,000 to 150,000. We *can* say that 50,000 more people were working in wage-employment in the later year than before. However, we *cannot* and *should not* say that 50,000 of the self-employed found wage-employment. The first is a statement about comparable cross sections, the second a statement about panel data changes. It may have been, for example, that over time 70,000 of the self-employed moved into wage-employment and 20,000 of the wage-employed moved into self-employment, producing a net increase in wage-employment of 50,000. To be able to make statements about gross flows (i.e. 70,000 moves from self-employment to wage-employment, 20,000 moves from wage-employment to self-employment), we must have panel data.

Such panel changes must be evaluated carefully. Personally, I have no hesitation in judging that the larger the number of positions in the upper rungs of the job ladder (in the previous example, the increase in wage-employment from 100,000 to 150,000), the better. However, I would not take a position on which is better: 50,000 moving up and no one moving down versus 70,000 moving up and 20,000 moving down; I see arguments on both sides.[4]

Disaggregation by work status can reveal a granularity that would otherwise have been missed. Recall that the World Bank study of Latin America concluded that the majority of independent workers (what in this chapter we are calling the self-employed) are working informally largely voluntarily, whereas the majority of informal salaried workers (in this chapter's terminology, informally wage-employed) appear to be working informally largely involuntarily (see Perry et al. 2007).

[4] For more on upward and downward movement and other mobility concepts, see Fields (2019a) as part of UNU-WIDER's forthcoming social mobility project (see Iversen et al. 2021).

When we are able to make use of panel data, as many of the country studies in this book do, we can quantify transitions and non-transitions between work status groups in general and the six-way work status variables in particular. Doing this is important for its own sake in understanding the extent of fixity or mobility between these categories, hence the subtitle of the Africa study by Danquah et al. (2019) 'Dead End or Steppingstone?'. Very recent papers by Danquah et al. (2019) and Raj et al. (2020) study transitions between the six work status groups. The lessons from the country studies are summarized in chapter 14 of this volume.

Another reason to analyse transitions between work status groups is to help explain the observed panel data changes in labour earnings and other economic magnitudes. These changes enable us to perform what I regard as the most important kind of mobility analysis: the study of directional income movements. (Directional income movements are the increases or decreases in dollars, log dollars, or some other measure of economic well-being.) From past research, we know that *change* in work status is an important determinant—and often the most important determinant—of the *change* in economic well-being of workers and their family.[5]

Knowing the magnitudes of transitions and non-transitions can provide insights into policy questions, to which we now turn.

3.4 Thinking about policy questions

> For every problem, there is a solution that is simple, neat—and wrong.
> —Variously attributed to Mark Twain, H.L. Mencken, Peter Drucker, and others

Much of our work is policy-relevant, including the chapters in this book. However, we need to be careful: few if any 'policy implications' are going to jump out at us.

First, if we ruminate about the preceding quotation, what is the problem we are trying to solve? Is it informality? Unemployment? Low labour market earnings? Poverty? Something else? I will assert that the overarching problem in the developing world is poverty and that informality is of interest because the informally employed are the lowest earners and, therefore, the most likely to be poor.

The data described in the preceding subsections—on single cross sections, comparable cross sections, and panel data analysis—are indispensable in thinking about policy. It would surely be helpful to know the distributions of employment by work status, marginal percentages, earnings ladders, work status transition

[5] For example, see Fields et al. (2003) for a study of Indonesia, South Africa, Spain, and Venezuela.

Fig. 2.5 Informal Workers in Mexico, India, and South Africa
Source: reproduced from Fields (2012).

matrices, earnings change data, tabulations and regressions involving personal characteristics, and much more.

I would also suggest an additional approach to data collection: asking working people. Consider the workers pictured in Fig. 2.5 (from Fields 2012):

We can ask them questions like these:

- Have you registered your backyard auto-mechanic shop with the government so that you can receive social security benefits? Why or why not?
- How much do you earn as a bicycle rickshaw driver? What could be done to enable you to earn more in this kind of work?
- Why are you earning your livelihood making and selling Zulu shields? Could you have been working in wage-employment instead?
- Are you able to move out of this work? Why or why not?

Now, let's think about policy choices. Here are two different policy syllogisms.

First:

- We want to help the poor.
- The poor work mainly on family farms and in family businesses.
- Therefore, we should invest our development resources in improving incomes where the poor are, on family farms and in family businesses.

And second:

- We want to help the poor.
- The poor will remain poor as long as they remain in poor work status groups.

- Family farms and family businesses pay poorly relative to wage-employment, particularly when the wage-employment is in enterprises registered with the government.
- Therefore, we should invest our development resources in creating new wage-employment in registered enterprises so that the poor can move to the parts of the economy where earnings and social protections are higher.

> These two arguments lead to precisely *opposite* conclusions. According to the first, the available resources should be used on family farms and family businesses. According to the second, the available resources should be used to create new wage employment in registered enterprises so that the poor can get *out* of family farms and family businesses.
>
> (Fields 2012: 92)

What should be done with the available resources? Use them for just the first? Just the second? Split them between the first and the second? Do something entirely different, like formalizing the informal or investing in education and skills development?

The simple answer is that *none* of these is *necessarily* the right policy choice. Policy recommendations need to be founded on a sounder basis such as social cost–benefit analysis or general equilibrium analysis. We owe it to people like those pictured to try.

References

Alaniz, E., T. H. Gindling, C. Mata, and D. Rojas (2020). 'Transforming Informal Work and Livelihoods in Costa Rica and Nicaragua'. WIDER Working Paper 2020/100. Helsinki: UNU-WIDER. https://doi.org/10.35188/UNU-WIDER/2020/857-3.

Banerjee, A. V., and E. Duflo (2007). 'The Economic Lives of the Poor'. *Journal of Economic Perspectives*, 21(1): 141–168. https://doi.org/10.1257/jep.21.1.141.

Banerjee, A. V., and E. Duflo (2011). *Poor Economics*. New York: PublicAffairs Press.

Basu, K. (1997). *Analytical Development Economics*. Cambridge, MA: MIT Press.

Basu, A., N. Chau, G. S. Fields, and R. Kanbur (2019). 'Job Creation in a Multi-Sector Labor Market Model for Developing Economies'. *Oxford Economic Papers*, 71(1): 119–144. https://doi.org/10.1093/oep/gpy029

Bonnet, F., J. Vanek, and M. Chen (2019). *Women and Men in the Informal Economy: A Statistical Brief*. Manchester: WIEGO.

Charmes, J. (2009). 'Concepts, Measurement, and Trends'. In J.P. Jutting and J.R. de Laiglesia (eds), *Is Informal Normal? Towards More and Better Jobs in Developing Countries*. Paris: OECD, pp. 27–62. https://doi.org/10.1787/9789264059245-4-en.

Cruces, G., G. S. Fields, D. Jaume, and M. Viollaz (2017). *Growth, Employment, and Poverty: Latin America in the 2000s*. Oxford: Oxford University Press. https://doi.org/10.1093/oso/9780198801085.001.0001.

Danquah, M., S. Schotte, and K. Sen (2019). 'Informal Work in Sub-Saharan Africa: Dead End or Steppingstone?'. WIDER Working Paper 2019/107. Helsinki: UNU-WIDER. https://doi.org/10.35188/UNU-WIDER/2019/743-9.

Fields, G. S. (1975). 'Rural–Urban Migration, Urban Unemployment and Underemployment, and Job Search Activity in LDCs'. *Journal of Development Economics*, 2(2): 165–187. https://doi.org/10.1016/0304-3878(75)90014-0.

Fields, G. S. (1990). 'Labour Market Modelling and the Urban Informal Sector: Theory and Evidence'. In D. Turnham, B. Salomé, and A. Schwarz (eds), *The Informal Sector Revisited*. Paris: Organisation for Economic Co-operation and Development (OECD), pp. 49–69 and 210–223.

Fields, G. S. (2009). 'Segmented Labor Market Models in Developing Countries'. In H. Kincaid and D. Ross (eds), *The Oxford Handbook of the Philosophy of Economic Science*. Oxford: Oxford University Press, pp. 476–509. Earlier version published as Fields, G.S. (2005). 'A Guide to Multisector Labor Market Models'. Social Protection Discussion Paper Series 0505. Washington, DC: World Bank.

Fields, G. S. (2012). *Working Hard, Working Poor: A Global Journey*. New York: Oxford University Press. https://doi.org/10.1093/acprof:oso/9780199794645.001.0001.

Fields, G. S. (2019a). 'Concepts of Social Mobility', WIDER Working Paper 2019/106. Helsinki: UNU-WIDER. https://doi.org/10.35188/UNU-WIDER/2019/742-2.

Fields, G. S. (2019b). *Employment and Development*. Oxford: Oxford University Press.

Fields, G. S. (2019c). 'Self-Employment and Poverty in Developing Countries'. *IZA World of Labor*, 1–10. rev. version. https://doi.org/10.15185/izawol.60.v2.

Fields, G. S., P. Cichello, S. Freije, M. Menéndez, and D. Newhouse (2003). 'Household Income Dynamics: A Four-Country Story'. *Journal of Development Studies*, 40(2): 30–54. https://doi.org/10.1080/00220380412331293757.

Ghose, A. K. (2003). *Jobs and Incomes in a Globalizing World*. Geneva: International Labour Organization (ILO).

Gindling, T. H., and D. Newhouse (2014). 'Self-Employment in the Developing World'. *World Development*, 56: 313–331. https://doi.org/10.1016/j.worlddev.2013.03.003.

Guha-Khasnobis, B., R. Kanbur, and E. Ostrom (2006). *Linking the Formal and Informal Economy: Concepts and Policies*. Oxford: Oxford University Press. https://doi.org/10.1093/0199204764.001.0001.

Günther, I., and A. Launov (2011). 'Informal Employment in Developing Countries: Opportunity or Last Resort?'. *Journal of Development Economics*, 97(1): 88–98. https://doi.org/10.1016/j.jdeveco.2011.01.001.

Herrera, J., M. Kuépié, C.J. Nordman, X. Oudin, and F. Roubaud (2012). 'Informal Sector and Informal Employment: Overview of Data for 11 Cities in 10 Developing Countries'. WIEGO Working Paper No. 9, January. Available at: https://www.wiego.org/sites/default/files/migrated/publications/files/Herrera_WIEGO_WP9.pdf (accessed 26 September 2022).

ILO (International Labour Organization) (2018). *Women and Men in the Informal Economy: A Statistical Picture*. Geneva: ILO.

ILO (2019). 'ILO Thesaurus: Informal Employment'. Available at: http://ilo.multites.net (accessed 13 January 2020).

Iversen, V., A. Krishna, and K. Sen (eds) (2021). *Social Mobility in Developing Countries: Concepts, Methods, and Determinants*. Oxford: Oxford University Press. Available at: https://www.wider.unu.edu/publication/social-mobility-developing-countries-0 (accessed 26 September 2022).

Kanbur, R. (2017). 'Informality: Causes, Consequences, and Policy Responses'. *Review of Development Economics*, 21(4): 939–961. https://doi.org/10.1111/rode.12321.

Kucera, D., and L. Roncolato (2008). 'Informal Employment: Two Contested Policy Issues'. *International Labour Review*, 147(4): 321–348. https://doi.org/10.1111/j.1564-913X.2008.00039.x.

LaPorta, R., and A. Shleifer (2014). 'Informality and Development'. *Journal of Economic Perspectives*, 28(3): 109–126. https://doi.org/10.1257/jep.28.3.109.

Levy, S. (2008). *Good Intentions, Bad Outcomes: Social Policy, Informality, and Economic Growth in Mexico*. Washington, DC: Brookings.

Levy, S. (2018). *Under-Rewarded Efforts: The Elusive Quest for Prosperity in Mexico*. Washington, DC: Inter-American Development Bank. https://doi.org/10.18235/0001189.

Maloney, W. F. (1999). 'Does Informality Imply Segmentation in Urban Labor Markets? Evidence from Sectoral Transitions in Mexico'. *World Bank Economic Review*, 13: 275–302. https://doi.org/10.1093/wber/13.2.275.

Maloney, W. F. (2004). 'Informality Revisited'. *World Development*, 32(7): 1159–1178. https://doi.org/10.1016/j.worlddev.2004.01.008.

Margolis, D. N. (2014). 'By Choice and by Necessity: Entrepreneurship and Self-Employment in the Developing World'. *European Journal of Development Research*, 26(4): 419–436. https://doi.org/10.1057/ejdr.2014.25.

Merotto, D., M. Weber, and R. Aterido (2018). *Pathways to Better Jobs in IDA Countries*. Washington, DC: World Bank. https://doi.org/10.1596/30594.

NCEUS (National Commission for Enterprises in the Unorganised Sector) (2009). *The Challenge of Employment in India: An Informal Economy Perspective*. New Delhi: NCEUS, Government of India.

Perry, G., W. Maloney, O. Arias, P. Fajnzylber, A. Mason, and J. Saavedra-Chanduvi (2007). *Informality: Exit and Exclusion*. Washington, DC: World Bank. https://doi.org/10.1596/978-0-8213-7092-6.

Poschke, M. (2013). 'Entrepreneurs Out of Necessity: A Snapshot'. *Applied Economics Letters*, 20: 658–663. https://doi.org/10.1080/13504851.2012.727968.

Raj, R. N., S. Schotte, and K. Sen (2020). 'Transitions between Informal and Formal Jobs in India: Patterns, Correlates, and Consequences'. WIDER Working Paper 2020/101. Helsinki: UNU-WIDER. https://doi.org/10.35188/UNU-WIDER/2020/858-0.

Squire, L. (1981). *Employment Policy in Developing Countries: A Survey of Issues and Evidence*. New York: Oxford University Press.

Thorbecke, E. (1973). 'The Employment Problem: A Critical Evaluation of Four ILO Comprehensive Country Reports'. *International Labour Review*, 107(5): 393–423.

Turnham, D. (1971). *The Employment Problem in Less Developed Countries*. Paris: OECD.

Udall, A. T., and S. Sinclair (1982). 'The 'Luxury Unemployment' Hypothesis: A Review of Recent Evidence'. *World Development*, 10(1): 49–62. https://doi.org/10.1016/0305-750X(82)90079-1.

WIEGO (Women in Informal Employment: Globalizing and Organizing) (2020). 'Informal Economy'. Available at: https://www.wiego.org/informal-economy (accessed 16 June 2020).

PART II

ASIA

3

Transforming informal work and livelihoods in China

Carl Lin, Linxiang Ye, and Wei Zhang

1. Introduction

The received wisdom that the informal sector is a place of residual employment for impoverished, marginalized, and vulnerable workers originates from early studies of the labour markets of low- and middle-income countries. From this traditional point of view, the informal sector has long been characterized as a hub for the poor and the vulnerable. The informal sector, however, can also be seen as a dynamic sector of budding entrepreneurs and the staging ground for the development of firms which may eventually employ a large number of workers (Alaniz et al. 2020). There has been some evidence that the informal sector may also help disadvantaged workers to become more competitive by gaining experience for accumulating human capital (Liang et al. 2016), meaning that the marked rise in informal employment globally, and particularly in China, has drawn attention to ambiguity in how informality should be conceived.

Before China began its economic reform and opening-up policies in 1978, the country viewed every sector as formal—no sector was informal under the socialist regime. During the transition from a planned economy to a market economy, informal employment has prevailed across the country. Although some studies have attempted to define informality and to examine informal employment in China (Cai and Wang 2004; Hu and Li 2006; Wan 2008), there is no generally accepted definition of the informal sector. This chapter addresses the ambiguity of the informal sector and explicitly takes into account the heterogeneity in the sector by distinguishing between the self-employed and the wage-employed and by dividing the informal sector into upper and lower tiers to estimate the effects of changing jobs on workers' earnings.[1] Previous studies have often used data sets that are either cross sections or lack information about rural–urban migrants. We use a nationally representative longitudinal data set which covers both urban and rural

[1] We present a method for assigning workers to such sectors in Fig. 3.1 and Table 3.1 and show the mean earnings of a job ladder by work status in Fig. 3.2 and Table 3.2. The work status dynamics in the case of China are presented in Tables C1–C3 in Appendix C in Lin et al. (2020).

Carl Lin, Linxiang Ye, and Wei Zhang, *Transforming informal work and livelihoods in China*. In: *The Job Ladder*. Edited by Gary S. Fields, T. H. Gindling, Kunal Sen, Michael Danquah, and Simone Schotte, Oxford University Press.
 DOI: 10.1093/oso/9780192867339.003.0003

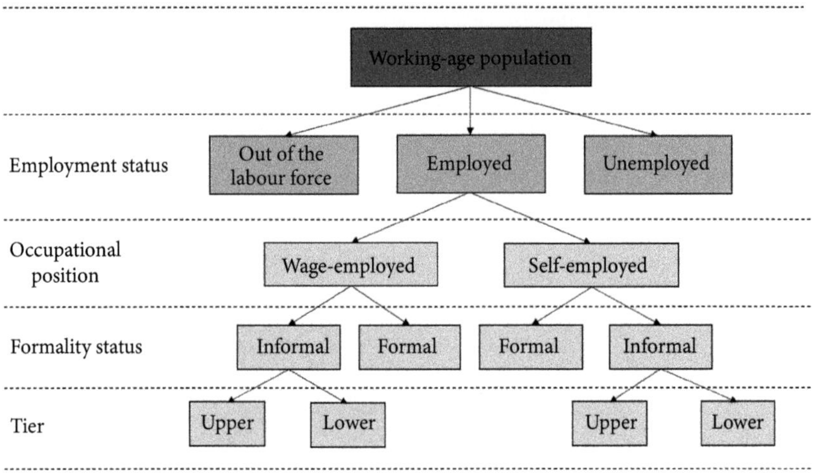

Fig. 3.1 Work status categorization: the case of China

Source: authors' elaboration based on China Family Panel Studies (CFPS) data (Institute of Social Science, Peking University 2018).

areas, containing 95 per cent of the Chinese population, to estimate the change in Chinese workers' livelihoods when they transition to different work status groups within or between formal and informal sectors.

Our work makes several contributions to the existing literature. First, China constitutes an important case study as it has the world's largest population and because of the vast size of its informal economy. Second, informal employment is a phenomenon among almost all Chinese rural–urban migrant workers—estimated at 290 million people in 2019 (National Bureau of Statistics of China 2019).[2] Our study adds to the limited evidence on the formal and informal employment of rural–urban migrants in China (Li and Tang 2002; Wan 2008, 2009) and offers an important lesson for other developing countries that are experiencing rapid rural–urban migration and urbanization. Other countries may not have the same formal structure of constraints imposed on rural–urban migrants, but if their urban infrastructures cannot keep up with the influx of new people, then migrant workers may be at similar risk of economic vulnerability and poor living standards. Third, women are disadvantaged in the Chinese labour market because of cultural norms and a prevailing preference for sons. From a gender perspective, we examine how job transitions can affect the earnings of female workers.

Policymakers are constrained by the lack of evidence on causes of informality and the most effective mechanism for reducing informality and strengthening

[2] According to our calculations using the 2014 China Family Panel Studies data set, informal employment among migrant workers (in cities) accounts for 81–86 per cent of their total employment, depending on the definition used. The figure is 93 per cent in rural areas.

Table 3.1 Work status definition and operationalization: the case of China

Work status group	Definition/operationalization
Formal self-employed	A person who is self-employed and pays work insurance (retirement pensions, medical insurance, unemployment insurance, work injury insurance, and maternity insurance) as an individual or a private business owner. Note that such work insurance belongs to work protection which has a higher protection level than New Rural Cooperative Medical Insurance and Urban Resident Basic Medical Insurance. Most Chinese residents, regardless of being employed or not, are included in the social protection system. It is therefore not straightforward to identify formal employment by whether they have work insurance in the case of China.
Upper-tier informal self-employed	A person who is self-employed in individual and private businesses in which the size of the work unit is equal to or greater than seven people or the self-employed who have college degrees or above and in job classes 1 (family agricultural work), 3 (agricultural work for other families), and 5 (non-agricultural casual workers).
Lower-tier informal self-employed	A person who is self-employed in the informal sector and has a high school degree or below. Farmers and individually owned small-scale businesses dominate this category.
Formal wage-employed	Wage workers whose employers provide them with work insurance such as retirement pensions, medical insurance, unemployment insurance, work injury insurance, and maternity insurance.
Upper-tier informal wage-employed	A person who works for wages in the formal sector (governments, party, people's organizations, military, state-owned and collectively owned public institutions, state-owned or state-controlled enterprises, companies with foreign capital investments or with investments from Hong Kong, Macao, Taiwan, or works in a firm employing seven more or people) but where the employer does not provide work insurance.
Lower-tier informal wage-employed	An employed worker in the informal sector where the work unit does not provide any work insurance. These individuals include, e.g. labourers employed by private businesses, agricultural workers, and non-agricultural casual workers.

Source: authors' elaboration based on CFPS data (Institute of Social Science, Peking University 2018).

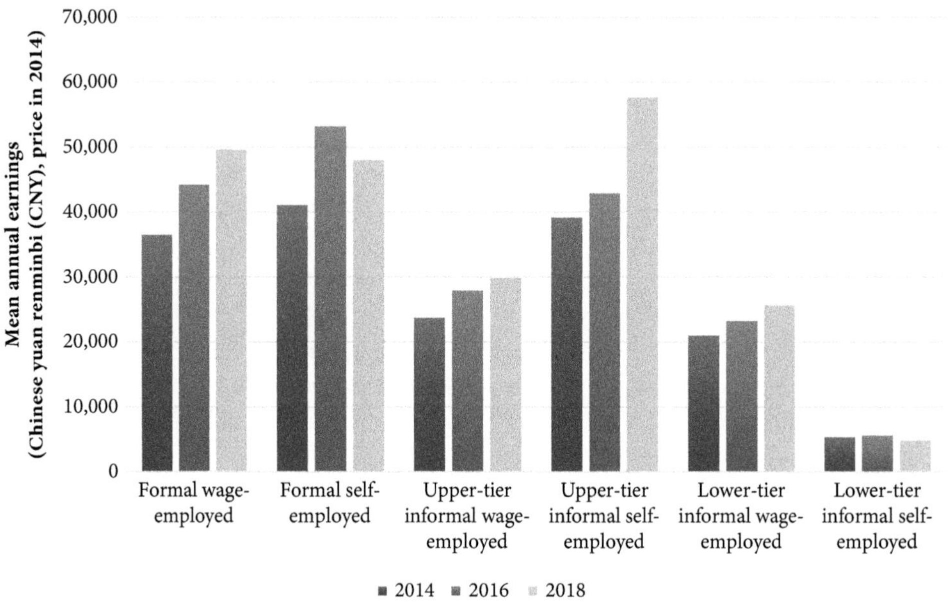

Fig. 3.2 Mean earnings by work status: the case of China

Note: Earnings of 2016 and 2018 are in 2014 prices.

Source: authors' calculations based on CFPS data (Institute of Social Science, Peking University 2018).

Table 3.2 Mean earnings by work status: the case of China

	Average annual earnings (CNY)		
	2014	**2016**	**2018**
Formal wage-employees	36,429.40	44,109.27	49,553.82
Formal self-employed	41,032.37	53,165.38	48,003.88
Upper-tier informal wage-employees	23,657.38	27,851.59	29,866.99
Upper-tier informal self-employed	39,107.29	42,837.14	57,631.67
Lower-tier informal wage-employees	20,971.44	23,167.24	25,637.84
Lower informal self-employed	5,338.44	5,556.78	4,825.13

Note: Mean annual earnings in the main job. Earnings of 2016 and 2018 are in 2014 prices.

Source: authors' calculations based on China Family Panel Studies (CFPS) data (Institute of Social Science, Peking University 2018).

decent work in the sector, especially for rural–urban migrants.[3] This chapter contributes to increasing the evidence on the heterogeneity of the informal economy

[3] To the best of our knowledge, Li (1999) and Liang et al. (2007) are the only two studies that examine the dynamics of movements between self-employment and wage-employees and between informal and formal employment in China. In particular, no one has examined transitions between a more nuanced definition of the informal sector which distinguishes between upper-tier and lower-tier informal sectors.

in China by using a nationally representative longitudinal survey of Chinese individuals, families, and communities in contemporary China. Our empirical framework allows us to control for a wide array of potential confounders to identify the causal effect of transitioning between different work status groups. We assess the magnitude of different earnings gaps within or between the informal and formal sectors using fixed-effects ordinary least squares (OLS) estimations. In particular, we separate the informal sector into upper and lower tiers. From the 37,868 observations covering the 2014–2018 period, this division shows that the lower-tier informal self-employed dominate the informal economy, with almost two-thirds of people working in the informal sector. The upper-tier informal wage-employed comprise 22 per cent, the lower-tier wage-employed comprise 13 per cent, and the upper-tier self-employed comprise about 1 per cent.

The literature claims that, in China, the informal economy had a significant role in sustaining high employment and inclusive economic growth during China's transition to a market economy from the early 1990s to the 2000s. We further show that transitioning from the informal sector to the formal sector, from self-employed to wage-employed, and from the lower tier to the upper tier helped to improve the livelihoods of Chinese workers after the country entered a 'new normal' stage of economic development.[4]

2. Literature

Approximately two billion women and men aged 15 and above—61.2 per cent of the world's employed population—earn their livelihoods in the informal economy (ILO 2018). These workers are denied decent working conditions not out of choice but because of a lack of job opportunities in the formal sector and a lack of other livelihood means and skills. The ILO (2018) estimated that 85.8 per cent of employment in Africa, 68.2 per cent in Asia and the Pacific, 68.6 per cent in the Arab States, 40 per cent in the Americas, and 25.1 per cent in Europe and Central Asia was informal.[5]

Kanbur (2017) reviewed studies from India and around the world and provided answers to questions relating to: the definition, magnitude, and trend of informality; the causes of and consequences for an increasing informal sector; and

[4] The Wikipedia page 'New Normal: 2012 China's economic slowdown' indicates that since 2012, China's economy has shown a marked slowdown, with growth rates declining from double-digit levels (before the 2008–2009 financial crisis) to around 7 per cent in 2014. In 2014, a statement by the President of China indicated that the country was entering a 'new normal'. The term was subsequently popularized by the press and came to refer to expectations of 7 per cent growth rates in China for the foreseeable future. It was indicative of the Chinese government's anticipation of moderate but perhaps more stable economic growth in the medium-to-long term. Available at: https://en.wikipedia.org/wiki/New_normal#2012_China%27s_economic_slowdown (accessed 19 August 2020).

[5] When excluding agricultural jobs, informal employment drops to 50.5 per cent globally. However, non-agricultural informal employment is still high in Africa, the Arab States, and Asia and the Pacific.

what workable and desirable policy responses to informality can be developed. He showed that over 80 per cent of Indian workers were employed in the informal sector despite India's high economic growth over the past 20 years and that there was no uniform trend of decreasing informality in Africa, Latin America, and South Asia. Using a theoretical model, he showed that state regulations, higher wages through development, and the evolution of technology were the main causes of non-declining informality, the consequences of which were linked to poverty. La Porta and Shleifer (2014) presented dual models of informality and showed consistent evidence that 'informal firms stay permanently informal, they hire informal workers for cash, buy their inputs for cash, and sell their products for cash, they are extremely unproductive, and they are unlikely to benefit much from becoming formal'. They suggested that economic growth can reduce informality, and their evidence strongly supports the prediction that as the economy develops, informality declines at a slow pace.

Nordman et al. (2016) used a four-wave panel data set from Madagascar covering the 2000–2004 period to estimate the magnitude of a variety of formal–informal-sector earnings gaps. They estimated standard earnings equations at various conditional quantiles over the earnings distribution and found that the sign and magnitude of the formal–informal-sector earnings gaps depended on workers' employment status and their relative positions in the earnings distribution. Their results showed that in many cases, such as the relatively low wages of formal-sector wage jobs, informal self-employed jobs have more or equal pay than formal wage jobs for men.

Hu and Yang (2001) and Hu and Li (2006) outlined the transition of formal and informal employment in urban areas in China from the mid-1990s to the early and mid-2000s, showing that informal employment was about 20 per cent of urban employment in 1995 and was expected to exceed 50 per cent by 2010. Xue and Gao (2012) used the 1 per cent census data to investigate the size, features, and earnings disparity of informal employment in urban China. They showed that informal employment made up as much as 59 per cent of China's urban employment and that the hourly earnings of formal workers were 1.65 times higher than those of informal workers. Cai and Wang (2004) attempted to interpret China's employment growth in the urban area from 1978 to 2003 and argued that urban informal employment was the product of China's rapidly developing labour market and was the main source of employment growth. Wu (2009) looked at the destination of China's informal employment and claimed that formalizing the labour market should not be the government's focus. He argued that the Chinese government should focus on policies that promote sustainable economic growth rather than forcing informal-sector employers and employees to switch to the formal sector by signing contracts.

Li and Tang (2002) used a data set from Beijing in 2002 to study Chinese rural–urban migrant workers in the informal sector. Their qualitative analysis suggested that the informal economy and informal employment of rural–urban migrants should not be viewed as entailing underground or illegal activities. Du and Wan (2014) used the China Urban Labor Survey in 2001, 2005, and 2010 to examine the effect of the informal employment of rural–urban migrants on poverty. Their results showed that the 5.65 per cent poverty rate of rural–urban migrants was higher than the poverty rate of local residents (4.15 per cent), and quantile regression estimations demonstrated that informal employment reduced the poverty rate for migrant workers. These findings are in line with the argument by Wu (2009) that policymakers should not plan to formalize the informal sector by understating the positive contribution of informal employment.

3. Data, descriptive statistics, and empirical strategy

3.1 Data

Our chapter uses the 2014, 2016, and 2018 China Family Panel Studies (CFPS)—China's first large-scale academically orientated longitudinal survey project—obtained from the Institute of Social Science Survey at Peking University to construct a three-year individual-level panel data set. We empirically examine the employment transitions between and within informal and formal sectors to study how job changes affect the livelihoods of Chinese workers. The CFPS carried out its baseline survey in 2010 and four waves of full-sample follow-up surveys in 2012, 2014, 2016, and 2018. Its baseline sample covers 25 out of 30 provinces, municipalities, and autonomous regions in China, which comprise 95 per cent of the Chinese population, making CFPS a nationally representative sample.[6] The 2010 baseline survey interviewed 14,960 households and 42,590 individuals (33,600 adults and 8,990 youths) covering urban and rural areas. As the survey questions that can identify formal and informal sectors are not available until 2014, we use the three waves (2014, 2016, and 2018) that consistently have this identifying information.

The CFPS surveys were carried out at three levels: the community level (villages and urban neighbourhood questionnaires), the family level (family roster and family questionnaires), and the individual level (adult and child questionnaires). We mainly use the adult questionnaire for individuals who were at least 16 years old at the time of the interviews. The job module in the adult questionnaire first asked individuals for their current employment status, that is, whether they were employed or had been employed since the previous

[6] The CFPS sample is drawn from 25 provinces, cities, and autonomous regions in mainland China (excluding Hong Kong, Macao, and Taiwan). Four autonomous regions (Xinjiang, Qinghai, Inner Mongolia, and Ningxia) and one province (Hainan) were not included in the survey.

interview (or during the past year). Individuals were asked whether they worked for wages or were self-employed and whether they worked in agriculture or in a non-agricultural job. The interviewees were then sorted into five job categories: (1) family agricultural work; (2) individual, private business, and other self-employment; (3) agricultural work for other families; (4) employed; and (5) non-agricultural casual workers.

The survey asked individuals specific job-related questions based on these five categories. Based on the method in Danquah et al. (2019), we used this information to divide interviewees into formal and informal workers and further distinguished between upper- and lower-tier informal jobs.

To identify formal and informal workers, we classified the workers in job classes (2) and (4) as having a job in the formal sector if the work unit provided work insurance (including retirement pensions, health insurance, unemployment insurance, work injury insurance, and maternity insurance) and housing provident funds or if the interviewee paid for insurance premiums as an individual or private-enterprise owner. Otherwise, we classified them as having an informal job. We viewed job classes (1), (3), and (5) as informal jobs and no job protection questions were asked.

To distinguish between upper- and lower-tier informal employment (wage-employed and self-employed), we made the following distinctions:

- The upper-tier informal wage-employed includes individuals working for wages in the formal sector (in government, party, people's organizations, military; state-owned and collectively owned public institutions; state-owned or state-controlled enterprises; companies in receipt of foreign capital investment or investment from Hong Kong, Macao, or Taiwan; or in firms employing seven or more people) but where their employers do not provide any work insurance.
- The upper-tier informal self-employed are self-employed persons in individual and private businesses in which the size of the work unit is equal to or greater than seven people or the self-employed are in job classes (1), (3), and (5) who have college degrees or above.
- The lower-tier informal wage-employed are wage workers in the informal sector whose work units do not provide any work insurance. For example, labourers in individual and private businesses, agricultural workers, and non-agricultural casual workers are in this category.
- The lower-tier informal self-employed are the self-employed in the informal sector who have high school degrees or below. This category is mainly made up of farmers and individually owned small-scale businesses.

In summary, we define six categories of workers split by employment status (wage-employed vs self-employed), formality status (formal vs informal), and the tier of work in the informal sector (upper vs lower) to estimate the effects on workers' earnings of transitions between and within different work status groups.[7]

3.2 Descriptive statistics

Table 3.3 shows the descriptive statistics of workers' characteristics for the years 2014, 2016, and 2018, which we use in estimating the earnings equations in section 3.3. Column 1 of Table 3.3 presents the means, standard deviations, minimums, and maximums for the pooled data, which contains 63,194 observations (22,293 in 2014, 21,531 in 2016, and 19,370 in 2018). For the pooled three years, 48 per cent of workers are male, 74 per cent have agricultural hukou status,[8] 49 per cent reside in urban areas, and the average age is 43.51 years. Ninety-one per cent of workers are of Han ethnicity, the largest ethnic group in China. With regard to marital status, 86 per cent are married with a spouse present. The average number of years of schooling is eight years, which is reasonable as the CFPS covers both rural and urban residents. About 8 per cent are Chinese Communist Party (CCP) members. Having CCP membership may help workers to change jobs in the Chinese context since many studies have found wage premiums for CCP membership (Bian and Logan 1996; Xie and Hannum 1996; Morduch and Sicular 2000; Lam 2003; Liu 2003; Li et al. 2007; Appleton et al. 2009) and on the attainment of elite occupation (Walder 1995; Li and Walder 2001). Approximately one-quarter of those observed have religious beliefs (Buddhism, Taoism, Muslim, and Christianity (including Roman Catholicism and Protestantism) or worship ancestors).

Next, in Table 3.4, we present work status by year and by the entire sample. Our study focuses on the number and share of the wage-employed and the self-employed in the formal and informal employed. As the numbers for each year in columns 3–5 of Table 3.4 are similar to the three-year pooled sample, we focus on the statistics from the pooled sample, which contain 63,194 observations. With regard to employment status, 1.28 per cent of workers are unemployed, 20.6 per cent are not in the labour force, and 78.12 per cent are employed. In the employed category, almost one-quarter (23.3 per cent) of workers in the pooled sample are in the formal sector, while about three-quarters (76.7 per cent) are in the informal sector. Among those employed in the formal sector, 92.78 per cent are

[7] Details of the work status definition and operationalization are in Appendix A. The transition matrices of work status by year, gender, hukou, and firm ownership are in Appendix figs D1–D6 in Lin et al. (2020).

[8] Note that every Chinese personal hukou status is categorized by type (agricultural vs non-agricultural) and by location (urban vs rural). A person inherits hukou status from parents at birth, including both hukou type and hukou location (Song 2014), and it is very difficult to change. We also divide the sample by agricultural and non-agricultural hukou status. The summary statistics for agricultural and non-agricultural work are in Appendix Table D1 in Lin et al. (2020).

Table 3.3 Summary statistics of workers' characteristics

	Pooled				2014				2016				2018			
	Mean	**SD**	**Min**	**Max**	**Mean**	**SD**	**Min**	**Max**	**Mean**	**SD**	**Min**	**Max**	**Mean**	**SD**	**Min**	**Max**
Male	0.48	0.5	0	1	0.47	0.5	0	1	0.48	0.5	0	1	0.48	0.5	0	1
Agricultural hukou	0.74	0.44	0	1	0.73	0.44	0	1	0.75	0.44	0	1	0.74	0.44	0	1
Urban	0.49	0.5	0	1	0.47	0.5	0	1	0.48	0.5	0	1	0.52	0.5	0	1
Age	43.51	12.51	16	64	42.98	12.86	16	64	43.36	12.55	16	64	44.28	12	16	64
Han ethnicity	0.91	0.28	0	1	0.92	0.28	0	1	0.91	0.28	0	1	0.91	0.29	0	1
Married	0.86	0.35	0	1	0.85	0.36	0	1	0.86	0.35	0	1	0.87	0.33	0	1
Education (year)	8.07	4.73	0	23	7.84	4.62	0	20	8.13	4.66	0	22	8.27	4.91	0	23
CCP member	0.08	0.27	0	1	0.06	0.24	0	1	0.08	0.27	0	1	0.09	0.29	0	1
Has religion	0.24	0.43	0	1	0.21	0.41	0	1	0.14	0.35	0	1	0.38	0.49	0	1
N		63,194				22,293				21,531				19,370		

Note: CCP denotes the Chinese Communist Party.
Source: authors' calculations based on CFPS data (Institute of Social Science, Peking University 2018).

Table 3.4 Work status by employment status, occupational position, formality status, and tier

	Pooled		2014		2016		2018	
	N	%	N	%	N	%	N	%
Total	63,194	100	22,293	100	21,531	100	19,370	100
Unemployed	809	1.28	314	1.41	278	1.29	217	1.12
Not in the labour force	13,016	20.60	4,875	21.87	4,357	20.24	3,784	19.54
Employed	49,369	78.12	17,104	76.72	16,896	78.47	15,369	79.34
Formal	11,501	23.30	3,568	20.86	3,694	21.86	4,239	27.58
Wage-employed	10,671	92.78	3,325	93.19	3,452	93.45	3,894	91.86
Self-employed	830	7.22	243	6.81	242	6.55	345	8.14
Informal	37,868	76.70	13,536	79.14	13,202	78.14	11,130	72.42
Upper-tier informal wage-employed	8,230	21.73	2,802	20.70	2,786	21.10	2,642	23.74
Upper-tier informal self-employed	350	0.92	116	0.86	125	0.95	109	0.98
Low-tier informal wage-employed	4,938	13.04	1,463	10.81	1,787	13.54	1,688	15.17
Low-tier informal self-employed	24,350	64.30	9,155	67.63	8,504	64.41	6,691	60.12

Source: authors' calculations based on CFPS data (Institute of Social Science, Peking University 2018).

wage-employed and only 7.22 per cent are self-employed, implying that wage-earning jobs dominate the formal economy. In the informal sector, 21.73 per cent of workers are upper-tier wage-employed and 13.04 per cent are lower-tier wage-employed. Self-employed workers make up a disproportionate share (64.3 per cent) of the lower-tier informal sector, but they comprise only 0.92 per cent of the upper-tier informal sector.

Table 3.5 presents the summary statistics for key variables in the earnings equations by work status. The average real annual earnings are CNY 20,020 over the 2014–2018 period. The self-employed in the formal sector have the highest annual earnings (CNY 47,470) but also the largest standard deviation. The self-employed in the upper-tier informal sector have the second-highest earnings (CNY 46,210) and the wage-employed in the formal sector have the third-highest

Table 3.5 Summary statistics of key variables in each work status, 2014–2018

	All		Formal				Informal								Unemployed		Not in the labour force	
							Upper-tier				Lower-tier							
			Self-employed		Wage-employed		Self-employed		Wage-employed		Self-employed		Wage-employed					
	Mean	SD	Mean	SD	Mean	SD	Mean	SD	Mean	SD	Mean	SD	Mean	SD	Mean	SD	Mean	SD
Annual earnings (CNY1000)	20.02	35.83	47.47	139.65	43.70	37.43	46.21	91.12	27.07	26.63	5.27	19.19	23.36	19.92	–		–	
Male	0.48	0.5	0.56	0.5	0.61	0.49	0.65	0.48	0.58	0.49	0.46	0.5	0.63	0.48	0.48	0.5	0.27	0.44
Agricultural hukou	0.74	0.44	0.56	0.5	0.44	0.5	0.58	0.49	0.73	0.45	0.95	0.22	0.79	0.4	0.59	0.49	0.61	0.49
Urban	0.49	0.5	0.75	0.44	0.76	0.43	0.69	0.46	0.57	0.49	0.24	0.43	0.53	0.5	0.69	0.46	0.62	0.49
Age	43.51	12.51	42.9	9.12	37.44	10.09	35.99	9.56	39.6	11.66	47.46	10.84	41.05	11.28	37.44	12.18	45.1	15.07
Han ethnicity	0.91	0.28	0.95	0.22	0.95	0.22	0.88	0.32	0.95	0.23	0.87	0.34	0.93	0.26	0.93	0.26	0.94	0.24
Married	0.86	0.35	0.93	0.25	0.81	0.39	0.87	0.34	0.81	0.39	0.92	0.27	0.86	0.35	0.71	0.45	0.81	0.39
Education	8.07	4.73	9.9	3.58	12.26	3.63	12.75	3.74	9.19	3.91	5.68	4.16	7.9	3.7	9.45	4.23	8.12	4.65
CCP member	0.08	0.27	0.09	0.28	0.19	0.39	0.1	0.3	0.08	0.26	0.05	0.21	0.04	0.2	0.04	0.2	0.06	0.23
Has religion	0.24	0.43	0.33	0.47	0.21	0.41	0.26	0.44	0.22	0.41	0.25	0.43	0.25	0.43	0.23	0.42	0.25	0.44
Size of the firm																		
1–10	0.34	0.47	0.88	0.32	0.1	0.3	0.78	0.42	0.17	0.38	1	0	1	0	–		–	
11–100	0.39	0.49	0.09	0.29	0.42	0.49	0.17	0.38	0.61	0.49	0	0	0	0	–		–	
101–500	0.17	0.37	0.01	0.12	0.27	0.44	0.04	0.19	0.16	0.36	0	0	0	0	–		–	
More than 500	0.11	0.31	0.01	0.1	0.21	0.41	0.01	0.12	0.06	0.25	0	0	0	0	–		–	

Area of activity																
1. Agriculture, forestry, animal, husbandry, and fishery	0.46	0.5	0	0.06	0.01	0.1	0.01	0.08	0.02	0.13	0.9	0.3	0.09	0.29	–	–
2. Mining	0.01	0.1	0	0.06	0.03	0.17	0.01	0.08	0.01	0.12	0	0.01	0	0.07	–	–
3. Manufacturing	0.14	0.35	0.15	0.36	0.32	0.47	0.16	0.37	0.32	0.47	0.01	0.12	0.1	0.3	–	–
4. Production and supply of electricity, gas, and water	0.01	0.09	0.01	0.09	0.03	0.16	0	0.05	0.01	0.12	0	0.01	0	0.05	–	–
5. Construction	0.06	0.23	0.05	0.22	0.05	0.23	0.07	0.25	0.17	0.38	0	0.06	0.13	0.33	–	–
6. Transportation, storage, and postal service	0.03	0.16	0.05	0.21	0.06	0.23	0.06	0.24	0.04	0.2	0	0.07	0.05	0.22	–	–
7. Information transmission, computer service, and software	0.01	0.09	0.01	0.09	0.03	0.16	0.01	0.09	0.01	0.1	0	0.01	0	0.06	–	–
8. Wholesale and retail	0.08	0.26	0.41	0.49	0.07	0.26	0.31	0.46	0.09	0.28	0.05	0.21	0.13	0.34	–	–
9. Hotel and catering service	0.03	0.18	0.16	0.37	0.02	0.14	0.16	0.37	0.07	0.25	0.02	0.13	0.06	0.24	–	–

Continued

Table 3.5 *Continued*

	All		Formal				Informal								Unemployed		Not in the labour force	
							Upper-tier				Lower-tier							
			Self-employed		Wage-employed		Self-employed		Wage-employed		Self-employed		Wage-employed					
	Mean	SD	Mean	SD	Mean	SD	Mean	SD	Mean	SD	Mean	SD	Mean	SD	Mean	SD	Mean	SD
10. Finance	0.01	0.11	0	0.06	0.04	0.19	0	0.05	0.02	0.13	0	0.01	0	0.05	–		–	
11. Real estate	0.01	0.1	0	0	0.02	0.15	0.01	0.12	0.03	0.16	0	0.01	0.01	0.11	–		–	
12. Rental and commercial service	0.01	0.12	0.03	0.16	0.03	0.18	0.04	0.19	0.02	0.15	0	0.04	0.02	0.13	–		–	
13. Scientific research, technical service, and geological prospecting	0	0.04	0	0	0.01	0.09	0	0	0	0.04	0	0	0	0.03	–		–	
14. Water resource, environment and public facility management	0.01	0.08	0	0.03	0.02	0.13	0	0.05	0.02	0.12	0	0	0	0.06	–		–	
15. Residential and other service industry	0.02	0.14	0.08	0.26	0.02	0.14	0.05	0.21	0.04	0.19	0.01	0.1	0.04	0.2	–		–	

16. Education	0.03	0.17	0.02	0.13	0.09	0.29	0.05	0.22	0.05	0.22	0	0.02	0.02	0.14	–	–
17. Health, social security, and public welfare	0.02	0.12	0.03	0.16	0.04	0.2	0.04	0.2	0.03	0.16	0	0.03	0.01	0.1	–	–
18. Culture, sports, and recreation	0.01	0.08	0.01	0.11	0.01	0.11	0.01	0.12	0.01	0.12	0	0.04	0.01	0.09	–	–
19. Public administration and social organization	0.03	0.17	0	0	0.1	0.29	0	0.05	0.04	0.2	0	0	0.01	0.1	–	–
20. Other industries	0.03	0.17	0	0	0	0.03	0	0	0	0.02	0	0	0.3	0.46	–	–
Employer type																
1. Government/party/people's organization	0.06	0.24			0.09	0.29			0.05	0.22			0.01	0.07		
2. State-owned/collectively owned public institution/research institute	0.09	0.29			0.16	0.36			0.06	0.23			0	0.06		

Continued

Table 3.5 *Continued*

	All		Formal				Informal								Unemployed		Not in the labour force	
							Upper-tier				Lower-tier							
			Self-employed		Wage-employed		Self-employed		Wage-employed		Self-employed		Wage-employed					
	Mean	SD	Mean	SD	Mean	SD	Mean	SD	Mean	SD	Mean	SD	Mean	SD	Mean	SD	Mean	SD
3. State-owned/state-controlled enterprise	0.13	0.34			0.22	0.42			0.08	0.27			0	0.06				
4. Private enterprise/individually owned business	0.58	0.49			0.43	0.49			0.76	0.43			0.58	0.49				
5. Enterprise invested by Hong Kong/Macao/Taiwan capital	0.03	0.18			0.06	0.24			0.01	0.12			0	0				
6. Other enterprise	0.01	0.09			0.01	0.11			0.01	0.07			0	0.04				
7. Individual/family	0.08	0.26			0	0			0	0			0.37	0.48				
8. Residential community committee/village committee/autonomous organization	0.02	0.13			0.02	0.13			0.02	0.14			0.02	0.14				
9. Other	0.01	0.1			0.01	0.09			0.01	0.09			0.01	0.12				

Note: CCP denotes the Chinese Communist Party.

earnings (CNY 43,700). The wage-employed in the upper-tier informal sector earn CNY 27,070 and CNY 23,360 in the lower-tier informal sector. However, self-employed workers in the lower-tier informal sector earn the least (CNY 5,270) of all work status groups. Male workers make up 48 per cent of the sample and are over-represented in the formal sector and the upper-tier informal sector, but they only constitute 46 per cent of the self-employed in the lower-tier informal sector.

With regard to hukou status, in the lower-tier informal sector, 95 per cent of the self-employed and 79 per cent of the wage-employed have an agricultural hukou. On average, less than 50 per cent of formal wage-employed workers have an agricultural hukou, which is the smallest among the six work categories. Over three-quarters of workers in the formal sector have an urban hukou, whereas less than one-quarter of the lower-tier informal self-employed have an urban hukou.

Most of the workers are of Han ethnicity (over 87 per cent of all six categories) and married (over 81 per cent of all six categories). The formal-sector wage-employed have an average of 12.26 years of schooling and the upper-tier informal self-employed have an average of 12.75 years of schooling. The lower-tier informal self-employed have the least number of years of schooling (5.68 years). With regard to CCP membership, 19 per cent of the formal wage-employed are CCP members, which is the highest of all categories. The upper-tier informal self-employed are next with 10 per cent being CCP members, followed by the lower-tier informal self-employed, 4–5 per cent of whom are CCP members. For religion, there is consistency across all informal worker categories, where about one-quarter of informal workers have a religious belief. The formal wage-employed is the lowest category (21 per cent) with religious beliefs and the formal self-employed has the highest number (33 per cent).

In relation to firm size, 34 per cent of workers are employed in firms with 1–10 employees, 39 per cent in firms with 11–100 employees, 17 per cent in firms with 101–500 employees, and 11 per cent work for large firms employing over 500 workers. As for area of activity, 46 per cent of workers are employed in agriculture, forestry, animal husbandry, and fishery. Overall, 90 per cent of the lower-tier informal self-employed work in this area. The second-largest category is manufacturing (14 per cent), where 32 per cent are formal wage-employed and upper-tier informal wage-employed. With regard to employer type, private enterprises and individually owned businesses have the largest share of workers (58 per cent) followed by 13 per cent for state-owned, state-controlled enterprises.

3.3 Empirical model

Our empirical model estimates fixed-effect regressions for the magnitude of different informal–formal earnings gaps with workers' earnings as the dependent variable. As the earnings data for some self-employed and the wage-employed in both the lower- and upper-tier informal sectors include non-positive values, we use the inverse hyperbolic sine (IHS or arcsinh) transformation to address the issue. This method has grown in popularity among applied econometricians because it is similar to a logarithm and allows zero-valued (and even negative valued) observations to be kept (Burbidge et al. 1988; MacKinnon and Magee 1990; Pence 2006). We compute elasticities based on the method by Bellemare and Wichman (2020). Besides the level of earnings, we transform the dependent variable by cube-root and concave log-like transformation methods, which allow non-positive values, as suggested by Ravallion (2017).

We define six categories of work status using the method in Danquah et al. (2019): formal wage-employed (FW), formal self-employed (FS), upper-tier informal wage-employed (UIW), upper-tier informal self-employed (UIS), lower-tier informal wage-employed (LIW), and lower-tier informal self-employed (LIS). Taking the formal wage-employed (FW) as the reference group, the estimated equation is:

$$y_{it} = \alpha + \beta_1 FS_{it} + \beta_2 UIW_{it} + \beta_3 UIS_{it} + \beta_4 LIW_{it} + \beta_5 LIS_{it} + X'_{it}\gamma + \lambda_i + T_t + \varepsilon_{it}, \tag{1}$$

where y_{it} is the earnings for worker i in year t and X is a vector of worker characteristics, which include age, age squared, years of schooling, dummies for sex, hukou status, urban residency, Han ethnicity, marital status, CCP membership, and religious beliefs. We include province fixed effects λ_i and year fixed effects T_t to control for unobserved heterogeneity. Industry fixed effects are included in the full set of control variables specification. ε_{it} is the error term. The estimated coefficients β_1 to β_5 are interpreted as a measure of the conditional earnings premium (or penalty) experienced by workers who change their work status between informal-sector jobs and formal-sector employment (or the reversal). For example, β_1 is interpreted as the conditional earnings gap between the formal self-employed and the formal wage-employed—the FS–FW gap. Likewise, β_2, β_3, β_4, and β_5 are the conditional earnings gaps for UIW–FW, UIS–FW, LIW–FW, and LIS–FW. Our identification of these conditional earnings gaps compares the earnings of movers and stayers and relies on our sample workers moving between the six work status groups from one year to the next. Standard errors are clustered at the province level.

To calculate the changes in earnings by work status transitions, we compute six cases of stayers and thirty cases of movers over a two-year period. For example, the changes in earnings for the six cases of stayers are:

$$E[y_{i2} - y_{i1} | FW_{i1} = 1, FW_{i2} = 1] = \Delta_1 \tag{2}$$

$$E[y_{i2} - y_{i1} | FS_{i1} = 1, FS_{i2} = 1] = \Delta_2 \tag{3}$$

$$E[y_{i2} - y_{i1} | UIW_{i1} = 1, UIW_{i2} = 1] = \Delta_3 \tag{4}$$

$$E[y_{i2} - y_{i1} | UIS_{i1} = 1, UIS_{i2} = 1] = \Delta_4 \tag{5}$$

$$E[y_{i2} - y_{i1}|LIW_{i1} = 1, LIW_{i2} = 1] = \Delta_5 \quad (6)$$

$$E[y_{i2} - y_{i1}|LIS_{i1} = 1, LIS_{i2} = 1] = \Delta_6 \quad (7)$$

Where $\Delta = (X'_{i2} - X'_{i1})\,\beta$. Equations (2)–(7) allow us to calculate changes in earnings for workers who do not change their work status from period 1 to period 2. For movers, if we take the formal wage-employed (FW) in period 1, for example, the five cases of moving are:

$$E[y_{i2} - y_{i1}|FW_{i1} = 1, FS_{i2} = 1] = \Delta_1 + \beta_1 \quad (8)$$

$$E[y_{i2} - y_{i1}|FW_{i1} = 1, UIW_{i2} = 1] = \Delta_1 + \beta_2 \quad (9)$$

$$E[y_{i2} - y_{i1}|FW_{i1} = 1, UIS_{i2} = 1] = \Delta_1 + \beta_3 \quad (10)$$

$$E[y_{i2} - y_{i1}|FW_{i1} = 1, LIW_{i2} = 1] = \Delta_1 + \beta_4 \quad (11)$$

$$E[y_{i2} - y_{i1}|FW_{i1} = 1, LIS_{i2} = 1] = \Delta_1 + \beta_5 \quad (12)$$

Equations (8)–(12) show the changes in earnings for those workers coming from the formal wage-employed (FW) and moving, respectively, into the formal self-employed (FS), the upper-tier informal wage-employed (UIW), the upper-tier informal self-employed (UIS), the lower-tier informal wage-employed (LIW), and the lower-tier informal self-employed (LIS). Likewise, the transitions of movers for FS, UIW, UIS, LIW, and LIS from period 1 to period 2 can be shown accordingly. Taken together, the changes in earnings for all 36 cases (six stayers and 30 movers), for example from period 1 to period 2, can be expressed as in Table 3.6.

Table 3.6 Changes in earnings from period 1 to period 2

		Period 2					
		FW	FS	UIW	UIS	LIW	LIS
Period 1	FW	Δ_1	$\Delta_1 + \beta_1$	$\Delta_1 + \beta_2$	$\Delta_1 + \beta_3$	$\Delta_1 + \beta_4$	$\Delta_1 + \beta_5$
	FS	$\Delta_2 - \beta_1$	Δ_2	$\Delta_2 - \beta_1 + \beta_2$	$\Delta_2 - \beta_1 + \beta_3$	$\Delta_2 - \beta_1 + \beta_4$	$\Delta_2 - \beta_1 + \beta_5$
	UIW	$\Delta_3 - \beta_2$	$\Delta_3 - \beta_2 + \beta_1$	Δ_3	$\Delta_3 - \beta_2 + \beta_3$	$\Delta_3 - \beta_2 + \beta_4$	$\Delta_3 - \beta_2 + \beta_5$
	UIS	$\Delta_4 - \beta_3$	$\Delta_4 - \beta_3 + \beta_1$	$\Delta_4 - \beta_3 + \beta_2$	Δ_4	$\Delta_4 - \beta_3 + \beta_4$	$\Delta_4 - \beta_3 + \beta_5$
	LIW	$\Delta_5 - \beta_4$	$\Delta_5 - \beta_4 + \beta_1$	$\Delta_5 - \beta_4 + \beta_2$	$\Delta_5 - \beta_4 + \beta_3$	Δ_5	$\Delta_5 - \beta_4 + \beta_5$
	LIS	$\Delta_6 - \beta_5$	$\Delta_6 - \beta_5 + \beta_1$	$\Delta_6 - \beta_5 + \beta_2$	$\Delta_6 - \beta_5 + \beta_3$	$\Delta_6 - \beta_5 + \beta_4$	Δ_6

Note: FW: formal wage-employed; FS: formal self-employed; UIW: upper-tier informal wage-employed; UIS: upper-tier informal self-employed; LIW: lower-tier informal wage-employed; LIS: lower-tier informal self-employed.
Source: authors' construction.

4. Earnings gaps, job transitions, and changes of livelihoods

4.1 Main results

In Table 3.7, we report the fixed-effects OLS results from estimating equation (1). The results in column 1 use levels of earnings as the dependent variable. To avoid the issue of non-positive earnings, column 2 adopts IHS-transformed earnings and column 3 takes on cube-root transformation. All models in the three columns use the formal wage-employed as the base category and include a full set of worker characteristics, year, province, and industry fixed effects.

Our preferred specification is the IHS-transformed earnings in column 2, which shows that in the formal sector, holding other variables constant, the self-employed (FS) earn 142 per cent less than the wage-employed. In the upper-tier informal sector, the wage-employed (UIW) earn 57 per cent less than the formal wage-employed (FW) and the self-employed (UIS) earn 159 per cent less than the formal wage-employed (FW). In the lower-tier informal sector, the wage-employed (LIW) earn 34 per cent less than the formal wage-employed (FW) and the largest earnings gap is between the lower-tier informal self-employed (LIS) and the formal wage-employed (FW), whereas LIS earn 235 per cent less than FW.

In column 1, which uses levels of earnings as the dependent variable, we find that the formal wage-employed (FW) earn CNY 6,314 less than the formal self-employed (FS) and CNY 1,104 less than the upper-tier informal self-employed, but the two estimates are statistically insignificant. On the other hand, the formal wage-employed (FW) have CNY 12,713 more annual earnings than the upper-tier informal wage-employed (UIW). The earnings gaps further increase to CNY 13,915 for the lower-tier informal wage-employed (LIW) and to CNY14,760 for the lower-tier informal self-employed (LIS). Column 3 presents the results using cube-root earnings. The estimated gap coefficients are all negative and statistically significant, which is in line with our preferred results in column 2, but column 3 should be interpreted with caution because of the much larger magnitudes.

The bottom part of Table 3.7 column 2—the IHS-transformed earnings—presents the estimated percentage change of earnings (semi-elasticities) when transitioning out of formal wage-employment (FW) to the other five work status groups, calculated using the method in Bellemare and Wichman (2020). For example, when the formal wage-employed (FW) switch to the formal self-employed (FS), earnings drop by 76 per cent. Similarly, earnings decline by 43 per cent when switching to the upper-tier informal wage-employed (UIW) and drop to 81 per cent when switching to the upper-tier informal self-employed (UIS). Finally, if the formal wage-employed (FW) switch to the lower-tier informal sector, earnings reduce by 29 per cent for the wage-employed (LIW) and by 91 per cent for the self-employed (LIS).

Table 3.7 Fixed-effects OLS estimates

Base category: Formal wage-employed (FW)	(1) Earnings (level)	(2) Earnings (inverse hyperbolic sine)	(3) Earnings (cube roots)
Formal self-employed	6,314.36	−1.42***	−3.94***
(FS)	(8,664.73)	(0.14)	(0.99)
Upper-tier informal wage-employed	−12,713.12***	−0.57***	−4.41***
(UIW)	(1,416.64)	(0.04)	(0.26)
Upper-tier informal self-employed	1,103.57	−1.59***	−4.13**
(UIS)	(5,322.00)	(0.43)	(1.60)
Lower-tier informal wage-employed	−13,915.17***	−0.34***	−4.31***
(LIW)	(1,485.06)	(0.09)	(0.38)
Lower-tier informal self-employed	−14,760.01***	−2.35***	−9.14***
(LIS)	(1,821.72)	(0.14)	(0.49)
Year fixed effects	Yes	Yes	Yes
Province fixed effects	Yes	Yes	Yes
Industry fixed effect	Yes	Yes	Yes
Observations	49,194	49,194	49,194
Adjusted R-squared	0.24	0.26	0.46
ξ(Earnings, FS)	–	−0.76	–
ξ(Earnings, UIW)	–	−0.43	–
ξ(Earnings, UIS)	–	−0.81	–
ξ(Earnings, LIW)	–	−0.29	–
ξ(Earnings, LIS)	–	−0.91	–

Note: Clustered robust standard errors at the province level in parentheses; * $p < 0.1$, ** $p < 0.05$, *** $p < 0.01$. All models include a full set of worker characteristics. The full set of regression results are reported in Appendix Table D2 of Lin et al. (2020). ξ (Earnings, work status) shows the percentage change of earnings (semi-elasticity) when transitioning from the formal wage-employed to another work status using the inverse hyperbolic sine (IHS or arcsinh) transformation.
Source: authors' calculation based on CFPS data (Institute of Social Science, Peking University 2018)

In short, we find a substantial decline in earnings when workers transition to a self-employed job. The largest earnings loss is for transitioning to the lower-tier informal sector, which reduces workers' annual earnings on average by 91 per cent, followed by 81 per cent for the upper-tier informal and 76 per cent for the formal sectors—a 10–15 percentage points difference. The reduction in earnings for transitioning to the lower-tier formal wage-employed is 29 per cent and increases to 43 per cent for the upper-tier formal wage-employed. Our interpretation is that, by definition, the upper-tier informal wage-employed hold jobs in the formal sector but without work insurance. The formal sector provides a better and stable working environment than those of the lower-tier informal wage-employed. The data shows that despite having lower earnings, the upper-tier informal wage-employed have higher levels of satisfaction with their jobs than the lower-tier wage-employed in relation to safety, promotion opportunities, and working environment.

Taken together, the fixed-effects OLS results show that the livelihoods of Chinese workers could be improved (i) by switching occupational position: from being self-employed to wage-employed and (ii) by changing tier: from the lower-tier informal self-employed to the upper-tier informal self-employed.

4.2 Gender

We present the estimated results by gender using the formal wage-employed as the base category and IHS-transformed earnings in columns 1 and 2 of Table 3.8. Compared to the formal wage-employed (FW), formal self-employed (FS) females earn 89 per cent less; upper-tier informal wage-employed (UIW) females earn 69 per cent less; upper-tier informal self-employed (UIS) females earn 195 per cent less; lower-tier informal wage-employed (LIW) females earn 59 per cent less; and lower-tier informal self-employed (LIS) females earn 208 per cent less. Likewise, for male workers, the formal wage-employed (FW) earn 189 per cent more than the formal self-employed (FS), 45 per cent more than the upper-tier informal wage-employed (UIW), 140 per cent more than the upper-tier informal self-employed (UIS), 13 per cent more than the lower-tier informal wage-employed (LIW),[9] and 260 per cent more than the lower-tier informal self-employed (LIS).

If the female formal wage-employed change job to work as self-employed in the next period, their earnings decline by 59 per cent. Their earnings also decrease by 49 per cent, 86 per cent, 45 per cent, and 88 per cent when switching jobs to UIW, UIS, LIW, and LIS, respectively. In the same way, the earnings of the male formal wage-employed decline by 85 per cent, 36 per cent, 77 per cent, 12 per cent, and 93 per cent when they move to FS, UIW, UIS, LIW, and LIS, respectively.

From a gender perspective, we find that the main results in section 4.1 still hold—transitioning out of self-employed jobs to wage-employment increases female workers' earnings by between 10 and 43 percentage points. For male workers, the difference is even larger—between 41 and 81 percentage points. With regard to the informal-sector tiers, the increase in earnings for the female self-employed who move from the lower-tier to the upper-tier is only 2 percentage points; within the wage-employed category, the same change results in a 4 percentage points increase. The transitions for male workers, however, are much larger (1–24 percentage point increases). This is because having a self-employed job

[9] Note that the coefficient for LIW (−0.13) is statistically insignificant.

Table 3.8 Fixed-effects OLS estimates by gender, hukou type, and hukou location

Base category: **Formal wage-employed (FW)**	**(1) Female**	**(2) Male**	**(3) Non-agricultural hukou**	**(4) Agricultural hukou**	**(5) Local**	**(6) Migrant**
Formal self-employed	−0.892***	−1.887***	−1.710***	−1.181***	−1.147***	−2.582***
(FS)	(0.160)	(0.231)	(0.231)	(0.149)	(0.146)	(0.561)
Upper-tier informal wage-employed	−0.689***	−0.447***	−0.548***	−0.543***	−0.535***	−0.614***
(UIW)	(0.069)	(0.045)	(0.040)	(0.049)	(0.036)	(0.092)
Upper-tier informal self-employed	−1.960**	−1.403***	−1.809***	−1.406***	−1.414***	−2.209***
(UIS)	(0.820)	(0.301)	(0.626)	(0.359)	(0.441)	(0.738)
Lower-tier informal wage-employed	−0.588***	−0.127	−0.814***	−0.192**	−0.275***	−0.521***
(LIW)	(0.128)	(0.085)	(0.124)	(0.086)	(0.086)	(0.170)
Lower-tier informal self-employed	−2.080***	−2.600***	−1.914***	−2.463***	−2.300***	−2.522***
(LIS)	(0.140)	(0.171)	(0.322)	(0.183)	(0.142)	(0.211)
Year fixed effects	Yes	Yes	Yes	Yes	Yes	Yes
Province fixed effects	Yes	Yes	Yes	Yes	Yes	Yes
Industry fixed effect	Yes	Yes	Yes	Yes	Yes	Yes
Observations	22,956	26,238	10,989	38,205	43,113	6,069
Adjusted R-squared	0.233	0.276	0.248	0.220	0.247	0.337
ξ(Earnings, FS)	−0.59	−0.85	−0.82	−0.70	−0.68	−0.92
ξ(Earnings, UIW)	−0.49	−0.36	−0.42	−0.42	−0.41	−0.46
ξ(Earnings, UIS)	−0.86	−0.77	−0.84	−0.77	−0.77	−0.89
ξ(Earnings, LIW)	−0.45	−0.12	−0.56	−0.18	−0.24	−0.41
ξ(Earnings, LIS)	−0.88	−0.93	−0.85	−0.92	−0.90	−0.92

Note: Dependent variable is inverse hyperbolic sine (IHS) earnings. Clustered robust standard errors at the province level in parentheses. All models include a full set of worker characteristics. The full set of regression results are reported in Appendix Tables D3 and D4 of Lin et al (2020). ξ (Earnings, work status) shows the percentage change (semi-elasticity) of earnings when transitioning from the formal wage-employed to another work status using the inverse hyperbolic sine (IHS or arcsinh) transformation; * $p < 0.1$, ** $p < 0.05$, *** $p < 0.01$.
Source: authors' calculation based on CFPS data (Institute of Social Science, Peking University 2018).

often means a higher risk of earnings and less job security. In the data, we find that the variance (or coefficient of variation) in earnings for men is higher than for women, implying that for male workers switching jobs will generally result in a larger change in earnings than for females.

4.3 Hukou status by type and location

Columns 3–6 of Table 3.8 show the results of hukou status by type (agricultural vs non-agricultural) and by location (local vs migrant). Compared to the formal wage-employed (FW), workers who have an agricultural hukou and work as formal self-employed (FS) have 118 per cent less earnings; likewise, the upper-tier informal wage-employed (UIW) have 54 per cent less earnings, the upper-tier informal self-employed (UIS) have 141 per cent less earnings, the lower-tier informal wage-employed (LIW) have 19 per cent less earnings, and the lower-tier informal self-employed (LIS) have 246 per cent less earnings. For workers who do not have an agricultural hukou, the formal wage-employed (FW) have 171 per cent more earnings than the formal self-employed (FS), 55 per cent more than the upper-tier informal wage-employed (UIW), 181 per cent more than the upper-tier informal self-employed (UIS), 81 per cent more than the lower-tier informal wage-employed (LIW), and 191 per cent more than the lower-tier informal self-employed (LIS).

If the formal wage-employed with an agricultural hukou change jobs to work as formal self-employed in the next period, then their earnings decline by 70 per cent. Their earnings also decrease by 42 per cent, 77 per cent, 18 per cent, and 92 per cent when switching jobs to UIW, UIS, LIW, and LIS, respectively. Similarly, the earnings of the formal wage-employed without an agricultural hukou decline by 82 per cent, 42 per cent, 84 per cent, 56 per cent, and 85 per cent when changing jobs to FS, UIW, UIS, LIW, and LIS, respectively. In short, the results by hukou type show the same findings, that is, that transitioning from being self-employed to wage workers and from being lower-tier informal self-employed to upper-tier informal self-employed increase earnings for both agricultural and non-agricultural hukou workers.

Our study is particularly interested in understanding how the livelihoods of rural–urban migrants may change when moving to different work status groups. Columns 5 and 6 of Table 3.8 show the results for local workers and migrant workers. For migrants who are formal wage-employed (FW), earnings are 258 per cent more than those of the formal self-employed (FS), 61 per cent more than the upper-tier informal wage-employed (UIW), 221 per cent more than the upper-tier informal self-employed (UIS), 52 per cent more than the lower-tier informal wage-employed (LIW), and 252 per cent more than the lower-tier informal self-employed (LIS). Likewise, for the local formal wage-employed, earnings are 115 per cent more than those of the formal self-employed (FS), 54 per cent more than the upper-tier informal wage-employed (UIW), 141 per cent more than the upper-tier informal self-employed (UIS), 28 per cent more than the lower-tier informal wage-employed (LIW), and 230 per cent more than the lower-tier informal self-employed (LIS).

If the migrant formal wage-employed (FW) change jobs and work as self-employed (FS) in the next period, their earnings decline by 92 per cent. Their earnings decrease by 46 per cent, 89 per cent, 41 per cent, and 92 per cent when switching to UIW, UIS, LIW, and LIS, respectively. Similarly, when the local formal wage-employed (FW) change jobs to formal self-employed (FS), their earnings decline by 68 per cent, by 41 per cent when changing to upper-tier informal wage-employed (UIW), and by 77 per cent when changing to upper-tier informal self-employed (UIS). If switching jobs to the lower-tier informal sector, earnings decline by 24 per cent when switching to wage-employed (LIW) and by 90 per cent when switching to self-employed (LIS).

In essence, the results show that, compared to local workers, migrants have larger earnings deficits between the formal wage-employed job and the other five categories of work status groups. Transitioning out of the formal wage-employed to all other work status groups reduces migrants' earnings substantially more than their local counterparts, especially for self-employed jobs (formal self-employed 92 per cent, upper-tier informal self-employed 89 per cent, and lower-tier informal self-employed 92 per cent). In other words, policymakers could enhance the livelihoods of migrants by revising—if eliminating is not entirely possible—the hukou system to close the rural–urban gap. Helping migrants to transition from the self-employed to the wage-employed can substantially increase their earnings (more than 50 percentage points from the estimation). Where migrants are working as self-employed in the informal sector, to improve their livelihoods, the government can also help them to move from the lower-tier to the upper-tier informal self-employed.

5. Conclusion and policy guidance

Since China began its economic reforms and open-door policy in 1978, the country has been experiencing remarkable economic growth, with people's living standards having increased more than tenfold in the past 40 years. Meanwhile, informality in China's labour market has also grown rapidly as the economy has developed. However, how transitioning jobs from the informal sector to the formal economy, or the reverse, affects the livelihoods of Chinese workers has remained unanswered. Our study fills this gap by using the latest three waves of a nationally representative longitudinal household survey data set to estimate the changes in earnings for wage earners and the self-employed within and between the informal and formal sectors.

Our findings show that the formal wage-employed have the highest earnings among all work status groups. We find that transitioning from the informal sector to the formal sector helps improve Chinese workers' livelihoods. In particular, switching from being self-employed to being wage-employed in either the formal or informal sector helps to increase earnings. The self-employed in the informal sector can also enhance their livelihoods by changing jobs from the lower tier to the upper tier. The results are consistent by gender (female vs male), hukou type (agricultural vs non-agricultural), and hukou location (local vs migrant).

Because of China's abundant labour supply in the informal sector—over 80 per cent of the 290 million rural–urban migrants—and insufficient labour demand in the formal sector, transitioning from the informal to the formal sector is practically difficult, though not impossible. In 2013, the Chinese Academy of Social Sciences proposed a blueprint for promoting urban–rural integration. It is one of the factor market integration plans (capital, labour, and information) in the government's policy guidelines for addressing the imbalanced development between rural and urban areas. First, our empirical findings are in line with the urban–rural integration plan in calling for improving factor markets, enhancing infrastructures, and creating more job opportunities in the formal sector to facilitate the movement from the informal to the formal sector and the flow from the lower tier to the upper tier. Second, our findings suggest that enforcement of and compliance with the 2008 Labor Contract Law should be strengthened. Under the law, the government mandates all employers to provide work insurance and pensions to employees, but noncompliance has been an issue (Giles et al. 2013). Offering social protection to the disadvantaged informal workers and the self-employed, as required by the law, can help enhance their livelihoods. Third, our findings suggest that there should be increased investment in human capital. Governments can provide education and training programmes to self-employed workers in the informal sector and the lower tier; human capital theory and our empirical results show that education plays a pivotal role in such workers' earnings.[10] Finally, we suggest that the hukou system should be revised or abolished. The institutional barrier of the hukou system has been discussed in numerous studies and has been criticized by commentators as the major culprit responsible for the increased urban–rural gap, rising income inequality, and threatened livelihoods.

Future research could extend the study through a distributional approach. Another potential extension would be to provide evidence of the effects on livelihoods for different types of firm ownership, especially the role played by state-owned enterprises and the thriving private firms during China's unprecedented economic transition.

[10] See Tables D2–D4 in Appendix D in Lin et al. (2020) for full estimation results.

References

Alaniz, E., T.H. Gindling, C. Mata, and D. Rojas (2020). 'Transforming Informal Work and Livelihoods in Costa Rica and Nicaragua'. WIDER Working Paper 100/2020. Helsinki: UNU-WIDER. https://doi.org/10.35188/UNU-WIDER/2020/857-3.

Appleton, S., J. Knight, L. Song, and Q. Xia (2009). 'The Economics of Communist Party Membership: The Curious Case of Rising Numbers and Wage Premium during China's Transition'. *Journal of Development Studies*, 45(2): 256–275. https://doi.org/10.1080/00220380802264739.

Bellemare, M.F., and C.J. Wichman (2020). 'Elasticities and the Inverse Hyperbolic Sine Transformation'. *Oxford Bulletin of Economics and Statistics*, 82(1): 50–61. https://doi.org/10.1111/obes.12325.

Bian, Y., and J.R. Logan (1996). 'Market Transition and the Persistence of Power: The Changing Stratification System in Urban China'. *American Sociological Review*, 61(5): 739–758. https://doi.org/10.2307/2096451.

Burbidge, J.B., L. Magee, and A.L. Robb (1988). 'Alternative Transformations to Handle Extreme Values of the Dependent Variable'. *Journal of the American Statistical Association*, 83(401): 123–127. https://doi.org/10.1080/01621459.1988.10478575.

Cai, F., and M. Wang (2004). 'Informal Employment and Labor Market Development—Interpreting China's Urban Employment Growth'. *Economics Dynamics*, 2: 24–28 (in Chinese).

Danquah, M., S. Schotte, and K. Sen (2019). 'Transforming Informal Work and Livelihoods'. Concept Note. Helsinki: UNU-WIDER.

Du, Y., and G. Wan (2014). 'The Effects of Urban Formal and Informal Employments in Urban on Poverty Reduction'. *Economics Dynamics*, 9: 88–97 (in Chinese).

Giles, J., D.Wang, and A. Park, (2013). 'Expanding Social Insurance Coverage in Urban China'. In C. Giulietti, K. Tatsiramos, and K.F. Zimmermann (eds), *Labor Market Issues in China* (*Research in Labor Economics, Vol. 37*), Emerald Group Publishing Limited, Bingley, 123–179.

Hu, A., and Z. Li (2006). 'China's Urban Informal Employment and Informal Sector during the Transition (1990–2004)'. *Journal of Tsinghua University (Philosophy and Social Science Edition)*, 3: 111–119 (in Chinese).

Hu, A., and Y. Yang (2001). 'Employment Mode Transitions: From Formal to Informal: An Analysis of China's Informal Employment'. *Management World*, 2: 69–78 (in Chinese).

Institute of Social Science, Peking University (2018). 'China Family Panel Studies (CFPS)'. Peking University Open Research Data Platform, V39. https://doi.org/10.18170/DVN/45LCSO.

ILO (International Labour Organization) (2018). *Women and Men in the Informal Economy: A Statistical Picture*. Geneva: ILO.

Kanbur, R. (2017). 'Informality: Causes, Consequences and Policy Responses'. *Review of Development Economics*, 21(4): 939–961. https://doi.org/10.1111/rode.12321.

La Porta, R., and A. Shleifer (2014). 'Informality and Development'. *Journal of Economic Perspectives*, 28(3): 109–126. https://doi.org/10.1257/jep.28.3.109.

Lam, K.-C. (2003). *Earnings Advantage of Party Members in Urban China*. Hong Kong: Business Research Centre, School of Business, Hong Kong Baptist University.

Li, B., and A.G. Walder (2001). 'Career Advancement as Party Patronage: Sponsored Mobility into the Chinese Administrative Elite, 1949–1996'. *American Journal of Sociology*, 106(5): 1371–1408. https://doi.org/10.1086/320816.

Li, H., P.W. Liu, J. Zhang, and N. Ma (2007). 'Economic Returns to Communist Party Membership: Evidence from Urban Chinese Twins'. *Economic Journal*, 117(523): 1504–1520. https://doi.org/10.1111/j.1468-0297.2007.02092.x.
Li, Q. (1999). 'Occupational Movements of China's Rural–Urban Migrants'. *Sociology Research*, 3: 95–103 (in Chinese).
Li, Q., and Z. Tang (2002). 'Rural–Urban Migrants and Informal Employment in Chinese Cities'. *Sociology Research*, 6: 13–25 (in Chinese).
Liang, X., Y. Lin, and D. Zhao (2007). 'Characteristics, Issues, and Countermeasures for Rural–Urban Migrants' Second Migration: A Migrant Survey from Zhejiang, Fujian, and Tianjin'. *China Social Sciences*, 3: 13–28 (in Chinese).
Liang, Z., S. Appleton, and L. Song (2016). 'Informal Employment in China: Trends, Patterns and Determinants of Entry'. IZA Discussion Paper 10139. Bonn: Institute of Labor Economics.
Lin, C., L. Ye, and W. Zhang (2020). 'Transforming Informal Work and Livelihoods in China'. WIDER Working Paper 2020/150. Helsinki: UNU-WIDER. https://doi.org/10.35188/UNU-WIDER/2020/907-5
Liu, Z. (2003). 'The Economic Impact and Determinants of Investment in Human and Political Capital in China'. *Economic Development and Cultural Change*, 51(4): 823–849. https://doi.org/10.1086/375570.
MacKinnon, J.G., and L. Magee (1990). 'Transforming the Dependent Variable in Regression Models'. *International Economic Review*, 31(2): 315–339. https://doi.org/10.2307/2526842.
Morduch, J., and T. Sicular (2000). 'Politics, Growth, and Inequality in Rural China: Does It Pay to Join the Party?'. *Journal of Public Economics*, 77(3): 331–356. https://doi.org/10.1016/S0047-2727(99)00121-8.
National Bureau of Statistics of China (2019). 'Report on the Dynamic Monitoring Survey of Migrant Population in Urban China'. Beijing: The National Population and Family Planning Commission.
Nordman, C.J., F. Rakotomanana, and F. Roubaud (2016). 'Informal Versus Formal: A Panel Data Analysis of Earnings Gaps in Madagascar'. *World Development*, 86: 1–17. https://doi.org/10.1016/j.worlddev.2016.05.006.
Pence, K.M. (2006). 'The Role of Wealth Transformations: An Application to Estimating the Effect of Tax Incentives on Saving'. *B.E. Journal of Economic Analysis & Policy*, 5(1): 1–26. https://doi.org/10.1515/1538-0645.1430.
Ravallion, M. (2017). 'A Concave Log-like Transformation Allowing Non-Positive Values'. *Economics Letters*, 161: 130–132. https://doi.org/10.1016/j.econlet.2017.09.019.
Song, Y. (2014). 'What Should Economists Know About the Current Chinese Hukou System?'. *China Economic Review*, 29: 200–212. https://doi.org/10.1016/j.chieco.2014.04.012.
Walder, A.G. (1995). 'Career Mobility and the Communist Political Order'. *American Sociological Review*, 60(3): 309–328. https://doi.org/10.2307/2096416.
Wan, X. (2008). 'Entry Conditions and Effects to the Formal Sector of Rural–Urban Migrants'. *Management World*, 1: 63–74 (in Chinese).
Wan, X. (2009). 'The Retrospection and Perspectives of Research on Informal Employment of Rural-Urban Migrants'. *Journal of Sun yat-sen University (Social Science Edition)*. 49(1): 159–170 (in Chinese).
Wu, Y. (2009). 'The Destination of Informal Employment'. *Economic Research*, 7: 91–106 (in Chinese).

Xie, Y., and E. Hannum (1996). 'Regional Variation in Earnings Inequality in Reform-Era Urban China'. *American Journal of Sociology*, 101(4): 950–992. https://doi.org/10.1086/230785.

Xue, J., and W. Gao (2012). 'Informal Employment in Urban China: Its Size, Features and Earning Disparity'. *Comparative Economic & Social Systems*, 16: 59–69 (in Chinese).

4

Moving up or down the job ladder in India

Examining informality–formality transitions

Rajesh Raj Natarajan, Simone Schotte, and Kunal Sen

1. Introduction

Among developing countries, India has the largest number of informal workers and a very high proportion of informal workers in the total workforce, at 83.5 per cent in 2017–2018 (NSSO 2019). The persistence of informality has been a puzzling feature of India's economic development pathway, given the rapid growth of the Indian economy since the early 1990s (Raj and Sen 2016; Bardhan 2018). Further, the persistence of informality in India makes the country 'atypical' among fast-growing Asian economies, most of which have seen a decline in the size of the informal sector in recent decades (McCaig and Pavcnik 2018). In addition, several studies have documented the heterogeneous nature of India's labour market and that both the self-employed and the wage-employed in informal work have upper-tier and lower-tier segments in India (see, in particular, Kannan and Papola 2007; NCEUS 2007). In this study, we ask: how likely is it for informal workers to transition to formal jobs and are reverse transitions possible? Do mobility patterns differ between self-employed and wage workers? Does lower-tier informal work provide a pathway for a better paid job? Or is it a dead-end activity with very limited possibility for upward mobility? How are education, caste, gender, and location of workers associated with mobility? And what are the implications of transitions for income gains or losses? We examine the patterns, correlates, and consequences of worker transition, both from informal to formal jobs and from lower-tier to upper-tier informal jobs, using a unique longitudinal data set for over 37,000 workers drawn from the India Human Development Survey (IHDS) of 2004–2005 and 2011–2012 (IHDS-1 and IHDS-2, respectively) conducted by the National Council of Applied Economic Research and the University of Maryland (see IHDS 2020).

There is a large existing scholarship on the informal sector in India, which has looked at both self-employment and wage-employment. Studies focusing on self-employment have examined the productivity implications of household and non-household enterprises (Marjit and Kar 2011; Kathuria et al. 2013; Mazumdar

Rajesh Raj Natarajan, Simone Schotte, and Kunal Sen, *Moving up or down the job ladder in India*. In: *The Job Ladder*. Edited by Gary S. Fields, T. H. Gindling, Kunal Sen, Michael Danquah, and Simone Schotte, Oxford University Press.
 DOI: 10.1093/oso/9780192867339.003.0004

and Sarkar 2013; Banerji et al. 2016; Raj and Sen 2016; Raj and Sen 2020). Studies focusing on wage-employment have tried to understand whether government regulations (such as labour laws) can explain why a formal firm may use informal workers instead of formal workers, the relationship between wage-employment and poverty, and the conditions of work among informal wage workers (Unni 1998; Unni and Rani 2003; Besley and Burgess 2004; NCEUS 2009; Saha et al. 2013; Barnes 2015; Kathuria and Raj 2016). However, these studies do not examine the possibility of workers transitioning from one work status to another as they mostly use repeated cross-sectional surveys of the National Sample Survey Office in New Delhi, India.[1] By using a nationally representative panel of workers, in both formal and informal jobs, over the period 2002/05–2011/12 and by implementing a classification of the work status of these workers (discussed in section 2), we are able to provide a rich characterization of the trajectories of workers across different tiers of the Indian labour market. The period of our analysis also coincides with the high growth episode of the Indian economy, when the average annual growth in gross domestic product was 8.4 per cent, the highest in the post-independence period, which allows us to examine whether India's rapid growth led to more informal workers moving to the formal sector as well as to increases in their earnings.

In the empirical analysis, we first document the transition probabilities of individuals across different work status. We then estimate multinomial logit models to examine the extent to which status choices and transition rates are correlated with individual and household-level characteristics, such as gender, age, education, geographic location, and social group. Finally, we estimate earnings equations to provide a quantitative assessment of the change in earnings that may occur when a worker moves from one work status to another.

Our results based on transition analysis suggest that self-employed workers exhibit relatively more mobility than wage workers. The movement out of existing status is more pronounced among formal self-employed workers and a majority of them transition downwards into the lower tier of the informal sector. Among the wage workers, we find high persistence rates for formal wage-employed and lower-tier informal wage-employed. The higher churn rate among the upper-tier informal wage-employed does offer some evidence towards upward mobility, with workers transitioning into formal wage-employment. However, we also find significant risk of downward mobility, with upper-tier informal salaried workers going into lower-tier informal employment. We also find that women, lower castes, less educated, and rural workers are less likely to move upwards in work status. As expected, our results do suggest substantial income gains for workers experiencing

[1] These are the Employment and Unemployment Survey and the Unincorporated Non-Agricultural Enterprises Survey.

upward transition. Overall, our results suggest that lower-tier informal workers, whether in self-employment or wage-employment, have limited upward transition possibilities and are in a 'dead-end' work status.

The rest of the chapter is divided into five sections. Section 2 presents a framework of analysis for the Indian labour market, considering the two-tiered nature of informal work. Section 3 presents the data and definitions of various employment status groups identified in the study. In section 4, we look at the composition of employment by work status and worker characteristics. We investigate the flow of workers between different work status groups using transition matrices in section 5. The results of our econometric analysis are also presented and discussed in this section. Section 6 concludes.

2. Work status classification in India

In this section, we discuss how we apply the schema proposed by Fields in Chapter 2 of the volume to the Indian context.

The social and economic structure of labour markets in India makes the schema particularly applicable to the Indian case. First, consider self-employment. In India, formal manufacturing firms need to register with the Indian Factories Act of 1948, which applies to manufacturing and requires registration of all enterprises with 10 or more workers if they use electricity and 20 or more workers if they do not (in effect, the latter requirement has become irrelevant as most firms in India use electricity; see Chatterjee and Kanbur 2014). Informal firms (i.e. firms that do not register with the Factories Act) can be of two types: enterprises that use hired labour (non-household enterprises) and enterprises that use only family labour (i.e. household enterprises). For the larger of the unregistered non-household enterprises, the decision not to formalize may be because these enterprises choose to avoid the occupational and health regulations that every formal firm needs to follow under the Indian Factories Act of 1948 (Kanbur 2017). For the smaller of the unregistered non-household enterprises, constraints to growth may be due to lack of availability of credit and skilled labour (Raj and Sen 2015). Unregistered non-household enterprises are significantly more productive than household enterprises in India and can be classified as upper-tier informal self-employed, while household enterprises can be classified as lower-tier informal self-employed (Raj and Sen 2016).

In the case of wage-employment, formal wage workers in India have permanent job contracts and are typically protected from job dismissal—especially in larger firms—under the Industrial Disputes Act, and have access to social security benefits (Saha et al. 2013). Upper-tier informal wage workers do not have the same job security as formal wage workers and can be employed in either formal or informal firms. However, they may enjoy de facto benefits such as subsidized meals and housing. They may also be workers in skilled jobs, which require some type of vocational training (such as those with degrees from national or regional vocational training institutes). Lower-tier informal wage workers, on the other hand, are free-entry occupations and are in unskilled work. In rural areas, these are mainly agricultural wage workers; in urban areas, these are mainly casual workers and day labourers, often in the construction sector. There is a wealth of anthropological and economic evidence that these occupations are at the bottom of the heap in India (see Harriss-White 2010). Agricultural labour in India has the highest poverty rates among all occupational groups (Gang et al. 2008) and lower castes in India's social hierarchy of labour are over-represented in this occupational group (Vaid 2012). This relationship between castes and specific occupations can be traced back to the *jajmani* system: a system of hereditary patron–client relationships between landed proprietors from the upper and middle castes and the bonded agricultural labourers from lower castes (Dumont 1970; Bayly 1999; Gang et al. 2016). Despite the reduction in the incidence of the worst forms of bonded labour and other coercive practices, the hereditary nature of the link between caste and occupation, especially in the lower rungs of the caste system, still persists in Indian society. In the case of construction labourers, these are workers who are often paid a daily wage below the minimum wage and who move from city to city searching for manual work in construction sites as 'footloose labour', as India's rapid growth led to a real estate boom (Breman 2012; Shah et al. 2018).

We now turn to a discussion of the data we use to study worker transition in India and how we operationalize the classification, as proposed by Fields in Chapter 2, in the Indian case.

3. Data source and work status classification

3.1 Data

The data for this study are drawn from the IHDS, conducted in 2004–2005 and again in 2011–2012 (henceforth referred to as 2005 and 2012, respectively; see IHDS 2020). This nationally representative, multi-topic survey collected information at both household and individual levels. In its first round in 2005, the survey covered 215,574 individuals from 41,554 households in 1,503 villages and 971 urban neighbourhoods across all states and union territories of India (with the exception of Andaman and Nicobar and Lakshadweep islands). More information on the data is provided in Natarajan et al. (2020). We made further adjustments to the data described in Natarajan et al. (2020). These adjustments left us with a balanced panel of 37,356 individuals.

The key to this study is to accurately define the work status of the worker. We base our definition of a worker on the minimum number of hours worked in a year. Following Dhanaraj and Mahambare (2019) and Lei et al. (2019), we fix this threshold at 240 hours, and those individuals who have reported to have put in at least 240 hours in a particular activity are counted as being in the workforce. Activities in this case constitute wage or salary work, animal care, or working on the household farm or business. Those who have worked for fewer than 240 hours are treated as unemployed. As mentioned earlier, we concentrate on workers engaged in non-farm activities and agricultural wage workers, although we also include farmers and the unemployed in robustness checks of our main findings.

In defining the 'activity status' of a worker, our study considers their main job, that is, the job where the worker has spent the maximum hours in the last year out of all the jobs they have worked on. As discussed in section 2, the transitional analysis in this chapter focuses on six mutually exclusive work status groups and does not consider unemployment. However, we do a robustness check of the transition analysis including unemployment as an additional status. The results of this additional exercise are not discussed in the chapter but are presented in Appendix A of Natarajan et al. (2020).

3.2 Work status classification

Based on the strategy discussed in section 2, we classify the workers into six mutually exclusive work status categories as explained in Table 4.1. We start with wage workers. Among the wage workers, those with permanent job contracts are classified as formal wage-employees. As mentioned in section 2, these workers enjoy labour law protection and are also entitled to social security benefits. Within the informal sector, the upper-tier wage-employment consists of workers in occupations that require some type of training and skills. As an approximation, we include workers who are employed in one of the following four occupations: professional, technical, and related workers (Divisions 0–1, Indian National Classification of Occupations (INCO) 1968); administrative, executive, and managerial workers (Division 2, INCO); clerical and related workers (Division 3, INCO); sales and service workers (Divisions 4–5, INCO); and production and related workers (Divisions 7–9, INCO).[2] Additionally, we also check whether these workers are entitled to de facto benefits such as meals or housing. All remaining workers, mainly agricultural, construction, and other manual labourers, are classified as 'lower-tier informal'.

[2] All these occupations require some prior skill and are therefore not 'free-entry' occupations (Howard and Prakash 2012).

Table 4.1 Work status classification

Category	Description
Formal wage-employees	All wage workers with permanent job contracts are classified as formal wage-employees. All permanent workers in India are offered labour law protection and are also entitled to social security benefits.
Upper-tier informal wage-employees	Informal wage workers are classified as upper-tier informal if they either work in occupations that require some type of training or receive some type of de facto benefit (such as meals or housing) from the employers.
Lower-tier informal wage-employees	All remaining informal workers are classified as lower-tier informal.
Formal self-employed	All self-employed workers who are in professions that require a high level of skills (Division 0–1, INCO), or employ 10 or more workers are classified as formal self-employed.
Upper-tier informal self-employed	All informal self-employed workers who employ fewer than 10 but at least one hired worker are classified as upper-tier informal. These also include workers who employ more than 10 workers but operate from home or from a mobile location.
Lower-tier informal self-employed	All informal self-employed workers who employ only household workers are classified as lower-tier informal self-employed. All contributing family workers are also included in this category.

Source: authors' compilation.

In the case of self-employed workers, we implement the formal–informal categorization of workers using the size of the businesses they own. Accordingly, all self-employed workers in non-farm businesses employing 10 or more workers are classified as formal self-employed. This definition is broadly in line with the official criterion used to classify firms in India. This criterion was laid down by the Factories Act of 1948, which demarcates all manufacturing firms employing 10 or more employees and using electric power as formal and those that fall below these cut-offs as informal sector firms (Besley and Burgess 2004).[3]

[3] One drawback of the India Human Development Survey (IHDS) data set is that it does not provide information on the number of workers employed by firms. Hence, using the information on the total wages paid to hired workers, we arrive at the number of hired workers. We first compute the average

Besides, we also treat all self-employed workers who are in professions that require a high level of skills as formal (Divisions 0–1, INCO). This category of occupations includes physicists, architects, engineers, technologists, physicians and surgeons, mathematicians, statisticians, economists, auditors, jurists, and teachers. Among the informal self-employed, all those who own businesses that employ fewer than 10 workers but at least one hired worker are classified as 'upper-tier informal'. These also include workers who are in businesses that employ hired workers but operate from home or from a mobile location. Self-employed workers who are in activities that employ only household workers are treated as lower-tier informal.[4] All contributing family workers are also included in this category. This is in line with the classification adopted by the surveys of the National Sample Survey Office in India, where they regard enterprises that employ household workers as own-account enterprises. These are the enterprises that form the bottom part of the manufacturing segment in the informal sector (Raj and Sen 2016).

We summarize the criteria adopted to classify the workers into six mutually exclusive work status groups in Table 4.1.

Our income estimates are derived from the main occupation, even though many individuals may have engaged in multiple jobs. We use the reported annual earnings, which are then converted to real values using the consumer price index at 2004–2005 prices. Only individuals who are working and have reported positive cash income are considered for the analysis. Following Danquah et al. (2019), we do not consider in-kind income and agricultural income generated by family farms for computing annual earnings.

4. Characteristics of workers in India's multi-tiered labour market

The shares of each labour work status for all individuals of working age (15–64 years) for 2005 and 2012 are presented in Table 4.2. The shares look similar between 2005 and 2012 except for notable changes in wage-employment. Table 4.2 shows that although informal employment makes up the major chunk of the total sample, it saw a slide from 90 per cent in 2005 to 85 per cent in 2012. The decline in

wage in each National Industrial Classification group from the total wage bill for each round of IHDS. We then estimate the number of hired workers by dividing the total wages paid to hired workers by the average wage. Using the number of hired workers, we then separate the formal businesses from the upper-tier informal ones. Accordingly, all workers who are part of the businesses that employ 10 or more workers are classified as formal and those who are employed in businesses with fewer than 10 workers are counted as upper-tier informal.

[4] We include workers in family farms under lower-tier informal, but they are excluded from most of our analysis.

Table 4.2 Distribution of workers by work status (percentage)

			2005	2012
(a) Proportion of employment by work status				
Self-employed	Formal		1.29	1.56
	Informal	Upper-tier	7.72	6.50
		Lower-tier	20.80	18.88
Wage-employed	Formal		9.24	13.81
	Informal	Upper-tier	29.33	21.70
		Lower-tier	31.62	37.55
Total number of observations			37,356	37,356
(b) Proportion of formal vs informal employment				
Formal			10.53	15.37
Informal		Upper-tier	37.05	28.20
		Lower-tier	52.42	56.43
Total			100	100
(c) Proportion of upper-tier informality in informal employment				
Upper-tier informal in total informal employment			41.41	33.32
Upper-tier informal in informal self-employment			27.08	25.60
Upper-tier informal in informal wage-employment			48.12	36.63

Note: We omit own farm work and animal care work and those who are unemployed from the final estimation. However, our lower-tier informal workers include agricultural wage labour. We used sample weights to arrive at these estimates.
Source: authors' estimates.

the share of upper-tier informal employment contributed to the overall drop in the contribution of the informal sector. The upper-tier of the informal sector reported a decline of about 8 per cent during this period. Although the upper tier declined in importance in both wage-employment and self-employment, it reported a steep fall of about 12 per cent in wage-employment. On the other hand, the significant gains in wage-employment led to formal-status employment increasing its contribution during this period.

When we look at each work status separately, we find that formal self-employment remains stable at around 1.5 per cent. Despite the fall in its share over the 2005–2012 period, lower-tier informal self-employment remains a substantially large segment in the self-employment category. The upper-tier—the second largest segment in the self-employment category—too finds its share declining marginally during this period. As is evident from Table 4.2, formal wage-employment reported substantial gains as the share of workers increased from 9.3 per cent to nearly 14 per cent during the study period. A similar increase in share is also noticed for lower-tier informal wage-employment. Maintaining its position as the single largest employer, this segment accommodates about 38 per cent of the workforce in the non-farm sector in 2012. Upper-tier informal wage-employment retains its position as the second largest work status but has registered an 8 per cent decline in its share over the 2005–2012 period. In summary, we observe significant increase in the share of workers in the formal status and more evidently in the wage-employment category. Evidence also points to the declining importance of upper-tier informal sector in both wage-employment and self-employment categories.

Table 4.3 provides a detailed analysis of the characteristics of the working-age population in each work status. To be specific, the table shows major differences in the characteristics of individuals of different status in the labour market. We consider three important individual attributes in Table 4.3, namely, age, gender, and geographical location. In general, self-employed workers are older than other workers in the non-farm sector (Table 4.3). The only exception is wage-employed in the formal sector, who are the oldest workers by average age. As Table 4.3 illustrates, the participation of workers is more skewed towards men—70 per cent of workers are men—and women are underrepresented in all work status groups. This finding is consonant with the studies indicating that women are increasingly underrepresented in the formal sector in comparison to their presence in the informal sector (Ghani et al. 2014). Our descriptive evidence points to a greater preponderance of self-employment and lower-tier informal employment among women. However, we also find a significant decline in the share of women in formal self-employment. This lends credence to the existing evidence that women tend to be more represented in the lower segment of the informal sector (Chen et al. 2006). Table 4.3 also points to geographic inequalities in the composition of jobs. A majority of about 70 per cent of non-farm workers are of rural origin. We find a significant share of urban workers in self-employment and formal wage-employment.

Education level is a crucial factor in aiding the transition from informal to formal employment (Benjamin and Mbaye 2014; ILO 2014). This is clearly evident from Table 4.4, which suggests a strong link between education levels and formal-sector employment. We find that better-educated workers are more represented in the formal sector while the less educated mostly end up in the informal sector. More than 70 per cent of formal-sector workers have secondary education or above, while a major chunk of informal-sector workers has only received primary education or have no schooling/education. This finding is perhaps consistent with the existing evidence that more educated workers are less likely to be employed in the informal sector (Shonchoy and Junankar 2014; Sheikh and Gaurav 2020). Sheikh and Gaurav (2020) found clear differences too in education levels between informal-sector and formal-sector workers, in favour of the latter. To sum up, our descriptive analysis broadly suggests that informality appears to be mostly evident among workers who are young, female, less educated, and who live in rural areas.

Table 4.3 Average worker characteristics by work status

Period	Self-employed			Wage-employed			Total
	Formal	Informal		Formal	Informal		
		Upper-tier	Lower-tier		Upper-tier	Lower-tier	
(a) Average age (years)							
2005	34.33	34.07	33.5	39.79	33.89	34.68	34.62
2012	42.22	42.53	42.27	42.6	40.51	41.83	41.79
(b) Share of female workers (%)							
2005	40.01	41.4	42.43	14.13	16.46	34.3	29.52
2012	37.99	41.91	43.21	15.59	17.82	32.02	29.52
(c) Share of urban workers (%)							
2005	39.83	50.08	39.6	54.22	31.81	0.08	29.43
2012	48.31	51.29	42.41	52.69	33.39	0.07	29.43

Note: We omit own farm work and animal care work and those who are unemployed from the final estimation. However, our lower-tier informal workers include agricultural wage labour. We used sample weights to arrive at these estimates.
Source: authors' estimates.

Table 4.4 Average worker characteristics by education level

Period	Self-employed			Wage-employed			Total
	Formal	Informal		Formal	Informal		
		Upper-tier	Lower-tier		Upper-tier	Lower-tier	
No schooling							
2005	10.69	15.69	25.37	9.64	33.55	54.74	34.67
2012	12.41	16.13	25.32	9.22	31.28	52.60	33.83
Lower primary							
2005	11.54	12.61	17.41	9.84	19.55	19.95	17.69
2012	9.51	13.55	18.33	9.34	21.31	21.24	18.38
Primary							
2005	5.90	10.00	9.39	5.83	9.58	7.87	8.64
2012	4.88	8.67	8.42	4.84	9.48	7.62	7.81
Secondary							
2005	24.22	33.40	30.95	33.60	25.51	14.12	24.38
2012	24.33	31.54	29.21	32.42	27.04	15.02	23.93
Higher secondary							
2005	16.96	15.53	11.21	15.31	7.14	2.86	8.16
2012	15.33	15.43	10.33	16.64	6.94	2.97	8.11
Graduation							
2005	30.68	12.76	5.67	25.78	4.68	0.46	6.46
2012	33.54	14.69	8.40	27.55	3.95	0.55	7.93

Note: We omit agricultural work and animal care work and those who are unemployed from the final estimation. However, our lower-tier informal workers include agricultural wage labour. We used sample weights to arrive at these estimates.
Source: authors' estimates.

5. Transitions in informal and formal employment

In this section, we first discuss the likelihood of workers moving from one work status to another using transition matrices. We then examine the correlates of worker mobility. Finally, we assess the income gains and losses that may take place when workers move from one work status to another.

5.1 Patterns in worker transition

How much movement is there among the work status groups in the non-farm sector in India? We examine this issue using the methodological tools discussed in Natarajan et al. (2020). In Table 4.5, we present probability estimates, defined as the probability of observing workers in a particular status at the end of the period, conditional on their employment status at the beginning of the period. In general, we observe considerable changes in employment status over the period 2004/05–2011/12. Close to half of the workers in our sample (47 per cent) change employment status during this period. Overall, the probabilities show that self-employed workers exhibit relatively more fluidity than wage workers. It is also evident from the table that there is very little movement of workers from wage-employment to self-employment. The findings also suggest that, in general, there is more mobility within self-employment and wage-employment than between these types of employment.

Job stability varies considerably across work status. For wage-employment, there is a lot of stickiness for formal and lower-tier informal work status. As is evident from Table 4.5, lower-tier informal wage workers report the highest retention rate, followed by formal wage workers. Nearly 73 per cent of the workers who worked in lower-tier informal wage-employment—the largest segment of our sample—retain the same work status in 2012. The finding of high persistence rates for lower-tier informal wage-employment perhaps indicates that these workers face significant challenges in changing jobs due to limited human capital and skills and insufficient working capital, especially for those wanting to move to self-employment. Among those who transitioned out, very few ended up (about 17 per cent) obtaining a salaried job in the upper-tier informal sector. The formal salaried workers, who account for 10 per cent of the total workers, too demonstrate a higher degree of immobility, with 65 per cent of them preferring to retain the same status. The most visible transition out of formal salaried employment is that into upper-tier informal wage-employment. Almost 17 per cent of the formal salaried workers moved into the upper-tier of wage-employment. Upper-tier informal wage workers are apparently the most mobile among wage workers, exhibiting a mixed transition pattern. While 38 per cent chose not to transition out, 32 per cent moved out as lower-tier wage workers, 16 per cent as formal salaried workers, and 10 per cent as lower-tier self-employed workers. Indeed, the higher turnover

Table 4.5 Transition matrix across work status groups

(a) Transition matrices								(b) Shares	
Employment status	Initial size (%)	Formal SE	Upper-tier informal SE	Lower-tier informal SE	Formal WE	Upper-tier informal WE	Lower-tier informal WE	% of individuals who remain in employment status	% of individuals who change employment status
Formal SE	1.29	29.16	8.8	25.42	14.34	10.51	11.77	0.38	0.91
Upper-tier informal SE	7.72	2.26	30.91	40.65	7.79	9.67	8.73	2.39	5.34
Lower-tier informal SE	20.79	2.12	12.37	48.41	5.96	14.01	17.13	10.06	10.73
Formal WE	9.24	1.3	2.51	6.34	64.96	17.08	7.81	6.01	3.23
Upper-tier informal WE	29.33	1.37	2.72	9.76	16.05	38.11	32.00	11.17	18.18
Lower-tier informal WE	31.62	0.14	1.25	6.01	3.42	16.28	72.90	23.05	8.57
Total	37,356	1.56	6.50	18.88	13.81	21.7	37.55	53.06	46.97

Note: SE = self-employed; WE = wage-employed. (i) Employment status in the base year and in the final year are presented in rows and columns, respectively. (ii) Initial size corresponds to the proportion of individuals who were in the particular employment status in the base year. (iii) The rows of the transition matrix sum to 1. (iv) The likelihood of staying in the same employment status conditional on the base-year employment status is highlighted in grey. (v) The share of those who remain in their employment status is the product of highlighted diagonals and initial size.
Source: authors' estimates based on India Human Development Survey (IHDS) data.

among upper-tier informal salaried workers offers some evidence of upward mobility, showing workers transitioning into formal wage-employment. At the same time, evidence also points to the existence of a significant risk of downward mobility, with upper-tier informal salaried workers going into lower-tier informal employment, either as wage earners or self-employed.

Turnover rates are highest among self-employed workers, implying that self-employment activities exhibit a lower degree of persistence than salaried jobs. The mobility out of existing status is more pronounced among formal self-employed workers, who form just 1.3 per cent of the total sample of workers. Nevertheless, they show a rather heterogeneous transition pattern. While those who remain in the status were confined to 29 per cent, 25 per cent experienced a downward transition to the lower tier of the informal self-employed and another 9 per cent to the upper tier. We do see some mobility out of formal self-employment into formal salaried jobs (14 per cent) and also to the upper tier and lower tier of wage-employment at 11 and 12 per cent, respectively. Separation rates are also very high among the self-employed in the upper-tier informal sector. The outflows from this segment are mostly to the lower tier of informal self-employment, indicating a deterioration in their work status. As Table 4.5 shows, the probability of transitioning from upper tier to lower tier stands at 41 per cent. We also find a high churning rate for workers in the lower-tier informal self-employed sector—the largest segment in the self-employed group accounting for 21 per cent of the workers in 2005. More than half of the workers (51 per cent) in this status opted to transition out. Of those who chose to move out, 26 per cent saw an upgradation in their status: 14 per cent as upper-tier informal wage-employed and 12 per cent as upper-tier informal self-employed. Another 17 per cent ended up as wage-employed in the lower tier of the informal sector.

The worker transition yields more or less a similar pattern when we include family farming under lower-tier informal self-employment activities in the destination state and introduce unemployment as an additional destination state.[5] Although we do see some movement of workers in every status into unemployment, the higher level of persistence of lower-tier informal wage-employment and formal-sector wage-employment is still evident in the overall transition pattern captured using the revised sub-sample of workers.

Our results based on an alternative classification, where we group together workers in wage-employment and self-employment to form three categories (namely, formal employment, upper-tier informal employment, and lower-tier informal employment), also show higher persistence of formal employment and lower-tier informal employment and lower persistence of upper-tier informal employment.[6]

[5] For the results, we refer the reader to an earlier version of this chapter, Natarajan et al. (2020).
[6] For results, please refer to the Appendix Table A2 of Natarajan et al. (2020).

We also find striking gender differences in transition (see Natarajan et al. 2020). Our results show that the degree of mobility is substantially lower among female workers than among male workers. We also find that mobility patterns for male workers are more or less similar to the transition probabilities for the total sample. As is the case with the total sample, we find higher retention rates among self-employed workers and higher rates of persistence among wage workers in the male sample. In the case of female workers, we find very high persistence rates for lower-tier informal wage-employment and formal wage-employment, and they are substantially higher than that of male workers.

5.2 Correlates of worker transition

Our preceding analysis suggests significant labour mobility across different work status groups. The next step in our empirical analysis is to locate the factors that might explain the transition between work status in the non-farm sector using the methodological tools discussed in Natarajan et al. (2020). In particular, in this section, we attempt to understand how the differences in individual and household attributes influence labour mobility across work status groups. The marginal effects of the multinomial logit model estimation yield the influence of selected explanatory variables on the probability of leaving the baseline work status for a certain destination status relative to the probability of not leaving the baseline status.[7] We test the robustness of our results by re-estimating the multinomial logit specification by including family farms and unemployment as additional status.[8] We also examine the coefficient estimates of worker characteristics using an ordered logit specification where we group together workers in wage-employment and self-employment to form three categories, namely, formal employment, upper-tier informal employment, and lower-tier informal employment.[9]

Figures 2–7 in Natarajan et al. (2020) present the average marginal effects on worker transitions by initial status in employment.[10] Here, we present the marginal effects of the transition from lower-tier informal self-employment (Fig. 4.1) and lower-tier informal wage-employment (Fig. 4.2) for illustrative purposes. Our results suggest a significant role for education, age, gender, social group, and geographical location in shaping mobility patterns. We find that education level plays a powerful role in explaining the mobility of workers from informal to formal status.

[7] For results, refer to Figures 2–7 and Appendix Table A3 of Natarajan et al. (2020).

[8] The results are presented in Appendix Table A4 of Natarajan et al. 2020.

[9] Results are not presented for brevity of space. Those who are interested may refer to the working paper version of this chapter (Appendix Table A5 in Natarajan et al. 2020).

[10] The regression results are presented in detail in Appendix Table A3 of Natarajan et al. (2020).

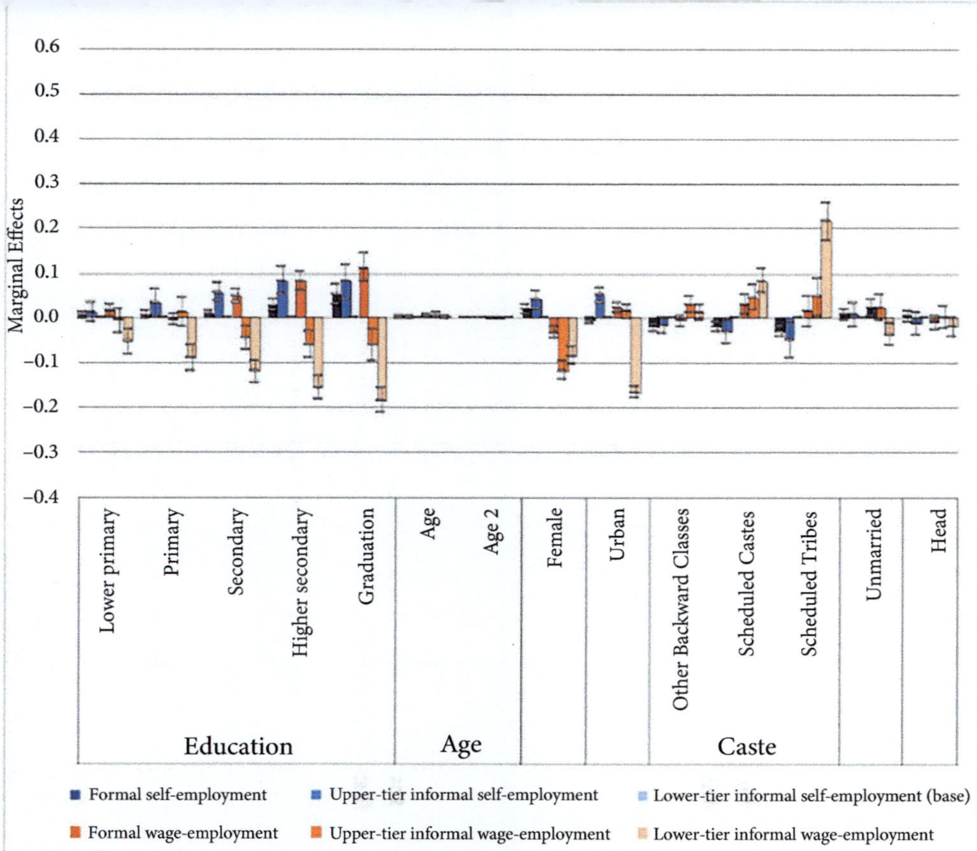

Fig. 4.1 Marginal effects for multinomial logistic regression: transitions from lower-tier informal self-employment

Source: authors' estimates.

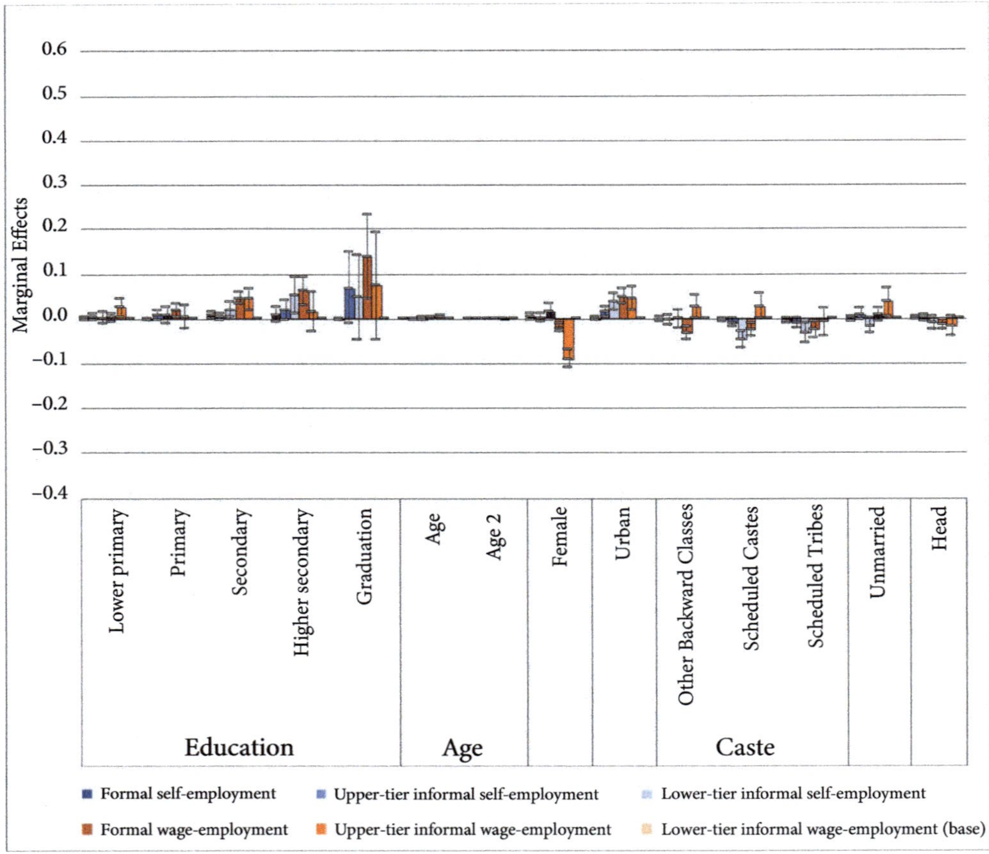

Fig. 4.2 Marginal effects for multinomial logistic regression: transitions from lower-tier informal wage-employment

Source: authors' estimates.

The education level significantly influences the probability of transition of workers from formal self-employment to formal wage-employment; the likelihood of formal self-employed transitioning to formal wage-employment increases with the level of education. Higher levels of education also increase the probability of upper-tier informal workers moving to formal employment and lower-tier informal workers moving to upper-tier informal employment. Overall, these findings highlight the importance of having skills, or human capital, which is one way workers can increase their chances of experiencing an upward transition in their work status. Moreover, our finding supports the existing evidence in the literature highlighting the critical role of education and human capital development in aiding the transition of an economy towards formality (Gong et al. 2004; La Porta and Shleifer 2014).

In the context of worker transitions, the gender of the worker appears to play a significant role. In particular, women exhibit a higher likelihood than men of transitioning from lower-tier informal self-employment to upper-tier informal and formal self-employment. However, a similar upward transition is not visible among women in wage-employment. In other words, compared with men, the likelihood of women making a favourable upward transition is less evident among salaried workers. Our results also suggest that the probability of female workers shifting from self-employment to wage-employment is low, but the reverse flow is much more common. In essence, our findings on gender corroborate the prevailing notion that women are significantly more likely than men to enter self-employment and less likely to enter wage-employment. This is more or less in line with the existing evidence that women are underrepresented in salaried work compared with self-employment in India (Neetha 2010). Given the traditional division of gender roles and the family responsibility of women in India, there is an increasing preference for flexible job options or part-time work among the women in India. Further, the costs of searching for jobs in the formal sector are likely to be higher for women than for men. It is argued that access to information about jobs is a constraint and social norms often dictate that women devote most of their time to domestic duties rather than looking for work (Fletcher et al. 2018).

5.3 Consequences of worker transition: income gains and losses

Our findings unambiguously point to substantial labour mobility across various work status groups in the non-farm sector in India. Does this labour mobility result in income gains? In other words, do workers experience significant wage gains as they transit across work status? In this section, we attempt to find an answer to this question, with the important caveat that earnings among self-employed are likely to be measured with error compared with earnings among wage-employed. We do this using the methodological tools discussed in Natarajan et al. (2020).

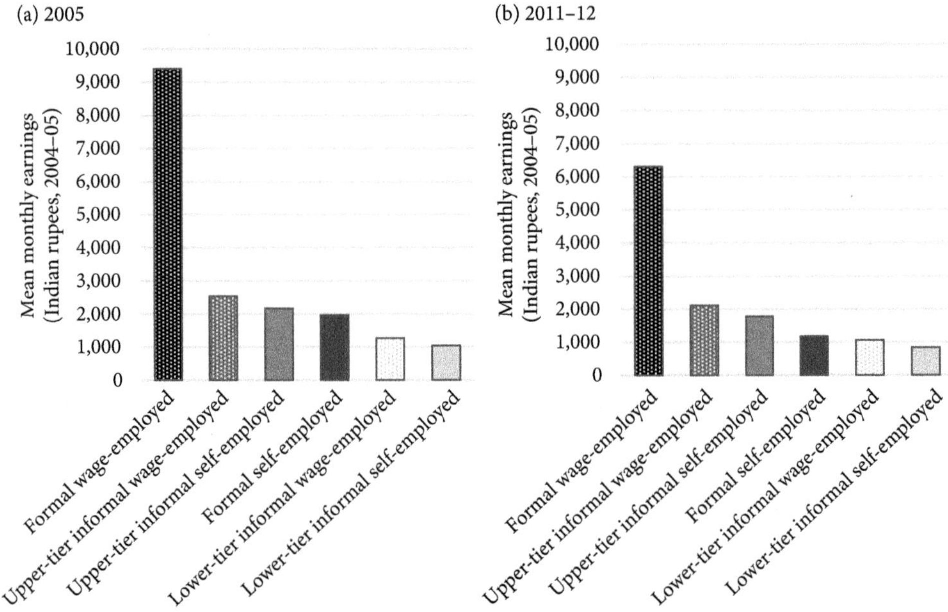

Fig. 4.3 Job ladder: Mean monthly earnings by work status
Source: authors' estimates based on Indian Human Development Survey (IHDS) data.

Before we discuss the regression results, we look at the differences in mean earnings across different work status groups and over time. We present the job ladder in Fig. 4.3, which depicts the mean earnings of workers in different labour market status groups to see whether mobility is systematically associated with changes in earnings.[11] The significantly higher wages for the formal wage-employment clearly explains why the formal wage workers tend to stay longer in the same status and turn out to be the ones most reluctant to leave the existing status. The finding also supports the traditional theory that formal salaried workers are paid significantly higher than their informal counterparts. Our results also endorse heterogeneity within informal employment as we find that the self-employed are often subject to lower wages compared with salaried ones. In addition, we find that upper-tier informal self-employed workers have somewhat higher earnings than formal self-employed workers, which may suggest that upper-tier jobs carrying a significant premium to compensate for the job security and other benefits of formal wage work, as has been found in the Latin American case (Maloney 2004).

Now, we discuss the main results where we investigate the effect of the transitions on worker's earnings. Following Danquah et al. (2019), we separately control for formality status and employment status. We present the detailed results in Natarajan et al. (2020), and Fig. 4.4 presents the visual representation of the results. Our results are more or less as expected. The gains in earnings over the period

[11] An important caveat here is that measurement errors are higher with self-employment earnings than wage earnings so that the earnings across the two categories may not be directly comparable.

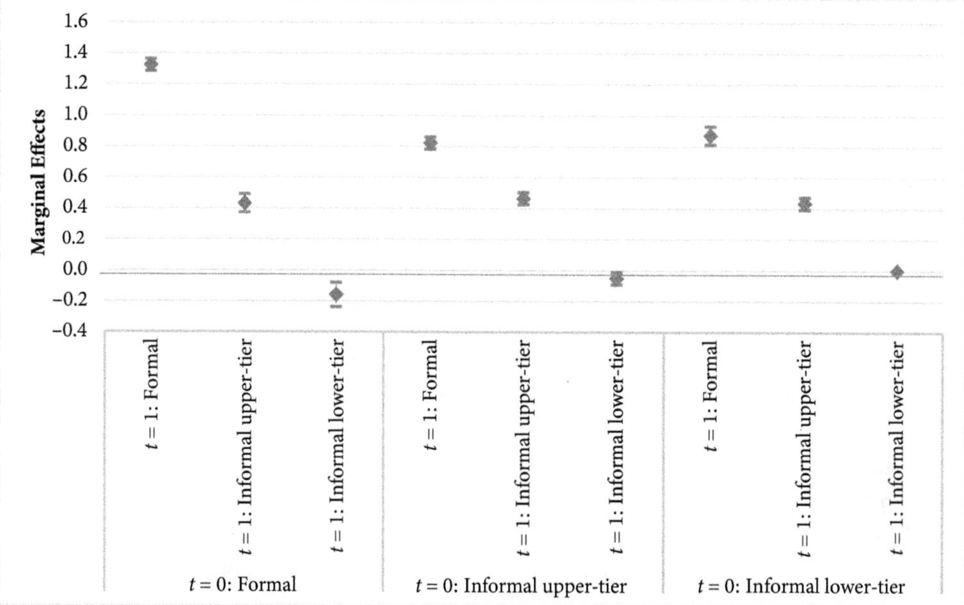

Fig. 4.4 Labour income dynamics
Source: authors' estimates.

2004/05–2011/12 are substantially higher for those who changed status from lower tier to upper tier or formal status than for those who did not change their status. We estimate that workers who transition from lower-tier informal employment to upper-tier informal employment and formal employment, on average experience a 33.1 and 63.9 per cent rise in earnings, respectively, relative to those who stay in the same category.

Thus, as one would expect, the rise in earnings is substantially higher for those who have made the transition to formal status (see Fig. 4.4). In other words, workers who made the transition to the formal sector from upper-tier and lower-tier informal status derived gains in earnings of similar magnitude. Further, positive income gains are also observed for those who transitioned from lower-tier to upper-tier informality compared with those who failed to make the transition. Expectedly, the largest inter-temporal change in earnings is reported by workers who continued to be in the formal sector.

6. Conclusions

This chapter examines the nature, magnitude, direction, and implications of employment transition patterns in India, the largest country in South Asia and the country with the highest levels of informality. We find significant worker mobility across different work status, although with limited entry into formal vis-à-vis informal employment. Overall, the transition probabilities suggest relatively more fluidity among self-employed workers than among wage workers. The findings also point to strong segmentation between wage-employment and self-employment. Our transition probabilities suggest that workers in formal self-employment are more likely to remain in that state or move into lower-tier self-employment than to move into wage-employment. Regarding the mobility pattern of informal self-employed workers, we do not find significant movement of workers from informal self-employment to formal self-employment.

The formal wage workers turned out to be the most reluctant to leave their state, endorsing the prevailing argument that workers regard formal wage-employment as the most desirable work status as they are intrinsically more secure and stable than those in the informal sector. There is also a relative absence of evidence supporting the possibility of reverse transition from formal wage-employment to formal or upper-tier informal self-employment, as is evident in some Latin American countries (Maloney 1999). Our findings thus refute the hypothesis that workers use formal wage-employment as an opportunity to upgrade the skill sets and generate savings so as to set up their own businesses in the upper tier of the informal sector. Upper-tier informal wage workers, on the other hand, exhibit a higher likelihood of moving into formal salaried jobs. This perhaps points to the possibility of formal employers using an informal employment relationship as a screening device to overcome information asymmetries and test workers' abilities before providing formal contracts, as some of the studies on sub-Saharan Africa suggest (Danquah et al. 2019).

Another noteworthy finding is the high persistence within the lower tier of informal wage-employment, with about three-quarters of workers in this segment not making the transition upwards. The higher retention rate of workers in this segment possibly shows that these workers face significant challenges in changing jobs due to limited human capital and skills and insufficient working capital, especially for those desiring to move to self-employment. Therefore, they are most likely to remain locked in a situation of inferior pay and conditions.

Our analysis on the correlates of labour market transitions suggests a significant role for age, gender, social group, and geographical location in shaping mobility patterns. In line with conventional wisdom, we find that the probability of transitioning into formal employment increases with years of schooling, implying that the more educated the worker the higher the probability of transitioning to a formal job. We also find a definite gender pattern in transitions as male workers are more likely to move into wage-employment while female workers are more likely to stay in self-employment. Finally, as we would expect in the context of India, the social group to which a worker belongs is found to influence worker mobility.

Our analysis on the implication of transitions on earnings suggests that the rise in earnings is substantially higher for those who have made the transition to formal status. Positive income gains are also observed for those who transitioned from lower-tier to upper-tier informality compared with those who failed to make the transition. As expected, the largest inter-temporal change in earnings is reported by workers who continued to be in the formal sector.

Overall, our results suggest that lower-tier informal workers, whether in self-employment or wage-employment, have limited upward transition possibilities and are in a dead-end work status. That this has happened in a high-growth phase of the Indian economy suggests that economic growth by itself may not make much material difference to reducing the high rates of informality in India and that direct state interventions that enhance the livelihoods of lower-tier informal workers may be necessary.

References

Banerji, S., R. S. N. Raj, and K. Sen (2016). 'Monitoring Costs, Credit Constraints and Entrepreneurship'. *Credit Constraints and Entrepreneurship, Manchester School*, 84(5): 573–599. https://doi.org/10.1111/manc.12122.

Bardhan, P. (2018). 'Reflections on Kalyan Sanyal's Rethinking Capitalist Development'. *Economic and Political Weekly*, 53(2): 19–22.

Barnes, T. (2015). *Informal Labour in Urban India: Three Cities, Three Journeys*. London and New York: Routledge. https://doi.org/10.4324/9781315737751.

Bayly, S. (1999). *Caste, Society and Politics in India: From the Eighteenth Century to the Modern Age*. Cambridge: Cambridge University Press. https://doi.org/10.1017/CHOL9780521264341.

Benjamin, N., and A. A. Mbaye (2014). 'Informality, Growth, and Development in Africa'. WIDER Working Paper 2014/52. Helsinki: UNU-WIDER. https://doi.org/10.35188/UNU-WIDER/2014/773-8.

Besley, T., and R. Burgess (2004). 'Can Labour Regulation Hinder Economic Performance? Evidence from India'. *Quarterly Journal of Economics*, 119(1): 91–134. https://doi.org/10.1162/003355304772839533.

Breman, J. (2012). *Footloose Labour: Working in India's Informal Economy*. Cambridge: Cambridge University Press.

Chatterjee, U., and R. Kanbur (2014). 'Regulation and Non-Compliance: Magnitudes and Patterns for India's Factories Act'. World Bank Other Operational Studies 16717. Washington, DC: World Bank. https://doi.org/10.1596/1813-9450-6755.

Chen, M., J. Vanek, and J. Heintz (2006). 'Informality, Gender and Poverty: A Global Picture'. *Economic and Political Weekly*, 41(21): 2131–2139.

Danquah, M., S. Schotte, and K. Sen (2019). 'Informal Work in Sub-Saharan Africa: Dead End or Steppingstone?'. WIDER Working Paper 2019/107. Helsinki: UNU-WIDER. https://doi.org/10.35188/UNU-WIDER/2019/743-9.

Dhanaraj, S., and V. Mahambare (2019). 'Family Structure, Education and Women's Employment in Rural India'. *World Development*, 115: 17–29. https://doi.org/10.1016/j.worlddev.2018.11.004.

Dumont, L (1970). *Homo Hierarchicus. The Caste System and Its Implications*. London: Paladin Press.

Fletcher, E., R. Pande, and C. Moore (2018). 'Women and Work in India: Descriptive Evidence and a Review of Potential Policies'. HKS Working Paper RWP18-004. Cambridge, MA: Harvard Kennedy School.

Gang, I., K. Sen, and M. -S. Yun (2008). 'Poverty in Rural India: Caste and Tribe'. *Review of Income and Wealth*, 54(1): 50–70. https://doi.org/10.1111/j.1475-4991.2007.00259.x.

Gang, I., K. Sen, and M. S. Yun (2016). 'Is Caste Destiny? Occupational Diversification among Dalits in Rural India'. *European Journal of Development Research*, 29(2): 476–492. https://doi.org/10.1057/s41287-016-0011-1.

Ghani, E., R. Kanbur, and S. D. O'Connell (2014). 'Urbanization and Agglomeration Benefits: Gender Differentiated Impacts on Enterprise Creation in India's Informal Sector'. Working Paper WP2014-04. Ithaca, New York: Charles H. Dyson School of Applied Economics and Management, Cornell University.

Gong, X., A. Van Soest, and E. Villagomez (2004). 'Mobility in the Urban Labor Market: A Panel Data Analysis for Mexico'. *Economic Development and Cultural Change*, 53(1): 1–36. https://doi.org/10.1086/423251.

Harriss-White, B. (2010). *India Working: Essays on Society and Economy*. Cambridge: Cambridge University Press.

Howard, L. L., and N. Prakash (2012). 'Do Employment Quotas Explain the Occupational Choices of Disadvantaged Minorities in India?'. *International Review of Applied Economics*, 26(4): 489–513. https://doi.org/10.1080/02692171.2011.619969.

IHDS (India Human Development Survey) (2020). 'IHDS Data: IHDS-1 and IHDS-2'. Available at: https://ihds.umd.edu (accessed November 2019).

ILO (2014). 'Transitioning from the Informal to the Formal Economy'. Report (V) 1. International Labour Conference 103rd Session. Geneva: ILO. Available at: https://www.ilo.org/wcmsp5/groups/public/---ed_norm/---relconf/documents/meetingdocument/wcms_218128.pdf (accessed August 2020).

Kanbur, R. (2017). 'Informality: Causes, Consequences and Policy Responses'. *Review of Development Economics*, 21: 939–961. https://doi.org/10.1111/rode.12321.

Kannan, K. P., and T. S. Papola (2007). 'Workers in the Informal Sector: Initiatives by India's National Commission for Enterprises in the Unorganized Sector (NCEUS)'. *International Labour Review*, 146(3–4): 321–329. https://doi.org/10.1111/j.1564-913X.2007.00018.x.

Kathuria, V., and R. S. N. Raj (2016). 'Do Informal Sector Wages Explain Rural Poverty? Evidence from India'. *Journal of Poverty*, 20(1): 73–101. https://doi.org/10.1080/10875549.2015.1094762.

Kathuria, V., R. S. N. Raj, and K. Sen (2013). 'The Effects of Economic Reforms on Manufacturing Dualism: Evidence from India'. *Journal of Comparative Economics*, 41: 1240–1262. https://doi.org/10.1016/j.jce.2012.10.003.

La Porta, R., and A. Shleifer (2014). 'Informality and Development'. *Journal of Economic Perspectives*, 28(3): 109–126. https://doi.org/10.1257/jep.28.3.109.

Lei, L., S. Desai, and R. Vanneman (2019), 'The Impact of Transportation Infrastructure on Women's Employment in India'. *Feminist Economics*, 25(4): 94–125. https://doi.org/10.1080/13545701.2019.1655162.

Maloney, W. F. (1999). 'Does Informality Imply Segmentation in Urban Labor Markets? Evidence from Sectoral Transitions in Mexico'. *World Bank Economic Review*, 13: 275–302. https://doi.org/10.1093/wber/13.2.275.

Maloney, W. F. (2004), 'Informality Revisited'. *World Development*, 32(7): 1159–1178. https://doi.org/10.1016/j.worlddev.2004.01.008.

Marjit, S., and S. Kar (2011). *The Outsiders: Economic Reform and Informal Labour in a Developing Economy*. New Delhi: Oxford University Press. https://doi.org/10.1093/acprof:oso/9780198071495.001.0001.

Mazumdar, D., and S. Sarkar (2013). *Manufacturing Enterprise in Asia: Size Structure and Economic Growth.* London and New York: Routledge.

McCaig, B., and N. Pavcnik (2018). 'Export Markets and Labor Allocation in a Low-Income Country'. *American Economic Review*, 108(7): 1899–1941. https://doi.org/10.1257/aer.20141096.

Natarajan, R. R., Schotte, S. and Sen, K. (2020), 'Transitions between Informal and Formal Jobs in India: Patterns, Correlates, and Consequences'. WIDER Working Paper 101/2020. Helsinki: UNU-WIDER.

NCEUS (National Commission for Enterprises in the Unorganized Sector) (2007). *Report on Conditions of Work and Promotion of Livelihoods in the Unorganised Sector.* New Delhi: National Commission for Enterprises in the Unorganised Sector (NCEUS), Government of India.

NCEUS (2009). *The Challenge of Employment in India: An Informal Economy Perspective.* New Delhi: National Commission for Enterprises in the Unorganised Sector (NCEUS), Government of India.

Neetha, N. (2010). 'Self-Employment of Women: Preference or Compulsion?'. *Social Change*, 40(2): 139–156. https://doi.org/10.1177/004908571004000203.

NSSO (National Sample Survey Office) (2019). *Periodic Labour Force Survey 2017–18.* New Delhi: Ministry of Statistics and Programme Implementation, Government of India.

Raj, R. S. N., and K. Sen (2015). 'Finance Constraints and Firm Transition in the Informal Sector: Evidence from Indian Manufacturing'. *Oxford Development Studies*, 43(1):123–143. https://doi.org/10.1080/13600818.2014.972352.

Raj, R. S. N., and K. Sen (2016). *Out of the Shadows? The Informal Manufacturing in Post-Reform India.* Delhi: Oxford University Press. https://doi.org/10.1093/acprof:oso/9780199460847.001.0001.

Raj, R. S. N., and K. Sen (2020). 'The "Missing Middle" Problem in Indian Manufacturing: What Role Do Institutions Play?'. *Economic and Political Weekly*, 55(16): 51–60.

Saha, B., K. Sen, and D. Maiti (2013). 'Trade Openness, Labour Institutions and Flexibilisation: Theory and Evidence from India'. *Labour Economics*, 24: 180–195. https://doi.org/10.1016/j.labeco.2013.08.008.

Shah, A., J. Lerche, R. Axelby, D. Benbabaali, B. Donegan, J. Raj, and V. Thakur (2018). *Ground Down by Earth: Tribe, Caste, Class and Inequality in Twenty-First Century India.* New Delhi: Oxford University Press.

Sheikh, R. A., and S. Gaurav (2020). 'Informal Work in India: A Tale of Two Definitions'. *European Journal of Development Research*, 32: 1105–1127. https://doi.org/10.1057/s41287-020-00258-z.

Shonchoy, A. S., and P. N. R. Junankar (2014). 'The Informal Labour Market in India: Transitory or Permanent Employment for Migrants?, *IZA Journal of Labor and Development*, 3: 9. https://doi.org/10.1186/2193-9020-3-9.

Unni, J. (1998). 'Employment and Wages in the Unorganised Sector: Issues in Wage Policy'. *Indian Journal of Labour Economics*, 41(4): 875–892.

Unni, J., and U. Rani (2003). 'Social Protection for Informal Workers in India: Insecurities, Instruments and Institutional Mechanisms'. *Development and Change*, 34(1): 127–161. https://doi.org/10.1111/1467-7660.00299.

Vaid, D. (2012). 'The Caste–Class Association in India: An Empirical Analysis'. *Asian Survey*, 52(2): 395–422. https://doi.org/10.1525/as.2012.52.2.395.

5

Progress and stagnation in the livelihood of informal workers in an emerging economy

Long-term evidence from Indonesia

Mayang Rizky, Daniel Suryadarma, and Asep Suryahadi

1. Introduction

A common characteristic among emerging economies is the existence of a large informal sector.[1] La Porta and Shleifer (2014) find that the informal sector makes up about 40 per cent of total economic activity in the poorest countries. The share is only about 15 per cent in the richest countries.

The existence of an informal sector can be explained by three main theories: exclusion, rational exit, and dual economy (Rothenberg et al. 2016). The exclusion theory argues that the informal sector exists because workers could not find jobs in the formal sector. The rational exit theory stipulates that the net benefits of joining the formal sector are negative. Finally, the dual economy theory states that the informal and formal sectors coexist; they produce different goods, have different productivity levels, pay different wage levels, and cater to different consumers.

The literature on emerging economies generally finds support for the dual economy theory. Workers and firms in the two sectors are different. Gindling and Newhouse (2012) and La Porta and Shleifer (2014) find that informal firms are small, unproductive, and stagnant. They argue that a better regulatory environment would not bring these firms into the formal sector. Rothenberg et al. (2016) evaluate an Indonesian government programme to ease firm registration. They find that the programme has negligible impact, mainly because informal firms are not interested in registering. Moreover, switching between sectors is rare. McCaig and Pavcnik (2015) find that only 17 per cent of informal workers switched to formal work in a four-year period, while de Mel et al. (2010) observe that less than 10

[1] We would like to thank reviewers from UNU–WIDER and seminar participants at the Australian National University for their comments and suggestions for this chapter. The views expressed are the views of the authors and do not necessarily reflect the views or policies of ADBI, ADB, its Board of Directors, or the governments they represent.

Mayang Rizky, Daniel Suryadarma, and Asep Suryahadi, *Progress and stagnation in the livelihood of informal workers in an emerging economy.* In: *The Job Ladder.* Edited by Gary S. Fields, T. H. Gindling, Kunal Sen, Michael Danquah, and Simone Schotte, Oxford University Press. © UNU-WIDER (2023). DOI: 10.1093/oso/9780192867339.003.0005 per cent of own-account workers in Sri Lanka grew to having employees within three years. Taken together, these findings support the dual economy theory.

In general, studies from emerging economies have two shortcomings. First, the heterogeneity of the informal sector—documented by Gunther and Launov (2012), among others—is often ignored. Second, the long-term livelihood of informal-sector workers and firms is rarely studied. Most studies in emerging economies rely on cross-sectional data sets. In Sri Lanka, de Mel et al. (2010) could only observe the same entrepreneurs for three years. In Viet Nam, available data sets allow McCaig and Pavcnik (2015) to follow individuals for only four years.

In this study, we use a rich household longitudinal data set from Indonesia that spans 19 years, from 1996 to 2014, to examine the livelihood of informal workers. The data also allow us to differentiate between low-tier and high-tier informal and formal workers. Finally, the data span a period in which Indonesia grew from a low-income to a middle-income country. Thus, we were able to examine changes in the proportion of low-tier informal workers as an economy grows.

In particular, we address the following research questions:

(1) What is the proportion of individuals whose first job is low-tier informal compared with those whose first job is high-tier informal, low-tier formal, or high-tier formal? What are the characteristics of individuals whose first job is low-tier informal compared with those whose first job is high-tier informal or formal?
(2) Has (1) changed over two decades as Indonesia has become a middle-income country?
(3) Among individuals whose first job was low-tier informal, what is the proportion of those who switch to other job types? Is the switch permanent or temporary? Does the path from low-tier informal to formal always go through high-tier informal? What are the characteristics of the individuals who managed to switch?
(4) What is the earnings premium of switching to either high-tier informal, low-tier formal, or high-tier formal jobs relative to staying in low-tier informal jobs?

2. Economic development and informal workers in Indonesia

After some tumultuous years during the 1960s, which culminated in a regime change, Indonesia started its economic development at the end of that decade. The new government was able to quickly restore macroeconomic stability and, awash with revenue from oil windfall, invested heavily in infrastructure. After that, Indonesia experienced high economic growth, averaging around 7 per cent annually, for the next three decades.

The mid-1980s witnessed a drop in international oil prices, which quickly dried up the government's coffers. Due to the inward-looking import substitution strategy adopted during the previous decade, Indonesian industries were inefficient and unable to compete in the international market. To deal with the dire situation, the government changed course quickly, adopting an export orientation strategy. The change in strategy was initiated through a large devaluation of the rupiah, whose exchange rate was pegged to the US dollar at that time. This was followed by various deregulation measures to make the economy more efficient. As a result, high economic growth was quickly restored.

This was brought to a sudden stop at the end of 1990s by the Asian financial crisis (AFC). Starting as a currency attack on Thailand's baht in 1997, the crisis quickly spread to other East Asian countries. Indonesia, whose political future was perceived as highly uncertain on account of its old and ailing president and lack of a clear successor, soon became the worst affected country. In 1998, the rupiah lost more than 80 per cent of its value in less than a year, prices skyrocketed (food prices rose by 120 per cent), and the economy contracted by an unprecedented 14 per cent.

The crisis brought a lot of changes. The country once again underwent a regime change as the authoritarian New Order government was toppled and Indonesia became a democratic country. Central and regional government leaders are now elected regularly by the people. Furthermore, pressure from the regions forced the new government to decentralize, both politically and fiscally. Regional autonomy was largely granted to the districts, bypassing the provinces.

The economy soon recovered from the crisis. The contraction in 1998 was followed by near zero economic growth in 1999, and in the new millennium the economy began to grow again, on average by around 6 per cent annually, helped by a commodity boom. The boom ended in 2011, slowing economic growth to around 5 per cent annually. The country's post-crisis economic growth is clearly lower than its pre-crisis level; nevertheless, the economy has grown steadily and respectably by world standards.

Throughout Indonesia's economic development, various social and economic indicators have steadily improved. Per capita income has increased, poverty has declined, education levels have risen, and access to basic services has improved. In the labour market, the proportion of informal workers in the total workforce has shown interesting trends. In general, higher per capita income and improvement in welfare are usually accompanied by a declining proportion of informal workers. This was true in Indonesia during the pre-crisis period. However, during the post-crisis period, this relationship did not hold. Even though the economy continued to grow and per capita income increased, the proportion of informal workers either increased or stagnated. Only after 2014 did the proportion of informal workers tend to decline again.

A deeper look at the labour market situation indicates that the reverse in the relationship between economic growth and the proportion of informal workers was largely due to the change in labour market regulations. During the pre-crisis period, labour movement was tightly regulated and only one labour union was allowed to operate. On the other hand, in the post-crisis period, the regulatory framework became pro-labour, resulting in high minimum wages and severance payments, complicated hiring-and-firing mechanisms, and mushrooming labour unions. This resulted in firms avoiding hiring workers, especially on a permanent basis, as much as possible. As a result, very little employment was created in the formal sector during this period. On the other hand, around 2 million new workers entered the labour market every year. Since there were few employment opportunities in the formal sector, most of them joined the informal sector, resulting in growing numbers of informal workers.

3. Data

3.1 The Indonesian Family Life Survey (IFLS)

Our primary data source is the Indonesian Family Life Survey (IFLS), a longitudinal socio-economic survey in Indonesia. There are five waves of the IFLS, all publicly available. The first wave, IFLS1, administered in 1993, was based on a sample of more than 22,000 individuals from 7,224 households across 321 sampling areas in 13 provinces. The data represented about 83 per cent of Indonesia's population in 1993. The other waves were fielded in 1997 (IFLS2), 2000 (IFLS3), 2007 (IFLS4), and 2014 (IFLS5). Household attrition is very low, at around 5 per cent for each wave. The latest wave, IFLS5, managed to survey 6,647 households that had been surveyed in all waves since 1993 (Strauss et al. 2016).

The IFLS consists of two sets of surveys: a household survey and a community survey. The community survey collects information regarding infrastructure at the level of the community, including health facilities, schools, roads, water supplies, and sanitation. The household survey collects both household- and individual-level information and includes data on each household member such as their education, employment, and health. Information relevant to this study includes labour market outcomes, education attainment, health outcomes, household expenditure, and demographic information.

Each IFLS collects labour market information on adults in respondent households since the previous survey. For example, in 1993, it collected labour market information since 1988. Thus, the whole five rounds of IFLS data contain annual labour market information on the same individuals from 1988 to 2014. However, the annual labour market outcomes module was modified in two ways between waves. First, IFLS3 was the first survey to differentiate between self-employment with and without employees; IFLS1 and IFLS2 make no such distinction, which is important in our study. Second, IFLS4 and IFLS5 did not record earnings, which means that we could only address the fourth research question with relatively short-term data covering seven years, that is, 1996–2000, 2007, and 2014. The following subsection provides more details.

3.2 Informal workers in IFLS

In this study, we use the last three rounds of the IFLS (2000, 2007, 2014). We start with the 2000 wave because (i) 94 per cent of answers on the year of starting work and occupation codes are missing in 1993 and (ii) the classification of work status in 1997 differs from the other waves: in IFLS 1993 and IFLS 2000 onwards, the classification of work status for self-employment type consists of self-employment without help, self-employment with the help of unpaid family/temporary worker(s), and self-employment with the help of permanent/regular worker(s). IFLS 1997, however, lumps them into only one category of self-employment.

The IFLS classifies workers as either employees or self-employed. Among the self-employed, as stated above, it indicates whether individuals are self-employed without help, with the help of unpaid family/temporary worker(s), or with the help of permanent/regular worker(s). Employees are specifically asked whether they work for the government, for a private company, or as an unpaid worker in the family business.

The IFLS provides information on each individual's type of work. There are two sources of information in the data: an occupation classification code and a list of daily primary duties. In each survey, the interviewer asks individuals about their occupation using open-ended questions. The answers, recorded as free text, are then coded using two-digit International Standard Text Code (ISTC) occupation codes. The IFLS team also assign one-digit sector codes to the open-ended answers on occupation.

In this study, we differentiate low-tier and high-tier informal workers through a classification of both work status and occupation type. Those who are employees of either the government or a private company, in any job type, are classified as formal workers. All those who are self-employed with the help of permanent/regular worker(s) are high-tier informal workers. Individuals whose work status is self-employed without help or self-employed with the help of unpaid family/temporary worker(s) and whose occupation type is professional, managerial, or official/administrative are also considered to be high-tier informal workers. The classification of high-tier informal workers is determined not only by the data on daily primary duties but also by the two-digit ISTC code. It includes occupation codes of 40 or less and codes 50, 60, 70, 80, and 90, which indicate a managerial level of workers in the service, agricultural, and production sectors. The rest of the self-employed without help or self-employed with the help of unpaid family/temporary worker(s) are considered to be low-tier informal workers, as are all unpaid family workers.

The classification of all employers as informal-sector workers may not be completely accurate. For example, employers whose businesses are formally registered with the government or taxed should be considered as formal, but, unfortunately, the IFLS does not collect such information. In the context of Indonesia, however, 96 per cent of micro firms (employing fewer than five people) and 93 per cent of small firms (employing between 5 and 19 people) are not taxed and can therefore be considered as informal (Rothenberg et al. 2016). This stylized fact supports our decision to consider individual employers as informal, rather than formal, workers. That said, this is an area for further study, once data become available.

We define all government employees or private-sector employees as formal workers. To distinguish between high-tier and low-tier formal, we use the same definition we use for informal workers: workers whose occupation type is professional, director, or official are considered to be high-tier formal. The rest are low-tier formal. Table 5.1 provides the classification matrix of types of workers based on work status and occupation type.

We apply the above definitions not only to an individual's current job but also to past jobs. Each wave of the IFLS provides information on individuals' employment before the survey: for example, IFLS 2000 gives information on individuals' annual employment in 1996–1999, IFLS 2007 on employment in 1999–2006, and IFLS 2014 on 2007–2015. We do not include 2015 employment in the analysis because of the higher rate of missing values in the occupation coding. Using this strategy, we can observe an individual's employment record for a maximum of 19 years from 1996 to 2014.

Other than current and past jobs, the IFLS also has a module on the first employment of individuals. Given the information on the first job's status and type, we can identify whether an individual started as a low-tier informal (LTI), high-tier informal (HTI), low-tier formal (LTF), or high-tier formal (HTF) worker using the same procedure. There is also information on the year of starting work. However, when we compared data from the first job module and data from the current and past jobs module, we found that 8 per cent of the occupation types were different. We therefore decided to use the informality type of first job supplemented by information from the latter module.

Individual characteristics

To identify the characteristics of individuals whose first jobs are LTI, HTI, LTF, or HTF, and the characteristics of individuals who switch tier or remain LTI workers, we include demographic characteristics such as age, years of schooling, height, and parental education. We use height as an indicator of early childhood health levels (Hatton et al. 2018), standardizing each individual's height data into a mean

Table 5.1 Definition of low-tier/high-tier and informal/formal workers

		Work status					
		Self-employed	**Self-employed with family member**	**Employer**	**Government employee**	**Private-sector employee**	**Unpaid family worker**
Occupation type	**Professional**	HTI	HTI	HTI	HTF	HTF	LTI
	Director or manager	HTI	HTI	HTI	HTF	HTF	LTI
	Official or administrative	HTI	HTI	HTI	HTF	HTF	LTI
	Sales	LTI	LTI	HTI	LTF	LTF	LTI
	Labour	LTI	LTI	HTI	LTF	LTF	LTI
	Production	LTI	LTI	HTI	LTF	LTF	LTI
	Transportation	LTI	LTI	HTI	LTF	LTF	LTI
	Unskilled	LTI	LTI	HTI	LTF	LTF	LTI

Note: LTI = low-tier informal; HTI = high-tier informal; LTF = low-tier formal; HTF = high-tier formal.
Source: authors' construction.

of zero and a standard deviation of one. The correlates also include urban versus rural residence.

For a subset of individuals (those between 7 and 24 years old in IFLS3), we have information on their mathematics and cognitive skills. We measure cognitive and mathematics skills using the results of the Raven's and maths tests provided in each wave of IFLS since 2000. The tests were administered for 7–14-year-olds and 15–24-year olds. The test design for the younger group consists of five primary-school-level arithmetic and five shape-matching problems. There are five (more complex) arithmetic and eight shape-matching problems for the older age group.

Community characteristics

To examine whether access to public services has an impact on first jobs, transitions into other types of job, and earnings, we include information on schools, health facilities, and roads. We do not measure these variables using the community survey in IFLS because more than 80 per cent of the sample has missing information on the community they are located in. We use the Potensi Desa (Village Potential Census) instead. Potensi Desa (Podes) is a village census carried out once every three or four years. It contains information on village-level characteristics from geographical location to infrastructures in the village.

We merge IFLS and Podes data. However, as village codes differ between IFLS and Podes, we use information on schools, health facilities, and roads from Podes at the district level. District-level school infrastructure comprises the average number of primary schools (SD) in the village, the average number of junior high schools (SMP) in the sub-district, and the average number of senior high schools (SMA) in the district. We differentiate district-level school infrastructure on the basis of its administration level in accordance with the Indonesian government policy of ensuring that all villages have at least one primary school, all sub-districts at least one junior high school, and all districts at least one senior high school. District-level health and road facilities are measured as a percentage of villages with a health centre and roads that are usable year round. We use Podes 2000, 2008, and 2014 to match with IFLS 2000, 2007, and 2014, respectively.

4. Method

In this study, our focus is on individual workers rather than firms. Specifically, we limit our sample to male workers in the non-agricultural sector. Given our focus on following individuals from the time they began working, we further restrict our sample to young workers (starting jobs a maximum of seven years before the wave administered). Finally, we limit our sample to those with no missing data on relevant variables. We use information on individuals' work status and occupation type to create four groups: low-tier informal workers, high-tier informal workers, low-tier formal workers, and high-tier formal workers.

The first and second research questions are tabulations by cohort and demographic characteristics across IFLS3 to IFLS5. To answer the third research question, our sample consists of individuals who began as a LTI workers either during 1996–2000 (observed in IFLS3) or during 2001–2007 (observed in IFLS4). To examine their characteristics, we use the same correlates as above but only using the year on the first job conditions to avoid reverse causality. We estimate a survival model since our data are censored on the right. We create the following outcome indicators: an indicator of switching to either HTI or formal employment, employment spells in each job type, and the number of switches between job type.

The fourth research question examines whether switching to HTI, LTF, or HTF jobs generates higher earnings compared with staying in LTI jobs. We build on the method used by Levine and Rubinstein (2017). Specifically, we estimate the following linear earnings equation:

$$y_{it} = \alpha + \beta_1 \mathrm{HTI}_{it} + \beta_2 \mathrm{LTF}_{it} + \beta_3 \mathrm{HTF}_{it} + \beta_X \mathrm{X}_{it} + \varepsilon_{it} \tag{1}$$

where the outcome variable y_{it} is the log hourly earnings of individual i in year t. Because log zero is undefined, we transform the log hourly earnings into inverse hyperbolic sine (IHS) form to allow the retention of zero-valued observations. Hourly earnings are calculated from individual i's wage and profit information divided by hours worked and adjusted using the consumer price index (CPI, 2012=100) from Statistics Indonesia.

In equation (1), HTI_{it} equals 1 if individual i in year t is an HTI worker and 0 otherwise; LTF_{it} equals 1 if individual i in year t is an LTF worker and 0 otherwise; HTF_{it} equals 1 if individual i in year t is an HTF worker and 0 otherwise. X_{it} is a vector of covariates consisting of individual i's age, years of schooling, cognitive and maths skills, height, residential location, parental education, whether individual i lives in an urban or rural area, and additional controls for public services in the district (schools, health centre, and road facilities), all at time t. Cognitive and maths test scores as well as heights are standardized. Parental education consists of two binary variables: whether father has more than six years of education (Yes = 1) and whether mother has more than six years of education (Yes = 1). Schools, health facilities, and roads are measured at district level. The vector of covariates also includes year, wave, and island fixed effects to control for trends in macroeconomic and regional differences that could affect the earnings. Finally, ε_{it} is the error term that can be decomposed into three components:

$$\varepsilon_{it} = \theta_i + \alpha_i(\mathrm{t}) + \varphi_{it} \tag{2}$$

where θ_i is the individual-specific and time-invariant component, $\alpha_i(t)$ is the time-varying individual influences, and φ_{it} is the individual-time shock to earnings. When excluding individual effects from equation (1), the estimated β_1, β_2, and β_3 parameters provide unbiased measures of the differences in residual earnings for individuals in HTI, LTF, or HTF jobs relative to LTI workers with similar traits included in X_{it}. When we include individual effects, we remove individual time-invariant unobserved heterogeneity and individual-level trend into the choice of job type. Therefore, the estimates for β_1, β_2, and β_3 yield unbiased estimates of the differences in residual earnings for individuals working in HTI, LTF, or HTF jobs relative to when they were an LTI worker. To obtain a clearer picture of these differences in residual earnings, we compare these estimated differences in earnings with the average earnings of LTI workers and provide the percentage difference to examine whether workers earn more when switching to HTI, LTF, or HTF work. We estimate the model using least squares and median regressions.

5. Results

5.1 First job informality

To address the first and second research questions, Fig. 5.1 shows the proportions of male workers, limited to those who worked in non-agricultural sectors, by the types of (in)formality of their first jobs and year of starting their first job. The figure clearly shows that, in non-agricultural sectors, the first jobs of male workers are predominantly LTF, that is, 70 per cent in 1996, significantly declining to 40 per cent in 2001, and stabilizing at around 60 per cent between 2009 and 2014. The decline in 2001 is most likely explained by the AFC. Among the remaining workers, the proportion whose first job was LTI was 15 per cent in 1996, more than doubling to 40 per cent in 2001, before following a fluctuating pattern between 2001 and 2014. The rate was at 27 per cent in 2014. The trend of first job as HTF was roughly consistent at around 10–13 per cent over the period. Finally, only around 1–2 per cent of workers' first jobs were HTI.

Looking at the 19-year trend, there is some evidence that the informal sector has declined as Indonesia's economy has grown. But the decline has been very slow. The share of workers whose first job was LTI increased by 80 per cent proportionally over the period that we observe. The impact of the 1998 AFC, which more than doubled the share of LTI first jobs, had yet to disappear by 2014. Over the period, the proportion of workers whose first job was LTF declined by 13.5 per cent proportionally. On the other hand, the share of workers whose first job was HTF increased by only 13 per cent. This trend is evidence that even if the informal sector appears to become smaller as an economy grows, the decline is very small and can be rapidly overturned by an economic crisis.

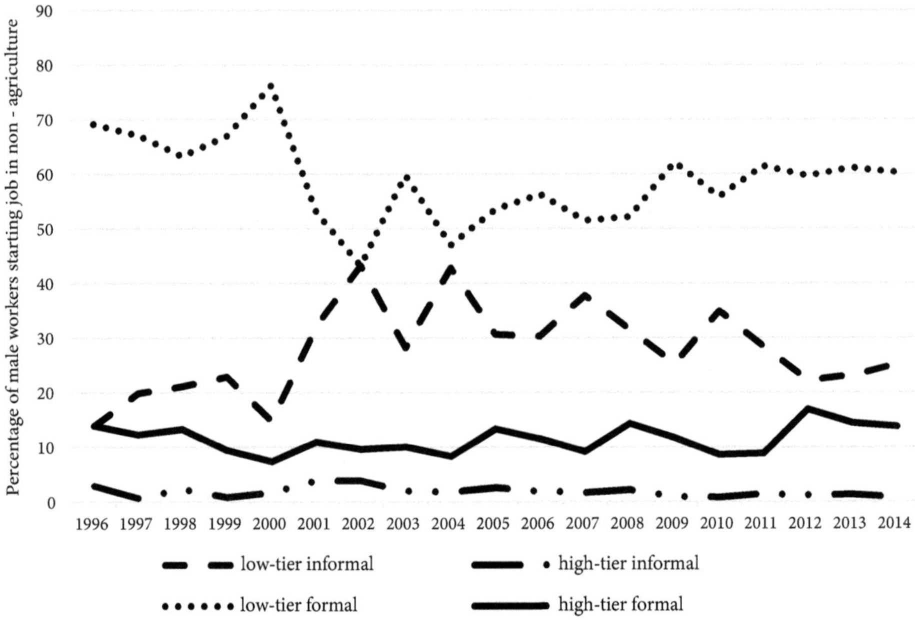

Fig. 5.1 Proportion of male workers starting jobs in non-agriculture in 1996–2014 by type of job

Note: Number of observations: 3,025.

Source: authors' construction based on data from the Indonesian Family Life Survey (IFLS) 2000, 2007, and 2014.

5.2 Sorting into first job types

We compare the characteristics of workers with different first jobs. Table 5.2 shows the mean characteristics, combining IFLS3, 4, and 5 (so covering first jobs from 1996 to 2014). On average, these workers started work when they were 22–26 years old. The average starting age of those who started as low-tier workers, either formal or informal, is similar. Those who started working as high-tier workers tended to start at slightly older ages, reflecting the fact that they remained in school about three years longer.

The cognitive and mathematics scores of those who started as low-tier workers, either informal or formal, are similar. Those who started as HTI or HTF workers also have similar mathematics and cognitive scores. Overall, those who started as HTI workers have the highest cognitive score, while those who started as HTF have the highest mathematics score. Comparing the formal and informal sectors as a whole, we find that those who started work in the formal sector have slightly higher cognitive and maths scores.

Using height as an indicator of early childhood health levels, we find that individuals who started as LTI workers are the shortest by almost 1 centimetre. This

Table 5.2 Mean characteristics of workers in the first job sample

	Informal		Total informal	Formal		Total formal	Total
	Low-tier	High-tier		Low-tier	High-tier		
Observations	841	53	894	1.778	353	2.141	3.025
	27.80%	1.75%	29.55%	58.78%	11.67%	70.45%	100.00%
Age	22.49	26.30	22.72	22.71	25.24	23.13	23.01
Years of schooling	9.25	12.08	9.41	10.10	12.89	10.56	10.22
Cognitive score	5.86	6.35	5.88	6.00	6.24	6.04	5.99
Maths score	1.90	2.19	1.91	2.00	2.39	2.06	2.01
Height (in cm)	162.65	163.25	162.69	163.48	164.04	163.57	163.31
Father's years of schooling	3.34	6.06	3.50	3.87	6.01	4.22	4.01
Mother's years of schooling	2.81	4.85	2.93	3.11	4.64	3.36	3.23
Urban	0.58	0.75	0.59	0.64	0.66	0.65	0.63
By district:							
Number of SD in village	4.37	4.82	4.40	4.81	5.11	4.86	4.72
Number of SMP in sub-district	11.65	11.47	11.64	12.51	13.22	12.63	12.34
Number of SMA in district	77.54	67.83	76.97	81.05	83.92	81.53	80.18
% villages in the district with:							
Health centre	0.18	0.21	0.18	0.22	0.24	0.23	0.21
Year-round roads	0.74	0.74	0.74	0.81	0.81	0.81	0.79

Note: The sample is restricted to male workers in non-agricultural sectors who started their first job between 1996 and 2014 and answered questions on their first job in IFLS 2000, 2007, and 2014.
Source: authors' construction based on data from IFLS 2000, 2007, and 2014. Variables on public services (schools, health, and road facilities) are derived from Podes data in 2000, 2008, and 2014.

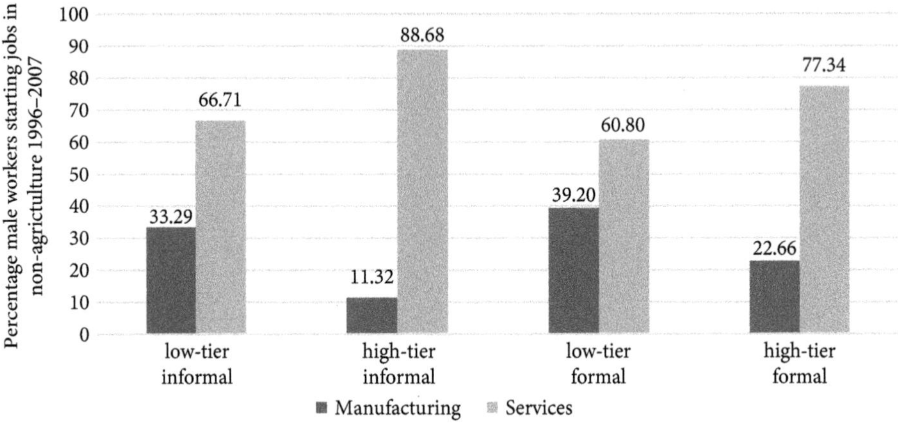

Fig. 5.2 Proportion of male workers starting jobs in 1996–2014 by industry and type of job

Note: Number of observations: 841 (LTI, low-tier informal).; 53 (HTI, high-tier informal); 1,778 (LTF, low-tier formal); 353 (HTF, high-tier formal).
Source: authors' construction based on data from IFLS 2000, 2007, and 2014.

information shows that those who begin as LTI workers have already faced worse conditions even from early in life.

The pattern in years of schooling of workers is also reflected in the patterns in their parents' years of schooling. High-tier workers, whether informal or formal, have the most educated parents. LTI workers have the least educated parents, on average by two years. Overall, the parents of these workers have only between two and four years of education, and the workers themselves have an average of nine years of schooling. Incidentally, the large intergenerational increase in educational attainment shows the Indonesian government's success in increasing access to education.

Figure 5.2 shows the sector that these workers started in. About 33–39 per cent of low-tier workers started work in manufacturing, the rest in services. In contrast, a large majority of high-tier workers began in the services sector. Among HTI workers, 87 per cent started in services. Comparing these figures, we see, again, that the main cleavage between workers is not between informal and formal but between low-tier and high-tier.

Next, we use a multinomial logit regression to examine whether individuals with different characteristics are more likely to enter the work force as LTI, HTI, LTF, or HTF workers. We assess the sorting into first job types using IFLS3, 4, and 5 for individuals who started work in 1996–2000, 2001–2007, and 2008–2014, respectively. The independent variables are listed in Table 5.2.

Table 5.3 shows the marginal effects at mean. First, older individuals are slightly more likely to have an HTF first job. An additional year of schooling is correlated

Table 5.3 Selection into types of first job, IFLS3, 4, and 5

	Informal		Formal	
	Low-tier (1)	High-tier (2)	Low-tier (3)	High-tier (4)
Age	−0.0027	−0.0002	0.0009	0.0020**
	(0.00169)	(0.00036)	(0.00161)	(0.00084)
Years of schooling	−0.0229***	0.0023***	−0.0056	0.0262***
	(0.00455)	(0.00048)	(0.00509)	(0.00430)
Cognitive score (standardized)	−0.0242**	−0.0000	0.0245**	−0.0003
	(0.01216)	(0.00392)	(0.01231)	(0.00772)
Maths score (standardized)	0.0019	−0.0001	−0.0222**	0.0205***
	(0.00887)	(0.00315)	(0.00955)	(0.00740)
Height (standardized)	−0.0151***	0.0001	0.0147	0.0003
	(0.00576)	(0.00120)	(0.01220)	(0.01139)
Urban (Yes = 1)	0.0106	0.0026	0.0243	−0.0375***
	(0.02084)	(0.00641)	(0.02645)	(0.01128)
Father has more than six years of education (Yes = 1)	−0.0238	−0.0055	−0.0136	0.0429***
	(0.02901)	(0.00566)	(0.02515)	(0.01474)
Mother has more than six years of education (Yes = 1)	0.0188	0.0088*	−0.0288	0.0012
	(0.02832)	(0.00493)	(0.03014)	(0.02105)
By district:				
Number of SD	0.0082	0.0008	−0.0135**	0.0045*
	(0.00936)	(0.00179)	(0.00765)	(0.00260)
Number of SMP	0.0038	−0.0001	−0.0037	−0.0001
	(0.00342)	(0.00071)	(0.00326)	(0.00186)
Number of SMA	−0.0000	−0.0001	0.0004**	−0.0000
	(0.00024)	(0.00008)	(0.00020)	(0.00006)
% village with health centre	−0.3055**	0.0054	0.3125***	−0.0124
	(0.13664)	(0.01529)	(0.10626)	(0.05286)
% village with year-round roads	−0.0269	−0.0206	0.1205***	−0.0730
	(0.11729)	(0.02071)	(0.18875)	(0.13249)
Observations	2,148	–	–	–
Pseudo R-squared	0.0909	–	–	–

Note: Sample is male workers in non-agricultural sectors who started working between 1996 and 2014; * $p < 0.10$, ** $p < 0.05$, *** $p < 0.01$. Coefficients come from a multinomial logit regression to estimate the probability of an individual working as LTI (low-tier informal), HTI (high-tier informal), LTF (low-tier formal), or HTF (high-tier formal). Estimations include year dummies on the first job, wave, and island fixed effects. Standard errors are in parentheses, clustered at province level.
Source: authors' construction based on data from IFLS 2000, 2007, and 2014.

with a 0.2–2.6 percentage point higher probability of working as a high-tier worker. Finally, having a more educated father is correlated with a 4.3 percentage point higher probability of starting as an HTF worker. Given that only 11 per cent of workers started in this category (Table 5.2), the benefit of having a more educated father is very large. This could be related to connections in employment or it could be that having a more educated father is a proxy for higher socio-economic status. Taller men are less likely to start as LTI workers. At 1.51 percentage points, however, the effect is relatively small. Workers with a higher cognitive score have a greater chance of starting work in LTF jobs and a smaller chance of starting in LTI jobs. Finally, a higher mathematics score increases the probability of starting in the HTF sector by 2 percentage points and reduces the probability of starting in the LTI sector by 2.2 percentage points.

Overall, the strong message from these estimates is that workers in LTI jobs are negatively selected. More favourable conditions increase the probability of working in the formal sector.

5.3 The extent of job switching

In this section, we observe the labour outcomes of workers who began working between 1996 and 2007. Among individuals whose first job was as an LTI worker, we find that 46 per cent remained as LTI workers through the next 8–19 years. About 7 per cent became HTI workers for at least one year, 37 per cent became LTF workers for at least one year, and 8 per cent became HTF workers for at least one year. These numbers show that switching out of LTI work happened about 50 per cent of the time, but the majority of those switches were to LTF work. High-tier work appears to have a high entry barrier for those who started as LTI workers.

Among the 54 per cent who switched to a different job type for at least one period, the mean duration spent as an HTI worker is 0.46 years. The mean duration spent as an LTF worker is 3.48 years and the mean as an HTF worker is 0.37 years. Given that we are observing a career of between 8 and 19 years, these means indicate a relatively short stint as a high-tier worker, either informal or formal. Figure 5.3 also shows that switches occur mostly in the first seven years of an individual's career.

When we look at the number of times these workers switch between types, we find that, on average, they switch three times. The average job spell (i.e. continuous number of years in a particular job type) is only 0.16 years as an HTI worker, 1.48 years as LTF, and 0.14 years as HTF. The switchers still have their longest job spell as LTI workers, with an average of 3.99 years.

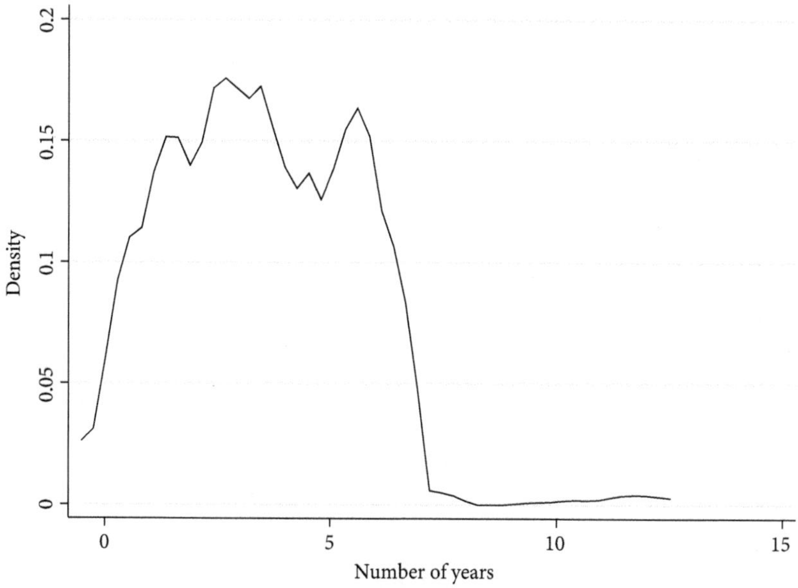

Fig. 5.3 Duration to switch of LTI first-job workers

Note: Number of observations: 529.

Source: authors' construction based on data from IFLS 2000, 2007, and 2014.

Of the switchers who became a formal worker for at least one period, only 4.3 per cent also experienced working in the HTI sector. Therefore, most men switched from LTI to formal-sector work without going through an HTI job. Our data show that most LTI workers, when they switch, become LTF workers. Almost none switch to high-tier work.

We next examine the characteristics of individuals who switch to a different job type for at least one year compared with those who do not switch. We use the same correlates as in Table 5.3. Table 5.4 shows that workers whose fathers are highly educated have a 35.5–51.5 percentage points higher probability of switching. Interestingly, height, mathematics skills, cognitive skills, and educational attainment have small correlations with switching. Only height is statistically significant.

5.4 Wage premium of switching from LTI work

Our results so far show that individuals who start as LTI workers very rarely switch to high-tier work. Of those who manage to switch, most become LTF workers. These results corroborate previous findings that support the dual economy theory

Table 5.4 Hazard ratio of switching from LTI work (IFLS3 and IFLS4)

	Switching (Yes = 1)		
	Weibull (2)	**Exponential** (3)	Cox (4)
Age	0.9756	0.9815	0.9771
	(0.02932)	(0.01565)	(0.02749)
Years of schooling	1.0052	1.0211	1.0059
	(0.03831)	(0.02662)	(0.03480)
Cognitive score (standardized)	1.0483	0.9982	1.0315
	(0.06472)	(0.05253)	(0.05894)
Maths score (standardized)	0.8721	0.9362	0.8992
	(0.08372)	(0.06118)	(0.07609)
Height (standardized)	0.9362**	0.9524**	0.9321**
	(0.02645)	(0.01944)	(0.02447)
Urban (Yes = 1)	1.1920	1.1235	1.1689
	(0.15341)	(0.10714)	(0.13724)
Father has more than six years of education (Yes = 1)	1.5148***	1.3553***	1.4966***
	(0.2221)	(0.1488)	(0.20554)
Mother has more than six years of education (Yes = 1)	0.8341	0.7905	0.8125
	(0.2957)	(0.18889)	(0.2493)
Community characteristics			
Number of SD in village	1.0298	1.0383	1.0392
	(0.06806)	(0.06203)	(0.70738)
Number of SMP in sub-district	1.0449	1.0181	1.0317
	(0.02994)	(0.02207)	(0.02723)
Number of SMA in district	0.9995	1.0011	0.9998
	(0.00139)	(0.00092)	(0.00128)
% village with health centre	0.0883***	0.1510**	0.1126**
	(0.08049)	(0.13272)	(0.10226)
% village with year-round roads	1.9302	1.0265	1.2364
	(4.20054)	(1.11631)	(1.77104)
Observations	299	299	299

Note: Sample is male workers in non-agricultural sectors who started working between 1996 and 2000 and 2001 and 2007; * $p < 0.10$, ** $p < 0.05$, *** $p < 0.01$. Columns (1)–(3) are hazard ratios to estimate the probability of individuals who started as LTI (low-tier informal) workers switching jobs. Column (1) is the hazard ratios generated by a survival model with Weibull distribution and Column (2) by a model with exponential distribution. Column (4) is the hazard ratios of the Cox proportional hazard model. The magnitude of the hazard ratio (<1 or >1) indicates whether the probability of switching is decreasing or increasing with the covariates. All regressions include wave and island fixed effects. Additional controls are schooling, health, and infrastructure variables. Standard errors are clustered at province level.

Source: authors' construction based on data from IFLS 2000, 2007, and 2014.

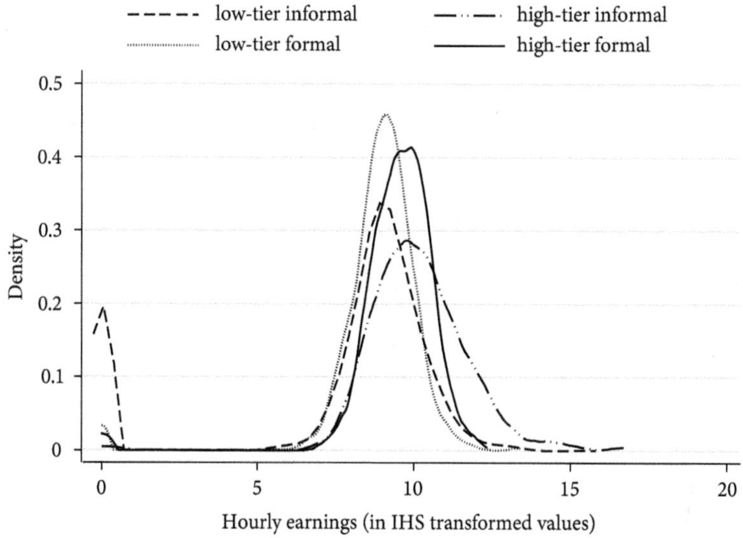

Fig. 5.4 Distribution of earnings by type of job

Note: Number of observations: 4,646.

Source: authors' construction based on data from IFLS 2000, 2007, and 2014.

but with a different nuance. It seems that the dual economy is divided between low-tier and high-tier work rather than informal and formal work. Individuals who started out as LTI workers can almost never switch to high-tier work but have a relatively good chance of switching to LTF work. If we consider low-tier as blue collar and high-tier as white collar work, the evidence shows that these sectors are disconnected in the sense that blue-collar workers almost never become white-collar workers.

However, the next question we ask is whether switching out of LTI work carries a wage premium. Figure 5.4 compares the distribution of hourly earnings by job types. We find that LTI and LTF workers have similar distributions. High-tier workers, in either informal or formal work, also have similar distributions. Similar to previous findings, the distinction appears to be more apparent between low-tier versus high-tier workers than informal versus formal workers.

Figure 5.5 shows the distribution of earnings of workers based on whether they switch out of LTI work or not. Note that the sample here comes from the IFLS labour market module rather than the first job module. The mean earnings of the switchers are higher regardless of the type of work they switch to. Also, the right tails of the earnings distributions are thicker. From the figure, it appears that switchers to high-tier work, whether informal or formal, earn the highest premium.

Table 5.5 shows the estimates. We focus on discussing the results with hourly earnings as the dependent variable. Note that, depending on whether we include

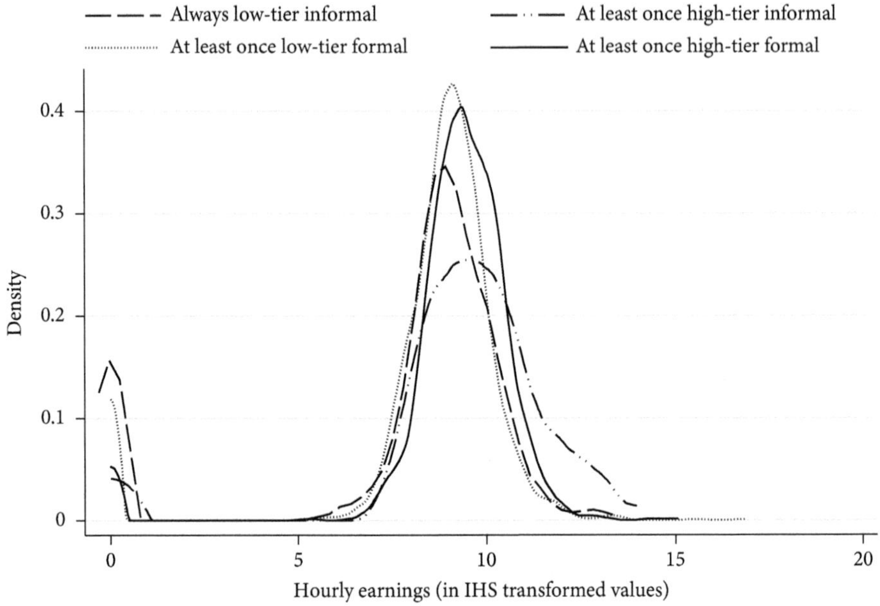

Fig. 5.5 Distribution of earnings by type of switching
Note: Number of observations: 4,646.
Source: authors' construction based on data from IFLS 2000, 2007, and 2014.

individual fixed effects, the results show different contexts. Column 1 shows the estimates without individual fixed effects, which show the differences in earnings for individuals with similar characteristics but different job types. We find that working as a non-LTI worker brings a large and statistically significant earnings premium. The premium is similar for formal jobs, either low-tier or high-tier, at almost 300 per cent. The premium for HTI work reaches 600 per cent.

Column 2 shows the results with individual fixed effects, which now show the earnings premium for individuals of switching from LTI ranging from 285 per cent to 335 per cent for switching to formal work (the difference between LTF and HTF work is not statistically significant) and being 524 per cent for switching to HTI work. Table 5.6 shows the median regression results.

In contrast to the stark earnings premiums for the average worker, the premiums for the median worker are much smaller. Again, the premium for LTF and HTF work is very similar at 42–52 per cent. The earnings premium for HTI work is about three times the earnings premium for formal work. These median regression results show that the enormous earnings premium shown in Table 5.5 is driven by outliers. In conclusion, however, it appears that switching out of LTI into LTF work is a feasible way to improve a worker's livelihood. Also, evidence shows that the LTF sector is relatively accessible to LTI workers.

Table 5.5 Wage premium of switching from LTI, OLS in levels

	IHS hourly earnings		IHS annual earnings	
	Levels		Levels	
	(1)	(2)	(3)	(4)
High-tier informal	2.0883***	1.9801***	3.1128***	2.5204***
	(0.26015)	(0.52584)	(0.26602)	(0.81805)
Low-tier formal	1.6099***	1.6767***	3.1996***	3.2817***
	(0.12899)	(0.24220)	(0.22053)	(0.42302)
High-tier formal	1.5612***	1.5791***	2.8499***	3.1535***
	(0.14896)	(0.28523)	(0.25293)	(0.47104)
Individual fixed effects	No	Yes	No	Yes
	% difference from LTI worker			
High-tier informal	607	524	2,048	1,042
Low-tier formal	300	335	2,253	2,462
High-tier formal	277	285	1,529	2,142
Observations	2,788	2,788	2,788	2,788
R-squared	0.1977	0.2042	0.2108	0.2247

Note: Sample is male workers in non-agricultural sectors starting work between 1996 and 2007. Observed earnings are from 1996 to 2000, 2007, and 2014; * $p < 0.10$, ** $p < 0.05$, *** $p < 0.01$. Earnings are calculated from wage and profit information and adjusted using the Consumer Price Index (CPI 2012 = 100) from *Badan Pusat Statistik* (Indonesian Statistics Agency). For the estimations, real earnings are transformed into IHS to include zero values. All regressions include variables on age, years of schooling, cognitive and maths scores, height, father and mother with more than six years' education, urban/rural location, schools, health, and road facilities in the districts, as well as year and island fixed effects.
Source: authors' construction based on data from IFLS 2000, 2007, and 2014.

6. Conclusion

Like other developing countries, Indonesia has a large informal sector. Of the total 125 million working population, about 57 per cent are informal workers. In the non-agriculture sectors, the proportion of informal workers has been around 50 per cent since 2000.

To understand the core drivers of informal worker dynamics, in this study, we focus on male informal workers in non-agricultural sectors and, instead of looking at the whole workforce, we focus on the first jobs of young workers. We also split the workers into low-tier and high-tier, including the latter to capture the fact that some work, either formal or informal, requires high skills and knowledge. Specifically, in this study, we measure the proportion of individuals whose first job is low-tier informal, high-tier informal, low-tier formal, and high-tier formal; compare their characteristics; calculate the number of low-tier informal workers who switch to a high-tier informal or formal job; identify the characteristics of those who switched; and estimate the earnings premium of switching.

Table 5.6 Effects of switching from LTI, median in levels

	IHS hourly earnings		IHS annual earnings	
	Levels		Levels	
	(1)	(2)	(3)	(4)
High-tier informal	0.8750***	1.9621	0.8356***	2.4478
	(0.17537)	(11.96927)	(0.11766)	(5.48840)
Low-tier formal	0.3534***	1.6626	0.5948***	3.2587
	(0.05289)	(4.2423)	(0.06522)	(2.01906)
High-tier formal	0.4165***	1.5615	0.6155***	3.1128
	(0.06542)	(5.53011)	(0.09210)	(2.51514)
Individual fixed effects	No	Yes	No	Yes
	% difference from LTI worker			
High-tier informal	140	–	131	–
Low-tier formal	42	–	81	–
High-tier formal	52	–	85	–
Observations	2,788	2,788	2,788	2,788
Pseudo R-squared	0.1182	–	0.1005	–

Note: Sample is male workers in non-agricultural sectors starting work between 1996 and 2007. Observed earnings are from 1996 to 2000, 2007, and 2014; * $p < 0.10$, ** $p < 0.05$, *** $p < 0.01$. Earnings are calculated from wage and profit information and adjusted using the Consumer Price Index (CPI 2012 = 100) from BPS. For the estimations, real earnings are transformed into IHS to include zero values. All regressions include variables on age, years of schooling, cognitive and maths scores, height, father and mother with more than six years' education, urban/rural location, schools, health, and road facilities in the districts, as well as year and island fixed effects.
Source: authors' construction based on data from IFLS 2000, 2007, and 2014.

We find that in non-agricultural sectors, the first jobs of male workers are predominantly formal; that is, between 60 and 80 per cent have formal jobs. Among the remaining workers, almost all start as low-tier informal workers. Only 1–2 per cent of workers have high-tier informal first jobs. The results from multinomial logit regression indicate that individuals are negatively selected into low-tier informal work. People who have higher education, have higher cognitive scores, and are taller are all less likely to start as low-tier informal workers.

Examining the trend of first jobs between 1996 and 2014, we find evidence that the informal sector appears to become smaller as an economy grows. However, the decline is very gradual and can be rapidly overturned by an economic crisis.

Among individuals whose first job was as a low-tier informal worker, almost half remained low-tier informal workers through the next 8–19 years, about 7 per cent became high-tier informal workers for at least one year, and 45 per cent became formal workers for at least one year, predominantly low-tier formal workers. Among the half who switched to a different job type for at least one period, the mean period spent as a high-tier informal worker is 0.46 years, the mean period as a low-tier formal worker 3.73 years, and the mean period as a high-tier formal worker 0.37 years. These indicate a relatively short stint as high-tier informal or formal workers. On average, these workers switch three times between types, the average job spell being similar to the average years employed.

In terms of the switching pattern, most individuals switched from low-tier informal to formal-sector work without going through a high-tier informal job. The characteristics of individuals who switched for at least one year indicate that workers whose fathers are highly educated have a significantly higher probability of switching. However, height, mathematics skills, cognitive skills, and education attainment have weak correlations with switching.

We find that the earnings premium that low-tier informal workers could gain by switching is large and statistically significant. Our median regression, which provides a more modest result, shows earnings premiums of between 42 and 52 per cent for observably similar workers in low-tier formal or high-tier formal work. The earnings premium for working in the high-tier informal sector is much higher at 140 per cent, but only about 7 per cent of workers who started out as low-tier informal workers were able to switch to this type of work.

Our findings imply two main points. First, low-tier informal workers are most likely to switch to low-tier formal work. Only a very small proportion are able to upgrade to high-tier informal work, although this is the route that most policymakers in developing countries appear to want low-tier informal workers to follow. Second, the earnings premium of switching to low-tier formal work is as high as 42 per cent. While it is still much lower than the earnings premium of switching to high-tier informal work, it seems that this is a more feasible route to improve the livelihoods of low-tier informal workers. Therefore, rather than creating policies that try to push low-tier informal-sector workers to become high-tier informal-sector workers, governments would be better advised to create jobs, albeit low-tier ones, that low-tier informal workers can apply for.

References

de Mel, S., D. McKenzie, and C. Woodruff (2010). 'Who are the Microenterprise Owners? Evidence from Sri Lanka on Tokman v. de Soto'. In J. Lerner and A. Schoar (eds), *International Differences in Entrepreneurship*. Chicago, IL: University of Chicago Press, 63–87.

Gindling, T. H., and D. Newhouse (2012). 'Self-Employment in the Developing World'. World Bank Policy Research Working Paper 6201. Washington, DC: World Bank. https://doi.org/10.1596/1813-9450-6201.

Gunther, I., and A. Launov (2012). 'Informal Employment in Developing Countries: Opportunity or Last Resort?' *Journal of Development Economics*, 97: 88–98. https://doi.org/10.1016/j.jdeveco.2011.01.001.

Hatton, T. J., R. Sparrow, D. Suryadarma, and P. van der Eng (2018). 'Fertility and the Health of Children in Indonesia'. *Economics and Human Biology*, 28(1): 67–78. https://doi.org/10.1016/j.ehb.2017.12.002.

La Porta, R., and A. Shleifer (2014). 'Informality and Development'. *Journal of Economic Perspectives*, 28(3): 109–126. https://doi.org/10.1257/jep.28.3.109.

Levine, R., and Y. Rubinstein (2017). 'Smart and Illicit: Who Becomes an Entrepreneur and Do They Earn More?' *Quarterly Journal of Economics*, 132(2): 963–1018. https://doi.org/10.1093/qje/qjw044.

McCaig, B., and N. Pavcnik (2015). 'Informal Employment in a Growing and Globalizing Low-Income Country'. *American Economic Review: Papers and Proceedings*, 105(5): 545–550. https://doi.org/10.1257/aer.p20151051.

Rothenberg, A. D., A. Gaduh, N. E. Burger, C. Chazali, I. Tjandraningsih, R. Radikun, C. Sutera, and S. Weilant (2016). 'Rethinking Indonesia's Informal Sector'. *World Development*, 80: 96–113. https://doi.org/10.1016/j.worlddev.2015.11.005.

Strauss, J., F. Witoelar, and B. Sikoki (2016). 'The Fifth Wave of the Indonesia Family Life Survey: Overview and Field Report'. RAND Working Paper WR-1143/1-NIA/NICHD. Santa Monica, CA: RAND Corporation. https://doi.org/10.7249/WR1143.1.

PART III
LATIN AMERICA

6

Transforming informal work and livelihoods in Costa Rica and Nicaragua

Enrique Alaniz, T. H. Gindling, Catherine Mata, and Diego Rojas

1. Introduction

Costa Rica and Nicaragua are neighbouring countries in Central America that present contrasting economic structures.[1] Most interesting for this chapter, Costa Rica has one of the most formal labour markets in Latin America, while Nicaragua has one of the least formal.

Informal work is often considered a place of residual employment for marginalized and vulnerable workers. However, it can also be seen as a dynamic sector of budding entrepreneurs: the staging ground for the development of firms that may eventually employ a large number of workers. As noted in Chapter 2, any analysis of informality must recognize this heterogeneity, differentiating between workers who are informal because of lack of formal employment opportunities ('lower-tier informal') and those who are self-employed or working in small firms voluntarily because of comparative advantage or preferences ('upper-tier informal'). Following the framework laid out in Chapter 2, we study the wages and labour mobility of heterogeneous informal work in Costa Rica and Nicaragua by dividing workers into six work status groups: formal self-employed, upper-tier informal self-employed, lower-tier informal self-employed, formal wage-employed, upper-tier informal wage-employed, and lower-tier wage-employed.

We estimate that more than 80 per cent of workers in Nicaragua are informal, while only 41 per cent of workers in Costa Rica are informal. Of these, fewer than 10 per cent of workers in Costa Rica are lower-tier informal, while 36 per cent are lower-tier informal in Nicaragua. The lower level of informality, and in particular lower-tier informal work, in Costa Rica compared to Nicaragua may be due to a variety of factors, including greater enforcement of social security taxes and other labour protection legislation (Gindling et al. 2015), higher gross domestic product (GDP) per capita, and public support for education, health, training, and other forms of human capital. GDP per capita in Costa Rica (US$ 19,762) is more than

[1] We are grateful to Kunal Sen, Simone Schotte, and Ira Gang for comments on earlier versions of this chapter.

Enrique Alaniz et al., *Transforming informal work and livelihoods in Costa Rica and Nicaragua.* In: *The Job Ladder.* Edited by Gary S. Fields, T. H. Gindling, Kunal Sen, Michael Danquah, and Simone Schotte, Oxford University Press.
 DOI: 10.1093/oso/9780192867339.003.0006

three times that in Nicaragua ($ 5,834) and poverty is half (1.4 per cent vs 3.2 per cent below $ 1.90/day, and 22 per cent vs 41 per cent at national poverty lines).[2] Public spending on the social sectors is higher in Costa Rica than in Nicaragua: 21 per cent of GDP in Costa Rica ($1,325 per capita) vs 14 per cent in Nicaragua ($157 per capita; Acosta et al. 2017).

2. Definitions and identification of the formal, upper-tier informal, and lower-tier informal work status groups

In this section, we describe the data and methodology used to identify which workers belong to which of the six different work status groups.

2.1 Data

Costa Rica

The data used in this analysis consist of a panel data set of individuals constructed from the 2011–2018 annual Costa Rican National Household Surveys (Encuesta Nacional de Hogares, or ENAHO, in Spanish). These household surveys are cross-sectional surveys that are conducted annually by the Costa Rican National Statistics and Census Institute. The ENAHO uses a rotating sample design whereby interviewers in one year return to approximately 75 per cent of the households interviewed in the previous year. Interviewers record a code identifying the address of each dwelling surveyed, which allows them to track dwellings that are surveyed in consecutive surveys. The Institute next checks that the same dwellings include the same households by comparing the personal characteristics of each household member (i.e. age, gender, education levels, etc.) for each consecutive year. Finally, using information on the personal characteristics of each member of each household, the Institute is able to match individuals across consecutive years. Using this strategy, the Institute has constructed seven year-to-year panel data sets of households and individuals (2011–2012, 2012–2013, 2013–2014, 2014–2015, 2015–2016, 2016–2017, and 2017–2018). Each year, 25 per cent of households are replaced in the sample; this implies that we will be able to follow, at most, 75 per cent of households from year to year, although in practice our sample is smaller. The year-to-year panels that we use include 37 per cent of all individuals between the ages of 15 and 65 who were interviewed in the ENAHO from 2011 to 2018.[3]

[2] World Bank World Development Indicators (2018) or most recent year. All dollar amounts are in current purchasing power parity (PPP) dollars.

[3] See Alaniz et al. (2020), which is an earlier version of this study, for additional detail on both the Costa Rican and Nicaraguan data used in this chapter.

Nicaragua

The primary data source used in this chapter for Nicaragua is a panel data set collected by the Fundación Internacional para el Desafío Económico Global (FIDEG), which follows households and household members from 2009 to 2017. The FIDEG survey is designed to measure poverty annually using household aggregate consumption as a welfare indicator and also includes data on household and individual characteristics, wages and other employment characteristics, access to some public services, and physical housing structure. It is a shorter version of the Living Standards Measurement Survey and the sample is a nationally representative panel of 1,700 households located in urban and rural areas throughout the country. The sample was designed using as the sampling frame the cartography of the Population and Dwellings Census conducted in 2005 by the National Institute of Statistics (INEC) and it is representative at national, urban, and rural levels; it is probabilistic and stratified. The primary sampling units are '*segmentos censales*' and the second-stage units are households within each segment. Eight households were selected in each segment using systematic sampling with random start.

In both Costa Rica and Nicaragua, we limit our samples to the working-age population, that is, those aged 15–65.

2.2 Identification of formal, upper-tier informal, and lower-tier informal work among wage-employees and the self-employed

Following the International Labour Organization (ILO) Thesaurus, our framework for identifying formal, upper-tier informal, and lower-tier informal workers is based on whether or not regulations and mandatory labour protections are complied with. Employers and workers who comply with all registration requirements and labour protections are identified as formal; those who comply with some but not all regulations and worker protections are upper-tier informal, and those who do not comply with any registration requirements or labour protections are lower-tier informal. In addition, we distinguish between wage-employees and the self-employed.

Costa Rica

In the ENAHO household surveys, wage-employees are self-identified as 'wage employees, un-paid assistants or private household workers' (including domestic servants). For private household wage-employees, the household (family) for whom they work is considered the employer. Wage-employees also include unpaid employees in family enterprises. We discuss first how we identify formal and the two types of informal wage-employees and then how we disaggregate formal and the two types of informal self-employed.

In the literature, informality may be defined relative to the employer or the worker. In this chapter, we focus on workers and follow the ILO Thesaurus definition of informal work as comprising 'all remunerative work (i.e. both self-employment and wage-employment) that is not registered, regulated or protected by existing legal or regulatory framework, as well as non-remunerative work undertaken in an income-producing enterprise' (ILO 2019). The common operationalization of 'not protected by the existing legal or regulatory framework' is whether or not the employer contributes to social security (through payroll taxes) for the employee. We follow this convention and identify formal wage-employees as those whose employers contribute to social security for the worker. This operationalization makes sense in Costa Rica as social security (which provides both health care and pensions) is the most widespread and desired social protection and payment of social security contributions is the most strongly enforced tax. Public-sector workers are also automatically included as formal-sector employees.

We identify upper-tier informal wage-employees as those whose employers comply with some but not all regulations and mandated worker protections. In Costa Rica, workers whose employers do not pay social security payroll taxes may still be covered by other labour protections. Other labour protections in Costa Rica include: sick leave, paid vacations, an *aguinaldo* (a mandated one-month salary bonus in December), overtime pay, worker compensation insurance, safety regulations, and maternal benefits. Our data include information on whether employees receive any of these other benefits. We identify as upper-tier informal employees those whose employers do not contribute to social security but who receive paid sick leave, paid vacations, work risk insurance, or the *aguinaldo*. We also include as upper-tier informal wage-employees those whose employers do not contribute to social security but who do have salary deductions for income taxes. Professional and technical wage-employees are also identified as upper-tier informal employees. We also identify wage-employees as upper-tier informal if they are covered by social security but their employers do not pay their payroll taxes—for example, if the employee is a direct dependant of someone whose employer does pay social security payroll taxes. A few people also pay directly for private insurance, which covers private clinics and hospitals but not social security clinics and hospitals. It is likely that many of these employees voluntarily forgo employer-subsidized social security in exchange for other forms of compensation such as higher wages. These workers are informal but are likely to be voluntarily so.

Lower-tier informal wage-employees are identified as those who are neither formal nor upper-tier informal wage-employees; that is, lower-tier informal wage-employees are those who receive no social security insurance or other labour protection benefits. These individuals could be employees in a firm, work in a private household, or work as an unpaid family member or they could be workers whose wage is paid in kind or in a single payment or per piece.

Self-employed workers are those who self-identify as own-account workers or owners of firms (employers). Self-employed workers in Costa Rica are legally required to be registered with both Costa Rica Social Security (CCSS) and the Ministry of Finance. Social security is mandated for all workers, including wage-employees and the self-employed. Self-employed workers pay under a 'special regime', which is the means by which they can contribute—and be affiliated—to the social security system in Costa Rica. This is needed because the 'normal' way that workers contribute to social security is through their employer, which self-employed workers do not have. The self-employed must pay both the employer and employee contributions to social security, although low-wage self-employed workers are subsidized by the government and therefore pay lower social security taxes.[4] Moreover, every private contractor is required to verify that a self-employed worker offering goods or services to their business is registered to both public institutions before contracting for any of their services. Each entity, the CCSS and the Ministry of Finance (known as the Hacienda in Costa Rica), is in charge of enforcing its own law and taxes, so it is possible for a self-employed worker to be registered with the CCSS but not with the Ministry of Finance (or vice versa).

For self-employed workers to fully comply with the law in Costa Rica, they must both pay into social security and be registered. We identify formal self-employed workers as those who follow all regulations: specifically, those who both contribute to social security *and* are registered. Workers are identified as registered if they are registered with the National Records or other public institution or keep formal accounts for reporting to the government.

Upper-tier informal self-employed are identified as those who comply with some but not all regulations—specifically, if they receive some type of social security health insurance (including through the special regime, as a direct dependant of an insured employee, insured by the government, or through private insurance) but are not registered with the Ministry of Finance or if they are registered with the Ministry of Finance but do not receive social security. Even if they are neither registered nor paying social security, other self-employed workers are classified as upper-tier informal self-employed if they are in a profession that requires post-secondary education, if they are employers with at least one employee, or if their place of work has a fixed premises.

[4] For instance, workers earning less than 78.85 per cent of the minimum wage pay 6.43 per cent of their income into the social security system under the special regime, workers earning between 78.85 per cent of and twice the minimum wage pay 9.3 per cent, workers earning between twice and four times the minimum wage pay 12.28 per cent, etc. The maximum social security tax for those in the special regime is 17.62 per cent of earnings (up to September 2017). This graduated payment scale by income is designed to encourage all self-employed workers, including the poor, to become enrolled into the social security system.

Lower-tier informal self-employed are identified as those who do not comply with any mandated government regulations—specifically, if they have no type of health insurance and are not registered, have no paid employees, and are not professional or technical workers. This includes those whose place of work has no fixed premises (i.e. they work in the owner's dwelling, are itinerant, or work on construction sites or agricultural plots).

Nicaragua

In the FIDEG survey, wage-employees are those who self-identify as an employee or a labourer (including domestic servants). Wage-employees also include unpaid employees in family enterprises.

As in Costa Rica, we follow the convention of identifying formal wage-employees as those whose employers contribute to social security for the worker. Other wage-employees are informal. Unlike in Costa Rica, the Nicaraguan data does not have information on other labour protections aside from social security and therefore our definitions of lower-tier and upper-tier informal wage-employees are not exactly the same in both countries. In Nicaragua, we identify lower-tier informal wage-employees as domestic servants and others working in private households. Upper-tier informal employees are all other employees whose employers do not contribute to social security.

Self-employed workers are those who self-identify as own-account workers or owners of firms (employers). Self-employed workers are not legally required to contribute to social security, but they can personally and voluntarily pay social security contributions through the '*seguro facultativo*'; however, we estimate that very few—approximately 2 per cent of self-employed workers—do so. Workers who do not contribute to social security still have access to local public health clinics.

Formal self-employed workers are those who are affiliated with social security in any capacity.[5] Upper-tier informal self-employed are defined as those who work in a unit with at least one wage-employee or who have private or other self-paid health insurance. Lower-tier informal self-employed are all other self-employed workers who have no health insurance (either social security or self-paid).

3. Descriptive analysis

In this section, we look at the characteristics of workers in each work status, including wages, poverty, education, age, and gender.

[5] Unlike in Costa Rica, the Nicaraguan data do not have information on whether self-employed workers are registered with other government agencies. Therefore, our measures of formal, upper-tier informal, and lower-tier informal self-employed in Nicaragua are not as nuanced as in Costa Rica.

3.1 Distribution by work status

Table 6.1 presents the distribution of workers (and those not in the labour force) in each work status for Costa Rica and Nicaragua. Overall, compared with Costa Rica, work in Nicaragua is less formal, with a much larger proportion of lower-tier informal workers. Formal work includes almost 60 per cent of workers in Costa Rica compared with 19 per cent in Nicaragua. While in both Costa Rica and Nicaragua upper-tier informal work accounts for a larger number of workers than lower-tier informal work, the overall proportion of lower-tier informality is very different; in Nicaragua, lower-tier informal work accounts for 36 per cent of workers, while, in Costa Rica, it accounts for only 9 per cent; this represents 43 per cent of informal workers in Nicaragua and 22 per cent in Costa Rica. In both countries, the proportion of workers who are wage-employees is higher than the proportion of self-employed workers, although the latter is larger in Nicaragua—38 per cent compared with 22 per cent in Costa Rica. The proportion of formal self-employment is particularly small in Nicaragua, at less than 1 per cent of workers, compared with over 5 per cent of workers in Costa Rica.

3.2 The job ladder

Figure 6.1 summarizes the 'job ladder' in Costa Rica and Nicaragua by comparing monthly earnings by work status. In both countries, there is a clear ordering: formal self-employment and formal wage-employment earn the most. Next comes upper-tier informal self-employment, followed by upper-tier informal wage-employment. At the bottom of the ladder comes lower-tier informal self-employment, with lower-tier informal wage-employment as the lowest-earning sector (although the differences between lower-tier self-employed and wage-employees are small).

3.3 Wage dynamics

Comparisons of average wages in each work status are an incomplete description of which are the best jobs for a given worker because the observed and unobserved characteristics of workers in each work status may be different. Average wages do not necessarily indicate the relative wages an observationally equivalent worker would earn in each work status. To address this issue, we use the panel nature of the data to examine whether wages for the same workers increase or decrease when these workers change work status, and we also adjust for observable worker characteristics. We adjust for changes in observable characteristics (education, vocational training, age, and gender) when workers change work status

Table 6.1 Percentage in each work and employment status for Costa Rica and Nicaragua

Costa Rica			**Working-age population**	**Labour force**	**All workers**	**Informal workers**	**Self-employed**	**Wage-employment**
Self-employed	Formal		3.1	5	5	–	24.2	–
	Informal	Upper-tier	7.9	13	14	33	61.7	–
		Lower-tier	1.8	3	3	8	14.1	–
Wage-employees	Formal		30.4	49	53		–	68
	Informal	Upper-tier	10.6	17	18	44	–	24
		Lower-tier	3.6	6	6	15	–	8
Not employed	Unemployed		5.0	8	–	–	–	–
	Full-time students		13.4	–	–	–	–	–
	Out of the labour force		24.1	–	–	–	–	–
Nicaragua			**Working-age population**	**Labour force**	**All workers**	**Informal workers**	**Self-employed**	**Wage-employment**
Self-employed	Formal		0.5	1	1	–	1.8	–
	Informal	Upper-tier	14.1	20	20	25	54.0	–
		Lower-tier	11.6	16	17	20	44.2	–
Wage-employees	Formal		12.1	17	18	–	–	28
	Informal	Upper-tier	17.8	25	26	32	–	42
		Lower-tier	12.9	18	19	23	–	30
Not employed	Unemployed		2.2	3	–	–	–	–
	Full-time students		6.6	–	–	–	–	–
	Out of the labour force		22.2	–	–	–	–	–

Source: authors' calculations based on the data described in section 2.1; for Costa Rica, average of ENAHO 2016, 2017, and 2018; for Nicaragua, average of FIDEG panel, 2009–2017.

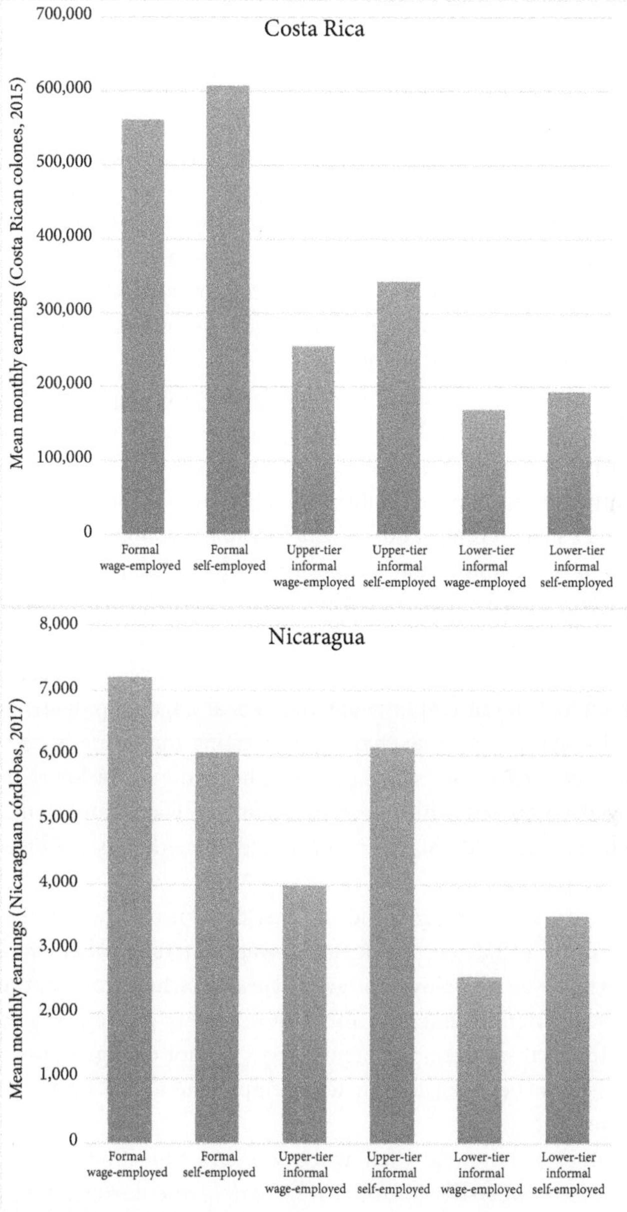

Fig. 6.1 Mean earnings by work status, Costa Rica and Nicaragua

Source: authors' calculations based on the data described in section 2.1.

with regression analysis of wage changes. We interpret a labour status as preferred if workers who transition from another wage status into that labour status experience an increase in earnings. For example, if wages increase when a worker moves from upper-tier informal wage-employment to formal wage-employment, this is evidence that formal wage-employment is preferred to upper-tier informal wage-employment. On the other hand, if there is no statistically significant change in wages when an upper-tier informal wage-employee moves to formal wage-employment, this is evidence that formal wage-employment is not necessarily preferred to upper-tier informal wage-employment, and vice versa. See the WIDER working paper version of this chapter (Alaniz et al. 2020) for a more formal description of the methodology.

Proportional changes in these adjusted hourly wages given changes in sectors are reported in Table 6.2 (the full wage equation results are presented later in Table 6.6). The wage dynamics suggest a somewhat different job ladder than do the mean earnings by work status. Probably the biggest difference is that the wage dynamics suggest that, in both Costa Rica and Nicaragua, wage-employment is preferred to self-employment within upper-tier informal work. For example, wages fall when workers transition from upper-tier informal wage-employment into upper-tier informal self-employment, while wages rise when the transition is in the opposite direction. In addition, in both Costa Rica and Nicaragua, transitions between formal self-employment and formal wage-employment do not lead to statistically significant wage changes, suggesting that there is no clear ordering between these two work status groups. The evidence for lower-tier informal self-employed compared with lower-tier informal wage-employed is that self-employment is preferred in Nicaragua but that neither is preferred in Costa Rica.[6]

In Costa Rica, the wage dynamics suggest that formal wage-employment has the best jobs: for all but one work status, wages increase when workers transition into formal wage-employment and wages fall when workers transition out of formal wage-employment into other work status groups. The exception is upper-tier informal wage-employment: wages do not change significantly when workers transition between formal wage-employment and upper-tier informal wage-employment.

On the other hand, wages fall when workers transition from formal self-employment into upper-tier informal wage-employment, suggesting that formal self-employment may be preferred. Upper-tier informal self-employment is the

[6] The differences between Fig. 6.1 and Table 6.2 may be because reported self-employed earnings include both returns to capital as well as returns to labour so that, at any point in time, the level of self-employed reported earnings may be higher than reported wage-employees even if returns to labour in the two labour status groups are the same. This measurement issue may have a smaller effect on earnings when wage-employees transition to self-employment.

Table 6.2 Adjusted monthly wage changes associated with transitions between working sectors

Costa Rica, 2011–2018	**1. Formal self-employed ($t+1$)**	**2. Upper-tier informal self-employed ($t+1$)**	**3. Lower-tier informal self-employed ($t+1$)**	**4. Formal wage-employee ($t+1$)**	**5. Upper-tier informal wage-employee ($t+1$)**	**6. Lower-tier informal wage-employee ($t+1$)**
1. Formal self-employed (t)	–	−0.158***	−0.399**	−0.0887	−0.195***	−0.337
	–	(0.0574)	(0.201)	(0.0851)	(0.0749)	(0.277)
2. Upper-tier informal self-employed (t)	0.216***	–	−0.0803	0.564***	0.173***	0.00218
	(0.0486)	–	(0.0672)	(0.0659)	(0.0571)	(0.129)
3. Lower-tier informal self-employed (t)	0.627***	0.0311	–	0.675***	0.363***	0.00127
	(0.149)	(0.0820)	–	(0.105)	(0.133)	(0.104)
4. Formal wage-employee (t)	−0.0933	−0.716***	−0.636***	–	−0.170***	−0.657***
	(0.0931)	(0.0671)	(0.0811)	–	(0.0259)	(0.0531)
5. Upper-tier informal wage-employee (t)	0.181**	−0.208***	−0.570***	0.235***	–	−0.334***
	(0.0795)	(0.0499)	(0.111)	(0.0297)	–	(0.0484)
6. Lower-tier informal wage-employee (t)	0.253	0.143	−0.125	0.624***	0.366***	–
	(0.358)	(0.140)	(0.0912)	(0.0613)	(0.0559)	–

Continued

Table 6.2 *Continued*

Nicaragua, 2010–17	1. Formal self-employed ($t+1$)	2. Upper-tier informal self-employed ($t+1$)	3. Lower-tier informal self-employed ($t+1$)	4. Formal wage-employee ($t+1$)	5. Upper-tier informal wage-employee ($t+1$)	6. Lower-tier informal wage-employee ($t+1$)
1. Formal self-employed (t)	–	0.423	0.199	0.063	0.240	NA
	–	(0.456)	(0.441)	(0.565)	(0.417)	–
2. Upper-tier informal self-employed (t)	0.138	–	-0.226^{***}	0.253^{**}	0.385^{***}	-0.325^{*}
	(0.167)	–	(0.061)	(0.130)	(0.068)	(0.160)
3. Lower-tier informal self-employed (t)	0.061	−0.002	–	0.183^{*}	0.255^{***}	-0.301^{***}
	(0.181)	(0.066)	–	(0.096)	(0.301)	(0.090)
4. Formal wage-employee (t)	−0.425	-0.333^{*}	−0.018	–	-0.112^{***}	-0.416^{***}
	(0.34)	(0.200)	(0.162)	–	(0.364)	(0.120)
5. Upper-tier informal wage-employee (t)	0.759^{*}	-0.593^{***}	-0.478^{***}	0.058^{*}	–	-0.133^{**}
	(0.424)	(0.094)	(0.089)	(0.033)	–	(0.068)
6. Lower-tier informal wage-employee (t)	0.328^{***}	0.037	0.621^{***}	0.231^{***}	0.163^{***}	–
	(0.094)	(0.196)	(0.116)	(0.089)	(0.072)	–

Note: Heteroskedasticity-robust standard errors in parentheses. Wage changes are relative to the wage if the workers stay in the same sector at both time t and $t+1$. OLS regressions include the following controls: log of wage at time t; lagged wage; age and its square; gender dummy; regional dummies; primary, secondary, and tertiary education dummies for time t; the change in these dummies between t and $t+1$; dummy for non-formal (vocational) education at time t; the change in this dummy between t and $t+1$; fluency in English at time t; change in fluency between t and $t+1$; and year dummies; * $p < 0.1$, ** $p < 0.05$, *** $p < 0.001$.

Source: authors' calculations based on the data described in section 2.1.

next most preferred. At the bottom of the job ladder are lower-tier informal workers.

In Nicaragua, the wage dynamics suggest that the most preferred jobs are also in formal wage-employment and formal self-employment. With the exception of formal self-employment, when workers transition into formal wage-employment wages increase. The next most preferred is upper-tier informal wage-employment: wages increase when other types of informal workers transition into this status and fall when workers transition from this status into other types of informality. The next most preferred is upper-tier informal self-employment: wages fall when workers in this status move to either lower-tier informal wage-employment or self-employment, followed by lower-tier informal self-employment. The least preferred is lower-tier informal wage-employment: transitions from this status into any other work status lead to higher wages, and transitions from any other work status into this status lead to lower wages.

3.4 Other characteristics of workers in each work status

In both Costa Rica and Nicaragua, lower-tier informal workers (self-employed and wage-employees) have the lowest education levels, formal workers (self-employed and wage-employees) have the highest education levels, and upper-tier informal workers are in between.

In both countries, self-employed workers have more vocational training than wage-employees at each work status. Among both the self-employed and wage-employees, formal workers have the most vocational training, followed by upper-tier informal workers, followed by lower-tier informal workers. The only exception is in Costa Rica, where formal wage-employees, formal self-employed, and upper-tier informal self-employed have similar average levels of vocational training.

In both Costa Rica and Nicaragua, lower-tier informal wage-employees tend to be young: 64 per cent of lower-tier informal wage-employees in Nicaragua and 48 per cent of lower-tier informal wage-employees are between 15 and 29. Self-employed workers in all work status groups tend to be older than wage-employees. For example, more than 38 per cent of upper-tier informal self-employed are age 50 or older, compared with fewer than 16 per cent of upper-tier informal wage-employees. In Costa Rica, 41 per cent of formal self-employed are 50 or older, while only 19 per cent of formal wage-employees are 50 or older.

The presence of women in each work status differs between Costa Rica and Nicaragua. In Costa Rica, the proportion of women is highest in upper-tier informal and lowest in lower-tier informal and formal self-employed. In Nicaragua, it is the opposite: the proportion of women is highest in lower-tier informal and lowest in upper-tier informal and formal self-employed. In both countries, formal wage-employment is in the middle. When we look only at women with young children, the results are more consistent across countries. In both countries, women with young children are over-represented in lower-tier informal work. For example, in Costa Rica, approximately 55 per cent of women with young children are found in lower-tier informal work status groups, while in every other work status this proportion is less than 45 per cent. In Nicaragua, the difference between the proportion of men and women with young children in lower-tier informal work is greater than in any other work status.

For each work status (except formal wage-employees), a larger proportion of workers is in agriculture in Nicaragua than in Costa Rica (see Table 6.3). In both Costa Rica and Nicaragua, the proportion of agricultural workers in lower-tier informal wage-employment is the highest (along with upper-tier self-employment in Nicaragua). In both countries, lower-tier informal wage-employees are also found in household service, and in Costa Rica, lower-tier informal wage-employees are also found in construction. In both Costa Rica and Nicaragua, the lowest proportion of agricultural workers is found in formal wage-employment.

Many Nicaraguans migrate to Costa Rica for work. In Costa Rica, Nicaraguan immigrants make up approximately 9 per cent of all workers and are concentrated in agriculture, construction, and household services (OECD and ILO 2018). Nicaraguan immigrants are disproportionally found in the lower-tier informality. We calculate that 14 per cent of lower-tier informal wage-employees and 12 per cent of lower-tier informal self-employed were born in Nicaragua. This compares to 7 per cent in formal wage-employment. Of course, because formal wage-employment comprises the majority of Costa Rican workers, the majority of Nicaraguan immigrants are also formal wage-employees.

A large proportion of formal wage-employees are in public/government employment (public administration, teaching, health care, social assistance, etc.). Public-sector workers make up about one-third of formal wage-employees in both Costa Rica and Nicaragua. However, because formal employment is larger in Costa Rica than in Nicaragua, this implies a different proportion of total workers: 16 per cent of workers in Costa Rica are public compared with only 4.5 per cent in Nicaragua.

Recall that a formal wage-employee is defined as one whose employer pays for social security health insurance. In Costa Rica, we find that if an employer pays for social security, then that employer is very likely to comply with other aspects of labour formality. For example, of formal wage-employees in Costa Rica, 95 per cent receive the *aguinaldo*, 90 per cent receive mandated sick days, and 91 per cent receive paid vacation. Consistent with this, other research that we have conducted in Costa Rica shows that policies designed to increase compliance with minimum wages can lead to more employers complying with other labour protections and therefore to more informal workers becoming formal (Gindling et al. 2015).

Table 6.3 Descriptive statistics by work status, Costa Rica and Nicaragua (percentages)

			Education							
			Primary incomplete	Primary complete	Secondary complete	Some tertiary	Non-formal vocational training	In agriculture	Born in Nicaragua	Poverty rate
Costa Rica, 2011–2018										
Self-employed	Formal		8	50	18	23	34	20	3	11.5
	Informal	Upper-tier	15	56	15	14	36	22	4	23.0
		Lower-tier	23	58	12	7	25	18	12	33.7
Wage-employees	Formal		7	40	19	34	36	12	7	6.7
	Informal	Upper-tier	17	61	13	9	25	19	8	22.2
		Lower-tier	23	61	12	4	17	27	14	35.7
Nicaragua, 2009–2017										
Self-employed	Formal		24	36	14	16	34	26		4.8
	Informal	Upper-tier	33	31	6	5	36	55		39.0
		Lower-tier	30	36	9	7	25	25		36.0
Wage-employees	Formal		9	37	18	32	36	7		23.6
	Informal	Upper-tier	27	37	11	7	25	48		48.0
		Lower-tier	27	43	10	6	17	51		44.5

Continued

Table 6.3 *Continued*

			Age					With children under 12	
			15–19	20–29	30–49	50 and above	Female	Male	Female
Costa Rica, 2011–2018									
Self-employed	Formal		0	6	53	41	19	40	33
	Informal	Upper-tier	1	9	47	42	42	36	44
		Lower-tier	2	18	53	27	26	40	54
Wage-employees	Formal		2	27	52	19	37	45	42
	Informal	Upper-tier	10	22	43	25	51	42	42
		Lower-tier	11	37	39	13	26	42	56
Nicaragua, 2009–2017									
Self-employed	Formal		2	9	33	57	52	61	69
	Informal	Upper-tier	3	12	52	34	36	72	70
		Lower-tier	5	20	46	29	55	67	70
Wage-employees	Formal		3	35	46	15	43	68	70
	Informal	Upper-tier	19	36	35	10	17	71	76
		Lower-tier	33	31	27	9	55	64	73

Source: authors' calculations based on the data described in section 2.1; for Costa Rica, average of 2011–2018 Costa Rica panel in 2015 colones; for Nicaragua, 2009–2017 FIDEG panel in 2017 córdobas.

Poverty rates for the household in which the worker lives have a similar ordering to monthly earnings. In Costa Rica, poverty rates are similar for the self-employed and wage-employees in each work status. Formal self-employed and wage-employees have the lowest poverty rates, followed by upper-tier informal self-employed and wage-employees, and lastly lower-tier informal self-employed and wage-employees. In Nicaragua, poverty rates are lower for the self-employed than for wage-employees in each work status. The poverty rankings by work status are therefore somewhat more complex than in Costa Rica. In Nicaragua, poverty rates are the lowest for formal self-employed, followed by formal wage-employees, followed by upper-tier informal self-employed; and poverty rates are higher for upper-tier informal wage-employees than for lower-tier informal self-employed (the opposite of Costa Rica). The highest poverty rate is for upper-tier informal wage-employees.

Considering all of the evidence together suggests that formal is the most preferred work status. Formal wage-employees are paid the most, have the lowest poverty rates, have more stable employment, are more likely to benefit from a range of labour protections, and have the highest education levels. The formal self-employed have similar earnings, poverty rates, and education levels. The next most preferred jobs are upper-tier informal (both wage-employment and self-employment), followed by lower-tier informal self-employment. Lower-tier informal wage-employment is the lowest-paid work status in both Nicaragua and Costa Rica.

4. Employment transitions

Table 6.4 presents P_{ij}, the proportion of those in each origin work status i at time t who transition to another work status j or remain in work status i in year $t + 1$.

A key question is whether lower-tier informality is a persistent state where, once entered, workers are stuck and unable to transition to better-paid work status groups. The transitions reported in Table 6.4 do not support the argument that individual lower-tier informal workers are stuck in lower-informal work in either Costa Rica or Nicaragua. In both countries, the proportion of workers who remain in the same work status from year to year is lower in lower-tier informal work than in any other work status. This is true in both countries and in both lower-tier informal work status groups. While many of the workers who transition out of lower-tier informality leave employment or transition into another lower-tier informal work status, most workers who do so transition to higher-paid work status groups. For example, 41 per cent of lower-tier informal wage-employees in year t in Costa Rica transition to either upper-tier informal or formal work status groups in year $t + 1$, compared with 31 per cent who transition to other work status groups or out of employment and 28 per cent who remain in lower-tier

Table 6.4 Year-to-year conditional probabilities of transition, as a percentage of the initial number in each status in year t

Costa Rica		$t+1 \rightarrow$	**Self-employed**			**Wage-employees**			**Not employed**			**Total**
			Formal	**Informal**		**Formal**	**Informal**		**Unemployed**	**Students**	**Out of labour force**	
		$t \downarrow$		**Upper-tier**	**Lower-tier**		**Upper-tier**	**Lower-tier**				
Self-employed	Formal		48.5	34.6	1.0	3.5	6.8	0.6	1.1	0.2	3.8	100.0
	Informal	Upper-tier	12.6	45.1	4.1	5.0	10.3	1.8	2.5	1.7	17.0	100.0
		Lower-tier	2.3	21.1	33.7	6.8	8.1	11.0	4.9	1.5	10.5	100.0
Wage-employees	Formal		0.4	1.4	0.5	86.5	3.5	1.5	3.0	0.7	2.5	100.0
	Informal	Upper-tier	2.2	8.4	1.3	12.7	42.4	5.9	5.4	5.3	16.5	100.0
		Lower-tier	0.6	4.5	5.8	15.2	20.7	27.9	9.9	4.3	11.2	100.0
Unemployed			0.6	4.7	2.4	22.3	11.0	7.9	22.8	9.8	18.6	100.0

Nicaragua		$t+1 \rightarrow$	**Self-employed**			**Wage-employees**			**Not employed**			**Total**
			Formal	**Informal**		**Formal**	**Informal**		**Unemployed**	**Students**	**Out of labour force**	
		$t \downarrow$		**Upper-tier**	**Lower-tier**		**Upper-tier**	**Lower-tier**				
Self-employed	Formal		18.0	29.5	16.4	9.0	6.6	4.1	0.0	0.0	16.4	100.0
	Informal	Upper-tier	0.9	56.6	15.2	1.7	9.8	6.3	0.8	0.3	8.5	100.0
		Lower-tier	0.8	20.5	40.0	2.4	10.8	7.6	1.4	0.8	15.7	100.0
Wage-employees	Formal		0.6	1.7	2.2	75.7	9.8	1.8	2.4	0.4	5.5	100.0
	Informal	Upper-tier	0.1	7.8	6.8	9.3	56.1	8.8	3.0	1.7	6.4	100.0
		Lower-tier	0.1	7.8	6.7	2.8	14.4	46.4	1.1	4.7	15.9	100.0
Unemployed			0.2	5.8	10.7	15.9	26.4	6.8	13.2	2.9	18.1	100.0

Source: authors' calculations based on (for Costa Rica) Costa Rican panel 2011–2017 and (for Nicaragua) FIDEG panel 2009–2017.

informal wage-employment. In Nicaragua, 25 per cent of lower-tier informal workers in year *t* transition to higher-paying work status groups in the next year, compared with 29 per cent who transition to other work status groups or out of employment. When workers move from lower-tier informal wage-employment, they are most likely to transition into upper-tier informal wage-employment: in Costa Rica, 21 per cent of workers who are lower-tier informal wage-employees in one year are upper-tier informal wage-employees in the next year; in Nicaragua, the proportion is 14 per cent. A few lower-tier informal workers also transition directly into formal wage-employment, although this is more common in Costa Rica than in Nicaragua: 15 per cent of lower-tier informal wage-employees transition directly into formal wage-employment in Costa Rica from year to year compared with 2.8 per cent in Nicaragua.[7] This difference between Costa Rica and Nicaragua is at least partly due to the larger proportion of formal wage-employees in Costa Rica.

Formal wage-employees have the least mobility into other wage status groups, which is what we would expect if formal wage-employment is rationed as predicted by the dualistic labour market segmentation model: 76 per cent in Nicaragua and 86 per cent in Costa Rica stay as formal wage-employees from year to year compared with less than 57 per cent who stay in any other wage status from year to year. Most of the formal wage-employees who do move out of formal wage-employment go into upper-tier informal wage-employment or out of the labour force (possibly retiring). We find that very few formal employees transition to lower-tier informal wage-employment or any type of self-employment. This finding is not consistent with some other studies from Latin America, which find evidence that workers use human capital obtained in formal wage-employment to successfully transition to self-employment (e.g. Maloney 2004).

Upper-tier informal wage-employees are more mobile than formal wage-employees but less mobile than lower-tier informal workers. In both Costa Rica and Nicaragua, when upper-tier informal wage-employees do change work status, they are more likely to transition into better-paid formal wage-employment than into lower-tier informal work. For example, 15 per cent of workers in upper-tier wage-employment in Costa Rica in one year are formal wage-employees the next; the proportion in Nicaragua is 9.3 per cent. This compares to 6 per cent of upper-tier informal wage-employees in Costa Rica and 8.8 per cent of upper-tier

[7] In Costa Rica, the proportion of lower-tier informal wage-employees who transition directly into formal work is actually higher than the proportion of upper-tier informal wage-employees who transition directly into formal work. However, because upper-tier informal wage-employment in Costa Rica is larger than lower-tier informal wage-employment, the *number* of workers who transition from upper-tier informal wage-employment into formal work (1,024 in our sample) is higher than the number who transition from lower-tier informal wage-employment into formal work (431 in our sample).

informal wage-employees in Nicaragua who transition into lower-paying informal wage-employment.

Those in the formal and upper-tier informal self-employed status groups are also reasonably mobile. In both countries, when the formal self-employed transition, they are most likely to move to upper-tier self-employment. The patterns of transitions out of upper-tier self-employment differ between Nicaragua and Costa Rica. In Costa Rica, upper-tier informal self-employed are most likely to transition up the job ladder into formal self-employment and upper-tier informal wage-employment. In Nicaragua, upper-tier informal self-employed are most likely to transition down into lower-tier informal self-employment, possibly due to the smaller size of formal wage-employment in Nicaragua compared to Costa Rica.

While we find that individual lower-tier and upper-tier informal workers have substantial mobility up the job ladder into higher-paying wage status groups, we also find that some workers transition down the job ladder into lower-paying work status groups. If mobility upwards is the same as mobility downwards, then the total number of informal workers might not change even if many individual workers transition into better-paying work status groups. However, this is not what we find. When we compare the *number* of transitions, we find that the number of workers who transition up the job ladder is greater than the number of workers who transition down the wage ladder. For example, in Nicaragua we found that 1,698 lower-tier informal workers in the sample transitioned into upper-tier informal work status groups, compared with 984 who transitioned from upper-tier informal into lower-tier informal. In Costa Rica, 1,101 workers in the sample transitioned from lower-tier informal work status groups into upper-tier informal work status groups, compared with 908 who transitioned from upper-tier informal work status groups into lower-tier informal work status groups. The number of transitions from upper-tier informal to formal work is also greater than the number who transition in the opposite direction. For example, in Nicaragua, 414 workers in our sample transitioned from upper-tier informal work into formal wage-employment compared with 302 who transitioned from formal to upper-tier informal wage-employment. In Costa Rica 1,024 workers transitioned up the job ladder into formal wage-employment compared with 812 who transitioned down the ladder into upper-tier informal wage-employment. Transitions between upper-tier informal self-employment and wage-employment and formal self-employment and wage-employment show similar patterns. There were also more transitions from lower-tier informal wage-employment into formal wage-employment than in the opposite direction (415 vs 340 in Costa Rica and 97 vs 54 in Nicaragua).

In summary, the transition matrices suggest that there is substantial mobility of individual workers from lower-tier informal into upper-tier informal, and from upper-tier informal into formal, and even mobility from lower-tier informal directly into formal work status. However, there is also substantial churning as workers move between upper-tier informal, lower-informal, and formal work status groups; but even with this churning, there are still more total transitions up the job ladder into higher-paying job status groups than down the ladder into lower-paying work status groups.

5. Characteristics correlated with improved work status and wages for informal workers

In this section, first we estimate work status transition equations to identify the observed characteristics associated with improved work status. Next, we use estimates of wage dynamics (wage change) equations to identify the observed characteristics that are correlated with increasing wages for those workers who remain in the same work status.

5.1 Characteristics correlated with transitions from informal employment into better work status groups

To provide evidence on improving the work and livelihoods of informal workers, we estimate equations that examine the correlates of transitions between sectors. In these estimated transition equations, we examine the impacts of personal characteristics (education and vocational training, age, gender), changes in personal characteristics, family-level variables (presence of a partner, number of children under 12 years old), changes in family-level variables, and public utilities that each individual has access to as government-provided public services (sanitation, potable water, and electricity).[8]

Although we estimate transitions between all work status groups, in Table 6.5 we present only a subset of the results—specifically, results of the employment transitions equations from lower-tier informal (combining self-employed and wage-employment) into upper-tier informal wage-employment, upper-tier informal self-employment, formal wage-employment, and formal self-employment. We also estimate employment transition equations for transitions between upper-tier informal work (combining self-employed and wage-employed) into formal wage-employment and formal self-employment.

The interpretation of the impact of changes in independent variables on transitions depends on whether those variables are levels or changes. For example, the education level of a worker was likely earned before that worker entered the

[8] We also control for year fixed effects. Further details on the methodology used in this section are available in the WIDER working paper version of this chapter (Alaniz et al. 2020).

Table 6.5 Estimation of the characteristics correlated with transitions from lower-tier and upper-tier informal status (self-employed and wage-employed) into the formal and upper-tier informal status

	Transitions from the lower-tier informal sectors			Transitions from the upper-tier informal sectors		
Independent variables (marginal probabilities are reported, standard errors in parentheses)	**To formal self-employed**	**To upper-tier informal self-employed**	**To formal wage-employee**	**To upper-tier informal wage-employee**	**To formal self-employed**	**To formal wage-employee**
(a) Costa Rica						
Age	0.00264**	0.0116***	0.000356	0.000795	0.0133***	0.00514***
	(0.00107)	(0.00288)	(0.00321)	(0.00333)	(0.00137)	(0.00134)
Age 2	−2.76e-05**	−0.000107***	−5.63e-05	−2.04e-05	−0.000139***	−0.000100***
	(1.27e-05)	(3.59e-05)	(4.36e-05)	(4.35e-05)	(1.58e-05)	(1.77e-05)
Female	−0.0124**	0.00126	−0.0459***	0.0563***	−0.0888***	−0.0524***
	(0.00560)	(0.0114)	(0.0134)	(0.0139)	(0.00531)	(0.00518)
Complete primary education	0.00747	0.0238*	0.0449**	−0.00848	0.0439***	−0.00558
	(0.00619)	(0.0141)	(0.0178)	(0.0173)	(0.00832)	(0.00896)
Complete secondary (academic and technical) education	0.0160**	0.0527***	0.0981***	0.00334	0.0621***	0.0263**
	(0.00784)	(0.0201)	(0.0223)	(0.0250)	(0.0101)	(0.0108)
Some tertiary and post-graduate education	0.0257***	0.0715***	0.108***	−0.0333	0.0992***	0.0390***
	(0.00860)	(0.0252)	(0.0284)	(0.0366)	(0.0103)	(0.0113)
Earn a primary education degree	0.00401	0.0382	0.0186	0.0655*	0.0209	−0.00193
	(0.0130)	(0.0273)	(0.0375)	(0.0335)	(0.0183)	(0.0200)
Earn a secondary education degree	0.0260***	0.0274	0.0173	−0.0898	0.0181	0.0240
	(0.00724)	(0.0370)	(0.0378)	(0.0600)	(0.0155)	(0.0156)
Earn some tertiary education	0.00524	0.0662*	−0.0618	0.0457	0.0300**	0.0269
	(0.0138)	(0.0393)	(0.0617)	(0.0635)	(0.0151)	(0.0174)
Non-formal vocational education	0.00254	0.0173	0.0426***	−0.0158	0.0162***	−0.00716
	(0.00484)	(0.0135)	(0.0139)	(0.0175)	(0.00517)	(0.00635)

Earn vocational education	0.00769	0.0358**	0.0570***	0.0287	0.0300***	0.0135*
	(0.00561)	(0.0174)	(0.0188)	(0.0225)	(0.00648)	(0.00818)
Fluency in English	0.00745	0.0272	−0.0413	−0.0908*	0.00621	0.0388***
	(0.00609)	(0.0266)	(0.0330)	(0.0476)	(0.00885)	(0.0102)
Increase fluency in English	0.00696	0.00862	0.0344	0.0540	0.0144	0.0444***
	(0.0146)	(0.0484)	(0.0461)	(0.0584)	(0.0139)	(0.0150)
Presence of a partner	0.0106**	0.0592***	0.0429***	−0.0110	0.0212***	−0.0148**
	(0.00435)	(0.0119)	(0.0138)	(0.0149)	(0.00565)	(0.00645)
Gain a partner	0.0123	0.0445	0.0526**	−0.0788**	0.0137	0.0204
	(0.01000)	(0.0288)	(0.0266)	(0.0398)	(0.0203)	(0.0170)
Lose a partner	−0.181***	−0.0266	0.0206	−0.0291	−0.0209	0.0263
	(0.0277)	(0.0338)	(0.0353)	(0.0448)	(0.0185)	(0.0177)
Number of children under 12 in household	−0.00136	−0.0100*	−0.0119*	0.00194	−0.00203	0.000489
	(0.00189)	(0.00550)	(0.00692)	(0.00656)	(0.00277)	(0.00346)
Change of children under 12	−0.00693*	−0.00132	−0.00308	0.00192	0.000201	0.00365
	(0.00382)	(0.00811)	(0.00941)	(0.0110)	(0.00468)	(0.00576)
Potable water	−0.00401	−0.0155	−0.0239	0.00985	−0.00317	0.0132
	(0.00567)	(0.0167)	(0.0177)	(0.0218)	(0.00720)	(0.00971)
Publicly provided sanitation system	0.000691	0.0139	0.00159	−0.0371*	−0.0131**	0.00802
	(0.00515)	(0.0140)	(0.0165)	(0.0193)	(0.00662)	(0.00730)
Central Valley	−0.00388	0.00286	0.000519	0.0434***	−0.00804*	0.0169***
	(0.00386)	(0.0104)	(0.0117)	(0.0132)	(0.00461)	(0.00547)
Time dummies	Yes	Yes	Yes	Yes	Yes	Yes
Observations	3,480	3,480	3,480	3,480	11,968	11,968

Continued

Table 6.5 *Continued*

Independent variables (marginal probabilities are reported, standard errors in parentheses)	Transitions from the lower-tier informal sectors			Transitions from the upper-tier informal sectors		
	To formal self-employed	To upper-tier informal self-employed	To formal wage-employee	To upper-tier informal wage-employee	To formal self-employed	To formal wage-employee
(b) Nicaragua						
Age	−0.0002	0.0182***	0.0016**	−0.0002	0.0001	−0.0004
	(0.0002)	(0.0019)	(0.0007)	(0.0002)	(0.0001)	(0.0011)
Age 2	0.000004*	−0.000193***	−0.000029***	0.000004	0.000000	−0.000014
	−0.000003	−0.000024	−0.000010	−0.000003	−0.000001	−0.000014
Female	0.0005	−0.0812***	−0.0061**	0.0005	0.0010**	−0.0053
	(0.0007)	(0.0087)	(0.0030)	(0.0007)	(0.0006)	(0.0045)
Complete primary education	0.0010	−0.0011	0.0086**	0.0010	0.0006	0.0102*
	(0.0011)	(0.0095)	(0.0043)	(0.0011)	(0.0006)	(0.0055)
Complete secondary (academic and technical) education	0.0034	−0.0043	0.0264***	0.0034	−0.0005	0.0246***
	(0.0038)	(0.0167)	(0.0102)	(0.0038)	(0.0005)	(0.0102)
Some tertiary and post-graduate education	0.0088***	−0.0112	0.0369***	0.0088	0.0037***	0.0713***
	(0.0070)	(0.0185)	(0.0135)	(0.0070)	(0.0031)	(0.0167)
Earn a primary education degree	0.0018	−0.0174	0.0225***	0.0018	0.0006	0.0067
	(0.0027)	(0.0170)	(0.0106)	(0.0027)	(0.0013)	(0.0103)
Earn a secondary education degree	0.0012	−0.0314	0.0058	0.0012	0.0045***	0.0013
	(0.0026)	(0.0212)	(0.0077)	(0.0026)	(0.0038)	(0.0106)
Earn some tertiary education	Omitted	−0.0578	0.0107	Omitted	0.0031	0.0631***
		(0.0276)	(0.0127)		(0.0059)	(0.0271)

Non-formal vocational education	0.0022*	−0.0142	0.0237***	0.0022	0.0008	0.0447***
	(0.0018)	(0.0121)	(0.0072)	(0.0018)	(0.0007)	(0.0084)
Earn vocational education	0.0019	0.0479***	0.0579***	0.0019	0.0024***	0.0597***
	(0.0021)	(0.0172)	(0.0118)	(0.0021)	(0.0016)	(0.0112)
Presence of a partner	0.0039***	0.0563***	−0.0018	0.0039	0.0008**	0.0109**
	(0.0016)	(0.0094)	(0.0034)	(0.0016)	(0.0005)	(0.0049)
Gain a partner	Omitted	0.0228	0.0096	Omitted	Omitted	0.0291**
	Omitted	(0.0265)	(0.0091)	Omitted		(0.0151)
Lose a partner	−0.0002	−0.0437*	−0.0075	−0.0002	0.0000	0.0250*
	(0.0017)	(0.0206)	(0.0069)	(0.0017)	(0.0009)	(0.0176)
Number of children under 12 in household	0.0001	0.0060**	0.0013	0.0001	0.0000	−0.0026
	(0.0003)	(0.0031)	(0.0011)	(0.0003)	(0.0004)	(0.0048)
Change of children under 12	0.0007*	0.0077	−0.0001	0.0007	0.0002**	−0.0004
	(0.0004)	(0.0053)	(0.0020)	(0.0004)	(0.0001)	(0.0017)
Potable water	0.0011	−0.0025	−0.0002	0.0011	0.0001	0.0005
	(0.0008)	(0.0093)	(0.0033)	(0.0008)	(0.0002)	(0.0028)
Electricity	Omitted	−0.0087	0.0003	Omitted	0.0003	0.0238***
		(0.0154)	(0.0062)		(0.0006)	(0.0063)
Publicly provided sanitation system	Omitted	−0.0428***	0.0090**	Omitted	0.0005	0.0360***
		(0.0115)	(0.0033)		(0.0004)	(0.0046)
Residential telephone	0.0010	0.0483***	0.0021	0.0010	0.0002	0.0021
	(0.0015)	(0.0215)	(0.0057)	(0.0015)	(0.0006)	(0.0080)
Time dummies	Yes	Yes	Yes	Yes	Yes	Yes
Observations	6,428	6,428	6,428	4,302	8,038	8,308

Note: Robust standard errors in parentheses; lower-tier informal sectors include informal self-employed and wage-employees results for transitions into unemployment, full-time student, and out of the labour force are not included in this table but are available from the authors; * $p < 0.1$, ** $p < 0.05$, *** $p < 0.01$.
Source: authors' calculations based on the data described in section 2.1.

labour force. If levels of education promote transitions, this might indicate that formal employers are simply choosing those who already have the most education (who are presumably the most productive) to hire into rationed high-wage jobs. On the other hand, if earning an education while employed promotes transitions into higher-wage work status groups, then this is stronger evidence that earning an education may increase the probability of a worker already employed in informal jobs transitioning to a higher-wage job. Changes in independent variables are under the control of workers and are therefore more useful for policymakers who are looking for policies to promote better jobs for informal workers.

In both Costa Rica and Nicaragua, earning vocational training (a change variable) increases the probability of a transition out of lower-tier informal work status groups into formal wage-employment and upper-tier informal self-employment. Earning a vocational education also increases the probability of a transition out of upper-tier informal work into both formal wage-employment and formal self-employment. Earning on-the-job vocational training is the most consistent correlate of transitioning from an informal sector into a better-paying sector and is therefore a possible focus of public policy.

In both Costa Rica and Nicaragua, higher education levels promote transitions from all informal work status groups into formal wage-employment. There is also evidence in both countries that earning a tertiary education promotes transitions from upper-tier informal into formal work and from lower-tier informal work into upper-tier informal work. In addition, earning a secondary education can promote transitions into formal self-employment.[9] Note that most workers enter the workforce with their primary and secondary education already at the highest levels they will reach. This may help to explain why earning a tertiary education has a bigger impact on the probability of transitioning into a better work status than does earning a primary education: more workers complete their tertiary education after entering the workforce. In summary, the evidence suggests that earning an education and having a higher education level are important correlates of an increase in the probability of transitioning from informal work into a better work status.

In both countries, an older age (a proxy for experience) promotes a transition from lower-tier informal work into upper-tier informal self-employment. In Costa Rica, an older age also promotes a transition from both lower-tier and upper-tier informal into formal self-employment. The impact of age/experience has diminishing marginal returns: the probability that a worker transitions into higher-paid self-employment is maximized around the upper 40s age group. In Costa Rica, older workers are also more likely to transition from upper-tier informality into

[9] Those who transition may be students who chose to work informally while in school as this may be more flexible to combine with their studies. They may be quite different from the 'average' informal worker.

formal wage-employment and self-employment. This suggests that workers who start out in informal work status groups may be gaining experience as lower-tier workers before becoming successfully self-employed.

As vocational training, formal education, and experience are forms of human capital, our results suggest that informal workers who increase their human capital on the job are more likely to transition into better work status groups.

Compared with men, women are less likely to transition from informal work into formal wage-employment and formal self-employment than men in both Costa Rica and Nicaragua. This suggests that women may be disadvantaged in their ability to obtain rationed formal employment.

Household structure also matters for transitions to better work status groups. For example, having a partner (i.e. spouse) is generally positively correlated with transitions from informal work into better work status groups.

5.2 Characteristics correlated with higher wages for workers who remain informal

Table 6.6 presents the full wage change regression results described in section 3.3 (and in the WIDER working paper version of this chapter). We do not present the coefficients on the variables that indicate changes in work status because these results are already reported in Table 6.2. The coefficients on the independent variables in Table 6.6 can be interpreted as the effect on the wage changes of workers in each work status if those workers remain in that work status. It is these correlates that we concentrate on in this subsection. In Nicaragua, earning vocational training increases the wages for upper-tier and lower-tier informal wage-employees who remain in those work status groups. In Costa Rica, fluency in English (which is the most popular programme in the National Apprentice Institute) also increases earnings for upper-tier and lower-tier informal wage-employees. This evidence suggests that providing vocational training to informal wage-employees could contribute to higher earnings for those who remain in that work status.

In both Costa Rica and Nicaragua, earning additional education while employed has little effect on the wages of workers who remain in lower-tier informal wage-employment. Earning a tertiary education increases earnings in lower-tier informal wage-employment but is not significant for any other types of education. However, other education levels are not significant correlates of earnings for those who remain informal in Nicaragua, although they are significant in Costa Rica (except for lower-tier informal wage-employment).

Age (a proxy for experience) is correlated with higher wages for those who remain in lower-tier informal wage-employment in Costa Rica but not in Nicaragua. In Nicaragua, age is correlated with higher wages for those who remain in informal self-employment and in upper-tier informal wage-employment but

Table 6.6 Wage change regressions, Costa Rica and Nicaragua

(a) Costa Rica	**Upper-tier informal self-employed**	**Lower-tier informal self-employed**	**Upper-tier informal wage-employment**	**Lower-tier informal wage-employment**
Log of hourly wage in *t*	−9.90e-05***	−0.000182***	−0.000163***	−0.000419***
	(1.01e-05)	(4.55e-05)	(1.45e-05)	(3.60e-05)
Age	−0.00589	0.00589	−0.00158	0.0224**
	(0.0121)	(0.0211)	(0.00515)	(0.0108)
Age squared	8.45e-05	−3.81e-05	4.49e-05	−0.000277*
	(0.000139)	(0.000258)	(6.48e-05)	(0.000148)
Female	−0.00712	0.0165	−0.0158	−0.00174
	(0.0418)	(0.106)	(0.0222)	(0.0526)
Complete primary education	−0.0111	0.145	0.0273	0.0376
	(0.0600)	(0.0881)	(0.0361)	(0.0527)
Complete secondary education	0.0739	0.0784	0.0747	0.141*
	(0.0790)	(0.148)	(0.0455)	(0.0819)
Some tertiary and postgraduate education	0.247***	0.392**	0.385***	0.256**
	(0.0776)	(0.168)	(0.0535)	(0.113)
Earn a primary education degree	−0.217	−0.0538	0.121	0.00498
	(0.132)	(0.209)	(0.0781)	(0.102)
Earn a secondary education degree	−0.0732	0.0473	0.0372	0.0884
	(0.127)	(0.182)	(0.0748)	(0.174)
Earn a tertiary education degree	−0.115	0.441	0.108*	0.584***
	(0.122)	(0.295)	(0.0629)	(0.209)
Vocational training	0.00657	−0.131*	−0.0463*	0.0162
	(0.0414)	(0.0794)	(0.0262)	(0.0546)
Earn training	−0.0112	0.124	−0.0129	0.0944
	(0.0667)	(0.114)	(0.0338)	(0.0737)
Fluency in English	0.149*	0.218	0.173***	0.232*
	(0.0831)	(0.178)	(0.0559)	(0.137)

Change in English fluency	0.0354	0.249	0.108	0.350
	(0.118)	(0.264)	(0.0709)	(0.291)
Central Valley	0.0236	−0.0439	0.0192	0.0164
	(0.0367)	(0.0746)	(0.0217)	(0.0402)
Year fixed effects	Yes	Yes	Yes	Yes
Wage status dummy variables	Yes	Yes	YES	Yes
	0.308	−0.0252	0.223**	0.0387
Constant	(0.260)	(0.441)	(0.105)	(0.199)
Observations	4,090	1,021	4,803	1,319
Adjusted R-squared	0.140	0.220	0.145	0.286

(b) Nicaragua

	Upper-tier informal self-employed	**Lower-tier informal self-employed**	**Upper-tier informal wage-employment**	**Lower-tier informal wage-employment**
Log of hourly wage in *t*	−0.5993***	−0.6635***	−0.6583***	−0.6227***
	(0.0203)	(0.0233)	(0.0309)	(0.0607)
Age	0.0575***	0.0503***	0.0138**	0.0159
	(0.0152)	(0.0129)	(0.0065)	(0.0147)
Age squared	−0.0006***	−0.0006***	−0.0002*	(0.0002)
	(0.0002)	(0.0002)	(0.0001)	(0.0002)
Female	0.0297	−0.0650	−0.0387	(0.1094)
	(0.0503)	(0.0505)	(0.0410)	(0.0852)
Complete primary education	0.2524***	0.1828***	0.1518***	0.0272
	(0.0553)	(0.0582)	(0.0310)	(0.0658)
Complete secondary education	0.2959***	0.3470***	0.2120***	0.0412
	(0.1032)	(0.0941)	(0.0455)	(0.0997)
Some tertiary and postgraduate education	0.7288***	0.5831***	0.4344***	0.2566**
	(0.1116)	(0.1141)	(0.0646)	(0.1216)

Continued

Table 6.6 *Continued*

	Upper-tier informal self-employed	Lower-tier informal self-employed	Upper-tier informal wage-employment	Lower-tier informal wage-employment
Earn a primary education degree	0.2846**	−0.0274	0.0851	0.1261
	(0.1205)	(0.1041)	(0.0671)	(0.1148)
Earn a secondary education degree	−0.2814*	0.0937	−0.0070	0.0986
	(0.1512)	(0.1494)	(0.0734)	(0.1210)
Earn a tertiary education degree	0.2475	0.3065	0.1304	−0.0693
	(0.2358)	(0.2501)	(0.0867)	(0.2808)
Vocational training	0.0356	−0.0901	0.0732	−0.0019
	(0.0591)	(0.0690)	(0.0480)	(0.1555)
Earn training	0.0187	−0.0194	0.1585***	0.2342***
	(0.0782)	(0.0890)	(0.0463)	(0.0904)
Year fixed effects	Yes	Yes	Yes	Yes
Wage status dummy variables	Yes	Yes	Yes	Yes
	0.3240	0.8683***	1.7201***	1.5497***
Constant	(0.3144)	(0.2663)	(0.1346)	(0.2871)
Observations	2,498	1,775	3,046	464
Adjusted R-squared	0.3332	0.3747	0.2799	0.348

Note: Robust standard errors in parentheses; * $p < 0.1$, ** $p < 0.05$, *** $p < 0.01$.
Source: authors' calculations based on the data described in section 2.

not in Costa Rica. Wage changes for those who remain informal do not differ between men and women.

In summary, we find evidence of few things that informal workers can do to positively affect their wages if they remain in the same informal work status. The strongest evidence of a variable increasing wages is related to vocational training, which is positively correlated with higher wages for those who remain informal.

6. Conclusions

Our results suggest that it is important to distinguish between lower-tier and upper-tier informal workers and between the self-employed and wage-employees.

Employment and wage transition patterns are different for different informal work status groups, as are the characteristics of workers in each work status and the characteristics of workers that are associated with moves up the job ladder.

We find that in both Costa Rica and Nicaragua, there is a clear ordering of work status groups. Earnings are highest for formal work (among both the self-employed and wage-employees), next-highest for upper-tier informal, and last for lower-tier informal. We also find that in both Nicaragua and Costa Rica, mobility out of the least favourable work status, lower-tier informal work, is greater than out of all other work status groups. There is also substantial mobility out of upper-tier informal work into formal work status. Formal wage-employment is the least mobile work status. This suggests that individual workers in Costa Rica and Nicaragua are not stuck in lower-tier informal work and that there is scope for promoting transitions from lower-tier and upper-tier informal work into better-paying work status groups.

While we find that individual lower-tier and upper-tier informal workers have substantial mobility up the job ladder into higher-paying wage status groups, we also find that some workers transition down the job ladder into lower-paying work status groups. If mobility upwards is the same as mobility downwards, then the total number of informal workers may not change even if many individual workers transition into better-paying work status groups. However, this is not what we find. When we compare the number of transitions, we find that the number of workers who transition up the job ladder is greater than the number of workers who transition down the wage ladder. The number of transitions from lower-tier informal work directly into formal work is greater in Costa Rica than in Nicaragua, at least partly due to the larger size of formal wage-employment and self-employment in Costa Rica.

Informal workers can improve earnings and livelihoods by moving to better work status groups or by staying as informal workers and improving their earnings. In both Costa Rica and Nicaragua, earning vocational training increases the probability of a transition out of lower-tier informal work status groups into upper-tier informal wage-employment and increases the probability of a transition out of upper-tier informal work into formal wage-employment and formal self-employment. In both countries, higher education levels promote transitions from all informal work status groups into formal wage-employment. There is also evidence in both countries that earning a tertiary education promotes transition from upper-tier informal into formal work and from lower-tier informal into upper-tier informal work. An older age (a proxy for experience) promotes transition from lower-tier informal work into upper-tier informal self-employment in both Costa Rica and Nicaragua and from upper-tier informal into formal self-employment and wage-employment in Costa Rica. As vocational training, formal education, and experience are forms of human capital, our results suggest that informal workers who increase their human capital on the job are more likely to transition into better work status groups. As the probability of transitioning to a better work status increases with age until the mid-to-upper 40s, these results also suggest that vocational training should be available not only for the young but also for informal workers throughout their prime working lives.

On the other hand, we find few things that informal workers can do to positively affect their wages if they stay informal. The strongest evidence is related to vocational training, which is positively correlated with higher wages for those who remain informal.

Promoting formalization of informal workers may also be possible through other government action. Costa Rica has been able to attain such a high proportion of workers whose employers pay social security taxes through a combination of increased enforcement among wage-employees and subsidies for low-income self-employed workers (Saenz et al. 2010; Gindling et al. 2015). In addition, work that we have done in Costa Rica shows that policies designed to increase compliance with some labour regulations, such as minimum wages, can lead to more employers complying with other labour protections and social security payroll taxes and therefore to more informal workers becoming formal (Gindling et al. 2015). These policies included public relations campaigns, increased enforcement, and incorporating workers into the enforcement process.

The strongest of our results suggest policies of providing vocational training to informal workers as a way of improving wages for those who remain informal and of promoting transitions into better-paying work status groups. Earning other types of human capital, such as formal education, also improves a worker's chances of transitioning into higher-paying work status. Overall, our results suggest that policies that promote investment in human capital for currently employed informal workers are an effective way to improve the livelihoods of informal workers in Costa Rica and Nicaragua.

References

Acosta, P., R. Almeida, T. H. Gindling, and C. L. Pena (2017). *Towards More Efficient and Effective Public Social Spending in Central America.* Washington, DC: World Bank. https://doi.org/10.1596/978-1-4648-1060-2.

Alaniz, E., T. H. Gindling, C. Mata, and D. Rojas (2020). 'Transforming Informal Work and Livelihoods in Costa Rica and Nicaragua'. WIDER working paper 2020/100. Helsinki: UNU-WIDER

Bosch, M., and W. Maloney (2010). 'Comparative Analysis of Labor Market Dynamics Using Markov Processes: An Application to Informality'. *Labour Economics*, 17(4): 621–631.

Gindling, T. H., N. Mossaad, and J. D. Trejos (2015). 'The Consequences of Increased Enforcement of Legal Minimum Wages in a Developing Country: An Evaluation of the Impact of the Campaña Nacional de Salarios Mínimos in Costa Rica'.

Industrial and Labor Relations Review, 68(3): 666–707. https://doi.org/10.1177/0019793915575703.

ILO (International Labour Organization) (2019). 'ILO Thesaurus: Informal Employment'. Available at: https://metadata.ilo.org/thesaurus.html (accessed 3 December 2019).

Maloney, W. (2004). 'Informality Revisited'. *World Development*, 32(7): 1159-1178.

OECD (Organisation for Economic Co-operation and Development) and ILO (2018). *How Immigrants Contribute to Costa Rica's Economy*. Paris: OECD Publishing. https://doi.org/10.1787/9789264303850-en.

Sáenz, M. del Rocio, J. L. Bermúdez, and M. Acosta (2010), 'Universal Coverage in a Middle Income Country: Costa Rica'. Background paper for the WHO 2010 World Health Report. Available at: https://www.who.int/publications/m/item/universal-coverage-in-a-middle-income-country-costa-rica (accessed 1 January 2022)

7

Informality, labour transitions, and the livelihoods of workers in Latin America

Roxana Maurizio and Ana Paula Monsalvo

1. Introduction

Since the 2000s, an increasing trend in labour formality has been observed in several Latin American countries. However, despite this positive evolution, informal employment continues to be one of the most distinctive characteristics in this region.

Informal employment is a very complex and heterogeneous phenomenon. It encompasses wage earners and self-employed, including employers and own-account workers. Likewise, informality may be found both in big firms and in micro-enterprises. However, the existence of a broad group of informal workers is mainly associated with a high presence of small, unstructured firms that operate with very low levels of productivity and competitiveness.

The main aim of this chapter is to carry out an in-depth study of the structural characteristics of the different segments of informal and formal workers and their changes during the new millennium in six Latin American countries—Argentina, Brazil, Ecuador, Mexico, Paraguay, and Peru—from a comparative and dynamic perspective. In particular, this study: (i) assesses the intensity of occupational turnover, focusing on the movements between informal and formal employment; (ii) estimates the likelihood of different segments of informal workers moving to a better position inside informal employment or to a formal occupation; and (iii) assesses the impacts of labour mobility on the wage dynamics. This selection of countries allows us to have a broad picture of the Latin American labour markets since they have occupational structures and dynamics that greatly differ from one another. Additionally, they account for about 70 per cent of the total population in the region.

Three aspects of this study are worth emphasizing. First, it resorts to information on labour transitions in addition to the more traditional cross-section analysis. In this regard, this document contributes to the scarce but growing literature on occupational mobility in Latin America.

Roxana Maurizio and Ana Paula Monsalvo, *Informality, labour transitions, and the livelihoods of workers in Latin America.* In: *The Job Ladder.* Edited by Gary S. Fields, T. H. Gindling, Kunal Sen, Michael Danquah, and Simone Schotte, Oxford University Press. DOI: 10.1093/oso/9780192867339.003.0007

Second, instead of focusing only on the dichotomy between formality and informality, we examine the heterogeneity of informal work, distinguishing between lower-tier and upper-tier informal workers. This differentiation allows us to assess whether informality is a last resort for the first segment of workers to earn income, while it is preferred over formal employment for the second segment.

Third, a comparative analysis is carried out with the six Latin American countries. Their differences regarding labour market structures and overall level of development provide insight for the analysis.

The results show that in all the countries considered, wages are the highest for formal workers and the lowest for lower-tier informal jobs. Two contrasting labour mobility patterns are found: on the one hand, the proportion of formal workers who maintain the work status of origin or move up the job ladder is significantly higher than the proportion who transition into lower-paying work status groups; on the other hand, despite the high labour turnover experienced by lower-tier informal wage-employees, most of them fail to move up the wage ladder.

Education strongly correlates with both higher probabilities of transiting to a better job and with higher wages, even in an informal occupation. In other words, informal workers who remain in this work status can still improve their wages with higher education.

These results are particularly important considering the high informality that still persists in the region and the close association between informality, low productivity, and low wages. Therefore, the findings provide useful guidance for the design of public policies aimed at reducing informality and enhancing the livelihoods of workers and families in the region.

The rest of this chapter is organized as follows. Section 2 details the sources of information and the identification of formal, upper-tier, and lower-tier informal workers in the countries under study. Section 3 describes the methodologies used. Section 4 analyses the evolution of labour formality during the 2000s. Section 5 identifies the patterns and characteristics of employment transitions. Section 6 assesses their impacts on wage dynamics. Section 7 concludes.

2. Data and measurement of informality

2.1 Data

Data used in this chapter come from regular household surveys carried out by the national statistical institutes of each country. Although these surveys are not longitudinal, their rotating panel sample allows flow data to be drawn from them. In such schemes, the total sample is divided into a certain number of household groups and each group remains in the sample for a given number of observation periods.

For Argentina, the data source is the Encuesta Permanente de Hogares (EPH) carried out by the Instituto Nacional de Estadística y Censos (INDEC). In the case of Brazil, data come from the Pesquisa Mensal de Emprego (PME) and the Pesquisa Nacional por Amostra de Domicilios Contínua (PNADC) conducted by the Instituto Brasileiro de Geografia e Estadistica (IBGE). The PME ended in 2015 and the PNADC began in 2012. In Ecuador, the Encuesta Nacional de Empleo, Desempleo y Subempleo (ENEMDU) is carried out by the Instituto Nacional de Estadística y Censos (INEC). The Encuesta Nacional de Ocupación y Empleo (ENOE) is the source of data for Mexico. It is conducted by the Instituto Nacional de Estadística y Geografía (INEGI). The Paraguayan Encuesta Continua de Empleo (ECE) is carried out by the Dirección General de Estadística, Encuestas y Censos. Finally, in the case of Peru, the Encuesta Nacional de Hogares (ENAHO) is the regular household survey conducted by the Instituto Nacional de Estadística e Informática (INEI).[1]

In all cases, the sample rotation schemes allow building yearly panel data. In order to obtain comparable data sets between countries, we included one transition for each individual. Since not all the surveys used are representative of each country as a whole, and given that labour markets in rural areas and urban centres may behave differently, our analysis only covers urban areas. To obtain sufficient observations, yearly panels have been pooled in each country so the results are the average for the period.

The period under analysis corresponds to the new millennium. However, specific years considered vary in each country according to data availability. In Argentina, all years between 2003 and 2019 are analysed, 2002–2019 for Brazil (2003–2015 PME, 2015–2019 PNADC), 2003–2019 for Ecuador, 2002–2019 for Peru, 2005–2019 for Mexico, and 2010–2017 for Paraguay.

Our study is restricted to male workers between 15 and 65 years of age and female workers between 15 and 60. The upper limits correspond to the compulsory retirement ages in the countries being analysed and we have used them in an attempt to minimize the bias that might come from the exit of older individuals from the labour force. Those individuals for whom information was incomplete or inconsistent regarding personal or occupational variables were removed from the sample.[2]

[1] For a more detailed description of the data, see Maurizio and Monsalvo (2021).

[2] There was no information in the databases that allowed us to differentiate loss of data due to attrition from that associated with the survey rotation scheme. However, we compared key descriptive statistics from panel and cross-section data and found no relevant differences between them.

2.2 Identification of formal, upper-tier, and lower-tier informal workers

The 15th and 17th International Conference of Labour Statistics (ICLS) of the International Labour Organization (ILO) have established the classification criteria for formal and informal workers. According to the 'productive approach', the *employment in the informal sector* is defined as the workers employed in small productive units that are not legally registered as firms, employ a reduced amount of capital, and make limited use of technology. However, given that household surveys do not inquire in depth into the characteristics of the firms, the ILO suggests adopting a measurement criterion based on the combination of occupational categories, occupation groups defined according to job qualifications, and the size of the firm. In this way, it is possible to identify the two major components of the informal sector: (i) family units comprising own-account workers and family workers and (ii) microenterprises comprising employers and wage earners in establishments with less than five employees. In the case of independent workers, only those with no professional skills (approximated by those individuals with incomplete university studies) are considered as part of the informal sector, as an operational way to leave only independent workers with low productivity in this sector.

Another perspective of informality focuses directly on job conditions. The 'job approach' associates informality with the evasion of labour regulations, defining *informal employment* as that of workers not covered by labour legislation.[3] When putting the job approach into practice, we seek to make comparable the formal wage-earners identification criterion, which does not necessarily imply the same empirical implementation in each country, given that household surveys capture this dimension in different ways. However, comparability is not very much affected because, although every country chooses different variables, they all share the same notion of informality, that is, the non-fulfilment or evasion of the labour legislation and social security regulations.

By combining these two approaches (and based on comparable available data across countries), this study identifies five different work status groups among workers:

[3] See ILO (2002); Hussmanns (2004).

Work status	Measurement
Formal wage-employees	Argentina: those who answer that their employers make payroll deductions to pay social security contributions Brazil: those who have signed a labour contract Paraguay, Mexico, and Peru: those enrolled in a pension system Ecuador: those indicating that they receive social insurance from the job
Upper-tier informal wage-employees	Informal wage-employees working in firms with more than five employees
Lower-tier informal wage-employees	Informal wage-employees working in firms with up to five employees
Formal self-employed	Owners in enterprises with more than five employees and professional own-account workers
Informal self-employed	Owners in enterprises with up to five employees, non-professional own-account workers, and unpaid family workers

Source: authors' compilation.

The identification of upper-tier informal wage-employees is somewhat different from that used in other chapters in this book. In particular, we use the definitions above to focus on a widespread phenomenon among informal workers in Latin America: informal employees working in formal firms (with more than five employees). In addition, due to the lack of comparable information across countries, the informal self-employed group is not separated into lower-tier and upper-tier.

3. Methodology

In addition to the descriptive analysis based on cross-section data, this study relies on econometric exercises from annual panel data. Starting with the dynamic analysis, the year-on-year transition matrices between different states (employed, unemployed, and inactive) and different work status groups are computed. Then, multinomial logit regressions are estimated in order to evaluate how these transitions vary according to observable workers attributes. Finally, wage dynamic equations are performed to estimate the impact of the mobility across work status groups on labour income changes.

3.1 Multinomial logit regressions

Multinomial logit regressions are estimated to identify the observed characteristics associated with changes in the initial work status, differentiating those attributes positively correlated with transitions into higher-paying occupations from those correlated with higher transits to lower-paying occupation. Specifically, from these regressions we estimate the probability of being in an employment status k at time $t = 1\,(S_{i1})$ depending on the initial work status at time $t = 0\,(S_{i0})$ and on observed individual characteristics (X_{i0}).
The statistical model can be formulated as follows:

$$\pi_{i1k} = P(S_{i1} = k|S_{i0}, X_{i0}) = \frac{e^{S_{i0}\theta_k + X_{i0}\beta_k}}{1 + \sum_{j=1}^{K} e^{S_{i0}\theta_j + X_{i0}\beta_j}} \quad (1)$$

where π_{i1k} represents the transition probability from the base status S_{i0} to status $S_{i1} = k$ for the individual i. Thus, the θ_k and β_k are the regression parameters associated to outcome status k.

Then, equation (1) can be expressed using the logit link for a generalized linear model (equation 2), in order to estimate the parameters:

$$log\left(\frac{\pi_{1k}}{\pi_{i1(k+1)}}\right) = S_{i0}\theta_k + X_{i0}\beta_k \quad (2)$$

We estimate employment transition equations between three work status groups: (i) formal wage-employees and formal self-employed; (ii) upper-tier informal wage-employees and (iii) lower-tier informal wage-employees and informal self-employed. In this way, we obtain three multinomial logit equations for each country under study, one for each work status and three outcomes in each one: stay in the same work status or transit to one of the other two possible status groups. For identifiability, the base category chosen is, in all cases, staying at the initial work status.

3.2 Wage dynamics regressions

After evaluating the characteristics associated with different patterns of labour mobility, we estimate the correlation between work status changes and wage dynamics, controlling for observable worker attributes. For this purpose, we regress the change in the logarithm of labour earnings between time $t = 0$ and time $t = 1\,(\Delta y_1)$, on the individual's initial log earnings (y_0), the initial worker characteristics like education, age, gender, branch of activity (X_0), and a set of dummies to model transitions from the initial job status to each one of the remaining status groups (D_{ij}). Our dynamic income model also considers fixed effects for year and region (equation 3).

$$\Delta y_{1i} = \beta_{0i} + \beta_{1i} y_{0i} + \beta_{2i} X_{0i} + \sum_j \vartheta_{ji} D_{ji} + \mu_i \tag{3}$$

The subscripts i and j represent lower tier informal, upper tier informal, and formal work status, and $i \neq j$. The base category i means the worker did not change his or her status between periods. The coefficients ϑ_{ji} can be interpreted as the premium or penalty when the worker moves from i work status to j work status relative to the worker who remains in the same work status i.

4. Evolution of labour informality and labour composition in Latin America during the 2000s

4.1 The labour formalization process

Latin America experienced a reducing trend in the informality rate among wage-employees during the new millennium. In the six countries under study, labour formalization meant an increase of around 12 percentage points (pp) in Argentina and 16 pp in Brazil in the formality rate among salaried workers. Even more intense was this process in Ecuador, Paraguay and Peru, where the share of formal workers grew between 18 pp and 22 pp. Mexico, on the contrary, only experienced a slight increase—about 2 pp—between the two ends of the period (Fig. 7.1).

The labour formalization process in these countries during the 2000s has been associated, on the one hand, with a greater dynamism in the generation of new jobs in a macroeconomic context characterized by a relatively high and stable growth rate and, on the other hand, to the implementation of specific public policies aimed at reducing the costs of informality through varied incentive mechanisms.

Indeed, the business cycle is a relevant factor to consider when analysing the drivers of the decline in labour informality. There are theoretical arguments on both the demand and supply sides of the labour market that account for the countercyclical nature of informality. The functioning of the labour market becomes more predictable as a result of sustained economic growth, thus favouring an increase in long-term contracts. In this context, formalization becomes more feasible. In addition, a period of sustained growth in labour demand might also lower the expected probability of layoffs and consequently the probability of employers having to face the costs of firing a formal worker. Hence, the incentives to maintain informal labour relations, associated with the relatively lower costs of staff reductions in downward phases of the business cycle, are reduced. In this context, employers can benefit from the positive effects of long-term labour relations: productivity increases as a result of the intensification of training activities and

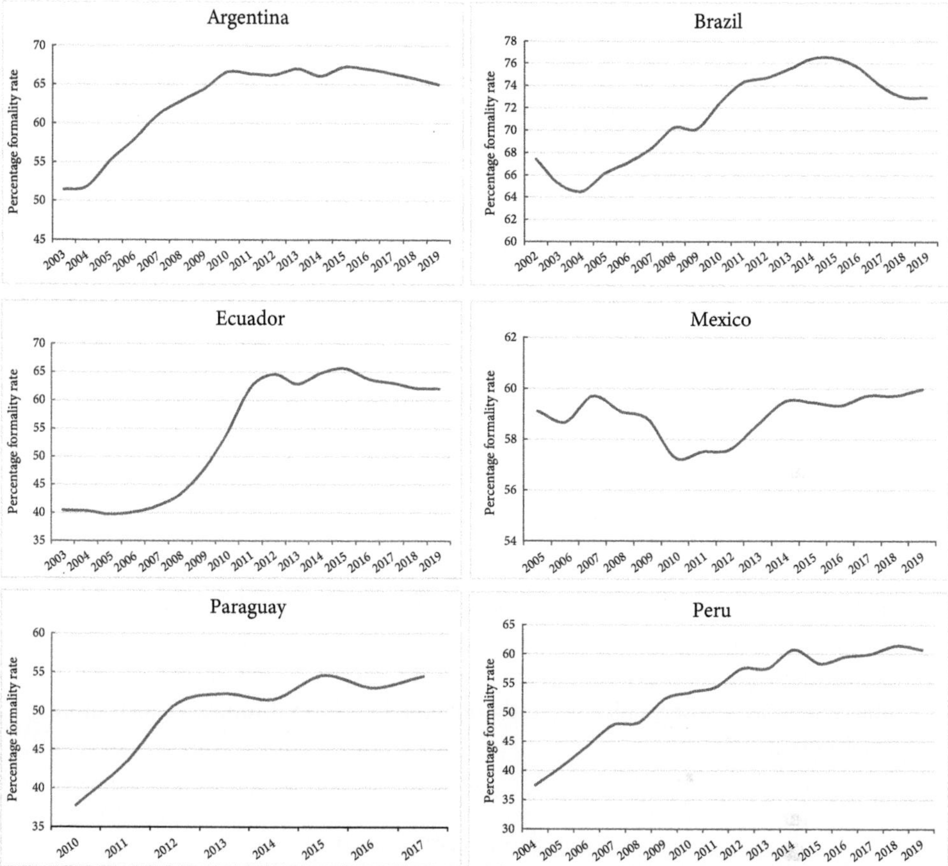

Fig. 7.1 Evolution in the formality rate among urban salaried employment during the 2000s

Source: authors' elaboration based on household surveys.

higher levels of job engagement. There is evidence regarding the positive impact of the economic cycle on formalization (Boeri and Garibaldi 2007; Bosch and Esteban-Pretel 2009; Corsueil and Foguel 2012).

Even when the evidence supports the procyclical behaviour of labour formality, economic growth seems a necessary but not sufficient condition. In particular, some of the specific policies implemented in these countries may also account for the process of formalization, among them, incentives for employment formalization and labour inspections. Some studies have found positive impacts of the reduction of employers' contributions or the simplification of administrative procedures to register workers on formal labour demand (Delgado et al. 2007; Fajnzylber et al. 2009; Castillo et al. 2012; Monteiro and Assunção 2012), while others have not found significant impacts (Chacaltana 2001, 2008; Cruces et al.

2010). In addition, the few studies evaluating the impact of inspection seem to confirm that they have a positive effect on labour market formality (Almeida and Carneiro 2009; Berg 2010; Ronconi 2010; the World Bank 2012; de Andrade et al. 2013).[4]

However, after the significant increase in labour formality in the countries under analysis (except Mexico), this process slowed down, stopped, or reversed in recent years, hand in hand with the weakening of the macroeconomic performance. As shown in Fig. 7.1, the turning point seems to have been around 2014/2015. In Argentina, after a certain stagnation of the formality rate between 2010 and 2015, it fell 2 pp between that year and 2019. A similar situation is observed in Ecuador, with a slowdown in the increase in formality between 2012 and 2015 and a subsequent reduction of 4 pp over the past four years.

These two contrasting phases are also observed in Brazil, where there was an increasing trend in formality until 2015 and a fall between 2015 and 2019 (−3.5pp). After the strong formalization process in Peru and Paraguay until 2014 and 2015, respectively, the proportion of formal workers remained relatively constant. Mexico experienced a different process from the rest of the countries considered. Initially, between 2007 and 2010, the formality rate reduced by 3 pp; then, it remained at this level until 2012 and then experienced a slight increase of 2 pp, mainly between 2012 and 2014. As mentioned, as a net result of these contrasting dynamics, the formality rate only increased by 2 pp throughout the period considered.

4.2 Labour composition

Behind these some common patterns, the composition of employment is highly heterogeneous among the countries considered in this study, which gives greater worth to the comparative analysis. As we can see in Fig. 7.2, Brazil exhibits the highest level of wage formality in salaried employment (73 per cent), followed by Argentina (65 per cent), Ecuador, Peru, and Mexico (about 60 per cent) and, finally, by Paraguay (54 per cent).

The ranking of countries, however, is somewhat different when considering the share of formality in total employment due to the dissimilar incidence of self-employment. While in Brazil and Argentina around half of the urban employed are formal wage earners, this value drops to 44 per cent and 41 per cent in Mexico and Paraguay, respectively, and to 36 per cent in Peru and Ecuador. Therefore, these figures show that formal wage earners, those covered by labour regulation, represent a small portion (at most half) of the total urban employed. In Ecuador and Peru, this group of workers is even lower numerically than non-salaried workers.

[4] ILO (2018) analyses policies implemented in Latin American countries supporting the process of labour formalization.

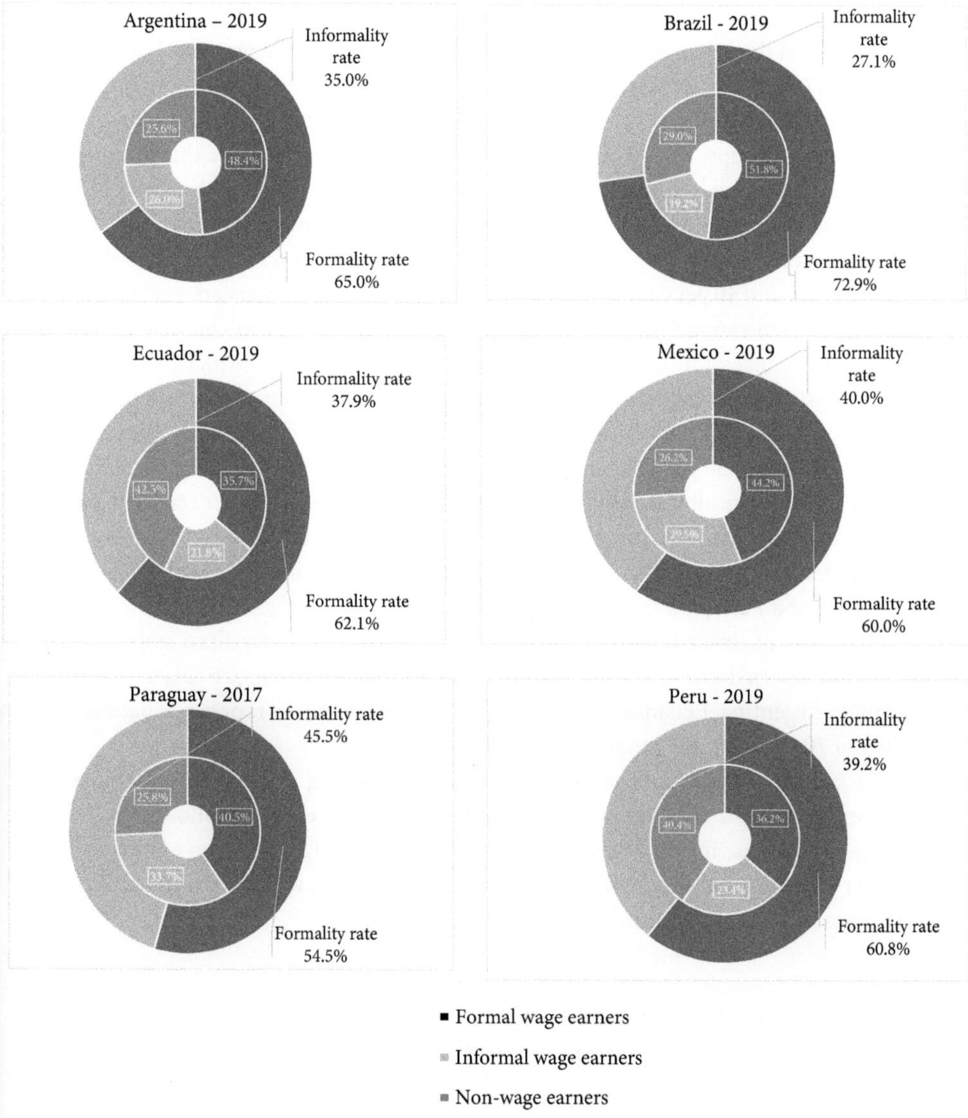

Fig. 7.2 Employment composition in six Latin American countries
Source: authors' elaboration based on household surveys.

The distribution of different groups of individuals across the five work status groups (formal wage-employment, upper-tier informal wage-employment, lower-tier informal wage-employment, formal self-employment and informal self-employment), unemployment, and labour also differs across country.

As already mentioned, employment in Brazil is more formal than the rest of the countries considered. Together, formal wage-employees and formal self-employed account for about 35 per cent of the working-age population (58 per cent of total workers). At the other end, these two groups of workers represent only 21 per cent in Peru (30 per cent of total workers).

Except in Peru, formal wage-employees are the biggest group among the five work status groups. In any case, the outlook is very alarming since this group of workers represents at most only half of total urban employment. This work status is followed by informal self-employed. They represent around 20 per cent of the total workers in Argentina, one-quarter in Brazil, Mexico, and Paraguay, one-third in Ecuador, and 40 per cent in Peru. Formal self-employed workers are a very small group, concentrating 5 per cent or less of total employment in all countries.

The relevance of informal non-salaried workers in the Latin American labour market is more evident within total informal workers (even more among self-employed workers), where they account for about 40 per cent in Argentina and Paraguay, about 50 per cent in Mexico, and more than half in Brazil, Ecuador, and Peru. In turn, although in all the countries they represent 80 per cent or more of the total self-employed workers, the proportion of formal self-employed workers is around 20 per cent in Argentina and Brazil, while it is 10 per cent or less in Ecuador and Paraguay.

The size of lower-tier informal wage-employment is larger than upper-tier informal salaried workers. The gap between these two groups is particularly significant in Argentina, Ecuador, and Mexico, where the first group represents between 50 and 70 per cent more than the second group.

In summary, with the exception of Peru, the ranking of work status groups according to their relative importance in total employment is as follows: formal wage-employees, informal self-employed, lower-tier informal wage-employees, upper-tier informal wage-employees, and formal self-employed. In Peru, the first two positions are exchanged, the rest being the same (Fig. 7.3).

4.3 Individual characteristics of workers and wages according to their status

As found in the empirical literature for Latin American countries (Bertranou and Casanova 2013; ILO 2014; Amarante and Arim 2015; Maurizio 2015; Maurizio and Vázquez 2019; Alaniz et al. 2020) education level is highly and positively correlated with formality.[5] In particular, formal workers are overrepresented among workers with complete university education (UC). On the contrary, informal non-salaried and lower-tier informal workers exhibit, on average, the lowest education levels (secondary incomplete or complete and university incomplete). Upper-tier informal wage-employees are in between.

[5] The analysis of this section is based on data included in Table A3 and A4 in Maurizio and Monsalvo (2021).

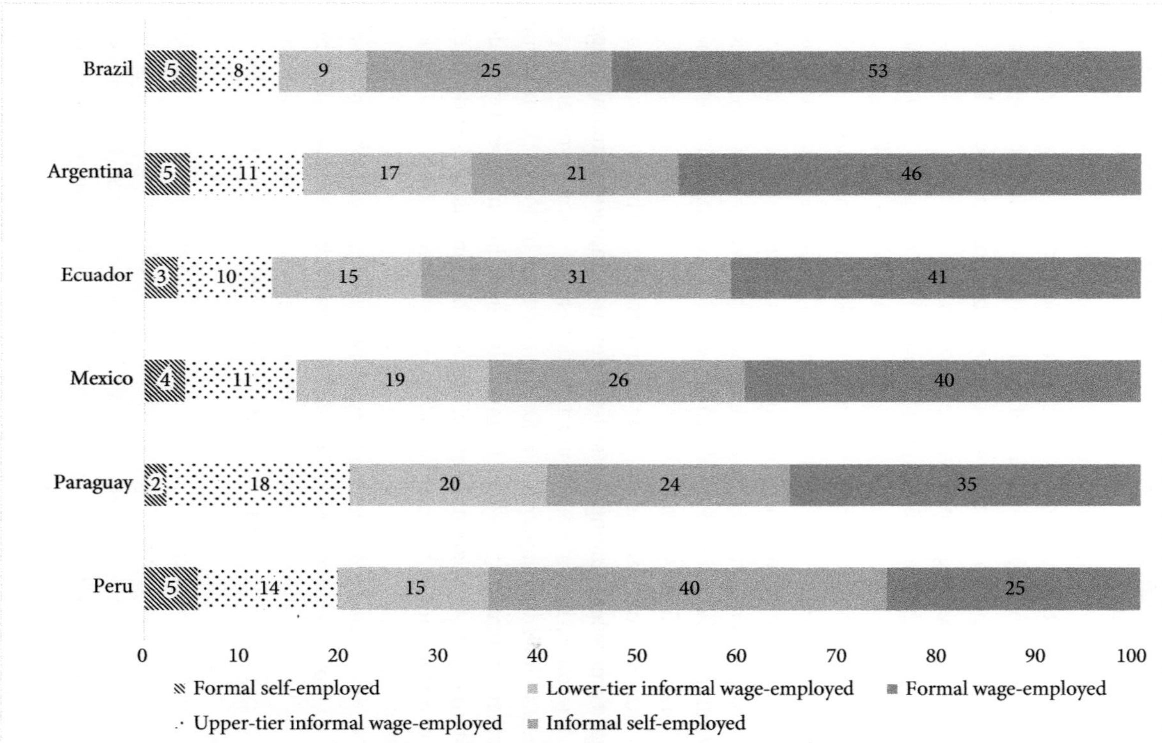

Fig. 7.3 Detailed employment composition in six Latin American countries

Note: Countries are ranked by the proportion of formal wage-employees in total employment.
Source: authors' elaboration based on household surveys.

Except in Ecuador, women are overrepresented among lower-tier informal wage-employment. However, the distribution of the other work categories significantly differs between countries. In Argentina and Brazil, the higher female presence in the informal lower tier is offset by the lower proportion of women among informal self-employed workers. As a consequence, the composition of the remaining work categories by gender is relatively similar to the proportion of women and men in total employment. On the contrary, in Ecuador, Mexico, Paraguay, and Peru, women are overrepresented among informal self-employed jobs. In all the countries, the proportion of men in upper-tier informal positions is higher than the proportion in total employment. In addition, only in Peru are men overrepresented among formal wage-employees.

As has been shown in previous studies (Bertranou and Maurizio 2011; Maurizio 2020), self-employment is not an 'entry door' to the labour market for young workers in Latin America. Rather, young people work mostly in informal salaried positions. On the contrary, the likelihood of formal employee or informal self-employment grows linearly with age: old workers are overrepresented in these two work status groups. In addition, there is a U-shaped behaviour in the association between age and formal salaried employment where its incidence is the highest among workers aged 25–45 years.

Informal workers earn lower wages than formal workers. This is verified both among wage earners and among the self-employed. In addition, among wage-employees, the mean hours worked are the highest for formal workers in all the countries, followed by upper-tier informal and then by lower tier informal salaried workers. Therefore, the gaps in monthly labour income are even wider than those found in hourly labour income. Among the non-salaried workers, the difference of working hours between formal and informal are (except in Paraguay) less significant.

Figure 7.4 shows the monthly wages by work category. In all the countries, formal self-employed workers are located at the upper tail of the wage distribution, followed by formal wage-employees. Depending on the country, the third position is occupied by the upper-tier informal wage-employees or by informal self-employed workers.

In order to test for statistically significant differences in average hourly earnings across these work status groups, Fig. 7.5 presents the coefficient of the fitted one-way ANOVA model, where the dependent variable is the log hourly earnings of each group of workers and the covariates are the work status dummies. The base category is formal wage-employment.

Results prove that formal self-employed exhibit the highest average hourly earnings, followed by formal wage-employees. This wage difference is significant in all the countries. Except in Paraguay, informality is associated with a statistically significant earning penalty, with lower-tier informal being the lowest-paying jobs. The gap between upper-tier informal wage-employees and informal self-employed is significant in Argentina, Brazil, and Mexico.

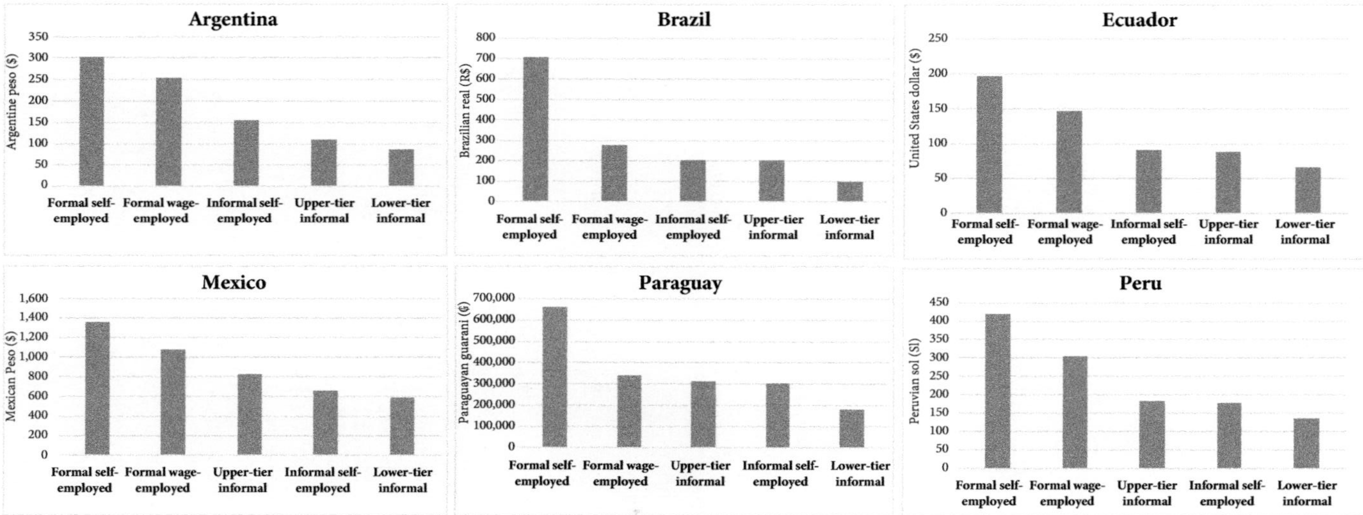

Fig. 7.4 Mean monthly wages by work status

Source: authors' elaboration based on household surveys.

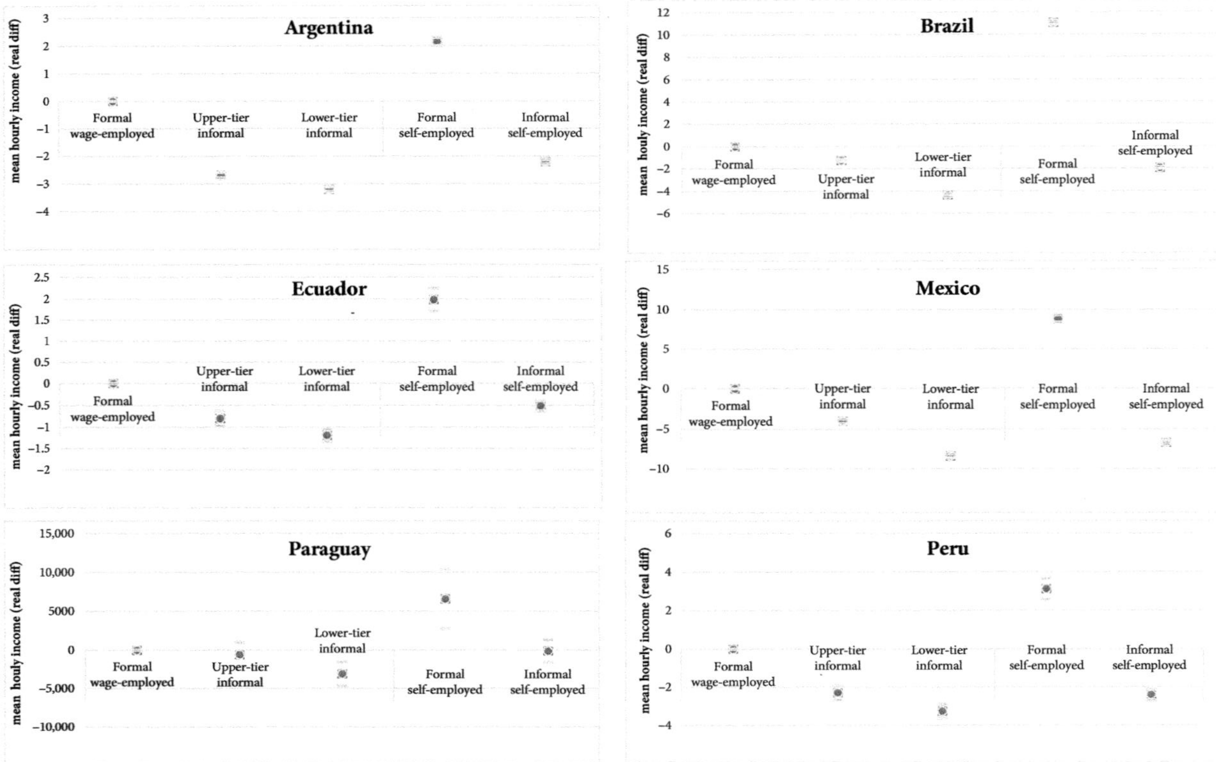

Fig. 7.5 ANOVA of mean hourly income across work status groups

Note: Coefficient estimates and 95 per cent confidence interval of fitted one-way ANOVA model of mean hourly labour income using formal wage-employees as the base category.
Source: authors' elaboration based on household surveys.

To sum up, the distribution of workers in each work status group is not random in any country. Prime-aged workers and those with a higher educational level are more likely to be formal than the rest of the workers. In turn, wages are statistically higher among formal than informal positions. Formal wage earners are, additionally, covered by labour legislation and receive social security benefits such as paid vacation, maternity leave, and future contributory pension, among others. Overall, this evidence suggests that formal is the most preferred job position. The following analysis will contribute to a better understanding of the characteristics and patterns of mobility of each work status.

5. Employment transitions

5.1 Transition matrices

Starting with the dynamic analysis, the year-on-year transition matrices between different states (employed, unemployed, and inactive) and different work status groups are analysed. Table 7.1 presents the average results for the whole period.

The first finding is that, as expected, formal workers in all the countries are more likely to remain in a formal job than the rest of workers. In particular, between 80 and 90 per cent of initially formal wage earners were still formal workers one year later. The higher occupational stability among formal wage earners may be explained by the existence of firing costs as well as by the fact that they are more concentrated in big, more stable, companies.

For the remaining 10–20 per cent, the most frequent destination after leaving a formal salaried position is upper-tier informal wage-employment in Mexico, Paraguay, and Peru or inactivity in Argentina, Brazil, and Ecuador. However, even in these three last countries, transitions between formality and upper-tier informality are common.

On the contrary, in all the countries, very few formal employees go into lower-tier informal salaried employment and even fewer to formal self-employment (at most, 2 per cent). Recall that formal self-employment is made up of professional own-accounts and employers in firms with five or more employees. Therefore, these types of transitions imply that a formal employee becomes an independent professional or employer of a medium or large firm. Therefore, it would not be easy for salaried employees without a university degree, in particular, to become employers of medium or large companies. This could explain why transitions to an informal self-employment position are more frequent, albeit very low. In any case, outflows from a formal salaried occupation to an informal wage position are, in all the countries, more important than those going into an independent occupation.

Informal wage-employees (both segments considered within this group) are the most mobile group of workers. Self-employed workers are in between. The

Table 7.1 Year-to-year conditional probabilities of transitions (percentage)

Country	Employment status in year t		Employment status in year $t+1$							
			Formal wage-employees	Informal wage-employees		Self-employed		Unemployed	Inactive	Total
				Upper-tier	Lower-tier	Formal	In formal			
Argentina	Formal wage-employees		87.4	2.7	2.4	0.8	1.8	1.9	2.9	100
	Informal wage-employees	Upper-tier	18.7	39.4	14.3	2.2	8.3	5.9	11.1	100
		Lower-tier	9.4	9.0	46.3	0.9	11.1	7.3	16.0	100
	Self-employed	Formal	8.2	5.2	3.0	59.0	17.0	2.1	5.6	100
		Informal	4.1	4.2	8.5	3.8	62.9	4.5	11.9	100
	Unemployed		10.4	8.5	13.8	1.3	11.2	26.5	28.4	100
	Inactive		2.5	2.8	5.6	0.5	4.3	6.1	78.1	100
Brazil	Formal wage-employees		79.0	2.6	2.2	0.9	2.6	5.8	6.9	100
	Informal wage-employees	Upper-tier	21.4	33.3	7.2	3.0	9.3	11.1	14.5	100
		Lower-tier	7.0	2.9	46.4	0.6	12.4	9.6	21.1	100
	Self-employed	Formal	3.7	2.4	1.0	71.2	13.8	2.6	5.3	100
		Informal	1.8	1.2	3.5	2.6	69.0	5.2	16.6	100
	Unemployed		7.1	2.9	5.5	1.4	10.4	41.8	30.9	100
	Inactive		1.2	0.8	2.2	0.4	5.6	8.8	81.1	100

Ecuador	Formal wage-employees		85.1	2.8	2.1	1.0	3.3	2.1	3.5	100
	Informal wage-employees	Upper-tier	22.1	33.9	18.5	1.5	12.1	4.4	7.6	100
		Lower-tier	9.4	10.8	44.5	0.7	19.8	4.5	10.3	100
	Self-employed	Formal	12.8	4.6	3.3	47.0	22.3	2.5	7.6	100
		Informal	3.8	3.4	8.2	2.3	67.0	2.2	13.1	100
	Unemployed		15.1	7.0	13.6	2.9	13.5	18.2	29.7	100
	Inactive		2.9	1.9	4.0	0.6	8.4	5.0	77.2	100
Mexico	Formal wage-employees		77.8	6.1	3.8	1.1	2.7	2.7	5.8	100
	Informal wage-employees	Upper-tier	26.5	30.9	16.3	1.9	7.9	4.1	12.4	100
		Lower-tier	8.5	9.2	49.1	0.8	13.4	3.3	15.7	100
	Self-employed	Formal	8.9	4.8	4.7	50.8	14.6	2.3	13.9	100
		Informal	4.1	3.5	10.5	2.4	59.6	1.6	18.2	100
	Unemployed		21.9	9.9	14.4	2.4	9.0	14.9	27.6	100
	Inactive		3.8	2.7	5.7	0.8	7.8	2.5	76.6	100

Continued

Table 7.1 *Continued*

Country	Employment status in year t		Employment status in year $t+1$							
			Formal wage-employees	Informal wage-employees		Self-employed		Unemployed	Inactive	Total
				Upper-tier	Lower-tier	Formal	In formal			
Paraguay	Formal wage-employees		86.8	5.0	1.5	0.2	2.5	2.1	1.9	100
	Informal wage-employees	Upper-tier	15.6	50.9	13.0	0.6	8.6	7.1	4.2	100
		Lower-tier	5.3	12.5	52.9	0.1	10.7	7.5	11.0	100
	Self-employed	Formal	5.2	5.0	2.2	36.8	42.7	6.6	1.5	100
		Informal	1.9	3.1	7.3	2.7	67.8	5.4	11.8	100
	Unemployed		9.8	16.5	18.0	0.5	7.8	27.8	19.6	100
	Inactive		2.3	4.0	8.0	0.2	7.9	9.5	68.2	100
Peru	Formal wage-employees		78.9	6.3	2.3	2.0	4.0	3.5	3.0	100
	Informal wage-employees	Upper-tier	20.5	36.9	13.1	2.0	11.3	5.7	10.6	100
		Lower-tier	6.2	14.3	43.5	1.0	17.4	5.4	12.3	100
	Self-employed	Formal	10.9	3.6	4.8	48.4	20.3	3.9	8.1	100
		Informal	2.9	4.0	5.6	3.0	70.5	3.3	10.6	100
	Unemployed		11.3	8.8	11.4	2.5	12.2	20.8	33.0	100
	Inactive		2.8	5.1	6.1	1.3	13.3	9.2	62.1	100

Note: Each row indicates work status in the initial year and each column indicates work status in the next year. The likelihood of staying in the same employment status conditional on the base year employment status is highlighted in grey.
Source: authors' elaboration based on household surveys.

lower labour stability of informal wage earners could be explained by the fact that they have low or no legal firing costs, thus making them attractive for employment in industries with unstable demand and for unstable occupations. Moreover, informal employees have a greater presence in small-scale firms, which are regularly exposed to risks that make them more vulnerable. As they operate with low capital/labour ratios, the decision to interrupt economic activity is easier.

Beyond this general outlook, in all the countries, upper-tier informal wage-employees are even more mobile not only than formal workers but also than lower-tier informal workers. Except in Paraguay, they are, indeed, the most unstable group of workers. Only about one-third of them stay in this work status from year to year in Brazil, Ecuador, and Mexico, 40 per cent in Argentina and Peru, and 50 per cent in Paraguay. These figures compare with 44 per cent and up to 53 per cent among lower-tier informal workers. It is striking that a better work status, at least in terms of average earnings, has less stability than another considered as worse.

However, upper-tier informal workers are more likely to transit into formal wage-employment than into lower-tier informal salaried employment. In fact, in all the countries, formal salaried employment is the most frequent destination for those workers. At least in part, this could be associated with the characteristics of the salaried formalization process observed in the region for most of the period under study. In particular, as found by Maurizio and Vázquez (2019) and Beccaria et al. (2021), a significant proportion of the new formal workers in Latin America actually became formal employees in the same job (in situ formalization); that is, a worker becomes formal, maintaining the same occupation between t and $t + 1$. In addition, a positive relationship is found between the probability of becoming formal and the size of the firm. Therefore, the low job stability of upper-tier informal workers did not always imply that they actually left the position but sometimes that they were formalized in the initial job. This may explain part of the 'apparent' transit from this work status to formality as this process was observed with greater intensity in medium and big companies.

Mobility patterns are very different in the case of lower-tier informal wage-employees, who, as shown before, are located at the lowest step of the job ladder. On the one hand, between 44 and 53 per cent of them remain in this work status for at least one year. On the other hand, when leaving this position, they are more likely to go into informal self-employment than any other work status. Less than 10 per cent of these workers move to formal salaried employment.

Between 60 and 70 per cent of those workers in an informal self-employed position (non-professional own-account, unpaid family worker, or employer in small enterprises) remain in this status over the following year. The most frequent destination for those workers who leave their initial occupation is inactivity. This was to be expected as the intermittence associated with certain typical occupations of such workers could imply that many of them do not actively seek a new job while 'waiting' for a new demand of their services or products.

On the contrary, most informal self-employed workers do not find formal jobs. Indeed, the percentage of transitions to a formal job is extremely low (less than 5 per cent) in all countries. This type of worker and the inactive people are the two groups of individuals with the least probability of moving towards formality, even lower than the unemployed. Instead, their options are limited to precarious wage-earning positions or another form of own-account employment, probably of low quality as well. Therefore, transits between the two categories of informality—informal self-employment and lower-tier salaried employment—are very frequent. In fact, for each of these categories, the other category is the main occupational destination after leaving the initial position.

Finally, given that in Latin America, including the countries concerned, unemployment spells are relatively short, basically because of a lack or low coverage of unemployment insurance, only about 15 –27 per cent of individuals who were initially unemployed remained so one year later. In most cases, this reflects the high number of transitions to inactivity (20–30 per cent) and informal jobs (13–35 per cent). In all cases, it is evident that although the unemployed quickly leave this initial state, this does not translate into intense entries into formality since, in almost all cases (except in Mexico), less than 16 per cent of those unemployed in one year are formal one year later. The same happens for the inactive people, for whom the probabilities of entering the workforce through a formal occupation are very low. As mentioned, transits between informal, self-employment, and inactivity are very frequent in all the countries.

This evidence allows us to evaluate whether informality is a persistent state or whether this is a stepping stone towards a better-paid occupation. Results suggest that there is significant labour turnover of workers from lower-tier informal salaried occupations. In fact, together with upper-tier informal wage-employees, these are the more mobile categories of workers. On the contrary, the informal self-employed exhibit a relatively high level (60–70 per cent) of job stability from year to year.

Complementary to this, the analysis of the destination after leaving the initial position is also revealing. Since the lower-tier informal wage-employees are in the worst-paying work status, their alternatives are only two: remaining in this type of occupation or transiting up the job ladder. More than half (between 52 and 67 per cent) are part of the first group, meaning that a lower share of informal workers improve their employment position by moving to a higher paying occupation: about 30–35 per cent in Brazil and Paraguay, 40 per cent in Argentina and Mexico, and about 48 per cent in Ecuador and Peru. This suggests that an important group of workers who were in this position in year t were in a better work status in year $t + 1$. However, even in the period under analysis, characterized by improvements in the labour markets and by a strong formalization process, most of them failed to move up the wage ladder. Further, as shown before, only a small proportion (less than one-third) of workers transitioned from a lower-tier informal wage job to a formal salaried position.

The higher stability of informal self-employment positions (most of them non-professional own-account workers), together with the high transits between these occupations and lower-tier informal wage-employment, result in a very low percentage of transits towards higher-paying job status (less than 13 per cent).

As mentioned, in all the countries, upper-tier informal wage-employees are more likely to transition into (or become in the initial job) formal wage-employment than into lower-tier informal salaried employment or informal self-employed. However, when we consider the stayers and those transiting into a worse work status, together they account for about two-thirds or more of total transitions.

Finally, for the two formal groups of workers (formal self-employed and formal wage-employees) the percentage of those who maintain their initial work status (and those formal wage-employees moving up the job ladder) is significantly higher than the share of workers transitioning into lower-paying work status groups (except in Paraguay, in the case of formal self-employed).

5.2 Characteristics associated with work status transitions

This heterogenous overview regarding labour turnover suggests that, in addition to the work status of origin, observed personal attributes are also associated with different probabilities of transiting into higher or lower-paying occupation.

For the multinomial logit regressions,[6] we collapsed employment transition equations into three work status groups: (i) formal wage-employees and formal self-employed, (ii) upper-tier informal wage-employees, and (iii) lower-tier informal wage-employees and informal self-employed.

With a few exceptions, education is a highly correlated factor with movements from low-paid informal positions to better-paid jobs. In particular, higher education promotes transits from lower-tier and upper-tier informal positions to formal positions. These results seem to be consistent with previous findings on the characteristics of the labour formalization in Latin America. For example, Maurizio (2016) found that skilled workers were benefited by this process with more intensity than the rest of the people.

Education also plays a role in improving the position within informality since it tends to correlate positively with transits from lower-tier to upper-tier informal jobs. Conversely, having a secondary or university level reduces the chances of leaving formality and moving towards either of the other two work status groups.

[6] The results of the multinomial logit regressions are detailed in Table A6 in Maurizio and Monsalvo (2021).

Therefore, the positive correlation between education and formality is observed through two channels: on the one hand, it contributes to a higher stability in formal jobs; on the other, it fosters entries to this kind of job.

In addition, in almost all cases, the linear coefficient of age (used as a proxy of general labour experience) is statistically significant and negative, and the quadratic coefficient is positive. This means that the prime-aged are more stable in formal jobs than the rest of workers. The role of education and age could be explained by the accumulation of specific human capital, which usually complements general human capital. Formal workers with higher educational levels tend to receive more specific training, and thus employers try to retain them.

Finally, gender is another dimension associated with different patterns of labour mobility. Except in Paraguay, men have more probabilities of moving towards a better position than women. This seems consistent with the greater difficulties that women have in the Latin American labour market, a stylized fact largely documented in the empirical literature for the region (ILO 2014; ECLAC and ILO 2019; Alaniz et al. 2020). However, unexpectedly, in Brazil, Ecuador, and Mexico, men also experience some type of movement in the opposite direction with greater intensity.

6. Wage dynamics

Finally, this section aims at evaluating the wage dynamics associated with labour turnover.[7] Figure 7.6 displays the estimated marginal effect on changes in log earnings by initial and destination employment status.

In almost all the countries, except in Paraguay, econometric results confirm the findings obtained from the descriptive analysis. The sign and the magnitude of the transition effect indicate that formal work status is preferred over upper-tier informal work, and the latter is preferred over a lower-tier informal job. In particular, the transit from formality to any other work status implies a loss of wage. This happens with greater intensity when workers move towards a lower-tier informal position or informal self-employment. On the contrary, transition from lower-tier informal employment to formality always increases wage. However, only in Argentina, Brazil, and Peru transits from lower tier to upper tier imply a true wage premium. Finally, upper-tier informal workers are the 'intermediate' group since they obtain an increase in wages when they move into a formal position, but they experience a wage reduction when they transit to lower-tier informal work.

In addition, in almost all the countries (except in Paraguay), gender dimension is statistically significant: women experience a wage penalty in all work status groups, suggesting wage discrimination against them. It is interesting, however, to

[7] This section is based on Table A7 in Maurizio and Monsalvo (2021).

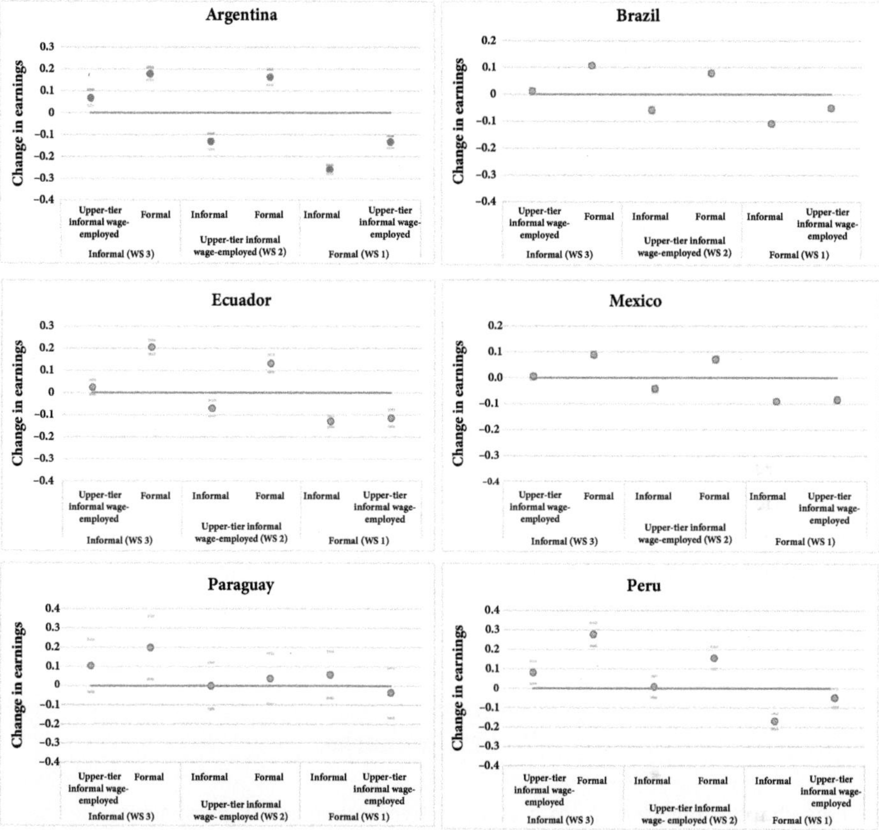

Fig. 7.6 Labour income dynamics

Note: Each point shows the estimated marginal effect on changes in log earnings by initial and destination employment state. The grey lines show the 95 per cent confidence intervals.
Source: authors' elaboration based on household surveys.

note that its magnitude grows as we move down the job ladder: the wage penalty reaches the highest value among lower-tier informal workers and the lowest level among formal workers. It contributes to intensifying the observed higher incidence of poverty and the working-poor phenomenon among women in the region (Maurizio 2018; Amarante and Colacce 2019).

As expected, education is one of the most relevant dimensions in wage determination. It positively correlates with wages in all work status groups. Again, returns to education are lower among formal workers than among low-paying informal jobs. Age is also correlated with higher wages (except in Paraguay and Peru, where some coefficients were not statistically significant). In Argentina, Brazil, Ecuador, and Mexico, this variable reaches the highest (lowest) positive influence in lower-tier informal and informal self-employed work status groups (formal jobs).

Therefore, wage gaps associated with different observable variables appear to be lower in formality than in informality. This seems to be consistent with the above-mentioned lower within-variance in the first group than in the second. Labour institutions, such as minimum wage or collective bargaining, and labour regulations could account for the lower wage dispersion among formal wage earners (Keifman and Maurizio 2014; Amarante and Arim 2015). In particular, to the extent that these institutions are binding and provide an income floor, they can reduce inequality within the group of workers covered by them.

At the same time, results show that informal workers who remain in the position of origin can improve their wages by increasing the level of education.

Finally, initial wage has a strong and negative impact on the change in earnings; that is, the higher the initial wage, the lower their real growth during the period under analysis. It is interesting to note that this is verified in a statistically significant way in each work status but with even greater intensity in the lowest categories of the job ladder. This pattern seems to be consistent with the reducing trend in inequality observed in Latin America and, in particular, in these countries over the 2000s (Cornia; 2012; Lustig et al. 2013; Maurizio and Vázquez 2016; ECLAC 2017).

7. Final remarks

This chapter analysed, from a comparative and dynamic perspective, the heterogeneity of formal and informal employment in six Latin American countries: Argentina, Brazil, Ecuador, Mexico, Paraguay, and Peru. This selection of countries allows us to have a broad picture of the Latin American labour markets since they have occupational structures and dynamics that greatly differ from one another. Additionally, they account for about 70 per cent of the total population in the region.

In particular, we have distinguished five work status groups: formal wage-employed, formal self-employed, upper-tier informal wage-employed, lower-tier informal wage-employed, and informal self-employed. We evaluated the intensity and patterns of the labour turnover between these work status groups and assessed its impact on wages.

In all the countries, formal workers earn the highest wages and lower-tier informal workers the lowest. Two contrasting labour mobility patterns were found: on the one hand, the proportion of formal workers who maintain the work status of origin or move up the job ladder is significantly higher than the proportion who transition into lower-paying work status groups; on the other hand, despite the high labour turnover experienced by lower-tier informal wage-employees, most of them fail to move up the wage ladder.

Education plays an important role by increasing the probability of transiting towards a better job and also by increasing wages, even in informal occupations. In other words, informal workers who remain in this work status can improve their wages by increasing their level of education.

Different types of public policies are needed to improve labour conditions in Latin American countries. As shown, after the significant increase in labour formality in the countries under analysis (except Mexico), this process slowed down, stopped, or reversed in recent years. This is particularly worrisome given that labour informality is far from being negligible in the region. Therefore, progress in employment formalization and the strengthening of labour institution policies are essential processes to allow jobs to become an effective mechanism to overcome poverty and achieve social protection.

In turn, efforts are required to increase investment in human capital. This should be complemented with a coherent system of training as well as other labour active policies. In order to progress towards an integrated training system which can effectively lead to improvements in global efficiency, labour careers, and labour conditions, a development path defined for the medium and long run is needed that generates continuous demand for greater human capital, either general or specific, which allows the offer of education and training to be reflected in higher wages and better working conditions. Finally, all these policies should be framed within an economic development strategy built on the basis of an integrated productive structure leading to high efficiency and systemic competitiveness.

References

Alaniz, E., T.H. Gindling, C. Mata, and D. Rojas (2020). 'Transforming Informal Work and Livelihoods in Costa Rica and Nicaragua'. WIDER Working Paper 2020/100. Helsinki: UNU-WIDER.

Almeida, R., and P. Carneiro (2009). 'Enforcement of Labor Regulation and Firm Performance'. *Journal of Comparative Economics*, 37(1): 28–46.

Amarante, V., and R. Arim (2015). Desigualdad e Informalidad. Un análisis de cinco experiencias latinoamericanas. Santiago de Chile: CEPAL–Ministerio de Asuntos Exteriores de Noruega.

Amarante, V., and M. Colacce (2019). 'Poverty and Gender in Latin America'. Paper presented at Eighth Society for the Study of Economic Inequality (ECINEQ) Conference.

Beccaria, L., R. Maurizio, and A. Monsalvo (2021). 'Labour Formalization and Inequality: The Distributive Impact of Labour Formalization in Latin America since 2000'. *Development and Change*, 53(1): 117–165. DOI: 10.1111/dech.12653 © 2021 International Institute of Social Studies.

Berg, J. (2010). 'Laws or Luck? Understanding Rising Formality in Brazil in the 2000s'. ILO Working Paper No. 5. Brasilia: International Labour Office.

Bertranou, F., and L. Casanova. (2013). *Informalidad laboral en Argentina: Segmentos críticos y políticas para la formalización*. Buenos Aires: Organización Internacional del Trabajo (OIT).

Bertranou, F. and R. Maurizio (2011). *Trabajadores Independientes, Mercado Laboral e Informalidad en Argentina*. Buenos Aires: OIT.

Boeri, T., and Garibaldi, P. (2007). 'Shadow Sorting'. In J. Frankel and C. Pissarides (eds), *NBER International Seminar on Macroeconomics 2005*. Cambridge, CA: MIT Press, pp. 125–163.

Bosch, M., and J. Esteban-Pretel (2009). 'Cyclical Informality and Unemployment'. Center for International Research on the Japanese Economy (CIRJE) Discussion Paper No. 613. Tokyo: CIRJE.

Castillo, V., S. Rojo Brizuela, and D. Schleser (2012). 'El impacto de las políticas laborales contracíclicas sobre el empleo asalariado registrado'. In Ministry of Labour, Employment and Social Security–International Labour Organization (MTEySS-ILO) (eds), *Macroeconomía, empleo e ingresos: debates y políticas en Argentina frente a la crisis internacional 2008–2009*. Buenos Aires: MTEySS-ILO, pp. 216–259.

Chacaltana, J. (2001). 'Reforma en la contratación y el despido en el Perú de los noventa'. *Revista Economía*, 24(48): 133–151.

Chacaltana, J. (2008). 'Una evaluación del régimen laboral especial para la microempresa en Perú, al cuarto año de vigencia'. Unpublished paper. Lima: ILO.

Cornia, A. (2012). 'Inequality Trends and Their Determinants: Latin America over 1990–2011'. WIDER Working Paper No. 9/2012. Helsinki: UNU-WIDER.

Corseuil, C. and M. Foguel (2012). 'Economic Expansion and Increase in Labour Market Formality: A Poaching Approach', *Revista Brasileira de Economia* 66(2): 207–224.

Cruces, G., S. Galiani, and S. Kidyba (2010). 'Payroll Taxes, Wages and Employment: Identification through Policy Changes'. Center of Distributive, Labor and Social Studies (CEDLAS) Working Paper No. 93. La Plata, Argentina: CEDLAS.

de Andrade, G., M. Bruhn and D. McKenzie (2013). 'A Helping Hand or the Long Arm of the Law? Experimental Evidence on what Governments Can Do to Formalize Firms'. Policy Research Working Paper No. 6435. Washington, DC: World Bank. https://openknowledge.worldbank.org/bitstream/handle/10986/16323/wps6435.pdf?sequence=1&isAllowed=y.

Delgado, G., A. Querino, A. Campos, F. Vaz, L. Rangel, and M. Stivali (2007). 'Avaliação do Simples: Implicações à Formalização Previdenciária'. Text for Discussion No. 1277, Brasilia: IPEA.

ECLAC (Economic Commission for Latin America and the Caribbean) (2017) *Social Panorama of Latin America 2016*. Santiago de Chile: ECLAC.

ECLAC and ILO (2019). 'Coyuntura Laboral en América Latina y el Caribe. Evolución y perspectivas de la participación laboral femenina en América Latina'. Paper No. 21. Santiago: ECLAC and ILO.

Fajnzylber, P., W. Maloney, and G. Rojas (2009). 'Does Formality Improve Micro-Firm Performance? Quasi-Experimental Evidence from the Brazilian SIMPLES Program'. Institute of Labor Economics (IZA) Discussion Paper No. 4531. Bonn: IZA.

Hussmanns, R. (2004). 'Measuring the Informal Economy: From Employment in the Informal Sector to Informal Employment'. Policy Integration Department Working Paper No. 53. Geneva: International Labour Organization.

ILO (International Labour Organization) (2002). 'Resolution concerning Decent Work and the Informal Economy'. Governing Body, 285th Session, Seventh item on the agenda, Geneva.

ILO (2014). *Thematic Labour Overview 1: Transition to Formality in Latin America and the Caribbean* (rev. edn). Lima: ILO, Regional Office for Latin America and the Caribbean.

ILO (2018). *Políticas de Formalización en América Latina. Avances y desafíos.* J. Salazar-Xirinachs and J. Chacaltana, (eds), Lima: ILO, Regional Office for Latin America and the Caribbean.

Keifman, S., and R. Maurizio (2014). 'Changes in Labour Market Conditions and Policies, and Their Impact on Wage Inequality during the Last Decade'. In G.A. Cornia (ed.), *Falling Inequality in Latin America: Policy Changes and Lessons.* Oxford University Press for UNU-WIDER. Oxford: Oxford University Press.

Lustig, N., L. Lopez-Calva, and E. Ortiz-Juarez (2013). 'Declining Inequality in Latin America in the 2000s: The Cases of Argentina, Brazil, and Mexico'. *World Development*, 44: 129–141.

Maurizio, R. (2015). 'Transitions to Formality and Declining Inequality: Argentina and Brazil in the 2000s'. *Journal of Development and Change*, 46(5): 1047–1079.

Maurizio, R. (2016). 'Labor Market and Income Distribution in Latin America in Times of Economic Growth: Advances and Shortcomings'. In M. Damill, M. Rapetti, and G. Rozewurcell (eds), *Macroeconomics and Development: Essays in Honour of Roberto Frenkel.* New York: Columbia University Press, pp. 159–187.

Maurizio, R. (2018). 'In-Work Poverty in Latin America. Prevalence, Driving Forces and Trends'. In H. Lohmann and I. Marx (eds), *Handbook of Research on In-Work Poverty.* Cheltenham: Edward Elgar Publishing, pp. 365–394.

Maurizio, R. (2020). 'Rotación ocupacional y calidad del empleo. El caso de los trabajadores independientes en América Latina'. *Revista Desarrollo Económico*, 60 (230): 27–58.

Maurizio, R., and A. Monsalvo (2021) 'Informality, Labour Transitions, and the Livelihoods of Workers in Latin America'. WIDER Working Paper No. 2021/19. Helsinki: UNU-WIDER.

Maurizio, R., and G. Vázquez (2016). 'Distribution Effects of the Minimum Wage in Four Latin American Countries: Argentina, Brazil, Chile and Uruguay'. *International Labour Review*, 155(1): 97–131.

Maurizio, R. and G. Vázquez (2019). 'Formal Salaried Employment Generation and Transition to Formality in Developing Countries. The Case of Latin America'. Employment Working Paper No. 251. Geneva: ILO.

Monteiro, J., and J. Assunção (2012). 'Coming Out of the Shadows? Estimating the Impact of Simplification and Tax Cut on Formality in Brazilian Microenterprises'. *Journal of Bureaucracy Development Economics*, 99(1): 105–115.

Ronconi, L. (2010). 'Enforcement and Compliance with Labor Regulations'. *Industrial and Labor Relations Review*, 63(4): 719–736.

World Bank (2012). 'Ecuador. Las caras de la informalidad'. Report No. 67808-EC. Lima: ILO, Regional Office for Latin America and the Caribbean.

8

Self-employment and labour market dynamics of men and women in El Salvador and Nicaragua

Enrique Alaniz, Alma Espino, and T. H. Gindling

1. Introduction

Men and women in developing economies have unequal access to good jobs. In this chapter, we focus on what factors help to achieve advantageous jobs in the labour markets of El Salvador and Nicaragua and whether those factors differ between men and women.[1] Specifically, we examine the influence of personal characteristics (such as education), family characteristics (such as the number of children), and job characteristics (such as the industry sector of employment) in determining whether a woman (or man) moves up into an advantageous labour market state from an unfavourable state.

Unlike most other chapters in this volume, we distinguish between rural and urban, men and women, and explicitly discuss transitions to and from unpaid domestic work, full-time students, and other states outside of the labour force. In examining the different labour market dynamics of men and women, it is important to consider transitions into and out of the labour force as many women move back and forth between unpaid domestic work and paid work throughout their lives.

In identifying 'advantageous' jobs, we recognize the heterogeneity of both self-employment and salaried employment, dividing the first into advantageous

[1] This study is based on empirical research originally supported by the Canadian International Development Research Center (IDRC) grant no. 107260-001, 'Better Jobs for Central American Women: Labor Market Dynamics in Nicaragua and El Salvador', which was awarded to the Fundación Internacional para el Desafío Económico Global (FIDEG), Managua, Nicaragua. The research project was directed by Enrique Alaniz of FIDEG. This research project involved collaboration between the authors, FIDEG in Nicaragua, and the Fundación Salvadoreno para el Desarrollo Económico y Social (FUSADES) in El Salvador. The research team at FUSADES included Margarita Beneke de Sanfelú, Susana Maria Delgado-Vides, José Andrés Oliva-Cepeda, and Lidia Elizabeth Vázquez. The research team at FIDEG included Enrique Alaniz and Gloria Carrión. We are grateful for useful suggestions from Alejandro Martínez-Cuenca and Carolina Robino. The methodology and preliminary discussions of the results presented in this chapter can be found in Alaniz et al. (2015) and Beneke de Sanfelú et al. (2015).

Enrique Alaniz, Alma Espino, and T. H. Gindling, *Self-employment and labour market dynamics of men and women in El Salvador and Nicaragua*. In: *The Job Ladder*. Edited by Gary S. Fields, T. H. Gindling, Kunal Sen, Michael Danquah, and Simone Schotte, Oxford University Press. © UNU-WIDER (2023). DOI: 10.1093/oso/9780192867339.003.0008 and unfavourable self-employment and the latter into formal and informal salaried employment. We consider three labour market states to be 'advantageous' ('*favorable*' in Spanish): (i) formal salaried employees, (ii) non-agricultural self-employed workers and employers with a decent income or an employer with a successful and growing firm, and (iii) agricultural self-employed workers or an employer with a decent income or an employer with a successful and growing firm.

Our results demonstrate that, in both countries, men are more likely to be found in advantageous labour market states compared to women. We find that there is substantial mobility of men and women between informal salaried employment and self-employment. For women, there is also substantial mobility between unpaid domestic work and these two states. On the other hand, we find very little mobility into formal salaried employment. Those who work as formal salaried employees tend to enter this sector soon after graduating from school (some after short periods as informal employees, unemployed, or unpaid family workers), and then remain in this sector for a long time. Very few older workers transition from unfavourable labour market states into formal salaried employment. For older workers, the most likely transition from an unfavourable state into an advantageous labour market state is into advantageous non-agricultural self-employment. Most of the advantageous non-agricultural self-employed are older workers who gained experience working as informal salaried workers or in unfavourable self-employment before succeeding as advantageous self-employed.

Our findings suggest that education is the most important personal characteristic promoting transition into non-agricultural advantageous labour market states and reducing transition out of advantageous labour market states. In particular, a tertiary (post-secondary) education is a strong predictor of whether a man or woman is found in and stays in the most advantageous labour market state, formal salaried employment. Along with a tertiary education, a secondary education also promotes advantageous self-employment.

A finding with relevance to public policy is that the provision of public services such as utilities (electricity, water, etc.) and health care significantly increase the probability that men or women will transition into advantageous non-agricultural self-employment. This suggests that providing these services to poor families could be an effective way to promote transition by the poor into advantageous non-agricultural self-employment.

Section 2 describes the panel data used in this chapter. Section 3 describes and compares the labour market characteristics of men and women in the Salvadoran and Nicaraguan labour markets. Section 4 uses the panel nature of our data to measure the degree to which men and women move from unfavourable states to advantageous labour market states and vice versa. Finally, Section 5 identifies the characteristics that determine whether or not men and women transition into or out of advantageous labour market states. Section 6 concludes and presents policy recommendations.

2. Data

2.1 Nicaragua

To study the labour market dynamics of women and men in Nicaragua, we use annual panel data collected by Fundación Internacional para el Desafío Económico Global (FIDEG) between 2009 and 2012. This data set allows us to follow women and men as they change jobs or as the characteristics of their jobs change. Consistent with official labour force statistics in Nicaragua and the availability of data, in our analysis, we consider anyone 10 years of age or older in Nicaragua.

We have observations on 10,766 individuals (male and female 10 years of age or older). For 28.6 per cent of these individuals, we have four years of panel data (the maximum); for 15.7 per cent, we have three years of data; for 20.0 per cent, we have two years of data; and for 35.8 per cent, we have only one year of data. In order to check the representativeness of the sample, we compared some basic characteristics of the workforce with those of the Nicaraguan Encuesta de Medición de Nivel de Vida carried out by the National Institute of Statistics in 2009. The distribution of the workers by economic activity, the distribution by employment status, and the unemployment rate are quite similar for the two samples. We find that the FIDEG's sample presents a higher labour force participation rate and higher percentage of employees working less than 40 hours per week.[2]

2.2 El Salvador

To study labour market dynamics in El Salvador, we created an annual panel data set using the Multipurpose Household Surveys (MHS) from the years 2008–2012. These survey data have been collected by the General Directorate of Statistics and Census (DIGESTYC) since 1975, although we only use the surveys from 2008 to 2012 because it is only in those years that the necessary variables are available to allow us to match individuals across surveys. Consistent with official labour force statistics in El Salvador and the availability of data, in our analysis, we consider only those 16 years of age or older. The MHS is based on a census mapping technique developed by DIGESTYC.

The division of segments allowed us to create year-to-year panels for the years 2008–2012. Our data effectively consists of four panel data sets, each of which

[2] These data are described in more detail in Alaniz, et al. (2019). Descriptive statistics on the analytical sample in Nicaragua and a comparison with the census can be found in the appendix of Alaniz et al. (2015).

follows households and individuals for two years (2008–2009, 2009–2010, 2010–2011 and 2011–2012). The sample used is restricted to the working-age population and contains 266,546 observations—122,403 males (45.9 per cent) and 144,143 females (54 per cent). From this sample, 165,360 belong to the economically active population—101,089 males (61.1 per cent) and 64,271 females (38.9 per cent).[3] On average, 23 per cent of the MHS observations were repeated the following year. In order to check the representativeness of the panel data sample, we compared some basic characteristics of the panel data with the full cross-sectional data set. The distribution of workers by gender, region of the country, economic activity, and the distribution by employment status are all similar in the panel and full data. Descriptive statistics on the panel data sample in El Salvador and a comparison to the full cross-sectional data set can be found in Beneke de Sanfeliu et al. (2015).

3. Women and men in the labour markets of El Salvador and Nicaragua

During the period that we study, in both El Salvador and Nicaragua, the labour market is characterized by low rates of unemployment, a high rate of underemployment, and a high degree of informality (see Table 8.1). For example, in El Salvador, only 29.1 per cent of employed workers are covered by social security and more than 55.6 per cent work in firms with five or fewer workers. In Nicaragua, these percentages demonstrate even less formality: 11.2 per cent covered by social security and 74.6 per cent in firms with five or fewer workers. Women are much less likely than men in both countries to be participants in the labour force, and if they are employed, women are more likely to be in precarious employment. For example, in Nicaragua, 55.7 per cent of employed women are underemployed in comparison to 34.3 per cent of men; 12.3 per cent of employed men are covered by social security, while only 10.3 per cent of employed women are covered; 41.3 per cent of employed women are self-employed compared to 30.6 per cent of men; and 19.3 per cent of women are unpaid family workers compared to 17.8 per cent of men.

In both countries, the level of education of the labour force is low compared to other countries in Latin America. In El Salvador, the mean worker has 7.6 years of education and only 13.3 per cent have any type of tertiary education, while in Nicaragua, the mean worker has only 5.9 years of education and only 8.7 per cent

[3] To create the panel data, we matched households, then household heads, and finally all the members of the household. This methodology considers key variables such as the segment number, geographical location, year of birth, and gender and age of each individual to create a unique identifier that allows a matching process of the head of household and the members living in the household for each home. We were able to match the same individuals across two consecutive years but cannot follow the same individuals for more than two years. Thus, our data effectively consists of four panel data sets, each of which follows households and individuals for two years (2008–2009, 2009–2010, 2010–2011 and 2011–2012).

Table 8.1 Selected labour market indicators and labour force characteristics, comparison by country (2008–2012)

	El Salvador (average 2008–2012)			Nicaragua (average 2009–2012)		
	All	Men	Women	All	Men	Women
Participation rate	62.8	81.2	47.4	63.4	79.3	47.8
Unemployment rate	6.6	8.1	4.5	3.4	3.6	3.3
Underemployment rate	27.2	25.1	30.0	42.7	34.2	55.7
Proportion working in firms with five or fewer employees	55.6	55.2	56.0	74.6	72.0	76.8
Proportion of workers insured by social security	29.1	29.2	29.0	11.2	12.3	10.3
Distribution of the labour force by economic sector:						
Agriculture and mining	22.2	33.8	5.7	38.5	52.6	16.2
Manufacturing/construction	20.6	21.9	18.7	16.9	15.3	19.4
Commerce	28.5	19.1	42.0	21.6	14.2	33.1
High-complexity services	17.4	18.6	15.8	9.4	9.5	9.2
Low-complexity services	11.3	6.6	18.0	13.7	8.4	22.0
Distribution of the labour force by employment status:						
Salaried employees	51.5	62.8	51.5	44.5	48.3	37.3
Owner	2.8	5.1	2.8	2.4	3.4	1.5
Self-employed	37.9	24.8	37.9	33.3	30.6	41.3
Unpaid	7.7	7.2	7.7	19.8	17.8	19.9
Distribution of the labour force by education level:						
No education	12.4	12.4	12.4	16.3	16.6	16.1
Primary	56.5	59.0	53.0	44.9	46.5	43.4
Secondary	17.8	17.1	18.8	30.1	28.8	31.3
Tertiary	13.3	11.5	15.8	8.7	8.2	9.1
Average years of schooling of the labour force	7.6	7.4	7.8	5.9	5.7	6.1

Source: authors' calculations based on the data described in section 3.

of the labour force has any type of tertiary education.[4] On average, women in the labour force have higher education levels than men. For example, in El Salvador,

[4] In 2009, in Argentina and Chile, the average education level of the population was 11 years of study; in Uruguay, in 2011, the average worker had 9.8 years of education, and in Mexico, it was 8.7 years of education (SEDLAC 2017).

Table 8.2 Gender wage gap

	El Salvador	Nicaragua
All	34.2	27.2
Salaried employees only	13.4	28.1
Adults (25–64 years)	37.4	28.7
Young (15–24 years)	24.6	21.4
Urban	32.9	36.1
Urban salaried adults	16.1	26.4

Note: The table shows the average percentage difference in the hourly wages of men and women, after controlling for education and potential experience.
Source: authors' calculations based on the data described in section 3.

women in the labour force have 7.8 years of education compared to 7.4 for men. It is also more likely that women in the labour force have some type of tertiary education compared to men.

The distribution of the employed by economic activity indicates that men are concentrated in agriculture, while women tend to work in commerce, services of low complexity, and manufacturing. Services of low complexity include personal and social services, domestic service, and services for the home. Highly complex services include public utilities (electricity, gas, and water), transport, telecommunications, financial services, and public administration.

Table 8.2 presents the gap in average hourly wages between men and women (measured as the percentage difference in the average hourly wage earned by men and women, controlling for education and potential experience). Women with the same education and experience earn less than men in both El Salvador and Nicaragua. In El Salvador, the average hourly wage of women is 34.2 per cent less than that of men; in Nicaragua, the average hourly wage of women is 27.2 per cent less than that of men.

4. The labour mobility of men and women in El Salvador and Nicaragua

In this section, we use individual-level panel data to study labour market dynamics with a focus on what factors help men and women to achieve advantageous jobs in the labour market. We consider three labour market states to be 'advantageous': (i) formal salaried employees, (ii) non-agricultural self-employed workers with a decent income, and (iii) agricultural self-employed workers with a decent income. In El Salvador, we define 'decent income' as a wage above the legal minimum wage; in Nicaragua, we define 'decent income' as household consumption spending above the poverty line. We examine the transitions into and out of these advantageous labour market states and other labour market and non-labour market states including informal salaried employment, unfavourable non-agricultural self-employment, unfavourable agricultural self-employment, unemployment, unpaid family work, and out of the labour force (distinguishing between those going to school, those engaged in unpaid domestic work, and those engaged in other activities).

Our definition of 'advantageous' labour market states is similar to the International Labour Organization (ILO) concept of 'decent work'. Two key components of the ILO concept of 'decent work' are social security and remunerative employment (Ghai 2003): 'Social security serves to meet people's urgent subsistence needs and to provide protection against contingencies, and as such is an important aspect of decent work' (Ghai 2003: 122). Our first advantageous labour market state is formal salaried employment, defined as paid employment where workers are insured by social security. Remunerative employment is work that pays sufficiently to allow a worker's family to live at an adequate level: 'For developing countries, a good indicator of remunerative work is provided by data on absolute poverty' (Ghai 2003: 119). The ILO suggests that a good indicator of whether workers do not have remunerative employment is the proportion of the working population earning below the household poverty line (Ghai 2003: 118). The definition of advantageous self-employment that we apply in Nicaragua includes those who live in a household with an income above the poverty line, while in El Salvador, advantageous self-employment includes those earning less than the minimum wage (which is set below the poverty line).[5] We do not use the term 'decent work' in this chapter because our measure of advantageous labour market states does not take into account other components that the ILO considers when defining decent work such as basic worker rights and social dialogue (i.e. access to collective bargaining). Box 8.1 describes how we identify each labour market state.

[5] We also construct a measure of 'advantageous' self-employment in El Salvador, which is based on whether or not the worker lives in a family with incomes below the poverty line. For comparison, tables using this definition are presented in the appendix of the WIDER working paper version of this chapter (Alaniz et al. 2019). In general, the conclusions about mobility using this alternative definition in El Salvador are the same as the conclusions reported in the body of this chapter. We do not highlight this alternative definition of 'advantageous' in El Salvador because we have more confidence in the wage and earnings data from El Salvador than in the income data. Neither the minimum wage definition nor the poverty line definition of 'advantageous' in El Salvador is identical to our definition of 'advantageous' in Nicaragua because we did not have access to the same variables in both countries (e.g. wages are not available in the Nicaraguan data, while household consumption is not available in the Salvadoran data). However, the fact that our results are similar using either definition (and in both countries) gives us confidence that our results are robust.

Box 8.1 Definitions of labour market states considered in this study

Advantageous:

1. **Formal salaried employees**: includes wage and salaried workers who are benefiting from social security, either employed full time or part-time. Compared to other labour market states, wages and household income are highest for formal salaried employees. This is the most advantageous labour market state by these measures.
2. **Advantageous non-agricultural self-employed**: includes self-employed workers who are not engaged in agriculture, with household per capita consumption above the poverty line (in Nicaragua) or whose labour earnings are greater than the legal minimum wage (in El Salvador). In Nicaragua, this category also includes employers of firms with five or more workers and employers of firms with fewer than five employees whose firm increased the number of employees last year. Advantageous non-agricultural self-employment is the second most advantageous labour market state in terms of wages and household income.
3. **Advantageous agricultural self-employed**: includes self-employed workers who are engaged in agriculture, with household per capita consumption above the poverty line (in Nicaragua) or whose labour earnings are greater than the legal minimum wage (in El Salvador). In Nicaragua, this category also includes employers of firms with five or more workers and employers of firms with fewer than five employees whose firm increased the number of employees last year.

Unfavourable:

4. **Informal salaried employees**: includes all wage and salaried employees not benefiting from social security.
5. **Unfavourable non-agricultural self-employed**: includes all self-employed workers and employers who are not engaged in agriculture and that do not meet the conditions to be classified as 'advantageous non-agricultural self-employment'.
6. **Unfavourable agricultural self-employed**: includes all self-employed workers and employers who are engaged in agriculture and that do not meet the conditions to be classified as 'advantageous agricultural self-employment'.

7. **Unpaid family worker**: includes any employed person who works without remuneration in a business, firm, or family farm.
8. **Unemployed**: defined as people who, over the past week or last month before the survey, looked for work or made efforts to install their own business or company. Similarly, those who were not working but already had jobs and were starting the next month are included in this category.

Not in the labour force:

9. **Student**: includes persons who are not part of the labour force and who report to be exclusively devoted to studying.
10. **Unpaid domestic work**: includes persons who are not part of the labour force who report to be exclusively devoted to domestic work. In Nicaragua, this category also includes those who report to be inactive because of any other reason (a small group). In El Salvador, those who report being inactive for any other reason constitute a larger group and we considered them as a separate category.
11. **Other inactive**: includes those who report not being in the labour force for any other reason. This last category includes those who are retired and young people who are neither working nor in school, plus the disabled (El Salvador only).

In terms of a job ladder, formal salaried employment and advantageous non-agricultural self-employment are the work states with the highest earnings in both countries, followed by advantageous agricultural self-employment. Next highest are informal salaried employment and unfavourable non-agricultural self-employment. Unfavourable agricultural self-employment is the work state with the lowest earnings in both countries.[6]

Figure 8.1 presents the distribution of men and women in these 11 states separately for El Salvador and Nicaragua. The most noticeable difference between men and women in both El Salvador and Nicaragua is that women are much more likely than men to be in unpaid domestic work. This difference between men and women is likely a consequence of the traditional expectation that wives will provide unpaid domestic care to children and other dependents, while husbands are expected to have full-time jobs outside of the home. A larger percentage

[6] In Nicaragua, mean monthly earnings were 5,498 2012 *córdobas* for formal salaried employees, 4,098 for advantageous non-agricultural self-employed, 3,225 for advantageous agricultural self-employed, 2,812 for unfavourable non-agricultural self employed, 2,651 for informal salaried employees, and 1,358 for unfavourable agricultural self-employed. In El Salvador, mean monthly earnings were 386 US dollars for formal salaried employees, 499 for advantageous non-agricultural self-employed, 242 for advantageous agricultural self-employed, 97 for unfavourable non-agricultural self employed, 185 for informal salaried employees, and 35 for unfavourable agricultural self-employed.

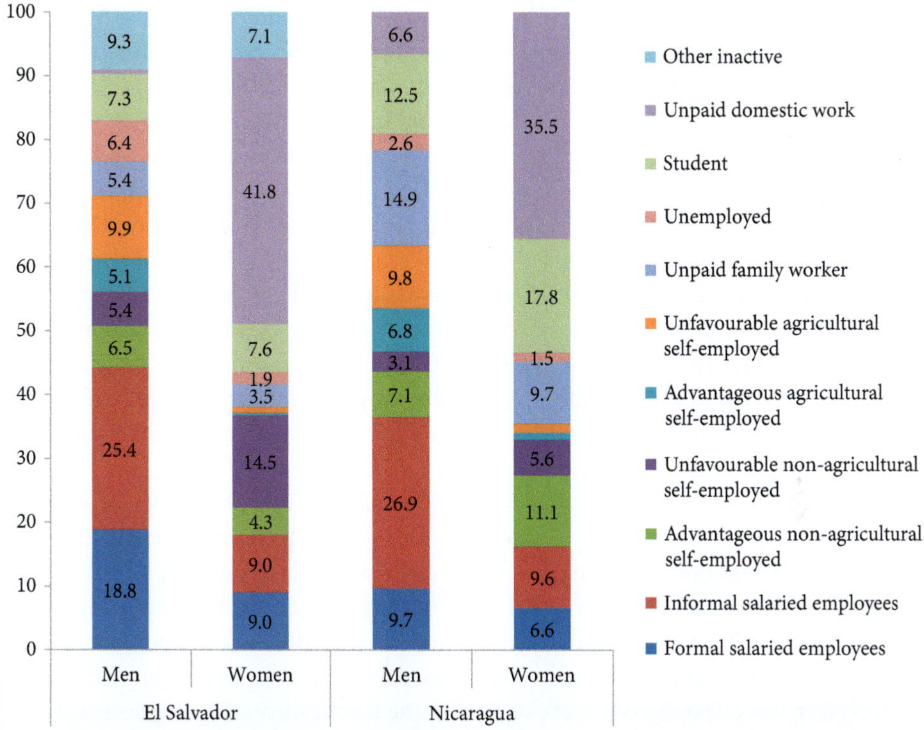

Fig. 8.1 Distribution of the working-age population according to their labour market state, comparison by country and gender
Source: authors' calculations based on the data described in section 3.

of women are in unpaid domestic work in El Salvador compared to Nicaragua. This may reflect a greater prevalence of these types of traditional family relationships between men and women in El Salvador compared to Nicaragua.

In both El Salvador and Nicaragua, men are more likely to be in advantageous labour market states compared to women. For example, men are more likely to be in formal salaried employment (the most advantageous labour market state). This is especially noticeable in El Salvador, where the formal sector is larger than in Nicaragua and men are almost twice as likely as women to be in this most advantageous sector. In El Salvador, it is more likely that men (compared to women) are in advantageous self-employment (non-agricultural or agricultural). In Nicaragua, where advantageous self-employed workers are those who live in families with incomes above the poverty line, it is more likely that women (compared to men) are in non-agricultural advantageous self-employment. This apparent inconsistency may be because in Nicaragua, many self-employed women live in households where the spouse earns above the poverty line but they earn very low wages themselves. The evidence from El Salvador supports this hypothesis; if we define 'advantageous' using the poverty line measure in both El Salvador and Nicaragua, then it is also true in El Salvador that women (compared to men) are more likely to be in advantageous self-employment (see the Appendix in the WIDER working paper version of this chapter, Alaniz et al. (2019)).

Women are more likely than men to be found in unfavourable non-agricultural self-employment in both Nicaragua and El Salvador. This may be because women in El Salvador and Nicaragua continue to have the primary responsibility for domestic work (childcare, etc.) even if they are working. Women may therefore be more likely to be in unfavourable self-employment in both El Salvador and Nicaragua because women value the flexibility of self-employment, in terms of hours and location of work, more than men. On the other hand, this may also reflect that the traditional division of labour between the sexes in Central America forces women into unfavourable employment, while men are free to spend more time searching for and working in advantageous labour market states.

While a substantial proportion of men are unemployed in both El Salvador and Nicaragua, few women are unemployed in either country. To be considered unemployed, one must not have a job and also be actively searching for a new one. It may be that when women lose their jobs, they do not spend very much time searching for a new one but rather move directly to unpaid domestic work or another sector, while men spend more time searching for advantageous employment before accepting less advantageous work or leaving the labour force. This suggests that policies focused on speeding up the transition from unemployment to advantageous employment are likely to have a larger impact on men than women (simply because a higher proportion of men are unemployed). On the other hand, policies focused on promoting the transition from unpaid domestic work into advantageous employment are likely to have a bigger impact on women than men (simply because more women are in this state).

Agriculture in both countries is dominated by men: almost no women are agricultural self-employed workers. This suggests that policies that promote advantageous agricultural self-employment will have little impact on the ability of women to obtain advantageous employment in El Salvador and Nicaragua.

A major focus of this study is to understand the mechanisms by which people in El Salvador and Nicaragua transition into and out of advantageous labour market states. Because we have panel data, which allows us to follow the same individuals and families from one year to the next, we can calculate how likely it is that a person will switch states (transitions). Figure 8.2 presents the magnitudes of mobility into each state; that is, Fig. 8.2 presents the proportion of our sample that transitions into each state from a different state the year before (excluded from Fig. 8.2 are those who remained in the same state). For men, the greatest mobility is into informal employment, followed by unemployment. For women, on the other hand, the greatest mobility is into unpaid domestic work, followed by non-agricultural self-employment (advantageous and unfavourable) and unpaid family work, then followed by informal employment. In both countries, there is

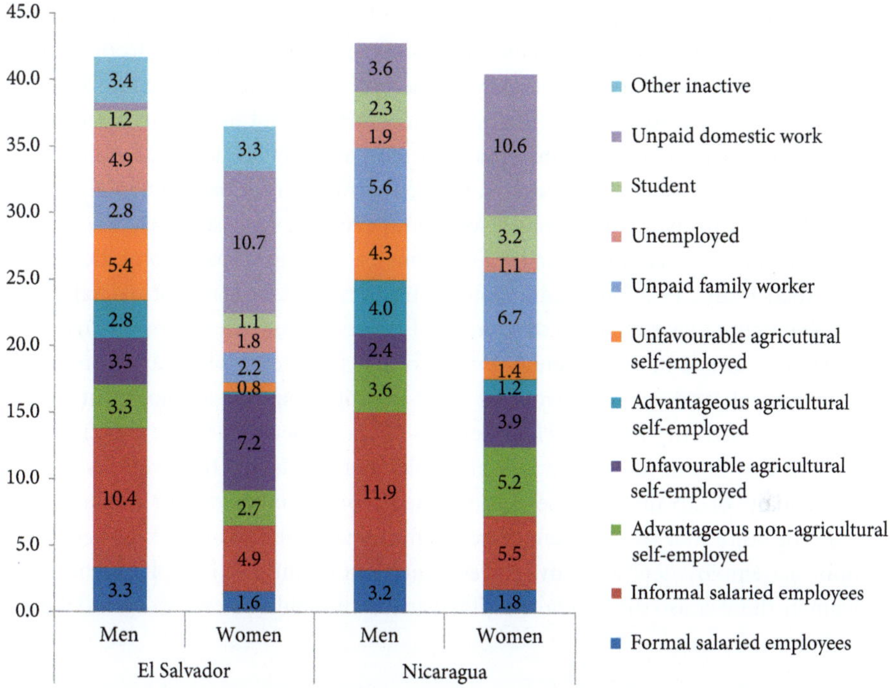

Fig. 8.2 Percentage of working-age population that transits to each state
Source: authors' calculations based on the data described in section 3.

less mobility of women into informal employment or unemployment and more mobility into self-employment compared to men. For women, there is more mobility into advantageous self-employment in Nicaragua compared to El Salvador. For both men and women, there is relatively little mobility into formal salaried employment.[7]

Figures 8.3a and b show the origins (one year before) of those found in the three advantageous labour market states. As noted before, there is very little mobility into or out of the most advantageous labour market state—formal salaried employment. Approximately 83 per cent (El Salvador) and 70 per cent (Nicaragua) of workers in formal salaried employment in one year were also in that sector the year before. This compares to approximately 40 per cent of men and 50 per cent of women (in both countries) who remain in advantageous non-agricultural

[7] The full transition matrices for both men and women and for both countries are presented in the appendix of the WIDER working paper version of this chapter (Alaniz et al. 2019). Using these tables, we also examined the relative magnitudes of the transitions out of advantageous labour market states. We do not present these figures in this chapter because the conclusions regarding mobility are the same as those in this paragraph; that is, the states that men and women are most likely to move into are also the states that men and woman are likely to move out of (see Tables A1–A4 in the WIDER working paper version of this chapter).

self-employment from one year to the next. Men and women who work as formal salaried employees tend to enter this sector soon after graduating from school (although not necessarily right away in the first year), and then remain in this sector. Of those who do enter formal salaried employment from other states, the largest number comes from informal salaried employment, followed by unemployment. Some women (but almost no men) also enter formal salaried employment directly from unpaid domestic work. Our evidence suggests that women may leave formal salaried employment for a time to take up unpaid domestic work and then return in a later year. Women may temporarily leave formal salaried employment to have children or for unpaid domestic work. Few men do this.

Almost no one of either gender enters formal salaried employment from self-employment, and very few workers enter advantageous self-employment from formal salaried employment. However, this does not mean that there is no mobility into and out of advantageous self-employment; it is just that workers move into and out of advantageous self-employment from other states. Our results show that, for both men and women, there is substantial mobility of workers between informal employment and advantageous non-agricultural self-employment. For women, there is also substantial mobility between unpaid domestic work and these

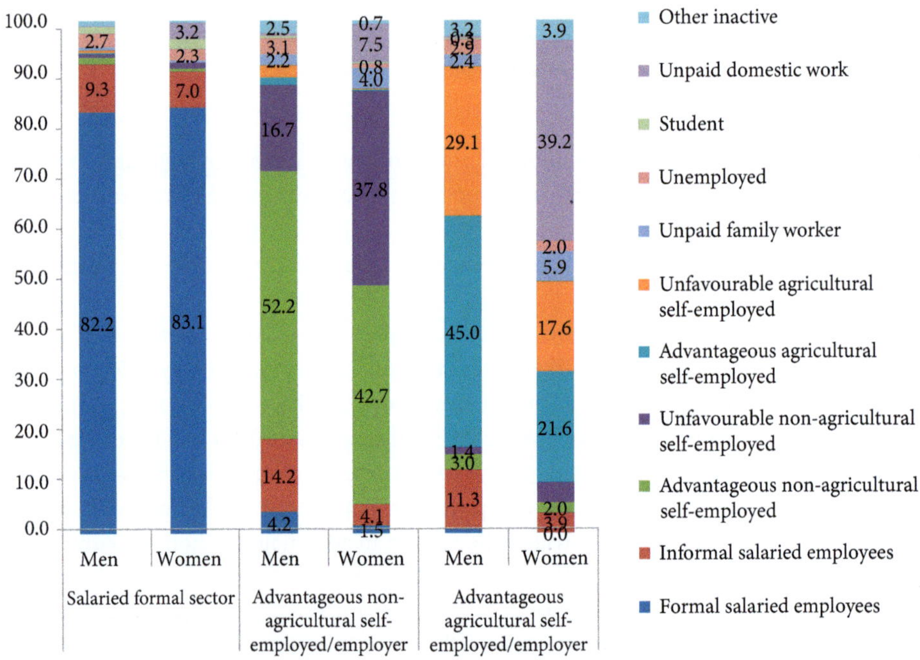

Fig. 8.3a Distribution of cases who transition into advantageous state according to their state of origin, comparison by gender, El Salvador

Source: authors' calculations based on the data described in section 3.

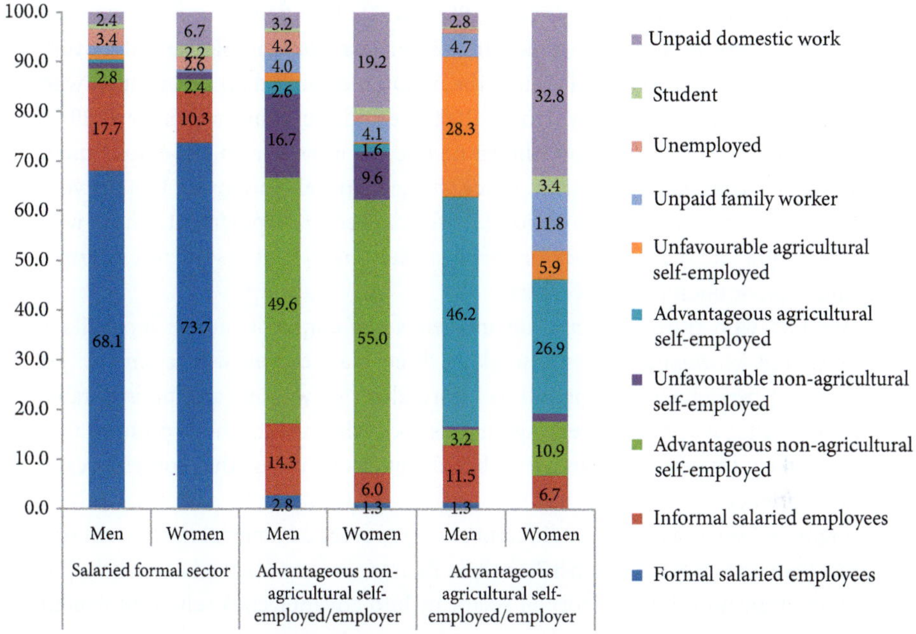

Fig. 8.3b Distribution of cases in each advantageous state according to their state of origin, comparison by gender, Nicaragua

Source: authors' calculations based on the data described in section 3.

two states—this is an important difference between men and women and reflects the fact that women have primary responsibility for childcare and other unpaid domestic work in both Nicaragua and El Salvador.

Most of the advantageous non-agricultural self-employed are older workers who gained experience working as informal salaried workers or unfavourable non-agricultural self-employment before succeeding as self-employed. As we will see, younger workers are more likely than older workers to transition into formal salaried employment, while, for older workers, the most likely transition into an advantageous labour market state is into advantageous non-agricultural self-employment. Men in advantageous non-agricultural self-employment are most likely to come from unfavourable self-employment (especially in El Salvador) or informal employment. In both El Salvador and Nicaragua, women in advantageous non-agricultural self-employment are also likely to come from unfavourable non-agricultural self-employment and informal employment. Women in advantageous self-employment are also likely to come from unpaid domestic work and unpaid family work.

Figures 8.2, 8.3a, and 8.3b summarize year-to-year moves by men and women between states. This may miss longer-term trends. In Nicaragua, we can follow the same individuals for longer than one year. Figure 8.4 presents the results of transitions over a three-year period (2009–2012). This figure confirms many of the conclusions from the year-to-year transition data. For example, we still see very little mobility into the formal sector; the majority of both men and women who are in formal salaried employment in 2009 are still found in that sector in 2012. Even over the four-year period, almost no one has moved from self-employment into formal salaried employment. Once workers are self-employed, there is very little chance that they will transition into formal-sector employment. Those who do transition into the formal sector are most likely to start out as students, informal employees, or unemployed workers.

Women who transition into advantageous self-employment are most likely to start out as unpaid domestic workers three years earlier, with a smaller yet significant percentage starting out as informal-sector workers and unfavourable non-agricultural self-employed. Again, this is consistent with the hypothesis that it is unlikely for self-employment to be advantageous unless the worker already has experience.

Figure 8.4 suggests a slightly different story about the advancement of recent students than do Figs 8.1, 8.2, and 8.3. In these figures, we found that it is not likely that workers transition into the formal sector or into advantageous self-employment

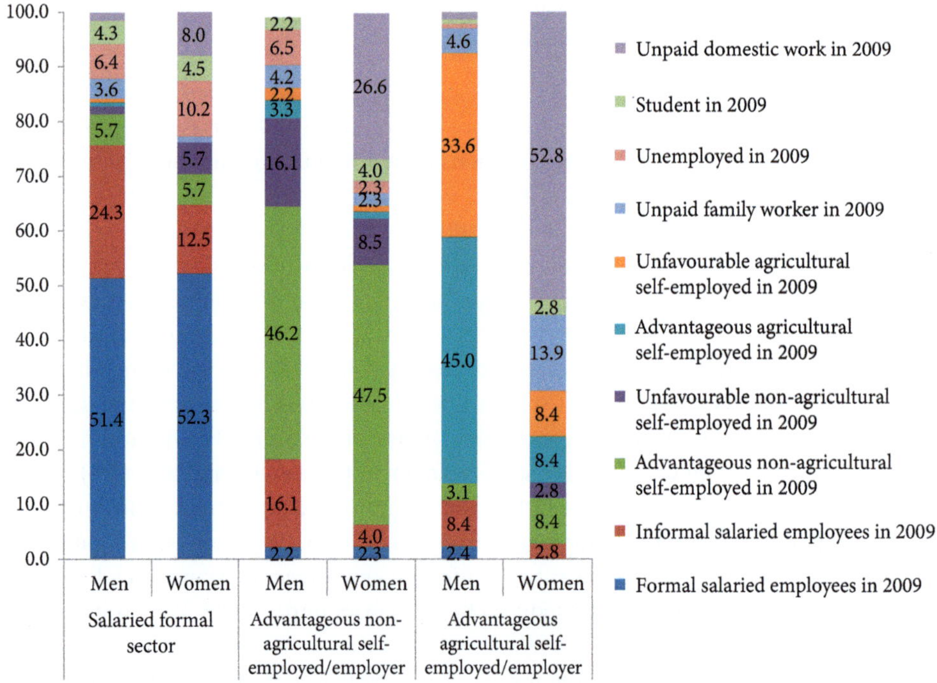

Fig. 8.4 Distribution of cases in each advantageous state in 2012, according to their initial state in 2009, comparison by gender, Nicaragua

Source: authors' calculations based on the data described in section 3.

directly from school. For both men and women, most students who leave school enter the informal sector or work as unpaid family workers the first year after leaving school (see the year-to-year transition matrices in the appendix). After three years, however, those who left school are much more likely to have become formal salaried employees and advantageous self-employed. These results suggest that men and women who leave school may take a short period of time before transitioning into salaried formal employment or advantageous self-employment. Both men and women may spend a short time unemployed and searching for work, as informal-sector employees or as unpaid family workers, before transitioning into the salaried formal sector or advantageous self-employment. Women are also likely to spend time out of the labour force directly following school before obtaining employment. This is consistent with the key role of education in obtaining formal salaried employment and advantageous self-employment, even though students may not find salaried formal employment immediately after graduation.

5. Variables correlated with mobility into advantageous labour market states

Next, we focus our study on the personal characteristics, family characteristics, and job characteristics that may help men and women to achieve advantageous jobs in the labour market. We use pooled data from El Salvador and Nicaragua and regression analysis to measure the impact of each personal, family, and job characteristic on the probability that a person moves up to an advantageous labour market state. Using a sample of workers in unfavourable states in time t, we estimate a probit equation of the form:

$$Prob(INADVANTit = 1) = f(\alpha o + X'it\beta + \sum_{t=1}^{T} \gamma_t YR_t + \mu_{it}). \qquad (1)$$

In this equation, $INADVANT_{it}$ equals one if the individual i is in an unfavourable state at time t but is in an advantageous state at time $t + 1$ and zero if the individual i is in an unfavourable state at time t and stays in an unfavourable state at time $t + 1$. We estimate equation (1) using probit regressions. X_{it} is the explanatory variables vector, which includes the variables described below in the text. In addition to these personal, family, and job characteristics, to control for year-specific factors such as aggregate supply and aggregate demand changes or design changes in the household surveys, we include a dummy variable for each year, YR_t. From the estimated coefficients, β_{it}, we can calculate the marginal impact of each explanatory variable on the probability of a transition from a not advantageous state to each advantageous labour market state.

The characteristics that we consider include: individual specific human capital variables (age, years of education); whether the individual lives in a high population density area; the relationship to the household head; change in the marital status, industry sector, household characteristics (number of young children, number of school age children, number of working-age household members, number of household members older than 65 years of age); whether the individual has access to public services (tube water and electricity); non-labour income of the family; and the amount of remittances.

According to previous studies, those with more human capital are more likely to be in the labour force and, if they work, are more likely to be full-time formal-sector employees (Duryea et al. 2006; Bosch and Maloney 2010; Cunningham and Bustos Salvagno 2011). We use age as a proxy for experience. Older workers with more experience (especially in the formal sector) are more likely to be successful entrepreneurs, while younger workers are more likely to be informal employees (Cunningham and Bustos Salvagno 2011). Some studies suggest that human capital is a more important factor in explaining success in the case of women entrepreneurs compared to men (Bardasi et al. 2011).

It has been argued that the reasons for becoming self-employed may differ between men and women; specifically, it has been argued that women become self-employed because they seek more flexible work schedules (Delmar and Davidson 2000). To examine this possibility, other explanatory variables include some that describe the structure of the family (marital status, number of young children, number of school-age children, number of working-age household members, and the household members older than 65 years of age). Others have argued that women start fewer businesses and are less successful than men because they have difficulty obtaining credit. If this were true, we would expect to find that women from households with higher income levels (and therefore with fewer restrictions for credit) tend to survive and grow as entrepreneurs. Therefore, we include non-labour income of the family and the amount of remittances.

It has also been found that the selection of economic activity differs between men and women entrepreneurs. Women entrepreneurs are predominantly concentrated in service activities, while men tend to be owners of companies engaged in manufacturing and construction activities (Bardasi et al. 2011). It has also been shown that in developing economies, women are less likely to operate in high-technology activities (Anna et al. 1999). To examine the role of the selection of economic activity as a determinant of success, the regressions include economic activity dummies as explanatory variables.

We also measure the impact of characteristics on the probability that a worker will leave an advantageous state. Specifically, using a sample of workers in advantageous states in time t, we estimate a probit equation of the form:

$$Prob(OUTADVANTit = 1) = f(\alpha o + X'it\beta + \sum_{t=1}^{T} \gamma_t YR_t + \mu_{it}). \quad (2)$$

In this equation, $OUTADVANT_{it}$ equals one if the individual i is in an advantageous state at time t but is not in an advantageous state at time $t + 1$ and zero if the individual i is in an advantageous state at time t and stays in advantageous state at time $t + 1$. X_{it} is the explanatory variables vector which includes the same variables as those in the previous estimated equation.

Our estimates of equations (1) and (2), estimated separately for men and women and for each advantageous labour market sector, are reported in Tables 8.3 and 8.4. A positive number in Table 8.3 indicates that an increase in the corresponding explanatory variable increases the probability of transitioning from an unfavourable state to each advantageous state indicated by the column of the table. A positive number in Table 8.4 indicates that an increase in the corresponding explanatory variable increases the probability of transitioning from an advantageous state to each unfavourable state indicated by the column of the table. In our discussion, we focus on those results that are statistically significant (which are starred, and where more stars indicate greater statistical significance).

Our findings suggest that education is the most important personal characteristic promoting transitions into non-agricultural advantageous labour market states and reducing transitions from advantageous labour market states. In particular, a complete secondary and a tertiary (post-secondary) education is a strong predictor of whether a man or woman transitions into and stays in the most advantageous labour market state—formal salaried employment. Both a tertiary education and a complete secondary education also promote advantageous non-agricultural self-employment.

The positive impact of education on transitions into advantageous labour market states is bigger for men than for women; that is, our results suggest that women need more education than men in order to get the same advantage in obtaining an advantageous labour market state. This result is consistent with Esquivel (2007), who finds that, on average, women in Latin America need substantially more education than men in order to obtain a job in the formal sector. This suggests that in El Salvador and Nicaragua even educated women are at a disadvantage relative to men when they seek to obtain advantageous employment.

Our results provide no evidence that education increases the probability of advantageous self-employment in agriculture. This does not mean that young people in rural areas do not benefit from education. More education increases the probability that everyone, including the children of farmers, enter non-agricultural advantageous labour market states.

Access to public services such as utilities (electricity, water, and electricity) significantly increases the probability that men or women will transition into advantageous non-agricultural self-employment.[8] This suggests that another policy to promote advantageous non-agricultural self-employment is for the government to provide these services to poor families.

[8] This result may be related to greater access to public services in urban areas compared to rural areas and the greater opportunities for urban workers (compared to rural workers) to transition to advantageous non-agricultural self-employment.

Table 8.3 Marginal effects on the probability of entering an advantageous state, comparison by gender

	Salaried formal sector		Advantageous non-agricultural self-employed		Advantageous agricultural self-employed	
	Men	Women	Men	Women	Men	Women
Number of observations	20,726	28,160	20,726	28,160	20,726	26,563
Pseudo R-squared	0.122	0.208	0.207	0.193	0.147	0.192
Log likelihood	−3,166	−2,007	−2,826	−3,527	−2,968	−589.3
Age	0.0037***	0.0007***	0.0033***	0.0030***	0.0031***	0.0002***
Age squared	−0.000049***	−0.00001***	−0.00003***	−0.00005***	−0.00003***	−0.000002***
Complete primary schooling	0.0153***	0.0057***	0.0066**	0.0071***	−0.0019	0.0003
Secondary schooling (incomplete)	0.0291***	0.0083***	0.0110***	0.0078***	−0.0062**	0.0001
Secondary schooling (complete)	0.0680***	0.0304***	0.0235***	0.0114***	−0.0051	0.0008
Some tertiary schooling	0.0881***	0.0443***	0.0230***	0.0178***	−0.0102***	Dropped
Household head	0.0025	−0.0004	0.0153***	0.0161***	0.0245***	0.0015
Spouse	0.0108	−0.0017**	0.0115*	0.0112***	0.0114	0.0002
Got married/found a companion	0.0100	0.0012	0.0066	0.0098	0.0004	0.0004
Got divorced/separated	0.0008	0.0046	0.0208**	0.0150**	−0.0079	0.0047*
High population density area	0.0176***	0.0065***	0.0023	0.0025	−0.0191***	−0.0010***
Manufacture/construction	0.0070**	0.0099***	0.0467***	0.0532***	−0.0199***	−0.0010***
Commerce	0.0152***	0.0023**	0.0727***	0.0869***	−0.0223***	−0.0010***
High-complexity services	0.0493***	0.0136***	0.0373***	0.0125***	−0.0175***	−0.0010***

Low-complexity services	0.0047***	0.0025***	0.0060***	0.0050***	−0.0065***	−0.0009
Young children (0–6 years old)	0.0015	−0.0001	0.0001	0.0005	0.0007	−0.0001
School-age children (7–18 years old)	−0.0002	−0.0004*	−0.0016***	−0.0010**	0.0001	−0.0001
Working-age members (19–65 years old)	0.0017**	0.0004*	−0.0002	−0.0010*	0.0009	−0.0001
Older members (older than 65 years)	−0.0015	−0.0011*	−0.0057***	−0.0009	0.0012	−0.0002
Tubed water inside the dwelling	0.0121***	0.0008	0.0073***	0.0028	−0.0062*	−0.0007
Tubed water outside the dwelling	0.0042*	0.0016**	0.0045***	0.0011	−0.0051**	0.0000
Electricity network	0.0011	0.0003	0.0125***	0.0115***	0.0011	−0.0018***
Total amount of monthly remittances	−0.2190**	0.0019	0.0122	0.0271	0.3120***	0.0115
Dummy Nicaragua	0.0166***	0.0081***	0.0391***	0.0774***	0.0066	0.0053**
Dummy 2010	0.0003	0.0001	0.0031	0.0017	0.0044*	0.0012*
Dummy 2011	−0.0028	0.0005	0.0033	0.0078***	0.0031	0.0002
Dummy 2010 *Nicaragua	−0.0038	−0.0029***	−0.0045	−0.0062***	−0.0013	−0.0004
Dummy 2011 *Nicaragua	0.0002	−0.0026***	−0.0102***	−0.0094***	0.0010	0.0009

Note: *significant at 10 per cent, **significant at 5 per cent, ***significant at 1 per cent.
Source: authors' calculations based on the data described in section 3.

Table 8.4 Marginal effects on the probability of leaving an advantageous state, comparison by gender

	Salaried formal sector		Advantageous non-agricultural self-employed		Advantageous agricultural self-employed	
	Men	**Women**	**Men**	**Women**	**Men**	**Women**
Number of observations	4,580	2,741	1,794	1,903	1,569	123
Pseudo R-squared	0.0805	0.0874	0.056	0.0448	0.0242	0.356
Log likelihood	−1873	−1041	−1155	−1260	−1060	−51.3
Age	−0.017***	−0.0246***	−0.0290***	−0.0221***	−0.0121**	−0.0389
Age squared	0.0002050***	0.000273***	0.0003160***	0.0002070***	0.0001140**	0.0003010
Complete primary schooling	0.014	0.0248	−0.0190	−0.0320	−0.1020**	−0.2700
Secondary schooling (incomplete)	−0.037**	−0.0437*	−0.0286	−0.0790**	−0.1010**	Dropped
Secondary schooling (complete)	−0.077***	−0.0467*	−0.0739*	−0.0692	−0.1620**	Dropped
Some tertiary schooling	−0.089***	−0.0747***	−0.1840***	−0.1090**	−0.1690*	Dropped
Household head	−0.119***	0.023	−0.1490***	−0.1290***	−0.1850***	0.1020
Spouse	−0.033	0.0281	−0.1510**	−0.0557	−0.0988	0.2980*
Got married/found a companion	−0.021	0.0106	−0.0738	0.0181	−0.0877	−0.0041
Got divorced/separated	0.060	0.0628	0.0404	−0.0826	−0.0049	−0.5710
High population density area	−0.014	−0.0245*	0.0337	−0.0006	0.0829	−0.0367
Manufacture/construction	−0.053**	−0.0955***	−0.0303	−0.1780***	Dropped	Dropped
Commerce	−0.033	−0.0566*	−0.1420**	−0.2400***	Dropped	Dropped

High-complexity services	−0.059***	−0.062**	−0.0565	−0.1090	Dropped	Dropped
Low-complexity services	−0.025***	−0.0351***	−0.0288*	−0.0532**	Dropped	Dropped
Young children (0–6 years old)	−0.004	0.0023	−0.0588***	−0.0036	−0.0162	0.0427
School-age children (7–18 years old)	0.006	0.00701	−0.0013	0.0031	0.0093	−0.0976**
Working-age members (19–65 years old)	−0.008*	−0.00178	0.0245**	0.0154	0.0010	0.1390***
Older members (older than 65 years)	0.002	0.0248*	−0.0310	−0.0038	0.0042	0.2570*
Tubed water inside the dwelling	−0.065*	−0.0365	−0.0577	−0.0582	−0.0666	−0.1240
Tubed water outside the dwelling	−0.012	−0.0145	−0.0775**	−0.0544	−0.0002	−0.1980
Electricity network	−0.025	−0.0253	−0.1380***	−0.1310***	−0.0155	0.1270
Total amount of monthly remittances	1.238	0.0152	−0.2860	−0.5590	−0.3910	−1.2070
Dummy Nicaragua	−0.077***	−0.0518	−0.0957	−0.2130***	−0.1010*	−0.8830***
Dummy 2010	−0.010	−0.0338**	0.0188	0.0454	0.0030	−0.2940
Dummy 2011	−0.029**	−0.0155	0.0565*	0.0643*	−0.0372	−0.6300***
Dummy 2010 *Nicaragua	0.045	0.0419	−0.0075	−0.0094	−0.0168	0.2940
Dummy 2011 *Nicaragua	0.103**	0.0341	−0.0158	−0.0339	0.0240	0.4200***

Note: Dropped/dropped because of collinearity or because it predicts success(failure) perfectly; *significant at 10 per cent, **significant at 5 per cent, ***significant at 1 per cent.
Source: authors' calculations based on the data described in section 3.

For both men and women, dependent children in a household reduces the probability of a transition into advantageous non-agricultural self-employment and increases the probability that a woman will leave advantageous non-agricultural self-employment.

In general, our results suggest that receiving more international remittances decreases the probability of men transitioning into formal salaried employment and decreases the probability that they will leave the private salaried employment. This may be because these workers are substituting leisure for labour now that the increase in non-labour income makes this affordable. On the other hand, remittances and other non-labour income promote advantageous agricultural self-employment for men; receiving more remittances and other non-labour income increases the probability of transitioning into advantageous agricultural self-employment and decreases the probability of transitioning out of this advantageous state. This may be because the inflow of money helps fund capital, inventories, or training for small businesses.

Older workers are more likely to become successfully self-employed than are younger workers; the probability of transitioning into advantageous self-employment increases with age until men are about 50 years old and women are about 30 years old. After the age of 30 for women and 50 for men, the probability of becoming successful in non-agricultural self-employment decreases with age. This suggests that the most likely age at which people enter advantageous non-agricultural self-employment for men is in the mid-to-late 40s. On the other hand, the age at which people are most likely to transition into the formal salaried sector is at a much lower age; the maximum probability of transitioning into the private formal sector is the high 30s for men and the low 30s for women. This again suggests that workers enter formal employment soon after leaving school, while those who are successful in self-employment gain experience first before becoming successful in non-agricultural self-employment. The probability that a worker leaves formal employment is largest for those in their mid-40s (for both men and women). This is also consistent with the conclusion that the best age to transition into advantageous self-employment is in the mid-to-late 40s.

For men and women, those who transition into both formal salaried employment and advantageous non-agricultural self-employment (and are least likely to transition out of these advantageous sectors) work in the industry sectors of manufacturing, construction, commerce, and services (vs agriculture, forestry, and mining). The magnitudes of the impact of sector of employment are similar for men and women except in high-complexity services. Our results imply that advantageous self-employed men are more likely than women to come from high-complexity services. This is consistent with Anna et al. (1999), who present evidence that in developing economies, entrepreneurial women are less likely to operate in high-technology activities.

6. Conclusions and policy implications

The most advantageous labour market state in El Salvador and Nicaragua is formal salaried employment. Those in this state are among the highest paid and have access to social security medical care. Most people enter this state soon after graduating from school and remain in this state for a long time; 80 per cent of formal employees in El Salvador and 70 per cent in Nicaragua remain as formal employees from year to year, and very few older workers transition from non-advantageous labour market states into formal salaried employment. A complete secondary and post-secondary (tertiary) education are particularly useful for obtaining formal salaried employment and significantly reduce the probability of leaving this work status. These results suggest that there should be clear efforts to reduce school drop-out rates, especially among girls, and to promote secondary school completion through alternative programmes for those already outside of the school system.

Improving educational outcomes for women is necessary but not sufficient to promote the success of women in the labour market. For example, our results suggest that women need higher levels of education than men in order to access advantageous formal salaried employment. Other factors also hold women back from obtaining advantageous employment. In our discussions with policymakers and civil society activists in El Salvador and Nicaragua, one barrier to the success of women in the labour market that was mentioned frequently was domestic violence against women. This suggests that programmes to change social norms against traditional stereotypes of the role of women are important for improving access of women to advantageous employment.

The focus of any policy to increase education levels will be on the young. Our results suggest that it is not likely that older people who are in informal salaried employment, self-employed, or are in unpaid domestic work will transition into formal salaried employment, even if they obtain more education. This suggests that most progress towards expanding advantageous employment, especially formal salaried employment, will be intergenerational; that is, those currently self-employed will not become formal-sector employees but their children may.

Our results suggest that access to electricity, potable water, sanitation, and schools is particularly important in promoting transitions from unfavourable states into all advantageous sectors. This suggests that it may be important for these public services to be widely provided.

Women who transition into advantageous self-employment are most likely to have unpaid domestic worker as a previous job, possibly their first job. This suggests that policies focused on promoting the transition from unpaid domestic work into advantageous employment, such as vocational training or assistance to stay in school, are likely to have a bigger impact on women than men (simply because more women are in this state).

While a substantial proportion of men are unemployed in both El Salvador and Nicaragua, few women are unemployed in either country. To be considered unemployed, one must not have a job and also be actively searching for a new one. It may be that when women lose their jobs, they do not spend very much time searching for a new one but rather move directly to unpaid domestic work or another sector, while men spend more time searching for advantageous employment before accepting less advantageous work or leaving the labour force. This suggests that policies focused on speeding up the transition from unemployment to advantageous employment, such as job search assistance, are likely to have a larger impact on men than women (simply because a higher proportion of men are unemployed).

Agriculture in both countries is dominated by men: almost no women are agricultural self-employed workers. This suggests that policies that promote advantageous agricultural self-employment will have little impact on the ability of women to obtain advantageous employment in El Salvador and Nicaragua.

Both men and women are more likely to transition into advantageous non-agricultural self-employment when they are older and have more working experience. For both men and women, those who transition into advantageous non-agricultural self-employment are most likely to come from informal employment or unfavourable non-agricultural self-employment and not formal salaried employment. These conclusions suggest that policies to promote advantageous self-employment should be targeted towards older workers who already have some relevant work experience and should target those currently working as informal employees or unfavourable non-agricultural self-employed and not formal salaried employees.

References

Alaniz, E., G. Carrión, and T.H. Gindling (2015). 'Moving In and Moving Up: Labor Market Dynamics of Women and Men in Nicaragua'. Fundación Internacional para el Desafío (FIDEG) Working paper 012014. Managua, Nicaragua: FIDEG.

Alaniz, E., A. Espino and T.H. Gindling (2019). 'Self-Employment And Labour Market Dynamics Of Men And Women In El Salvador And Nicaragua'. WIDER Working Paper 2019/97. Helsinki: UNU-WIDER.

Anna, A.L., G.N. Chandler, E. Jansen, and N.P. Mero (1999). 'Women Business Owners in Traditional and Non-traditional Industries'. *Journal of Business Venturing*, 5(3): 279–303.

Bardasi, E., S. Sabarwal, and K. Terrell (2011). 'How Do Female Entrepreneurs Perform? Evidence from Three Developing Regions'. *Small Business Economics*, 37: 414–441. https://doi.org/10.1007/s11187-011-9374-z.

Beneke de Sanfelú, M., T.H. Gindling, L.E. Vázquez, J.A. Oliva Cepeda, and S.M. Delgado Vides (2015). 'Moving In and Moving Up: Labor Market Dynamics of Women and Men in El Salvador'. FIDEG Working Paper 022014. Managua, Nicaragua: FIDEG.

Bosch, M., and W. Maloney (2010). 'Comparative Analysis of Labor Market Dynamics Using Markov Processes: An Application to Informality'. *Labour Economics*, 17(4): 621–631.

Cunningham, W., and J. Bustos Salvagno (2011). 'Youth Employment Transitions in Latin America'. Policy Research Working Paper No. 5521. Washington, DC: World Bank.

Delmar, F., and P. Davidson (2000). 'Where Do They Come From? Prevalence and Characteristics of Nascent Entrepreneurs'. *Entrepreneurship and Regional Development*, 12: 1–23.

Duryea, S., G. Marquez, C. Pages, and S. Scarpetta (2006). 'For Better or Worse? Job and Earnings Mobility in Nine Middle- and Low-Income Countries'. In S.M. Collins and C. Graham (eds), *Brookings Trade Forum 2006: Global Labor Markets?* Washington, DC: Brookings Institution Press: 187–209.

Esquivel, V. (2007). 'Género y Diferenciales de Salarios en la Argentina'. In: M. Novick and H.Palomino (coordinators), *Estructura Productiva y Empleo: Un Enfoque Transversal.* Buenos Aires: Ministerio de Trabajo, Empleo y Seguridad Social: 363–392.

SEDLAC (2017). 'Socio-Economic Data Base for Latin America and the Caribbean'. Available at: www.cedlas.econo.unlp.edu.ar/wp/en/estadisticas/sedlac (accessed 27 September 2022).

9

Informal work in urban Mexico

Characteristics, dynamics, and workers' preferences

Robert Duval-Hernández

1. Introduction

In urban Mexico, around half of the employed population works in informal jobs.[1] This large group of informal workers is, however, far from homogeneous. Not only do they differ among themselves in terms of socio-economic characteristics, but they also have different reasons for being informally employed.

This chapter has two goals. First, it studies the heterogeneity in employment in urban Mexico, analysing the different employment status groups that characterize it as well as the dynamics across such status groups. Second, it uses a special module of the 2015 Labour Force Survey to distinguish the workers that participate voluntarily in informal employment from those that are informal due to a lack of better options in the market. More specifically, it estimates the share of informal workers that would rather be in formal wage-employment and it describes their characteristics.

Like other studies in this volume, the present chapter distinguishes between six different work status groups: formal wage-employment, formal self-employment, upper-tier informal wage work, upper-tier informal self-employment, lower-tier informal wage work and lower-tier informal self-employment (see Chapter 2 for a discussion of this typology).

The analysis of the different employment status groups reveals the existence of a job ladder, where better-paying jobs are found in formal employment, followed by those in the upper tier of informal employment, while at the bottom of the ladder are the lower-tier jobs. About half of the employed urban population are formally employed, almost one-third are in lower-tier informal jobs, and the rest are in upper-tier informal jobs. Eight out of nine formal workers are wage-employees. In contrast, one in three informal workers are in self-employment, irrespective of tier.

[1] I would like to thank Gary S. Fields, T. H. Gindling, Kunal Sen, Simone Schotte, Michael Danquah, and seminar participants at the project workshops as well as two anonymous referees for their valuable comments. The opinions and views here expressed are my own and do not represent those of my employer or of UNU-WIDER.

Robert Duval-Hernández, *Informal work in urban Mexico.* In: *The Job Ladder.* Edited by Gary S. Fields, T. H. Gindling, Kunal Sen, Michael Danquah, and Simone Schotte, Oxford University Press. © UNU-WIDER (2023).
DOI: 10.1093/oso/9780192867339.003.0009

As one moves down the job ladder, the workers' years of schooling decrease on average. In addition, within each segment (formal, upper-tier, and lower-tier) the self-employed have higher earnings than the corresponding wage-employees in their segment, probably because the self-employed are older and because their reported earnings likely capture payments to both labour and capital productive factors.

The analysis of employment and earnings dynamics over the course of a year show that there is little employment mobility at the top (formal) and bottom (lower tier) of the job ladder. An analysis of the conditional correlates of employment transitions indicates that lower-tier wage-employment serves as an entry state to the labour market, while transitions into self-employment increase with age. Males are more likely to experience upward transitions in the job ladder, and this is particularly true for married men, while the opposite occurs for married women. Schooling is a strong correlate of accessing formal jobs and, as expected, movements up the job ladder involve positive earnings changes.

The analysis of stated preferences reveals that around 80 per cent of the respondents who lack social security coverage would prefer to have a job with such benefits, even if that entailed having to pay the corresponding contributions for them. As argued below, this number likely reflects a preference for the entire set of characteristics that accompany a formal job rather than a preference for social security coverage per se, and this suggests that a large fraction of the urban informal workers in Mexico are not voluntarily so.

In summary, the results from the analysis of stated preferences for formal wage-employment contrast with the view put forward by a strand of the literature which considers that most informal workers in Mexico prefer an informal job over a formal one (see, for instance, Maloney 1999, 2004). Not only are urban Mexican labour markets stratified along very heterogeneous status groups, but also a large fraction of workers would rather move out of informal employment.

The rest of the chapter is organized as follows. Section 2 presents an overview of the structure of urban labour markets in Mexico. In section 3, the analysis of employment and earnings dynamics is presented. Section 4 discusses the evidence on the valuation of formal jobs and section 5 concludes.

2. A descriptive view of Mexican urban labour markets

This section presents an overview of the structure of Mexican urban labour markets, with an emphasis on the heterogeneity of the different segments it comprises. More precisely, it presents the main characteristics of six types of workers: formal wage-employees, formal self-employed, upper-tier wage-employees, upper-tier self-employed, lower-tier wage-employees, and lower-tier self-employed. As discussed in Chapter 2 of this volume, this taxonomy has three defining dimensions, namely: (i) it distinguishes between formal and informal status; (ii) it distinguishes between wage-employees and the self-employed; and (iii) it creates two tiers (upper and lower) within the informal status, where the upper tier is more likely composed of informal work with higher remunerations, with barriers to entry and, therefore, this tier is more likely to be a segment of the market where workers participate voluntarily.

The operationalization of these categories for the Mexican case is summarized in Table 9.1. While there is no universal definition of what constitutes an 'informal job', in the case of Mexico, two dimensions have been used as defining characteristics to establish whether a job is formal or not.[2] In the case of wage-employees, the defining criterion for distinguishing between formal and informal workers is whether the job offers social security coverage. For the self-employed,

Table 9.1 Work status definition and operationalization, the case of Mexico

Work status group	Definition/operationalization
Formal self-employed	These are the self-employed (own-account or owners) who operate a business registered with tax authorities and with fixed work premises. Also, all employers (with at least one employee) in the agricultural sector enter this category.
Upper-tier informal self-employed	These (own-account and owners) are those who voluntarily enrol for social security coverage (through the government or have private insurance), or work in a profession that requires post-secondary or vocational education, or they are employers with at least one employee, or their place of work has fixed premises.
Lower-tier informal self-employed	These include all other self-employed not in the above two categories. This includes all self-employed working in agriculture.
Formal wage-employees	These include those whose employers contribute to social security, except if the employer itself is a non-registered business (i.e. the firm is not registered with tax authorities and does not have fixed work premises).
Upper-tier informal wage-employees	These are wage-employees whose employers do not contribute to social security (or if they do, the employer itself is a non-registered business) *but* who receive other benefits such as paid annual leave, profit sharing, (government-sponsored) housing credit, day-care facilities, private insurance (life or health), saving funds, time for parental care, or *aguinaldo* (mandatory one-month salary bonus in December), or work in a profession that requires post-secondary or vocational education, or they have a permanent contract.
Lower-tier informal wage-employees	These include all other employees. Also, all unpaid workers are included in this category.

Source: author's illustration.

[2] See, for instance, Levy (2018). See also Fields (2011) and Ruppert Bulmer (2018) for thoughtful discussions of the many definitions that the term 'informality' takes in the literature.

the formality status of a business is determined by whether it is registered with tax authorities and has fixed work premises (see, for instance, INEGI 2014).[3] This second criterion is relevant because Mexican law does not mandate self-employed individuals to register themselves for social security coverage.[4]

The self-employed in the upper tier are those who: (i) are employers (i.e. with employees of their own), (ii) have a place of work with fixed premises, (iii) voluntarily enrol in a social security scheme, or (iv) work in an occupation that requires post-secondary education.[5] Similarly, wage-employees in the upper tier are those in skilled occupations, those with a permanent contract, or those who, although they do not receive social security coverage, receive other fringe benefits at work. All other informal workers are classified in their corresponding lower tier, depending on whether they are wage-employees or self-employed.[6]

Table 9.2 presents descriptive statistics for a representative sample of the different worker categories outlined above, as well as for the unemployed and those out of the labour force in large urban areas in 2015.[7] The table shows that about half of the employed population are formally employed, almost one-third are in lower-tier informal jobs, and the rest are in upper-tier informal jobs. Most formal workers are wage-employees, as the self-employed represent only one-ninth of the formal employed population. In contrast, one in three informal jobs are in self-employment, irrespective of tier.

The self-employed are, on average, 10 years older than wage-employees, and there are more males in formal employment and upper-tier self-employment, while the gender distribution is more balanced in the other segments of the market and among the unemployed. Schooling decreases monotonically as one moves down the job ladder from formal employment to upper-tier and, last, to

[3] A registered self-employed person working in a business without fixed work premises is classified as informal. In addition, all employers in agriculture with at least one employee are considered formal. In this chapter, this type of employer is less relevant as it focuses its analysis only on large urban areas. The criteria for distinguishing formal work are those used by the Mexican Statistical Agency, Instituto Nacional de Estadística y Geografía (INEGI 2014) in agreement with the guidelines set by the International Labour Organization (ILO). It should be noted that under the classification adopted by INEGI, there can be informal workers employed in the formal sector but not the other way around. A business is considered part of the formal sector if it is a registered entity for legal and tax purposes. For more details, see INEGI (2014).

[4] They can register voluntarily in a government-sponsored social security scheme. Few of them do so, however.

[5] I use the Labour Force Survey to find the four-digit occupations where the majority of workers have post-secondary or vocational education. These include most of the managerial, professional, and technical occupations of the International Standard Classification of Occupations (ISCO) classification, and a few select others.

[6] All unpaid employees are classified as lower-tier informal wage-employees.

[7] The data used for this table is the Labour Force Survey (Encuesta Nacional de Ocupación y Empleo, ENOE) (INEGI 2015a) and I use geographical and temporal criteria to make it comparable with the module that is analysed in section 4 of the chapter. Large, urban centres are those with a population of 100,000 or more. Comparable statistics for the entire country are available upon request from the author. To the extent that informality has been traditionally conceived as being an urban phenomenon, little is lost through this narrower geographical focus. Furthermore, the module which enquires about preferences for social security in section 4 is representative only at the level of large, urban centres. All the estimates in this chapter are weighted using sampling weights.

Table 9.2 Descriptive statistics of Mexican labour markets, 2015, large urban centres

	Formal employment		Upper-tier informal		Lower-tier informal		Unemployed	Out of labour force
	Wage-employed	Self-employed	Wage-employed	Self-employed	Wage-employed	Self-employed		
Percentage	46.9	5.8	10.1	5.6	20.3	11.3	5.2	39.0
Years of age	37.9	46.6	36.2	45.1	36.6	46.6	32.5	41.6
Male (%)	60.2	71.7	54.2	67.3	55.0	54.2	56.7	29.0
Years of schooling	12.3	13.2	11.1	10.1	8.7	8.2	11.4	9.3
Schooling level (%)								
Elementary	8.6	10.5	16.9	25.8	30.7	38.0	10.8	26.82
Intermediate	54.4	37.2	52.8	53.3	61.8	55.4	60.3	56.1
Higher	37.0	52.4	30.2	20.9	7.5	6.6	28.9	17.08
Enrolled in school (%)	5.2	2.2	10.0	3.0	10.0	2.1	10.8	29.5
Married (%)	46.9	64.7	34.3	54.4	36.1	50.3	24.0	39.8
Occupation (%)								
Managers	7.5	12.1	3.4	1.5	0.1	0.0		
Professionals	28.7	34.4	34.9	35.0	1.4	0.0		
Clerical	15.6	0.7	12.1	1.4	2.3	0.1		
Sales	10.5	29.7	10.0	26.3	19.7	27.8		
Services	8.5	8.0	8.2	12.6	11.9	9.8		
Manual	4.2	10.0	7.3	20.0	13.4	28.6		
Operators	15.0	3.5	6.4	0.9	11.1	7.5		

Elementary	10.1	1.6	17.7	2.4	40.2	26.2
Industry (%)						
Primary	1.4	1.3	0.7	0.0	1.7	2.4
Construction	4.4	4.6	5.8	12.4	11.9	11.1
Manufacturing	23.2	8.4	10.8	10.1	13.2	9.7
Trade	15.9	31.2	11.5	26.9	22.1	44.0
Communication	6.1	4.9	3.7	0.7	9.2	8.1
Business services	13.5	21.9	16.4	10.3	3.5	3.5
Education	10.5	1.5	7.6	4.1	0.6	0.0
Health	6.1	7.0	6.1	3.0	0.8	0.0
Personal services	8.3	19.2	32.3	32.6	36.2	21.3
Public admin.	10.7	0.0	5.1	0.0	0.7	0.0
Public sector (%)	24.9	0.0	9.9	0.0	1.7	0.0
Social security (%)	100	0.1	0.0	0.0	0.0	0.0
Earnings	7,576	10,598	5,201	5,589	3,085	3,667

Note: The definitions of the different work status groups follow the criteria in Table 9.1. The percentages are the shares of total employment in columns 1–6, the unemployment rate in column 7, and the population out of the labour force as a percentage of the total working-age population in column 8. Earnings are measured in 2015 Mexican pesos per month and include individuals with zero earnings. All estimates use sampling weights.
Source: author's calculations based on ENOE 2nd quarter 2015, large urban areas for individuals aged fifteen years and more (INEGI 2015a).

lower-tier informal employment. However, the unemployed are not the least-educated workers, and they have comparable education levels to those of workers in the upper-tier informal segment. This indicates that, in Mexico, the unemployed are not necessarily the worst-off workers but, rather, a group that can 'afford' to keep searching for better jobs without having to enter into informal employment as a last-resort option. Also, very few self-employed are still enrolled in school, while this share is 10 per cent among informal wage-employees. Finally, the statistics show that informal wage-employees are more likely to be single than the rest of the employed population.

In terms of occupation and industry, certain categories, such as managerial, professional, and clerical occupations, as well as jobs in manufacturing, business services, education, and health are over-represented in the formal and upper-tier segments of the market. In contrast, jobs in personal services are over-represented in informal employment, especially at the lower tier. As expected, most public-sector workers are formal, but even this sector hires some wage-employees informally. Finally, as previously mentioned, only a small fraction of the formal self-employed voluntarily choose to contribute to a social security scheme.

The last row of Table 9.2 presents the average earnings for each group of workers. These numbers are reproduced in Fig. 9.1. Two patterns are visible in the figure. First, earnings fall as one moves down the job ladder and, second, within

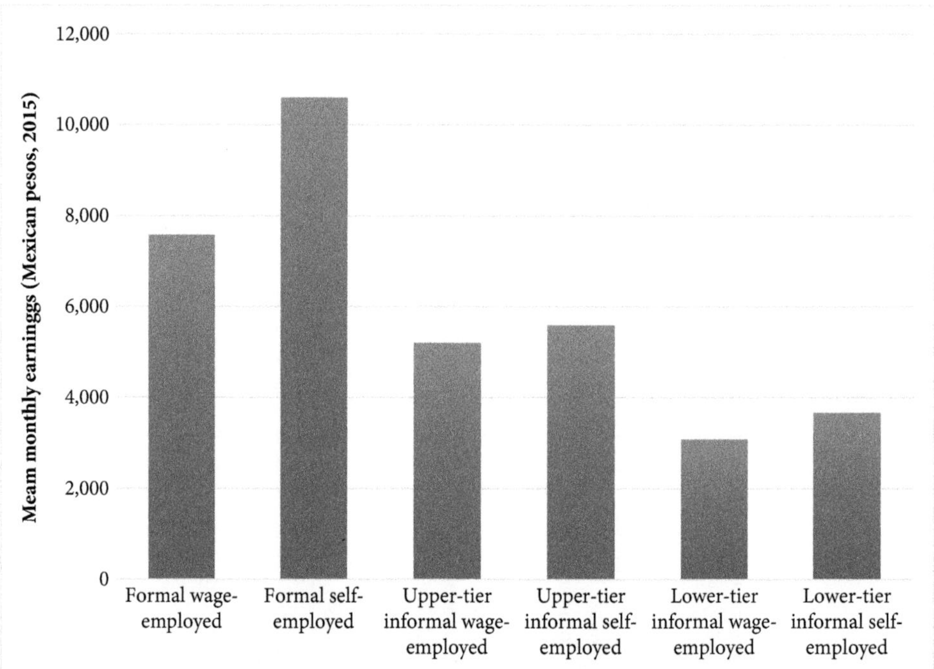

Fig. 9.1 Mean earnings by work status

Note: All estimates use sampling weights.
Source: author's calculations based on ENOE 2nd quarter 2015, large urban areas (INEGI 2015a).

each segment (formal, upper-tier, and lower-tier), the self-employed have higher earnings than the corresponding wage-employees in their segment. There may be two reasons for this last pattern: first, on average, the self-employed are older and thus have more experience; and second, their reported earnings likely capture payments to both labour and capital productive factors, especially for those self-employed operating in the formal sector.

3. Employment transitions and earnings dynamics

The descriptive analysis of section 2 can be complemented by studying the transitions across the six employment status groups under consideration. Table 9.3 presents panel data evidence on these transitions over a period of one year for those workers who were employed during both the initial and final periods.[8] Several interesting findings arise from this table. First, formal wage-employees have the highest share of stayers among all groups (87.4 per cent), reflecting the greater job security enjoyed by these workers and the fact that they are at the top of the job ladder and are therefore less likely to change jobs willingly. In contrast, the greatest turnover is found among upper-tier informal workers, with about 34 per cent staying in their original employment category after one year.[9] Of the upper-tier movers, about half move down the job ladder to lower-tier informal employment. The fact that lower-tier informal workers have a large share of stayers, second only to formal wage-employees, implies that not only do these workers have the worst jobs, but they also have a small chance of moving out to a better segment of the market.[10]

The individual-level correlates of these transitions are analysed through the estimation of multinomial logit models, one for each initial employment status. The dependent variable in these models is a categorical variable of the six employment status destinations one year later. The correlates studied are age (and its square), gender and marital status and their interaction, years of education, and enrolment in school. In addition, the models include a set of city dummies to control for local labour market conditions. To facilitate the interpretation of the results of the models, instead of directly presenting the parameter estimates, Figs 9.2–9.4 present the average marginal effects for each correlate. These effects measure the average change in a given transition probability when a correlate increases marginally or, in the case of a discrete correlate, when this variable changes values, holding other factors constant.[11]

[8] A full transition matrix, including transitions into unemployment and out of the labour force, is available from the author upon request.

[9] This fraction of stayers increases to around 40 per cent if we consider transitions between wage-employment and self-employment *within the same tier*.

[10] More specifically, around 58 per cent of lower-tier informal workers remain in their original employment category, and this fraction increases to around 66–77 per cent if we consider transitions between wage-employment and self-employment *within the same tier*.

[11] The original parameter estimates of the multinomial logit models are available upon request from the author.

Table 9.3 One-year transitions across work status

				1st quarter 2016						Share of stayers
				Self-employed			Wage-employed			
				Formal	Informal		Formal	Informal		
					Upper-tier	Lower-tier		Upper-tier	Lower-tier	
1st quarter 2015	Self-employed	Formal		52.73	15.28	7.11	10.13	6.04	8.71	3.54
		Informal	Upper-tier	18.47	35.26	16.99	5.81	6.77	16.7	1.94
			Lower-tier	5.78	8.68	59.2	6.5	2.21	17.64	5.97
	Wage-employed	Formal		0.96	0.87	1.63	87.44	5.11	3.99	44.42
		Informal	Upper-tier	2.94	3.57	2.83	27.84	33.92	28.89	3.2
			Lower-tier	4.5	3.99	9.54	12.84	12.02	57.11	9.96
	Total			6.69	5.32	10.15	50.94	8.9	18	69.03

Note: All estimates use sampling weights.
Source: author's calculations based on ENOE 1st quarter 2015 and 2016, large urban areas (INEGI 2015a).

For each correlate, there are 36 average marginal effects, one for each possible transition between the six work status groups. These effects are presented in the following way. Figure 9.2 presents the results pertaining to the marginal effects of age, Fig. 9.3 presents the marginal effects of gender and marital status, and finally, Fig. 9.4 presents the marginal effects of the schooling variables.[12]

The estimates presented in Fig. 9.2 indicate that the probability of transiting from upper-tier self-employment into formal self-employment increases with age, especially for middle-age and older workers. Furthermore, the probability of remaining in self-employment at a given tier increases with age. The probability of moving into formal wage-employment falls with age, except for young workers in upper-tier self-employment and older workers in upper-tier wage-employment. The probability of remaining as a formal wage worker also increases with age among young and middle-aged workers. Finally, the probability of remaining in or transiting into lower-tier wage-employment decreases with age, indicating that this status is an entry state into the labour market.[13]

Regarding the effects of gender, Fig. 9.3 shows that men are more likely than women to remain in formal self-employment, while women are more likely to transit from formal self-employment into upper-tier self-employment. Men are also more likely than women to transit between self-employment and wage-employment in the lower tier, while women are more likely to remain in their initial type of employment within the lower tier. Finally, men in formal and upper-tier wage-employment are less likely than women to remain in their original employment states.

Figure 9.3 also presents the effects associated with marital status, separately for each gender. Most of these effects are, however, very imprecisely estimated. Among the patterns that are statistically significant (at the 95 per cent level), it is often observed that married men are more likely to experience a movement up the job ladder than single men. For women, the opposite is true; namely, relative to single women, married women are more likely to experience movements down the job ladder.

The average marginal effects of years of schooling in Fig. 9.4 show that this variable has a strong positive association with either transiting into or remaining in formal employment and is negatively correlated with transitions into the lower-tier status groups. Finally, workers enrolling in school over the panel year are less likely to transit into formal employment, and the initially formal self-employed that enrol in school are more likely to transit into lower-tier self-employment. In most cases, school enrolment is negatively associated with transitions from self-employment into wage-employment, probably because the latter does not offer the flexibility in schedules required by those attending school.

[12] The average marginal effects for age are reported at three different levels of age since this variable enters in a quadratic polynomial in the multinomial logit estimations.

[13] This finding is consistent with evidence that informal wage jobs serve to screen low-skilled young workers (see, for instance, Cano-Urbina 2015).

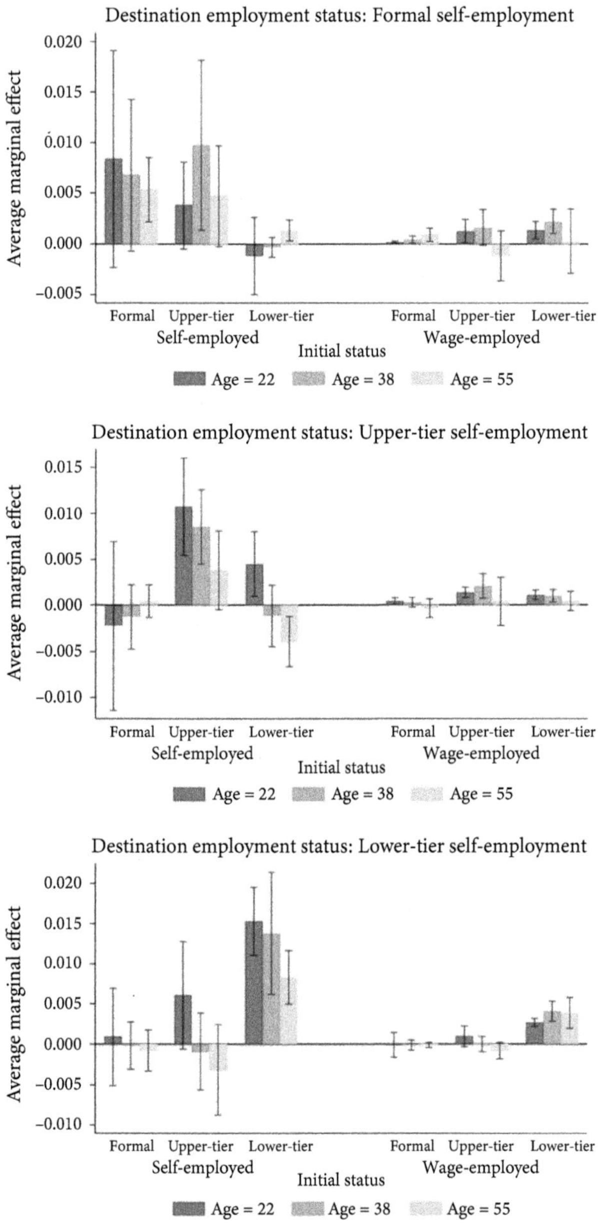

Fig. 9.2 Average marginal effects of years of age in multinomial logit models

Note: Range plot indicates 95 per cent confidence interval with standard errors robust to clustering at the city level.
Source: author's calculations based on ENOE 1st quarter 2015 and 2016, large urban areas (INEGI 2015a).

Fig. 9.2 *continued*

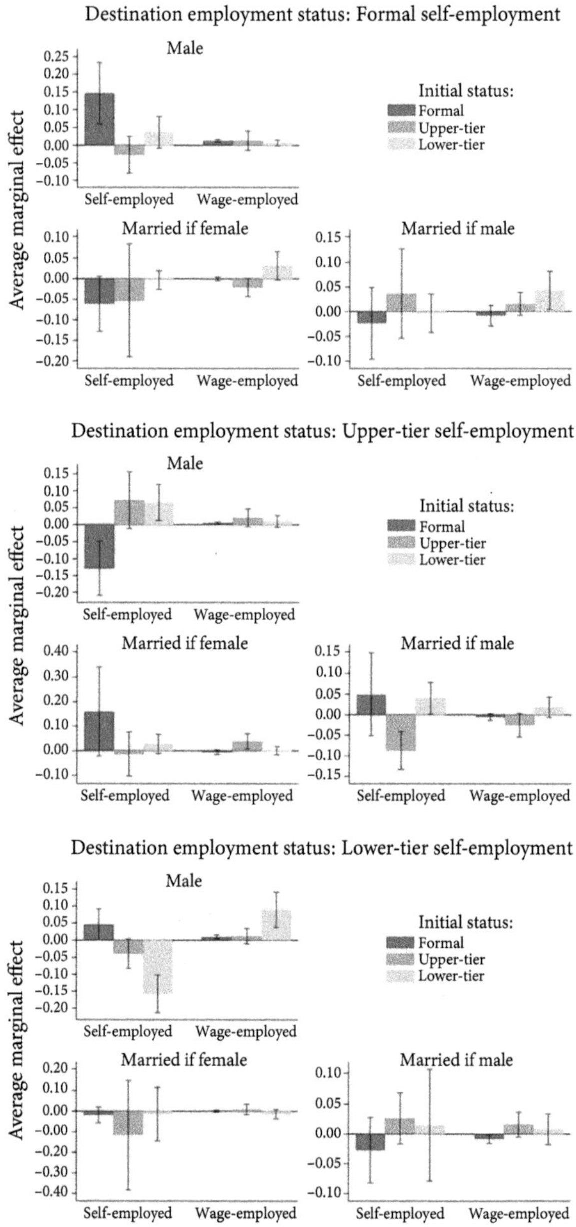

Fig. 9.3 Average marginal effects of gender and marital status in multinomial logit models

Note: Range plot indicates 95 per cent confidence interval with standard errors robust to clustering at the city level.

Source: author's calculations based on ENOE 1st quarter 2015 and 2016, large urban areas (INEGI 2015a).

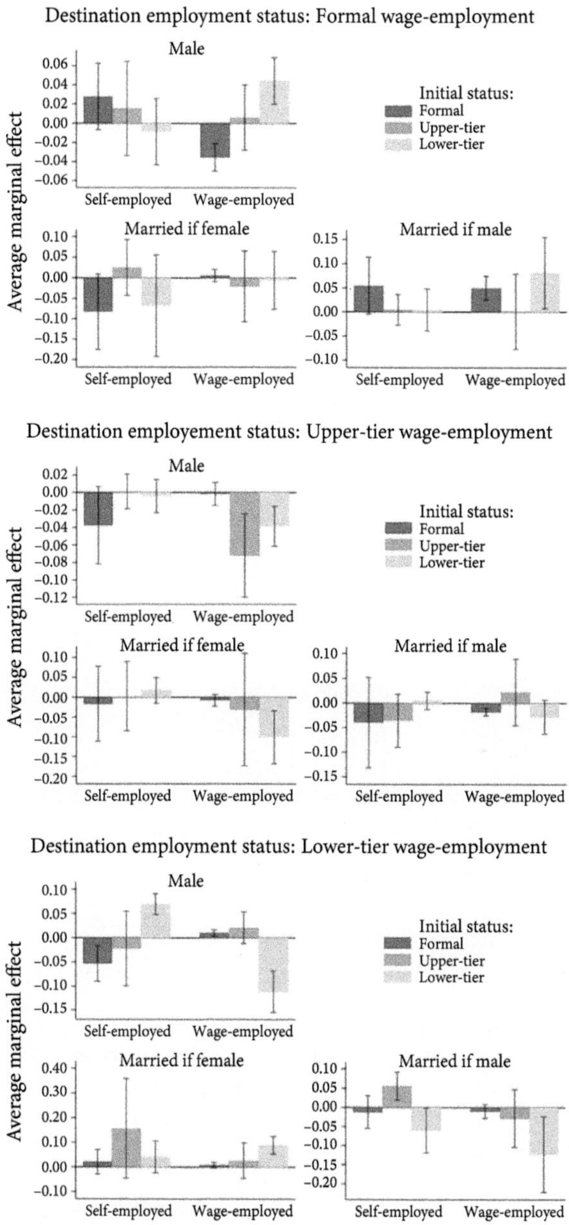

Fig. 9.3 *continued*

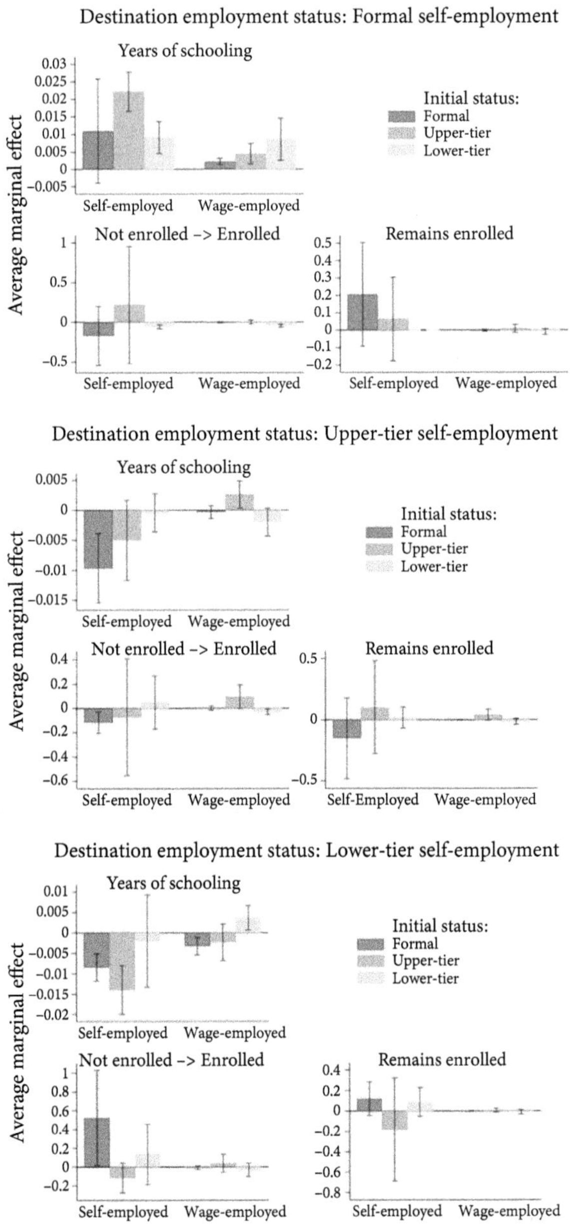

Fig. 9.4 Average marginal effects of schooling variables in multinomial logit models

Note: Range plot indicates 95 per cent confidence interval with standard errors robust to clustering at the city level.
Source: author's calculations based on ENOE 1st quarter 2015 and 2016, large urban areas (INEGI 2015a).

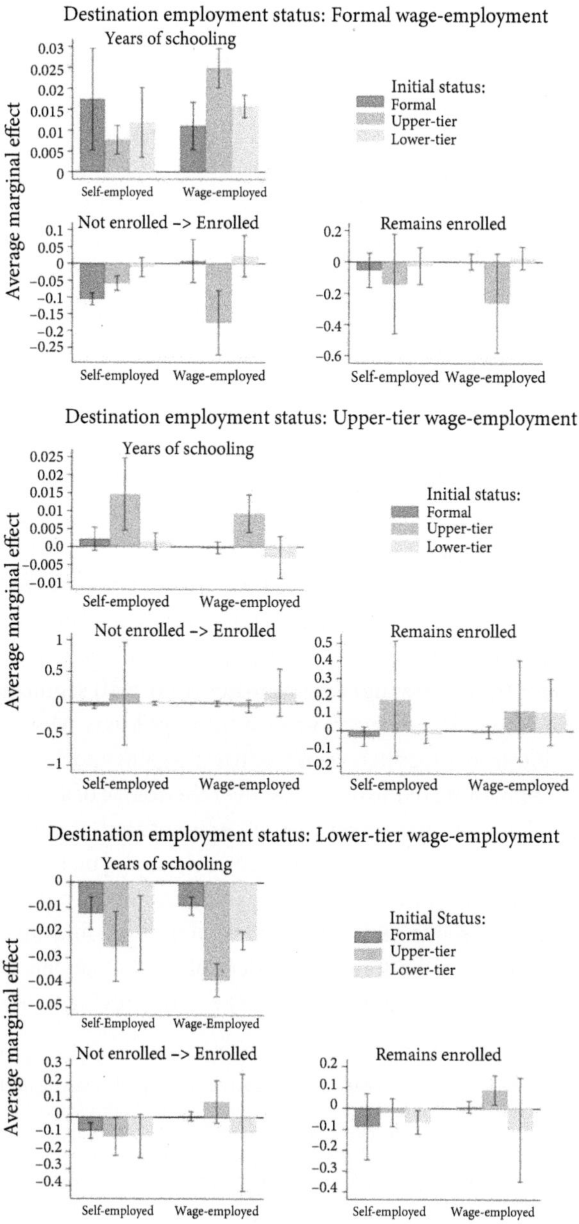

Fig. 9.4 *continued*

To complement the analysis of employment transitions, Table 9.4 presents the earnings changes associated with such transitions. Three different estimates of earnings changes are analysed. The first one, labelled 'Unconditional', is the average change in log earnings between the initial and final period in the one-year panel for each of the 36 transitions between the six employment status groups. A second measure, dubbed 'Conditional', reports the corresponding log earnings changes after adjusting for age, gender, marital status, years of schooling, school enrolment status, city-level dummies, and initial (log) earnings.[14] Finally, a third specification, labelled 'Selectivity', performs a Heckman-type selectivity correction to control for the potential selectivity bias arising due to the high fraction of non-reporting of earnings in the sample.[15]

While the different estimates of earnings changes lead to different predictions, whenever the earnings changes of a given transition are statistically different from zero for more than one method, they share the same sign. Another regularity observed in Table 9.4 is that the estimates from the selectivity-adjusted model are always smaller (i.e. less positive, or more negative) than the ones from the conditional linear regressions.

Turning to the specific patterns of earnings changes, it is observed that whenever the log-earnings changes of workers transiting into formal employment are statistically different from zero, they have a positive sign in all but one case. The opposite occurs for transitions into the lower-tier (informal) segment of the market, as these transitions almost always involve earnings losses. Movements up the job ladder from lower to upper tiers involve earnings gains and so do the earnings changes of those remaining in the upper tier over the course of a year. Movements from formal employment into upper-tier self-employment are accompanied by earnings losses; however, transitions from formal employment into upper-tier wage-employment involve gains according to the Conditional model.

Taking stock of the results presented in this section, we find little job mobility at the top (formal) and bottom (lower tier) of the job ladder. Instead, most workers in the middle of the ladder (upper tier) end up moving to other segments

[14] The adjustment is made through a linear regression of log-earnings changes on initial log earnings, a second-order age polynomial, gender interacted with marital status, years of education, dummies for enrolment in school over both periods, city-level dummies, and a set of dummy variables for each employment transition. The reported estimates are the predicted values of this regression when separately setting each of the employment transition dummies to 1 (and the others to zero), while averaging the other covariates over the sample.

[15] Around half the observations (weighted) are lost due to non-reporting of earnings in either the initial or the final period. Furthermore, this pattern is not random, as non-reporting increases steeply with the years of education, indicating that higher-income workers refuse to report their earnings. The selectivity-adjustment model estimates in the main equation a specification similar to the one of the Conditional model described above, and the selection equation includes as regressors age (in a second-order polynomial), gender interacted with marital status, years of education (in a second-order polynomial), dummies for enrolment in school over both periods, the dependency ratio at the household level, city-level dummies, and a set of dummy variables for each employment transition. The original estimates for all regressions are available from the author upon request.

Table 9.4 One-year changes in log earnings

				1st quarter 2016					
				Self-employed			Wage-employed		
				Formal	Informal		Formal	Informal	
					Upper-tier	Lower-tier		Upper-tier	Lower-tier
1st quarter 2015	Self-employed	Formal	Unconditional	0.09	−0.20*	−0.04	0.02	0.28**	−1.53***
			Conditional	0.33***	−0.02	0.06	0.32**	0.28***	−1.25**
			Selectivity	−0.003	−0.34*	−0.16*	−0.02	0.02	−2.06***
		Informal, Upper-tier	Unconditional	0.08	0.19***	−0.27	0.21**	0.28**	−1.14**
			Conditional	0.26*	0.18***	−0.16	0.30**	0.41***	−1.14**
			Selectivity	−0.03	−0.09	−0.45**	−0.003	0.06	−1.44***
		Informal, Lower-tier	Unconditional	−0.07	0.16	0.05	0.14**	0.24	−1.14***
			Conditional	0.17*	0.21*	−0.02	0.11**	0.29*	−1.12***
			Selectivity	−0.17	−0.06	−0.23***	−0.07	0.14	−1.21***
	Wage-employed	Formal	Unconditional	0.21	−0.38***	−0.25**	0.01**	−0.04	−0.41*
			Conditional	0.45***	−0.12	−0.13	0.27***	0.16***	−0.32
			Selectivity	0.07	−0.31***	−0.36***	−0.003	−0.16	−0.55***
		Informal, Upper-tier	Unconditional	−0.05	0.82**	−0.06	0.08	−0.05	−0.18
			Conditional	0.04	0.85***	0.03	0.24***	0.15***	−0.12
			Selectivity	−0.44*	0.69**	−0.24	−0.04	−0.07	−0.31**
		Informal, Lower-tier	Unconditional	1.61*	1.71*	1.40***	0.85***	0.66**	−0.16*
			Conditional	1.05**	0.87*	0.64***	0.60***	0.46***	−0.88***
			Selectivity	0.75	0.64	0.36*	0.37***	0.24	−1.07***

Note: Unconditional: average change in log earnings; conditional: log-earnings change controlling for age, gender, marital status, and schooling variables in linear regression; Selectivity: conditional log-earnings changes after correcting for selectivity bias due to non-reporting of earnings; * $p < 0.10$, ** $p < 0.05$, *** $p < 0.01$ based on standard errors robust to clustering at the city level. Earnings are in real terms at prices of February 2015.
Source: author's calculations based on ENOE 1st quarter 2015 and 2016, large urban areas (INEGI 2015a).

of the market. The analysis of the correlates of employment transitions indicate that lower-tier wage-employment serves as an entry state to the labour market, while transitions into self-employment increase with age. However, as formal wage workers become older the probability of transiting into self-employment increases by a very small amount. Therefore, the findings provide partial support to the hypothesis that workers enter informal wage jobs, until they gain access to better remunerated formal jobs, and eventually finish their career in self-employment (see, for instance, Maloney, 2004 and Duval Hernandez and Orraca 2011). The analysis also reveals that males are more likely to experience transitions up the job ladder, and this is particularly true for married men, while the opposite occurs for married women. Finally, schooling is a strong correlate of accessing jobs at the top of the ladder. As expected, movements up the job ladder are accompanied by positive earnings changes, and the opposite is true for movements down the ladder.

While the analysis of transitions provides valuable information about how likely it is for some workers to be trapped in poor-quality employment, it does not answer the question of how many of the stayers in a given employment status do so voluntarily rather than because of a lack of opportunities elsewhere in the market. To answer this, it is necessary to have information about workers' preferences for certain types of jobs. In the remainder of the chapter, I analyse a special module of the 2015 Labour Force Survey (INEGI 2015b) which contains this type of information.

4. Voluntary versus involuntary informal employment

In the second quarter of 2015, the Mexican Labour Force Survey was supplemented by a module inquiring about the employment trajectories of workers in large urban areas and their contribution to and valuation of social security protection.[16] The MOTRAL module (after its acronym in Spanish) was applied to a representative sample of workers aged 18–54 who were either employed or had previous labour market experience. This target population represented around 90 per cent of the labour force in large, urban centres and 60 per cent of the overall urban labour force in 2015.[17]

This module included the following key question: 'Do you think it is better to have a job with social security, even if you have to make payments to be eligible for

[16] The supplementary module is the Módulo de Trayectorias Laborales (MOTRAL) 2015 and its data can be publicly accessed online (see INEGI 2015b). A similar module was also applied in 2012, but, in that edition, the key variable used in the analysis next was not included.

[17] The individuals interviewed in the module also answered the traditional Labour Force Survey, and the two data sets can therefore be linked, as is done here, in order to have a richer set of variables.

it?'[18] This question is central to the analysis because most labour surveys contain information on the sector of employment but they do not collect information on the types of jobs workers value. Without this piece of information, researchers have no choice but to try to infer through indirect methods what fraction of the informal workforce is so because of a lack of options rather than by choice.

Given that having social security coverage is the defining characteristic of formal wage-employment in Mexico, this variable can be used as a proxy for the value workers give to this type of employment. Comparing this variable to the current type of job (formal or informal) can help us to approximate the fraction of involuntary informal workers.

Table 9.5 shows the percentage of the employed population who report preferring a job covered by social security protection and the main reason for valuing this protection among those who prefer jobs with social security coverage. The first column shows that across all employment status groups the vast majority respond affirmatively to the question of whether they prefer to have a job with coverage.

The highest proportion of positive responses are found among the lower-tier self-employed and the formal wage-employees, with affirmative answers from about 85 per cent of the respondents. In contrast, the lowest share of workers who answer this question affirmatively is found in the upper-tier informal, where 'only' about 74 per cent of workers answer affirmatively. The table also shows that among those respondents who prefer jobs with coverage, the most-valued attributes of social security protection are usually health and pension benefits.[19]

The bottom rows of Table 9.5 compare the responses of workers in the upper tier of the market with those in the lower tier, separately for wage-employees and the self-employed. While upper-tier workers are less likely to prefer covered jobs, the difference is only significant for the self-employed. Also, among those who prefer covered jobs, respondents in the upper-tier value more health benefits relative to respondents in the lower-tier.

Table 9.6 compares the characteristics of respondents depending on whether they have social security coverage in their job and on whether they would prefer to have a job with coverage. The table shows that the age and gender composition is more or less homogeneous across groups except for workers with coverage who do not value their social security benefits (in column 2), who are predominantly male. Workers with coverage are more educated than those without coverage and, within each group (with coverage or without coverage), respondents who do not value social security are slightly more educated than those who value it.[20] Workers

[18] The original question reads: '¿Considera que es mejor tener un empleo con seguridad social, aunque tenga que realizar pagos para tener derecho a ella?'.

[19] Specifically, the survey asked respondents to rank the value of the five attributes listed in columns 2–6 of Table 9.5. In Mexico, formal workers have very limited unemployment benefits and, probably because of this, the access to such benefits was not listed in the MOTRAL questionnaire as a reason for valuing social security coverage.

[20] Furthermore, workers without coverage are more likely to still be enrolled in school.

Table 9.5 Preference for jobs with social security

	Prefers job with social security [1]	Most-valued attribute of social security: Health insurance [2]	Pension [3]	Life insurance [4]	Housing benefits [5]	Disability benefits [6]
Formal employment						
Wage-employment	83.6	46.2	22.8	13.2	13.7	4.2
Self-employment	77.7	44.5	25.2	16.4	6.8	7.1
Informal employment						
Upper-tier						
Wage-employment	73.7	55.2	15.3	11.5	10.2	7.8
Self-employment	75.3	52.2	14.3	4.5	25.3	3.7
Lower-tier						
Wage-employment	79.3	41.3	14.1	21.3	16.4	6.9
Self-employment	86.3	39.4	19.8	13.6	19.4	7.8
Difference in responses upper–lower tier						
Wage-employment	−5.5	13.9*	1.2	−9.8***	−6.2	0.9
	(5.31)	(6.95)	(3.63)	(3.25)	(4.20)	(1.24)
Self-employment	−11.1***	12.9***	−5.5**	−9.1***	5.8	−4.1
	(3.17)	(3.13)	(2.40)	(1.88)	(6.88)	(3.66)

Note: Column 1 reports the percentage of individuals who consider it is better to have a job with social security benefits, even if one must pay to be entitled to such benefits. Columns 2–6 show the most-valued reason for preferring social security. The numbers in these columns are the row percentages of respondents selecting a given reason among those individuals who declare preferring a job with social security coverage. All estimates use sampling weights. The estimates listed under the 'Difference in Responses' panel of the table correspond to the estimates for the upper tier minus those of the lower-tier averages, separately for the wage-employed and self-employed; * $p < 0.10$, ** $p < 0.05$, *** $p < 0.01$ based on standard errors (in parentheses) robust to clustering at the city level.
Source: author's calculations based on MOTRAL 2015 (INEGI 2015b) and ENOE 2nd quarter 2015 (INEGI 2015a).

without coverage who do not value social security benefits are less likely to be married and have the lowest earnings of all groups. In contrast, the group that exhibits higher average earnings is the workers with coverage who do not value social security coverage.

While the question on the valuation of jobs with social security benefits is a new useful piece of information, its interpretation requires careful thought. One problem with the wording of this question is that it does not distinguishes between a preference over social security benefits alone and a broader preference for formal

Table 9.6 Characteristics of employed population in 2015 MOTRAL module

	Has social security		Does not have social security	
	Wants social security [1]	Does not want social security [2]	Wants social security [3]	Does not want social security [4]
Years of age	37.1	35.4	38.4	37.1
Male (%)	48.2	63.0	48.4	49.7
Years of schooling	11.8	12.4	9.9	10.7
Enrolled in school (%)	3.9	2.9	6.1	6.3
Married (%)	45.1	42.5	44.7	32.7
Earnings (monthly Mexican Pesos)	7,456	9,167	4,461	3,652
Share of employment	43.5	8.9	38.3	9.3
No. of observations (unweighted)	1,906	393	1,759	439

Note: Unless otherwise stated, all numbers are averages across the different employment groups. All estimates use sampling weights.
Source: author's calculations based on MOTRAL 2015 (INEGI 2015b) and ENOE 2nd quarter 2015 (INEGI 2015a).

employment, including all the characteristics that it comprises, such as higher wages and greater job security, in addition to social security benefits.[21]

This limitation in the wording of the question can be problematic if some workers answer stating their preference over social security benefits *exclusively* and not their overall preference for a formal job, which, in the context of this chapter, is the object of interest. For instance, 16 per cent of formal wage-employees state not valuing social security benefits (see Table 9.5); still, it is clear they prefer formal to informal employment *in general* as otherwise they would voluntarily move to an informal job. In other words, they remain in formal employment because of other job qualities such as higher wages, greater job security, and generally better working conditions.[22]

Since, in general, formal jobs are better than informal ones across several dimensions, such as pay, job security, and work conditions, there is a smaller risk of misclassifying a worker as involuntary informal when in fact his or her answer to the valuation question reflected a preference over social security benefits exclusively and not over a formal job in general. It is, of course, possible that

[21] Neither does the MOTRAL survey inquire about the reservation wages that informal workers have with respect to a formal wage job.

[22] This interpretation is corroborated by the descriptive evidence in column 2 of Table 9.6 which shows that workers with coverage who do not value social security coverage are, on average, more educated than the others and have the highest average earnings of all groups.

some informal workers prefer to remain informally employed because of a greater flexibility in work schedules, a valuation for being 'their own boss', and so on. If such workers were to answer the valuation question based on their preference over social security benefits only, and not over formal jobs in general, then one would misclassify them as involuntary informal. However, Levy (2008) argues that for many low-income workers, such as those in lower-tier employment, the net benefits package offered by the social security system is not necessarily superior to the benefits available through non-contributory social protection schemes. If this argument is correct, it should therefore be unlikely that informal workers declare valuing covered jobs based on their preference over social security benefits *alone* and not because of a preference for formal employment in general.[23]

In Duval-Hernández (2020), I provide additional evidence using ancillary information from a survey on micro-entrepreneurs conducted in 2012. That survey asked self-employed individuals whether they would accept a wage job with a similar income to their current one but in which they had access to social security and/or pension benefits. Around 60 per cent of the respondents declared they would accept such formal wage-employment, and this proportion increases monotonically as we move down the job ladder. These results support the evidence presented in Table 9.5 and suggest that a large proportion of the informal self-employed would rather be in formal wage-employment.

In that paper, I also analyse how socio-demographic characteristics of the worker relate to the willingness to have a covered job and the probability of obtaining one within the framework of a structural econometric model. The findings of that estimation indicate that the traditional division of labour at home is a likely culprit, limiting both the willingness of females to seek formal wage-employment and their probability of being hired in such jobs. Also, the level of education of a worker is positively associated with his or her chances of being hired in a formal job and of earning a higher income from it.

Given the previous discussion, one can regard those informal workers who consider it better to have a job with social security coverage as involuntarily employed in their current job. Under this interpretation, based on the figures in Table 9.6, involuntary informal workers make up 38 per cent of the employed and 80 per cent of the employed without social security, while the voluntary informal comprise 9 per cent of the employed and about 20 per cent of the uncovered workers.[24]

[23] The fact that very few self-employed voluntarily enrol for social security coverage (as permitted by the law) indicates that few of them value social security benefits per se, given their current employment. Therefore, those self-employed that declare preferring a job with coverage, answer based on an overall comparison between being self-employed and being a formal wage-employee.

[24] Specifically, in columns 3 and 4 of Table 9.6 it is reported that 38.3 per cent of the sample are involuntary informal and 9.3 per cent are voluntary informal. Therefore, of the total informal population (which represents 47.6 per cent of the sample), 80 per cent are involuntary informal (i.e. 38.3/47.6). The same proportion of involuntary informal workers would arise if we defined formality not just by social security coverage but if we also included the formal self-employed among them.

Column 1 of Table 9.5 shows that this proportion of involuntary informal is high, irrespective of employment status. In fact, there is no immediate one-to-one association between being voluntarily in informal employment and being in the upper tier of the market since a large proportion of the upper-tier informal workers still consider jobs with coverage to be preferable. This can occur if some workers have a comparative advantage in being employed formally, while, at the same time, having an absolute advantage in both types of employment. Therefore, if they are unable to obtain a formal job, they find an upper-tier informal job.

This high proportion of involuntary informal workers contrasts with the view put forward by a strand of the informality literature which considers Mexican labour markets to be mainly composed of voluntary workers (see, for instance, Maloney 1999, 2004; Bosch and Maloney 2010). This literature reaches this conclusion mainly based on an analysis of the patterns of sector transitions over the business cycle rather than from the direct measurement of workers' stated preferences, as this chapter does.[25] Sector transitions over the business cycle, while interesting on their own, only provide indirect evidence about the preferred sector of employment of a given worker. Furthermore, sector transitions, by definition, do not tell us anything about the preferred jobs of stayers as they may remain in their initial job either because they are satisfied with it or because they face significant barriers to accessing a better job elsewhere.

Our results also contrast with the argument that informality is high in Mexico because many workers find the benefits associated with social security not worth the taxes that have to be paid to obtain them (Levy 2008). While it is possible that some informal workers do not value such benefits per se, the answers in the MOTRAL module survey indicate that a large proportion of informal workers would prefer to be employed as wage-employees in a formal job with better pay and working conditions.

To conclude this section, it is worth mentioning that a few studies in other Latin American countries have exploited valuation questions similar to the one used in this chapter, where workers are explicitly asked whether they would prefer to have a formal job (see Soares 2004 and Contreras et.al. 2017). The proportion of involuntary informal wage workers in Brazil is similar to the one found in this chapter. However, the proportions of involuntary self-employed in Brazil and Chile are substantially lower than those found in Mexico.[26]

[25] Maloney (2004) presents results on the reasons reported by the self-employed for leaving their last job. This information, however, does not directly inquire their preferences over formal employment and, by construction, excludes all informal wage workers, which, as shown in Table 9.2, nowadays represent two-thirds of informal employment.

[26] Other papers in the literature have tried to estimate the proportion of involuntary informal workers in Mexico using structural econometric methods. However, the estimates arising from these indirect methods vary widely depending on the econometric specification used. For a discussion of this literature, see Duval-Hernández (2020). For a novel application to Costa Rica and Nicaragua, see Alaniz, et.al., (2021).

In general, there is room for more extensive use of these types of counterfactual questions to complement the information regularly collected by the labour surveys. For example, Ulyssea (2011) argues that the analysis of traditional variables such as wages, job transitions, and durations is insufficient to identify whether labour markets are segmented or integrated. Therefore, incorporating information about preferences seems a fruitful way to enhance our understanding of the workings of the labour markets in developing countries.

5. Conclusions

The analysis presented in this chapter shows very heterogeneous forms of employment in urban Mexico. The traditional divides between formal and informal jobs and between wage-employment and self-employment are not enough to characterize the labour market. Instead, even within informal employment, one can distinguish between better-quality jobs (the upper tier) and the rest (the lower tier). The various employment status groups that can be formed by interacting all the above dimensions indicate important differences in the composition of the workforce as well as in their employment and earnings dynamics.

Of particular concern are the working conditions of those in the lower tier of informal employment. Not only do they have the lowest level of earnings and few, if any, additional fringe benefits, but also their mobility to higher rungs of the job ladder is very limited.

Furthermore, the analysis of a unique data set with information about the stated preferences regarding type of employment indicates that almost 80 per cent of informal workers consider it preferable to be employed in a formal job. This suggests that many of the urban informal workers are in this sector because of a lack of better options. In spite of the diversity characterizing the various work status groups identified in the chapter, there is an overwhelming preference for formal wage-employment across the various segments of the market.

Structural econometric estimations in a companion study (Duval-Hernandez, 2020) identify two important factors that affect the workers' access to formal wage-employment, namely, the division of housework at the household level and the levels of human capital. Therefore, policies that seek to encourage formal wage-employment from the supply side of the labour market need to consider how they can affect these two dimensions. Such policies could include the expansion of access to higher education and incentivizing the provision of market substitutes to home production so as to encourage female participation in the labour market in general and in formal employment in particular.

References

Alaniz, E., T. H. Gindling, C. Mata, and D. Rojas (2021). 'Heterogeneous Informality in Costa Rica and Nicaragua.' WIDER Working Paper No. 2021/50. Helsinki: UNU-WIDER.

Bosch, M., and W.F. Maloney (2010). 'Comparative Analysis of Labor Market Dynamics Using Markov Processes: An Application to Informality'. *Labour Economics*, 17(4): 621–631. https://doi.org/10.1016/j.labeco.2010.01.005.

Cano-Urbina, J. (2015). 'The Role of the Informal Sector in the Early Careers of Less-Educated Workers'. *Journal of Development Economics*, 112, 33–55. https://doi.org/10.1016/j.jdeveco.2014.10.002.

Contreras, D., R. Gillmore, and E. Puentes (2017). 'Self-Employment and Queues for Wage Work: Evidence from Chile'. *Journal of International Development*, 24(4): 473–499. https://doi.org/10.1002/jid.3074.

Duval-Hernández, R. (2020). 'By Choice or By Force? Uncovering the Nature of Informal Employment in Urban Mexico'. WIDER Working Paper No. 2020/151. Helsinki: UNU-WIDER.

Duval Hernández, R., and P. Orraca Romano (2011). 'Análisis por cohortes de la participación laboral en México (1987–2009)'. *El Trimestre Económico*, LXXVIII(2): 343–375. http://dx.doi.org/10.20430/ete.v78i310.37.

Fields, G.S. (2011). '"Informality": It's Time to Stop Being Alice-in-Wonderland-ish'. Women in Informal Employment: Globalizing and Organizing (WIEGO) Research Paper. Manchester: WIEGO. https://www.wiego.org/publications/%E2%80%9Cinformality%E2%80%9D-it%E2%80%99s-time-stop-being-alice-wonderland-ish

INEGI (Instituto Nacional de Estadística y Geografía) (2014). *La informalidad laboral: Encuesta Nacional de Ocupación y Empleo: marco conceptual y metodológico.* Aguascalientes: INEGI.

INEGI (2015a). 'Encuesta Nacional de Ocupación y Empleo, población de 15 años y más de edad'. Available at: https://www.inegi.org.mx/programas/enoe/15ymas (accessed 1 November 2018).

INEGI (2015b). 'Módulo de Trayectorias Laborales (MOTRAL) 2015'. Available at: https://www.inegi.org.mx/programas/motral/2015 (accessed 1 July 2019).

Levy, S. (2008). *Good Intentions, Bad Outcomes: Social Policy, Informality, and Economic Growth in Mexico.* Washington, DC: Brookings Institution Press.

Levy, S. (2018). *Under-Rewarded Efforts: The Elusive Quest for Prosperity in Mexico.* Washington, DC: Inter-American Development Bank. https://doi.org/10.18235/0001189.

Maloney, W.F. (1999). 'Does Informality Imply Segmentation in Urban Labor Markets? Evidence from Sectoral Transitions in Mexico'. *World Bank Economic Review*, 13(2): 275–302. https://doi.org/10.1093/wber/13.2.275.

Maloney, W.F. (2004). 'Informality Revisited'. *World Development*, 32(7): 1159–1178. https://doi.org/10.1016/j.worlddev.2004.01.008.

Ruppert Bulmer, E. (2018) 'Defining Informality vs Mitigating Its Negative Effects'. *IZA World of Labor*, 442: 1–12. https://doi.org/10.15185/izawol.442.

Soares, F.V. (2004). 'Do Informal Workers Queue for Formal Jobs in Brazil?' Texto para Discussão # 1021. Rio de Janeiro: IPEA.

Ulyssea, G. (2011). 'The Formal–Informal Labor Market Segmentation Hypothesis Revisited'. *Brazilian Review of Econometrics*, 30(2): 311. https://doi.org/10.12660/bre.v30n22010.3467.

PART IV
SUB-SAHARAN AFRICA

10

The dynamics of off-farm self-employment in the West African Sahel

Sènakpon Fidèle Ange Dedehouanou and Didier Yélognissè Alia

1. Introduction

In most developing countries, wage jobs are elusive (Fox et al. 2016). Studies show that less than 5 per cent of working-age individuals in sub-Saharan Africa (SSA) have a formal public wage job (Banerjee and Duflo 2007). The vast majority of individuals, especially those living in rural areas, derive their livelihood from agriculture. However, the agricultural sector coexists with a vibrant non-farm sector. Thus, the majority of African workers in both urban and rural areas are involved in some kind of non-farm self-employment. These workers choose non-farm entrepreneurship through the creation and the management of small businesses as a strategy to boost their income and enable them to mitigate unexpected shocks[1] to their livelihood because of the high-risk nature of the agricultural sector and limited options in the formal employment sectors (Nagler and Naudé 2017). Thus, the non-farm economy has been shown to have the potential to spur economic growth and poverty reduction (Fox and Sohnesen 2012). Yet, in most African countries it is characterized by a high level of informality with a large proportion of self-employed workers (Gollin 2008; La Porta and Shleifer 2014; ILO 2018).

Self-employed work consists mainly in small business activities, mostly involving workers with low skills and little opportunity to find decent salaried employment. Most non-farm businesses are small, and, in many cases, they are owned by a single individual who is both the investor and the manager (McCaig and Pavcnik 2015). These non-farm self-employed workers are heterogeneous in many dimensions including the sectors of activity in which they operate, the structure of the business activity, the growth potential of the business, and their likelihood of becoming formal workers (Bruhn and McKenzie 2014). The most vulnerable of these businesses are found in rural areas and face numerous constraints to expansion and growth (Bekele and Worku 2008).

[1] Defined as events that cause an unexpected loss of revenue from non-agricultural and salaried activity, negatively affecting the household's financial capital potential.

Sènakpon Fidèle Ange Dedehouanou and Didier Yélognissè Alia, *The dynamics of off-farm self-employment in the West African Sahel*. In: *The Job Ladder*. Edited by Gary S. Fields, T. H. Gindling, Kunal Sen, Michael Danquah, and Simone Schotte, Oxford University Press. © UNU-WIDER (2023). DOI: 10.1093/oso/9780192867339.003.0010

Another feature of non-farm self-employed workers in African and other developing countries is that they are generally engaged in unregistered business activities and it is unclear whether moving to formality would improve their performance (McKenzie and Sakho 2010; Campos et al. 2018). Although the importance of entrepreneurship for poverty reduction is acknowledged (Benjamin and Mbaye 2012; McCaig and Pavcnik 2015; Mhando and Kiggundu 2018), there is a concern that self-employment in Africa is generally survivalist or necessity-driven (Williams and Youssef 2014). How to bring self-employed workers out of informality is thus a continuing concern of policymakers, development practitioners, and researchers alike. The recent COVID-19 pandemic has renewed the question of informal work in SSA as the pandemic is deemed likely to be more detrimental to informal workers (Balde et al. 2020; Danquah et al. 2020).

While several studies have clearly documented the importance of non-farm self-employment, advances still need to be made in the literature related to the understanding of its heterogeneity and dynamics (McCaig and Pavcnik 2015). We add to the literature that acknowledges the existence of heterogeneities in informal work and accounts for the division of informal employment work into upper-tier and lower-tier in Central America and anglophone Africa (Danquah et al. 2019; Alaniz et al. 2020). In this chapter, we analyse the dynamics of non-farm self-employment in two West Africa Sahel countries—Mali and Niger. We differentiate non-farm self-employed workers according to three distinct work status groups: formal self-employed workers, lower-tier informal self-employed workers, and upper-tier informal self-employed workers. We examine the profile of these workers and take advantage of the panel nature of Niger data to extend our analysis to mobility between work status groups and the factors explaining the transition to a higher work status.

Our three-fold distinction in formality status is justified by the mixed literature showing that the transition from low-return to high-return non-farm employment is welfare improving (Bezu and Barrett 2012), that inducing more self-employment into formality will not necessarily lead to positive changes in workers' performance (McKenzie and Sakho 2010; McCaig and Nanowski 2019), and that most of the non-farm self-employed workers in developing countries are reported to be informal (Nagler and Naudé 2017) yet have a potential for growing their business activities (Fox and Sohnesen 2012). An understanding of the heterogeneities governing non-farm self-employment could thus inform effective specific policy interventions towards the informal sector.

Given widespread evidence of a gender gap in non-farm entrepreneurship (Jayachandran 2020), we also conduct the analyses through a gendered lens, asking whether there are systemic differences between female workers and male workers.

Finally, the literature is skewed towards specific regions and countries, creating a risk of distorting understanding of the functioning of non-farm self-employment across many settings. Our focus on the West African Sahel—a region that has received little attention in the literature so far—adds to the body of evidence on informal self-employment. We complement the literature on Latin America, South Asia, and Eastern and Southern Africa by studying two West African countries, Niger and Mali, which are among the poorest in the world and face important development challenges, thus also adding to understanding of the dynamics of self-employment in fragile and conflict-affected countries. Specifically, our study adds to the work of Grimm et al. (2012) on the informal sector in seven capital cities in francophone West Africa, including Niger and Mali, which shows the existence of self-employed workers with the potential to become formal entrepreneurs as they share the same business characteristics as these. We leverage the recent availability of rich nationally representative data for these two countries—Mali and Niger—to analyse work status groups in both urban and rural locations. Besides examining the factors related to the characteristics of self-employed workers and their business activity that might explain the transition between work status groups, we also seek to establish how such a transition responds to the occurrence of shocks.

The remainder of the chapter is structured as follows. In section 2, we provide a brief overview of the broader literature into which this study fits. We then describe the data sets and their main features in section 3. In section 4, we present some descriptive results on work status, the profile of self-employed workers, and the characteristics of their business activities in the two countries of study. Section 5 focuses on the analysis of employment dynamics. We then offer concluding remarks in section 6.

2. Related literature

Our study, focusing on the West African Sahel, sits at the intersection of two large and growing strands of the literature. The first deals with informal microenterprises in developing countries (Bennett 2010; McCaig and Pavcnik 2015). A recent review by Jayachandran (2020), extending previous reviews, has documented several areas this literature has explored, including the role of access to capital and business training, the importance of barriers to hiring and formalization, and gender differences in the profile and performance of firms. It is widely believed that individuals in developing countries face steep challenges in starting businesses, which are therefore constrained to remain informal, with few prospects for growth. Many of these individuals are self-employed by necessity rather than self-employed as a calling (Jayachandran 2020). Our study is directly related to this literature in that we characterize both the profile of self-employed workers and the enterprises they work in, including the gender dimension.

The second strand of the literature our study ties into concerns the factors explaining the dynamics of off-farm employment in low- and middle-income countries. Nagler and Naudé (2017) and, more recently, Van den Broeck and Kilic (2019) explore this question using the World Bank's Living Standards Measurement Study—Integrated Surveys on Agriculture (LSMS—ISA) data for Ethiopia, Malawi, Nigeria, Tanzania, and Uganda.[2] They find that the drivers of entering off-farm employment and staying in it are country- and gender-specific and include vulnerability to shocks. Our study also uses the World Bank's LSMS—ISA, but it considers an extra dimension of off-farm employment dynamics other than entry into or exit from off-farm employment.

Our study categorizes workers into informal self-employment status groups and studies their transition between status groups with a focus on the drivers of growth from lower-tier informal self-employment to either upper-tier informal or formal self-employment. Our approach is related to Grimm et al. (2012), which studied non-farm employment in seven capital cities in francophone West Africa and showed that a substantial share of self-employed workers are 'survivalists', whose business skills and entrepreneurial behaviour resemble those of formal entrepreneurs.

It also aligns with recent studies in Central America and SSA (Danquah et al. 2019; Alaniz et al. 2020) that have examined employment movement within and between formal and informal work status groups. Using data from Ghana, South Africa, Tanzania, and Uganda, Danquah et al. (2019) found significant heterogeneity among lower-tier and upper-tier informal self-employed workers, the latter finding it difficult to make the transition to formal employment. This is contrary to the situation in Costa Rica and Nicaragua, where self-employed workers have not been found stuck in lower-tier informal work (Alaniz et al. 2020), showing the necessity to study informal work dynamics in different contexts. The study of Danquah et al. (2019) focused on SSA but was limited to anglophone Africa. Benjamin and Mbaye (2012) and Grimm et al. (2012) analysed the informal sector in francophone West Africa and made a distinction between large and small informal firms. However, the authors focused only on the urban informal sector in some capital cities. Our study, in contrast, uses nationally representative recent data covering both urban and rural workers over multiple periods, allowing us to study employment dynamics in a region, the West African Sahel, that has hitherto received little attention in the literature.

3. Data sources, samples, and unit of analysis

We primarily use data from the LSMS—ISA in Mali and Niger. We use data from two survey rounds for Mali (2014 and 2017) and two survey rounds for Niger

[2] The data were collected by the National Bureau of Statistics in collaboration with the World Bank and can be downloaded from https://microdata.worldbank.org/index.php/catalog/lsms.

(2011 and 2014). The data for Mali are repeated cross-sectional data with different households interviewed in the two rounds. The data for Niger are panel data with the same households interviewed in both rounds. Both surveys collected rich household-, individual-, firm-, and community-level information, and the samples for each country are nationally representative.

In this study, we focus on the samples of off-farm self-employed workers, which are the unit of analysis. Off-farm self-employed workers are individual household members involved, during the twelve months prior to the surveys, in a self-employment/entrepreneurship (non-agricultural) activity, either as own-account workers or as owners (employers). The samples we use for Mali consist of 2,675 workers in 2014 and 952 workers in 2017. The samples used for Niger consist of 3,727 workers in 2011 and 2,885 workers in 2014. For the purpose of the analysis of the employment dynamics, we additionally construct, with the Niger database, a balanced panel of 1,465 off-farm self-employed workers in 2011 and 2014, based on the same identifiers of households and household members tracked in these two years of surveys.

The structure of the samples has the advantage of allowing a comparison of statistics across location and over time. We can determine whether the data present the same picture within the same context for the same subjects in different years (the Niger case in both survey rounds), within different contexts for different subjects in the same year (Niger and Mali cases for the 2014 survey round), and within the same context for different subjects in different years (Mali case in the two survey rounds).

4. Off-farm self-employment work and earnings in Mali and Niger

4.1 Business activities and formality status of self-employed workers

Table 10.1 presents the characteristics of the activities self-employed workers were involved in during the 12 months prior to the surveys. Statistics are presented for the total samples of each survey round, for sub-samples in urban and rural areas, and for sub-samples of self-employed women and men, with significant differences between the last two groups tested using bivariate regressions with sampling weights.

Table 10.1 shows that self-employment work in Niger and Mali is, overall, predominantly own-account-based work. Yet, some differences exist between the two countries. Only a tiny proportion of self-employed workers in Niger share their proprietorship with a non-household member (at most, 2 per cent), whereas in Mali, the percentage of self-employed workers that co-own their business activities with external household members amounted in 2014 to 11 per cent and in 2017 to 22 per cent in rural zones and 21 per cent among self-employed men. We

Table 10.1 Characteristics of self-employment work and formality status

	First survey round					Second survey round				
	All	Rural	Urban	Women	Men	All	Rural	Urban	Women	Men
Niger	**2011 (N = 3727)**					**2014 (N = 2885)**				
Co-owns the business	0.01	0.01	0.02	0.01	0.02*	0.02	0.02	0.02	0.01	0.02***
Age of business (years)	9.74	10.38	8.77	8.66	10.70***	10.32	10.42	10.20	8.79	11.55***
Location: fixed dwelling	0.44	0.49	0.38	0.71	0.21***	0.39	0.41	0.36	0.64	0.19***
Location: fixed outside	0.25	0.18	0.35	0.14	0.35***	0.25	0.18	0.34	0.15	0.34***
Location: mobile	0.30	0.33	0.27	0.15	0.44***	0.36	0.41	0.29	0.21	0.48***
Salaried workers (#)	0.14	0.04	0.27	0.08	0.19***	0.17	0.05	0.31	0.06	0.26***
Has registered workers	0.00	0.00	0.01	0.00	0.00	0.01	0.00	0.02	0.01	0.01
Has no salaried worker	0.96	0.97	0.93	0.98	0.94***	0.94	0.97	0.89	0.97	0.91***
Registered	0.05	0.02	0.10	0.04	0.06	0.02	0.00	0.05	0.00	0.04***
Formal	0.04	0.02	0.08	0.03	0.05	0.02	0.00	0.03	0.00	0.03***
Upper-tier informal	0.25	0.20	0.34	0.16	0.34***	0.27	0.20	0.36	0.17	0.36***
Lower-tier informal	0.70	0.79	0.58	0.81	0.61***	0.71	0.80	0.60	0.83	0.61***
Mali	**2014 (N = 2675)**					**2017 (N = 952)**				
Co-owns the business	0.10	0.11	0.10	0.08	0.11*	0.18	0.22	0.16	0.14	0.21***
Age of business (years)	9.83	10.00	9.65	8.95	10.50***	10.12	8.67	10.69	8.57	11.27***
Location: fixed dwelling	0.33	0.41	0.24	0.46	0.22***	0.38	0.59	0.28	0.51	0.28***
Location: fixed outside	0.29	0.18	0.40	0.21	0.35***	0.38	0.24	0.45	0.24	0.49***
Location: mobile	0.39	0.41	0.36	0.33	0.43***	0.24	0.18	0.27	0.25	0.23
Salaried workers (#)	0.31	0.26	0.35	0.18	0.40***	0.68	0.87	0.59	0.40	0.90***
Has registered workers	0.01	0.01	0.02	0.01	0.02*	Na	Na	Na	Na	Na
Has no salaried worker	0.90	0.91	0.88	0.94	0.86***	0.76	0.75	0.77	0.84	0.70***
Registered	0.07	0.04	0.09	0.04	0.09***	Na	Na	Na	Na	Na
Formal	0.05	0.03	0.07	0.03	0.07***	Na	Na	Na	Na	Na
Upper-tier informal	0.29	0.22	0.37	0.23	0.34***	0.51	0.42	0.55	0.34	0.63***
Lower-tier informal	0.65	0.75	0.56	0.74	0.59***	0.49	0.58	0.45	0.66	0.37***

Note: 'Na' means 'not available' due to missing data on the related variables. Significant differences across gender are tested using bivariate regressions with sampling weights. Significant levels are indicated by * $p < 0.10$, ** $p < 0.05$,*** $p < 0.01$.

note that in both Niger and Mali, self-employed workers generally persist in their activities for a long period as the average age of their businesses is 10 years. Women entered self-employment later than men in both countries and years.

Another key characteristic of self-employed workers in these two countries is the location of their business activities. Close to half of the self-employed workers in the samples operate at a fixed location, either in the household's dwelling or in an outside building. Slightly more than one-third of them are mobile, with no fixed location. There is substantial heterogeneity across gender and place of residence within each country. A high share of self-employed women operate in a fixed location, with a more pronounced picture in Niger (64–71 per cent) than in Mali (46–51 per cent). This confirms the notion that self-employed women in developing countries tend to operate in the household dwelling to reduce costs and to more easily combine family life with business activity (Amin 2010; Babbitt et al. 2015). As a consequence, they are likely to sort into low-return home-based economic activities (Bruhn 2009; Berge and Pires 2015).

We should note that hiring external workers is marginal in the study context. Self-employed workers essentially employ family labour to assist them. Only a handful of self-employed workers—mostly women and in rural areas—hired salaried workers (generally ranging from two to four), only a small share of them being formally registered in the national social security fund (henceforth NSSF).[3] Few self-employed workers followed the standard business practice of keeping an accounting system or a commercial register to record all transactions, and very few enterprises had a fiscal identification number (what we define as 'registered'); most of those that did were managed by men and located in urban areas. These statistics show the informal character of most self-employment in these countries, as in developing countries in general (La Porta and Shleifer 2014; Jayachandran 2020).

Based on the figures shown in Table 10.1, we classified self-employed workers in three work status groups (Table 10.A1 in the appendix), differentiating between formal self-employed, upper-tier informal self-employed and lower-tier informal self-employed, in accordance with the International Labour Organization's definition of informal employment (ILO 2018). The formal self-employed are defined as own-account workers (with no salaried workers) who (i) have kept written accounts, (ii) have a commercial register, or (iii) have a fiscal identification number. They also include business owners and employers (those with at least one employee) who have observed at least one of these three regulations and registered their employees in the NSSF. Upper-tier informal self-employed workers are identified as those who do not comply with the above regulations but whose operations are in fixed premises outside the dwelling. Lower-tier informal

[3] Niger's fund is called the Caisse Nationale de Sécurité Sociale and Mali's the Caisse Malienne de Sécurité Sociale.

self-employed workers are identified as those who do not comply with the above regulations but whose operations are in their dwelling or who are itinerant/mobile. Note that self-employed workers are divided into informal work status groups only for the second survey round in Mali due to missing data on variables related to registration.

The share of self-employed workers found in each work status is presented at the bottom of Table 10.1 for each country. The majority of self-employed workers are in the lower-tier informal work status in both countries, with a higher percentage found in Niger. In both countries, self-employed women and self-employed workers in rural areas are mostly found in the lower-tier informal work status, contrary to their male counterparts and workers in urban areas, who are found mostly in the formal and upper-tier informal work status groups.

In Table 10.2, we report summary statistics on the profile of the self-employed workers and the main branch of activity they were operating in, according to their work status. We also present results of a test for differences between means of the variables between lower-tier informal and upper-tier informal self-employed, using bivariate regressions with sampling weights. The figures in Table 10.2 indicate that the majority of self-employed workers in the two study countries are adults aged 25–64 years, predominantly in the lower-tier informal work status, the average age being 38–42 years. A small proportion of workers are young (aged 15–24) or old adults (aged 65 and above), with a greater proportion of them employed in the lower-tier informal work status in both countries. Women are fairly represented among the self-employed workers, with, again, a greater proportion in the lower-tier work status, the difference being statistically significant. We also note that a majority of workers are heads of households, significantly found in upper-tier informal or formal work status groups.

Table 10.2 also shows that 20–52 per cent of self-employed workers in Niger have at least a primary education, that is, between two and seven years of education.[4] It is observed in both countries that most self-employed workers are able to read or write in at least one language and that the educated are more represented in the formal and upper-tier informal work status groups in that order of importance. In Mali, youth and adult self-employed workers (aged 15–64) and those who have some formal education are equally found in both informal status groups.

The distribution of self-employed workers by their main branch of activity indicates that most self-employed workers operate in sales (39–58 per cent), both in Niger and in Mali. The second predominant branch of activities is services in Niger (25–32 per cent) and manufacturing and construction in Mali (21–38 per cent). Self-employed workers operating in food processing are found mostly in the lower-tier informal status in both countries.

[4] The survey in Mali did not collect data on the level of education of the self-employed. Instead, we have used the information on the question of whether they studied in a school or on a private course.

Table 10.2 Self-employed workers' profiles and branch of activity by work status

	First survey round				Second survey round			
		Work status				Work status		
	All	Formal	Upper-tier informal	Lower-tier informal	All	Formal	Upper-tier informal	Lower-tier informal
	2011				**2014**			
Niger (N = #)	(3,727)	(157)	(949)	(2621)	(2,885)	(50)	(787)	(2,048)
Self-employed woman	0.46	0.39	0.29	0.53***	0.45	0.12	0.28	0.52***
Self-employed married	0.79	0.83	0.79	0.78	0.81	0.88	0.83	0.80
Self-employed head of household	0.52	0.61	0.68	0.46***	0.55	0.78	0.70	0.49***
Age of self-employed (mean)	39.71	42.94	38.87	39.82	41.71	43.44	41.84	41.62
15–24 years	0.12	0.09	0.11	0.12	0.08	0.08	0.06	0.09**
25–34 years	0.29	0.20	0.30	0.29	0.27	0.10	0.26	0.27
35–64 years	0.53	0.61	0.55	0.52	0.59	0.78	0.63	0.57***
65+ years	0.06	0.10	0.03	0.07***	0.06	0.04	0.05	0.07**
Self-employed can read or write	0.32	0.44	0.37	0.29***	0.35	0.72	0.45	0.31***
Education of self-employed (years)	2.23	3.48	2.72	1.98***	2.22	7.10	3.04	1.78***
Self-employed has at least primary education level	0.25	0.34	0.29	0.23***	0.24	0.52	0.33	0.20***
Branch of activity: food processing	0.14	0.11	0.12	0.15***	0.13	0.04	0.09	0.14***
Branch of activity: manufacture/construction	0.20	0.11	0.17	0.21	0.17	0.06	0.13	0.19
Branch of activity: sales	0.42	0.52	0.46	0.39***	0.43	0.58	0.51	0.40***
Branch of activity: services	0.25	0.25	0.25	0.25	0.27	0.32	0.27	0.27

Continued

Table 10.2 *Continued*

	First survey round				Second survey round			
		Work status				Work status		
	All	Formal	Upper-tier informal	Lower-tier informal	All	Formal	Upper-tier informal	Lower-tier informal
	2014				**2017**			
Mali (N = #)	(2,675)	(120)	(790)	(1765)	(952)		(482)	(470)
Self-employed woman	0.45	0.23	0.34	0.51***	0.43	Na	0.28	0.58***
Self-employed married	0.80	0.86	0.81	0.80	0.82	Na	0.82	0.82
Self-employed head of HH	0.46	0.61	0.56	0.40***	0.44	Na	0.51	0.36***
Age of self-employed (mean)	40.28	40.27	40.15	40.34	40.86	Na	41.01	40.69
15–24 years	0.12	0.11	0.11	0.13	0.10	Na	0.10	0.11
25–34 years	0.25	0.26	0.25	0.24	0.25	Na	0.25	0.25
35–64 years	0.57	0.60	0.59	0.56	0.58	Na	0.59	0.57
65+ years	0.06	0.03	0.05	0.07*	0.06	Na	0.06	0.07
Self-employed can read or write	0.37	0.58	0.41	0.33**	0.49	Na	0.53	0.44***
Self-employed has studied in formal school	0.32	0.53	0.35	0.29	0.43	Na	0.46	0.40
Branch of activity: food processing	0.01	0.00	0.01	0.01	0.04	Na	0.03	0.05**
Branch of activity: manufacture/construction	0.35	0.21	0.30	0.38	0.30	Na	0.27	0.33
Branch of activity: sales	0.46	0.56	0.52	0.42*	0.48	Na	0.51	0.45**
Branch of activity: services	0.18	0.23	0.17	0.18	0.18	Na	0.20	0.17

Note: 'Na' means 'not available' due to missing data on variables related to formal work status (see Table 10.1). Significant differences across informal work status groups are tested using bivariate regressions and sampling weights. Significant levels are indicated by * $p < 0.10$, ** $p < 0.05$, *** $p<0.01$.
Source: authors' calculations based on LSMS–ISA data for Mali and Niger.

4.2 Earnings and dispersal in earnings-related variables

Figure 10.1 presents the earnings (gross revenue) from self-employment in Niger and Mali. Average earnings are calculated for each country on the pooled sample (two rounds combined), adjusted for inflation and converted to 2017 US dollar values. Observations with zero earnings and with outlier values are not considered.

Figure 10.1 shows the same trend in monthly average earnings in both countries: on average, formal self-employment work pays more than informal work of either status. Within the informal work status groups, upper-tier informal self-employed workers earn more than lower-tier informal self-employed workers.

Table 10.3 summarizes the earnings disaggregated by gender of self-employed workers and the branches of their activity. Overall, the trend observed above is consistent within the disaggregated groups of self-employed workers. In addition, irrespective of work status, self-employed men earn higher revenues in both countries. This echoes the common trend observed in SSA and Latin American countries (Bruhn 2009; Nix et al. 2015). Regarding branches of activity, formal work status offers the highest earnings in both countries within all branches except food processing, where high incomes are also observed in the upper-tier informal work status. Note, however, that the difference in average earnings between

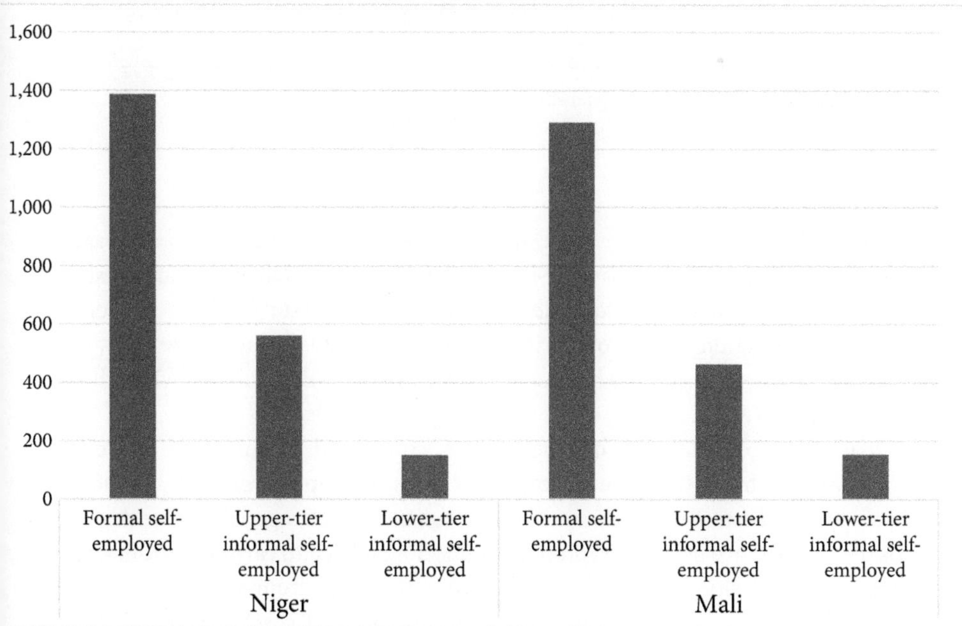

Fig. 10.1 Mean earnings by work status, Niger and Mali

Source: authors' illustration based on Living Standards Measurement Study–Integrated Surveys on Agriculture (LSMS–ISA) data for Mali and Niger.

Table 10.3 Average monthly earnings from self-employment, by gender and branch of activity (US$ 2017)

	All self-employed workers	By gender of self-employed worker		By branch of activity			
		Women	Men	Food processing	Manufacture and construction	Sales	Services
Niger	**(N = 6,418)**						
All enterprises	274.46	97.53	410.81	151.41	169.99	456.10	135.80
Formal	1,386.62	415.28	1,935.35	385.32	1,418.92	1,966.97	659.25
Upper-tier informal	559.94	173.70	685.77	392.39	434.71	799.39	266.97
Lower-tier informal	151.05	78.52	222.40	97.51	61.62	261.62	81.98
Mali	**(N = 2,414)**						
All enterprises	352.63	132.38	553.41	136.28	274.00	434.08	290.76
Formal	1,290.40	249.48	1,571.39	52.24	2247.72	988.57	590.20
Upper-tier informal	462.22	168.83	620.61	448.48	331.64	544.36	424.39
Lower-tier informal	153.90	90.43	232.23	94.13	106.31	175.98	197.27

Note: Statistics are presented on the pooled sample (two rounds combined).
Source: authors' calculations based on LSMS–ISA data for Mali and Niger.

the formal and the upper-tier work status groups is slight. Note also that average earnings in the formal status (upper-tier informal status) in Mali may be underestimated (overestimated) as the data derive only from the first survey, for the reasons explained in section 3. The comparison within work status groups shows that, in most cases, sales generate the highest average incomes when compared with other activities.

It must be remembered that the workers considered in our study are self-employed—either own-account workers or owners (employers)—and, as such, likely to bear costs. With this in mind, we explore the heterogeneity in work status observed above using two additional indicators related to earnings: profit and labour productivity. Profit is defined as the net revenue from self-employment activity, which equals the gross revenue minus the total cost of operating the activity. We define labour productivity as the gross revenue divided by the number of workers used in operating the activity, including family labour and the owner. Figure 10.2 shows the dispersal of profit and labour productivity by work status in the two countries using the pooled data with the two rounds combined and kernel density estimates.

Figure 10.2 shows large differences in profit and labour productivity between work status groups, with more pronounced trends in Mali for both profit and labour productivity, and, within Niger, for labour productivity. Overall, lower-tier informal (formal/upper-tier informal) self-employed workers have lower (higher) profits and labour productivity—a finding consistent with our expectation and evidence reported in previous studies (Benjamin and Mbaye 2012; Bezu and Barrett 2012). Differences in the educational level of the workers may be one explanation for this. Based on the assumption that managerial capacity is important for productivity, Nagler and Naudé (2017), using LSMS—ISA data for four

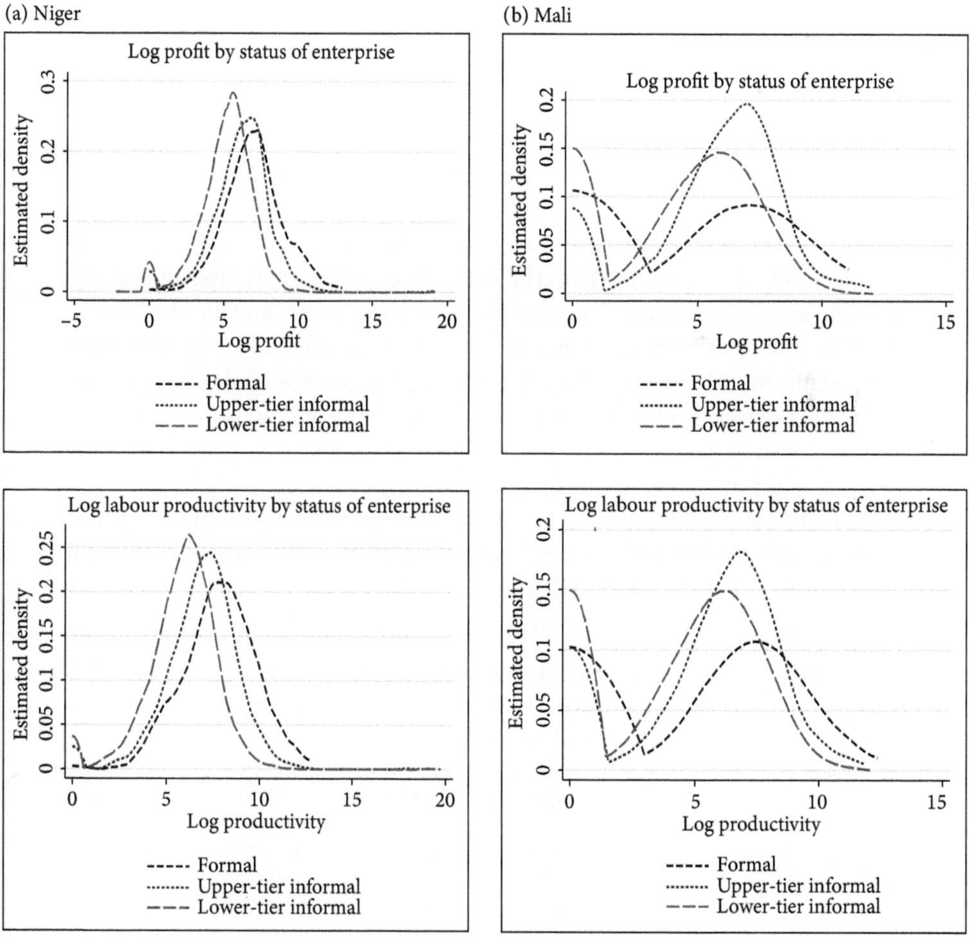

Fig. 10.2 Profit and productivity dispersal by work status

Source: authors' illustration based on LSMS–ISA data for Mali and Niger.

anglophone African countries, found that literate self-employed workers, proxied by the ability to read and write, operate more productively. This is consistent with our data as we found that self-employed workers who were able to read and write were more represented in the formal and upper-tier informal work status groups in both countries (Table 10.2). The labour productivity pattern is also consistent among self-employed women and men but with more dispersal and wider variance for women (Figure 10.A1).

5. The dynamics of off-farm self-employment work

We also analysed the transition of self-employed workers from one work status to another between the two survey rounds. As explained in section 3 on data, we focused on the panel database of Niger with the 1,465 identical self-employed workers followed in the two surveys.

5.1 Transition probabilities and livelihoods

Table 10.4 reports the transition probabilities between different work status groups in Niger from 2011 to 2014. The cells in the shaded area of the table indicate the percentage of self-employed moving from work status i in 2011 to work status j in 2014. The rows refer to the number of self-employed workers in each initial work status in 2011 and sum to 100 per cent. The column totals thus show the percentage of self-employed workers who moved into work status j in 2014. The proportion of workers who stayed in their initial work status is calculated as the product of the transition matrix diagonals and the initial share of workers.

Table 10.4 shows that more than half of self-employed workers did not change work status in 2014 (66.75 per cent), the majority of the stayers being found in the lower-tier informal status (49.76 per cent). However, looking at the transitions

Table 10.4 Transition probabilities for self-employed workers in Niger (percentage)

	Work status in 2014				
Work status in 2011	**Formal**	**Upper-tier informal**	**Lower-tier informal**	**Total % (N)**	**Share of stayers %**
Formal	13.41	41.46	45.12	100 (82)	0.75
Upper-tier informal	3.26	51.74	45	100 (460)	16.24
Lower-tier informal	0.98	20.04	78.98	100 (923)	49.76
Total %	2.39	31.19	66.42	100 (1465)	66.75

Source: authors' calculation based on LSMS–ISA data for Niger.

between work status groups, there is a non-negligible proportion of self-employed workers that moved from their initial work status to alternatives. Of the 923 self-employed in the lower-tier informal work status in 2011, 20.04 per cent and 0.98 per cent were able to transit to upper-tier informal work status and formal work status, respectively. Of the 460 self-employed in the upper-tier informal work status in 2011, 3.26 per cent were able to transit to formal work status. The frequency of self-employed workers exiting the upper-tier informal and formal status groups is higher than the frequency of upper-tier informal self-employed workers entering the formal work status, suggesting the difficulty of moving to a higher work status and the existence of factors or forces pushing or maintaining self-employed workers in a lower work status. This tendency may be explained by workers' gender and household-related factors.

We therefore first disaggregate the transition matrix by the sex of self-employed workers. Table 10.5 shows that the percentage of self-employed women that moved to the lower-tier informal work status is even higher and the percentage of self-employed women that transited to a higher work status is even lower than those observed in the whole sample of self-employed workers. This transition movement is contrary to that observed for self-employed men (Table 10.5).

Second, we compare the mean initial household endowment (human and physical capital) across work status groups in the first survey round (Table 10.6). Human capital consists of labour and education. Labour is defined as the number of adult household members. Education is defined as the shares of adult household members having a primary education level versus having at least a secondary level of education. Physical capital are land per adult equivalent, tropical livestock unit,

Table 10.5 Transition probabilities by sex of self-employed workers in Niger (percentage)

	Work status in 2014				
Work status in 2011	**Formal**	**Upper-tier informal**	**Lower-tier informal**	**Total % (N)**	**Share of stayers %**
Self-employed women					
Formal	4.17	4.17	91.67	100 (24)	0.18
Upper-tier informal	1.87	37.38	60.75	100 (107)	7.05
Lower-tier informal	0	11.93	88.07	100 (436)	67.72
Total %	0.53	16.4	83.07	100 (567)	74.95
Self-employed men					
Formal	17.24	56.9	25.86	100 (58)	1.11
Upper-tier informal	3.68	56.09	40.23	100 (353)	22.05
Lower-tier informal	1.85	27.31	70.84	100 (487)	38.42
Total %	3.56	40.53	55.9	100 (898)	61.58

Source: authors' calculations based on LSMS–ISA data for Niger.

Table 10.6 Initial household endowment by work status in Niger in 2011

	Work status in 2011					
	Formal (82)		Upper-tier informal (460)		Lower-tier informal (923)	
	Mean	SE	Mean	SE	Mean	SE
Adult household members (#)	3.70	0.25**	3.16	0.13	3.05	0.06
Adult with primary education (share)	0.17	0.03*	0.14	0.01	0.12	0.01
Adult above primary education (share)	0.09	0.02	0.09	0.01**	0.06	0.01
Livestock (tropical livestock unit)	3.24	0.80	3.02	0.43	2.68	0.17
Land holding (hectares)	3.96	0.67**	4.76	1.11	4.68	0.25
Value of assets owned (in 1,000 FCFA)	359.8	74.0***	375.8	202.4***	250.5	108.0

Note: 'SE' means standard errors. Significant differences between the higher work status groups and the lower-tier informal work status are tested using bivariate regressions and sampling weights. Significant levels are indicated by * $p < 0.10$, ** $p < 0.05$, *** $p < 0.01$.
Source: authors' calculations based on LSMS–ISA data for Niger.

Table 10.7 Initial household endowment by transition into lower-tier informal work status

	Formal and upper-tier informal work status groups (493)			
	Stayed (249)		Moved (244)	
	Mean	SE	Mean	SE
Adult household members (#)	3.43	0.23	3.08	0.13
Adult with primary education (share)	0.17	0.02	0.12	0.02**
Adult above primary education (share)	0.13	0.02	0.06	0.01***
Livestock (tropical livestock unit)	3.38	0.87	3.02	0.35
Land holding (hectares)	0.74	0.11	1.77	0.57*
Value of assets (in 1,000 FCFA)	97.95	20.87	29.80	3.64***

Note: 'SE' means standard errors. Significant differences are tested using bivariate regressions and sampling weights. Significant levels are indicated by * $p < 0.10$. ** $p < 0.05$, *** $p < 0.01$.
Source: authors' calculations based on LSMS–ISA data for Niger.

and per adult equivalent value of household assets such as vehicles, dwelling, furniture, and appliances. Table 10.6 shows that households in the formal work status have significantly higher human capital (labour and adult share with a primary education level), higher assets, and lower land endowments than those in the informal work status groups. Households in the upper-tier informal work status have a significantly higher adult share above a primary education level and higher assets than those in the lower-tier informal work status.

Overall, self-employed workers initially in the higher work status groups possessed significantly higher household human and physical capital than self-employed workers initially in the lower-tier informal work status. Moreover, compared with those who stayed in their initial work status in 2014, formal and upper-tier informal self-employed workers who transited into the lower-tier informal work status had significantly lower mean initial household endowments of education and assets (Table 10.7). This supports the finding in the non-farm employment literature that possession or accumulation of capital is necessary for low-return non-farm employment to enter high-return non-farm employment (Bezu and Barrett 2012).

5.2 The correlates of moving into upper-tier informal and formal work status groups

We next determine the factors that explain the transition of self-employed workers from the lower-tier informal work status to formal and upper-tier informal work status groups. We pull the samples of formal and upper-tier informal work status groups together because of the small sample size of the former. We thus estimate the probability of self-employed workers moving from the lower-tier informal work status in the first panel round to a higher work status in the second panel round as:

$$P(\textit{moved into}\ \text{formal or upper-tier in formal work status}_{i,\,2014} = 1 \mid \text{being in lower-tier in formal work status}_{i,\,2011} = 1) = \alpha X_{i,2011} + u_{i,2014} \qquad (1)$$

where α is a vector of the parameters to be estimated and u_i the error terms. X_i is a set of explanatory variables defined at the previous survey round (2011) to reduce potential reverse causality bias. These variables are human and physical capital, worker and household characteristics, and shocks experienced by the households during the 12 months prior to the second survey round. Regarding financial capital, the data set for Niger did not record any questions that might allow an assessment of access to finance, except information on the main source of financing self-employment work, recorded only in the second round of the survey. According to this 2014 survey round, financing stemmed mostly from savings and gifts from parents and relatives (88 per cent of the 1,465 self-employed workers of our panel data). Only in a few cases (5 per cent) did financing come from a loan. We therefore use household income from non-employment work as a proxy for access to financial capital.

The model (1) is estimated using a probit regression. The model was run on the sample of lower-tier informal self-employed workers in 2011 and explains why some moved to a higher work status while others did not transit at all. Results are presented in Table 10.8 with different specifications, first including only household characteristics (column 1), then adding other businesses activity characteristics (column 2), community variables (column 3), shocks experienced by the households the workers belong to (column 4), and interaction between some shocks and wealth variables (column 5). Standard errors are adjusted for cluster within households in all regressions.

Table 10.8 shows that workers' gender and age are significantly correlated with moving into formal and upper-tier informal work status. Self-employed men in the lower-tier informal work status are more likely than women to move out of this work status. Most self-employed women operate their businesses from a fixed dwelling, which is a specific characteristic of the lower-tier informal work status. As those who generally take care of the family, they may not be able to move their business activities to fixed locations outside the dwelling, where most upper-tier informal workers run their business activities. Compared with the other age groups, younger and older self-employed workers are also less likely to move out of the lower-tier informal worker status.

Household characteristics and initial wealth endowment are also drivers of the transition movement. Lower-tier informal self-employed workers belonging to households with a higher share of dependants are less likely to exit the lower-tier informal work status. More dependants in the household may indicate low availability of the potential labour endowment required for higher work status groups. Self-employed workers belonging to the Haoussa ethnicity (whose members have historically been principally involved in marketing activities) are more likely to transit into the formal and upper-tier informal work status groups, suggesting the positive role of social capital not only in off-farm businesses development in Niger (Dedehouanou et al. 2018) but also in off-farm employment dynamics.

Initial asset holdings in terms of wealth are positively associated with transition out of lower-tier work status, consistent with previous results found in Ethiopia (Bezu and Barrett 2012). Initial earnings from self-employment are likely to induce a move out of the lower-tier informal work status to a higher work status, probably because more productive self-employed workers have a potential to grow their business activity and are thus able to become employers and comply with the regulations formal and upper-tier informal self-employed workers are subject to. This is in line with the study by McCaig and Pavcnik (2017), which showed that initially performant self-employed workers in Viet Nam are more likely to become formal workers and employers.

An increase in household non-labour income itself is less likely to make lower-tier informal self-employed workers transit. However, in column 5, the coefficient of the interaction term between income shock and initial household non-labour income is positive. Thus, for lower-tier informal self-employed workers belonging

Table 10.8 Probit estimation of correlates of moving into upper-tier informal or formal work status

	(1)	(2)	(3)	(4)	(5)
Workerss is male	0.837***	0.815***	0.790***	0.810***	0.843***
	(0.178)	(0.188)	(0.188)	(0.187)	(0.185)
Worker is married	−0.161	−0.153	−0.141	−0.217	−0.238
	(0.225)	(0.234)	(0.234)	(0.241)	(0.242)
Age of worker: 25–34 years (ref. 15–24 years)	0.885**	0.942**	0.921**	0.894**	0.811**
	(0.395)	(0.397)	(0.406)	(0.398)	(0.406)
Age of worker: 35–64 years	0.896**	0.847**	0.837**	0.817**	0.735*
	(0.364)	(0.378)	(0.383)	(0.373)	(0.383)
Age of worker: 65+ years	−0.258	−0.430	−0.411	−0.394	−0.463
	(0.429)	(0.482)	(0.483)	(0.477)	(0.491)
Education of worker (years)	0.013	0.013	0.011	0.014	0.016
	(0.030)	(0.032)	(0.031)	(0.030)	(0.030)
Worker can read or write in any language	−0.180	−0.168	−0.141	−0.160	−0.172
	(0.173)	(0.177)	(0.176)	(0.173)	(0.174)
Number of adults in household	−0.034	−0.028	−0.033	−0.025	−0.014
	(0.047)	(0.050)	(0.049)	(0.049)	(0.050)
Number of dependants in household	−0.072***	−0.071**	−0.074***	−0.074***	−0.073***
	(0.028)	(0.028)	(0.028)	(0.027)	(0.028)
Adult with primary education (share)	0.361	0.351	0.376	0.361	0.352
	(0.352)	(0.368)	(0.365)	(0.379)	(0.377)
Adult above primary education (share)	−0.562	−0.638	−0.709	−0.647	−0.767
	(0.502)	(0.506)	(0.507)	(0.491)	(0.501)
Ethnicity: Haoussa	0.396**	0.353*	0.369*	0.348*	0.371*
	(0.200)	(0.208)	(0.208)	(0.211)	(0.218)

Continued

Table 10.8 *Continued*

	(1)	(2)	(3)	(4)	(5)
Ethnicity: Djema	−0.327	−0.359	−0.271	−0.335	−0.330
	(0.245)	(0.256)	(0.252)	(0.256)	(0.259)
Ethnicity: Touareg	−0.085	−0.134	−0.092	−0.173	−0.155
	(0.295)	(0.314)	(0.315)	(0.315)	(0.316)
Wealth (index)	0.071*	0.071*	0.073*	0.076*	0.105**
	(0.043)	(0.043)	(0.043)	(0.043)	(0.044)
Livestock (tropical units)	0.007	−0.001	−0.003	−0.003	−0.032
	(0.015)	(0.015)	(0.015)	(0.016)	(0.024)
Log (non-labour income)	−0.024**	−0.027**	−0.026**	−0.028**	−0.032**
	(0.012)	(0.012)	(0.012)	(0.012)	(0.013)
Age of business activity (years)	–	0.011	0.012	0.011	0.009
	–	(0.008)	(0.008)	(0.008)	(0.008)
Log (annual earnings from self-employment)	–	0.059**	0.065**	0.063**	0.063**
	–	(0.029)	(0.030)	(0.030)	(0.031)
Distance (km) to nearest major road	–	–	0.010	0.011	0.010
	–	–	(0.007)	(0.007)	(0.007)
Distance to nearest market	–	–	0.001	0.002	0.002
	–	–	(0.002)	(0.002)	(0.002)
Finance institution exists in community	–	–	−0.201	−0.156	−0.107
	–	–	(0.206)	(0.210)	(0.208)
Community radio exists in community	–	–	0.359	0.392	0.438*
	–	–	(0.242)	(0.242)	(0.246)
Public transport passes through community	–	–	0.017	0.038	0.018
	–	–	(0.151)	(0.148)	(0.149)

Geographical shock: drought/flood	–	–	–	0.282^{*}	−0.100
	–	–	–	(0.149)	(0.209)
Idiosyncratic shock: death/illness	–	–	–	0.231	0.206
	–	–	–	(0.172)	(0.173)
Price shock: food, input, output	–	–	–	0.089	0.108
	–	–	–	(0.143)	(0.143)
Income shock: loss of revenue from non-farm activity	–	–	–	-0.444^{*}	-0.978^{***}
	–	–	–	(0.228)	(0.300)
Geographical shock *Wealth	–	–	–	–	-0.210^{*}
	–	–	–	–	(0.122)
Geographical shock *Livestock	–	–	–	–	0.083^{**}
	–	–	–	–	(0.040)
Income shock *Log (non-labour income)	–	–	–	–	0.079^{**}
	–	–	–	–	(0.040)
Rural	-0.604^{***}	-0.596^{***}	-0.752^{***}	-0.805^{***}	-0.820^{***}
	(0.166)	(0.172)	(0.214)	(0.214)	(0.218)
Constant	-1.423^{**}	-2.195^{***}	-2.540^{***}	-2.423^{***}	-2.431^{***}
	(0.556)	(0.600)	(0.668)	(0.695)	(0.724)
Number of observations	923	876	876	876	876
McFadden's (Pseudo) R-squared	0.17	0.18	0.19	0.21	0.22
Log pseudolikelihood	−281,990.87	−268,787.17	−266,202.55	−260,913.19	−256,898.51

Note: Wealth index is calculated as the first principal component of household assets such as vehicles, dwelling, furniture, and appliances. Region dummies are included in the regressions. Survey weights were used. Standard errors, adjusted for clusters within household, in parentheses. Explanatory variables are lagged with three time periods (from the first survey round 2011). Significant levels are indicated by * $p < 0.10$, ** $p < 0.05$, *** $p < 0.01$.
Source: authors' calculations based on LSMS–ISA data for Niger.

to households that have experienced an income shock, higher initial household non-labour income is deemed to be a factor likely to favour transition into formal and upper-tier informal work status groups. This suggests the role of non-labour income in mitigating income shocks that might otherwise keep workers in the lower-tier informal work status.

Covariate shocks also affect the transition movement. For lower-tier informal self-employed workers belonging to households that have experienced natural disasters such as floods, droughts, or pest infestations, a higher initial livestock endowment is positively related to movement into a higher work status. The existence of a community radio in the village or neighbourhood is likely to favour transition out the lower-tier work status, suggesting the importance of information transfer in employment dynamics.

Table 10.9 presents heterogenous results by sex of self-employed worker and by geographical location of business activity. As the age of both female and male self-employed workers increases, the likelihood of the transition into a higher status group increases but with a return effect as age reaches a certain level. There are some significant differences between female and male lower-tier informal self-employed workers in terms of the factors moving them into higher status groups. Table 10.9 shows that married men are more likely than married women to transit out of the lower-tier informal work status. Literate men, members of households with a higher share of dependants, and men living in rural areas are less likely to move out of the lower-tier informal work status. Men with a long history of self-employment, men belonging to the Haoussa ethnicity, and men living in households with a high initial level of wealth are more likely to transit to higher work status groups. Compared with male business owners, where no significant results are found, performant female workers with previously or initially high annual business revenues are more likely to move into a higher work status. Information transfer is also an important factor in the transition out of the lower-tier informal status for self-employed women. For female workers belonging to households that have experienced negative consequences of aggregate shocks, higher initial wealth (livestock) endowment is negatively (positively) related to the transition to higher status groups, suggesting the mitigating role of livestock over wealth.

Examining the results disaggregated by location, Table 10.9 also shows significant differences in terms of human capital, financial capital, and shocks. Regarding labour, urban self-employed workers with a high initial household labour endowment are less likely to move out of the lower-tier informal work status. Rural self-employed workers with a high initial household share of dependants are also less likely to move out of the lowest work status. Education—even primary school completion—is a significant factor explaining the likelihood of self-employed workers transiting into the formal and upper-tier informal work

Table 10.9 Probit estimation of correlates of moving into upper-tier informal or formal work status groups, by sex of workers and location

	By sex of self-employed worker		By location	
	Men	Women	Urban	Rural
Worker is male	–	–	1.411***	0.776***
	–	–	(0.220)	(0.262)
Worker is married	0.866**	−0.430	−0.167	−0.336
	(0.391)	(0.297)	(0.252)	(0.449)
Age of worker	0.108**	0.105**	0.123***	0.142***
	(0.045)	(0.052)	(0.045)	(0.050)
Age of worker square	−0.001***	−0.001*	−0.001**	−0.002***
	(0.000)	(0.001)	(0.000)	(0.001)
Education of worker (years)	0.046	−0.014	−0.010	0.043
	(0.039)	(0.042)	(0.033)	(0.049)
Worker can read or write in any language	−0.379*	0.069	−0.358	−0.127
	(0.203)	(0.338)	(0.244)	(0.229)
Number of adults in household	0.070	−0.030	−0.163**	0.015
	(0.076)	(0.064)	(0.063)	(0.078)
Number of dependants in household	−0.097***	−0.050	0.037	−0.144***
	(0.037)	(0.042)	(0.039)	(0.038)
Adult with primary education (share)	−0.285	0.670	1.142***	−0.088
	(0.474)	(0.424)	(0.410)	(0.646)
Adult above primary education (share)	−0.945	−0.635	0.684	−1.963*
	(0.774)	(0.685)	(0.539)	(1.095)
Ethnicity: Haoussa	0.764***	−0.222	−0.098	1.165***
	(0.274)	(0.348)	(0.285)	(0.398)
Ethnicity: Djema	−0.373	−0.301	−0.123	0.273
	(0.344)	(0.384)	(0.327)	(0.460)
Ethnicity: Touareg	−0.295	0.548	0.036	0.369
	(0.351)	(0.506)	(0.380)	(0.534)
Wealth (index)	0.203*	0.016	0.095**	0.261*
	(0.106)	(0.060)	(0.045)	(0.135)
Livestock (tropical units)	−0.015	−0.107	−0.020	−0.053
	(0.027)	(0.069)	(0.043)	(0.035)
Log (non-labour income)	−0.041**	−0.045*	−0.019	−0.036**
	(0.017)	(0.025)	(0.019)	(0.017)
Age of business activity (years)	0.021**	−0.016	−0.010	0.017
	(0.010)	(0.015)	(0.013)	(0.011)
Log (annual earnings from self-employment)	0.058	0.156**	0.109***	0.044
	(0.040)	(0.071)	(0.042)	(0.046)

Continued

Table 10.9 *Continued*

	By sex of self-employed worker		By location	
	Men	Women	Urban	Rural
Distance (km) to nearest major road	0.011 (0.009)	−0.012 (0.014)	−0.066 (0.091)	0.009 (0.008)
Distance to nearest market	0.005* (0.003)	0.000 (0.004)	0.007 (0.004)	0.003 (0.003)
Finance institution exists in community	−0.057 (0.292)	−0.386 (0.368)	0.152 (0.224)	−0.154 (0.539)
Community radio exists in community	0.036 (0.324)	0.835** (0.371)	−0.236 (0.321)	1.214*** (0.423)
Public transport passes through community	−0.031 (0.193)	−0.169 (0.290)	0.268 (0.254)	0.043 (0.191)
Geographical shock: drought/flood	0.220 (0.269)	−2.127*** (0.815)	−0.229 (0.344)	−0.222 (0.366)
Idiosyncratic shock: death/illness	0.130 (0.245)	0.302 (0.332)	−0.513* (0.264)	0.479** (0.227)
Price shock: food, input, output	0.232 (0.194)	−0.257 (0.293)	−0.081 (0.207)	0.148 (0.186)
Income shock: loss of revenue from non-farm activity	−0.791** (0.332)	−2.457*** (0.666)	−0.366 (0.329)	−3.251* (1.896)
Geographical shock *Wealth	−0.121 (0.162)	−1.397** (0.550)	−0.001 (0.135)	−0.344 (0.222)
Geographical shock *Livestock	0.062 (0.055)	0.216** (0.084)	−0.233 (0.226)	0.124** (0.053)
Income shock *Log (non-labour income)	0.085* (0.052)	0.193*** (0.062)	−0.017 (0.041)	0.327* (0.188)
Rural	−1.219*** (0.293)	−0.078 (0.318)	– –	– –
Constant	−4.342*** (1.405)	−5.112*** (1.529)	−6.142*** (1.419)	−5.409*** (1.452)
Number of observations	466	403	344	532
McFadden's (Pseudo) R-squared	0.25	0.33	0.32	0.27
Log pseudolikelihood	−171,397.59	−54,192.48	−54,877.8	−174,404.61

Note: Wealth index is calculated as the first principal component of household assets such as vehicles, dwelling, furniture, and appliances. Region dummies are included in the regressions. Survey weights were used. Standard errors, adjusted for clusters within household, in parentheses. Explanatory variables are lagged with three time periods (from the first survey round 2011). Significant levels are indicated by * $p < 0.10$, ** $p < 0.05$, *** $p < 0.01$.
Source: authors' calculations based on LSMS–ISA data for Niger.

status groups, especially in urban areas. High initial/previous annual income from self-employment in urban zones is positively correlated with the likelihood of transiting to a higher work status. Unexpected idiosyncratic shocks are likely to cause urban self-employed workers to stay and rural self-employed workers to transit.

6. Conclusions

Evidence that the majority of self-employment work in most developing countries remains informal has prompted several attempts to encourage formalization reforms, with mixed results (McKenzie and Sakho 2010; Bruhn and McKenzie 2014; McCaig and Nanowski 2019). We have addressed the nature of informal self-employment work in two fragile and conflict-affected countries in the West African Sahel—Mali and Niger. In doing so, we have gone beyond the duality of formal versus informal employment that is common in the literature. We have differentiated informal non-farm self-employed workers into lower-tier and upper-tier work status groups and have analysed mobility, and the factors explaining it, between work status groups.

We find that a key characteristic of self-employed workers is the location of their business activities, with more than one-third of workers employed in mobile/itinerant microenterprises. Given that this type of business requires low capital and skills, it is not surprising that the majority of self-employed workers are found in the lower-tier informal work status, especially in Niger (70 per cent). Self-employed women, self-employed workers in rural areas, youth and young adult self-employed workers (aged 15–24), and older adult self-employed workers (aged 65 and above) are mostly found in the lower-tier informal status in Niger and Mali. Although, in both countries, most self-employed workers are able to read or write at least one language, educated workers are more represented in the formal and upper-tier informal work status groups. On average, monthly average earnings are higher in the formal work status than in the informal work status groups. Within the informal status groups, upper-tier informal self-employed workers earn more than lower-tier informal self-employed workers. The comparison within work status groups shows that, in most cases, activities involving sales generate the highest average incomes within, compared with other activities.

We also found that more than half of self-employed workers did not change their work status between survey rounds, the majority of the 'stayers' being in the lower-tier informal status. The transition out of upper-tier informal and formal work status groups is higher than the transition into these 'high' work status groups, suggesting the existence of factors or forces pushing or maintaining self-employed workers in the 'low' work status. Overall, self-employed workers initially in higher work status groups possess significantly higher household human and physical capital than those initially in the lower-tier informal work status, suggesting that possession of human and physical capital is necessary for self-employed workers to transit out of the lower-tier informal work status. Consistent with the regression results, we found that household characteristics, initial asset holdings, and initial earnings from self-employment are drivers of the transition out of the lower-tier informal work status. The regression results showed the mitigating role of household non-labour income on income shocks (unexpected loss of revenue from non-agricultural and salaried activities) that might prevent self-employed workers from moving out of the lower-tier informal work status.

Finally, we found significant differences between urban and rural workers and between women and men in the lower-tier informal status in terms of the factors likely to move them into higher status groups. Self-employed men with a high initial level of wealth are more likely to transit. Rural self-employed workers and self-employed women with a high initial annual business revenue are also more likely to move up. For rural workers belonging to households that have experienced negative consequences of aggregate shocks and income shocks, a higher initial livestock endowment and non-labour income are factors that may prevent them from remaining stuck in the lower-tier informal work status.

These results indicate the heterogeneity of the groups of self-employed workers found in the lower-tier informal work status. These groups of individuals are the most vulnerable to shocks affecting their business activities. Given that the movement from the lower-tier informal work status to the upper-tier informal and formal work status groups is likely to be welfare improving, the results stress the importance of taking into account these specific groups of workers in designing policy interventions for transforming informal work and livelihoods—a fact further emphasized by the recent COVID-19 pandemic (Balde et al. 2020; Danquah et al. 2020). Household-related factors such as asset holdings, livestock endowment, and non-labour income, may play a role in helping these vulnerable groups transit to a higher work status, even in the event of shocks.

References

Alaniz, E., T.H. Gindling, C. Mata, and D. Rojas (2020). 'Transforming Informal Work and Livelihoods in Costa Rica and Nicaragua'. WIDER Working Paper No. 2020/100. Helsinki: UNU-WIDER. https://doi.org/10.35188/UNU-WIDER/2020/857-3.

Amin, M. (2010). 'Necessity vs. Opportunity: Entrepreneurs in the Informal Sector'. Enterprise note 17. Washington, DC: World Bank Group.

Babbitt, L.G., D. Brown, and N. Mazaheri (2015). 'Gender, Entrepreneurship, and the Formal–Informal Dilemma: Evidence from Indonesia'. *World Development*, 72: 163–174. https://doi.org/10.1016/j.worlddev.2015.02.019.

Balde, R., M. Boly, and E. Avenyo (2020). 'Labour Market Effects of Covid-19 in Sub-Saharan Africa: An Informality Lens from Burkina Faso, Mali, and Senegal'. United Nations University-Maastricht Economic and Social Research Institute on

Innovation and Technology (UNU-MERIT) Working Paper No. 2020–022. Maastricht: UNU-MERIT.

Banerjee, A.V., and E. Duflo (2007). 'The Economic Lives of the Poor'. *Journal of Economic Perspectives*, 21(1): 141–167. https://doi.org/10.1257/jep.21.1.141.

Bekele, E., and Z. Worku (2008). 'Factors that Affect the Long-Term Survival of Micro, Small and Medium Enterprises in Ethiopia'. *South African Journal of Economics*, 7(3): 548–568. https://doi.org/10.1111/j.1813-6982.2008.00207.x.

Benjamin, N., and A.A. Mbaye (2012). *The Informal Sector in Francophone Africa: Firm Size, Productivity and Institutions*. Washington, DC: The World Bank. https://doi.org/10.1596/978-0-8213-9537-0.

Bennett, J. (2010). 'Informal Firms in Developing Countries: Entrepreneurial Stepping Stone or Consolation Prize?' *Small Business Economics*, 34(1): 53–63. https://doi.org/10.1007/s11187-009-9194-6.

Berge, L.I.O., and A.J.G. Pires (2015). 'Gender, Social Norms, and Entrepreneurship'. SNF Working Paper No. 05/15. Bergen: Samfunns- og næringslivsforskning AS (Centre for Applied Research at NHH). Available at: https://openaccess.nhh.no/nhh-xmlui/bitstream/handle/11250/295765/A05_15.pdf?sequence=1&isAllowed=y (accessed 19 October 2020).

Bezu, S., and C. Barrett (2012). 'Employment Dynamics in the Rural Nonfarm Sector in Ethiopia: Do the Poor Have Time on Their Side?' *Journal of Development Studies*, 48(9): 1223–1240. https://doi.org/10.1080/00220388.2012.671476.

Bruhn, M. (2009). 'Female-Owned Firms in Latin America: Characteristics, Performance, and Obstacles to Growth'. Policy Research Working Paper No. 5122. Washington, DC: World Bank. https://doi.org/10.1596/1813-9450-5122.

Bruhn, M., and D. McKenzie (2014). 'Entry Regulation and the Formalization of Microenterprises in Developing Countries'. *World Bank Research Observer*, 29: 186–201. https://doi.org/10.1093/wbro/lku002.

Campos, F.M.L., M.P. Goldstein, and D.J. McKenzie (2018). 'How Should the Government Bring Small Firms into the Formal System? Experimental Evidence from Malawi'. Policy Research Working Paper No. 8601. Washington, DC: World Bank Group. https://doi.org/10.1596/1813-9450-8601.

Danquah, M., S. Schotte, and K. Sen (2019). 'Informal Work in Sub-Saharan Africa: Dead End or Stepping Stone?' WIDER Working Paper No. 2019/107. Helsinki: UNU-WIDER. https://doi.org/10.35188/UNU-WIDER/2019/743-9.

Danquah, M., S. Schotte, and K. Sen (2020). 'COVID-19 and Employment: Insights from the Sub-Saharan African Experience'. WIDER Background Note No. 7/2020. Helsinki: UNU-WIDER. Available at: https://www.wider.unu.edu/sites/default/files/Publications/Background-note/PDF/bn2020-7-covid-19-employment-subSaharan-Africa.pdf (accessed 19 October 2020).

Dedehouanou, S.F.A., A. Araar, A. Ousseini, A.L Harouna, and M. Jabir (2018). 'Spillovers from Off-Farm Self-Employment Opportunities in Rural Niger'. *World Development*, 105: 428–442. https://doi.org/10.1016/j.worlddev.2017. 12.005.

Fox, L., and T.P. Sohnesen (2012). 'Household Enterprises in Sub-Saharan Africa: Why They Matter for Growth, Jobs, and Livelihoods'. Policy Research Working Paper No. 6184. Washington, DC: World Bank Africa Region Poverty Reduction and Economic Management Unit. https://doi.org/10.1596/1813-9450-6184.

Fox, L., L.W. Senbet, and W. Simbanegavi (2016). 'Youth Employment in Sub-Saharan Africa: Challenges, Constraints and Opportunities'. *Journal of African Economies*, 25(1): i3–i15. https://doi.org/10.1093/jae/ejv027.

Gollin, D. (2008). 'Nobody's Business but My Own: Self-Employment and Small Enterprise in Economic Development'. *Journal of Monetary Economics*, 55(2): 219–233. https://doi.org/10.1016/j.jmoneco.2007.11.003.

Grimm, M., P. Knorringa, and J. Lay (2012). 'Constrained Gazelles: High Potentials in West Africa's Informal Economy'. *World Development*, 40: 1352–1368. https://doi.org/10.1016/j.worlddev.2012.03.009.

ILO (International Labour Organization) (2018). *Women and Men in the Informal Economy: A Statistical Picture* (3rd edn). Geneva: International Labour Office.

Jayachandran, S. (2020). 'Microentrepreneurship in Developing Countries'. National Bureau of Economic Research (NBER) Working Paper 26661. Cambridge, MA: NBER. https://doi.org/10.3386/w26661.

La Porta, R.L., and A. Shleifer (2014). 'Informality and Development'. *Journal of Economic Perspectives*, 28: 109–126. Available at: https://pubs.aeaweb.org/doi/pdfplus/10.1257/jep.28.3.109 (accessed 19 October 2020).

McCaig, B., and J. Nanowski (2019). 'Business Formalisation in Vietnam'. *Journal of Development Studies*, 55(5): 805–821. https://doi.org/10.1080/00220388.2018.1475646.

McCaig, B., and N. Pavcnik (2015). 'Informal Employment in a Growing and Globalizing Low-Income Country'. *American Economic Review*, 105(5): 545–550. https://doi.org/10.1257/aer.p20151051.

McCaig, B., and N. Pavcnik (2017). 'Out with the Old and Unproductive, in with the New and Similarly Unproductive: Microenterprise Dynamics in a Growing Low-Income Economy'. GLM|LIC Working Paper No. 23. Bonn: Institute of Labour Economics.

McKenzie, D., and Y.S. Sakho (2010). 'Does It Pay Firms to Register for Taxes? The Impact of Formality on Firm Profitability'. *Journal of Development Economics*, 91: 15–24. https://doi.org/10.1016/j.jdeveco.2009.02.003.

Mhando, P.C., and M.N. Kiggundu (2018). 'Introduction to Special Issue—Managing Africa's Informal Economy: Research, Practice and Advocacy'. *Africa Journal of Management*, 4(3): 219–224. https://doi.org/10.1080/23322373.2018.1518837.

Nagler, P., and W. Naudé (2017). 'Non-Farm Entrepreneurship in Rural Sub-Saharan Africa: New Empirical Evidence'. *Food Policy*, 67: 175–191. https://doi.org/10.1016/j.foodpol.2016.09.019.

Nix, E., E. Gamberoni, and R. Heath (2015). 'Bridging the Gender Gap: Identifying What Is Holding Self-Employed Women Back in Ghana, Rwanda, Tanzania, and the Republic of Congo'. *World Bank Economic Review*, 30: 501–512. https://doi.org/10.1093/wber/lhv046.

Van den Broeck, G., and T. Kilic (2019). 'Dynamics of Off-Farm Employment in Sub-Saharan Africa: A Gender Perspective'. *World Development*, 119: 81–99. https://doi.org/10.1016/j.worlddev.2019.03.008.

Williams, C.C., and Y.A. Youssef (2014). 'Is Informal Sector Entrepreneurship Necessity- or Opportunity-Driven? Some Lessons from Urban Brazil'. *Global Business and Management Research*, 3: 41–53. https://doi.org/10.5430/bmr.v3n1p41.

Appendix

Table 10.A1 Work status groups

Work status group	Definition/operationalization
1. Formal	We identify formal self-employed workers as own-account workers (with no salary) that (i) keep written accounts, (ii) have a commercial register, or (iii) hold a fiscal identification number given by the Directorate General of Taxes (DGI). We also include owners or employers (with at least one salaried worker) that follow at least one of the above regulations and have additionally registered worker(s) in the national social security fund.
2. Upper-tier informal	Upper-tier informal self-employed are identified as those who do not comply with the above regulations (in 1) but operate their businesses in fixed premises outside the dwelling.
3. Lower-tier informal	These are self-employed workers that do not comply with the above regulations (in 1) but have no fixed business premises (outside the owner's dwelling) or are itinerant/mobile.

Source: authors' illustration based on LSMS–ISA data for Mali and Niger.

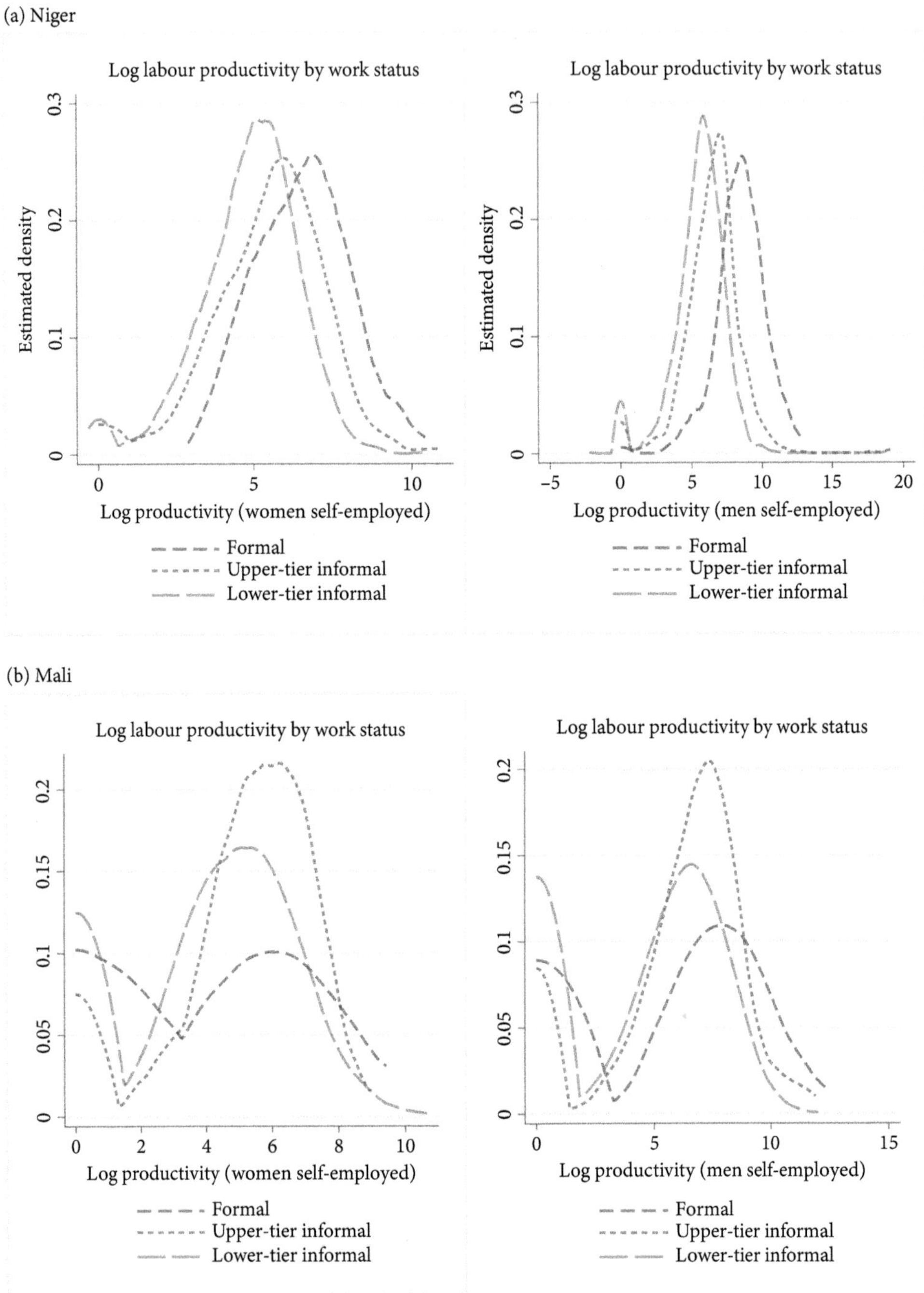

Fig. 10.A1 Labour productivity dispersal by gender of self-employed worker

Source: authors' illustration based on LSMS–ISA data for Mali and Niger.

11

Informal–formal workers' transition in Nigeria

A livelihood analysis

Abiodun O. Folawewo and Olusegun A. Orija

1. Introduction

In many African countries, especially in Nigeria, not only is the informal sector large, but it is also a major absorber of labour (Jerome 1996; Folawewo 2013; Medina et al. 2017).[1] The size of the sector is also growing across European countries (Adame and Tuesta 2017; Beręsewicz and Nikulin 2018). As indicated by the International Labour Organization (ILO 2018), on average, about 60 per cent of informal employment in Africa is within the informal sector. Furthermore, the informal sector accounts for about 65 per cent of gross domestic product (GDP) in Nigeria (NBS 2010; Medina et al. 2017). Generally, the growth of the sector has been driven by slow economic development, poor economic performance, and shrinkage of formal-sector jobs (Carr and Chen 2001; ILO 2004; Lapeyre 2017).

The informal sector in the Nigerian economy is spread across both rural and urban areas and covers several economic activities. Hence, the informal sector is a vital source of livelihood[2] for the vast majority of citizens. As in many other developing countries, the Nigerian informal sector is characterized by low productivity, low wages, absence of social security, low capital and inadequate finance, and a lack or inadequate coverage of official institutional regulations (ILO 2017, 2018). This has led to a situation where informal-sector employment is precarious and securing decent and sustainable jobs in the sector is not guaranteed. Similarly, while the informal sector cushions the unemployment effect for the majority of people that are either unable to secure jobs in or are laid off from the formal sector, several factors hinder the movement of workers from the informal sector back to the formal sector (Maloney 1999; Krstić and Sanfey 2006; Tansel and Kan 2012a).

[1] We are grateful for the support of UNU–WIDER and analysis assistance from Noah Olasheinde. Any errors in the study are solely those of the authors.

[2] Generally, livelihood is defined as all forms of human strategies, capacities, resources, and activities involved in making a living (see, e.g. Chambers and Conway 1992; Ellis 2000; UNDP—IRP 2011).

Abiodun O. Folawewo and Olusegun A. Orija, *Informal–formal workers' transition in Nigeria*. In: *The Job Ladder*. Edited by Gary S. Fields, T. H. Gindling, Kunal Sen, Michael Danquah, and Simone Schotte, Oxford University Press.
 DOI: 10.1093/oso/9780192867339.003.0011

Informal employment in Nigeria can be categorized as self-employment in agricultural and non-agricultural activities, as unpaid family business, and as salaried employment. This reflects the heterogeneous nature of the informal sector. In line with this heterogeneity, the ILO (2019) classifies employment by formality status (i.e. whether formal or informal employment) and by work status in terms of wage-employment and self-employment. Each of these categories has peculiarities, but income and wage inequality is a common feature. Consequently, mobility across different jobs within the informal sector is often pronounced, albeit with some constraints. Given the significant employment role of the informal sector, we use a panel of national household survey data to conduct an empirical analysis of the relationship between the informal sector and livelihood and of the dynamic movements into and out of various forms of informal employment. Specific attention is focused on the nature and factors affecting workers' transition between informal and formal employment.

We apply a binary logit model to a national General Household Survey (GHS) panel data set for 2010–2011, 2012–2013, and 2015–2016. We find that informal employment has a more positive impact on workers' livelihoods. Our results also show a very high dynamic of worker transition within the different types of informal employment, especially among the lower-tier segments. We further find a likelihood of workers' movement from informal to formal employment, this likelihood being higher among the upper-tier informal wage-employed. Our findings also reveal a higher probability of workers' transition from informal employment to formal employment than from formal to informal.

The rest of the chapter is made up of six sections. Section 2 provides an overview of the Nigerian labour market, where the regulatory framework and wage and employment issues are discussed. In section 3, a brief exploration of extant literature on informal–formal employment transition is made. Section 4 is devoted to a description of the methodological approach and sources of data used in the study. A descriptive data analysis is presented in section 5, and a discussion of the regression results in section 6. Finally, in section 7, policy recommendations and concluding remarks are provided.

2. Overview of the Nigerian labour market

The Nigerian labour market is characterized by heterogeneity and dualism, which are the general features of most African and developing countries' labour markets (Harris and Todaro 1970; Aminu 2010; Fields 2011). Its dualistic nature is reflected in a rural–urban as well as a formal–informal dichotomy. The formal labour market comprises public-sector organizations and large private firms, while the informal segment is made up of micro, small, and medium-scale enterprises, petty trades, and other forms of individual economic activity. Essentially, the formal and informal sectors differ in terms of governance and regulatory framework, employment process, employees' compensation (wage determination), and productivity.

The governance of labour matters in Nigeria follows a tripartite framework involving the government (the Federal Ministry of Labour and Employment (FMLE) and allied agencies), employers (represented by Nigeria's Employers Consultative Association (NECA)), and workers (represented by their umbrella unions, the Nigeria Labour Congress (NLC) and Trade Union Congress (TUC)). Labour market relations are controlled by a variety of regulations. The Labour Act (Decree) No. 21 of 1974 and its subsequent amendments, such as the Labour Act 1990 and Labour Act 2004, is complemented by the many international labour standards that Nigeria has ratified and domesticated, while the Trade Unions Act (Cap. T14 L.F.N 2004) provides guidelines for the formation of trade unions, which generally advocate workers' rights and welfare. Another form of regulation guiding interactions among players within the Nigerian labour market is the Trade Disputes Act 2004 (Cap. T8 L.F.N). In addition, several minimum wage laws have been implemented in the country in recent years, the latest being the National Minimum Wage (Amendment) Act 2011 and 2019. All these Acts and regulatory frameworks are set up to facilitate a smooth relationship and to resolve conflicts that may arise between employers and employees.

Rules and regulations emanating from the legislation governing operations within the labour market are, however, usually poorly implemented and most often ineffective. Moreover, they cover only part of the labour market, the large informal segment being uncovered. In the public sector, rules and regulations are complied with, but in the private sector, the compliance level is low due to poor monitoring and implementation (Folawewo 2016). This has also allowed a lack of adherence to employment and compensation laws among employers across all market sectors. Workers are therefore subject to exploitation, casualization, lack of adequate protection, and job insecurity (Nwaka 2016).

In the informal sector, where adherence to official regulations is even poorer than in the formal sector, hiring (employment) procedures are often based on personal contact without any formal contractual agreement. This results in job insecurity, employers having the freedom to fire employees at will, and poor remuneration—usually below the national minimum wage. Similarly, inadequate health-and-safety measures and environmental hazards are more prevalent in the informal sector, where workers in all sectors are confronted with unsatisfactory welfare facilities, practically non-existent occupational health services, and other challenges (Forastieri 1999; Nwaka 2016). Because of the poor remuneration and working conditions in the informal sector, workers often transit from the informal to the formal sector, while there is little reverse transition—usually brought about by retirement or retrenchment from formal jobs (Nwaka 2016; Roberts 2016).

In recent times, the informal sector has witnessed rapid growth due to poor economic performance and lack of growth in the formal sector (Folawewo 2016; Medina et al. 2017). This shows that the informal sector serves as a reservoir of workers who are readily available for formal employment once the opportunity is provided. The transition of workers within informal activities is also common, especially among workers moving from informal salaried employment to self-employment, and between self-employment in agricultural activities and non-agricultural activities. Consequently, sectoral workers' transition predicated on differential working conditions is a regular feature of the Nigerian labour market.

3. Literature review

Theoretical distinctions between the formal and informal sectors and explanations for workers' transition between the two sectors can be found within market dualism (segmented labour market) and modernization theories (Harris and Todaro 1970; Perry et al. 2007). The dual labour market/segmented theory posits that the existence of minimum wages and other forms of compensation in the organized (formal) segment of the labour market attracts workers to it. However, due to limited space and job availability, workers that are unable to secure employment in the organized segment are pushed into the unorganized or informal sector, where they are forced to accept the prevailing working conditions. The modernization theory, on the other hand, argues that the dichotomy between the formal and informal sectors is brought about by the development process. In the early stage of development, informal activities usually surpass formal, but, as the economy develops, the formal or modern economic sector begins to grow and informal activities (production units) gradually fizzle out (Perry et al. 2007; Hillenkamp et al. 2013). The modernization theory therefore suggests that informality is a consequence of underdevelopment or a failure of modernization. Both the segmented labour market and modernization theories are regarded as orthodox.

A more recent view is based on institutional theory, which opines that existing institutional arrangements may affect livelihoods as well as labour transition. This view argues that the complex interactions between the formal and informal economy are affected by institutions and social norms (Perry et al. 2007; Hillenkamp et al. 2013). Institutional arrangements affect interaction and economic activity through their effects on contracts, property rights, and social networks. Institutional arrangements often lead to the formalization of economic activities and subsequently cause movement of workers from the informal to the formal sector (Lapeyre 2017).

In all, the theoretical expositions on the formal–informal segmentation of the labour market are suggestive that the formal sector is preferable to the informal because of the perceived better working conditions such as higher compensation, job security, and availability of employment protection legislation (EPL). Consequently, informal employment is seen as a temporary expedient, and workers seek to transit from it to formal employment. Empirical literature on the informal–formal transition has, however, been polarized along two strands. On the one hand, informal employment is seen as voluntary and subject to workers' willingness and preference (Maloney 1999, 2004; Bosch and Maloney 2010; Fields 2019). On the other hand, informal employment is seen as involuntary, with workers being forced into it (de Soto 2000).

Recent literature has shown that both the orthodox and institutional theories fail to adequately capture the heterogeneity within job status; hence, the extent of dynamic mobility across different employment may not be fully measured. Thus, in line with the ILO's employment characterization (ILO 2019), formal employment cuts across both the formal and the informal sectors. In this regard, the formality status of employment is determined by the conditions surrounding different types of work, such as coverage of EPL and the availability of social and job security. With regard to work status, employment can also be classified into wage-employment or self-employment. This view leads to six categories of employment: formal wage-employment, formal self-employment, upper-tier informal wage-employment, lower-tier informal wage-employment, upper-tier self-employment, and lower-tier self-employment (Danquah et al. 2019; ILO 2019).

There is divergent empirical evidence in relation to the potential for and ability of workers to transit across the various job categories. This is due to differential country features, time periods, and methodological approaches. While showing that informality is a major source of livelihood for most Mexican workers, Biles (2008) argues that there is high mobility of workers both within informal activities and between informal and formal employment, with evidence of voluntary transition from the formal to the informal sector. In line with this, several other studies on workers' mobility have noticed high rates of mobility across formal and informal salaried jobs and a low rate between formal salaried jobs and self-employment (Maloney 1999; IDB 2004; Pagés and Stampini 2009; Bosch and Maloney 2010; Mahmud 2017). One common submission from all the studies is that voluntary transition from formal to informal is a possibility.

Some other studies have investigated the determinants of workers' transition across sectors. Several factors have been found to affect the probability of mobility and transitions both within and between sectors. Individual and household characteristics such as education and intrinsic demographics, experience and wage differential, and location are among the crucial factors influencing mobility (Krstić and Sanfey 2006; Tansel and Ozdemir 2015; Núñez 2017; Bereęsewicz and Nikulin 2018). In terms of within-sector/employment type transition, the sector of economic activities has been shown to play a significant role. For example, there is a high probability of transition from informal employment to regular employment within the formal sector, and salaried employees are more likely to transit to self-employment in the informal sector (Tansel and Kan 2012b; de la Parra 2017; Gutierrez et al. 2019).

Other recent studies have shown comprehensive dynamism in formal–informal workers' transition between ILO employment classifications. Bosch and Maloney (2010) studied Latin American countries (Argentina, Brazil, and Mexico) and evidenced a high rate of transition among informal self-employed and wage-employed workers and between upper-tier self-employed and formal self-employed workers. While confirming that workers transit from informal to formal employment, Danquah et al. (2019) also argued that gender plays a crucial role in the participation of workers in formal versus informal employment. Specifically, they showed that, on average, women in three African countries—Ghana, South Africa, and Tanzania—prefer informal lower-tier self-employment and upper-tier informal wage-employment.

The increasing extent of informal employment and its importance to livelihood has been the preoccupation of many studies in recent times. In particular, institutional and structural features and the cyclical nature of the economy are found to affect the size and importance of the informal sector. In this connection, shrinkage in formal jobs and growing unemployment are major drivers of informal-sector employment (Ndiweni et al. 2014; Hovsha and Meyer 2015; de la Parra 2017; ILO 2018; Albertini et al. 2019). Stringent labour regulations and restrictions are also argued to be major contributory factors to labour transition and the significant role of the informal sector in livelihood (Timalsina 2011; Tshuma and Jari 2013).

4. Methodology and data

The impact of the informal and formal sectors on livelihood is evaluated using descriptive analysis. This involves measuring the percentage of individuals engaged in various employment types and analysing the characteristics of such individuals. The analysis of workers' transition within and between informal and formal employment is situated within the framework of a logistic probability model. Unlike Tansel and Kan (2012a, b), we employed a standard binary logistic model to investigate the probability of workers' mobility across different informal employment types and between informal and formal employment. This methodology is preferred as it enables us to evaluate the effect of individual workers' characteristics on their ability to transit from one form of employment to another over a given period. In this case, a worker's movement from one specific form of employment to another is treated as 1 and no movement as 0. The fact that the regressors are either categorical or continuous in nature further justifies the suitability of the binary logistic model.

If we assume the log odds of a worker's transition as $p = P(Y = 1)$, given the worker's characteristics, then the standard logistic model can be specified as:

$$l = log_b \frac{P}{1-P} = \beta_0 + \beta_i Z_i \tag{1}$$

where b is the base of the logarithm and Z_i is the vector of the individual worker's characteristics. The odds of transition are recovered by expressing the log odds in exponential form as follows:

$$\frac{P}{1-P} = b^{\beta_0 + \beta_i Z_i}. \tag{2}$$

Consequently, results from the logistic model estimations are reported in odds ratios, unless otherwise indicated. The logit model is estimated in such a way that it comprehensively reflects workers' transition across different occupational positions and work status groups. Thus, the logit model is estimated for two forms of occupational position, that is, whether a worker is self-employed or engaged in wage-employment. The occupational position is embedded in the formality status of the job—whether such a position is formal or informal employment. Informal employment is further classified into upper and lower tiers.

The dependent variable in each regression is measured as a categorical variable that assumes the value of 1 if an individual transits from a particular activity or employment in period t to a reference activity in the subsequent period, $t+1$, and 0 if the individual does not transit to the reference employment. In the descriptive analysis, it is also recognized that workers are not unlikely to engage in more than one economic activity, that is, more than one type of employment. However, for ease of analysis, in the logistic regression, workers are restricted to a particular type of job at a given time; that is, the major form of employment (main economic activity and source of income) of an individual is used as the employment type for that individual in a particular wave. Workers' characteristics in the base period are also used in the regression analysis. For example, the age of a worker in Wave 1 is used for movement from Wave 1 to Wave 2, and the age in Wave 2 is used when analysing movement from Wave 2 to Wave 3.

In order to effectively capture workers' transition among jobs, the GHS data set for 2010–2011 (Wave 1), 2012–2013 (Wave 2), and 2015–2016 (Wave 3) is used. The GHS is a panel survey covering 5,000 households across all the geopolitical zones of the country. The GHS is conducted over two different periods: post-planting and post-harvesting. The post-harvesting data set is used in this study as it contains information on both agricultural and non-agricultural activities, unlike the post-planting data set, which concentrates on agricultural and farming activities.

Given the limitations of the data set, which does not contain vital information such as business registration or workers' training other than formal education, clarification of the method of classification and measurement of different occupational positions and employment status groups is pertinent. All public-sector (government) and large private firm/organization employment that is covered by official labour market regulations—such as recruitment and dismissal, compensation, and other EPL—is classified as formal and falls under 'wage employment'. Since the GHS data do not include information on business registration, participation in the National Health Insurance Scheme (NHIS) is used as an additional criterion for determination of the formality status of an employment. Thus, workers are also said to be in formal employment if they make NHIS contributions, whether they are self-employed or in wage-employment. Forms of employment that are neither covered by any official regulations nor linked to NHIS contributions are regarded as informal, irrespective of whether they are self-employment or wage-employment.

Within informal employment, the educational level of workers is used as the distinguishing factor for whether they belong to the upper or lower tier. As noted earlier and supported by the literature (e.g. Gutierrez et al. 2019), a majority of informal workers have little education; consequently, workers with secondary education and below are categorized as lower-tier informal workers, while those with post-secondary and tertiary education are classified as upper-tier.

5. Baseline descriptive data analysis

As a means of achieving the objectives of the study, empirical analysis is carried out in three stages. First, a descriptive analysis of unemployed and employed individuals across the three waves of the data set is done. Second, a regression analysis of the impact of various work status groups on livelihood is performed using earnings as a key indicator of livelihood. The third phase of the analysis involves an examination of the dynamic movement of workers within the different informal jobs and an evaluation of their ability to move from informal activities to formal employment.

Two sets of data are used: the number of individuals before data matching is used for the basic descriptive analysis (see Folawewo and Orija 2020: Table 11.A1), while the number of individuals after data matching is used for both the transition and the regression analyses (see Folawewo and Orija 2020: Table 11.A2). The matched data set consists of household members that appear in all three waves of the GHS, as shown by the household roster identifiers in the data set.

5.1 Workers' characteristics

We begin by looking at the characteristics of the unemployed, who account for 7.3 per cent of household members on average (see Folawewo and Orija 2020: Table 11.A1). It is observed that more male household members were unemployed than females (50.3 per cent as against 49.7 per cent; see Folawewo and Orija 2020: Table 11.A3). The percentage (62.0) of unemployed household members within the age bracket 18–30 was higher than that of those aged 31–60 (28.7), which confirms the generally high rate of youth unemployment in the country. On average, the percentage of unemployed household members across the data set was highest among those with secondary education (42.4), followed by those with tertiary education (24.0), those without formal education (no schooling) having the least (3.4). This explains the high rate of joblessness among secondary school-leavers and post-secondary institution graduates in the country. The percentage of the unemployed was also higher for rural dwellers (56.3) than urban (43.47), an indication of the higher rate of unemployment in the rural centres, which often leads to a high rate of rural–urban migration.

It is shown that in terms of the occupational position of household members, more individuals were engaged in self-employment (67.4 per cent on average) than were wage-employed (32.6 per cent; see Folawewo and Orija 2020: Table 11.A1). It can be seen that while self-employment rose throughout the period under study, the reverse is the case for wage-employment. Within the self-employed, the average percentages for informal lower-tier, informal upper-tier, and formal employed were 95.6, 4.2, and 0.2, respectively. For wage-employed individuals, formal employment accounted for an average of 60.0 per cent, while the proportions of lower-tier and upper-tier informal workers were 37.2 and 2.8, respectively. This shows that the bulk of wage-employed workers could be found in formal employment, while informally employed individuals dominated self-employment. Furthermore, lower-tier workers constituted the larger proportion of the informally employed (for both self-employed and wage-employment) with an average of 93.9 per cent, the remaining 6.1 per cent being upper-tier. On the whole, in terms of formality status and irrespective of whether self-employed or wage-employed, a majority of household members were engaged in informal employment: an average of 83.8 per cent compared with 16.2 per cent in formal employment. Thus, aggregately, in terms of employment opportunities, the informal sector provides a better livelihood than the formal sector for households in Nigeria.

The occupational position of workers reflects the fact that, on average across all waves, males were more engaged in wage-employment (54.7 per cent) than their female counterparts (45.3 per cent; see Folawewo and Orija 2020: Table 11.A4). A further disaggregation by work status indicates that formal wage-employment was dominated by males: an average of 63.7 per cent as against 36.3 per cent for females (see Folawewo and Orija 2020: Tables 11.A5–7). Females were more prevalent in

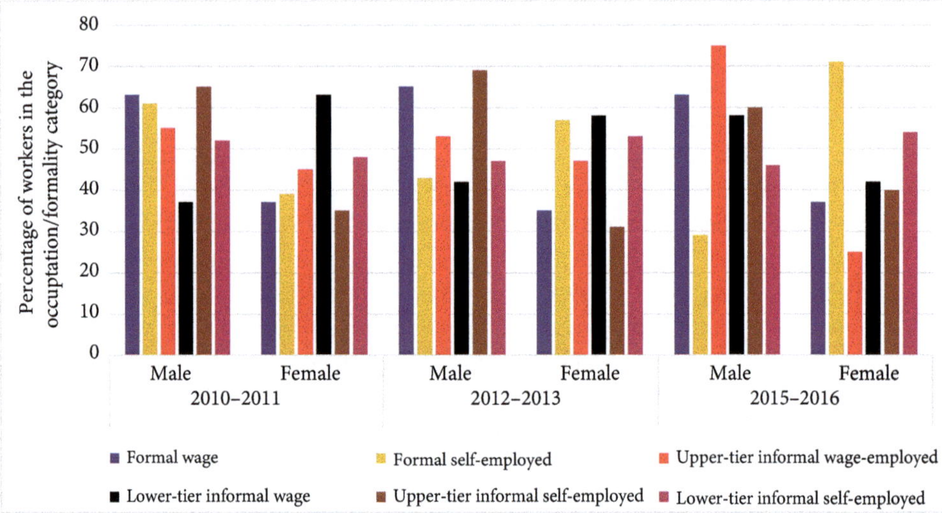

Fig. 11.1 Gender distribution of workers by occupational and formality status
Source: authors' computation from the National Bureau of Statistics General Household Survey (NBS GHS) data sets.

informal self-employment (55.7 per cent) than males (44.3 per cent). Upper-tier informal wage-employment was dominated by males (61 per cent compared with 39 per cent for females). Conversely, the lower-tier informal wage-employed were predominantly females, with an average of 54.3 per cent compared with 45.7 per cent for males across the three waves. In addition, there was a higher percentage of males (64.7) in upper-tier informal self-employment than females (35.3); on the other hand, informal lower-tier self-employment had a higher proportion of females (51.7) than males (48.3). Thus, in Nigeria's setting, male workers are more prominent in the upper tier of informal employment, whereas females are more prevalent in the lower tier, as depicted in Fig. 11.1.

As shown in Fig. 11.2, the educational distribution of workers reflects the fact that those without any formal education (no schooling) could mainly be found in self-employment (19.7 per cent of all workers on average), with relatively few in wage-employment (6.7 per cent). The proportion of self-employed workers with primary education (39.0) was more than that of the wage-employed (25.0). The average percentage of wage-employed workers with secondary education was 32.2 as against 31.0 per cent for the self-employed. Workers with tertiary education were dominant in wage-employment (36.0 per cent) as opposed to self-employment (10.3 per cent). This implies that workers with a low level of education are concentrated in self-employment; however, as workers move up the education ladder they become more engaged in wage-employment.

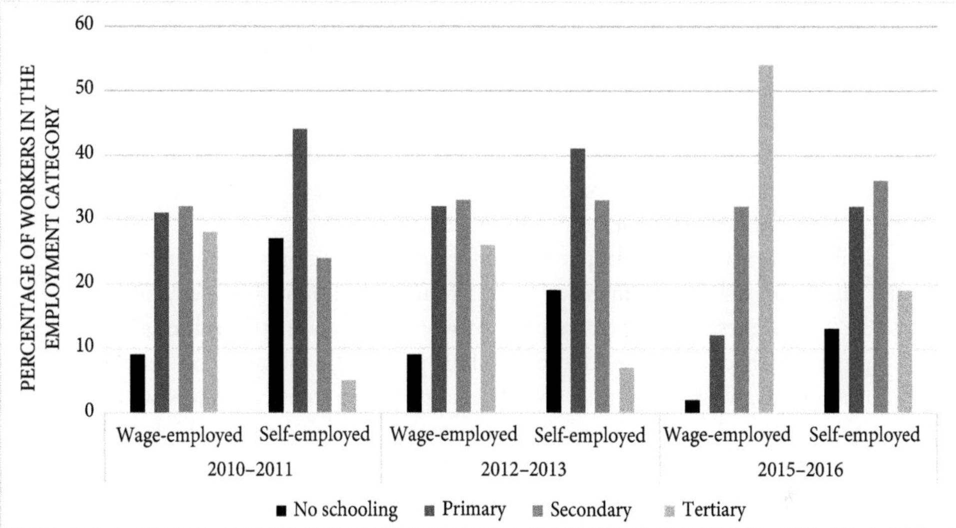

Fig. 11.2 Educational distribution of workers by occupational position

Note: Wage = wage-employed and self = self-employed.
Source: authors' computation from NBS GHS data sets.

Fig. 11.3 Average proportion of workers' education across occupational position and formality status

Source: authors' computation from NBS GHS data sets.

A further breakdown of the education distribution of workers by work status (Fig. 11.3) reveals that on average, formal wage-employment was dominated by workers with tertiary education (49.7 per cent), followed by secondary education (30.3 per cent) and primary education (16.3 per cent). Across all waves, formal self-employment was dominated by workers with secondary education (45.7 per cent), followed by those with primary education (33.3 per cent), tertiary education (11.7 per cent), and no education (9.3 per cent).

Strikingly, workers in upper-tier informal wage-employment and upper-tier informal self-employment all had tertiary education (100 per cent—Fig. 11.3). The highest average percentage of workers in lower-tier informal wage-employment had primary education (46.3 per cent), followed by secondary education (44.3 per cent), and no schooling (9.3 per cent). Workers with primary education dominated lower-tier informal self-employment (44.3 per cent), followed by secondary education (33.0 per cent), and those without education (22.7 per cent).

In terms of the earnings of workers across work status groups (Table 11.1), we found that formal wage-employed workers received the highest average monthly earnings (NGN 92,573; equivalent to US$ 493.20). The second-highest average monthly earnings were received by the upper-tier informal wage-employed (NGN 62,782/US$ 334.48), followed by the upper-tier informal self-employed (NGN 52,735/US$ 280.95) and the formal self-employed (NGN 52,110/US$ 277.50). The lowest monthly earnings were received by lower-tier informal wage-employed workers, with an average of NGN 31,761 (US$ 169.21). Average workers' earnings are shown pictorially in Fig. 11.4, from which it is obvious that while formal wage-employment and upper-tier informal wage-employment deliver better welfare and livelihood to workers in terms of income, both lower-tier informal self-employment and lower-tier informal wage-employment have minimal impact on workers' livelihoods.

5.2 Transition of workers across work status groups

Before examining the nature of transition among workers across work status groups, we first describe their initial distribution across such status groups. Table 11.2 presents the proportions of individuals in the different employment status groups in the three survey waves. The lower-tier informal self-employed had the highest average proportion of 61.4 per cent, followed by the formal wage-employed (17.4 per cent) and lower-tier informal wage-employed (17.2 per cent).

According to Table 11.3 (panel A), about 22.2 per cent of workers transited from formal self-employment in Wave 1 to lower-tier informal self-employment in Wave 2. Similarly, 22.2, 11.1, and 44.4 per cent of formal self-employed in Wave 1 transformed to formal wage-employed, informal upper-tier wage-employed, and informal lower-tier wage-employed status, respectively, in Wave 2. Consequently, no formal self-employed workers in Wave 1 maintained the same status in Wave 2 as they were all able to transit to other forms of employment. Of the upper-tier informal wage-employed in Wave 1, the total proportion of those who were able to move to different employment types in Wave 2 was 46.5 per cent, a majority transiting to upper-tier informal wage-employment (28.3 per cent of the total). Thus, the share of stayers (i.e. those who remained in their initial employment position)—calculated as the product of the highlighted diagonals and initial size[3]—in the first wave was 1.2. Out of the lower-tier informal self-employed in Wave 1, 0.1 per cent were able to move to formal self-employment, 0.8 per

Table 11.1 Mean workers' earnings by occupational position and formality status

	Average monthly earnings (Nigerian naira, NGN)			
	2010/11	2012/13	2015/16	Average
Formal self-employed	60,913	43,898	51,520	52,110
Formal wage-employed	115,916	82,898	78,906	92,573
Upper-tier informal self-employed	54,598	52,574	51,033	52,735
Upper-tier informal wage-employed	88,905	72,442	27,000	62,782
Lower-tier informal self-employed	43,761	51,700	48,486	47,983
Lower-tier informal wage-employed	32,860	47,823	14,600	31,761

Source: authors' computation from the National Bureau of Statistics General Household Survey (NBS GHS) data sets.

Table 11.2 Proportion of workers by work status across waves

	2010/11	2012/13	2015/16
Self-employment			
Formal	0.2	0.1	0.2
Informal upper-tier	2.3	1.7	3.9
Informal lower-tier	59.7	45.7	78.9
Wage-employment			
Formal	19.1	16.2	16.9
Informal upper-tier	1.3	2.4	0.04
Informal lower-tier	17.4	33.9	0.1
Total	4,384 (100.0)	4,436 (100.0)	4,450 (100.0)

Source: authors' computation from GHS data set.

[3] The percentage of workers that moved from a particular work status in wave $t + 1$ multiplied by the initial number of workers in that same work status in time t, divided by 100.

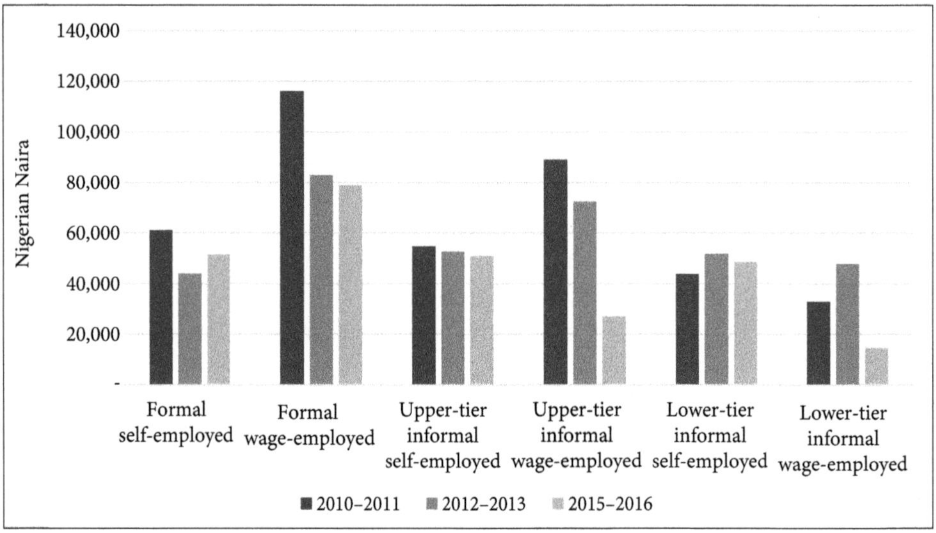

Fig. 11.4 Mean monthly earnings by work status (Nigerian naira, NGN)
Source: authors' computation from NBS GHS data sets.

cent to upper-tier informal self-employment, and 2.8 per cent to formal wage-employment, whilst 34.8 per cent transited to lower-tier informal self-employment by Wave 2. The share of stayers was 36.5 per cent, a reflection of the low probability of transition for that category of workers in Wave 1.

With regard to the movement of workers away from wage-employment between Waves 1 and 2, 16.2 per cent migrated to lower-tier informal self-employment and 2.6 per cent to upper-tier informal self-employment. The proportion of workers who maintained their Wave 1 status within formal wage-employment was 68.8 per cent, while 8.6 per cent transited to lower-tier informal wage-employment and 3.8 per cent migrated to upper-tier informal wage-employment. Therefore, the proportion of those that stayed in formal wage-employment was 13.2 per cent. Furthermore, 10.7 per cent of workers moved away from upper-tier informal wage-employment to upper-tier informal self-employment, 1.8 per cent moved to formal self-employment, and 53.6 per cent transited to formal wage-employment. A total of 33.9 per cent maintained their original work status, leading to a 0.4 per cent share of stayers. Table 11.3 (panel A) also indicates a low probability of transition for lower-tier informal wage-employed workers as only 39.8 per cent of them were able to move to other employment by Wave 2, while 60.1 per cent remained in their initial work status, that is, 10.5 per cent being stayers.

As for the transition of workers across Waves 2–3, Table 11.3 (panel B) shows that 50 per cent of workers retained their Wave 2 job status within formal

Table 11.3 Workers' transition matrices across work status groups and waves

Panel A

				Wave $t = 2$					Share of stayers
				Self-employed			Wage-employed		
				Formal	Informal		Formal	Informal	
					Upper-tier	Lower-tier		Upper-tier	Lower-tier	
Wave $t = 1$	Self-employed	Formal		0	0	22.2	22.2	11.1	44.4	0.0
		Informal	Upper-tier	0	53.5	0	18.2	28.3	0	1.2
			Lower-tier	0.1	0.8	61.2	2.8	0.34	34.8	36.5
	Wage-employed	Formal		0	2.6	16.2	68.8	3.8	8.6	13.2
		Informal	Upper-tier	1.8	10.7	0	53.6	33.9	0	0.4
			Lower-tier	0.1	0	32.5	5.6	1.6	60.1	10.5
	Total			0.1	1.7	45.7	16.2	2.4	33.9	61.8

Panel B

				Wave $t = 3$						Share of stayers
				Self-employed			Wage-employed			
				Formal	Informal		Formal	Informal		
					Upper-tier	Lower-tier		Upper-tier	Lower-tier	
Wave $t = 2$	Self-employed	Formal		50	0	0	50	0	0	0.05
		Informal	Upper-tier	0	82.7	0	17.3	0	0	1.4
			Lower-tier	0.2	0	97.4	2.4	0	0.05	44.5
	Wage-employed	Formal		0.4	4	12.6	82.7	0.1	0.1	13.4
		Informal	Upper-tier	0	32.7	0	27.1	40.2	0	1.0
			Lower-tier	0.1	1.7	92.8	4.1	0.1	1.3	0.4
	Total			0.2	3.9	78.9	16.9	0.04	0.1	60.8

Note: The sum of each row is 100 per cent and each cell represents the distribution of workers at the row's wave. The share of stayers represents those who remained in their initial employment position, which is calculated as the product of the highlighted diagonals and initial size (the percentage of workers that moved from a particular work status in wave $t + 1$ multiplied by the initial number of workers in that same work status in time t, divided by 100).
Source: authors' computation from GHS data set.

self-employment, while the remaining 50 per cent transited to formal wage-employment. Consequently, the proportion of stayers in formal self-employment was 0.05. About 82.7 per cent of workers retained their Wave 2 upper-tier informal self-employment status as against the 17.3 per cent that moved to formal wage-employment by Wave 3; that is, the share of stayers in upper-tier informal self-employment was 1.4 per cent. The percentage of workers who maintained their status as informal lower-tier self-employed was 97.4, as only 0.2, 2.4, and 0.05 per cent migrated to formal self-employment, formal wage-employment, and lower-tier informal wage-employment, respectively, by Wave 3. This gives a proportion of stayers of 44.5 per cent for self-employed informal lower-tier.

The transition of workers from wage-employment shows that 0.4 per cent moved from formal wage-employment to formal self-employment, 4.0 per cent migrated to upper-tier informal self-employment, and 12.6 per cent to lower-tier informal self-employment. The percentage of those that changed from formal wage-employment to both upper-tier and lower-tier informal wage-employment was 0.1. The percentage of formal wage-employed in Wave 2 that remained was 82.7, which translates to 13.4 per cent stayers. Furthermore, 32.7 and 27.1 per cent of upper-tier informal wage-employed workers in Wave 2 migrated to upper-tier informal self-employment and formal wage-employment, respectively, by Wave 3. The remaining 40.2 per cent upper-tier informal wage-employed retained their status, yielding a proportion of 1.0 stayers. A very large percentage (92.8) of Wave 2 lower-tier informal wage-employed workers transited to lower-tier informal self-employment by Wave 3, while 5.9 of the remainers moved into other forms of employment. Therefore, only 1.3 per cent of lower-tier informal wage-employed individuals in Wave 2 stayed in that status in Wave 3, equivalent to a proportion of 0.4 per cent of stayers.

A notable issue arising from Tables 11.2 and 11.3 is the inconsistency in the transition pattern, especially from wave 2 to 3, and specifically within the different wage-employments. This observed phenomenon is because of the data set used for the analysis. First, the GHS 2015–2016 (Wave 3) is a bit different from the two previous waves (Waves 1 and 2) in terms of the total number of households and individuals covered as well as the prevailing socio-economic situation under which the survey was generated. The survey was conducted during economic recession and a period of high-level unemployment. Second, the transition matrix reflects the proportion of individuals that transited from one wave to the other and from their initial (original) employment status to another across the waves. Finally, the definition and measurement of the different work status groups classification used herein also contributed to the seemingly observed inconsistences.

Overall, we found that, on average and across all waves, the probability of transiting from formal employment, whether self-employment or wage-employment, to informal employment was low. Similarly, the probability of moving from informal to formal employment was very slim and even slimmer (and minimal) for lower-tier workers. In addition, upper-tier informal wage-employed workers appeared to have better chances of transiting to formal wage-employment. Conversely, there was a high rate of workers' transition within informal employment, in particular from lower-tier wage-employment to lower-tier self-employment. Observably, due to their low level of education, the bulk of lower-tier informal self-employed workers are locked down and unable to transit.

6. Regression results

6.1 Informal sector and livelihood

The descriptive analyses have shown that the informal sector accounts for the bulk of total employment in the country (about 80 per cent), as depicted by the GHS data set. The importance and contribution of the sector to workers' livelihoods is further investigated with regression estimates using earnings as a measure of livelihood. Regression results on the impact of various characteristics and work status groups on workers' earnings are presented in Table 11.4. The results for Wave 1 (model 1) indicate that both age of worker and its squares have no significant effect on earnings. However, as we move from one wave to the next, age becomes more important in earnings determination. Gender and marital status of workers also have significant positive effects on earnings, specifically when such workers are male and married. It is also found that all levels of education influence earnings significantly in positive ways. Of importance is that the more an individual climbs the education ladder, the higher their earnings rise. The results further indicate that urban residence is a crucial factor in the determination of earnings.

Turning to the impact of the different work status groups and employment categories on livelihood, results show that all have significant positive effects on earnings. With reference to self-employment, the impact of each of the two tiers of informal employment (upper and lower) outweigh that of formal employment, the lower tier having the most effect. Within wage-employment, across the three waves, informal lower-tier has the most significant impact on earnings, but the impact of formal wage-employment is greater than that of informal upper-tier. By implication, formal wage-employment has more relevance to livelihood than formal self-employment. Not surprisingly, both lower-tier informal self-employment and wage-employment have an overwhelmingly greater impact on livelihood than all other job categories. This is further confirmation of the importance to livelihood of the informal sector in Nigeria.

Table 11.4 Livelihood regression results

Variables	1	2	3
Age	0.001	0.021**	0.058***
	(0.420)	(2.231)	(7.281)
Age squared	−0.000	−0.000	−0.001***
	(−0.259)	(−1.580)	(−6.248)
Male	0.446***	0.350***	0.206***
	(8.662)	(12.007)	(8.489)
Married	0.984***	0.159***	0.333***
	(13.095)	(3.325)	(8.238)
Education			
Primary	0.260***	0.139***	0.023
	(4.227)	(3.808)	(0.735)
Secondary	0.644***	0.246***	0.247***
	(9.093)	(6.257)	(7.492)
Tertiary	2.392***	0.769***	0.803***
	(19.171)	(10.977)	(14.294)
Work status			
Formal self–employed	7.208***	10.391***	10.220***
	(11.803)	(22.134)	(37.290)
Upper–tier informal self–employed	5.263***	9.849***	9.639***
	(22.991)	(77.849)	(122.256)
Lower–tier informal self–employed	7.359***	10.585***	10.332***
	(71.365)	(168.709)	(209.925)
Formal wage-employed	4.219***	9.886***	9.757***
	(35.641)	(139.507)	(178.219)
Upper–tier informal wage-employed	4.968***	9.544***	4.242***
	(16.907)	(79.013)	(8.343)
Lower–tier informal wage-employed	6.310***	9.549***	2.313***
	(52.907)	(146.160)	(9.796)
Urban	0.469***	0.092***	0.182***
	(7.792)	(2.832)	(6.848)
Constant	1.530***	−0.775***	−1.467***
	(13.939)	(−4.568)	(−10.362)
Observations	10,798	7,967	7,724
Adjusted R-squared	0.383	0.811	0.883
F–statistics	480.5***	2443***	4167***

Note: 1, 2, and 3 represent Wave 1 (2010/11), Wave 2 (2012/13), and Wave 3 (2015/16) models; * $p < 0.1$, ** $p < 0.05$, *** $p < 0.01$. *T*-statistics in parentheses. Dependent variable is workers' earnings.
Source: authors' calculations based on NBS GHS survey data sets.

6.2 Dynamic transitions within informal employment

The dynamic movement of workers within informal employment is analysed by examining the probability of transiting from one form of informal activity to another across the different waves. Dynamic transitions within the informal sector are subject to many factors (see Folawewo and Orija 2020: Table 11.A8). The probability of movement of workers between different forms of informal employment from Wave 1 to Wave 2 is given in models (1)–(3), while the likelihood regression results for transition from Wave 2 to Wave 3 are presented in models (4)–(7).

The results show that the likelihood of transition from lower-tier self-employment to lower-tier wage-employment becomes higher as the age of a worker increases. In terms of gender, male workers are less likely to transit from lower-tier self-employment to lower-tier wage-employment. Level of education is found to be an important factor that increases the chance of worker transition from lower-tier self-employment to lower-tier wage-employment, workers with primary education having a better transition chance than those with secondary education. Marital status and geographical location are also important factors that influence the probability of transition from lower-tier self-employment to lower-tier wage-employment, with a higher probability for married and urban dwellers. The likelihood of workers' movement from upper-tier self-employment to upper-tier wage-employment is significantly influenced by age and geographical location. The transition of workers from lower-tier wage-employment to lower-tier self-employment between two waves is determined by their gender, educational level, marital status, and geographical location. However, the more educated a worker is, the less likely they are to move from lower-tier wage-employment to lower-tier self-employment.

The results of workers' transition within the various informal employment status groups from Wave 2 to Wave 3 indicate that education and marital status have important effects on the transition from lower-tier self-employment to upper-tier self-employment. The probability of transiting from lower-tier wage-employment to lower-tier self-employment is significantly determined by gender, education, and marital status, the probability reducing for males and those with secondary education. Only secondary education and marital status appear to be important factors affecting the likelihood of transition from lower-tier wage-employment to upper-tier self-employment. There is no factor that has a significant effect on workers' transition from upper-tier wage-employment to upper-tier self-employment.

Overall, we find that workers are most likely to transit from an initial position of lower-tier self-employment to lower-tier wage-employment or from upper-tier self-employment to upper-tier wage-employment, particularly from Wave 1 to Wave 2. We also see a very low probability of transition for lower-tier wage-employed workers to lower-tier self-employed; there is a slight increase in the probability from Wave 2 to Wave 3, and this is significantly influenced by educational level, especially for females. There is also little likelihood of transition from both lower-tier and upper-tier wage-employment to upper-tier self-employment. Consequently, we can say that there is a highly dynamic workers' transition movement within the different types of informal employment, especially among the lower-tier segments, which corroborates Bosch and Maloney's (2010) results.

6.3 Formal–informal employment transition

Analysis of transitions of workers between informal and formal employment is done at both aggregate and disaggregated data levels by looking at the possibility of reverse transitions; that is, we examine the likelihood of transition from formal to informal employment as well as from informal to formal. The results of the transition from informal to formal employment at aggregate data level show that age, gender, and education are significant factors in such a transition (see Folawewo and Orija 2020: Table 11.A9). Specifically, the results indicate that as workers grow older, their likelihood of transiting from informal to formal employment becomes higher between Wave 1 and Wave 2 but lower between Wave 2 and Wave 3. Male workers have higher odds of transiting from informal to formal employment than their female counterparts across all waves. This indicates that men have better access to formal employment than women. The likelihood of transition becomes higher as the level of education rises from primary to secondary and tertiary, suggesting education as a major constraint to movement from informal to formal employment. The likelihood of transition from formal to informal employment is affected by similar factors to that of movement from informal to formal but it is slimmer.

The results of our analysis of the transition of workers from different forms of informal to formal employment across waves (disaggregated data analysis) are given in Folawewo and Orija (2020: Table 11.A10). It can be observed that across all waves, workers in the lower-tier segment of both informal self-employment and wage-employment are likely to transit to formal wage-employment, the likelihood being significant for male workers and those with secondary education. Obviously, there is also a likelihood of upper-tier informal wage-employed workers transiting to formal wage-employment from Wave 2 to Wave 3, this likelihood being higher than for lower-tier workers. This finding is consistent with Danquah et al.'s (2019) evidence from four sub-Saharan African countries (Ghana, South Africa, Tanzania, and Uganda).

The logistic regression results for movement of workers from formal wage-employment to different types of informal employment is affected by age, gender, education, and location (see Folawewo and Orija 2020: Table 11.A11, model 1). The results suggest that there is a very low chance of transition for workers from formal wage-employment to lower-tier informal self-employment across all waves. This chance is even lower for male workers and those with secondary and tertiary education. A higher chance of movement from formal wage-employment to lower-tier informal wage-employment can be observed between Wave 1 and Wave 2. Furthermore, the likelihood of workers transiting from formal wage-employment to upper-tier informal formal wage-employment is much lower than the movement to both lower-tier informal self-employment and lower-tier wage-employment. Our results are similar to those of Danquah et al. (2019) but differ from Bosch and Maloney (2010) and Slonimczyk and Gimpelson (2015).

In general, our results reveal that while the likelihood of workers moving from informal to formal employment is high, the reverse is the case for movement from formal to informal employment. It is also found that both self-employed and wage-employed informal workers have a good chance of transiting to formal wage-employment, the upper-tier wage-employed having a better chance. On the other hand, there is little or no likelihood of the formal wage-employed transiting to upper-tier informal self-employment. We also find no likelihood of formal self-employed workers transiting to formal wage-employment.

7. Conclusions

In this study, we examined the impact of informal and formal employment on livelihood in Nigeria. We also analysed the dynamic movements of workers across different employment types within the informal sector as well as the factors that determine the probability of workers' transition from informal to formal employment and vice versa. Three waves of the Nigerian GHS survey data were used, that is, 2010–2011, 2012–2013, and 2015–2016. The data were analysed using binary logistic regression.

The descriptive analysis indicates that the informal sector plays a more significant role with respect to its impact on workers' livelihoods as more workers are engaged in informal employment than in the formal sector. In addition, informal employment has assumed an upward trend over time, while there has been a continuous decline in formal employment. Furthermore, we find that self-employment is the dominant form of employment in Nigeria, the lower-tier informal segment providing the largest chunk of employment. We also find that, while highly educated individuals are concentrated in formal wage-employment, relatively few of them are in upper-tier informal wage-employment and formal self-employment. Of importance is the fact that a majority of the informal self-employed and informal wage-employed lack social security coverage, which makes them vulnerable. This indicates the need for policy frameworks that ensure the provision of social security and a safety net for the large pool of workers found in informal employment, whether self-employed or wage-employed.

Further analysis of the data reveals that formal wage-employed and upper-tier informal wage-employed workers are better off than workers in other forms of self-employment and wage-employment as they earn higher incomes. This suggests the imperative for policymakers to design income support programmes for low-income workers, with particular reference to the lower-tier informal self-employed and wage-employed. Another important finding of our study is the constraint imposed by a low level of education on lower-tier informal self-employed and lower-tier informal wage-employed workers, which prevents them from transiting to formal employment. Consequently, an education upgrade becomes pertinent for this set of workers—through either continuous education or on-the-job training.

As expected, we find a high rate of dynamic movement of workers within the various forms of informal employment, particularly among lower-tier workers in both self-employment and wage-employment. The study further shows that both self-employed and wage-employed informal workers have the likelihood of transiting to formal employment. However, the chance of moving from informal to formal employment is much higher for upper-tier wage-employed workers. More importantly, whereas there is a high chance of transition for workers from informal employment to formal, the chance is much lower for the reverse transition from formal to informal employment. An important policy implication of these findings is the need for the creation of better working conditions for informal workers. This would greatly enhance the welfare of informal workers and encourage them to stay within their employment, given the limited employment opportunities in the formal sector.

References

Adame, V., and D. Tuesta (2017). 'The Labyrinth of the Informal Economy: Measurement Strategies and Impacts'. BBVA Research Working Paper No. 17–18. Madrid: BBVA Research Group.

Albertini, J., A. Poirier, and T. Sopraseuth (2019). 'Informal Work along the Business Cycle: Evidence from Argentina'. GATE Working Paper Series WP No. 1916. Lyon: Groupe d'Analyse et de Théorie Economique. https://doi.org/10.2139/ssrn.3373045.

Aminu, A. (2010). *Determinants of Participation and Earnings in Wage Employment in Nigeria*. Nairobi: African Economic Research Consortium (AERC).

Beręsewicz, M., and D. Nikulin (2018). 'Informal Employment in Poland: An Empirical Spatial Analysis'. Spatial Economic Analysis. [online] https://doi.org/10.1080/17421772.2018.1438648.

Biles, J.J. (2008). 'Informal Work and Livelihoods in Mexico: Getting By or Getting Ahead?' *The Professional Geographer*, 60(4): 541–555. https://doi.org/10.1080/00330120802288743.

Bosch, M., and W. Maloney (2010). 'Comparative Analysis of Labor Market Dynamics Using Markov Processes: An Application to Informality'. *Labour Economics*, 17(4): 621–631. https://doi.org/10.1016/j.labeco.2010.01.005.

Carr, M., and M.A. Chen (2001). *Globalization and the Informal Economy: How Global Trade and Investment Impact on the Working Poor*. Geneva: International Labour Organization.

Chambers, R., and G. Conway (1992).'Sustainable Rural Livelihoods: Practical Concepts for the 21st Century'. Institute of Development Studies (IDS) Discussion Paper No. 296. Brighton: IDS.

Danquah, M., S. Schotte, and S. Kunal (2019). 'Informal Work in Sub-Saharan Africa: Dead End or Steppingstone?'. UNU-WIDER Working Paper No. 2019/107. Helsinki: UNU-WIDER. https://doi.org/10.35188/UNU-WIDER/2019/743-9.

de la Parra, B.S. (2017). *Cyclical Behavior of Informal Employment and Self-Employment in Mexico*. St Louis, MI: Federal Reserve Bank of St. Louis.

de Soto, H. (2000). *The Mystery of Capital: Why Capitalism Triumphs in the West and Fails Everywhere Else*. New York: Basic Books.

Ellis, F. (2000). *Rural Livelihoods and Diversity in Developing Countries*. Oxford: Oxford University Press.

Fields, G.S. (2011). 'Labour Market Analysis for Developing Countries'. *Labour Economics*, 18: S16–S22. https://doi.org/10.1016/j.labeco.2011.09.005.

Fields, G.S. (2019). *Employment and Development: How Work Can Lead from and into Poverty*. Oxford: Oxford University Press. https://doi.org/10.1093/oso/9780198815501.001.0001.

Folawewo, A.O. (2013). *The Informal Labour Market in Developing Countries*. Ibadan: Hope Publications.

Folawewo, A.O. (2016). 'Institutions, Regulatory Framework and Labour Market Outcomes in Nigeria'. *Journal of Social and Economic Development*, 18(1–2): 67–84. https://doi.org/10.1007/s40847-016-0028-5.

Folawewo, A.O., and O.A Orija (2020). 'Informal–Formal Workers' Transition in Nigeria: A Livelihood Analysis'. WIDER Working Paper No. 2020/146. Helsinki: UNU-WIDER. https://doi.org/10.35188/UNU-WIDER.

Forastieri, V. (1999). 'Improvement of Working Conditions and Environment in the Informal Sector through Safety and Health Measures'. Available at: https://www.ilo.org/global/topics/safety-and-health-at-work/resources-library/publications/WCMS_110306/lang--en/index.htm (accessed 2 November 2020).

Gutierrez, I.A., K.B. Kumar, M. Mahmud, F. Munshi, and S. Nataraj (2019). 'Transitions between Informal and Formal Employment: Results from a Worker Survey in Bangladesh'. *IZA Journal of Development and Migration*, 9(3): 1–27. https://doi.org/10.1186/s40176-019-0141-2.

Harris, J.R., and M.P. Todaro (1970). 'Migration, Unemployment and Development: A Two-Sector Analysis'. *American Economic Review*, 60(March): 126–142.

Hillenkamp, I., F. Lapeyre, and A. Lemaître (2013). *Securing Livelihoods: Informal Economy Practices and Institutions*. Oxford: Oxford University Press. https://doi.org/10.1093/acprof:oso/9780199687015.001.0001.

Hovsha, J., and A. Meyer (2015). 'The Informal Economy and Sustainable Livelihoods'. *Journal of the Helen Suzman Foundation*, 75(1): 1–5.

IDB (Inter-American Development Bank) (2004). 'Good Jobs Wanted: Labor Markets in Latin America. Economic and Social Progress in Latin America Report (IPES)'. Washington, DC: Inter-American Development Bank.

ILO (International Labour Organization) (2004). *The Informal Economy and Workers in Nepal. International Labour Organization*, Series 1. Kathmandu: International Labour Organization.

ILO (2017). *World Social Protection Report 2017–19: Universal Social Protection to Achieve the Sustainable Development Goals*. Geneva: International Labour Organization.

ILO (2018). *Women and Men in the Informal Economy: A Statistical Picture* (3rd edn). Geneva: International Labour Organization.

ILO (2019). *ILO Thesaurus: Informal Employment*. Geneva: International Labour Organization. Available at: https://metadata.ilo.org/thesaurus/936921656.html (accessed 16 October 2020).

Jerome, T.A. (1996). 'Creating an Enabling Environment for the Informal Sector in the Post-Adjustment Era in Nigeria'. In *The Nigerian Economic Society, Beyond Adjustment: Management of the Nigerian Economy*. Ibadan: The Nigerian Economic Society, 331–337.

Krstić, G., and P. Sanfey (2006). 'Mobility, Poverty and Well-Being among the Informally Employed in Bosnia and Herzegovina'. Working Paper No. 101. London: European Bank for Reconstruction and Development.

Lapeyre, F. (2017). *Transition from the Informal to the Formal Economy: Guiding Principles and Policy Guidelines for the Ufm*. Barcelona: International Labour Organization.

Mahmud, M. (2017). 'Transitions between Informal and Formal Employment: Results from a Worker Survey in Bangladesh'. BIDS Research Paper. Bangladesh: BIDS.

Maloney, W. (1999). 'Does Informality Imply Segmentation in Urban Labor Markets? Evidence from Sectoral Transitions in Mexico'. *World Bank Economic Review*, 13(3), 275–302. https://doi.org/10.1093/wber/13.2.275.

Maloney, W. (2004). 'Informality Revisited'. *World Development*, 32(7): 24–41. https://doi.org/10.1016/j.worlddev.2004.01.008.

Medina, L., A.J. Onelis, and M. Cangul (2017). 'The Informal Economy in Sub-Saharan Africa: Size and Determinants'. IMF Working Paper No. WP/17/156. Washington, DC: International Monetary Fund. https://doi.org/10.5089/9781484305942.001.

NBS (National Bureau of Statistics) (2010). *National Manpower Stock and Employment Generation Survey: Household and Micro-Enterprise (Informal Sector)*. Abuja: National Bureau of Statistics.

Ndiweni, N.J., S. Mashonganyika, N. Ncube, and N. Dube (2014). 'Informal Economy as a Source of Livelihood in Zimbabwean Urban Areas: The Case of Bulawayo Metropolitan Province'. *International Journal of Scientific and Research Publications*, 4(1): 1–8.

Núñez, A.P.V. (2017). 'Analysis of Formal–Informal Transitions in the Ecuadorian Labour Market'. United Nations Economic Commission for Latin America and the Caribbean (CEPAL) Review No. 123. Santiago: CEPAL.

Nwaka, I.D. (2016). 'Heterogeneity in the Nigerian Labour Market: Exploring the Wage Gap'. Unpublished Ph.D. thesis. Gazimağusa, Northern Cyprus: The Eastern Mediterranean University.

Pagés, C., and M. Stampini (2009). 'No Education, No Good Jobs? Evidence on the Relationship between Education and Labour Market Segmentation'. *Journal of Comparative Economics*, 37(2): 387–401. https://doi.org/10.1016/j.jce.2009.05.002.

Perry, G.E., W.F. Maloney, O.S. Arias, P. Fajnzylber, A.D. Mason., and J. Saavedra-Chanduvi (2007). 'Informality Exit and Exclusion'. Washington, DC: The World Bank. https://doi.org/10.1596/978-0-8213-7092-6.

Roberts, R.E. (2016). 'Harnessing the Informal Sector for Growth in Nigeria'. [online] Available at: https://rebeccaidd.wordpress.com/2016/03/29/harnessing-the-informal-sector-for-growth-in-nigeria (accessed 22 October 2020).

Slonimczyk, F., and V. Gimpelson (2015). 'Informality and Mobility: Evidence from Russian Panel Data'. *Economics of Transition*, 23(2): 299–341. https://doi.org/10.1111/ecot.12064.

Tansel, A., and E.O. Kan (2012a). 'Labour Mobility across the Formal/Informal Divide in Turkey: Evidence from Individual Level Data'. Institute of Labor Economics (IZA) Discussion Paper No. 6271. Bonn: Institute of Labour Economics. https://doi.org/10.2139/ssrn.1978291.

Tansel, A., and E.O. Kan (2012b). 'The Formal/Informal Employment Earnings Gap: Evidence from Turkey'. IZA Discussion Paper No. 6556. Bonn: Institute of Labour Economics. https://doi.org/10.2139/ssrn.2049336

Tansel, A., and Z.A. Ozdemir (2015). 'Determinants of Transitions across Formal/Informal Sectors in Egypt'. IZA Discussion Paper 8773. Bonn: Institute of Labour Economics. https://doi.org/10.2139/ssrn.2547146.

Timalsina, K.P. (2011). 'An Urban Informal Economy: Livelihood Opportunity to Poor or Challenges for Urban Governance'. *Global Journal of Human Social Science*, 11(2): 24–32.

Tshuma, M.C., and B. Jari (2013). 'The Informal Sector as a Source of Household Income: The Case of Alice Town in the Eastern Cape Province of South Africa'. *Journal of African Studies and Development*, 5(8): 250–260.

UNDP—IRP (United Nations Development Programme—International Recovery Platform) (2011). 'Guidance Note on Recovery: Livelihood'. Geneva: UNDP—IRP. Available at: https://www.unisdr.org/files/16771_16771guidancenoteonrecoveryliveliho.pdf (accessed 22 October 2020).

12

Informal–formal transitions in work status in sub-Saharan Africa

A comparative perspective

Michael Danquah, Simone Schotte, and Kunal Sen

1. Introduction

In many sub-Saharan African countries, informal forms of economic activity is the norm as it captures over 90 per cent of all economic units (ILO 2018). Most businesses in sub-Saharan Africa (SSA) are informal in the way they operate, and major and essential economic activities such as public transport operations, market centres, and food processing are dominated by informal businesses (see Sacchetto et al., 2020). Informal economic activity in SSA is not limited to some sectors or aspects of the economy—it is far reaching, covering all genders, age groups, and sectors. For instance, a census of business establishments in Ghana shows that 90 per cent of businesses in Ghana are informal (GSS 2015). Informal activities also contribute significantly to economic growth—with estimates ranging from 30 to 65 per cent of gross domestic product (GDP) in many SSA countries (Charmes 2016). Following from the patterns of structural change in many SSA countries, where we see labour moving out of agriculture into informal jobs in both services and manufacturing, it is expected that informalization may increase in the future (Rodrik 2016).

As discussed in Chapter 1, there is an increasing consensus in recent theoretical and empirical studies that recognizes the extent of heterogeneity in informal work (see, e.g. Perry et al. 2007; Echevin and Murtin 2009; Chen 2012; Grimm et al. 2012; De Vreyer and Roubaud 2013; Radchenko 2017; Basu et al. 2018). For example, within informal wage-employment, one may observe workers employed as casual labourers in poorly paid unskilled jobs, at the lower end, along with skilled workers employed in better-paid jobs that are not covered by labour legislation or social protection provisions but nevertheless require some professional training to obtain these jobs. Similarly, within informal self-employment, one may observe subsistence own-account or household entrepreneurs, often referred to as 'penniless entrepreneurs' (see Banerjee and Duflo 2007) or the 'reluctant

Michael Danquah, Simone Schotte, and Kunal Sen, *Informal–formal transitions in work status in sub-Saharan Africa.* In: *The Job Ladder.* Edited by Gary S. Fields, T. H. Gindling, Kunal Sen, Michael Danquah, and Simone Schotte, Oxford University Press. © UNU-WIDER (2023). DOI: 10.1093/oso/9780192867339.003.0012 self-employed' (see Basu et al. 2018), along with larger and more productive non-household enterprises employing hired labour, sometimes referred to as 'constrained gazelles' and 'top performers' (see Grimm et al. 2012). This internal duality between a 'lower-tier' and a 'upper-tier' in informality can be observed both in wage-employment and self-employment.

A key issue concerning the persistence of informality in the labour markets of many SSA countries is whether informality itself—especially in lower-tier work—is a persistent state such that the most disadvantaged workers are locked in a situation of inferior pay and conditions or whether informality is a transient state that all workers are roughly equally likely to experience at some point throughout their working life. Closely related to this is the question of whether informal employment provides a 'stepping stone' towards formal positions or, on the contrary, presents a 'dead end' without better job perspectives, with the result that informal workers either stay in this position or drop out of the labour force (Slonimczyk and Gimpelson 2015).

In this chapter, we examine the likelihood of workers moving from lower-tier to upper-tier informal work and to formal work (and vice versa), as well as the earning implications of such transitions, using comparable panel data for four countries in SSA—Ghana, South Africa, Tanzania, and Uganda. Our results show high persistence in the lower-tier segment of informality, where self-employed workers in particular tend to remain locked in a situation of inferior pay and conditions. Informal wage jobs, by contrast, can present a stepping stone into formal employment relationships, especially for those in the more dynamic upper-tier segment. We find a relatively strong segmentation between wage-employment and self-employment in the SSA case, with few workers exiting formal or upper-informal wage-employment for self-employment. Finally, we also find a significant earnings gain for workers who make the transition from lower-tier employment to upper-tier employment.

This chapter contributes significantly to the discussions on the nature, magnitude, and direction of employment transition patterns in the informal economy in SSA, where our knowledge of such transitions is limited. A strength of our analysis is the comparative nature of our study, which allows us to assess whether the patterns of transitions that we observe is specific to one country context or holds true for other countries in our sample. The location of the countries in our study—in Western Africa (Ghana), Eastern Africa (Tanzania and Uganda), and Southern Africa (South Africa)—provides a basis for making generalizable claims on the patterns of mobility within and across the informal economy in SSA. The four are among the few SSA countries for which at least two waves of household panel data are available and where variable definitions can be harmonized across countries.

The chapter is organized as follows. Section 2 presents a brief description of the data, work status classification, and methodology, whilst section 3 describes the patterns of employment mobility using transition matrices. Section 4 presents the results from the econometric analysis and section 5 concludes.

2. Data, work status classification, and methodology

This study is based on the employment modules of living standard household surveys from four SSA countries: Ghana (Ghana Socioeconomic Panel Survey, GSPS), South Africa (National Income Dynamics Study, NIDS), Tanzania (Tanzania National Panel Study, TZNPS), and Uganda (Uganda National Panel Study, UNPS). In addition to the geographic focus on SSA, the choice of countries is based on the share of employment outside of smallholder agriculture and the availability of at least two recent waves of nationally representative panel data with individual-level information on demographic characteristics, labour earnings, and employment, including direct or indirect information concerning the individual's formality status in employment. For reasons of data availability and cross-country comparability, we focus the analysis on the two most recent waves of panel data available in each of the four countries under study. The data were collected between 2010 and 2017 with a two-to-four-year time gap between panel waves.[1] The sample is restricted to workers in prime working age (15–64 years old). We convert the labour earnings reported for different time periods to monthly earnings based on reported working times.[2]

The work status classification schema for identifying formality status and tiers for both wage-employment and self-employment follows the earlier description in Chapters 1 and 2 of this book and can also be found in Danquah et al. (2019). The detailed presentation of the methodology outlining the analysis of employment transitions, labour income dynamics, and initial employment and attrition is also available in Danquah et al. (2019).

3. Descriptive analysis

A key strength of our analysis is its comparative nature. The countries included in our study cover different regions—Western Africa (Ghana), Eastern Africa (Tanzania and Uganda), and Southern Africa (South Africa)—as well as the different levels of development—including middle-income (South Africa), lower middle-income (Ghana), and low-income (Tanzania and Uganda) countries.

[1] A full reference to the sources of the data for the four countries are available in Danquah et al. (2019).

[2] All income data is deflated to 2010 prices and, for reasons of cross-country comparability, converted to international dollars using the World Bank's purchasing power parity conversion factor for private consumption. Income levels above the 99th percentile of the distribution are considered outliers and replaced by the cut-off value. Only individuals working and reporting strictly positive cash income are included, whereas in-kind income is not taken into consideration. Agricultural income generated by family farms is excluded from the analysis as data on agricultural revenues and costs are relatively noisy.

In this section, we assess the differences and commonalities in the composition of employment across these four countries, both from a static and dynamic perspective.

3.1 Composition of employment

The summary statistics presented in Table 12.1 show the aggregated distribution of workers in employment by work status. As widely established in the literature, the

Table 12.1 Distribution of workers by work status (percentage)

(a) Proportion of employment by work status

			Ghana	South Africa	Tanzania	Uganda
Wage-employed	Formal		13.2	56.7	11.7	11.7
	Informal	Upper-tier	5.3	8.9	3.3	10.8
		Lower-tier	18.9	21.4	28.6	26.0
Self-employed	Formal		8.9	4.0	9.1	3.1
	Informal	Upper-tier	11.9	5.4	3.9	5.8
		Lower-tier	41.8	3.7	43.4	42.6
Total			100	100	100	100

(b) Proportion of formal vs informal employment

		Ghana	South Africa	Tanzania	Uganda
Formal		22.1	60.6	20.7	14.9
Informal	Upper-tier	17.2	14.3	7.2	16.6
	Lower-tier	60.7	25.1	72.0	68.6
Total		100	100	100	100

(c) Proportion of upper-tier informality in informal employment

	Ghana	South Africa	Tanzania	Uganda
Upper informal in total informal employment	22.1	36.4	9.1	19.4
Upper informal in informal self-employment	22.2	59.7	8.2	11.9
Upper informal in informal wage-employment	22.0	29.4	10.5	29.4

Note: For each country, summary statistics are compiled for the initial wave of panel study under study. Workers employed on family farms have been excluded from the analysis.
Source: authors' calculations based on survey data from Ghana Socioeconomic Panel Survey (GSPS) 2009–2010, Tanzania National Panel Survey (TZNPS) 2010–2011, Uganda National Panel Study (UNPS) 2010–2011, and National Income Dynamics Study (NIDS) 2014–2015.

Table 12.2 Change in distribution of workers by work status, balanced panel

(a) Change (ppts) in proportion of employment by work status

			Ghana	South Africa	Tanzania	Uganda
	Formal		1.7	−0.4	5.0	−2.7
Wage-employed	Informal	Upper-tier	−2.5	1.6	−2.4	0.0
		Lower-tier	−3.8	−3.3	−0.4	0.7
	Formal		0.8	2.0	−2.8	1.3
Self-employed	Informal	Upper-tier	−1.5	−0.5	0.7	0.5
		Lower-tier	5.3	0.6	−0.1	0.3

(b) Change (ppts) in proportion of formal and informal employment

		Ghana	South Africa	Tanzania	Uganda
Formal		2.5	1.5	2.3	−1.5
Informal	Upper-tier	−4.0	1.1	−1.7	0.5
	Lower-tier	1.5	−2.6	−0.5	1.0

(c) Change (ppts) in proportion of self-employment

	Ghana	South Africa	Tanzania	Uganda
Self-employed	4.6	2.1	−2.2	2.1

Source: authors' calculations based on survey data from GSPS 2009/10–2013/14, TZNPS 2010/11–2012/13, UNPS 2010/11–2011/12, and NIDS 2014/15–2017.

composition of the workforce in South Africa differs remarkably from the employment structure observed in poorer SSA countries. In South Africa, we observe that 60.6 per cent of those in non-farm employment are formally employed (see Table 12.1). By contrast, in Ghana and Tanzania, only about 20 per cent and, in Uganda, 16.6 per cent of those employed in non-farm activities are in formal employment, which means that about 80 per cent of the non-farm employment in these three countries is informal. Most of the informal workers in these three countries are in lower-tier informal self-employment, accounting for more than 40 per cent of all non-farm employment. The latter share would be yet substantially larger if family farms were included in the analysis (forming part of the lower-tier segment of informality), raising the informality rate in Tanzania and Uganda to just above 90 per cent. Complementary tables on the proportion of employment by work status, including family farms and unemployment, is available in Danquah et al. (2019).

The main difference thus consists in the relative absence of lower-tier informal self-employment in South Africa compared to the three other countries. This difference can be attributed to two factors. First, South Africa's economy provides relatively more employment opportunities in the formal economy. Second, in South Africa, a larger share of workers can afford to be openly unemployed (23.3 per cent) compared to the three poorer countries (below 2 per cent), where workers revert to survivalist self-employment strategies in the absence of other job opportunities and sufficiently developed social protection systems.

We observe no large changes in these country-level employment structures between survey waves (see Table 12.2). In Ghana, South Africa, and Uganda, the share of individuals in self-employment in the balanced panel (workers employed in non-farm activities in both panel waves) moderately increased, while it slightly decreased in Tanzania. Ghana, South Africa, and Tanzania show an increase in the aggregate rate of formal employment among the balanced panel by 1.5–2.5 percentage points (ppts). In Ghana and Tanzania, this was mainly driven by a rise in the share of formal wage-employment, mirrored by a decline in the upper-tier segment of informal wage work. By contrast, in South Africa and Uganda, we see an expansion in formal self-employment, accompanied by a moderate decline in formal wage-employment. These relatively small changes in aggregate shares tend to mask substantial mobility of workers across employment categories, which is discussed in section 4.

Table 12.3 presents three additional descriptive features of our data. First, we find that informal employment is more common among younger workers. Second, women tend to be under-represented in formal wage-employment and self-employment and to be importantly over-represented in lower-tier informal employment. Finally, workers with secondary or tertiary education are over-represented in formal employment, while workers who have either no education or only completed primary schooling are dominantly found in informal employment.

We also analyse labour market earnings across the six aggregate groups and work status groups for all countries. The mean monthly earnings (in 2005 PPPs) for the six aggregate groups for all four countries shows that formally employed workers earn more than informally employed workers. Wage-employees earn more on average than the self-employed, whilst upper-tier informal workers earn more than lower-tier informal workers (see Fig. 12.1).

Disaggregating further using the six work status groups, the job ladder in Fig. 12.2 shows the mean monthly earnings (in 2005 PPPs) by work status for Ghana, South Africa, Tanzania, and Uganda. The highest earning status in Ghana, South Africa, and Tanzania is the formal wage-employed whilst the informal upper-tier self-employed has the highest earning in Uganda. Across all countries, the lowest earning status is the lower-tier informal self-employed.

Table 12.3 Average worker characteristics by work status

(a) Average age (years)

			Ghana	South Africa	Tanzania	Uganda
Wage-employed	Formal		43.5	37.5	40.5	36.1
			(0.53)	(0.16)	(0.52)	(0.71)
	Informal	Upper-tier	36.4	35.6	33.4	34.7
			(0.82)	(0.37)	(1.00)	(0.84)
		Lower-tier	38.4	35.4	30.3	30.5
			(0.46)	(0.25)	(0.35)	(0.53)
Self-employed	Formal		41.5	41.3	37.5	34.8
			(0.64)	(0.72)	(0.54)	(1.29)
	Informal	Upper-tier	40.3	40.2	34.7	38.8
			(0.53)	(0.54)	(0.83)	(0.95)
		Lower-tier	40.8	38.6	31.0	34.8
			(0.29)	(0.69)	(0.33)	(0.47)
Total			40.5	37.2	32.7	34.1
			(0.19)	(0.12)	(0.20)	(0.29)

(b) Share of female workers (%)

			Ghana	South Africa	Tanzania	Uganda
Wage-employed	Formal		33.7	41.5	32.5	41.3
			(2.41)	(0.75)	(2.15)	(3.77)
	Informal	Upper-tier	30.0	57.0	35.5	34.3
			(3.55)	(1.65)	(4.33)	(3.80)
		Lower-tier	33.8	44.3	34.0	26.8
			(1.91)	(1.09)	(1.55)	(2.12)
Self-employed	Formal		47.9	45.8	36.0	39.7
			(3.24)	(3.00)	(2.83)	(6.60)
	Informal	Upper-tier	50.0	40.3	25.4	29.4
			(2.67)	(2.25)	(3.73)	(4.25)
		Lower-tier	81.7	58.4	63.9	47.9
			(1.08)	(2.96)	(1.31)	(1.85)
Total			56.8	44.2	46.7	38.9
			(0.90)	(0.55)	(0.87)	(1.19)

(c) Share of workers with secondary or tertiary education (%)

			Ghana	South Africa	Tanzania	Uganda
Wage-employed	Formal		52.2	63.7	36.4	60.1

Continued

Table 12.3 *Continued*

			(3.02)	(0.74)	(2.29)	(3.88)
	Informal	Upper-tier	37.8	55.5	39.9	59.7
			(4.04)	(1.66)	(4.76)	(4.09)
		Lower-tier	19.1	28.0	1.2	11.8
			(1.76)	(0.98)	(0.36)	(1.66)
Self-employed	Formal		18.6	69.3	2.4	42.9
			(2.80)	(2.78)	(0.91)	(6.74)
	Informal	Upper-tier	10.0	28.6	3.3	37.3
			(1.82)	(2.07)	(1.56)	(4.59)
		Lower-tier	8.3	33.0	1.7	12.2
			(0.95)	(2.82)	(0.38)	(1.29)
Total			19.0	52.5	7.1	25.8
			(0.83)	(0.55)	(0.47)	(1.13)

Note: For each country, summary statistics are compiled for the initial wave of panel study under study. Standard errors of mean values in parentheses.
Source: authors' calculations based on survey data from GSPS 2009–2010, TZNPS 2010–2011, UNPS 2010–2011, and NIDS 2014–2015.

3.2 Patterns of transitions

We now move from the preceding static assessment to a dynamic perspective. The transition matrices in Table 12.4 report the probabilities with which workers are observed in a certain work status at the end of the period, conditional on their initial state. Accordingly, the elements in the main diagonal give the probabilities of staying in the same work status, while the elements outside the main diagonal give the probabilities of moving to a different work status. The share of stayers, defined as the proportion of workers who remain in their work status, is calculated as the product of the highlighted diagonals and the initial share of workers in the respective category. We observe the highest employment mobility in Ghana, where just about 50 per cent of all initially employed individuals were observed in the same work status at the end of the period. In the other three countries, the same was true for about 60 per cent of all workers.

The transition patterns vary considerably across countries. However, a commonality observed is that employment stability tends to be highest among the formally wage-employed. This may partly be attributed to these jobs being regulated and protected by existing legal standards. In South Africa and Tanzania, around 80 per cent of all workers in formal wage-employment remain in this work status from one survey wave to the next. This share is somewhat lower in Ghana, at 65.1 per cent, and lowest in Uganda, at 48.3 per cent.

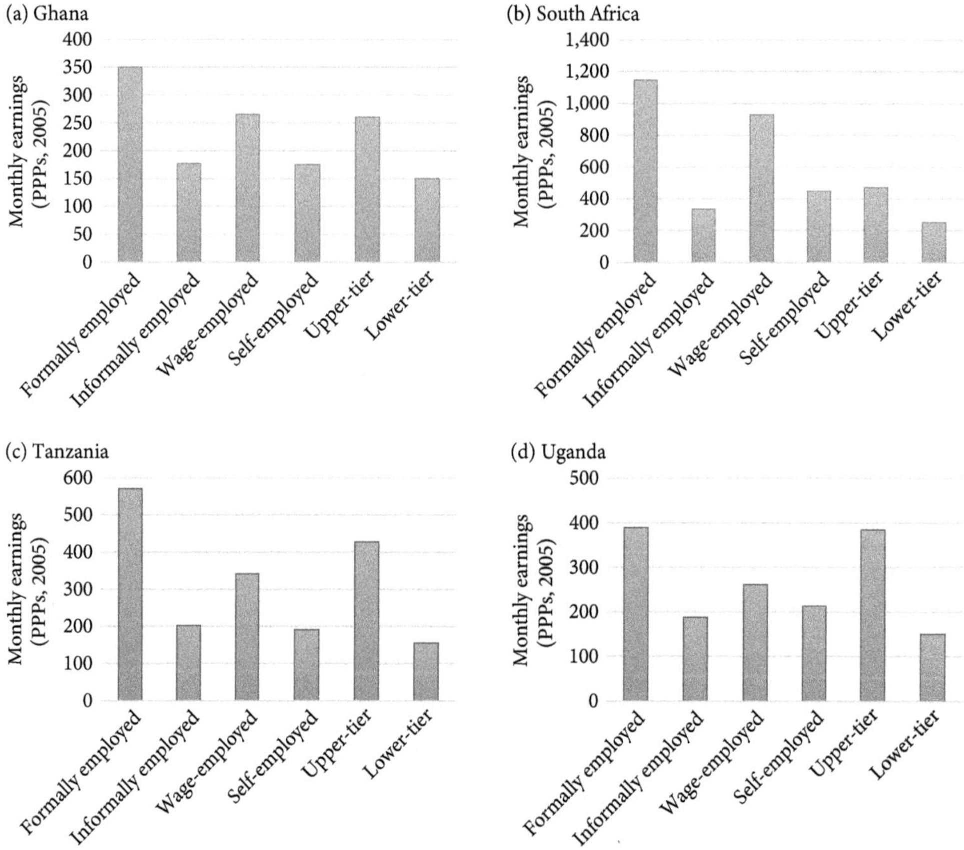

Fig. 12.1 Mean monthly labour earnings (in PPPs, 2005) across six aggregate groups

Note: For each country, summary statistics are compiled for the initial wave of panel study under study. Standard errors of mean values in parentheses.

Source: authors' calculations based on survey data from Ghana Socioeconomic Panel Survey (GSPS) 2009/10–2013/14, Tanzania National Panel Survey (TZNPS) 2010/11–2012/13, Uganda National Panel Study (UNPS) 2010/11–2011/12, and National Income Dynamics Study (NIDS) 2014/15–2017.

Labour turnover tends to be higher in formal self-employment, with important differences observed across countries. In South Africa, among the formally self-employed, 50.8 per cent stay in this state, 13 per cent move into formal wage-employment, 23 per cent move into upper-tier informality, and only 13.2 per cent move into lower-tier informality (being either self-employed or wage-employed). On the contrary, only around 30 per cent of the formally self-employed in Ghana, Tanzania, and Uganda remain in formal self-employment from one survey wave to the next, while up to 40 per cent move into lower-tier informal self-employment. While these movements may partly be explained by reporting errors, business instability is assumed to also play a major role.

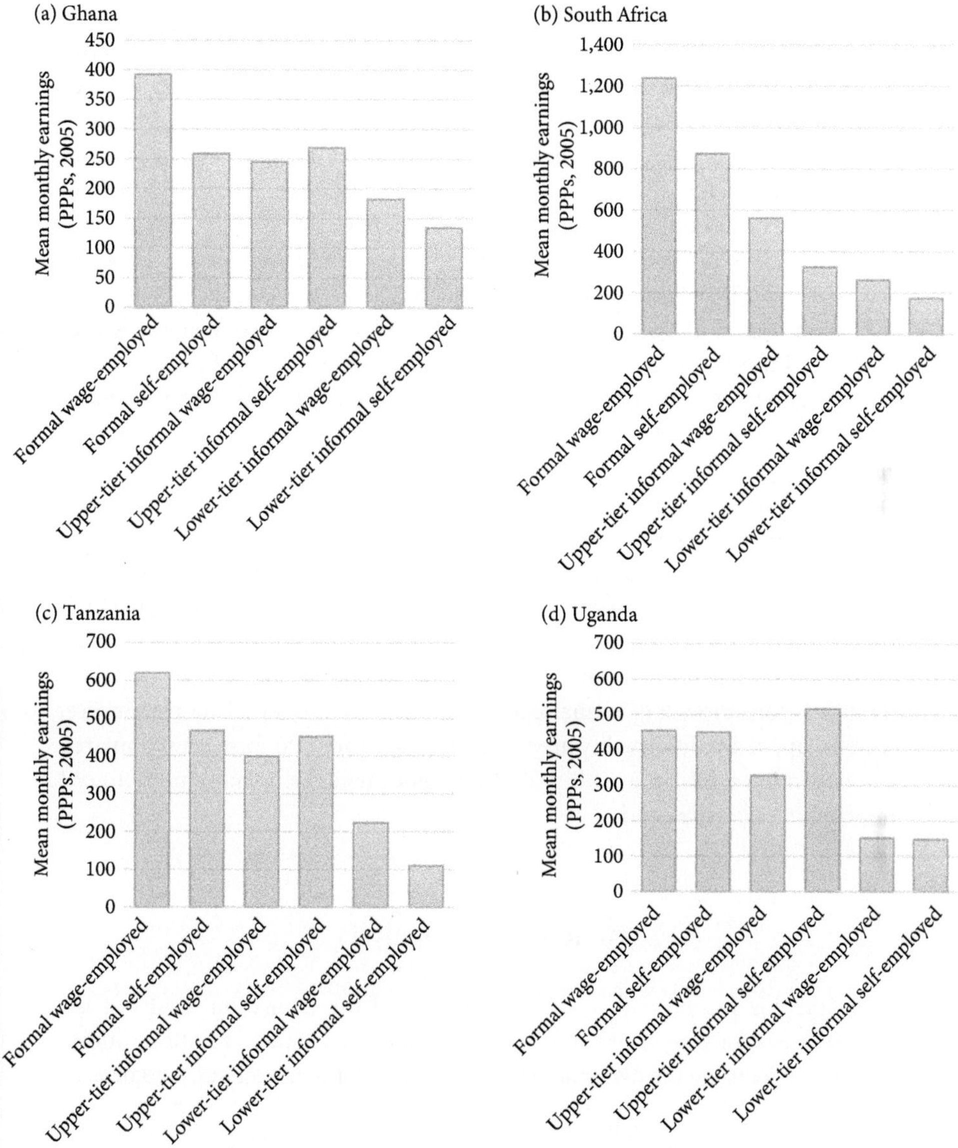

Fig. 12.2 Mean monthly labour earnings (in PPPs, 2005) across six work status groups

Note: For each country, summary statistics are compiled for the initial wave of panel study under study. Standard errors of mean values in parentheses.
Source: authors' calculations based on survey data from Ghana Socioeconomic Panel Survey (GSPS) 2009/10–2013/14, Tanzania National Panel Survey (TZNPS) 2010/11–2012/13, Uganda National Panel Study (UNPS) 2010/11–2011/12, and National Income Dynamics Study (NIDS) 2014/15–2017.

Furthermore, in Ghana, Tanzania, and Uganda, we observe high stability within lower-tier informal self-employment, with around two-thirds of the respective workers staying in this segment. The 'stickiness' in this segment reflects the limited alternative job opportunities available to workers in this group. Notably, when including family farming under lower-tier informal self-employment activities in the destination state, we observe an even higher level of persistence in this segment. Hence, a non-negligible share of workers may draw on a combination of self-employment in agriculture and in lower-tier non-agricultural informality (see Danquah et al. 2019 for additional information).

In Tanzania and Uganda, we observe a similar level of stagnation within lower-tier informal wage-employment, with about 80 per cent of the respective workers either remaining in this category or moving into lower-tier informal self-employment. In Ghana and South Africa, higher mobility out of lower-tier informal wage-employment into formal wage-employment is observed, suggesting that for about 20 per cent of all workers in this group, lower-tier informal wage-employment can present a stepping stone into formal employment relationships. This may imply that workers take on informal employment to gain work experience (either voluntarily or due to the limited supply of formal (or regular) job opportunities) before moving into better-paying activities. It may also reflect information asymmetries, where employers first employ workers informally to test their abilities before providing formal contracts. Furthermore, in all four countries, those in upper-tier informality are more likely to move into formality compared to those in lower-tier informality. This difference tends to be more pronounced among the wage-employed.

4. Regression analysis

We begin this section with a short discussion of the estimation results of the selected equations capturing initial employment and panel retention. Subsequently, we focus on the dynamics in employment status and labour income.

4.1 Initial employment and attrition

The subset of workers who were employed in non-farm activities in the initial panel wave, as opposed to working on a family farm or being unemployed, ranges from 78.1 per cent in South Africa, 51.7 per cent in Ghana, and 34 per cent in Uganda to 33.2 per cent in Tanzania. Panel retention rates among the active workforce are highest in South Africa (75.9 per cent) and lowest in Tanzania (69.1 per cent).

Table 12.4 Transition matrices across work status groups

(a) Ghana

				Wave $t = 1$						Share of Stayers
				Wage-employed			Self-employed			
				Formal	Informal		Formal	Informal		
					Upper-tier	Lower-tier		Upper-tier	Lower-tier	
Wave $t = 0$	Wage-employed	Formal		65.1	6.9	9.6	4.3	3.6	10.6	8.6
		Informal	Upper-tier	33.0	11.8	23.7	2.5	3.2	25.8	0.6
			Lower-tier	21.7	5.3	32.2	7.5	6.4	26.9	6.1
	Self-employed	Formal		2.1	3.4	12.1	29.5	15.8	37.1	2.6
		Informal	Upper-tier	4.0	2.5	15.2	14.7	44.7	18.9	5.3
			Lower-tier	2.1	2.0	15.8	6.8	6.3	67.2	28.1
	Total			21.0	4.5	18.4	9.1	11.2	35.8	51.3

Continued

Table 12.4 *Continued*

(b) South Africa

				Wave $t = 1$						Share of Stayers
				Wage-employed			Self-employed			
				Formal	Informal		Formal	Informal		
					Upper-tier	Lower-tier		Upper-tier	Lower-tier	
	Wage-employed	Formal		83.3	7.1	5.8	2.2	1.1	0.5	47.2
		Informal	Upper-tier	50.1	25.1	14.7	6.0	1.0	3.1	2.2
			Lower-tier	26.4	13.1	47.7	4.7	3.9	4.3	10.2
Wave $t = 0$	Self-employed	Formal		13.0	9.7	5.1	50.8	13.3	8.1	2.0
		Informal	Upper-tier	12.2	11.1	19.5	16.1	23.5	17.6	1.3
			Lower-tier	14.7	6.2	16.8	6.9	24.6	30.8	1.1
	Total			63.4	9.9	14.9	5.2	3.4	3.1	64.0

(c) Tanzania

				Wave $t = 1$						Share of Stayers
				Wage-employed			Self-employed			
				Formal	Informal		Formal	Informal		
					Upper-tier	Lower-tier		Upper-tier	Lower-tier	
	Wage-employed	Formal		79.7	4.4	9.7	1.5	1.0	3.6	9.3
		Informal	Upper-tier	45.8	5.8	33.1	6.5	2.9	6.0	0.2
			Lower-tier	14.8	0.9	62.4	2.9	3.5	15.5	17.9
Wave $t = 0$	Self-employed	Formal		2.0	0.0	5.0	31.7	18.2	43.1	2.9
		Informal	Upper-tier	4.5	0.0	21.8	15.2	23.1	35.4	0.9
			Lower-tier	5.8	1.5	15.3	8.3	4.1	64.9	28.2
	Total			22.2	1.8	27.3	8.6	6.0	34.2	59.3

(d) Uganda

				Wave $t = 1$						Share of Stayers
				Wage-employed			Self-employed			
				Formal	Informal		Formal	Informal		
					Upper-tier	Lower-tier		Upper-tier	Lower-tier	
	Wage-employed	Formal		58.0	27.0	8.1	5.2	0.0	1.7	6.8
		Informal	Upper-tier	20.0	48.3	14.1	5.7	6.1	5.9	5.2
			Lower-tier	4.7	6.2	68.3	2.7	4.3	13.9	17.7
Wave $t = 0$	Self-employed	Formal		2.7	0.0	10.5	20.7	15.0	51.1	0.6
		Informal	Upper-tier	0.0	4.6	5.0	13.9	39.8	36.8	2.3
			Lower-tier	2.2	1.0	11.9	4.4	7.2	73.2	31.2
	Total			14.8	13.3	24.3	5.7	7.9	34.1	63.9

Note: Each row indicates work status in the base period, and each column in transition matrices indicates work status in the next period; transition matrix rows sum to 100. The likelihood of staying in the same employment status conditional on the base year employment status is highlighted in grey. The share of stayers (proportion of workers who remain in their work status) is calculated as the product of highlighted diagonals and initial size.

Source: authors' calculations based on survey data from GSPS 2009/10–2013/14, TZNPS 2010/11–2012/13, UNPS 2010/11–2011/12, and NIDS 2014/15–2017.

For the propensity of initial employment in non-farm activities, we use a binary variable identifying household heads (as opposed to other household members) as an instrument. Across countries, heads of household are significantly more likely to be initially employed in non-farm activities, while the variable is validly excludable from the main employment transition equation.

Finding a valid instrument for the propensity of panel retention that is available across countries proved difficult. Following a similar approach to Schotte et al. (2018), for South Africa, Tanzania, and Uganda—where at least one previous wave of panel data is available—we use a binary variable indicating whether the respondent was a sample member in the previous survey wave. In Ghana, identification relies on the non-linear form of the inverse Mills ratio. A full description of the estimation strategy and additional results are available in Danquah et al. (2019).

4.2 Employment transitions

Table 12.5 presents the conditional transition probabilities estimated from the multinomial logit regression. The average marginal effects in each column are calculated by destination work status in $t = 1$. The reference status that is used as both transitions' starting point and destination is lower-tier informal self-employment. We pool the data for all countries so that the displayed results present cross-country average marginal effects. To ensure that the somewhat different employment structure and transition patterns observed in South Africa compared to the three other countries are not driving the results (see section 3.1), we re-estimate the regression excluding South Africa, finding largely similar results. We also test how our results change when including family farms (under lower-tier informal self-employment) and unemployment as additional destination states and further explore the coefficient estimates of our control variables using a condensed ordered logit specification. All the regression estimates are provided in Danquah et al. (2019).

The average marginal effects on initial work status reported in the upper panel of Table 12.5 can be read similarly to the conditional transition probabilities of a transition matrix.[3] In this sense, the coefficient estimates on being in employment state $k = \{1, \ldots, 5\}$ at time $t = 1$, conditional on being observed in the same state k at time $t = 0$ (main diagonal) give an indication of the degree of persistence or state dependence in employment status that is not explained by differences in education, age, gender, and geographic location (Gong et al. 2004; Liu 2015).

[3] The likelihood ratio test rejects the null hypothesis that the dynamic factors play no role; that is, the lagged labour states are jointly significant (p-value of 0.0000) and also, in most cases, individually significant.

Table 12.5 Employment transitions

Multinomial logistic regression			**No. of observations**	=	**7,816**
Average marginal effects on work status in $t = 1$			**Log likelihood**	=	**–7851.1291**
Base outcome: lower-tier informal wage-employed			**Pseudo R-squared**	=	**0.3353**

VARIABLES	**(1) Formal wage-employed**	**(2) Upper-tier informal wage-employed**	**(3) Lower-tier informal wage-employed**	**(4) Formal self-employed**	**(5) Upper-tier informal self-employed**
Work status in $t = 0$ (base: lower-tier informal self-employed)					
(1) Formal wage-employed	0.628***	0.037**	–0.066**	–0.128***	–0.096***
	(0.028)	(0.016)	(0.033)	(0.014)	(0.029)
(2) Upper-tier informal wage-employed	0.293***	0.192***	0.044	–0.099***	–0.078***
	(0.026)	(0.015)	(0.033)	(0.014)	(0.028)
(3) Lower-tier informal wage-employed	0.153***	0.062**	0.264***	–0.104***	–0.062**
	(0.008)	(0.024)	(0.042)	(0.016)	(0.025)
(4) Formal self-employed	–0.045*	–0.007	–0.079***	0.227***	0.043
	(0.026)	(0.023)	(0.020)	(0.033)	(0.044)
(5) Upper-tier informal self-employed	–0.012	0.028	–0.023	0.016	0.201***
	(0.024)	(0.022)	(0.030)	(0.014)	(0.056)
Level of education (base: no schooling)					
Primary	0.053***	0.001	–0.089***	0.023***	0.001
	(0.018)	(0.009)	(0.025)	(0.006)	(0.004)

Continued

Table 12.5 *Continued*

Multinomial logistic regression			**No. of observations**	**=**	**7,816**
Average marginal effects on work status in $t = 1$			**Log likelihood**	**=**	**–7851.1291**
Base outcome: lower-tier informal wage-employed			**Pseudo R-squared**	**=**	**0.3353**

VARIABLES	**(1) Formal wage-employed**	**(2) Upper-tier informal wage-employed**	**(3) Lower-tier informal wage-employed**	**(4) Formal self-employed**	**(5) Upper-tier informal self-employed**
Post-primary	0.121***	0.011	–0.160***	0.050***	0.004
	(0.023)	(0.026)	(0.033)	(0.005)	(0.005)
Secondary	0.196***	0.008	–0.223***	0.052***	–0.002
	(0.025)	(0.022)	(0.034)	(0.003)	(0.012)
Post-secondary	0.246***	0.026	–0.283***	0.096***	–0.000
	(0.028)	(0.022)	(0.036)	(0.020)	(0.012)
Tertiary	0.342***	–0.001	–0.337***	0.107***	–0.016
	(0.024)	(0.019)	(0.041)	(0.038)	(0.020)
Age	0.003	–0.002	–0.010***	0.006	0.000
	(0.003)	(0.002)	(0.003)	(0.004)	(0.002)
Age squared (x0.01)	–0.002	0.002	0.009***	–0.006	–0.001
	(0.004)	(0.003)	(0.003)	(0.005)	(0.003)
Female	–0.037***	0.029***	–0.008	–0.021***	–0.016***
	(0.009)	(0.003)	(0.011)	(0.005)	(0.001)
Urban	0.029***	–0.027***	0.015	0.007	–0.013***
	(0.006)	(0.007)	(0.018)	(0.009)	(0.004)

Country (base: Ghana)					
South Africa	0.122***	0.037***	0.005	−0.010	−0.020***
	(0.006)	(0.007)	(0.012)	(0.006)	(0.003)
Tanzania	0.112***	−0.033***	−0.019***	0.017***	−0.036***
	(0.018)	(0.004)	(0.006)	(0.002)	(0.005)
Uganda	−0.106***	0.099***	0.011	−0.018***	0.007***
	(0.005)	(0.010)	(0.007)	(0.002)	(0.002)
Sample selection					
Panel retention	−0.044**	−0.019**	−0.026*	−0.007	−0.009
from $t = 0$ to $t = 1$	(0.020)	(0.009)	(0.015)	(0.011)	(0.013)
Employed (non-farm)	0.011	−0.002	0.010	0.005	−0.025**
in $t = 0$	(0.012)	(0.021)	(0.022)	(0.014)	(0.010)

Note: * $p < 0.1$, ** $p < 0.05$, *** $p < 0.01$. Standard errors clustered at the country level in parentheses.
Source: authors' calculations based on survey data from GSPS 2009/10–2013/14, TZNPS 2010/11–2012/13, UNPS 2010/11–2011/12, and NIDS 2014/15–2017.

Interestingly, we find a relatively strong segmentation between wage-employment and self-employment. Workers in formal self-employment are most likely to remain in this state or move into informal self-employment. By contrast, transitions from formal self-employment to formal wage-employment are rare and even less likely to occur than a move from lower informal to formal wage-employment. Similarly, we find a high degree of persistence in formal wage-employment, which is expected given the prevalence of permanent contracts in this groups.

More surprising is the observation that workers originating from formal wage jobs do not display an elevated likelihood of moving into formal or upper-tier informal self-employment, as some of the literature on Latin America would suggest (Maloney 1999; Bosch and Maloney 2010). Our evidence thus does not lend support to the hypothesis that workers use the human capital acquired in formal wage jobs to set up own businesses and benefit from greater flexibility and independence. While workers in lower-tier informal wage jobs are more likely than other wage workers to move into self-employment, we still observe an important extent of segregation between wage-employment and self-employment, even in the lower-tier of informality.

As expected, workers in upper-tier informal jobs have significantly higher chances of moving into formal wage jobs than those in the lower tier. It is worthwhile noting that the same does not apply within self-employment, where lower-tier and upper-tier informal workers display a similar (not statistically different) conditional likelihood to formalize. However, this does not imply that both groups face the same obstacles to formalization, which in the upper tier may partly be explained by choice.

We find that even after controlling for differences in education, location, age, and initial work status, women are less likely than men to be formally employed. They are more likely to engage in lower-tier informal self-employment or to work in upper-tier informal wage jobs, which excludes them from the social protection benefits associated with formal wage-employment. This may partly be explained by a higher preference for more flexible job arrangements but may also be attributable to the difficulty of females finding jobs in the formal economy. Our results, obtained using the ordered logit specification, confirm that women, on average, face a higher likelihood of dropping out of formal jobs and slip into upper-tier and particularly lower-tier informality more often than men (see Danquah et al. 2019 for details).

Moreover, we find that higher levels of education are associated with a higher likelihood of working formally (see Table 12.5). When excluding South Africa from the sample, we furthermore observe that higher levels of education are associated with a higher likelihood of being in upper-tier rather than lower-tier informal wage-employment. Interestingly, the correlation between educational attainment and formality status is stronger in wage-employment than in self-employment.

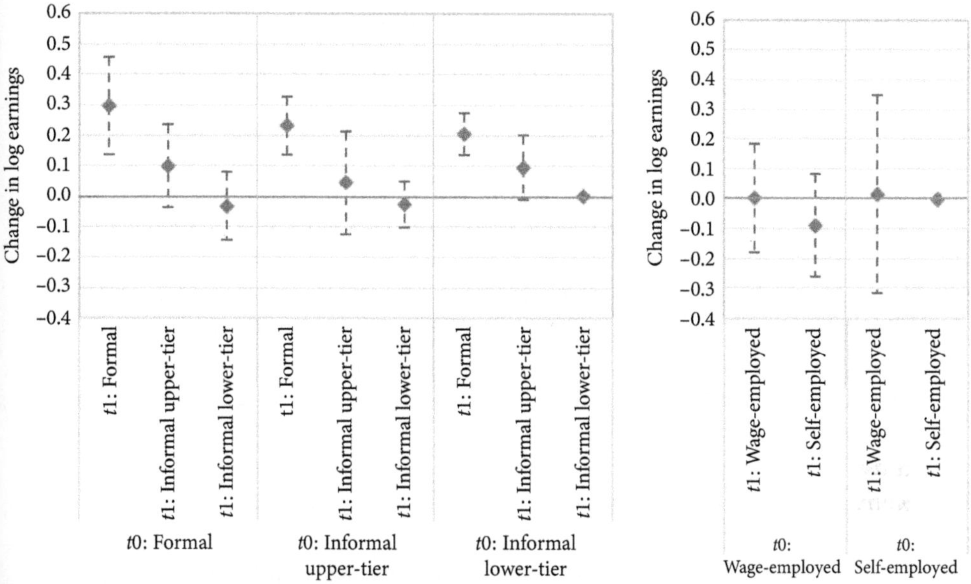

Fig. 12.3 Labour income dynamics

Note: Each point shows the estimated marginal effect on changes in log earnings by initial and destination employment state, with 'Informal lower' and 'Wage-employed' being the base categories. The dashed lines show the 95 per cent confidence intervals.
Source: authors' calculations based on survey data from Ghana Socioeconomic Panel Survey (GSPS) 2009/10–2013/14, Tanzania National Panel Survey (TZNPS) 2010/11–2012/13, Uganda National Panel Study (UNPS) 2010/11–2011/12, and National Income Dynamics Study (NIDS) 2014/15–2017.

From this, we conclude that the lack of schooling presents an important barrier to attaining formal or upper-tier informal wage jobs, while, on the business side, other barriers, such as access to credit, may play an additional role.

4.3 Labour income dynamics

Finally, we investigate changes in labour earnings by initial and destination work status. The main estimated effects are displayed in Fig. 12.3. To keep the number of transition categories manageable for illustrative purposes, we separately control for formality status and tier (formal vs upper-tier informal vs lower-tier informal) and occupational position (wage-employment vs self-employment). The observed patterns are consistent with an alternative specification that splits the sample by initial work status. The full regression results are presented in Danquah et al. (2019).

We estimate that workers who transition from lower-tier informal employment to upper-tier informal employment on average experience a 9.5 per cent rise in earnings relative to those who stay in the same category. As expected, a larger positive earnings effect of 20.6 per cent is found for those who move into formal employment. These effects are somewhat smaller than the coefficients estimates derived from the fixed-effects panel regression model.[4] Based on our findings, we cannot reject the hypothesis that the earnings premium (or penalty) associated with moving from one work status to another is symmetric to the penalty (or premium) associated with the reverse move.

All other things being equal, the largest inter-temporal change in earnings is experienced by those who were initially in formal employment and sustained this status over time. This may partly be attributable to unobserved individual characteristics of workers in this group but may also reflect a premium on experience in this labour market segment. Interestingly, while workers moving from formal to upper-tier informal employment experience a less favourable change in earnings compared to those who remain formal, they still tend to be better off than those who were already initially in upper-tier informal employment and maintained this status.

Furthermore, we observe that transitions from self-employment to wage-employment are not significantly associated with an earnings premium. Transition from wage-employment to self-employment tend to come with an earnings penalty, which, however, is not statistically significant.

5. Conclusions

Using panel data from Ghana, South Africa, Tanzania, and Uganda, this chapter offered a comparative perspective on the composition of employment in four SSA countries and documented the transition patterns between formal and informal employment and across different forms of informality, distinguishing between wage-employment and self-employment. Our analysis revealed that the distinction between lower-tier and upper-tier informal work is consequential in terms of both employment and earnings dynamics. We found that, for most workers, informal work, especially in the lower tier, rather presents a 'dead end' than a 'stepping stone'. This particularly applies to workers in lower-tier informal self-employment, who often remain in this position of inferior pay and conditions. Across countries, upper-tier informality presents a more dynamic state, with a higher proportion of workers formalizing than in the lower tier. However, when controlling for differences in educational attainment and other worker characteristics, the gap in the likelihood of moving into formal self-employment from either upper-tier

[4] These suggest that, on average, upper-tier informal employment is associated with an earnings premium of 18.3 per cent and formal employment with an earnings premium of 31.4 per cent compared to lower-tier informality.

or lower-tier informal self-employment shrinks and becomes insignificant. On the contrary, workers in upper-tier informal wage jobs have significantly higher chances of moving into formal wage jobs than those in the lower tier. This result may partly be explained by formal employers using an informal employment relationship as a screening device before providing formal contracts. Moreover, we find that workers who transition from lower-tier to upper-tier informal employment on average experience a rise in earnings. This positive earnings effect is yet larger for those who move into formal employment.

As expected, employment stability tends to be highest among the formally wage-employed. This can be attributed to these jobs being regulated and protected by existing legal standards. By contrast, formal self-employment is a much more dynamic state, with particularly high mobility into lower-tier informal self-employment being observed in Ghana, Tanzania, and Uganda. While these movements may partly be explained by reporting errors, business instability probably plays a major role. Interestingly, we find a relatively strong segmentation between wage-employment and self-employment; that is, transitions between self-employment and wage-employment are comparatively rare and mainly occur in the lower tier of informality. Exiting formal or upper-informal wage-employment for self-employment is not common, particularly among better-educated workers.

Following from the findings, policymakers would first need to recognize the heterogeneity in informal work and devise policies that are not necessarily a 'one-size-fits-all' approach to the informal economy. Second, given the limited alternative job opportunities available, particularly to those in lower-tier informal self-employment, our findings suggest that specific policy measures that seek to enhance the livelihoods of workers in this most disadvantaged segment may be more relevant in the sub-Saharan context as compared to policies that aim to reduce the regulatory barriers to formalization.

References

Banerjee, A.V., and E. Duflo (2007). 'The Economic Lives of the Poor'. *Journal of Economic Perspectives*, 21(1): 141–168.

Banerjee, S., Raj, R.S.N. and Sen, K. (2016). 'Monitoring Costs'. *Credit Constraints and Entrepreneurship, Manchester School*, 84(5): 573–599.

Basu, A.K., N.H. Chau, G.S. Fields, and R. Kanbur (2018). 'Job Creation in a Multi-Sector Labour Market Model for Developing Economies'. *Oxford Economic Papers*, 71(1): 119–144.

Beusch, E., and A. van Soest, A. (2019). 'A Dynamic Multinomial Model of Self-employment in the Netherlands'. Available at: https://www.instituutgak.nl/wp-content/uploads/2019/03/2014-528_P01.pdf (accessed 13 May 2020).

Bosch, M., and W. Maloney (2010). 'Comparative Analysis of Labor Market Dynamics Using Markov Processes: An Application to Informality'. *Labour Economics*, 17(4): 621–631.

Charmes, J. (2016) 'The Informal Economy: Definitions, Size, Contribution and Main Characteristics'. In E. Kraemer-Mbula & S. Wunsch-Vincent (Eds.), *The Informal Economy in Developing Nations: Hidden Engine of Innovation?* Cambridge: Cambridge University Press, 13–52. doi:10.1017/CBO9781316662076.006

Chen, M.A. (2012). 'The Informal Economy: Definitions, Theories and Policies'. Women in Informal Employment: Globalizing and Organizing (WIEGO) Working Paper No. 1. Cambridge, MA: WIEGO.

Danquah, M., S. Schotte, and K. Sen (2019). 'Informal Work in Sub-Saharan Africa: Dead End or Steppingstone?'. WIDER Working Paper No. 107/2019. Helsinki: UNU-WIDER. https://doi.org/10.35188/UNU-WIDER.

De Vreyer, P., and F. Roubaud (eds) (2013). *Urban Labor Markets in Sub-Saharan Africa*. Washington, DC: World Bank.

Echevin, D., and F. Murtin (2009). 'What Determines Productivity in Senegal? Sectoral Disparities and the Dual Labour Market'. *Journal of Development Studies*, 45(10): 1707–1730.

Gong, X., A. Van Soest, and E. Villagomez (2004). 'Mobility in the Urban Labor Market: A Panel Data Analysis for Mexico'. *Economic Development and Cultural Change*, 53(1): 1–36.

Grimm, M., P. Knorringa, and J. Lay (2012). 'Constrained Gazelles: High Potentials in West Africa's Informal Economy'. *World Development*, 40(7): 1352–1368.

GSS (Ghana Statistical Service) (2015). *Integrated Business Establishment Survey: Summary Report*. Accra: GSS.

ILO (International Labour Organization) (2018). *Women and Men in the Informal Economy: A Statistical Picture* (3rd edn). Geneva: ILO.

Liu, X. (2015). *Methods and Applications of Longitudinal Data Analysis*. Amsterdam: Elsevier.

Maloney, W.F. (1999). 'Does Informality Imply Segmentation in Urban Labor Markets? Evidence from Sectoral Transitions in Mexico'. *World Bank Economic Review*, 13: 275–302.

Perry, G., W. Maloney, O. Arias, P. Fajnzylber, A. Mason, and J. Saavedra-Chanduvi (2007). *Informality: Exit and Exclusion*. Washington, DC: World Bank.

Radchenko, N. (2017). 'Informal Employment in Developing Economies: Multiple Heterogeneity'. *Journal of Development Studies*, 53(4): 495–513.

Rodrik, D. (2016). 'Premature Deindustrialization'. *Journal of Economic Growth*, 21(1): 1–33.

Sacchetto, C., E. Daniel, M. Danquah, and H. Telli (2020). 'Informality and COVID-19 in sub-Sarahan Africa'. Policy Brief. London: IGC Publications.

Schotte, S., R. Zizzamia, and M. Leibbrandt (2018). 'A Poverty Dynamics Approach to Social Stratification: The South African Case'. *World Development*, 110: 88–103.

Slonimczyk, F., and V. Gimpelson (2015). 'Informality and Mobility: Evidence from Russian Panel Data'. *Economics of Transition*, 23(2): 299–341.

PART V

NORTH AFRICA AND THE MIDDLE EAST

13

The evolution of vulnerable employment in Egypt, Jordan, and Tunisia

Shireen AlAzzawi and Vladimir Hlasny

1. Introduction

Youths in the Middle East and North Africa (MENA) face notoriously precarious employment prospects. Youth unemployment there is the highest in the world, at 23 per cent in Arab states and 30 per cent in Northern Africa in 2019.[1] Youth unemployment in the Arab states was also the fastest growing in the world, increasing from 19.5 to 23 per cent, between 2012 and 2020.[2] Unemployment among young women in the region is more than twice that of young men, reaching 42 per cent, and has been growing at a much faster rate than that of young men (ILO 2020b).

While youth unemployment is a major problem in the region, a more alarming issue is that even those who are employed tend to work in vulnerable jobs that are informal, lacking job security and stability, paid leave, social and health insurance, and safety (WEF 2012). The share of youth in informal employment is as high as 85 per cent in Arab states (87.5 per cent in northern Africa), far higher than that for adults (61 per cent) (ILO 2020a). Arab states have the highest youth–adult gap in the world in terms of informal employment, which reflects the worsening labour market conditions available to youths compared to older cohorts. Such vulnerabilities are often closely associated with and reinforce multiple dimensions of social and economic deprivation, as well as entrenched inequality of opportunity and income, and may persist across generations.

There are a number of well-known structural faults in the MENA region's labour markets that stem primarily from the strong state of duality between 'good' formal jobs, in both the public and private sectors, and 'bad' informal jobs. This duality is a direct result of the state-led industrialization model that existed in the 1950s through the 1970s in most of these economies. This contract started

[1] The International Labour Organization (ILO) defines 'Arab states' as consisting of the Arab countries in Asia and reports separate statistics for North African Arab countries.

[2] Youth unemployment in Northern Africa stayed almost the same between 2012 and 2020 (ILO 2020a).

Shireen AlAzzawi and Vladimir Hlasny, *The evolution of vulnerable employment in Egypt, Jordan, and Tunisia.* In: *The Job Ladder.* Edited by Gary S. Fields, T. H. Gindling, Kunal Sen, Michael Danquah, and Simone Schotte, Oxford University Press. © UNU-WIDER (2023). DOI: 10.1093/oso/9780192867339.003.0013 to fray and disappear by the 1980s, following exchange rate and budget crises that forced most of these economies to move towards neoliberal economic development. The availability of formal public-sector jobs gradually declined over the next several decades without a parallel increase in formal private-sector jobs, leaving new labour market entrants at a considerable disadvantage compared to older cohorts (Assaad 2014). In Egypt, Jordan, and Tunisia, for example, job creation and access to formal jobs have all deteriorated over the past several decades, while the share of irregular wage work has increased (Assaad and Krafft 2015; Assaad et al. 2019; Shahen et al. 2020).

Restrictive employment contract laws and high ratios of formal minimum wages to mean wages in some MENA countries push down labour demand and are harmful to employment (Agénor et al. 2004). At the same time, the large pool of unemployed workers aspiring to formal jobs empowers large corporate employers to exert power over their hiring, restraining employment. Recent studies for Egypt and Jordan have concluded that the type of higher education, a measure of human capital and skill, has a lower effect on the employers' choice of the limited number of hires from large applicant pools than circumstances such as background and social class (Krafft and Assaad 2016; Assaad et al. 2018). The aspiration of attaining a public-sector job discourages young MENA workers of higher socioeconomic standing from considering lower-quality jobs (Assaad et al. 2010; Egel and Salehi-Isfahani 2010). By contrast, those without the advantage of connections must make do with informal and irregular private-sector jobs or are forced to migrate to sustain their livelihoods (Binzel 2011; Hlasny and AlAzzawi 2018).

International development agencies—such as the World Bank, ILO, and United Nations Development Programme—have long recognized the value of accounting for work status within employment. When most jobs available to a particular group are informal jobs, members of the group face a higher level of instability and risk in various aspects of their lives. It is therefore crucial to study the prevalence of such vulnerable jobs and their evolution over time.

In this chapter, we contribute to the literature by examining the prevalence, incidence, and evolution of vulnerable employment in three MENA countries—Egypt (1998, 2006, 2012, 2018), Jordan (2010–2016), and Tunisia (2014)—during periods of far-reaching economic and social change.[3] We utilize panel labour market data spanning twenty years in Egypt (from the Egypt Labour Market Panel Survey (ELMPS) for the years 1998, 2006, 2012, and 2018), six years in Jordan (from the Jordan Labour Market Panel Surveys (JLMPS) for 2010 and 2016), and

[3] This chapter is an extension of our previous Economic Research Forum working paper (AlAzzawi and Hlasny 2018) by extending the analysis to an additional country (Tunisia) and adding results for the most recent data for Egypt (2018). In addition, it utilizes different definitions of youth and non-youth and extends the static and dynamic analysis in several dimensions.

retrospective labour market data for Tunisia (from the Tunisian Labour Market Panel Survey (TLMPS) for 2014) (OAMDI 2019).

In Egypt, the period under study was initially characterized by a strong push towards economic reform, trade opening, and privatization of publicly owned firms, followed by the 2008 economic crisis and a surge of popular discontent leading to the 2011 uprising and the 2011–2014 political changes. The 2018 survey followed a series of significant currency devaluations in January 2013, March 2016, and notably November 2016, which hit the most vulnerable households particularly hard (AlAzzawi and Hlasny 2019a). In Jordan, the period under study started with widespread discontent due to worsening living conditions and spans the post-Arab Spring period and civil war in Syria, when Jordan absorbed a large fraction of refugees, representing a sizeable shock to its labour market. In Tunisia, the period under study is in the immediate aftermath of the Jasmine revolution in the winter of 2010–2011, at a time when the political situation had largely stabilized and the economy was steadily growing, raising the hope that youth employment prospects would improve (Stampini and Verdier-Chouchane 2011).

These data allow both static and dynamic analysis of workers' vulnerability at multiple points in their careers and enable us to differentiate between cohorts by age and gender. We are able to follow the same individuals over time, examining the dynamics of starting out in a vulnerable job and the prospects of eventually exiting into a decent job.

The rest of this chapter is organized as follows. We first review relevant literature, data sources, and concept definitions in sections 2 and 3. Section 4 describes the empirical approaches taken to isolate the driving factors of individuals' employment vulnerability and employment mobility, directly followed by the presentation of our findings. Section 5 reiterates the key conclusions and policy implications.

2. Related literature

The unemployment rate among MENA region youths is the highest and fastest-growing relative to other world regions (Pieters 2013). Kabbani and Kothari (2005) confirmed that MENA region youths faced poor employment prospects and that societal and enterprise social norms and childbearing breaks from the labour market contributed to the particularly precarious conditions for women. More recent research has relied on survey microdata to assess the outcomes of various social groups. Majbouri (2017) contrasted mobility in expenditures per capita in Egypt and Jordan and found mobility in Egypt to be low in absolute terms as well as compared to Jordan.

Assaad and Krafft (2015) used ELMPS 1998–2012 data to assess labour market conditions for workers of all ages. They identified large differences in working conditions, job stability, and risk of falling into poverty across workers of different employment types. Informal workers were among the most vulnerable. Assaad and Krafft (2014) analysed youth workers' transitions from school to the labour market. Workers' employment prospects were found to be constrained by non-meritocratic recruiting practices by employers and a skills mismatch. Women's personal circumstances, such as family resources and childbearing plans, also affected their labour market achievements.

Public-sector jobs have diminished in recent years as the main employment type in Egypt and Tunisia, signalling the governments' efforts to reform and rewrite the social contract in light of economic challenges (El-Haddad 2020). At the same time, private-sector positions have become less likely to confer benefits and contracts (Amer 2012, 2015; Assaad 2012). The prospect of public-sector employment is particularly low among Egyptian youths as the legal age for hiring in the public sector has increased and employers have been explicitly encouraged to hire older workers. The role of connections in securing public-sector jobs in Egypt has also grown since the 1990s for both men and women (Barsoum and Abdalla 2020).

In Jordan, young workers are highly immobile and unable to transition from informal to formal jobs, although they can move between formal private- and public-sector jobs. Jordanian women are particularly vulnerable because of the diminishing public-sector employment, lack of accommodation for their needs in private-sector jobs, and sluggish reform of labour laws (Mryyan 2012; Assaad et al. 2014). The share of youths not in employment, education, or training is high compared to developing countries in other world regions for both sexes but particularly for females (Pieters 2013). Meanwhile, vulnerability in employment has various socio-economic repercussions for the MENA region, including for youths' economic well-being, marriage prospects, education, mental health, and the prevalence of conflict and violence (Fehling et al. 2016; Ehab 2019).

Our study contributes by examining the drivers of vulnerable employment among young workers and their prospects for job mobility. We assess the impact of workers' circumstances and labour market experience on their wage earnings, their prospect of attaining a decent first job, and their prospect of attaining better jobs in the following years. Multiple waves of high-quality panel surveys for Egypt (four waves) and Jordan (two waves) and one wave for Tunisia are used to gauge workers' circumstances, follow the outcomes of workers over time, and link the outcomes of fathers to those of their offspring. To our knowledge, this is the only study that examines the dynamics of vulnerable employment among MENA youths.

3. Data used

Our data are from the 1998, 2006, 2012, and 2018 waves of the ELMPS, the 2010 and 2016 waves of the JLMPS, and the 2014 TLMPS. These high-quality representative labour market surveys were conducted, harmonized, and made available by the Economic Research Forum (ERF) (OAMDI 2019).[4] These data are ideal for our analysis as they cover workers' labour earnings, occupation, education, household assets, various demographics, and linked information about their parents.

3.1 Employment vulnerability

The first task of this study is to identify measures that capture the monetary and non-monetary aspects of workers' vulnerability in the labour market. Using the panel dimension of our surveys, we compare youth and non-youth workers in the initial period and how their outcomes evolved in later years.

We classify workers as vulnerably employed if they engage in unpaid family work, self-employment (without employing others), irregular wage work (casual or seasonal work), or informal private-sector work (defined as lacking a contract or social security). These workers share undesirable working conditions including a lack of contracts, lack of benefits, low job security, and a lack of any form of social protection from shocks.[5]

Our analysis distinguishes between youth (aged 15–29)[6] and non-youth workers (aged 30–59) and follows the respective groups across ranges of years. The 1998 cohort of Egyptian workers are followed over eight years, to 2006 (when the youths were 23–37 years of age); after another six years, to 2012 (when they were 29–43); and after another six years, to 2018 (when they were 35–49). We therefore follow the '1998 youths' over an extensive part of their careers. We follow the '2006 Egyptian youths' across six years, to 2012, when they were 21–35, and to 2018, when they were 27–41. The '2012 Egyptian youths' are followed to 2018, when they were 21–35. We also follow the '2010 Jordanian youths' over the next six years, to 2016, when they were 21–35. The comparison group encompasses those aged 30–59 in each survey wave, who are followed across six years in Jordan and up to 20 years in Egypt.

[4] See the appendix in AlAzzawi and Hlasny (2020) for a detailed description of the surveys used in the analysis.

[5] The World Bank (2020) defines the vulnerably employed group as the sum total of unpaid family workers and the self-employed. This is a lower bound of our definition. Danquah et al. (2019), addressing informal employment, included all irregular, unpaid, and self-employment, notably excluding self-employment in registered businesses. As we acknowledge, however, business registration information is not available in our data sets. Moreover, the bulk of self-employment in the MENA region is deemed to be precarious, so this study considers all the self-employed (without employing others) to be vulnerable.

[6] We extend the age of youths to encompass workers who were 15–29 instead of the traditional 15–24. Many youths are students or military draftees until their early 20s. Restricting the age to below 24 would disregard the working status of these youths.

4. Main analysis and results

The following sections appraise workers' employment status and mobility in detail and estimate the bearing of workers' circumstances on these outcomes. The corresponding analytical approaches are briefly introduced in each section, followed directly by a discussion of their results.

4.1 Static analysis of employment status and vulnerability

We first briefly describe workers' current employment sector, distinguishing youth versus older cohorts and males versus females. This analysis encompasses those who were unemployed and those out of the labour force as these status groups are particularly prevalent among women.[7] We find that in Egypt, overall, youths are less likely to have formal job, whether public or private, than older men, while women, both youth and non-youth, were overwhelmingly out of the labour force altogether, except for a small minority of older women in formal employment. The likelihood of formal employment declined steadily over the twenty years under consideration for all groups, while that of the vulnerable job categories decreased steadily for men. Women largely stayed out of the labour force.

A slightly better employment picture emerged initially for Jordan with young men being equally likely to have formal jobs as older men but slightly more likely to be in vulnerable jobs. By 2016, however, the share of young men in vulnerable employment had shrunk dramatically and instead the share out of the labour force increased to over 25 per cent. As in Egypt, most Jordanian women stayed out of the labour force unless they were in the small group formally employed. In Tunisia, youths were substantially more likely to be unemployed than to be in any other employment status, both compared to older men and compared to both Egypt and Jordan. Women were, once again, mostly out of the labour force regardless of age.

Mean monthly earnings of workers in each employment status for youths and non-youths (see AlAzzawi and Hlasny 2020: Table 13.1a) also confirm that youths are disadvantaged in terms of earnings compared to non-youths in every employment status and especially in vulnerable employment categories.

4.2 Dynamic analysis of employment outcomes

Next, cross-tabulations between two sets of outcomes allow us to gauge workers' performance as a function of their pre-existing circumstances. Workers' current employment status is linked to their past employment status (Fig. 13.1)

[7] See AlAzzawi and Hlasny (2020: Figs 13.A1a–d for Egyptian youth in 1998–2018, A2a–b for Jordan, A2c for Tunisia).

(a) 1998–2006 Egypt

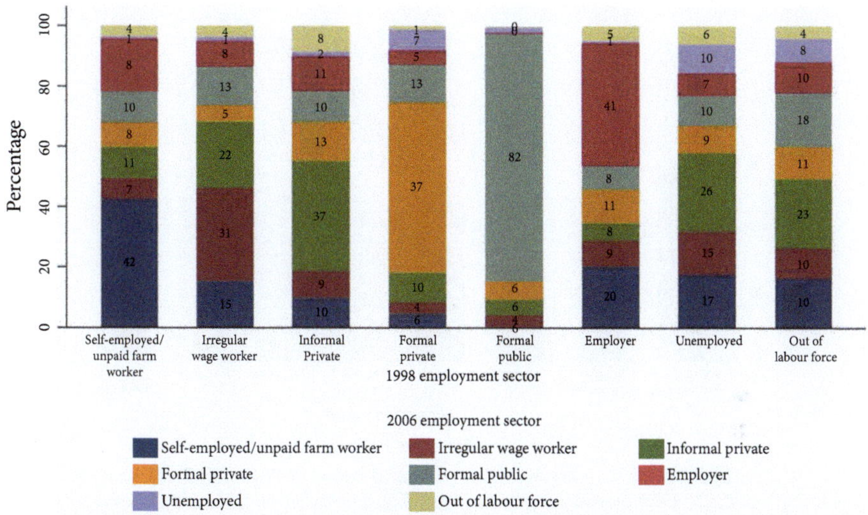

(b) 2006–2012 Egypt

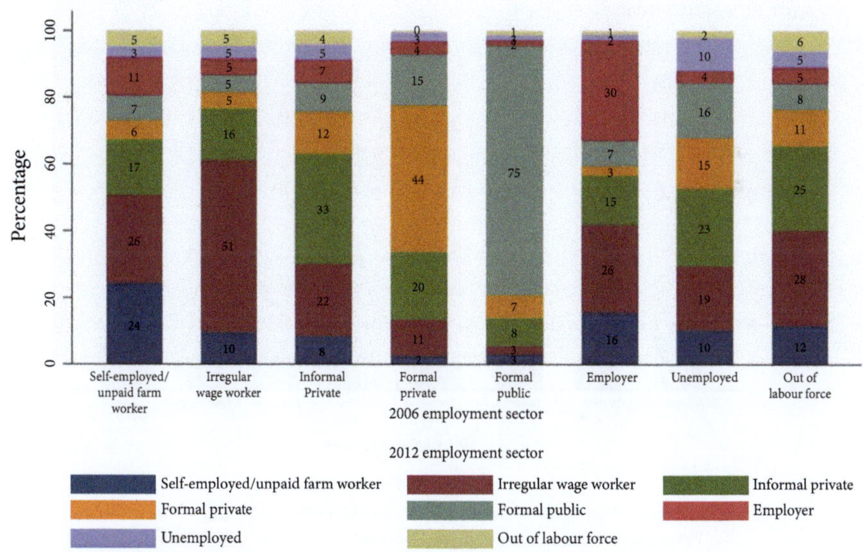

Fig. 13.1 Employment sector transitions, male non-student youth

Source: authors' illustrations based on the Egypt Labour Market Panel Survey (ELMPS) 1998–2018, the Jordan Labor Market Panel Survey (JLMPS) 2010–2016, and the Tunisia Labor Market Panel Survey (TLMPS) 2014 (OAMDI 2019).

(c) 2012–2018 Egypt

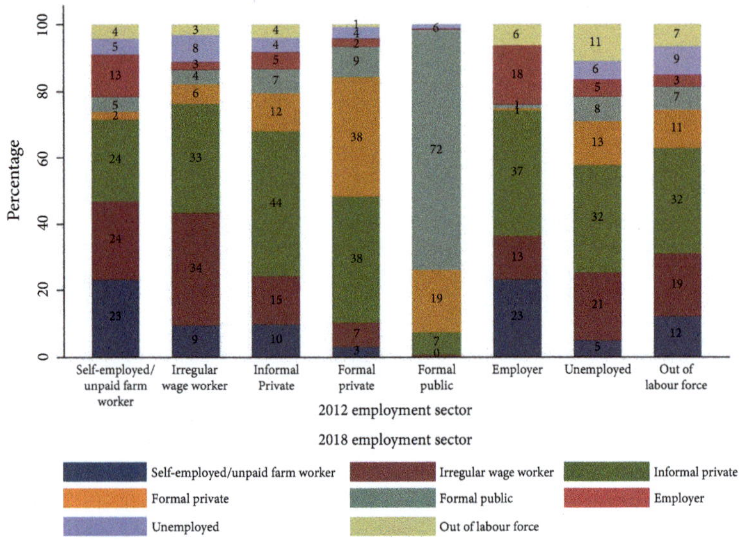

(d) 2010–2016 Jordan

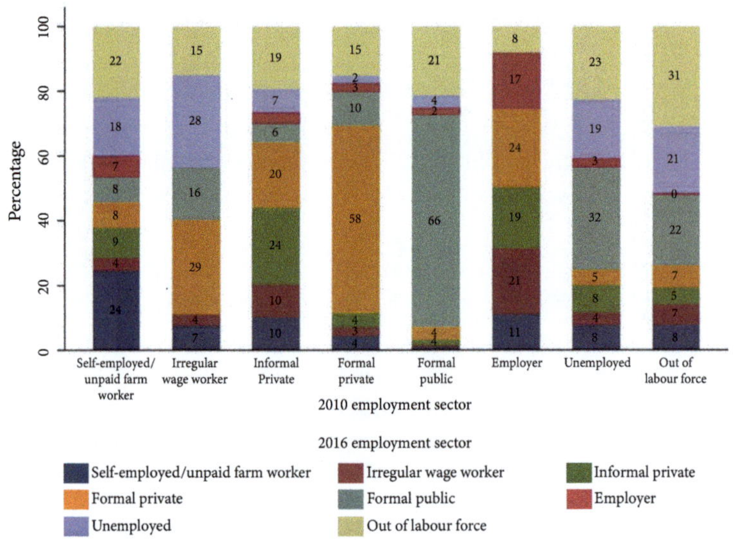

Fig. 13.1 *continued*

(e) 2011–2014 Tunisia

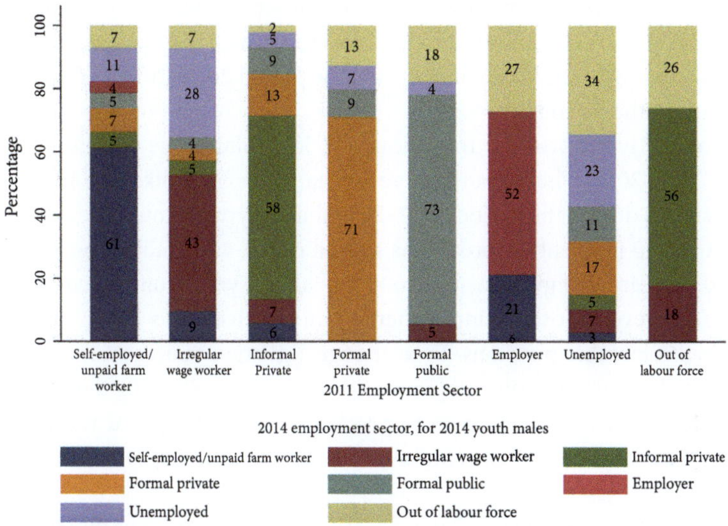

Fig. 13.1 *continued*

Figure 13.1 reports the employment transitions for 1998 Egyptian male youths in the year 2006 (Fig. 13.1i), 2006 male youths in 2012 (Fig. 13.1ii), and 2012 male youths in 2018 (Fig. 13.1iii). Figure 13.1iv shows this for 2010 Jordanian male youths in 2016.[8] The results for Egypt (Figs 13.1i–iii) show very weak intertemporal mobility to formal public- or private-sector jobs. Between 56 and 68 per cent of those in vulnerable employment in 1998 remained so by 2006. At the same time, 66–88 per cent of those who started in formal jobs in 1998 had kept them in 2006. With the benefit of hindsight, young graduates in 1998 who aspired to eventually find decent work would have been advised to hold out in their search of formal jobs—that is, if they had the luxury of choice. By remaining unemployed or out of the labour force, they had a 19–29 per cent probability of finding formal jobs by 2006, compared to an 18–23 per cent probability if they had accepted informal work in 1998.

Between 2006 and 2012, the prospect of transitioning from an informal job to a formal job was similarly slim (10–21 per cent) and even lower than among the unemployed or economically inactive workers (19–31 per cent). At the same time, the prospect of formal job workers keeping their status was high (59–82 per cent). Between 2012 and 2018, the situation deteriorated even further, with over 75 per cent of those who started out in 2012 in a vulnerable job unable to exit it by 2018

[8] Longer-term transitions for Egyptian youths mapping their employment transitions from 1998 to 2012 and from 2006 to 2018 also reveal a very high level of persistence of employment vulnerability, even after such long work experience. See AlAzzawi and Hlasny (2020: Fig. 13.A3.)

and, even more alarming, over 40 per cent (65 per cent) of those who had formal private jobs (were employers) in 2012 moving to vulnerable jobs by 2018. The prospect of transitioning from informal to formal jobs was somewhat higher during the period 1998–2006 than during the period 2006–2012. It declined once again during the period 2006–2018.

Figure 13.1iv reports the transitions for Jordanian male youths during the period 2010–2016. These youths were substantially more likely to move to formal positions during the period 2010–2016 than Egyptian youths across all years. Fewer than 40 per cent of Jordanians started out in vulnerable jobs, while more than 60 per cent of Egyptians did so across all the years considered. Many Jordanians, however, chose unemployment or an inactive status in 2016 rather than accepting vulnerable positions. Even though Egyptian youths were worse off in terms of being stuck in vulnerable jobs, Jordanians were leaving the labour force all together instead of holding on to precarious employment. At the same time, almost 70 per cent of formally employed workers in 2010 kept their formal status in 2016.

Only one survey wave is available for Tunisia (Fig. 13.1v), but this survey contains retrospective questions regarding workers' employment and student status in 2011. Tunisian youths were as unlikely to move to formal jobs during the period 2011–2014 as Egyptians during the period 2006–2012. Of the 46 per cent of Tunisian young men who started in vulnerable jobs over this period, only 15 per cent moved on to formal private- or public-sector jobs, while 62 per cent remained in vulnerable positions and 23 per cent became unemployed or exited the labour force. At the same time, of the 17 per cent of formally employed male youths in 2011, 76 per cent kept their formal status in 2014.

4.3 Cross vulnerabilities: parents' wealth and education versus job outcomes

We next evaluate the association between household wealth or parents' education, on the one hand, and workers' current employment status, on the other. Following a growing body of literature, we use principal component analysis to impute households' wealth as an alternative indicator of workers' circumstances and vulnerability (AlAzzawi and Hlasny 2019b; Hlasny and AlAzzawi 2019).

Egyptian youths (Figs 13.2i–2vii) from lower wealth-quintile families are shown to have been more likely to end up with vulnerable employment, particularly irregular wage and informal work (Figs 13.2i–iv). Formal employment was most prevalent among the wealthiest quintile. Interestingly, there were more unemployed and inactive male youths in the middle quintile in 1998 and 2006 compared to 2012, when middle-wealth youths were more prone to accept informal and particularly

(a) 1998 Egypt

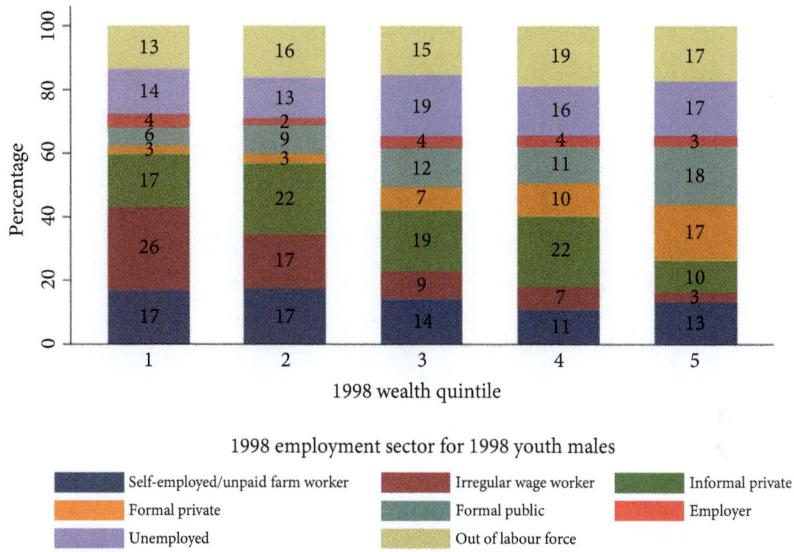

(b) 2006 Egypt

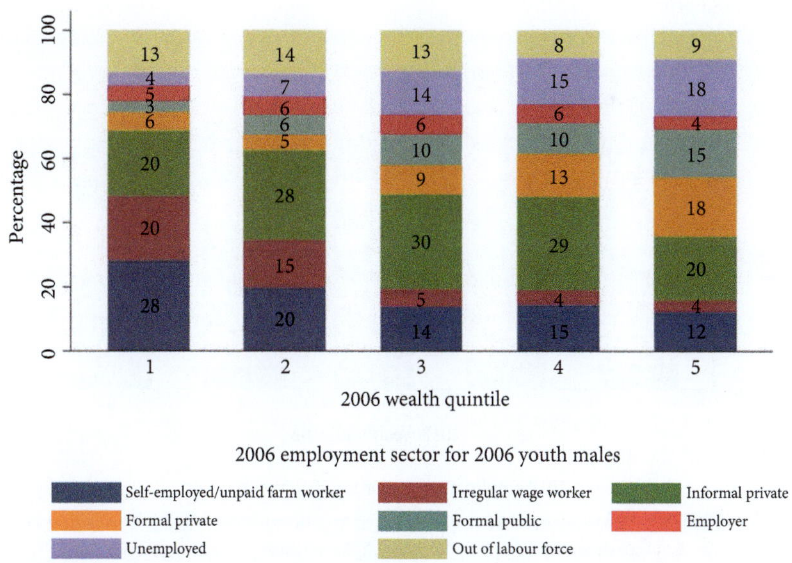

Fig. 13.2 Employment sector by household wealth quintiles, for youth males
Source: authors' illustrations based on ELMPS 1998–2018, JLMPS 2010–2016, and TLMPS 2014 (OAMDI 2019).

(c) 2012 Egypt

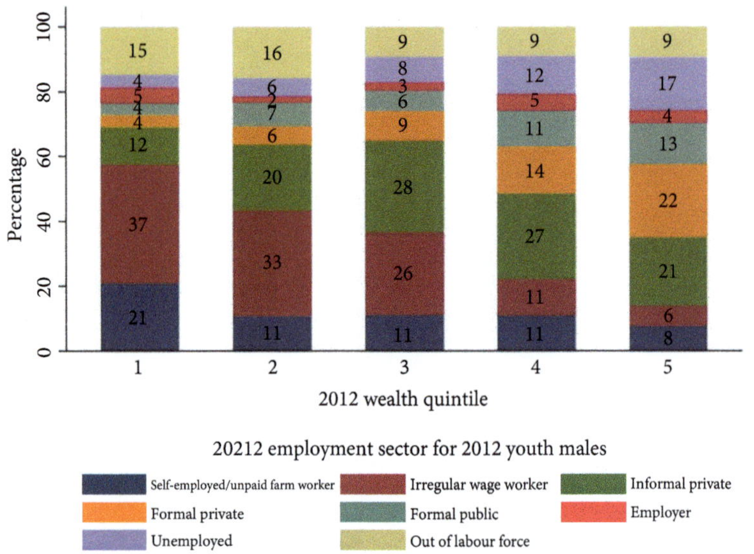

(d) 2018 Egypt

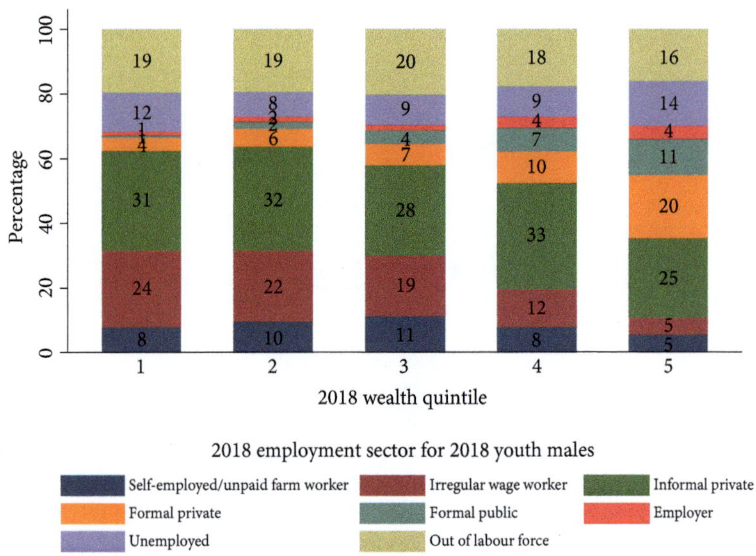

Fig. 13.2 *continued*

(e) 2010 Jordan

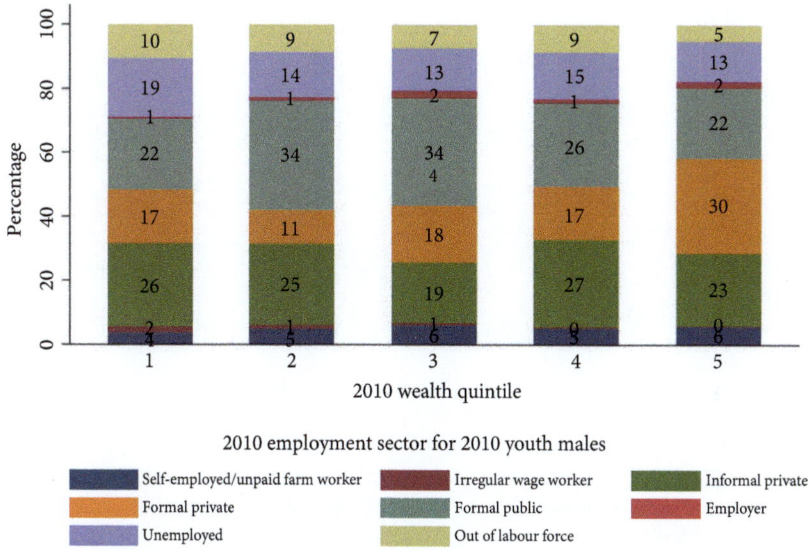

(f) 2016 Jordan

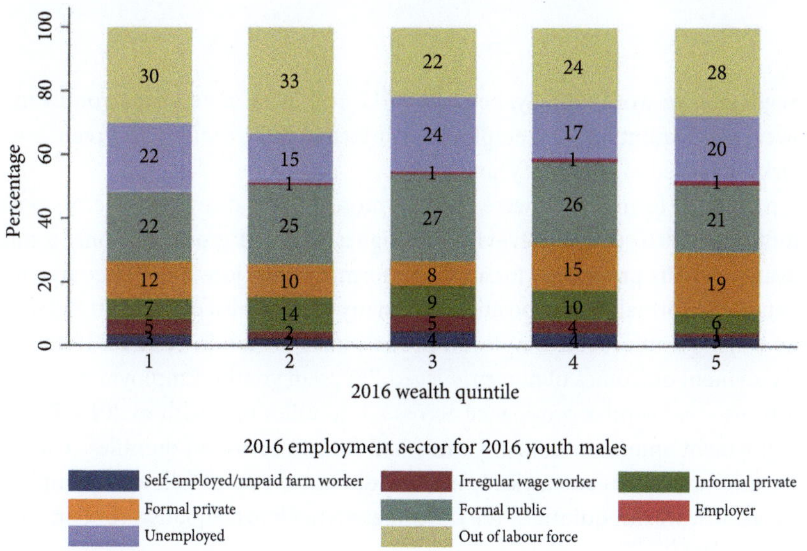

Fig. 13.2 *continued*

(g) 2014 Tunisia

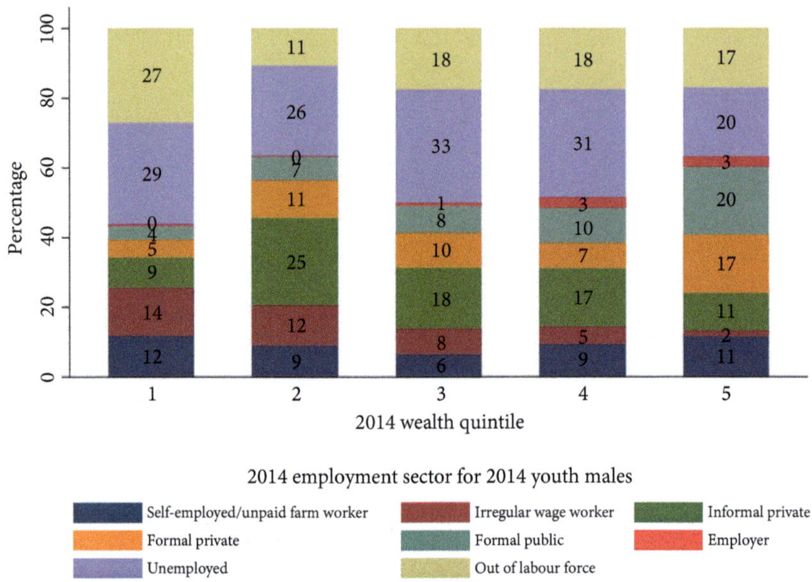

Fig. 13.2 *continued*

irregular wage work. Finally, between 2012 and 2018 more of the youths in the lower wealth quintiles were employed in informal private jobs than irregular wage work compared to previous years.

In Jordan, formal jobs were slightly more evenly distributed across wealth quintiles in 2010 (Figs 13.2v–vi). The highest-quintile group had only a minor advantage in its propensity for attaining formal public jobs but a large advantage in attaining formal private positions. As many as one-third of youth in the second and third quintiles were employed in the public sector, in contrast to the poor employment outcomes of non-privileged Egyptian youths. Employment vulnerability also had similar prevalence across all quintiles of wealth in 2010. By 2016, employment among Jordanian youths had shrunk across all quintiles. The share of unemployed and economically inactive did not appear to follow any simple pattern against wealth quintiles: the outcomes were almost equally prevalent across all quintiles.

In Tunisia (Fig. 13.2vii), the share of young workers who were either unemployed or inactive was much higher for the lower quintiles (and compared to the 1998–2018 Egypt and 2010 Jordan cohorts). The prevalence of formal jobs was only significantly different for the top wealth quintile, which again points to a high degree of inequality of access to good jobs.

The relationship between fathers' education and children's employment outcomes (not shown to save on space) reveals a relatively similar pattern, with father's education being far more important in Egypt than in Jordan and Tunisia as a determinant of employment status.[9]

4.4 Earnings vulnerability

We next assess the labour *income* vulnerability of Egyptian and Jordanian youths. We use current labour market earnings for regular wage workers to evaluate the prevalence of low labour earnings and earnings mobility. This analysis cannot be performed for Tunisia as only one point in time is available.

For Egypt and Jordan, we use two benchmarks to identify low earnings: a relative one, based on belonging to the lowest earnings quintile, and an absolute one, based on comparing labour earnings to a government-set low earnings line (LEL). The LELs are taken from official poverty lines (PL) obtained from Jordanian DOS (2010), the World Bank (2016), and CAPMAS (2018). To compute an individual-level monthly LEL, the annual PL/capita is divided by 12 and multiplied by the household-level dependency ratio as each worker typically supports more than one family member.[10]

Table 13.1 shows vulnerability in labour earnings according to both the relative and absolute benchmarks, distinguishing young and older workers. According to the LELs, across all years in Egypt, youths are 1.5–2.5 times more likely than non-youths to have labour earnings among the lowest quintile or to be low earners.

In Jordan in 2010, youths were also twice as likely to be in the lowest quintile or low earners relative to the LEL. By 2016, this had changed, however, and there was no significant difference between youths and non-youths. For both categories, there was a one in four chance of being in the bottom quintile and about 3 per cent were earning below the LEL. In Tunisia, youths were also at a significant relative disadvantage compared to non-youths, with 1.5 times as many in the bottom quintile as non-youths. For both categories, about 4 per cent were earning below the LEL.

[9] See AlAzzawi and Hlasny (2020: Fig. 133) and accompanying discussion for full details. We also examine the long-term persistence of employment vulnerability across the years, given their initial family wealth and their father's education, 6–20 years prior. For Egypt, we find that even after a long period of work experience, both family wealth and father's education play an extremely large role in workers' employment outcomes. For Jordan, higher wealth was also associated with higher employment vulnerability 6 years later but also higher unemployment and inactivity, while father's education did not seem to play a very prominent role in employment status. (We cannot perform the same analysis for Tunisia since we only have one survey wave.) These results are available in AlAzzawi and Hlasny (2020: Figs A4, A5).

[10] See appendix in AlAzzawi and Hlasny (2020) for detailed information on the poverty lines and construction of the LELs for each country.

Table 13.1 Relative and absolute earnings vulnerability (percentage)

		Non-student youths: 15–29	Non-youths: 30–59	All
Country	*Relative earnings vulnerability: lowest quintile*			
Egypt	1998 earnings	29.73	13.61	19.23
	2006 earnings	34.87	13.13	21.28
	2012 earnings	26.70	16.30	19.89
	2018 earnings	28.22	16.87	20.15
Jordan	2010 earnings	29.01	15.69	21.35
	2016 earnings	26.55	25.49	25.85
Tunisia	2014 earnings	28.90	17.29	20.41
	Absolute earnings vulnerability: low earners compared to LEL			
Egypt	1998 earnings	18.11	6.90	10.71
	2006 earnings	14.38	5.33	8.69
	2012 earnings	9.30	5.72	6.93
	2018 earnings	10.14	8.11	8.65
Jordan	2010 earnings	4.02	1.35	2.49
	2016 earnings	2.36	2.91	2.73
Tunisia	2014 earnings	4.82	3.90	4.15

Source: authors' calculations based on ELMPS 1998–2018, JLMPS 2010–2016, TLMPS 2014 (OAMDI 2019).

4.5 The effects of workers' circumstances on employment outcomes

To investigate the standalone role of workers' various circumstances, we estimate multinomial logistic regressions of workers' employment status on the conditions in their youth, 6–20 years prior (Assaad et al. 2014; Assaad and Krafft 2014). The contribution of this study is to analyse the detailed occupational distribution among youths and non-youths separately using longitudinal data in pooled surveys. We thus derive the changes in labour market prospects for youths and non-youths over time, mitigate the potential endogeneity of workers' circumstances by using their backgrounds from previous survey waves, and mitigate heteroskedasticity in the estimations due to latent heterogeneity across workers.

Multinomial logit regressions are used to fit the probability that an individual will attain a specific value of a dependent variable—here, employment status—compared to the probability of a baseline value—remaining economically inactive. This baseline was selected as a natural state among fresh graduates contemplating whether to begin job hunting and can be thought of as the least-preferred state, which is helpful for interpreting regression parameters. The model takes the values of regressors, estimates outcome-specific parameters on those regressors using maximum likelihood, and computes the probabilities of all the alternative outcomes. The outcome with the greatest probability of occurring is set as the estimated outcome.

Tables 13.2–13.4 report the main regression specifications estimated on pooled surveys for each country, separately for youth and non-youth workers for Egypt, Jordan, and Tunisia. Table 13.2 shows the estimates for the pooled 2006–2018 ELMPSs, where workers' employment outcomes in 2006–2018 are linked to their circumstances in 1998, 2006, or 2012. As expected, workers' employment prospects are associated positively with their age, albeit with a slowly diminishing rate. Female workers have significantly lower employment prospects than men in all types of jobs and even have a lower probability of being unemployed relative to their high risk of being out of the labour force.

Being literate and having a higher educational attainment increases the prospect of attaining formal employment in the public or private sector but has a surprisingly modest effect on other types of employment. Above-intermediate education has the strongest effect across most employment types. Formal employment is the only occupation status where higher education offers systematically positive and significant (marginal) returns among youth as well as non-youth workers, so that secondary and tertiary school graduates have the highest odds of being employed there. Interestingly, the secondary- and tertiary-educated workers also have a high risk of being unemployed, suggesting that these workers may be rejecting inferior opportunities in search of formal employment. Among female workers, education typically offers higher returns in terms of their prospects of being economically active than among men because most education–gender interaction terms—except for the model of unpaid family work but including the model of unemployment—are positive. The effect is strongest for the prospects of formal employment and unemployment and at the above-intermediate and tertiary education level. As, for men, this suggests that higher-educated women join the labour force but shun inferior job opportunities in search of formal employment.

Several results stand out related to workers' family backgrounds. Household wealth has a negative effect on workers' employment prospects, except for the prospect of becoming an employer, where it has no effect. Interestingly, the wealth effect is as high among non-youth workers as among youths. Family wealth thus has lifelong implications for workers' employment. Fathers' education and employment status, by contrast, play a greater role in the employment prospects of youth workers. Fathers' higher education is associated with a lower probability of informal employment and self-employment among their offspring, especially among youths. Fathers' employment status has a strong effect on children's employment prospects, with the interesting finding that fathers who are employers are more likely to have children who are self-employed or unpaid family workers or who become employers themselves. These children are significantly less likely to hold formal or informal paid work or to be searching for work.

Table 13.2 Multinomial logit regressions on pooled ELMPS 2006–2018 data, youth v. non-youth

	Youth					Non-youth				
	Self-employed/ unpaid family worker	**Informal + irregular**	**Public + formal private**	**Employer**	**Unemployed**	**Self-employed/ unpaid family worker**	**Informal + irregular**	**Public+ formal private**	**Employer**	**Unemployed**
Age–min (age)	0.423***	0.580***	0.666***	0.740***	0.222***	0.191***	0.215***	0.290***	0.286***	0.244***
	(0.041)	(0.041)	(0.045)	(0.056)	(0.045)	(0.040)	(0.049)	(0.040)	(0.054)	(0.070)
Age–min (age) squared	−0.011***	−0.017***	−0.016***	−0.018***	−0.007***	−0.003***	−0.005***	−0.004***	−0.005***	−0.005***
	(0.001)	(0.002)	(0.002)	(0.002)	(0.002)	(0.001)	(0.001)	(0.001)	(0.001)	(0.001)
Female = 1	−3.099***	−5.776***	−5.412***	−5.943***	−3.242***	−2.818***	−5.328***	−5.900***	−5.390***	−3.758***
	(0.189)	(0.225)	(0.411)	(0.377)	(0.326)	(0.131)	(0.161)	(0.237)	(0.179)	(0.299)
Reads and writes	0.409	0.516**	1.324***	0.625*	1.028***	0.165	−0.193	0.682***	−0.052	0.188
	(0.309)	(0.262)	(0.323)	(0.340)	(0.397)	(0.216)	(0.200)	(0.206)	(0.203)	(0.360)
Less than intermediate	0.033	0.098	0.737***	0.063	−0.043	0.224	−0.305*	0.937***	−0.290	0.519*
	(0.219)	(0.192)	(0.242)	(0.252)	(0.339)	(0.185)	(0.174)	(0.184)	(0.181)	(0.311)
Intermediate	−0.155	−0.129	0.994***	−0.239	0.387	0.516**	0.236	2.072***	−0.027	0.574*
	(0.182)	(0.162)	(0.207)	(0.224)	(0.306)	(0.200)	(0.190)	(0.207)	(0.204)	(0.304)
Above intermediate	1.032***	0.782**	2.664***	0.817***	1.779***	1.192***	0.126	2.475***	0.011	1.938***
	(0.352)	(0.322)	(0.339)	(0.401)	(0.428)	(0.422)	(0.421)	(0.399)	(0.443)	(0.578)
University +	0.242	0.046	2.055***	0.196	1.844***	0.369	−0.261	2.767***	0.226	0.873**
	(0.226)	(0.196)	(0.233)	(0.272)	(0.322)	(0.267)	(0.264)	(0.259)	(0.270)	(0.410)

Reads and writes x female	−0.855**	0.566	−1.315	0.475	0.288	−0.451	0.225	1.230***	−0.736	0.278
	(0.405)	(0.433)	(0.925)	(1.060)	(0.507)	(0.297)	(0.446)	(0.434)	(0.650)	(0.609)
Less than intern x female	0.098	0.345	0.325	−0.478	1.129***	−0.968***	0.477	1.017***	−0.038	0.713
	(0.277)	(0.315)	(0.504)	(0.624)	(0.409)	(0.240)	(0.295)	(0.347)	(0.400)	(0.438)
Intermediate x female	−0.090	1.201***	1.896***	0.587	2.385***	−0.850***	−0.142	2.521***	−0.413	2.068***
	(0.221)	(0.253)	(0.423)	(0.502)	(0.341)	(0.229)	(0.280)	(0.282)	(0.349)	(0.369)
Above intern x female	−2.051***	1.171***	1.446***	0.695	1.648***	−2.552***	−0.390	2.707***	−0.407	1.260*
	(0.635)	(0.452)	(0.524)	(0.821)	(0.470)	(0.832)	(0.851)	(0.462)	(0.863)	(0.679)
University x female	−0.462	2.793***	3.364***	0.964	2.167***	−1.128**	1.347***	3.401***	0.441	2.555***
	(0.317)	(0.283)	(0.430)	(0.590)	(0.351)	(0.547)	(0.442)	(0.310)	(0.531)	(0.448)
Household wealth	−0.174***	−0.351***	−0.101**	−0.087	−0.140***	−0.195***	−0.441***	−0.150***	0.110	−0.357***
	(0.054)	(0.046)	(0.050)	(0.080)	(0.051)	(0.052)	(0.061)	(0.058)	(0.070)	(0.094)
Household size	0.059***	0.056***	0.012	−0.038	−0.001	0.024	−0.016	−0.057***	0.011	−0.062*
	(0.014)	(0.013)	(0.014)	(0.023)	(0.013)	(0.017)	(0.021)	(0.019)	(0.020)	(0.032)
Female-headed head of household	−0.088	0.239***	0.085	0.269*	0.139	−0.023	0.233*	0.148	0.355**	0.194
	(0.106)	(0.088)	(0.090)	(0.149)	(0.087)	(0.119)	(0.140)	(0.115)	(0.171)	(0.187)

Continued

Table 13.2 *Continued*

	Youth					Non-youth				
	Self-employed/ unpaid family worker	**Informal + irregular**	**Public + formal private**	**Employer**	**Unemployed**	**Self-employed/ unpaid family worker**	**Informal + irregular**	**Public+ formal private**	**Employer**	**Unemployed**
Highest years of education in household	−0.054***	−0.083***	−0.019	−0.060***	−0.050***	−0.032**	−0.039***	−0.009	−0.024	−0.042*
	(0.014)	(0.013)	(0.015)	(0.022)	(0.016)	(0.013)	(0.014)	(0.017)	(0.017)	(0.023)
Father reads and writes	−0.115	−0.127	−0.017	0.026	−0.034	−0.033	−0.073	0.094	−0.011	−0.101
	(0.093)	(0.081)	(0.088)	(0.134)	(0.093)	(0.086)	(0.099)	(0.087)	(0.104)	(0.147)
Father < intermediate	−0.217*	−0.164*	−0.019	−0.123	0.023	−0.047	−0.259*	0.090	0.089	0.040
	(0.118)	(0.096)	(0.101)	(0.167)	(0.102)	(0.135)	(0.149)	(0.116)	(0.166)	(0.198)
Father < intermediate +	−0.324**	−0.490***	−0.011	−0.079	0.010	−0.215	−0.263	−0.000	−0.003	−0.003
	(0.141)	(0.107)	(0.107)	(0.199)	(0.104)	(0.190)	(0.209)	(0.134)	(0.213)	(0.234)
Father university +	−0.849***	−0.692***	−0.007	−0.353	−0.208	0.102	−0.560*	−0.229	0.512*	−0.055
	(0.221)	(0.148)	(0.136)	(0.266)	(0.139)	(0.273)	(0.326)	(0.178)	(0.284)	(0.384)
Father employer	0.562***	−0.198**	−0.371***	0.719***	−0.225***	0.413***	−0.105	−0.059	0.715***	−0.190
	(0.085)	(0.077)	(0.085)	(0.124)	(0.086)	(0.076)	(0.088)	(0.073)	(0.095)	(0.149)
Father self-employed	0.228**	−0.165*	−0.385***	0.179	−0.212**	0.226**	−0.071	−0.268***	0.248**	0.087
	(0.112)	(0.099)	(0.109)	(0.169)	(0.104)	(0.093)	(0.110)	(0.093)	(0.118)	(0.181)

Father unpaid family worker/non-employed	−0.127	0.219*	0.180	0.114	0.204	−0.100	0.350	−0.145	−0.237	−0.092
	(0.174)	(0.130)	(0.135)	(0.238)	(0.130)	(0.284)	(0.279)	(0.254)	(0.391)	(0.392)
Rural residence	0.007	0.086	0.122	−0.080	0.158*	−0.004	−0.011	0.002	0.064	0.138
	(0.105)	(0.091)	(0.097)	(0.155)	(0.091)	(0.104)	(0.117)	(0.103)	(0.131)	(0.169)
Cairo, Alexandria	0.359	−0.272*	0.172	0.120	0.290**	−0.155	0.016	−0.061	−0.090	0.002
	(0.240)	(0.143)	(0.129)	(0.268)	(0.140)	(0.195)	(0.178)	(0.151)	(0.215)	(0.239)
Urban lower-tier	0.989***	0.020	−0.050	0.414*	0.738***	0.620***	0.239	0.319**	0.829***	0.249
	(0.201)	(0.124)	(0.125)	(0.225)	(0.126)	(0.158)	(0.171)	(0.151)	(0.186)	(0.214)
Urban upper-tier, rural lower-tier	1.012***	−0.271**	0.019	0.510**	0.392***	0.472***	0.085	0.522***	0.922***	0.220
	(0.196)	(0.123)	(0.119)	(0.220)	(0.127)	(0.161)	(0.166)	(0.142)	(0.183)	(0.213)
Rural upper-tier	1.023***	−0.377**	−0.231	0.536**	−0.059	0.517***	0.092	0.367**	0.948***	−0.403
	(0.223)	(0.155)	(0.159)	(0.271)	(0.164)	(0.192)	(0.202)	(0.173)	(0.220)	(0.276)
Round 2012	−0.504***	0.239***	−0.364***	−0.391***	−0.269***	−0.180**	0.313***	−0.502***	−0.607***	0.274
	(0.088)	(0.083)	(0.074)	(0.128)	(0.083)	(0.080)	(0.113)	(0.070)	(0.093)	(0.224)
Round 2018	−0.755***	0.075	−1.115***	−1.338***	−0.523***	−0.312***	0.537***	−0.951***	−1.120***	0.811***
	(0.098)	(0.090)	(0.087)	(0.155)	(0.091)	(0.094)	(0.117)	(0.088)	(0.110)	(0.213)

Continued

Table 13.2 *Continued*

	Youth					Non-youth				
	Self-employed/ unpaid family worker	**Informal + irregular**	**Public + formal private**	**Employer**	**Unemployed**	**Self-employed/ unpaid family worker**	**Informal + irregular**	**Public+ formal private**	**Employer**	**Unemployed**
Constant	-3.388^{***}	-2.102^{***}	-5.264^{***}	-5.939^{***}	-2.061^{***}	-1.843^{***}	−0.406	-3.210^{***}	-3.176^{***}	-3.456^{***}
	(0.395)	(0.359)	(0.396)	(0.554)	(0.421)	(0.629)	(0.789)	(0.643)	(0.864)	(1.048)
Observations	24,295	24,295	24,295	24,295	24,295	21,424	21,424	21,424	21,424	21,424
Clusters	8889	8889	8889	8889	8889	8281	8281	8281	8281	8281
Chi-squared	7102	7102	7102	7102	7102	6637	6637	6637	6637	6637
Pseudo R-squared	0.278	0.278	0.278	0.278	0.278	0.329	0.329	0.329	0.329	0.329

Note: Samples weighted using individual-level weights. Standard errors clustered at household level are in parentheses; * $p < 0.1$, ** $p < 0.05$, *** $p < 0.01$. Workers' status as 'youth' and all household-level variables are lagged by one survey wave to estimate the effect of workers' circumstances in their youth on their subsequent outcomes.
Source: authors' calculations based on ELMPS 1998–2018 (OAMDI 2019).

There are clear regional disparities in employment prospects, with workers from urban lower and urban upper governorates having better prospects, especially among non-youth workers. Workers from rural areas are more likely to become self-employed or unpaid family workers or to serve as employers, but these results are insignificant when country regions are controlled for. Finally, there is strong evidence that employment prospects for formal employment, self-employment, and becoming employers deteriorated between 2006 and 2012. As the odds of becoming informal/irregular workers significantly increased, some youth workers gave up on their job search and remained out of the labour force, while non-youth workers joined the ranks of the unemployed.

Table 13.3 reports the same regressions on the 2010–2016 surveys for Jordan. The workers' employment outcomes are taken from the 2016 wave, while their circumstances and youth status are taken from the 2010 wave. As in Egypt, workers' employment prospects are strongly and positively associated with their age, particularly their likelihood of becoming employers of others. This effect of age diminishes only very slowly. Women are again substantially less likely to hold any type of employment, but the male–female gaps in the employment likelihoods are much lower in Jordan than in Egypt.

Education confers a systematically positive benefit in terms of the likelihood of decent employment, which is very significant for formal employment and for the prospect of becoming an employer. In contrast to Egypt, in Jordan, we find that even primary and secondary education has a clear positive impact on youth workers' odds of labour market participation. Higher education levels are associated only with a higher likelihood of formal employment. Those with less than intermediate education have a comparable likelihood of labour market participation as college graduates. The benefit of advanced education comes from a significantly improved prospect of formal employment. Among women, university education appears to have a stronger effect on their employment prospects, particularly on formal employment and on the likelihood of searching for work. Some parameters on the gender–education interaction terms and on household-head gender are large, suggesting that collinearity among covariates or a few influential observations, particularly when pursued by many explanatory variables, may be causing problems. This occurs particularly in models of the prospects of becoming an employer or self-employed, where the sample of women is relatively small. The absolute sizes of the relevant parameters must therefore be viewed with caution.

Among household circumstances, household wealth has a negative effect on workers' employment prospects, except for becoming an employer, where it has a strong positive effect. The wealth effect on the odds of attaining formal or informal employment, or of searching for jobs, is negative in Jordan. Like in Egypt, the wealth effect appears to be as strong or even stronger among non-youth workers, suggesting that initial family wealth is relevant throughout workers' careers. Fathers' education, on the other hand, has a weak effect on employment prospects,

Table 13.3 Multinomial logit regressions on JLMPS16, separating youth and non-youth

	Youth					Non-youth				
	Self-employed/ unpaid family worker	Informal + irregular	Public + formal private	Employer	Unemployed	Self-employed/ unpaid family worker	Informal + irregular	Public + formal private	Employer	Unemployed
Age–min (age)	0.999**	0.550***	0.887***	0.919***	1.109***	0.699***	0.446**	0.641***	0.997***	0.210
	(0.416)	(0.148)	(0.267)	(0.301)	(0.236)	(0.247)	(0.209)	(0.136)	(0.361)	(0.132)
Age–min (age) squared	−0.014*	−0.007***	−0.013***	−0.011**	−0.020***	−0.008***	−0.005**	−0.008***	−0.011***	−0.003**
	(0.007)	(0.002)	(0.005)	(0.005)	(0.004)	(0.003)	(0.002)	(0.001)	(0.004)	(0.002)
Female = 1	−4.711***	−3.876***	−4.270***	−6.412***	−1.920***	−4.616***	−3.606***	−3.271***	−5.650***	−2.351***
	(0.504)	(0.319)	(0.211)	(1.060)	(0.199)	(0.388)	(0.346)	(0.172)	(0.737)	(0.236)
Reads and writes	1.420**	0.498	1.352***	1.629	−0.041	0.210	−0.689	0.361	−0.282	−0.967*
	(0.642)	(0.499)	(0.474)	(1.097)	(0.432)	(0.504)	(0.552)	(0.412)	(0.755)	(0.510)
Less than intermediate	1.298**	0.790	2.144***	0.790	0.200	−0.158	−0.099	0.738*	−0.710	−0.845*
	(0.646)	(0.497)	(0.446)	(1.112)	(0.398)	(0.529)	(0.539)	(0.404)	(0.776)	(0.491)
Secondary education	0.485	0.785	2.177***	0.819	0.373	−0.029	−0.795	1.386***	−0.737	−0.589
	(0.749)	(0.532)	(0.461)	(1.150)	(0.407)	(0.563)	(0.604)	(0.416)	(0.797)	(0.519)
University +	0.229	−0.437	1.944***	−1.223	0.319	0.537	−1.088	2.410***	−0.836	−0.430
	(0.760)	(0.629)	(0.515)	(1.311)	(0.468)	(0.731)	(0.783)	(0.498)	(0.935)	(0.734)
University x female	2.172**	2.183***	3.112***	−14.244***	1.715***	−19.500***	1.825	1.336***	1.880	1.445**
	(1.030)	(0.603)	(0.313)	(1.236)	(0.343)	(0.604)	(1.285)	(0.355)	(1.404)	(0.647)
Household wealth	0.015	−0.114	−0.038	0.568**	−0.122	0.283*	−0.104	−0.206**	0.784***	−0.309*
	(0.201)	(0.134)	(0.096)	(0.279)	(0.102)	(0.156)	(0.172)	(0.099)	(0.280)	(0.175)
Household size	0.028	−0.010	0.056**	0.132*	0.071**	−0.089	0.036	−0.110***	0.010	−0.026
	(0.063)	(0.043)	(0.027)	(0.067)	(0.031)	(0.054)	(0.054)	(0.036)	(0.073)	(0.056)

Female-headed head of household	−0.335 (0.538)	0.502 (0.374)	0.540* (0.285)	1.125 (0.800)	0.626* (0.347)	−20.387*** (0.447)	−20.766*** (0.297)	0.120 (0.341)	−19.632*** (0.536)	0.565 (0.531)
Highest years of education in household	−0.060 (0.072)	−0.096** (0.048)	−0.003 (0.035)	−0.075 (0.120)	0.047 (0.040)	−0.076 (0.050)	0.015 (0.051)	0.084** (0.035)	−0.023 (0.070)	0.112** (0.055)
Father reads and writes	0.696 (0.440)	0.233 (0.307)	0.182 (0.212)	1.513* (0.870)	0.092 (0.218)	0.007 (0.252)	0.147 (0.250)	0.170 (0.150)	0.354 (0.315)	0.041 (0.242)
Father < intermediate	0.040 (0.615)	0.822** (0.363)	0.397 (0.243)	0.754 (1.087)	0.458* (0.240)	0.217 (1.328)	1.348 (1.029)	0.567 (0.752)	−19.643*** (0.862)	0.734 (0.802)
Father intermediate +	0.547 (0.530)	0.499 (0.345)	0.327 (0.237)	2.098** (0.946)	0.128 (0.241)	0.725* (0.416)	0.390 (0.445)	−0.323 (0.271)	0.625 (0.699)	0.212 (0.396)
Father university +	0.594 (0.718)	0.996** (0.484)	0.347 (0.289)	2.028* (1.140)	0.361 (0.310)	1.188** (0.519)	0.022 (0.756)	−0.210 (0.348)	1.603** (0.787)	0.466 (0.554)
Father employer	0.542 (0.515)	0.480 (0.367)	−0.007 (0.284)	1.495** (0.663)	−0.270 (0.334)	0.273 (0.388)	0.240 (0.446)	−0.569** (0.246)	0.487 (0.588)	0.164 (0.437)
Father self-employed/ unpaid family worker	0.856** (0.349)	0.230 (0.246)	−0.045 (0.191)	1.269** (0.512)	0.021 (0.209)	0.386 (0.251)	0.317 (0.253)	−0.256 (0.165)	0.809** (0.316)	−0.580** (0.258)
Father non-employed	0.562 (0.532)	−0.447 (0.502)	−0.275 (0.308)	0.955 (0.874)	−0.421 (0.390)	−0.138 (0.556)	0.281 (0.520)	0.117 (0.291)	0.460 (0.945)	0.073 (0.542)
Rural residence	−0.657* (0.356)	−0.841*** (0.236)	0.200 (0.132)	−0.556 (0.596)	−0.002 (0.150)	−0.376* (0.225)	−0.739*** (0.249)	−0.021 (0.140)	−1.180*** (0.384)	−0.531** (0.239)
North region	−0.384 (0.292)	−0.254 (0.211)	0.472*** (0.140)	0.667 (0.444)	0.730*** (0.165)	0.208 (0.213)	−0.536** (0.239)	0.549*** (0.142)	0.878*** (0.295)	1.173*** (0.260)

Continued

Table 13.3 *Continued*

	Youth					Non-youth				
	Self-employed/ unpaid family worker	Informal + irregular	Public + formal private	Employer	Unemployed	Self-employed/ unpaid family worker	Informal + irregular	Public + formal private	Employer	Unemployed
South region	−0.860*	−0.377	1.242***	1.841**	1.698***	−0.617	−1.420***	0.413*	−0.601	1.077***
	(0.510)	(0.344)	(0.209)	(0.807)	(0.247)	(0.417)	(0.397)	(0.212)	(0.471)	(0.309)
Constant	−3.754***	−0.819	−2.787***	−8.310***	−0.849	−3.707*	−2.549	−3.439***	−8.237**	−2.253*
	(1.127)	(0.849)	(0.725)	(1.796)	(0.730)	(2.182)	(1.678)	(1.147)	(3.220)	(1.221)
Observations	3,597	3,597	3,597	3,597	3,597	3,429	3,429	3,429	3,429	3,429
Chi-squared	4896	4896	4896	4896	4896	33949	33949	33949	33949	33949
Pseudo R-squared	0.241	0.241	0.241	0.241	0.241	0.287	0.287	0.287	0.287	0.287

Note: Samples weighted using individual-level weights. Standard errors robust to arbitrary heteroskedasticity are in parentheses; * $p < 0.1$, ** $p < 0.05$, *** $p < 0.01$. Workers' status as 'youth' and all household-level variables are lagged by one survey wave to estimate the effect of workers' circumstances in their youth on their subsequent outcomes.

Source: authors' calculations based on JLMPS 2010–2016 (OAMDI 2019).

without any consistent patterns. Fathers' employment type also has a weak effect on the likelihood of their offspring's employment status, even though there is some evidence of intergenerational transmission of employment status. Fathers' employment type has the greatest impact on the likelihood of similar employment types among their offspring. Children of economically inactive fathers have weak odds of working or searching for jobs. Fathers who are self-employed or employers are particularly likely to have children who are self-employed/unpaid or employers and less likely to have children working in the formal sector or being unemployed.

Like in Egypt, we find a great regional disparity in employment prospects between the Central region (baseline) and the North and South regions and between urban and rural areas. Workers in the North and South regions have significantly higher odds of landing formal jobs and of searching for work and have lower odds of being self-employed or having an informal job. In rural areas, workers are substantially less likely to be self-employed or an employer, have an informal job, or be searching for a job. Urban workers appear to have higher odds of being unemployed. The availability of decent jobs relative to the pool of applicants aspiring to get them is lower in urban areas. This may be the effect of an influx of refugees on the availability of informal and other unskilled jobs.

Finally, Table 13.4 reports on the same regressions as those estimated on the 2014 survey for Tunisia. Because only one survey wave is available, all covariates are taken from the same year, with the exception of youth status (taken from six years prior, i.e. 2008), residence (urban/rural and region of birthplace), and fathers' characteristics when the worker was aged 15. We again find a strong positive but diminishing effect of age on employment (as well as unemployment) prospects, and a strong negative effect of being female. Workers' higher education is strongly and positively associated with formal employment. Interestingly, among youth workers, higher education is associated negatively with becoming self-employed or an employer and positively with unemployment, while among non-youth workers, the opposite is the case. Among youths, women's return to education in terms of the odds of formal employment is lower than among men, while it is higher among older workers. On the other hand, higher-educated young women are less likely to remain unemployed than their male counterparts, while the opposite is true among higher-educated older women.

Household wealth increases the prospect of becoming an employer and lowers the risk of irregular employment and unemployment. Like in Egypt and Jordan, the wealth effect is highly persistent across youth and non-youth ages. Fathers' education is negatively correlated with the risk of unemployment, but little can be said about its effect on other employment status groups because the parameters appear to be implausibly high. Data problems, including a small sample of highly educated fathers or incidental collinearity with other covariates, are likely at play. Like in Egypt and Jordan, fathers' self-employment or status as an employer has a strong positive effect on their offspring's own self-employment or employer status.

Table 13.4 Multinomial logit regressions on TLMPS14, separating youth and non-youth

	Youth					Non-youth				
	Self-employed/ unpaid family worker	Informal + irregular	Public + formal private	Employer	Unemployed	Self-employed/ unpaid family worker	Informal + irregular	Public + Formal private	Employer	Unemployed
Age–min (age)	1.541***	0.561*	1.353***	1.924**	0.955***	0.379***	0.380***	0.716***	0.760***	0.346***
	(0.423)	(0.324)	(0.278)	(0.775)	(0.270)	(0.048)	(0.048)	(0.057)	(0.122)	(0.062)
Age–min (age) squared	−0.026***	−0.009	−0.022***	−0.030**	−0.017***	−0.004***	−0.005***	−0.008***	−0.009***	−0.005***
	(0.008)	(0.006)	(0.005)	(0.013)	(0.005)	(0.001)	(0.001)	(0.001)	(0.001)	(0.001)
Female = 1	−1.732***	−2.273***	−1.572***	−2.212***	−0.939***	−3.220***	−3.763***	−4.024***	−5.217***	−3.429***
	(0.331)	(0.330)	(0.249)	(0.839)	(0.267)	(0.251)	(0.268)	(0.270)	(0.809)	(0.320)
Reads and writes	0.112	1.161***	0.431	−0.127	0.254	0.359	0.321	1.253***	0.605	0.411
	(0.343)	(0.393)	(0.391)	(0.796)	(0.369)	(0.231)	(0.227)	(0.250)	(0.551)	(0.318)
Primary	1.816***	2.268***	1.756***	1.797***	1.941***	0.696**	0.252	1.352***	1.384**	0.152
	(0.431)	(0.450)	(0.458)	(0.884)	(0.453)	(0.327)	(0.292)	(0.323)	(0.590)	(0.390)
Preparatory	0.789	1.591***	1.580***	1.212	1.586***	0.141	−0.874**	1.065***	0.526	−1.273***
	(0.532)	(0.514)	(0.505)	(0.916)	(0.529)	(0.362)	(0.342)	(0.345)	(0.741)	(0.483)
Secondary	−0.112	0.353	1.461***	0.481	1.205**	−0.940**	−2.022***	1.444***	0.147	−2.139***
	(0.553)	(0.568)	(0.488)	(0.951)	(0.484)	(0.439)	(0.464)	(0.356)	(0.654)	(0.622)
University short cycle	−0.828	0.041	1.465***	−2.432*	1.231***	−21.897***	−2.857**	3.027***	1.205	−1.697*
	(0.657)	(0.602)	(0.479)	(1.322)	(0.451)	(0.512)	(1.171)	(0.553)	(1.044)	(0.925)
University long cycle +	−24.032***	−0.479	1.575***	−2.732**	1.384***	1.240	1.689**	5.301***	3.122***	2.564***
	(0.509)	(0.700)	(0.507)	(1.359)	(0.489)	(1.147)	(0.825)	(0.714)	(1.082)	(0.859)
Less than intermediate × female	−2.170***	−1.947***	−0.792*	−23.003***	−2.067***	−0.484	0.230	0.250	−0.879	0.434
	(0.581)	(0.549)	(0.455)	(1.085)	(0.548)	(0.442)	(0.414)	(0.407)	(1.330)	(0.485)

Intermediate × female	−0.830 (0.727)	−1.040* (0.626)	−0.759 (0.511)	−2.061 (1.514)	−1.440*** (0.526)	0.171 (0.545)	1.132 (0.770)	1.288*** (0.446)	1.416 (1.187)	1.455** (0.589)
University × female	−1.236 (0.769)	0.236 (0.673)	−0.530 (0.464)	−22.877*** (1.224)	−0.163 (0.458)	0.991 (0.668)	1.981*** (0.754)	1.605*** (0.409)	−19.021*** (0.878)	2.852*** (0.793)
Household wealth	0.011 (0.185)	−0.778*** (0.200)	0.041 (0.115)	0.767*** (0.296)	−0.378*** (0.142)	−0.357** (0.146)	−0.558*** (0.147)	0.035 (0.100)	0.638*** (0.231)	−0.682*** (0.195)
Household size	0.040 (0.068)	−0.057 (0.064)	−0.154*** (0.055)	−0.327** (0.139)	0.040 (0.052)	0.029 (0.051)	−0.017 (0.052)	0.038 (0.053)	−0.058 (0.101)	−0.076 (0.061)
Female headed head of household	−0.390 (0.571)	−0.346 (0.424)	−0.234 (0.350)	−1.087 (1.199)	−0.200 (0.358)	0.523 (0.382)	0.312 (0.365)	0.910** (0.371)	0.312 (1.197)	0.232 (0.346)
Highest ears of education in household	0.083** (0.033)	0.028 (0.030)	0.011 (0.030)	0.166*** (0.057)	0.070** (0.031)	−0.018 (0.023)	−0.004 (0.022)	−0.025 (0.022)	0.010 (0.037)	0.046 (0.032)
Father reads and writes	−0.001 (0.380)	0.286 (0.322)	0.331 (0.343)	−23.358*** (1.363)	0.745*** (0.279)	0.210 (0.409)	0.139 (0.379)	−0.631 (0.672)	−20.045*** (0.516)	0.712* (0.368)
Father primary	−0.448 (0.296)	0.128 (0.256)	0.098 (0.208)	−0.569 (0.708)	−0.429* (0.230)	0.023 (0.223)	−0.013 (0.200)	0.100 (0.181)	0.166 (0.397)	0.282 (0.287)
Father preparatory	0.093 (0.497)	0.131 (0.348)	−0.145 (0.279)	0.446 (0.738)	−0.180 (0.271)	−0.101 (0.645)	0.046 (0.557)	0.242 (0.325)	−0.409 (0.770)	−0.487 (0.571)
Father university short cycle	0.404 (0.968)	−0.027 (1.152)	0.781 (0.700)	3.025*** (1.169)	−0.509 (0.785)	−20.748*** (0.476)	0.276 (1.026)	−0.121 (0.840)	−22.292*** (1.311)	−0.416 (1.156)
Father university long cycle	−22.797*** (0.757)	−0.398 (1.169)	0.072 (0.498)	−22.446*** (1.017)	−1.059 (0.841)	−21.261*** (0.553)	−22.056*** (0.558)	−0.763 (0.782)	−20.833*** (0.879)	−0.843 (1.270)

Continued

Table 13.4 *Continued*

	Youth					Non-youth				
	Self-employed/ unpaid family worker	Informal + irregular	Public + formal private	Employer	Unemployed	Self-employed/ unpaid family worker	Informal + irregular	Public + Formal private	Employer	Unemployed
Father	2.209	−23.076***	−0.613	−23.265***	−25.022***	−23.697***	3.962***	−25.585***	−25.766***	−24.508***
post-graduate	(1.703)	(0.923)	(0.890)	(2.245)	(0.703)	(0.893)	(1.297)	(0.766)	(1.297)	(0.978)
Father	1.143**	0.206	0.322	1.993***	−0.706*	0.772***	−0.788*	−1.227***	1.096**	−0.832*
employer	(0.528)	(0.387)	(0.320)	(0.602)	(0.422)	(0.279)	(0.405)	(0.291)	(0.427)	(0.503)
Father self-	0.674**	−0.142	−0.299	0.064	−0.251	1.029***	−0.219	−0.249	−0.343	−0.031
employed/unpaid family worker	(0.270)	(0.243)	(0.248)	(0.682)	(0.240)	(0.168)	(0.174)	(0.161)	(0.382)	(0.249)
Father non-	−0.054	−0.541	−0.769***	−2.112**	−0.377	0.208	−0.851**	−0.247	−0.584	−0.289
employed	(0.362)	(0.333)	(0.281)	(1.036)	(0.256)	(0.447)	(0.333)	(0.384)	(0.786)	(0.335)
Rural	0.783***	−0.307	−0.061	−0.245	−0.323*	0.098	−0.044	−0.011	0.433	−0.029
birthplace	(0.253)	(0.208)	(0.191)	(0.448)	(0.188)	(0.189)	(0.195)	(0.171)	(0.298)	(0.204)
Nabeul,	1.063*	0.450	0.643**	2.955**	0.710**	0.130	−0.198	0.375*	−0.617	−0.028
Zaghouan, Bizerte	(0.642)	(0.358)	(0.257)	(1.157)	(0.297)	(0.379)	(0.266)	(0.225)	(0.508)	(0.438)
Beja,	1.867***	−0.588	−0.538*	−20.737***	0.437	1.398***	−0.020	0.437*	−0.206	−0.070
Jendouba, Le kef, Siliana	(0.559)	(0.385)	(0.319)	(1.303)	(0.332)	(0.344)	(0.286)	(0.260)	(0.602)	(0.400)
Sousse,	1.385**	0.483	−0.150	2.223*	0.320	1.031***	0.330	0.235	0.150	0.141
Monastir, Mahdia, Sfax	(0.604)	(0.347)	(0.262)	(1.171)	(0.306)	(0.366)	(0.296)	(0.252)	(0.480)	(0.369)

Kairouan, Kasserine, Sidi Bouzide	1.032	0.251	−0.393	2.178	0.925***	0.068	0.028	−0.084	−0.520	0.374
	(0.638)	(0.413)	(0.311)	(1.354)	(0.338)	(0.367)	(0.291)	(0.292)	(0.585)	(0.371)
Gabes, Mednine, Tataouine	1.700***	0.186	−0.154	2.662**	0.278	0.700*	−0.060	0.165	0.242	0.110
	(0.604)	(0.357)	(0.305)	(1.275)	(0.300)	(0.418)	(0.293)	(0.278)	(0.562)	(0.413)
Gafsa, Tozeur, Kebili	2.589***	0.772*	0.289	3.233**	−0.008	1.133***	−0.351	0.197	0.455	1.200**
	(0.630)	(0.431)	(0.373)	(1.481)	(0.401)	(0.412)	(0.443)	(0.325)	(0.657)	(0.551)
Constant	−3.559***	−1.317*	−0.712	−6.663***	−1.376**	−3.221***	−0.222	−4.419***	−5.899***	−0.690
	(0.993)	(0.794)	(0.718)	(1.851)	(0.699)	(0.584)	(0.486)	(0.579)	(1.113)	(0.687)
Observations	2,371	2,371	2,371	2,371	2,371	4,543	4,543	4,543	4,543	4,543
Chi-squared	42,106	42,106	42,106	42,106	42,106	54,025	54,025	54,025	54,025	54,025
Pseuddo R-squared	0.230	0.230	0.230	0.230	0.230	0.330	0.330	0.330	0.330	0.330

Note: Samples weighted using individual-level weights. Standard errors robust to arbitrary heteroskedasticity are in parentheses; * $p < 0.1$, ** $p < 0.05$, *** $p < 0.01$. Workers' status as 'youth' is lagged by six years (i.e. 'youth' are 21–35 years old in 2014) and region and rural/urban residence are from workers' birthplace to estimate the effect of workers' circumstances in their youth on their subsequent outcomes.

Source: authors' calculations based on TLMPS 2014 (OAMDI 2019).

Finally, workers from rural areas are more likely to be self-employed or unpaid family workers and less likely to remain unemployed.

When the smoothed probabilities of all employment status groups by age, level of education, or wealth index score are plotted,[11] the figures show that, in Egypt, the prospect of informal employment falls with workers' ages and the prospect of formal employment continuously rises. In Jordan and Tunisia, by contrast, the likelihood of formal employment peaks around age 40 and falls thereafter and that of informal employment stagnates throughout workers' lives.

In addition to the baseline models in Table 13.2–13.4, estimations were conducted as robustness checks of the sample composition and of the dynamics in workers' employment trends. To address the question of job transition from vulnerable employment, we restricted the samples in Table 13.2–13.4 to those who were vulnerable in the prior period (previous survey wave in Egypt and Jordan, first previous employment status in Tunisia). The results show that the risk factors for transition out of vulnerability to various employment sectors are somewhat different to those for the general population of workers (regression results available on request; predicted lines shown in Fig. 13.3). Parameter sizes change systematically from their levels in Table 13.2–13.4 because of the sample restriction but are generally less significant because of the smaller sample sizes. We find that higher education is more strongly associated with upward mobility, while higher household wealth, rural residence, and having a female household head are all associated negatively with upward mobility. These parameters are not too far apart from those in Table 13.2–13.4 because the restriction does not affect a large share of male workers who started their youth lives in informal, irregular, or self-employment. Those starting in formal jobs or as employers can be seen as outliers who do not affect the predicted parameters too much.

Figure 13.3 shows that among vulnerably employed men, the odds of formal employment are significantly lower than in the general sample of all men, and the odds of informal/irregular employment are significantly higher. Among all men, we have seen that the odds of formal employment rise sharply with age and begin to dominate all other employment status groups by the ages of 28–39 in Egypt and by the ages of 22–26 in Jordan and Tunisia. By contrast, among men initially employed in vulnerable occupations, the odds of formal employment are much flatter and never dominate the odds of informal employment. In Egypt, they are half as high or lower than the odds of informal employment across all ages. In Tunisia, they are half as high until the age of 42, and then gradually approach the odds of informal employment by the age of 56. In Jordan, the odds of formal employment are nearly as high as the odds of informal employment

[11] See AlAzzawi and Hlasny (2020: Figs 4, A6–A8).

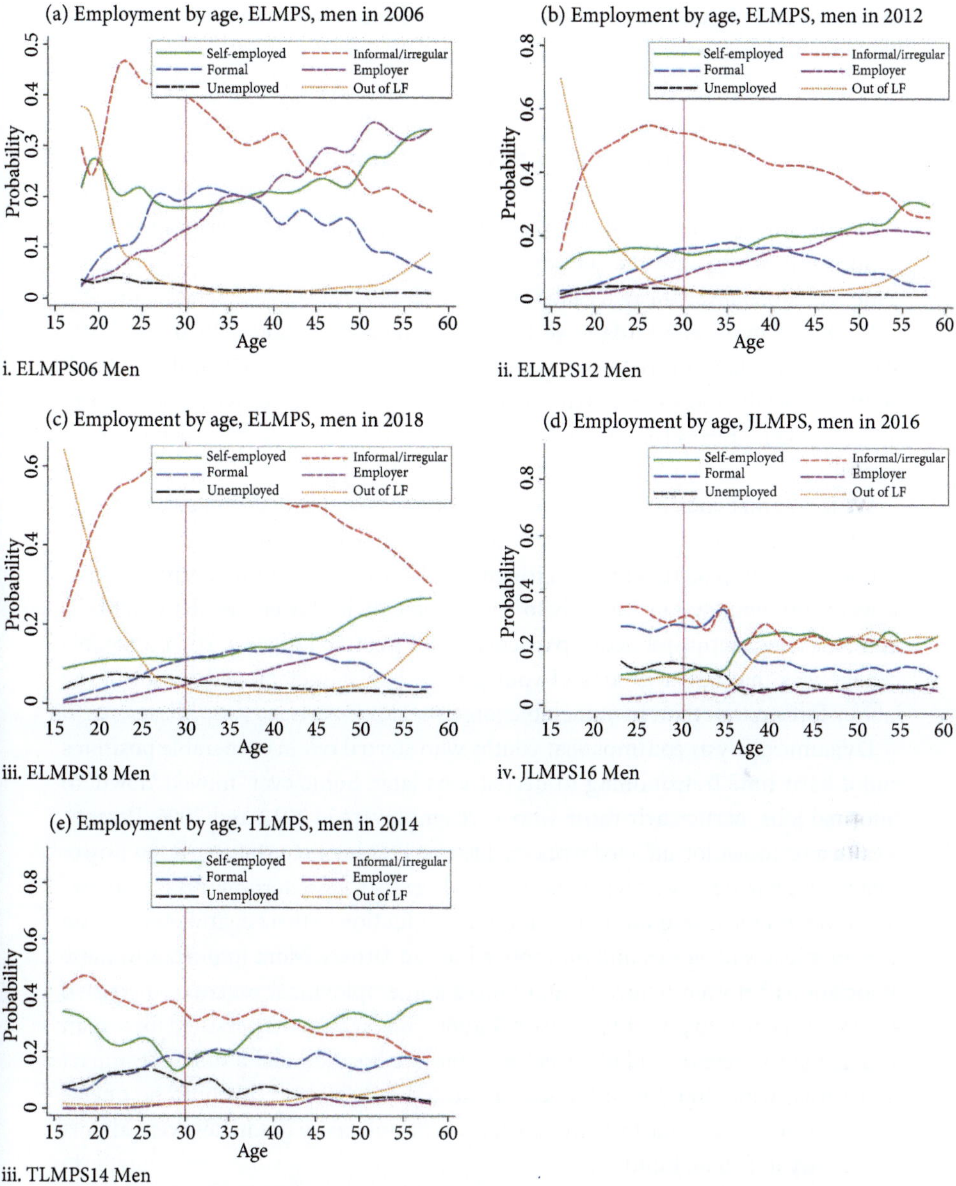

Fig. 13.3 Predicted probability of transition from vulnerability among men, by age

Source: authors' illustrations based on predictions from multinomial regression results based on ELMPS 2006–2018, TLMPS 2014, and JLMPS 2016 (OAMDI 2019).

until the age of 36 and fall to two-thirds of the odds of informality for higher-age workers.[12]

5. Conclusions and policy implications

We studied youth vulnerabilities in Egypt, Jordan, and Tunisia in terms of employment status groups and the set of protections afforded to workers. We relied on panel data to analyse the outcomes of youths in 1998, 2006, 2012, and all the way to 2018 in Egypt. For Jordan, we tracked individuals between 2010 and 2016. We only had data for 2014 for Tunisia but were still able to examine vulnerability statically and over a span of three years, as well as cross vulnerabilities using workers' birthplace, father's education and employment, and household wealth.

We found that youths in all three countries were disadvantaged in terms of their employment status, with most youths landing vulnerable positions including self-employment, unpaid family work, irregular wage work, or informal private-sector work. Youth employment is likely to be associated with lower pay and this likelihood increases across the years, particularly in Egypt. In Jordan in 2016, a notable change was that larger groups of youths were either unemployed or out of the labour force rather than in vulnerable jobs.

Dynamic analysis confirms that youths who started out in vulnerable positions had a hard time transitioning to decent jobs later. Some even moved 'down' to informal jobs, particularly those who were employers in 2012 and 2006. Parents' wealth and education affected workers' lifetime employment status groups. Lower wealth and having less-educated fathers were very strong determinants of vulnerable employment. There was a clear and stark reduction in this negative association at higher levels of wealth and for more educated fathers. More importantly, these associations between family circumstances and employment outcomes persisted even years later—20 years in the case of Egypt. Similar patterns persisted for Jordan and Tunisia in terms of family wealth. Fathers' education had a different impact in Tunisia, with children of the least-educated fathers more likely to be unemployed or to remain inactive, while children of university graduates were almost exclusively in formal jobs.

Multinomial logit regressions confirm that youth workers were less likely to obtain good jobs than older workers. Comparing the regression results for Egypt,

[12] The models for Egypt were estimated with random effects, and even with fixed effects, to limit the effects of unobserved heterogeneity across workers. As an alternative to the models restricted to initially vulnerably employed workers (Fig. 13.3), dynamic models were considered using prior labour market experience as a factor influencing current job. These models suffer from potential endogeneity of the prior labour market experience.

Jordan, and Tunisia, we found many consistencies in the demographic distribution across different types of jobs. College graduates in all three countries had a high probability of remaining unemployed, perhaps hoping to land formal private or public employment. While workers could rely on consistent returns to education through prospects for better employment, substantial differences in the returns existed between males and females, and females remained most likely to be out of the labour force. Family wealth helped to explain workers' career-long job mobility, while parental education and employment mattered mostly in workers' youth.

These results suggest that, even among wage jobs, work may be informal, low-security, and low-pay. It is crucial not to limit attention to unemployment and self-employment rates as youth employment indicators. If the objective of youth programmes is to secure decent work for young people, then productivity, compensation, social protection, occupational safety, health, and job security need to be reviewed.

Our results inform policymakers about the vital support systems needed for vulnerable workers, especially youths, the poor, and those with less educated parents. They provide insights into the challenges young people face and the inefficiencies in matching formal jobs with talent, as family wealth and socio-economic background still dominate individual skills and effort. We hope these results can be used to create a better framework for aligning skill supply with demand and to create more acceptable working conditions in the informal and formal sectors to facilitate worker mobility and greater economic efficiency.

References

Agénor, P.-R., H.T. Jensen, M. Nabli, and T. Yousef (2004). 'Labor Market Reforms, Growth, and Unemployment in Labor-Exporting Countries in the Middle East and North Africa'. Social Protection Working Paper No. 3328. Washington, DC: World Bank. https://doi.org/10.1596/1813-9450-3328.

AlAzzawi, S., and V. Hlasny (2018). 'Youth Vulnerability in Egypt and Jordan'. ERF Working Paper No. 1275. Cairo: Economic Research Forum.

AlAzzawi, S., and V. Hlasny (2019a). 'Disparities in the Cost of Living Changes after a Large-Scale Devaluation: The Case of Egypt 2016'. *Topics in Middle Eastern and African Economies*, 21(2): 1–32.

AlAzzawi, S., and V. Hlasny (2019b). 'Household Asset Wealth and Female Labor Supply in MENA'. *Quarterly Review of Economics and Finance*, 73: 3–13. https://doi.org/10.1016/j.qref.2019.08.002.

AlAzzawi, S. and V. Hlasny (2020). 'Vulnerable Employment of Egyptian, Jordanian, and Tunisian Youth: Trends and Determinants'. WIDER Working Paper No. 2020/166. Helsinki: UNU-WIDER.

Amer, M. (2012). 'The School-to-Work Transition of Jordanian Youth'. ERF Working Paper No. 686. Cairo: Economic Research Forum.

Amer, M. (2015). 'Patterns of Labor Market Insertion in Egypt, 1998–2012'. In R. Assaad and C. Krafft (eds), *The Egyptian Labor Market in an Era of Revolution*. Oxford: Oxford University Press, 70–89. https://doi.org/10.1093/acprof:oso/9780198737254.003.0004.

Assaad, R. (2012). 'The Structure and Evolution of Employment in Jordan'. ERF Working Paper No. 674. Cairo: Economic Research Forum.

Assaad, R. (2014). 'Making Sense of Arab Labor Markets: The Enduring Legacy of Dualism'. *IZA Journal of Labor and Development*, 3(1): 1–25. https://doi.org/10.1186/2193-9020-3-6.

Assaad, R., and C. Krafft (2014). 'Youth Transitions in Egypt: School, Work, and Family Formation in an Era of Changing Opportunities'. Silatech Working Paper No. 14–1. Doha: Silatech.

Assaad, R., and C. Krafft (2015). 'The Structure and Evolution of Employment in Egypt: 1998–2012'. In R. Assaad and C. Krafft (eds), *The Egyptian Labor Market in an Era of Revolution*. Oxford: Oxford University Press, 27–51. https://doi.org/10.1093/acprof:oso/9780198737254.001.0001.

Assaad, R., C. Binzel, and M. Gadallah (2010). 'Transitions to Employment and Marriage among Young Men in Egypt'. *Middle East Development Journal*, 2(1): 39–88. https://doi.org/10.1142/S1793812010000162.

Assaad, R., R. Hendy, and S. Yassin (2014). 'Gender and the Jordanian Labor Market'. In R. Assaad (ed.), *The Jordanian Labour Market in the New Millennium*. Oxford: Oxford University Press, 105–143. https://doi.org/10.1093/acprof:oso/9780198702054.001.0001.

Assaad, R., C. Krafft, and D. Salehi-Isfahani (2018). 'Does the Type of Higher Education Affect Labor Market Outcomes? Evidence from Egypt and Jordan'. *Higher Education*, 75(6): 945–995. https://doi.org/10.1007/s10734-017-0179-0.

Assaad, R., C. Krafft, and C. Salemi (2019). 'Socioeconomic Status and the Changing Nature of the School-to-Work Transition in Egypt, Jordan, and Tunisia'. ERF Working Paper No. 1287. Cairo: Economic Research Forum.

Barsoum, G., and D. Abdalla (2020). 'Still the Employer of Choice: Evolution of Public Sector Employment in Egypt'. ERF Working Paper No. 1386. Cairo: Economic Research Forum.

Binzel, C. (2011). 'Decline in Social Mobility: Unfulfilled Aspirations among Egypt's Educated Youth'. Institute of Labor Economics (IZA) Discussion Paper No. 6139. Bonn: IZA.

CAPMAS (Central Agency for Public Mobilization and Statistics) (2018). *Egypt in Figures*. Cairo: CAPMAS.

Danquah, M., S. Schotte, and K. Sen (2019). 'Informal Work in Sub-Saharan Africa: Dead End or Stepping Stones?'. WIDER Working Paper No. 2019/107. Helsinki: UNU-WIDER. https://doi.org/10.35188/UNU-WIDER/2019/743-9.

DOS (Jordanian Department of Statistics) (2010). *Poverty Status in Jordan*. Amman: DOS.

Egel, D., and D. Salehi-Isfahani (2010). 'Youth Transitions to Employment and Marriage in Iran: Evidence from the School to Work Transition Survey'. *Middle East Development Journal*, 2(1): 89–120. https://doi.org/10.1142/S1793812010000198.

Ehab, M. (2019). 'Employment Transitions of Youth and Health Implications in Egypt'. ERF Working Paper 1355. Cairo: Economic Research Forum.

El-Haddad, A. (2020). 'Redefining the Social Contract in the Wake of the Arab Spring: The Experiences of Egypt, Morocco and Tunisia'. *World Development*, 127(104774). https://doi.org/10.1016/j.worlddev.2019.104774.

Fehling M., Z.M. Jarrah, M.E. Tiernan, S. Albezreh, M.J. VanRooyen, A. Alhokair, and B.D. Nelson (2016). 'Youth in Crisis in the Middle East and North Africa: A Systematic Literature Review and Focused Landscape Analysis'. *Eastern Mediterranean Health Journal*, 21(12): 916–930. https://doi.org/10.26719/2015.21.12.916.

Hlasny, V., and S. AlAzzawi (2018). 'Return Migration and Socioeconomic Mobility in MENA: Evidence from Labor Market Panel Surveys'. WIDER Working Paper No. 2018/35. Helsinki: UNU-WIDER. https://doi.org/10.35188/UNU-WIDER/2018/477-3.

Hlasny, V., and S. AlAzzawi (2019). 'Asset Inequality in MENA: The Missing Dimension?'. *Quarterly Review of Economic and Finance*, 73: 44–55. https://doi.org/10.1016/j.qref.2018.07.010.

ILO (International Labour Organization) (2020a). 'Global Employment Trends for Youth 2020: Africa'. Available at: https://www.ilo.org/wcmsp5/groups/public/---dgreports/---dcomm/documents/briefingnote/wcms_737670.pdf (accessed 25 November 2020).

ILO (International Labour Organization) (2020b). 'Global Employment Trends for Youth 2020: Arab States'. Available at: https://www.ilo.org/wcmsp5/groups/public/---dgreports/---dcomm/documents/briefingnote/wcms_737672.pdf (accessed 25 November 2020).

Kabbani, N., and E. Kothari (2005). 'Youth Employment in the MENA Region: A Situational Assessment'. Social Protection Discussion Paper No. 534. Washington, DC: World Bank.

Krafft, C., and R. Assaad (2016). 'Inequality of Opportunity in the Labor Market for Higher Education Graduates in Egypt and Jordan'. In I. Diwan and A. Galal (eds), *The Middle East Economies in Times of Transition*. International Economic Association Series. London: Palgrave Macmillan, 159–185. https://doi.org/10.1007/978-1-137-52977-0_6.

Majbouri, M. (2017). 'Income Mobility and the Arab Spring: The Case of Egypt and Jordan'. *Applied Economics Letters*, 24(15): 1070–1074. https://doi.org/10.1080/13504851.2016.1254332.

Mryyan, N. (2012). 'Demographics, Labor Force Participation and Unemployment in Jordan'. ERF Working Paper No. 670. Cairo: Economic Research Forum.

OAMDI (Open Access Micro Data Initiative) (2019). 'Labor Market Panel Surveys (LMPS)'. Version 2.0 of Licensed Data Files; ELMPS 1998, 2006, 2012, 2018 panel v.2.0; JLMPS 2010, 2016 panel v.1.1; TLMPS 2014 v.2.0. Cairo: Economic Research Forum. Available at: https://erf.org.eg/oamdi (accessed 27 November 2020).

Pieters, J. (2013). 'Youth Employment in Developing Countries'. Background Paper No. DCI-EDUC/2012/310-255. Luxembourg: European Commission.

Shahen, M.E., K. Kotani, M. Kakinaka, and S. Managi (2020). 'Wage and Labor Mobility between Public, Formal Private and Informal Private Sectors in a Developing Country'. *Economic Analysis and Policy*, 68: 101–113. https://doi.org/10.1016/j.eap.2020.09.006.

Stampini, M., and A. Verdier-Chouchane (2011) 'Labor Market Dynamics in Tunisia: The Issue of Youth Unemployment'. IZA Discussion Paper No. 5611. Bonn: IZA.

WEF (World Economic Forum) (2012). *Addressing the 100 Million Youth Challenge: Perspectives on Youth Employment in the Arab World in 2012.* Geneva: World Economic Forum.

World Bank (2016). 'Tunisia Poverty Assessment 2015'. World Bank Other Operational Studies No. 24410, Washington, DC: World Bank.

World Bank (2020). 'Metadata Glossary: Vulnerable Employment, World Bank Databank'. Available at: https://databank.worldbank.org/metadataglossary/world-development-indicators/series/SL.EMP.VULN.ZS (accessed 27 November 2020).

PART VI

LESSONS LEARNT

14

How to transform informal work and livelihoods?

Lessons learnt and policy options

Gary S. Fields, T. H. Gindling, Kunal Sen, Michael Danquah, and Simone Schotte

1. Introduction

The 11 case studies presented in this book offer a comparative perspective on the composition of employment in 22 countries spanning Asia, Latin America (LA), sub-Saharan Africa (SSA), and the Middle East and North Africa (MENA). Each chapter characterizes the composition of employment in the specific country contexts, documents the transition patterns between formal and informal employment, and across different forms of informality, distinguishing between wage-employment and self-employment. The broad drivers of transitions between different work status groups, as well the implications of moving from one work status to another, in terms of income gains and losses, are also examined.

What can be learnt from each of these analyses? What are the bigger-picture patterns that relate the findings? And what are the options for policies that could improve the livelihoods of lower-tier informal workers? These are the three core questions guiding this concluding chapter.

2. Summary of lessons learnt: country-by-country findings

The study on China, Chapter 3, shows that mobility was low at the top (formal wage-employees) and the bottom (lower-tier informal self-employed) of the job ladder, the latter particularly having little chance to move up to higher levels. More than two-thirds of formal wage-employees remained in their respective level and they were least likely to move down to lower levels. The lower-tier informal self-employed had little chance (about 3 per cent) to move up and the majority of them (79 per cent) remained at the same level. Over the period 2014–2018, about 5 per cent of lower-tier informal workers moved up to the formal work status, 7 per cent of them moved up to the upper-tier informal work, and 78 per cent of them stayed

Gary S. Fields et al., *How to transform informal work and livelihoods?*. In: *The Job Ladder*. Edited by Gary S. Fields, T. H. Gindling, Kunal Sen, Michael Danquah, and Simone Schotte, Oxford University Press. © UNU-WIDER (2023). DOI: 10.1093/oso/9780192867339.003.0014 put, while less than 1 per cent became unemployed and 9 per cent dropped out the labour force. Over the same period, 25 per cent of upper-tier informal workers moved up to formal work, 33 per cent of them remained in the same status, and 27 per cent of them moved down to the lower-tier informal work, while 2 per cent became unemployed and 14 per cent left the labour force.

Workers in the formal work status earn more than those in the informal. In the formal work status, self-employed workers have higher mean earnings than wage-employees over the 2014–2018 period. Over the 2014–2018 period, on average, the formal self-employed have the highest annual earnings of all work status groups; on the other hand, lower-tier self-employed informal workers earn the least of all work status groups. Using fixed-effects models, the authors study earnings gains or losses when transitioning between work status groups. They find that age, gender, marital status, and years of schooling are statistically significant in determining earnings in general. They also find a substantial decline in earnings when workers transition from formal wage-employment to a self-employed job. The largest earnings loss is for transitioning from formal wage-employment to lower-tier informal, which reduces workers' annual earnings on average by 91 per cent, followed by 81 per cent for the upper-tier informal and 76 per cent for the formal, a 10–15 percentage points difference.

Investigating the case of India, Chapter 4 finds clear differences in movement from one work status to another between wage-employed and self-employed workers, with self-employment being the more dynamic state. While about one-third of the formal self-employed remain in the same work status, one-quarter experience a downward transition to the lower tier of the informal self-employed. In the case of upper-tier informal self-employed, the chapter finds that 2 per cent formalize, while around 40 per cent of workers transition to lower-tier self-employment work status. There is high upward mobility among lower-tier informal self-employed, with about half moving out of their current work status. In contrast to the high rates of movement from one work status to another among the self-employed, the chapter finds high rates of persistence among formal wage-employed and lower-tier informal wage-employed. Three-quarters of the workers who work in the lower-tier informal wage-employment—the largest segment of the India sample—retain the same work status.[1] Formal wage-employed also demonstrate a higher degree of immobility, with 65 per cent of them retaining the same status.[2]

[1] A majority of lower-tier informal wage-employed are agricultural wage labourers, who remain in farm employment for much of their working lives (Natarajan et al. 2020). This occupational group also show very low inter-generational upward mobility, with their children also likely to be in the same work status (Iversen et al. 2017).

[2] A possible reason for the persistence of the work status of formal wage-employees could be the provision of lifetime tenure for public-sector employees and for private-sector employees under the Industrial Disputes Act of 1947 in India, which provides one of the most protective employment legislation in the developing world (Saha et al. 2013).

Using multinomial logit models to examine the correlates of mobility, the chapter finds that increases in the level of education of the worker increases the probability of transitioning to a formal job. Further, male workers are more likely to move into wage-employment, while female workers are more likely to stay in self-employment. There is a steep gradient in the job ladder, with formal wage-employed earning the most among all the six work status groups. The largest inter-temporal change in earnings is reported by workers who continued to be in formal employment.

Analysing long-term panel data from Indonesia, Chapter 5 analyses transitions between low-tier and high-tier formal (wage-) employment and low-tier and high-tier informal (self-) employment. The chapter shows that transitions in work status are common among workers, except for those in the low-tier informal jobs. Specifically, 81 per cent of low-tier informal workers in 1996 stay in that job type through the next 8–19 years, 12 per cent move up to low-tier formal, 4.5 per cent to high-tier informal, and 2.2 per cent to high-tier formal. At the same time, the authors observe large entry rates into low-tier informal employment. Out of those in high-tier informal work, 76 per cent move down to low-tier informality, while only 11 per cent sustain their position. Out of those in low-tier formal work, 36 per cent remain in the same position, 54 per cent move into low-tier informal work, and 8 per cent move up to high-tier formal jobs. Finally, among those in high-tier formal work, 46 per cent remain in the same position, while 20 per cent decline into low-tier formal work and 29 per cent fall into low-tier informal work.

The results from multinomial logit regression indicate that individuals are negatively selected into low-tier informal work. More favourable conditions, such as higher education, higher cognitive skills, and age, increase the probability of being in formal employment. Using survival and the Cox proportional hazard model, the chapter shows that workers whose fathers are highly educated have a higher probability of switching between different work status groups. The average monthly earnings by work status provides a clear pattern of the job ladder. Low-tier informal workers earn the lowest, followed by low-tier formal, high-tier formal, and high-tier informal workers. The rise in earnings is substantially higher for those who have made the transition to formal status. Workers who made the transition to formality from either upper-tier informality or lower-tier informality exhibit approximately equal earnings gains. Further, positive income gains are also observed for those who transitioned from lower-tier to upper-tier informality compared with those who failed to make the transition. However, the largest inter-temporal gain in earnings is reported by workers who continued to be in formal employment.

Assessing data from Nicaragua and Costa Rica, Chapter 6 finds that in both countries earnings are highest for formal work, next for upper-tier informal, and lowest for lower-tier informal. This chapter also presents estimates of how wages change when workers change work status groups. With one exception, these wage transitions are consistent with the ordering above. The exception is upper-tier informal wage-employment; wages do not change significantly when workers transition between formal wage-employment and upper-tier informal wage-employment. This may be seen as evidence that upper-tier informal wage-employment is in part voluntary.

Mobility out of lower-tier informal work is higher than out of any other work status. Most workers who leave lower-tier informality transition to higher-paid work status groups. This may be seen as evidence that lower-tier informality is a not a persistent state for many lower-tier informal workers. In general, even with some churning back and forth between work status groups, there are still more total transitions up the job ladder than down the ladder.

Multinomial logits are estimated that compare year-to-year changes in work status to year-to-year changes in individual characteristics. The strongest result suggests policies that provide vocational training to informal workers as a way of improving wages for those who remain informal and of promoting transitions into better-paying work status groups. Transitions from all types of informality into formality are more common in Costa Rica than in Nicaragua, partly due to the larger proportion of formal workers within Costa Rica (58 per cent of workers in Costa Rica are formal vs 19 per cent in Nicaragua).

Providing comparative evidence on Argentina, Brazil, Ecuador, Mexico, Paraguay, and Peru, Chapter 7 finds formal wage earners to display the highest levels of stability. This may be explained by the existence of firing costs as well as by the fact that they are more concentrated in big, more stable, companies. The most frequent destination after leaving a formal salaried position is upper-tier informal wage-employment in Mexico, Paraguay, and Peru, or inactivity in Argentina, Brazil, and Ecuador. However, even in these three last countries, transitions between formality and upper-tier informality are common. On the contrary, in all the countries, very few formal employees transition into lower-tier informal salaried employment and even fewer to formal self-employment (at most 2 per cent). Informal wage-employees (considered both segments within this group) are the most mobile group of workers. Self-employed workers are in between. The lower labour stability of informal wage earners could be explained by the fact that they have low or no legal firing costs, thus making them attractive for employment in industries with unstable demand and for unstable occupations.

Beyond this general outlook, in all the countries analysed in this chapter, upper-tier informal wage-employees are even more mobile not only than formal workers but also than lower-tier informal workers. Except for Paraguay, they are, indeed, the most mobile group of workers. Only about one-third of them stay in this work status from year to year in Brazil, Ecuador, and Mexico; 40 per cent in Argentina and Peru; and 50 per cent in Paraguay. Upper-tier informal wage-employees are more likely to transition into formal wage-employment than into lower-tier informal salaried employment. Mobility patterns are very different in the case of lower-tier informal wage-employees who, as shown before, are located at the lowest step of the job ladder.

In all the countries analysed in this chapter, formal self-employed workers are located at the upper tail of the wage distribution, followed by formal wage-employees. Depending on the country, the third position is occupied by the upper-tier informal wage-employees or by informal self-employed workers.

To sum up, the distribution of workers in each work status is not random in any of the countries studied in this chapter. Prime-aged workers and those with a higher educational level are more likely to be formal than the rest of workers. In turn, wages are statistically higher among formal than informal positions. The results of the multinomial logit regressions shows that education is a highly correlated factor with movements from low-paid informal positions to better-paid jobs. In addition, in almost all cases, the linear coefficient of age (used as a proxy of general labour experience) indicates that the primed-aged are more stable in formal jobs than the other workers. Finally, except in Paraguay, men have higher probabilities of moving towards a better position than women. In almost all the countries, except in Paraguay, the transits from formality to any other work status implies a loss of wages. Upper-tier informal workers are the 'intermediate' group since they obtain an increase in wages when they move into a formal position but they experience a wage reduction when they transit to lower-tier informal work.

Chapter 8 examines the labour market dynamics of men and women in El Salvador and Nicaragua, focusing on the factors that help men and women move into an advantageous labour market state from an unfavourable state. The mobility patterns in the two countries show that workers in wage-employment have the least mobility: 89 per cent of formal and 71 per cent of informal wage-employees in El Salvador stay in the same work status from one year to the next, while, in Nicaragua, the same applies to 83 per cent and 72 per cent, respectively. There is little mobility between self-employment and formal wage-employment in either country. In this way, one could argue that once workers become unfavourably self-employed, they remain 'stuck' in self-employment. Of those who do enter formal salaried employment from other states, the largest number come from informal salaried employment, followed by unemployment. Some women (but almost no men) also enter formal salaried employment directly from unpaid domestic work.

Using pooled data from El Salvador and Nicaragua, the findings from the regression analysis suggest that education levels are the most important personal characteristic promoting transitions into non-agricultural advantageous labour market states[3] and reducing transitions out of advantageous labour market states. Access to public services such as utilities (electricity, water, and electricity) significantly increases the probability that men or women will transition into advantageous

[3] This chapter identifies 'advantageous' states to be formal wage-employees and self-employed workers with a decent income or owners of successful and growing firms.

non-agricultural self-employment. The results suggest that receiving more remittances decreases the probability of men (but not women) transitioning into formal wage-employment and decreases the probability that they will leave formal wage-employment. Older workers are more likely to become successfully self-employed than are younger workers.

Studying employment mobility in Mexico, Chapter 9 finds that formal wage-employees have the highest share of stayers among all groups (87.4 per cent), reflecting the greater job security enjoyed by these workers and the fact that they are at the top of the job ladder and are therefore less likely to change jobs willingly. In contrast, the greatest turnover is found among upper-tier informal workers, with about 34 per cent staying in this segment after one year. Of the upper-tier movers, about half move down the job ladder to lower-tier informal employment. The fact that lower-tier informal workers have a large share of stayers (around 58 per cent), implies that not only do these workers have the worst jobs but they also have a relatively small chance of moving out to a better segment of the market. The proportion of lower-tier workers that have moved up to higher levels is 23 per cent and 33 per cent for lower-tier self-employed and wage-employed, respectively. Earnings fall as one moves down the job ladder and, within each segment (formal, upper-tier, and lower-tier) the self-employed have higher earnings than the corresponding wage-employees in their segment.

The multinomial logit analysis of the age profiles of employment transitions indicate that lower-tier wage-employment serves as an entry state to the labour market, and transitions into self-employment tend to increase with age. However, as formal wage workers become older the probability of transiting into self-employment increases by a very small amount. The analysis also reveals that males are more likely to experience transitions up the job ladder, and this is particularly true for married men, while the opposite occurs for married women. Finally, schooling is a strong correlate of accessing jobs at the top of the ladder. Movements up the job ladder from lower to upper tiers involve earnings gains and so do the earnings changes of those remaining in the upper tier over the course of a year. Movements from formal employment into the upper-tier self-employment are accompanied by earnings losses. However, transitions from formal employment into upper-tier wage-employment involve earnings gains for some of the econometric models.

Chapter 10 uses detailed household-level data to analyse off-farm self-employment dynamics in Mali and Niger. In Niger, two-thirds (67 per cent) of self-employed workers did not change work status in 2014, with the majority of the stayers being found in the lower-tier informal status (50 per cent). One in five workers moved from informal lower-tier to informal upper-tier status. A larger share (45 per cent) of workers moved in the opposite direction. Only 1 per cent of lower-tier informal workers were able to transition to formal work compared to 3 per cent of upper-tier informal workers. More importantly, the small share of workers in formality shrunk further over time, with half of them sliding into lower-tier informality. In both Mali and Niger, the higher a worker in the job ladder, the higher are the earnings. Workers in formal self-employment earn more than twice the income of workers in informal work status. Among informal workers, the earnings of those in upper-tier employment status is substantially higher than the earnings of those in lower-tier work status.

In Niger, where panel data is available, the authors estimate the probability of self-employed workers moving from lower-tier informality in the first panel round to a higher work status in the second panel round. The findings show that workers' gender and age are significantly correlated with moving into formal and upper-tier informal work status. Self-employed men in lower-tier informal work are more likely than women to move out of this work status. Compared with the other age groups, younger and older self-employed workers are also less likely to move out of the lower-tier informal worker status. Household characteristics and initial wealth endowment are also drivers of the transitions. Initial asset holdings in terms of wealth are positively associated with transitions out of lower-tier informality.

The mobility patterns in Nigeria over the 2010–2016 period, assessed in Chapter 11, illustrate high levels of downward mobility out of formal self-employment: 22 per cent of formally self-employed workers transition into lower-tier informal self-employment and 44 per cent move into lower-tier informal wage-employment. At the same time, 22 per cent moved into formal wage-employment and 11 per cent moved into informal upper-tier wage-employment. Of the upper-tier informal wage-employed, 46.5 per cent moved into different work status groups. Out of the lower-tier informal self-employed, just a small proportion were able to move to upper-tier informal self-employment and to formal self-employment. Movements to formal wage-employment over the period was also minimal.

In terms of the earnings of workers across work status groups, the authors found that formal wage-employed workers received the highest average monthly earnings. The second-highest average monthly earnings were received by the upper-tier informal wage-employed, followed by the upper-tier informal self-employed and the formal self-employed. The lowest monthly earnings were received by lower-tier informal wage-employees. The logit regressions showed that education, marital status, and initial employment status are major drivers of transition between different work status.

Providing a comparative assessment across four SSA countries, Chapter 12 finds that transition patterns vary considerably across countries. However, a common finding is that employment stability tends to be highest among the formally wage-employed. In South Africa and Tanzania, around 80 per cent of all workers in formal wage-employment remain in this work status from one survey wave to the next. This share is somewhat lower in Ghana, at 65 per cent, and lowest in Uganda, at 48 per cent. Labour turnover tends to be higher in formal self-employment, with important differences observed across countries. In South Africa, among the formally self-employed, 51 per cent stay in this state, 13 per cent move into formal wage-employment, 23 per cent move into upper-tier informality, and only 13 per cent move into lower-tier informality (being either self-employed or wage-employed). On the contrary, only around 30 per cent of the formally self-employed in Ghana, Tanzania, and Uganda remain in formal self-employment from one survey wave to the next, while up to 40 per cent move into lower-tier informal self-employment. While these movements may partly be explained by reporting errors, business instability may also play a role. Furthermore, in Ghana, Tanzania, and Uganda, we observe high stability within lower-tier informal self-employment, with around two-thirds of the respective workers staying in this segment.

The 'stickiness' in this segment reflects the limited alternative job opportunities available to workers in this group. In Tanzania and Uganda, the authors observe a similar level of stagnation within lower-tier informal wage-employment, with about 80 per cent of the respective workers either remaining in this category or moving into lower-tier informal self-employment. In Ghana and South Africa, higher mobility out of lower-tier informal wage-employment into formal wage-employment is observed, suggesting that, for about 20 per cent of all workers in this group, lower-tier informal wage-employment can present a stepping stone into formal employment relationships. Furthermore, in all four countries, those in upper-tier informality are more likely to move into formality compared to those in lower-tier informality.

In terms of mean monthly earnings, formal workers earn more than informal workers, wage-employees earn more than the self-employed, and upper-tier informal workers earn more than lower-tier informal workers. Formal wage-employees are the highest-earning category in Ghana, South Africa, and Tanzania, while informal upper-tier self-employed have the highest earnings in Uganda. Across all countries, the lowest earning status is the lower-tier informal self-employed.

Using multinomial logistic regression for the analysis, the chapter finds that higher levels of education are associated with a higher likelihood of working formally. The correlation between educational attainment and formality status is stronger in wage-employment than in self-employment. Ceteris paribus, the largest inter-temporal change in earnings is experienced by those who were initially in formal employment and sustained this status over time. This may partly be attributable to unobserved individual characteristics of workers in this group but may also reflect a premium on experience in this labour market segment. While workers moving from formal to upper-tier informal employment experience a less favourable change in earnings compared to those who remain formal, they still tend to be better off than those who were already initially in upper-tier informal employment and maintained this status. Furthermore, it is observed that transitions from self-employment to wage-employment are not significantly associated with an earnings gain. Transition from wage-employment to self-employment tend to come with an earnings penalty, which, however, is not statistically significant.

Providing comparative evidence on Egypt, Tunisia, and Jordan, Chapter 13 shows that very few youths transition from vulnerable jobs[4] to non-vulnerable ones (formal public/private and employers) once they start out in the labour market in a vulnerable job. This is true even after 20 years in the case of Egypt. Tunisian youth also face precarious working conditions and low probability of transition. Jordanian youth are in somewhat better circumstances, but they are also more likely to exit the labour force altogether than to take on informal jobs. Socio-economic status as measured by family wealth, father's education, or father's occupation is a strong determinant of vulnerable employment, with those of higher socio-economic status likely to end up in non-vulnerable jobs and stay in them while those of lower socio-economic status rarely move up to better jobs.

3. Comparative perspective

Not all chapters in this book are able to examine all six work status groups in every country (see Appendix A for further details of the work status classifications used in all the country chapters). Two work status groups are identified in almost all countries: formal wage-employment and formal self-employment. Moreover, most chapters identify at least one lower-tier informal work status, even though not all chapters identify lower-tier informal work in both wage-employment and self-employment (e.g. Chapter 7 combines upper-tier and lower-tier informal self-employment). In the MENA countries (Jordan, Egypt, Tunisia), specific types of lower-tier informal workers, such as unpaid family workers, informal private-sector workers, and irregular workers, are separately identified.

The full six work status categories are reported for 10 countries (China, India, Costa Rica, Mexico, and Nicaragua in Latin America; Nigeria, Ghana, South Africa, Tanzania, and Uganda in SSA). In an additional five Latin American countries (Argentina, Brazil, Ecuador, Paraguay, and Peru) upper-tier and lower-tier self-employment are combined, but all other work status categories are reported. In Mali and Niger, only self-employed workers are considered. In El Salvador, self-employed informal workers are separated into lower-tier informal and upper-tier informal, but informal wage-employees are not. The work status categories reported in Indonesia and the three MENA countries (Jordan, Egypt, and Tunisia) differ in important aspects from the work status categories used in the other countries studied, which makes many comparisons between these countries and the other countries in the book difficult.

[4] These are jobs that are informal, lacking job security and stability, paid leave, social and health insurance, and safety (World Economic Forum 2012).

3.1 Distribution of workers between work status groups

Formal wage-employment is the largest work status in South Africa and in all Latin American countries studied except for Nicaragua, ranging from 25 per cent in Peru to 57 per cent in South Africa (Table 14.1). The share of formal wage-employment in China, India, and the SSA countries studied is much smaller, ranging from 9 per cent (India) to 22 per cent (China). Based on these patterns, it appears that formal wage-employment is generally larger in countries with higher average incomes compared to countries with lower average incomes.

Formal self-employment typically comprises only a small share of the workforce in all countries, ranging from 0 per cent in Nigeria to 9 per cent in Ghana and Tanzania.

Upper-tier informal wage-employment is larger in China, India, and in all of the middle-income Latin American countries (except for the country with the lowest income, Nicaragua) than in the SSA countries (except for the country with the highest income, South Africa). This pattern is not true for upper-tier informal self-employed, where in some SSA countries (Ghana, Mali, and Niger) this work status is larger than in Latin America, China, or India. This pattern suggests that upper-tier informal wage-employment tends to be a larger work status in middle-income countries compared to lower-income countries.

Lower-tier informal self-employment, which is generally characterized by low earnings and high levels of persistence, is a much larger work status in China and SSA (except for South Africa) than in India and Latin America. The share of workers who are in lower-tier informal self-employed in SSA (excluding South Africa) ranges from 42 per cent (Ghana) to 70 per cent (Niger), while in Latin America, the country where this work status is the largest (Nicaragua) includes only 17 per cent of workers.

On the other hand, lower-tier informal wage-employment is higher in China, India, and Latin America than in SSA. However, in all countries except for India and Nicaragua, lower-tier informal wage-employment still encompasses a relatively small proportion of all workers.

3.2 The job ladder

In almost all countries, the order of the work categories from highest wages to lowest wages is: (i) formal, (ii) upper-tier informal, and (iii) lower-tier informal. There are no clear distinctions between self-employed and wage-employees among formal and upper-tier informal workers. See Appendix B, where we present figures of job ladders for all the countries covered in the book.

Table 14.1 Share of workers by work status classifications

		Formal self-employed	Upper-tier informal self-employed	Lower-tier informal self-employed	Formal wage-employed	Upper-tier informal wage-employed	Lower-tier informal wage-employed
Asia	China (Ch. 3)	2	1	49	22	17	10
	India (Ch. 4)	1	8	21	9	29	32
	Indonesia (Ch. 5)	–	–	–	–	–	–
Latin America	Argentina (Ch. 7)	5	21		46	11	17
	Brazil (Ch. 7)	5	25		53	8	9
	Costa Rica (Ch. 6)	5	14	3	53	18	6
	Ecuador (Ch. 7)	3	31		41	10	15
	El Salvador (Ch. 8)	–		–	–	–	
	Mexico (Ch. 9)	6	6	11	47	10	20
	Nicaragua (Ch. 6)	1	20	17	18	26	19
	Paraguay (Ch. 7)	2	24		35	18	20
	Peru (Ch. 7)	5	40		25	14	15

Continued

Table 14.1 *Continued*

		Formal self-employed	Upper-tier informal self-employed	Lower-tier informal self-employed	Formal wage-employed	Upper-tier informal wage-employed	Lower-tier informal wage-employed
MENA	Egypt (Ch. 13)	–	–	–	–	–	–
	Jordan (Ch. 13)	–	–	–	–	–	–
	Tunisia (Ch. 13)	–	–	–	–	–	–
Sub-Saharan Africa	Ghana (Ch. 12)	9	12	42	13	5	19
	Mali (Ch. 10)	5	29	65	–	–	–
	Niger (Ch. 10)	4	25	70	–	–	–
	Nigeria (Ch. 11)	0	2	60	19	1	17
	South Africa (Ch. 12)	4	5	4	57	9	21
	Tanzania (Ch. 12)	9	4	43	12	3	29
	Uganda (Ch. 12)	3	6	43	12	11	26

Note: The work status classifications used in chapters 5, 8, and 13 are too country-specific to allow for full comparability across all categories. For Mexico, Chapter 9 identifies all six status groups, while Chapter 7 combines upper-tier and lower-tier informal self-employment. The distribution of workers across status groups is in a similar range in both chapters.

Source: authors' compilation based on country studies.

Table 14.2 Work status with highest average earnings

Work status	ASIA	Latin America	MENA	Sub-Saharan Africa
Formal self-employed	China	Argentina, Brazil, Costa Rica, Ecuador, Mexico, Paraguay, Peru		Mali, Niger
Formal wage-employed	India	Nicaragua	Egypt (private), Jordan (private), Tunisia (public)	Ghana, Nigeria, South Africa, Tanzania
Upper-tier informal self-employed	Indonesia (higher-tier informal)	El Salvador (advantageous non-agricultural)	–	Uganda

Source: authors' compilation based on country studies.

Formal wage-employees and formal self-employed are at the top of the wage ladder (Table 14.2). Average wages in these formal work status groups are higher than the average wages in any of the other four informal work status groups in 19 of the 22 countries covered in this book (the exceptions are Indonesia, El Salvador, and Uganda, where the highest wages are in upper-tier informal self-employment). For the different types of formal workers, average wages are highest in formal self-employment in 10 countries and highest in formal wage-employment in 9 countries (Table 14.2). Whether the formal self-employed or formal wage-employed workers report higher earnings is subject to substantial regional variation. Out of the 10 countries where formal self-employed workers lead the earnings ranking, 7 are located in Latin America. In SSA and MENA, by contrast, formal wage-employees tend to be at the top of the earnings ladder (see Table 14.2).

Formal self-employment typically comprises only a small share of the workforce. For example, in countries where formal self-employment constitutes the highest-paying work status, it only comprises 2 per cent (China and Paraguay) to 6 per cent (Mexico) of total employment. Because of the small sample size for this status, comparisons of the earnings of formal self-employed and formal wage-employed workers should be interpreted with care.

The average earnings of both upper-tier informal self-employed and wage-employees tend to be above the earnings of lower-tier informal self-employed and wage-employees. As noted, in all but 3 of 22 countries, upper-tier informal wage-employees earn less than formal workers. This is not consistent with the hypothesis that upper-tier informal wage-employees voluntarily forgo social

Table 14.3 Work status with lowest average earnings

Work status	ASIA	Latin America	MENA	Sub-Saharan Africa
(Lower-tier) informal self-employed	China, India, Indonesia (lower-tier informal)	El Salvador (unfavourable agricultural), Mexico	Egypt (unpaid family worker)	Mali, Niger, Ghana, South Africa, Tanzania, Uganda[c]
(Lower-tier) informal wage-employed	–	Argentina,[a] Brazil,[a] Costa Rica, Ecuador[a], Nicaragua[b], Paraguaya, Peru[a]	Jordan (irregular), Tunisia (informal private)	Nigeria

Notes: [a] Average earnings for upper-tier and lower-tier informal self-employment are grouped together in these five Latin American countries. [b] For Nicaragua, chapter 6 identifies lower-tier informal wage-employment as the lowest paying category, while Chapter 8 identifies unfavourable agricultural self-employment as the least paid status. [c] For Uganda, average earnings are virtually identical in lower-tier informal self-employment and wage-employment.
Source: authors' compilation based on country studies.

security and other labour protections of formal work in exchange for higher earnings as informal workers. Upper-tier informal wage-employees and upper-tier informal self-employees tend to have similar earnings.

Generally, the lowest-paid work status groups are either lower-tier informal self-employed or lower tier informal wage-employees (Table 14.3). Some regional patterns appear in Table 14.3. In the Asian and large parts of the Central American and SSA cases, the lowest average pay is recorded in lower-tier informal self-employment. In the South American cases, as well as in Costa Rica, Jordan, Tunisia, and Nigeria, we see the lowest average earnings in lower-tier informal wage-employment. However, it is important to note that upper-tier and lower-tier informal self-employed wages are grouped together in most of the Latin American countries (Argentina, Brazil, Ecuador, Paraguay, and Peru) and so these observed regional patterns may misrepresent the Latin American pattern.

3.3 Transitions between work status groups

One of the key questions at the centre of this project is whether lower-tier informal work is a dead end where, once workers enter, there is little chance of moving up the job ladder. Examining transitions between work status groups, we find some evidence of this, especially among the lower-tier informal self-employed (see Appendix C, where we present the transition matrices by country and region).

In 12 of 15 countries where comparisons are possible, lower-tier informal self-employment has the first or second highest rates of persistence (where persistence is defined as a relatively high conditional probability of staying in the initial work status).

However, this broader pattern is subject to substantial cross-country heterogeneity. The highest persistence rates in lower-tier informal self-employment are observed in China (86 per cent), Indonesia (81 per cent), Niger (79 per cent), Nigeria (61 per cent), Ghana (67 per cent), Tanzania (65 per cent), and Uganda (73 per cent) and the lowest in Costa Rica (34 per cent), Nicaragua (34 per cent), and South Africa (31 per cent), followed by India (48 per cent). Thus, in one group of countries (China, Indonesia, Niger, Nigeria, Ghana, Tanzania, and Uganda), lower-tier informal self-employment appears to be mostly a dead end with few alternative opportunities, whereas in another group of countries (South Africa, Costa Rica, Nicaragua, and India), informal self-employment appears to be a more temporary and dynamic state, with greater options for upward mobility.

Overall, more workers appear to remain 'stuck' in lower-tier informal self-employment than in lower-tier informal wage-employment. In 10 countries where the comparison is possible, persistence rates are higher in lower-tier informal self-employment, while in only 3 countries, persistence rates are higher in lower-tier informal wage-employment. In lower-tier informal wage-employment, the highest persistence rates are observed in Mexico (49–57 per cent) and Paraguay (53 per cent) and the lowest in Costa Rica (28 per cent). While the chapter on Mexico argues that lower-tier informal workers have a small chance of moving to a better segment of the market, in Costa Rica and Nicaragua, mobility out of lower-tier informal wage work is higher than out of any other work status, indicating substantial upward mobility as most of these workers transition to higher-paid work status groups. In most of the SSA countries covered, there is also similar within-regional heterogeneity in mobility patterns. While in Tanzania and Uganda, 80 per cent of the respective workers either remain in this category or move into lower-tier informal self-employment, in Ghana and South Africa, higher upward mobility is observed, suggesting that lower-tier informal wage-employment can present a stepping stone into formal employment relationships. The higher entry rate into formal employment in Ghana and South Africa compared to Tanzania and Uganda may be associated with the countries' higher level of development and higher availability of formal wage jobs.

In almost all countries, formal wage-employment is the most persistent work status. This is true in 13 of 18 countries where comparisons are possible. This is consistent with formal wage-employment as the most preferred work status where workers are unlikely to leave voluntarily once they obtain employment. The high persistence in this status may also be attributed to the nature of the employment relationship—usually defined in terms of having a written, permanent work contract with social security entitlements, indicating higher turnover costs—as well as the typical engagement in larger-scale private companies or government jobs, which may provide a more stable work environment. Formal self-employment, which tends to be the smallest work status, displays relatively lower persistence compared to formal wage-employment, indicating higher risks of downward shifts. An exception from this rule is Brazil, where 71 per cent of formally self-employed workers sustain their position.

Across regions, we observe upper-tier informality, especially upper-tier informal wage-employment, to be the least persistent work status. In 12 of 15 countries where the comparison is possible, upper-tier informal wage-employment is the first or second most mobile work status. Across regions, upper-tier informal wage-employment can present a stepping stone into formal wage-employment, with an average transition rate from upper-tier informal into formal wage-employment of about 20 per cent reported across the Asian and Latin American countries and 35 per cent for the SSA case studies. However, transitions out of upper-tier informality present not only opportunities for upward mobility but also risks for downward slides with more or less equal probabilities. Transitions out of upper-tier informal wage-employment are more likely down the job ladder than up the job ladder in seven countries, but more likely up the job ladder in six countries. Movements from upper-tier informal self-employment to formal self-employment occur less frequently but, with an average rate of 10 per cent compared to 4 per cent, are still more frequent than transitions from lower-tier informal to formal self-employment.

Concerning the personal worker-level characteristics that can be associated with mobility patterns, first, the education level of a worker is consistently mentioned as one of the key factors associated with upward transitions into better-paying work status groups. Education also tends to be positively associated with employment stability in higher-wage work status groups and a lower risk of downward shifts. Second, most studies find that men display higher chances of moving towards better positions than women. Particularly married men display a higher likelihood to climb the job ladder, while the opposite is true for married women. Moreover, male workers are more likely to move into wage-employment, while female workers are more likely to stay in self-employment. Considering that self-employment offers more flexible working times, this may reflect a preference or constraint. Third, workers in prime working age appear to hold the most favourable positions in most contexts. In some countries, lower-tier wage-employment appears to serve as an entry point to the labour market for young workers, while transitions into self-employment tend to increase with age. Household wealth in terms of assets is furthermore positively associated with transitions out of lower-tier informality. Even though assets can benefit household production, this relationship may be explained by third factors and does not warrant causal claims.

3.4 Limitations of the empirical analysis

Two features of our book make it particularly noteworthy but also point to some limitations of our empirical analysis. First, our book is perhaps the first of its kind in examining heterogeneity within informal work by applying a common conceptual framework and empirical methodology across a diverse range of countries across Africa, Asia, and Latin America. The fact that we can do like-for-like comparisons using a common conceptual approach to categorizing formal and informal employment is a strength of our empirical analysis and aids greatly in gleaning the comparative findings that we have presented in this section. However, to implement the work status classifications introduced in Chapter 1 of the book, the authors of the country chapters had to rely on existing secondary data sources such as labour force surveys. As noted in the beginning of this section, our ideal-type classification of the six work status groups could not be implemented in all the countries due to data limitations. Specifically, the available data was not granular enough in some country contexts to sufficiently distinguish between lower-tier and upper-tier informal employment. Our book points to the need for labour force surveys in developing countries to obtain information on occupations of workers that can differentiate between formal, lower-tier, and upper-tier informal employment, and between self-employment and wage-employment with sufficient accuracy.

Second, we were able to document transition patterns across different formality and work status groups as well as to explore the possible factors that may explain transitions across work status as all country studies were able to use panel data of two or more waves. The availability of panel data is scarce in low- and middle-income countries. A key contribution of the book is that authors are able to assess patterns and correlates of labour market transitions with such data, which would not be possible if we had to rely on cross-sectional data. However, for several of the countries, the panel data lacked representativeness at the national level, given the relatively small number of workers that were surveyed initially or could be followed in the panels. In addition, the relatively few waves of panel data that were available, especially for SSA, did not allow us to infer whether the movement of workers from one work status to another was temporary (due to business cycle-related factors) or more permanent. Therefore, it is critical that we have panel data that follows workers over time, with larger representativeness, and over longer periods, especially for low-income countries. We hope that the book can serve as a call to arms for data-collecting agencies like national statistical organizations and multilateral development agencies, such the World Bank, to compile such panel data for developing country labour markets.

4. Some policy options suggested by the chapters

The chapter authors were asked for the key policy recommendations of their findings. The answers were often quite nuanced, and their emphases differed considerably across the different chapters.

Here, we summarize the recommendations across several dimensions. One regional difference bears mention at the outset. In the Africa chapters, formal job creation did not receive as much attention as in Asia and Latin America. This may be because formal wage-employment is such a small percentage of total employment in Africa, with the notable exception of South Africa.

4.1 Economic growth

Economic growth was suggested by many. Some country studies suggest that economic growth, by itself, may not be sufficient for improving the livelihoods of lower-tier informal workers. For example, the India study characterized lower-tier informal workers as being in a dead-end work status, despite the high-growth phase of the economy, leading the authors to conclude that direct state interventions that enhance the livelihoods of lower-tier informal workers may be necessary. The Latin America chapter called for economic growth to be complemented with a coherent system of investment in education and training, as well as other active labour market policies.

4.2 Raising the earnings of the lower-tier self-employed

Raising the earnings of the lower-tier self-employed was the most common policy recommendation. The specific suggestions varied from place to place:

> In Ghana, South Africa, Tanzania, and Uganda, policies should not be one size fits all. Given the limited alternative job opportunities for those working informally, the authors recommend (1) focus on policy measures to enhance the livelihoods of those workers where they are and (2) do not emphasize policies that aim to reduce the regulatory barriers to formalization (see chapter 12, Danquah et al. this volume).

In Nigeria, given the limited employment opportunities in the formal sector, the authors suggest that creating better working conditions for informal workers would greatly enhance their welfare and encourage them to stay within their employment.

In Mali and Niger, the focus of the policy recommendations is transforming informal work and livelihoods. Specifically, (i) addressing household-related factors such as asset holdings, livestock endowment, and non-labour income; and (ii) promoting and strengthening non-farm employment.

4.3 Creating more formal jobs for those down the job ladder to move into

The recommendations for China include: recognizing the insufficient labour demand in the formal sector and therefore creating more formal jobs; creating more wage-employment, as opposed to self-employment; these results are consistent by gender (female vs male), hukou type (agriculture vs non-agriculture), and hukou location (local vs migrant); these recommendations are consistent with China's urban–rural integration plan.

In Indonesia, the authors suggest that, rather than creating policies that try to push low-tier informal-sector workers to become high-tier informal-sector workers, government would be better advised to create jobs, albeit lower-tier ones, that lower-tier informal workers can apply for.

In Mexico, the author states that 'many of the urban informal workers are in this sector because of a lack of better options [...] There is an overwhelming preference for formal wage jobs across the various segments of the market.' The study distinguishes between the worker's decision to apply for formal wage jobs and the hiring decisions of formal firms, noting that policies that seek to encourage formal wage-employment from the supply side of the labour market need to consider how they can affect these two dimensions—for example, expanding access to higher education as well as encouraging female participation in formal employment through the provision of market substitutes to home production.

4.4 Providing those on the bottom of the job ladder with more human capital

The study of six Latin American countries calls for increased investment in human capital, including 'a coherent system of training' and other active labour market policies.

The chapters on Costa Rica, Nicaragua, and El Salvador distinguish between levels and changes. Changes in formal education are a statistically insignificant determinant of whether or not a worker transitions up the job ladder, probably because few workers earn more formal education after they enter the labour force. On the other hand, many workers participate in vocational training after entering the labour force. In Costa Rica, Nicaragua, and El Salvador, it is found that earning vocational training and investment in human capital after entering the labour force promotes both transitions up the job ladder and improvements in the earnings of those who remain in lower-tier work. Vocational training policy should focus on experienced workers. It should target those currently working as informal employees, not formal wage-employees. In addition, the authors urge that efforts be made to reduce school drop-out rates, especially among girls, and to promote secondary school completion through alternative programmes for those already outside of the school system.

In China, the chapter calls for education and training programmes to self-employed workers in the informal sector and the lower tier.

4.5 Formalizing the upper-tier informal and increasing the enforcement of labour protections

Our framework in this book suggests that upper-tier informal workers may be informal voluntarily, willing to forego social security and other labour protections in exchange for higher wages or the flexibility of informal work. For example, in India and Latin America, upper-tier informal wage-employees are often employed in formal firms and work alongside workers who have social security and other labour protections. This suggests that one appropriate strategy for promoting formality is to increase enforcement of labour protection laws in formal firms and among upper-tier informal wage-employees. Such policies are likely to be most effective in countries where the upper-tier wage-employees are a large percentage of workers. Indeed, the country studies which suggest this policy as a way to promote formality are China and Latin America, regions where our country studies find that upper-tier wage-employment is common (especially compared to SSA).

In six Latin American countries, given that the increase in labour formality has slowed down, progress in employment formalization and the strengthening of labour institutions policies are identified as essential mechanisms to overcome poverty and achieve social protection.

In Costa Rica, increase compliance with labour regulations with respect to labour protections and social security payroll taxes, thereby enabling informal workers to become formal.

In China, enforce compliance with the 2008 Labour Contract Law, which mandates that employers provide work insurance and pensions to employees.

4.6 Other country-specific and region-specific measures

In North Africa, a particularly pressing issue is the employment problem facing young people. The study of Egypt, Jordan, and Tunisia highlights the need for support systems for vulnerable workers, especially youths, the poor, and those with less educated parents. It also calls for aligning skill supply with demand and creating more acceptable working conditions in the informal and formal sectors.

In El Salvador and Nicaragua, recommendations were made specifically for women by getting them out of domestic work. There, women cannot be helped by promoting advantageous agricultural self-employment because agriculture in both countries is dominated by men.

In China, the authors suggest that to enable movements from lower-tier to upper-tier self-employment the government should create the conditions for the integration of rural and urban markets, as suggested in the government's policy guidelines for addressing the imbalanced development between rural and urban areas. The authors also suggest that an additional policy to help integrate rural and urban labour markets is to abolish or revise the hukou system, which ties the provision of social services, such as education and health care, to the region and city where a person is born (even if they migrate from rural to urban areas).

References

Iversen,V., A. Krishna, and K. Sen (2017). 'Rags to Riches? Intergenerational Occupational Mobility in India'. *Economic and Political Weekly*, 52(4): 107–114.

Natarajan, R. R., S. Schotte, and K. Sen (2020). 'Transitions between Informal and Formal Jobs in India: Patterns, Correlates, and Consequences'. WIDER Working Paper No. 101/2020, Helsinki: UNU-WIDER.

Saha, B., K. Sen, and D. Maiti (2013). 'Trade Open-ness, Labour Institutions and Flexibilisation: Theory and Evidence from India'. *Labour Economics*, 24(2): 180–195.

WEF (World Economic Forum) (2012). *Addressing the 100 Million Youth Challenge: Perspectives on Youth Employment in the Arab World in 2012*. Geneva: World Economic Forum.

APPENDIX A

Work status definition and operationalization

II. ASIA

3. Transforming informal work and livelihoods in China

Carl Lin, Linxiang Ye, and Wei Zhang

Work status group	Definition/operationalization
Formal self-employed	A person who is self-employed and pays work insurance (retirement pensions, medical insurance, unemployment insurance, work injury insurance, and maternity insurance) as an individual or a private business owner. Note that such work insurance belongs to work protection which has a higher protection level than New Rural Cooperative Medical Insurance and Urban Resident Basic Medical Insurance. Most Chinese residents, regardless of being employed or not, are included in the social protection system. It is therefore not straightforward to identify formal employment by whether they have work insurance in the case of China.
Upper-tier informal self-employed	A person who is self-employed in individual and private businesses in which the size of the work unit is equal to or greater than seven people. Or the self-employed who have college degrees or above and in job classes 1 (family agricultural work), 3 (agricultural work for other families), and 5 (non-agricultural casual workers).
Lower-tier informal self-employed	A person who is self-employed in the informal sector and has a high-school diploma or below. Farmers and individually-owned small-scale businesses dominate this category.
Formal wage-employed	The formal wage-employed are wage workers whose employers provide them with work insurance such as retirement pensions, medical insurance, unemployment insurance, work injury insurance, and maternity insurance.
Upper-tier informal wage-employed	A person who works for wages in the formal sector (governments, party, people's organizations, military, state-owned and collectively owned public institutions, state-owned or state-controlled enterprises, companies with foreign capital investments or with investments from Hong Kong, Macao, Taiwan, or working in a firm employing seven or more people) but where the employer does not provide work insurance.
Lower-tier informal wage-employed	An employed worker in the informal sector where the work unit does not provide any work insurance. These individuals include, for example, labourers employed by private businesses, agricultural workers, and non-agricultural casual workers.

4. Moving up or down the job ladder in India: examining informality–formality transitions

Rajesh Raj Natarajan, Simone Schotte, and Kunal Sen

Work status group	Definition/operationalization
Formal self-employed	All wage workers with permanent job contracts are classified as formal wage-employees. All permanent workers in India are offered labour law protection and are also entitled to social security benefits.
Upper-tier informal self-employed	Informal wage workers are classified as upper-tier informal if they either work in occupations that require some type of training or receive some type of de facto benefit (such as meals or housing) from employers.
Lower-tier informal self-employed	All remaining informal workers are classified as lower-tier informal.
Formal wage-employed	All self-employed workers who are in professions that require a high level of skill (Division 0–1, INCO), or employ 10 or more workers are classified as formal self-employed.
Upper-tier informal wage-employed	All informal self-employed workers who employ fewer than 10 but at least one hired worker are classified as upper-tier informal. These also include workers who employ more than 10 workers but operate from home or from a mobile location.
Lower-tier informal wage-employed	All informal self-employed workers who employ only household workers are classified as lower-tier informal self-employed. All contributing family workers are also included in this category.

5. Progress and stagnation in the livelihood of informal workers in an emerging economy: long-term evidence from Indonesia

Mayang Rizky, Daniel Suryadarma, and Asep Suryahadi

Work status group	Definition/operationalization
Low-tier informal	We identify low-tier informal workers as workers who are self-employed without help or self-employed with the help of unpaid family/temporary workers and with work types in sales, labour, production, transportation, and unskilled. All unpaid family workers are also considered to be low-tier informal workers.

Continued

Continued

Work status group	Definition/operationalization
High-tier informal	Those who are self-employed with the help of permanent/regular worker(s) are high-tier informal workers. Workers who are self-employed without help or self-employed with the help of unpaid family/temporary worker(s) and whose work type is professional, managerial, or official/administrative are also considered to be high-tier informal workers. The classification of high-tier informal workers is determined not only by the data on daily primary duties but also by the two-digit occupation code. It includes codes of 40 or less and codes 50, 60, 70, 80, and 90, which indicate a managerial level of workers in the service, agricultural, and production sectors.
Low-tier formal	Those who are employees of either the government or a private company, in any job type, are classified as formal workers. Employees whose work type is sales, labour, production, transportation, and unskilled are considered to be low-tier formal.
High-tier formal	Those who are employees of either the government or a private company and whose work type is professional, managerial, or official/administrative are considered to be high-tier formal.

III. LATIN AMERICA

6. Transforming informal work and livelihoods in Costa Rica and Nicaragua

Enrique Alaniz, T. H. Gindling, Catherine Mata, and Diego Rojas

Work status group	Costa Rica	Nicaragua
Formal self-employed	We identify formal self-employed workers as the self-employed (own-account or owners) who follow all regulations—specifically, those who both contribute to social security and are registered. Workers are identified as registered if they are registered in the National Records or other public institution or keep formal accounts for reporting to the government.	Formal self-employed workers are those who are affiliated with social security in any capacity.

Upper-tier informal self-employed	These are identified as those who comply with some but not all regulations—specifically, the self-employed (own-account and owners) who are registered or receive some type of social security health insurance (including the special regime, as a direct dependent of an insured employee, insured by the government, or with private insurance) but are not both registered and receiving social security. Even if they are neither registered nor receiving social security, other self-employed workers are classified as upper-tier informal self-employed if they are in a profession that requires post-secondary or vocational education, if they are employers with at least one employee, or if their place of work has a fixed premises.	Upper-tier informal self-employed are defined as those who work in a unit with at least one wage-employee or who have private or other self-paid health insurance.
Lower-tier informal self-employed	These are self-employed workers who have no type of health insurance and are not registered, have no paid employees, and are not professional or technical workers. They include those whose place of work has no fixed premises (i.e. they work in the owner's dwelling, are itinerant, or work on construction sites or agricultural plots).	Lower-tier informal self-employed are all other self-employed workers who have no health insurance (either social security or self-paid).
Formal wage-employees	These are wage-employees whose employers contribute to social security or who are public-sector employees.	These are wage-employees whose employers contribute to social security for the worker or who are public-sector employees.
Upper-tier informal wage-employees	These are wage-employees whose employers do not contribute to social security but who have social security health insurance as a dependant of someone who is directly insured; who pay through the 'special regime' or '*cuota voluntaria*'; who are insured by the state or private insurance;	Upper-tier informal employees are all employees who are neither formal nor lower-tier informal.

Continued

Continued

Work status group	Costa Rica	Nicaragua
	or who receive other mandated benefits such as paid annual leave, paid sick leave, work risk insurance, or *aguinaldo* (mandated one-month salary bonus in December) or from whose salary income taxes are deducted; or who are professional or technical employees.	
Lower-tier informal wage-employees	These are all other employees—that is, lower-tier informal employees have no health insurance and receive no other labour protection benefits.	Lower-tier informal wage-employees are identified as domestic servants and others working in a private household.

Source: authors' construction based on ILO (2019).

7. Informality, labour transitions, and the livelihoods of workers in Latin America

Roxana Maurizio and Ana Paula Monsalvo

Work status	Measurement
Formal wage-employees	Argentina: includes those who answer that their employers make payroll deductions to pay social security contributions. Brazil: includes those who have signed a labour contract. Paraguay, Mexico, and Peru: includes those enrolled in a pension system. Ecuador: includes those indicating that they receive social insurance from the job.
Upper-tier informal wage-employees	These are informal wage-employees working in firms with more than five employees
Lower-tier informal wage-employees	These are informal wage-employees working in firms with up to five employees
Formal self-employed	These are owners in enterprises with more than five employees and professional own-account workers
Informal self-employed	These are owners in enterprises with up to five employees, non-professional own-account workers, and unpaid family workers.

8. Self-employment and labour market dynamics of men and women in El Salvador and Nicaragua

Enrique Alaniz, Alma Espino, and T. H. Gindling

Work status group	Definition/organization
Formal wage-employees	Both in Nicaragua and El Salvador, this category includes wage and salaried workers who are benefiting from social security and are either employed full time or part time.
Informal wage-employees (upper-tier and lower-tier informal wage-employees)	In both countries, this category includes all wage-employees not benefiting from social security.
Advantageous non-agricultural self-employed (formal and upper-tier informal non-agricultural self-employed)	In Nicaragua, this category includes self-employed workers who are not engaged in agriculture with household per capita consumption above the poverty line. It also includes employers of firms with five or more workers and employers of firms with fewer than five employees whose firm increased the number of employees in the past year. In El Salvador, this category includes self-employed workers who are not engaged in agriculture and whose labour earnings are greater than the legal minimum wage.
Advantageous agricultural self-employed (formal and upper-tier informal agricultural self-employed)	In Nicaragua, this category includes self-employed workers who are engaged in agriculture with household per capita consumption above the poverty line. It also includes employers of firms with five or more workers and employers of firms with fewer than five employees whose firm increased the number of employees in the past year. In El Salvador, this category includes self-employed workers who are engaged in agriculture and whose labour earnings are greater than the legal minimum wage.
Unfavourable non-agricultural self-employed (lower-tier informal non-agricultural self-employed)	In both countries, this category includes all self-employed workers and employers who are not engaged in agriculture and do not meet the conditions to be classified as 'advantageous non-agricultural self-employment'.
Unfavourable agricultural self-employed (lower-tier informal agricultural self-employed)	In both countries, this category includes all self-employed workers and employers who are engaged in agriculture and do not meet the conditions to be classified as 'advantageous agricultural self-employment'.

Continued

Continued

Work status group	Definition/organization
Unpaid family worker	In both countries, this category includes any employed person who works without remuneration in a business, firm, or family farm.
Unemployed	In both countries, this category includes people who, over the past week or month before the survey, looked for work or made efforts to install their own business or company. Similarly, those who were not working but already had jobs and were starting the next month are included in this category.

9. Informal work in urban Mexico: characteristics, dynamics, and workers' preferences

Robert Duval-Hernández

Work status group	Definition/operationalization
Formal self-employed	These are the self-employed (own-account or owners) who operate a business registered with tax authorities and with fixed work premises. Also, all employers (with at least one employee) in the agricultural sector enter this category.
Upper-tier informal self-employed	Upper-tier informal self-employed (own-account and owners) are those who voluntarily enrol for social security coverage (through the government or have private insurance) or work in a profession that requires post-secondary or vocational education, or they are employers with at least one employee, or if their place of work has fixed premises.
Lower-tier informal self-employed	These are all other self-employed not in the above two categories. This includes all self-employed working in agriculture.
Formal wage-employees	These are wage-employees whose employers contribute to social security, except if the employer itself is a non-registered business (i.e. the firm is not registered with tax authorities and does not have fixed work premises).
Upper-tier informal wage-employees	These are wage-employees whose employers do not contribute to social security (or if they do, the employer itself is a non-registered business) *but* who receive other benefits such as paid annual leave, profit-sharing, (government-sponsored) housing credit, day-care facilities, private insurance (life or health), saving funds, time for parental care, or *aguinaldo* (mandatory one-month salary bonus in December), or work in a profession that requires post-secondary or vocational education, or they have a permanent contract.
Lower-tier informal wage-employees	These are all other employees. Also, all unpaid workers are included in this category.

IV. SUB-SAHARAN AFRICA

10. The dynamics of off-farm self-employment in the West African Sahel

Sènakpon Fidèle Ange Dedehouanou and Didier Y. Alia

Work status group	Definition/operationalization
Formal self-employed (1)	We identify formal self-employed workers as own-account workers (with no salary) that (i) keep written accounts, (ii) have a commercial register, or (iii) hold a fiscal identification number given by the Directorate General of Taxes (DGI). We also include owners or employers (with at least one salaried worker) that follow at least one of the above regulations and have additionally registered worker(s) in the national social security fund.
Upper-tier informal self-employed (2)	Upper-tier informal self-employed are identified as those who do not comply with the above regulations (in 1) but operate their businesses in fixed premises outside the dwelling.
Lower-tier informal self-employed (3)	These are self-employed workers that do not comply with the above regulations (in 1) but have no fixed business premises (outside the owner's dwelling) or are itinerant/mobile.

11. Informal–formal workers' transition in Nigeria: a livelihood analysis

Abiodun O. Folawewo and Olusegun A. Orija

Work status group	Definition/operationalization
Formal wage-employees	These are workers in public-sector (government) and large private firm/organization employment that are covered by official labour market regulations such as recruitment and dismissal, compensation, and other forms of employment protection laws (EPL) and have National Health Insurance Scheme (NHIS) coverage.
Formal self-employed	Since the Global Human Settlement (GHS) data do not include information on business registration, participation in the NHIS is used as an important criterion for determination of the formality status of an employment. Thus, workers who are self-employed (own-account and owners) but have NHIS are classified as formal self-employed.

Continued

Continued

Work status group	Definition/operationalization
Upper-tier informal wage-employees	Within informal employment, the educational level of workers is used as the distinguishing factor for whether they belong to the upper or lower tier. As noted earlier and supported by the literature (e.g. Gutierrez et al. 2019), a majority of informal workers have little education; consequently, informal salary (wage-employed) workers with post-secondary and tertiary education and without NHIS are classified as upper-tier informal wage-employees.
Lower-tier informal wage-employees	These are salary (wage-employed) workers with secondary education and below who work in business organizations outside of public-sector and large private firms/organizations and without NHIS contribution are regarded as lower-tier informal wage-employees.
Upper-tier self-employed	Workers who are self-employed (own-account and owners) and have post-secondary and tertiary education are classified as upper-tier informal self-employed.
Lower-tier self-employed	These workers who are self-employed (own-account and owners) with secondary education and below are identified as lower-tier self-employed.

12. Informal–formal transitions in work status in sub-Saharan Africa: a comparative perspective

Michael Danquah, Simone Schotte, and Kunal Sen

Work status group	Definition/operationalization
Formal self-employed	These are workers (own-account or owners) with business activities that are registered with national state authorities (e.g. with social security, sales, or income tax authorities).
Upper-tier informal self-employed	These are workers (own-account or owners) with unregistered business activities who either employ at least one person (who is not a household member) or who are in activities that require some type of professional training (defined as International Standard Classification of Operations (ISCO) groups 1–4, covering managers, professionals, technicians, and clerks).
Lower-tier informal self-employed	All other self-employed workers not in the above two categories are classified as lower informal. This includes all contributing family workers, irrespective of the nature of the enterprise. Workers in smallholder agriculture (family farms) would be classified as lower informal but have been excluded from the main analysis presented in this chapter.

Formal wage-employed	These are employees who contribute to social security.
Upper-tier informal wage-employed	Wage workers not covered by social protection provisions who are in professions that require some type of professional training (ISCO groups 1–4) are classified as upper informal. In addition, wage workers who report having a written employment agreement and/or are entitled to de facto benefits such as paid sick or maternity leave fall into this category.
Lower-tier informal wage-employed	All other wage workers not in the above two categories are classified as lower informal wage-employed.

V. NORTH AFRICA AND THE MIDDLE EAST

13. The evolution of vulnerable employment in Egypt, Jordan, and Tunisia

Shireen AlAzzawi and Vladimír Hlásny

Non-vulnerable employment	**Formal private**	Private-sector workers with either social security or a contract in the past three months
	Formal public	Public-sector and government workers with either social security or a contract in the past three months
	Employer	Employers, who employ others, where no information on formality status of the establishment was available in the survey
Vulnerable employment	**Self-employed**	Self-employed, without employing others, where no information on formality status of the establishment was available in the survey
	Unpaid family worker	People who work without pay in a market-orientated establishment operated by a related person living in the same household
	Irregular wage worker	Workers who receive wages on a daily basis or are in temporary employment
	Informal private	Private-sector workers who either lack social security or had not had a contract in the past three months

APPENDIX B

The job ladder

II. ASIA

3. Transforming informal work and livelihoods in China

Carl Lin, Linxiang Ye, and Wei Zhang

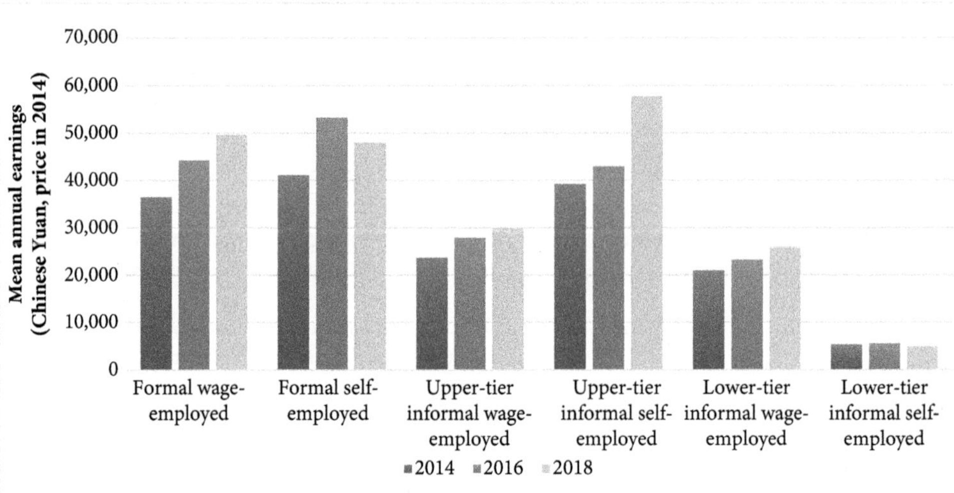

Fig. B.3 Mean earnings by work status: the case of China

Note: Earnings of 2016 and 2018 are in 2014 prices.
Source: authors' calculations based on China Family Panel Studies (CFPS) data (Institute of Social Science, Peking University 2018).

4. Moving up or down the job ladder in India: examining informality–formality transitions

Rajesh Raj Natarajan, Simone Schotte, and Kunal Sen

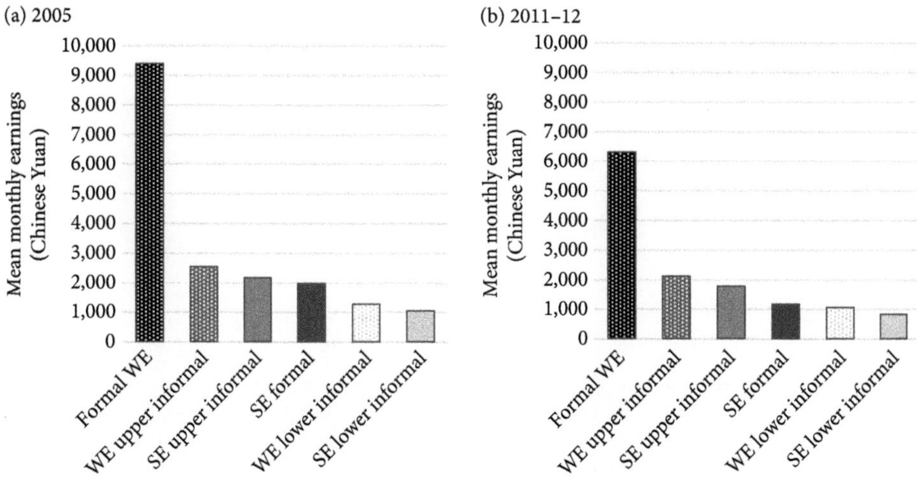

Fig. B.4 Mean monthly earnings by work status (2004–2005, Indian Rupees)
Source: authors' calculations based on IHDS data.

5. Progress and stagnation in the livelihood of informal workers in an emerging economy: long-term evidence from Indonesia

Mayang Rizky, Daniel Suryadarma, and Asep Suryahadi

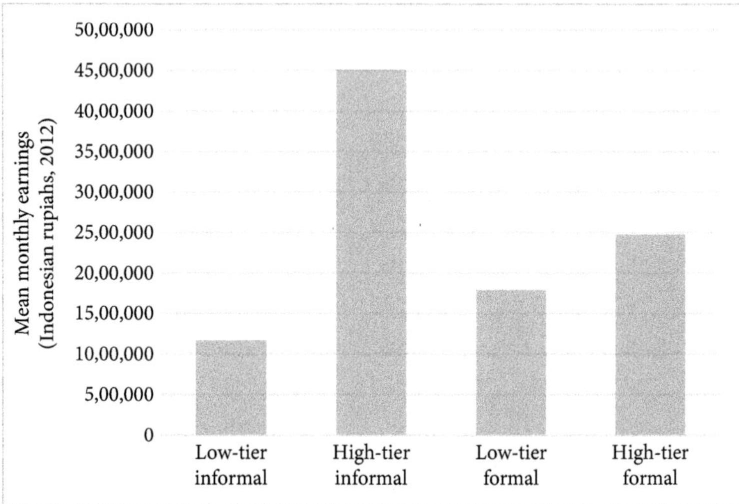

Fig. B.5 Mean earnings by work status: the case of Indonesia
Note: Mean monthly earning in main job, 2014.
Source: authors' calculation based on Indonesian Family Life Survey (IFLS5) 2014.

III. LATIN AMERICA

6. Transforming informal work and livelihoods in Costa Rica and Nicaragua

Enrique Alaniz, T. H. Gindling, Catherine Mata, and Diego Rojas

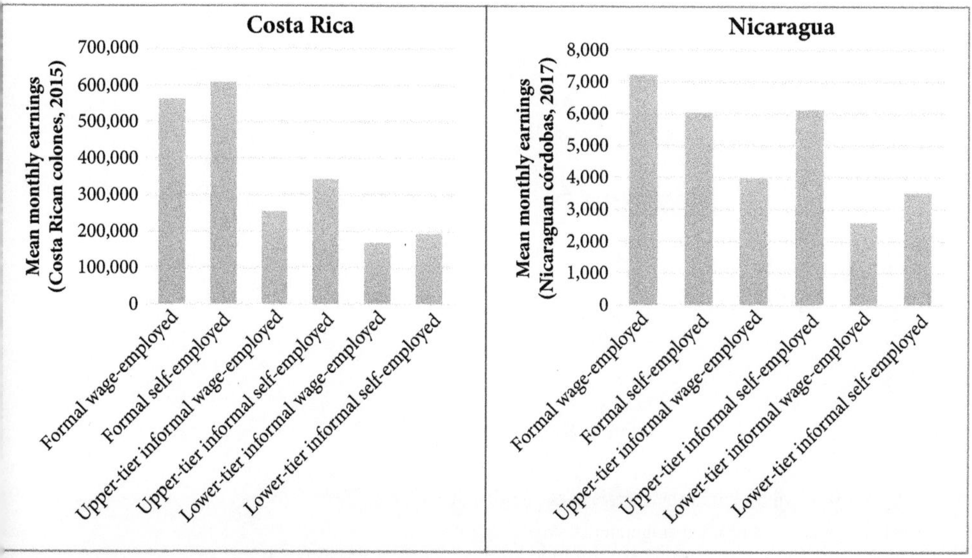

Fig. B.6 Mean earnings by work status: Costa Rica and Nicaragua

Source: authors' calculations based on the data described in section 2.1.

7. Informality, labour transitions, and the livelihoods of workers in Latin America

Roxana Maurizio and Ana Paula Monsalvo

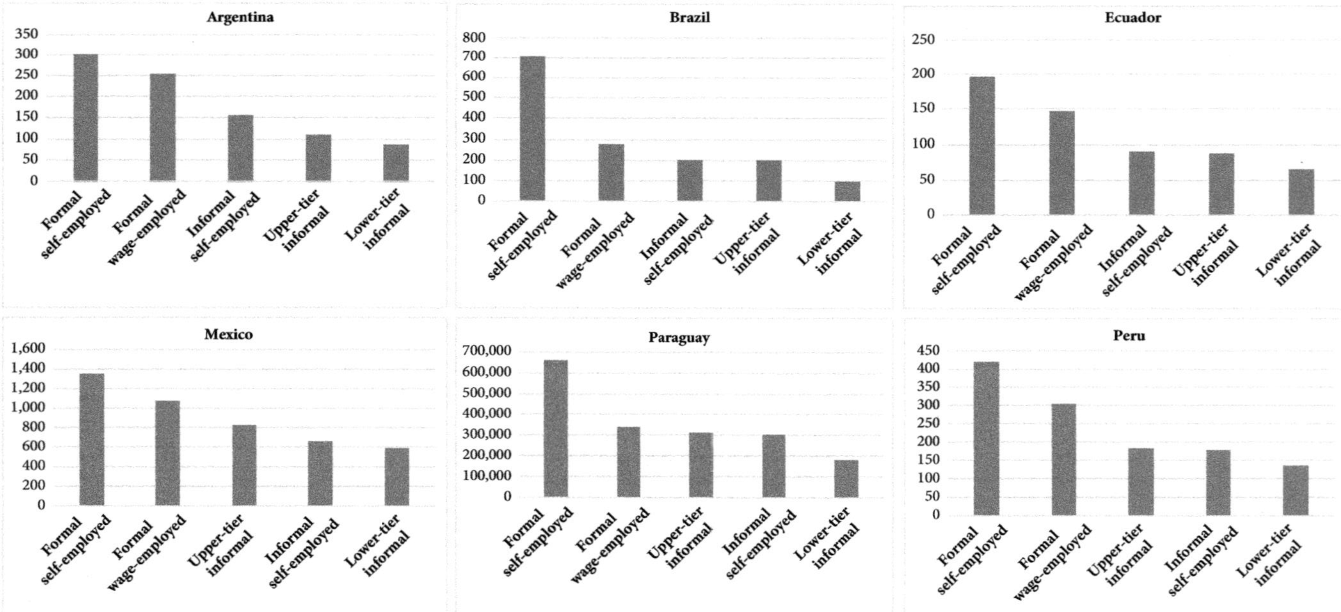

Fig. B.7 Mean monthly wages by work status
Source: authors' elaboration based on household surveys.

8. Self-employment and labour market dynamics of men and women in El Salvador and Nicaragua

Enrique Alaniz, Alma Espino, and T. H. Gindling

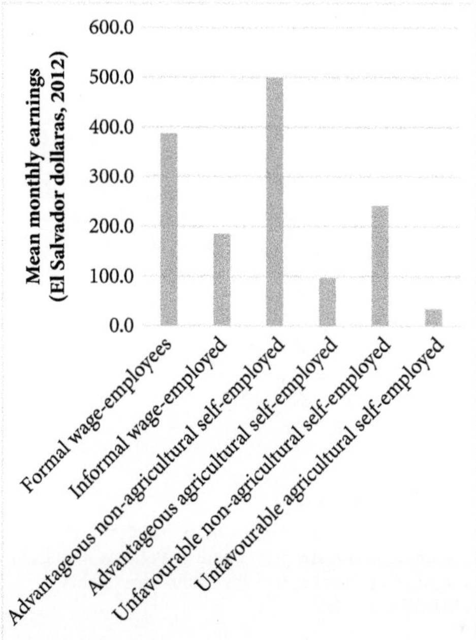

Fig. B.8a El Salvador

Source: authors' calculations from the 2008–2012 Encuesta de Hogares de Propósitos Múltiples (EHPM).

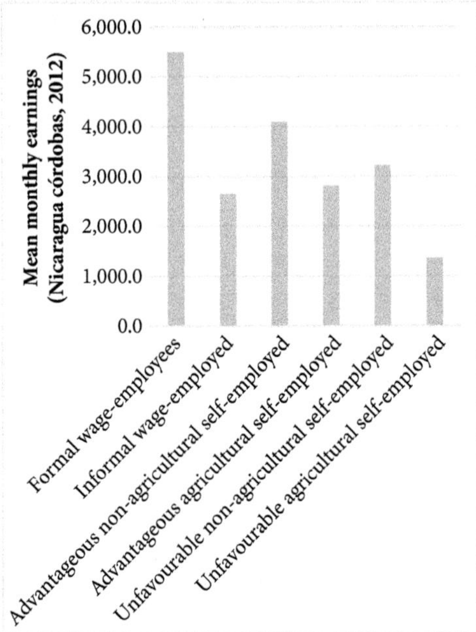

Fig. B.8b Nicaragua

Source: authors' calculations from the 2009–2012 Encuesta de Hogares para Medir la Pobreza–Fundación Internacional para el Desafio Económica Global (EHMP–FIDEG).

9. Informal work in urban Mexico: characteristics, dynamics, and workers' preferences

Robert Duval-Hernández

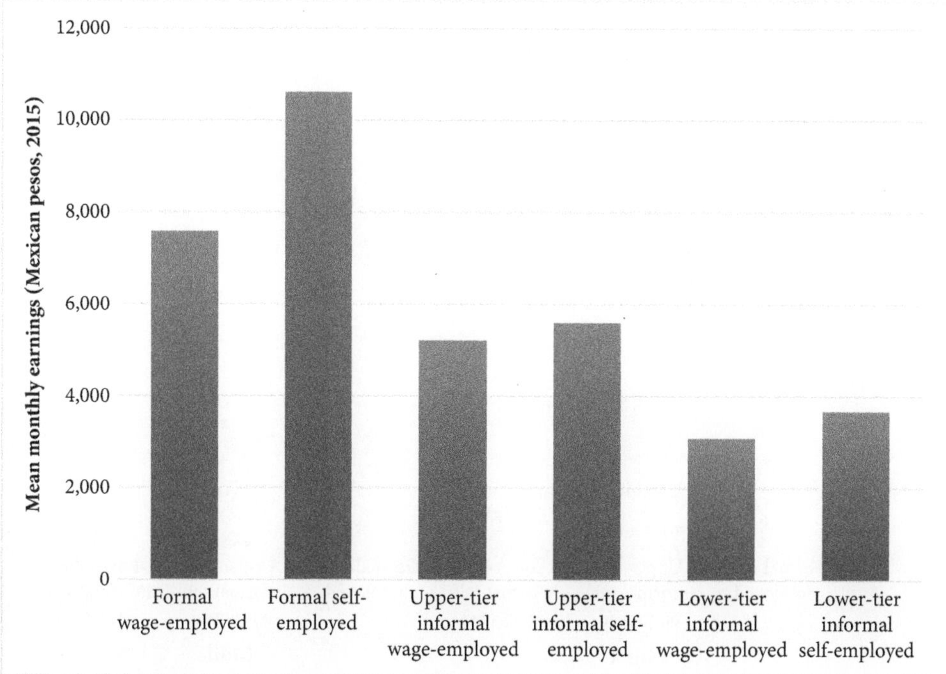

Fig. B.9 Mean earnings by work status

Note: All estimates use sampling weights.

Source: author's calculations based on ENOE 2nd Quarter 2015, large urban areas (INEGI 2015b).

IV. SUB-SAHARAN AFRICA

10. The dynamics of off-farm self-employment in the West African Sahel

Sènakpon Fidèle Ange Dedehouanou and Didier Y. Alia

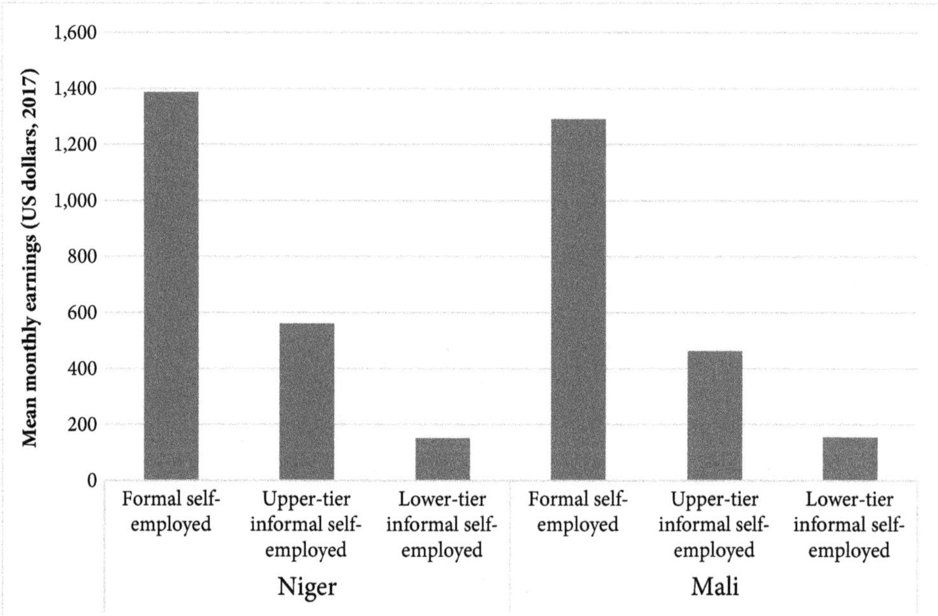

Fig. B.10 Mean earnings by work status, Niger and Mali
Source: authors' illustration based on LSMS-ISA data for Mali and Niger

11. Informal–formal workers' transition in Nigeria: a livelihood analysis

Abiodun O. Folawewo and Olusegun A. Orija

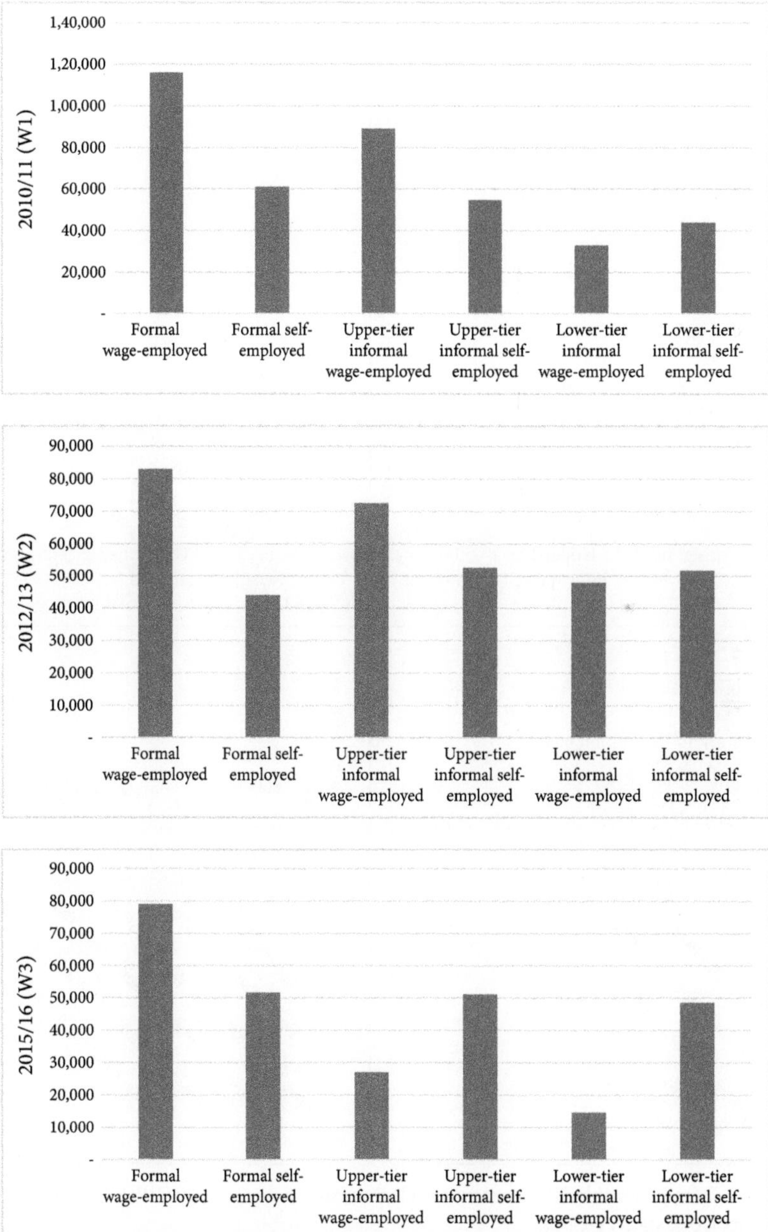

Fig. B.11 Informal-formal workers transition in Nigeria: a livelihood analysis
Source: authors' computation from NBS GHS datasets.

12. Informal–formal transitions in work status in sub-Saharan Africa: a comparative perspective

Michael Danquah, Simone Schotte, and Kunal Sen

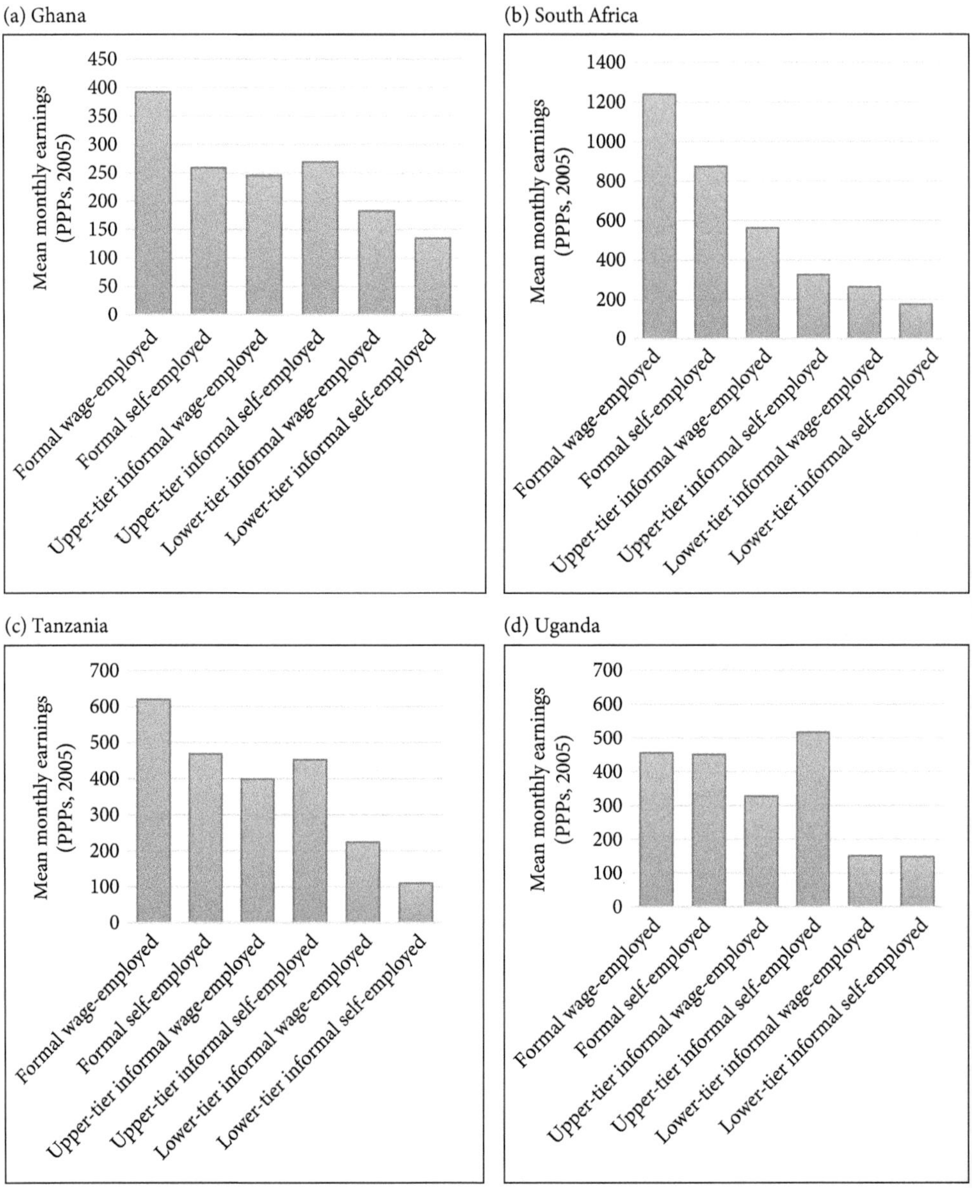

Fig. B.12 Mean monthly labour earnings (Purchasing power parity (PPPs), in 2005) across six work status groups

Note: For each country, summary statistics are compiled for the initial wave of panel study under study. Standard errors of mean values in parentheses. *Source*: authors' own calculations based on survey data from Ghana Socio-Economic Panel Survey (GSPS) 2009/10–2013/14, National Income Dynamics Study (NIDS) 2014/15–2017, Tanzania National Panel Survey (TZNPS) 2010/11–2012/13, and Uganda National Panel Study (UNPS) 2010/11–2011/12.

V. NORTH AFRICA AND THE MIDDLE EAST

13. The evolution of vulnerable employment in Egypt, Jordan, and Tunisia

Shireen AlAzzawi and Vladimír Hlásny

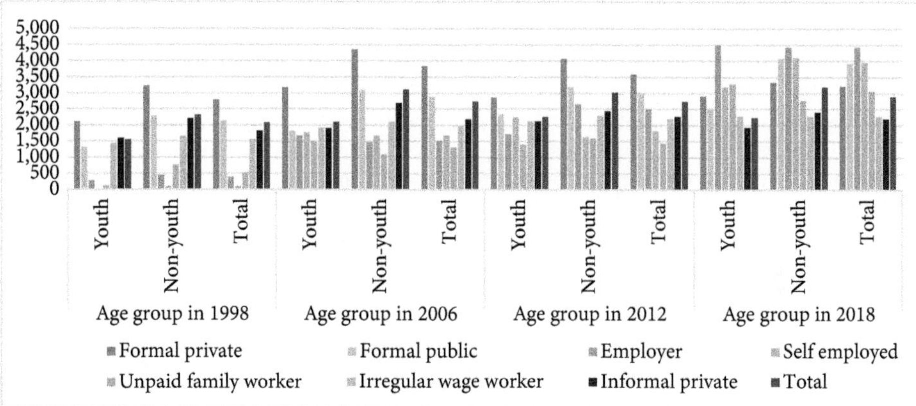

Fig. B.13a Egypt: Mean income by employment status and age 1998–2018 in real 2018 Egyptian pounds (EGP)

Source: authors' illustrations based on the Egypt Labour Market Panel Survey (ELMPS) 1998–2018, the Jordan Labor Market Panel Survey (JLMPS) 2010–2016, and the Tunisia Labor Market Panel Survey (TLMPS) 2014 (OAMDI 2019).

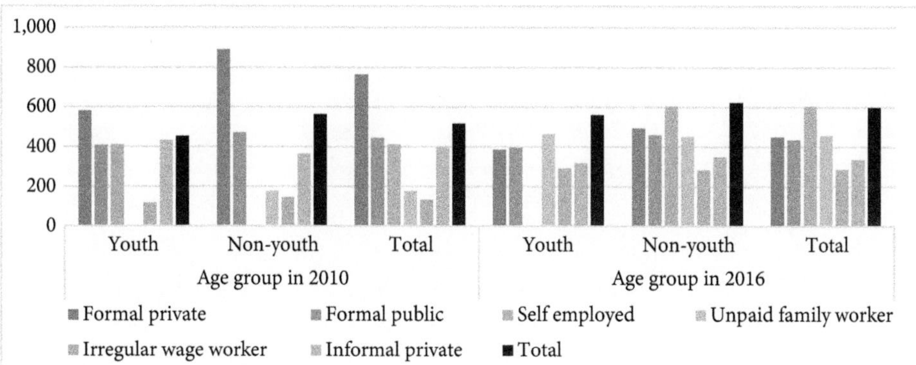

Fig. B.13b Jordan: Mean income by employment status and age 2010–2016 in real 2016 Jordanian dollars (JD)

Source: authors' illustrations based on ELMPS 1998–2018, JLMPS 2010–2016, TLMPS 2014 (OAMDI 2019).

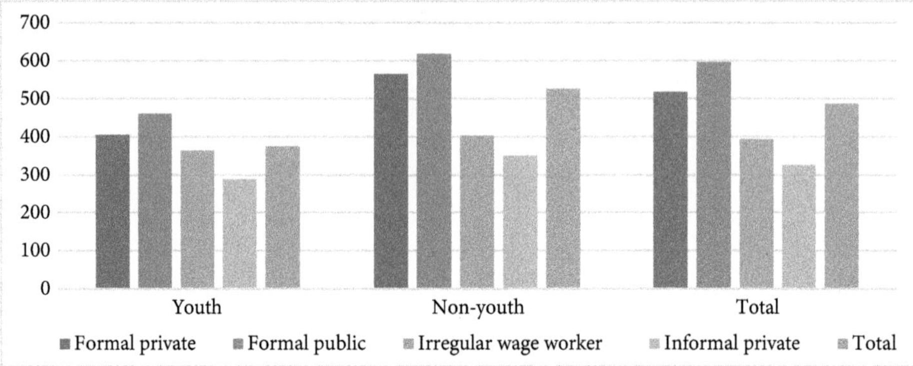

Fig. B.13c Tunisia: Mean income by employment status and age in 2014 Tunisian dollars (TD)

Source: authors' illustrations based on ELMPS 1998–2018, JLMPS 2010–2016, TLMPS 2014 (OAMDI 2019).

APPENDIX C

Work status dynamics

II. ASIA

3. Transforming informal work and livelihoods in China

Carl Lin, Linxiang Ye, and Wei Zhang

Table C.3a Transition matrices across work status groups from 2014 to 2016: the case of China

				Year = 2016						Share of stayers
				Self-employed			Wage-employed			
				Formal	Informal		Formal	Informal		
					Upper-tier%	Lower-tier%		Upper-tier%	Lower-tier%	
Year = 2014	Self-employed	Formal		86.2	0.0	4.6	8.0	1.1	0.0	1.0
		Informal	Upper-tier	0.0	57.9	2.6	7.9	28.9	2.6	0.3
			Lower-tier	0.1	0.0	94.0	1.0	2.1	2.8	54.8
	Wage-employed	Formal		0.5	0.1	2.8	89.6	5.4	1.5	17.7
		Informal	Upper-tier	0.3	1.3	13.5	7.8	68.8	8.3	9.5
			Lower-tier	0.4	0.2	19.9	5.3	11.8	62.5	4.1
	Total			1.2	0.5	58.5	19.8	12.7	7.2	87.4

Source: authors' calculations based on China Family Panel Studies (CFPS) data (Institute of Social Science, Peking University, 2018).

Table C.3b Transition matrices across work status groups from 2016 to 2018: the case of China

				Year = 2018						Share of stayers
				Self-employed			Wage-employed			
				Formal	Informal		Formal	Informal		
					Upper-tier%	Lower-tier%		Upper-tier%	Lower-tier%	
Year = 2016	Self-employed	Formal		29.0	6.5	44.1	7.5	4.3	8.6	0.4
		Informal	Upper-tier	18.4	42.1	13.2	2.6	10.5	13.2	0.2
			Lower-tier	2.1	0.3	88.7	1.9	3.8	3.2	51.9
	Wage-employed	Formal		0.5	0.1	2.7	79.9	13.0	3.7	15.8
		Informal	Upper-tier	0.5	0.4	8.5	29.2	46.4	15.0	5.9
			Lower-tier	0.9	0.2	14.4	12.9	26.0	45.6	3.3
	Total			1.9	0.6	55.2	21.7	12.7	7.9	77.5

Source: authors' calculations based on China Family Panel Studies (CFPS) data (Institute of Social Science, Peking University, 2018).

Table C.3c Transition matrices across work status groups from 2014 to 2018: the case of China

				Year = 2018						Share of stayers
				Self-employed			Wage-employed			
				Formal	Informal		Formal	Informal		
					Upper-tier%	Lower-tier%		Upper-tier%	Lower-tier%	
Year = 2014	Self-employed	Formal		28.7	6.9	44.8	8.0	5.7	5.7	0.3
		Informal	Upper-tier	15.8	36.8	5.3	21.1	7.9	13.2	0.2
			Lower-tier	1.9	0.2	86.2	2.7	4.9	4.1	50.2
	Wage-employed	Formal		0.7	0.2	4.2	76.9	14.2	3.8	15.2
		Informal	Upper-tier	1.1	0.5	17.4	27.8	38.2	15.0	5.3
			Lower-tier	2.0	0.8	18.7	13.6	25.6	39.4	2.6
	Total			1.9	0.6	55.2	21.7	12.7	7.9	73.8

Source: authors' calculations based on CFPS data (Institute of Social Science, Peking University, 2018).

4. Moving up or down the job ladder in India: examining informality–formality transitions

Rajesh Raj Natarajan, Simone Schotte, and Kunal Sen

Table C.4 Transition matrices across work status groups in India

		A. Transition matrices						B. Shares	
Employment status	**Initial size (%)**	**Formal SE**	**Upper-tier informal SE**	**Lower-tier informal SE**	**Formal WE**	**Upper-tier informal WE**	**Lower-tier informal WE**	**% of individuals who remain in employment status**	**% of individuals who change employment status**
Formal SE	1.29	29.16	8.8	25.42	14.34	10.51	11.77	0.38	0.91
Upper-tier informal SE	7.72	2.26	30.91	40.65	7.79	9.67	8.73	2.39	5.34
Lower-tier informal SE	20.79	2.12	12.37	48.41	5.96	14.01	17.13	10.06	10.73
Formal WE	9.24	1.3	2.51	6.34	64.96	17.08	7.81	6.01	3.23
Upper-tier informal WE	29.33	1.37	2.72	9.76	16.05	38.11	32.00	11.17	18.18
Lower-tier informal WE	31.62	0.14	1.25	6.01	3.42	16.28	72.90	23.05	8.57
Total	37.356	1.56	6.50	18.88	13.81	21.7	37.55	53.06	46.97

Note: SE, self-employment; WE, wage-employment. (i) Employment status in the base year and in the final year are presented in rows and columns, respectively. (ii) Initial size corresponds to the proportion of individuals who were in the particular employment status in the base year. (iii) The rows of the transition matrix add up to 1. (iv) The likelihood of staying in the same employment status conditional on the base-year employment status is highlighted in grey. (v) The share of those who remain in their employment status is the product of highlighted diagonals and initial size.
Source: authors' estimates based on India Human Development Survey (IHDS) data.

5. Progress and stagnation in the livelihood of informal workers in an emerging economy: long-term evidence from Indonesia

Mayang Rizky, Daniel Suryadarma, and Asep Suryahadi

Table C.5 Progress and stagnation in the livelihood of informal workers in an emerging economy: long-term evidence from Indonesia

			2014			
			Informal		Formal	
			Low-tier%	High-tier%	Low-tier%	High-tier%
1996	Informal	Low-tier	81.4	4.5	11.9	2.2
		High-tier	75.8	11.4	8.5	4.3
	Formal	Low-tier	53.6	2.8	35.8	7.8
		High-tier	29.1	4.6	20.3	46.0
Total			63.6	4.2	22.7	9.5

Source: authors' construction based on data from IFLS 2000, 2007, and 2014.

III. LATIN AMERICA

6. Transforming informal work and livelihoods in Costa Rica and Nicaragua

Enrique Alaniz, T. H. Gindling, Catherine Mata, and Diego Rojas

Table C.6 Year-to-year conditional probabilities of transition as a percentage of the initial number in each status in year *t*

Costa Rica		$t+1 \rightarrow$	Self-employed			Wage-employees			Not employed			Total
			Formal	Informal		Formal	Informal		Unemployed	Students	Out of labour force	
		$t \downarrow$		Upper-tier%	Lower-tier%		Upper-tier%	Lower-tier%				
Self-employed	Formal		48.5	34.6	1.0	3.5	6.8	0.6	1.1	0.2	3.8	100.0
	Informal	Upper-tier	12.6	45.1	4.1	5.0	10.3	1.8	2.5	1.7	17.0	100.0
		Lower-tier	2.3	21.1	33.7	6.8	8.1	11.0	4.9	1.5	10.5	100.0
Wage-employees	Formal		0.4	1.4	0.5	86.5	3.5	1.5	3.0	0.7	2.5	100.0
	Informal	Upper-tier	2.2	8.4	1.3	12.7	42.4	5.9	5.4	5.3	16.5	100.0
		Lower-tier	0.6	4.5	5.8	15.2	20.7	27.9	9.9	4.3	11.2	100.0
Unemployed			0.6	4.7	2.4	22.3	11.0	7.9	22.8	9.8	18.6	100.0

Continued

Table C.6 *Continued*

Nicaragua		$t+1$ →	Self-employed			Wage-employees			Not employed			Total
			Formal	Informal		Formal	Informal		Unemployed	Students	Out of labour force	
		t ↓		Upper-tier	Lower-tier		Upper-tier	Lower-tier				
Self-employed	Formal		18.0	29.5	16.4	9.0	6.6	4.1	0.0	0.0	16.4	100.0
	Informal	Upper-tier	0.9	56.6	15.2	1.7	9.8	6.3	0.8	0.3	8.5	100.0
		Lower-tier	0.8	20.5	40.0	2.4	10.8	7.6	1.4	0.8	15.7	100.0
Wage-employees	Formal		0.6	1.7	2.2	75.7	9.8	1.8	2.4	0.4	5.5	100.0
	Informal	Upper-tier	0.1	7.8	6.8	9.3	56.1	8.8	3.0	1.7	6.4	100.0
		Lower-tier	0.1	7.8	6.7	2.8	14.4	46.4	1.1	4.7	15.9	100.0
Unemployed			0.2	5.8	10.7	15.9	26.4	6.8	13.2	2.9	18.1	100.0

Source: authors' calculations based on (for Costa Rica) Costa Rican panel 2011–2017 and (for Nicaragua) Fundación Internacional para el Desafío Económico Global (FIDEG) panel 2009–2017.

Table C.7 Year-to-year conditional probabilities of transitions (percentage)

Country	Employment status in year *t*		Employment status in year *t* + 1							
			Formal wage-employees	Informal wage-employees		Self-employed		Unemployed	Inactive	Total
				Upper-tier%	Lower-tier%	Formal	Informal			
Argentina	Formal wage-employees		87.4	2.7	2.4	0.8	1.8	1.9	2.9	100
	Informal	Upper-tier	18.7	39.4	14.3	2.2	8.3	5.9	11.1	100
	wage-employees	Lower-tier	9.4	9.0	46.3	0.9	11.1	7.3	16.0	100
	Self-employed	Formal Informal	8.2	5.2	3.0	59.0	17.0	2.1	5.6	100
			4.1	4.2	8.5	3.8	62.9	4.5	11.9	100
	Unemployed		10.4	8.5	13.8	1.3	11.2	26.5	28.4	100
	Inactive		2.5	2.8	5.6	0.5	4.3	6.1	78.1	100
Brazil	Formal wage-employees		79.0	2.6	2.2	0.9	2.6	5.8	6.9	100
	Informal	Upper-tier	21.4	33.3	7.2	3.0	9.3	11.1	14.5	100
	wage-employees	Lower-tier	7.0	2.9	46.4	0.6	12.4	9.6	21.1	100
	Self-employed	Formal	3.7	2.4	1.0	71.2	13.8	2.6	5.3	100
		Informal	1.8	1.2	3.5	2.6	69.0	5.2	16.6	100
	Unemployed		7.1	2.9	5.5	1.4	10.4	41.8	30.9	100
	Inactive		1.2	0.8	2.2	0.4	5.6	8.8	81.1	100

Continued

Table C.7 *Continued*

Country	Employment status in year t		Employment status in year $t+1$: Formal wage-employees	Informal wage-employees		Self-employed		Unemployed	Inactive	Total
				Upper-tier%	Lower-tier%	Formal	Informal			
Ecuador	Formal wage-employees		85.1	2.8	2.1	1.0	3.3	2.1	3.5	100
	Informal	Upper-tier	22.1	33.9	18.5	1.5	12.1	4.4	7.6	100
	wage-employees	Lower-tier	9.4	10.8	44.5	0.7	19.8	4.5	10.3	100
	Self-employed	Formal	12.8	4.6	3.3	47.0	22.3	2.5	7.6	100
		Informal	3.8	3.4	8.2	2.3	67.0	2.2	13.1	100
	Unemployed		15.1	7.0	13.6	2.9	13.5	18.2	29.7	100
	Inactive		2.9	1.9	4.0	0.6	8.4	5.0	77.2	100
Mexico	Formal wage-employees		77.8	6.1	3.8	1.1	2.7	2.7	5.8	100
	Informal	Upper-tier	26.5	30.9	16.3	1.9	7.9	4.1	12.4	100
	wage-employees	Lower-tier	8.5	9.2	49.1	0.8	13.4	3.3	15.7	100
	Self-employed	Formal	8.9	4.8	4.7	50.8	14.6	2.3	13.9	100
		Informal	4.1	3.5	10.5	2.4	59.6	1.6	18.2	100
	Unemployed		21.9	9.9	14.4	2.4	9.0	14.9	27.6	100
	Inactive		3.8	2.7	5.7	0.8	7.8	2.5	76.6	100

Paraguay	Formal wage-employees		86.8	5.0	1.5	0.2	2.5	2.1	1.9	100
	Informal	Upper-tier	15.6	50.9	13.0	0.6	8.6	7.1	4.2	100
	wage-employees	Lower-tier	5.3	12.5	52.9	0.1	10.7	7.5	11.0	100
	Self-employed	Formal	5.2	5.0	2.2	36.8	42.7	6.6	1.5	100
		Informal	1.9	3.1	7.3	2.7	67.8	5.4	11.8	100
	Unemployed		9.8	16.5	18.0	0.5	7.8	27.8	19.6	100
	Inactive		2.3	4.0	8.0	0.2	7.9	9.5	68.2	100
Peru	Formal wage-employees		78.9	6.3	2.3	2.0	4.0	3.5	3.0	100
	Informal	Upper-tier	20.5	36.9	13.1	2.0	11.3	5.7	10.6	100
	wage-employees	Lower-tier	6.2	14.3	43.5	1.0	17.4	5.4	12.3	100
	Self-employed	Formal	10.9	3.6	4.8	48.4	20.3	3.9	8.1	100
		Informal	2.9	4.0	5.6	3.0	70.5	3.3	10.6	100
	Unemployed		11.3	8.8	11.4	2.5	12.2	20.8	33.0	100
	Inactive		2.8	5.1	6.1	1.3	13.3	9.2	62.1	100

Source: Argentina: Encuesta Permanente de Hogares (EPH), 2019.
Brazil: Pesquisa Mensal de Emprego (PME) (IBGE 2016) and the Pesquisa Nacional por Amostra de Domicilios Contínua (PNADC) (IBGE 2020).
Ecuador: Encuesta Nacional de Empleo, Desempleo y Subempleo (ENEMDU), 2017.
Mexico: Encuesta Nacional de Ocupación y Empleo (ENOE), 2019.
Paraguay: Paraguayan Encuesta Continua de Empleo (ECE), 2017.
Peru: the Encuesta Nacional de Hogares (ENAHO),2022.

8. Self-employment and labour market dynamics of men and women in El Salvador and Nicaragua

Enrique Alaniz, Alma Espino, and T. H. Gindling

Table C.8a Transition matrices across work status groups: the case of El Salvador

				Wave $t = 1$					
				Self-employed				Wage-employed	
				Non-agriculture		Agriculture		Formal	Informal
				Advantageous	Unfavourable	Advantageous	Unfavourable		
Wave $t = 0$	Self-employed	Non-agriculture	Advantageous	56.6	27.4	1.5	1.8	2.9	9.8
			Unfavourable	19.1	63.9	0.5	2.3	1.7	12.6
		Agriculture	Advantageous	2.6	3.4	49.8	29.7	0.9	13.7
			Unfavourable	1.9	3.9	17.0	54.7	1.1	21.5
	Wage-employed	Formal		1.4	1.3	0.2	0.6	89.2	7.4
		Informal		4.1	7.2	2.0	6.6	8.6	71.5
	Total			11.3	17.0	4.9	9.2	28.3	29.3

Source: Multipurpose Household Surveys (MHS), 2008-2012 by General Directorate of Statistics and Census (DIGESTYC).

Table C.8b Transition matrices across work status groups: the case of Nicaragua

				Wave $t = 1$					
				Self-employed				Wage-employed	
				Non-agriculture		Agriculture		Formal	Informal
				Advantageous	Unfavourable	Advantageous	Unfavourable		
Wave $t = 0$	Self-employed	Non-agriculture	Advantageous	66.1	14.6	2.8	0.4	3.0	13.2
			Unfavourable	32.5	45.5	1.0	3.3	2.9	14.7
		Agriculture	Advantageous	5.2	1.2	53.2	26.7	1.0	12.9
			Unfavourable	1.5	3.1	19.7	58.5	0.9	16.2
	Wage-employed	Formal		2.4	0.8	0.7	0.7	82.7	12.8
		Informal		6.5	3.7	3.7	5.1	9.4	71.6
	Total			18.4	8.6	9.4	12.5	18.6	32.5

Source: Fundación Internacional para el Desafío Económico Global (FIDEG).

9. Informal work in urban Mexico: characteristics, dynamics, and workers' preferences

Robert Duval-Hernández

Table C.9 One-year transitions across work status

				1st quarter 2016						Share of stayers
				Self-employed			Wage-employed			
				Formal	Informal		Formal	Informal		
					Upper-tier	Lower-tier		Upper-tier	Lower-tier	
1st quarter 2015	Self-employed	Formal		52.73	15.28	7.11	10.13	6.04	8.71	3.54
		Informal	Upper-tier	18.47	35.26	16.99	5.81	6.77	16.7	1.94
			Lower-tier	5.78	8.68	59.2	6.5	2.21	17.64	5.97
	Wage-employed	Formal		0.96	0.87	1.63	87.44	5.11	3.99	44.42
		Informal	Upper-tier	2.94	3.57	2.83	27.84	33.92	28.89	3.2
			Lower-tier	4.5	3.99	9.54	12.84	12.02	57.11	9.96
	Total			6.69	5.32	10.15	50.94	8.9	18	69.03

Source: authors' calculations based on ENOE 1st Quarter 2015 and 2016, urban areas (INEGI 2015b).

IV. SUB-SAHARAN AFRICA

10. The dynamics of off-farm self-employment in the West African Sahel

Sènakpon Fidèle Ange Dedehouanou and Didier Y. Alia

Table C.10 Transition probabilities for self-employed workers in Niger (in %)

				Wave 2014 Self-employed		
				Formal	**Informal**	
					Upper-tier	**Lower-tier**
Wave 2011	Self-employed	Formal		13.41	41.46	45.12
		Informal	Upper-tier	3.26	51.74	45
			Lower-tier	0.98	20.04	78.98
	Total%			2.39	31.19	66.42

Source: authors' calculation based on LSMS-ISA data for Niger.

11. Informal–formal workers' transition in Nigeria: a livelihood analysis

Abiodun O. Folawewo and Olusegun A. Orija

Table C.11 Workers' transition matrices across work status groups and waves: the case of Nigeria

Panel A

				Wave $t = 2$						Share of stayers
				Self-employed			Wage-employed			
					Informal			Informal		
				Formal	Upper-tier%	Lower-tier%	Formal	Upper-tier%	Lower-tier%	
Wave $t = 1$	Self-employed	Formal		0	0	22.2	22.2	11.1	44.4	0.0
		Informal	Upper-tier	0	53.5	0	18.2	28.3	0	1.2
			Lower-tier	0.1	0.8	61.2	2.8	0.34	34.8	36.5
	Wage-employed	Formal		0	2.6	16.2	68.8	3.8	8.6	13.2
		Informal	Upper-tier	1.8	10.7	0	53.6	33.9	0	0.4
			Lower-tier	0.1	0	32.5	5.6	1.6	60.1	10.5
	Total			0.1	1.7	45.7	16.2	2.4	33.9	61.8

Panel B

				Wave $t = 3$						Share of stayers
				Self-employed			Wage-employed			
				Formal	Informal		Formal	Informal		
					Upper-tier	Lower-tier		Upper-tier	Lower-tier	
Wave $t = 2$	Self-employed	Formal		50	0	0	50	0	0	0.05
		Informal	Upper-tier	0	82.7	0	17.3	0	0	1.4
			Lower-tier	0.2	0	97.4	2.4	0	0.05	44.5
	Wage-employed	Formal		0.4	4	12.6	82.7	0.1	0.1	13.4
		Informal	Upper-tier	0	32.7	0	27.1	40.2	0	1.0
			Lower-tier	0.1	1.7	92.8	4.1	0.1	1.3	0.4
	Total			0.2	3.9	78.9	16.9	0.04	0.1	60.8

Note: The sum of the transition matrix row (excluding the share of stayers) is 100 per cent and each cell represents the distribution of workers at the row's wave. The share of stayers represents those who remained in their initial employment position, which is calculated as the product of the highlighted diagonals and initial size (the percentage of workers that moved from a particular work status in wave $t + 1$ multiplied by the initial number of workers in that same work status in time t, divided by 100).
Source: authors' computation from Global Human Settlement (GHS) data set.

Table C.12 Transition matrices across work status groups

(a) Ghana

				Wave $t = 1$						Share of stayers
				Wage-employed			Self-employed			
				Formal	Informal		Formal	Informal		
					Upper-tier	Lower-tier		Upper-tier	Lower-tier	
Wave $t = 0$	Wage-employed	Formal		65.1	6.9	9.6	4.3	3.6	10.6	8.6
		Informal	Upper-tier	33.0	11.8	23.7	2.5	3.2	25.8	0.6
			Lower-tier	21.7	5.3	32.2	7.5	6.4	26.9	6.1
	Self-employed	Formal		2.1	3.4	12.1	29.5	15.8	37.1	2.6
		Informal	Upper-tier	4.0	2.5	15.2	14.7	44.7	18.9	5.3
			Lower-tier	2.1	2.0	15.8	6.8	6.3	67.2	28.1
	Total			21.0	4.5	18.4	9.1	11.2	35.8	51.3

(b) South Africa

				Wave $t = 1$						Share of stayers
				Wage-employed			Self-employed			
				Formal	Informal		Formal	Informal		
					Upper-tier	Lower-tier		Upper-tier	Lower-tier	
Wave $t = 0$	Wage-employed	Formal		83.3	7.1	5.8	2.2	1.1	0.5	47.2
		Informal	Upper-tier	50.1	25.1	14.7	6.0	1.0	3.1	2.2
			Lower-tier	26.4	13.1	47.7	4.7	3.9	4.3	10.2
	Self-employed	Formal		13.0	9.7	5.1	50.8	13.3	8.1	2.0
		Informal	Upper-tier	12.2	11.1	19.5	16.1	23.5	17.6	1.3
			Lower-tier	14.7	6.2	16.8	6.9	24.6	30.8	1.1
	Total			63.4	9.9	14.9	5.2	3.4	3.1	64.0

Continued

Table C.12 *Continued*

(c) Tanzania

				Wave $t = 1$						Share of stayers
				Wage-employed			Self-employed			
				Formal	Informal		Formal	Informal		
					Upper-tier	Lower-tier		Upper-tier	Lower-tier	
Wave $t = 0$	Wage-employed	Formal		79.7	4.4	9.7	1.5	1.0	3.6	9.3
		Informal	Upper-tier	45.8	5.8	33.1	6.5	2.9	6.0	0.2
			Lower-tier	14.8	0.9	62.4	2.9	3.5	15.5	17.9
	Self-employed	Formal		2.0	0.0	5.0	31.7	18.2	43.1	2.9
		Informal	Upper-tier	4.5	0.0	21.8	15.2	23.1	35.4	0.9
			Lower-tier	5.8	1.5	15.3	8.3	4.1	64.9	28.2
	Total			22.2	1.8	27.3	8.6	6.0	34.2	59.3

(d) Uganda

				Wave $t = 1$						Share of stayers
				Wage-employed			Self-employed			
				Formal	Informal		Formal	Informal		
					Upper-tier	Lower-tier		Upper-tier	Lower-tier	
Wave $t = 0$	Wage-employed	Formal		58.0	27.0	8.1	5.2	0.0	1.7	6.8
		Informal	Upper-tier	20.0	48.3	14.1	5.7	6.1	5.9	5.2
			Lower-tier	4.7	6.2	68.3	2.7	4.3	13.9	17.7
	Self-employed	Formal		2.7	0.0	10.5	20.7	15.0	51.1	0.6
		Informal	Upper-tier	0.0	4.6	5.0	13.9	39.8	36.8	2.3
			Lower-tier	2.2	1.0	11.9	4.4	7.2	73.2	31.2
	Total			14.8	13.3	24.3	5.7	7.9	34.1	63.9

Note: Each row indicates work status in the base period, and each column in transition matrices indicates work status in the next period; transition matrix rows sum to 100. The likelihood of staying in the same employment status conditional on the base-year employment status is highlighted in grey. The share of stayers (proportion of workers who remain in their work status) is calculated as the product of highlighted diagonals and initial size. *Source:* authors' own calculations based on survey data from Ghana Socio-Economic Panel Survey (GSPS) 2009/10–2013/14, Tanzania National Panel Survey (TZNPS) 2010/11–2012/13, Uganda National Panel Study (UNPS) 2010/11–2011/12, and National Income Dynamics Study (NIDS) 2014/15–2017.

V. NORTH AFRICA AND THE MIDDLE EAST

13. The evolution of vulnerable employment in Egypt, Jordan, and Tunisia

Shireen AlAzzawi and Vladimír Hlásny

Table C.13a Transition matrices across work status groups: the case of Egypt

	Self-empl/ unpaid family worker	Irregular wage work	Informal private	Formal private	Formal public	Employer	Unemployed	Out of labour force	Total
1998									
Self-employed/ unpaid family worker	42.49	6.83	10.6	8.01	10.26	17.56	0.66	3.6	100
Irregular wage work	15.29	30.99	21.95	5.5	12.76	8.49	1.39	3.63	100
Informal private	9.74	8.95	36.5	12.89	10.41	11.38	1.67	8.46	100
Formal private	4.54	3.78	9.91	56.41	12.64	4.71	6.93	1.11	100
Formal public	0.21	3.94	5.23	5.97	82.17	0.37	1.74	0.37	100
Employer	20.21	8.77	5.95	10.98	7.89	40.64	0.7	4.86	100
Unemployed	17.49	14.57	25.98	8.91	10.13	7.37	9.55	5.99	100
Out of labour force	16.31	10.01	23.08	10.71	17.82	10.13	7.67	4.14	100
Total	17.22	12.39	20.08	11.73	18.51	10.75	4.0	4.57	100

	Self-empl/ unpaid fam	Irregular wage work	Informal private	Formal private	Formal public	Employer	Unemployed	Out of labour force	Total
2006									
Self-employed/unpaid family worker	24.2	26.46	16.67	5.64	7.49	11.49	3.19	4.86	100
Irregular wage work	9.55	51.48	15.64	4.83	5.01	5.11	3.68	4.71	100
Informal private	8.46	21.52	33.16	12.38	8.54	7.13	4.62	4.18	100
Formal private	2.49	10.78	20.43	43.77	15.36	4.01	2.69	0.48	100
Formal public	2.99	2.51	8.5	6.77	74.56	1.78	1.52	1.38	100
Employer	15.6	26.24	14.82	2.85	7.49	30.1	1.8	1.09	100
Unemployed	10.32	19.07	23.39	15.18	16.33	3.72	9.91	2.07	100
Out of labour force	11.68	28.44	25.39	10.18	7.74	5.01	4.83	6.12	100
Total	11.6	24.3	22.07	12.24	14.13	7.77	4.24	3.65	100

Continued

Table C.13a *Continued*

	Self-empl/ unpaid family worker	Irregular wage work	Informal private	Formal private	Formal public	Employer	Unemployed	Out of labour force	Total
2012									
Self-employed/unpaid family worker	26.27	21.27	24.78	3.44	3.15	11.75	5.48	3.87	100
Irregular wage work	9.05	34.16	31.27	5.92	4.0	3.3	7.35	4.96	100
Informal private	8.44	15.58	45.4	10.44	6.23	4.33	4.07	5.51	100
Formal private	4.54	7.72	29.7	42.27	7.63	3.94	3.43	0.77	100
Formal public	1.06	1.51	10.91	14.8	68.45	0.2	1.46	1.61	100
Employer	12.34	16.82	35.56	2.84	4.4	25.66	1.51	0.86	100
Unemployed	4.1	14.25	30.56	19.02	8.91	3.44	11.54	8.18	100
Out of labour force	10.51	19.01	33.61	9.81	8.03	4.4	4.45	10.18	100
Total	10.18	19.55	31.91	11.99	10.52	5.57	5.33	4.95	100

Source: Egypt Labour Market Panel Survey (ELMPS), 1998, 2006, 2012, and 2018.

Table C.13b Transition matrices across work status groups: the case of Jordan

	Self-empl/unpaid family worker	Irregular wage work	Informal private	Formal private	Formal public	Employer	Unemployed	Out of labour force	Total
2010									
Self-employed/unpaid family worker	24.44	4.13	9.28	7.78	7.83	6.62	17.96	21.96	100
Irregular wage work	7.41	3.68	0	29.26	16.22	0	28.39	15.04	100
Informal private	10.04	10.28	23.7	20.29	5.62	3.52	7.21	19.33	100
Formal private	4.3	2.74	4.35	57.97	10.38	2.74	2.29	15.24	100
Formal public	0.93	0.55	1.63	4.08	65.4	2.25	3.86	21.3	100
Employer	10.92	20.62	18.71	24.1	0	17.4	0	8.27	100
Unemployed	7.54	4.01	8.58	4.74	31.64	2.76	18.11	22.61	100
Out of labour force	7.71	6.51	5.06	6.98	21.69	0.44	20.61	31.01	100
Total	6.3	4.46	8.48	18.19	30.25	2.97	8.78	20.57	100

Source: Jordan Labour Market Panel Surveys (JLMPS) for 2010 and 2016.

Table C.13c Transition matrices across work status groups: the case of Tunisia

	2014								
	Self-empl/ unpaid family worker	**Irregular wage work**	**Informal private**	**Formal private**	**Formal public**	**Employer**	**Unemployed**	**Out of labour force**	**Total**
2011									
Self-empl/unpaid family worker	57.61	16.93	8.61	0	0	4.82	12.02	0	100
Irregular wage work	0	61.25	8.75	0	3.51	0	24.95	1.54	100
Informal private	3.79	6.49	68.1	0	0	0	16.78	4.84	100
Formal private	4.67	4.47	12.83	29.33	0	0	48.7	0	100
Formal public	3.33	4.8	9.37	3.84	42.97	0	35.69	0	100
Employer	21.73	0	0	0	0	78.7	0	0	100
Unemployed	5.81	28.73	3.97	2.65	1.84	0	57.0	0	100
Out of labour force	3.23	6.27	1.48	3.89	7.1	3.05	73.58	1.4	100
Total	9.1	17.26	14.34	5.99	7.85	2.21	42.19	1.06	100

Source: Tunisian Labour Market Panel Survey (TLMPS) for 2014).

Index

Note: Tables, figures, and boxes are indicated by an italic *t*, *f*, and *b* following the page number.